TO MARKET, TO MARKET

Reinventing Indianapolis

Edited by

Ingrid Ritchie
and
Sheila Suess Kennedy

University Pres
Lanham · New York · Oxford

Copyright © 2001 by
Ingrid Ritchie and Sheila Suess Kennedy

University Press of America,® Inc.
4720 Boston Way
Lanham, Maryland 20706

12 Hid's Copse Rd.
Cumnor Hill, Oxford OX2 9JJ

Library of Congress Cataloging-in-Publication Data

To market, to market : reinventing Indianapolis /
edited by Ingrid Ritchie and Sheila Suess Kennedy.
p.   cm
Includes bibliographical references and index.
1. Municipal government—Indiana—Indianapolis. 2. Human services—
Contracting out—Indiana—Indianapolis. 3. Privatization—Indiana—
Indianapolis. 4. Indianapolis (Ind.)—Economic conditions.
5. Indianapolis (Ind.)—Social conditions. I. Ritchie, Ingrid.
II. Kennedy, Sheila Suess.
HD4606.I6 T6   2001   338.9772'5205—dc21   2001027031 CIP

ISBN 0-7618-1981-9 (cloth: alk. paper)
ISBN 0-7618-1982-7 (pbk. : alk. paper)

Dedicated to

Johanna, Mayme, and Georgia

—I.R.

Table of Contents

Part Three: Service Delivery in the Privatized City

Part Four: "Marketizing" Public Assets

Foreword

Well, there's apples.and oranges.and, what? Peaches? Comparing and contrasting can be hard work. Those of us who watch cities closely for a living (or out of obsession), have had no shortage of characters, geniuses, technocrats, populists, noble failures and outright incompetents working out of America's big City Halls in the last fifty years. During decades of breathtaking decline and occasional renewal, cities have been blessed and cursed with chief executives of their own choosing.

Can you compare Riordan to Bradley to Yorty in Los Angeles? Can you really contrast Giuliani to Koch to Beame in New York? Did the world stand still in a way to allow valid conclusions to be drawn from comparisons of Daley to Washington and Byrne (and another Daley) in Chicago?

The questions are important ones, but useful answers are elusive. The variables of urban life. population shifts, regional economic health, the sympathies of other levels of government. are in constant flux. Talented and ambitious urban chief executives may find their best laid plans unraveling in the face of a national economic downturn, a sudden period of tight credit, or a hostile legislature in the capital. Conversely, the public perceptions of mayors can be shaped by good times set into motion by predecessors, the fruition of careful housekeeping, or the continued rise of the ambient mood that is the work of people far from the mayor's office.

However, this kind of assessment, for all its challenge, need not be consigned to the realms of academic musing, or become a parlor game akin to comparing Willie Mays, Duke Snider, and Mickey Mantle in

1950s New York. The book you are holding in your hands is a bold and creative piece of scholarship, taking on the devilishly difficult task of comparing the tenures of a growing city over a 30-year period. With care and precision, Indianapolis' trajectory from the era of gas lines to the World Wide Web is detailed, quantified, and compared.

In the particular case of Indianapolis, the comparison is particularly intriguing, since the city was arguably blessed with competent and well-supported mayors over an unusually long period of time. Few New Yorkers harbor nostalgia for the chaos and meltdown of Abraham Beame's tenure. Many Chicagoans who speak with affection for Jane Byrne also never wanted her to be mayor again. Today, after less than a year in office, Mayor Anthony Williams of Washington, DC has few people longing for Marion Barry. Indianapolis makes the work of contrast that much harder an intriguing way. There is no "slam dunk" case. Its three last mayors were Republicans. None practiced the politics of charisma over competence. Unlike mayors in any number of east coast and Midwest cities, Indianapolis mayors were not called upon to find a dignified and solvent way to manage decline. Their city was the cultural, recreational, economic, and governmental core of a growing metropolitan area.

Richard Lugar was able to parlay his time in city hall to a national reputation as a United States senator. Bill Hudnut was a leader among American mayors, enjoyed strong bipartisan support, and played a big role in transforming his city's skyline. Stephen Goldsmith tenure was a perfect expression of the tenor of his time: as Americans questioned old assumptions about government services and public employment, he tried to make government a market-disciplined institution. His influence is widespread. Goldsmith is quoted by other mayors, and has become one of presidential candidate George W. Bush's senior domestic policy advisors.

Since the riots, fires, and re-segregation of the 1960s, The Mayor has changed in ways no less fundamental than The City. The populist paterfamilias, the urban clan leader of an earlier period has receded steadily, to be replaced by a politician stressing management skills, competence, and the balance sheet over bread and circuses. "Vote for me because I am one of you!" is an appeal not heard as often in the run-up to election day. City-dwellers are more likely to hear something like "Vote for me because I am smart, hard-working, and results-oriented." Such appeals carry little in the way of ideological heat. Mayors are becoming post-party and post-politics elected leaders.

So while it is worthy of notice that Indianapolis is now run by a Democrat, it doesn't matter an awful lot that Los Angeles, and New York are run by Republicans, or that Richard M. Daley in Chicago or Anthony Williams in the District of Columbia are Democrats. There is little identifiable partisanship, and more in the way of creating strategic alliances, in the 21st century mayor's office. Modern civil service laws and waves of government reform have meant fewer and fewer jobs in the gift of the Mayor, removing them even further from the old ways of patronage and party power. The changes at City Hall haven't stopped there. Title One and its dangerous relatives, Model Cities, "slum clearance," and Urban Renewal have also moved from the scene, meaning mayors get fewer chances to pose with chromed shovels and hard hats, or conference table-covering plaster models of projects that are going to remake square miles of the urban body in one massive sweep.

The Federal government's Faustian bargain with the city, roughly rendered as "You take in the poor and I'll help pay the bills," also lapsed, leaving urban chief executives with fixed and fearsome costs and a shrinking number of willing partners to help shoulder the burdens. This has happened at a time when questions are asked from the Oval Office to the kitchen table about what people want government to do for them, and what they are willing to pay for. Getting the relationship right between the individual and the state is the day-to-day project of post-Reagan America. As the government leader closest to the people, the mayor is whipsawed by sentiment and expectation far more than the president ever will be.

Politicians at all levels of government have painted themselves into a rhetorical corner. One of the most reliable applause lines in modern political rhetoric since the 1970s has been to suggest that government is bad. Meaning flawed fundamentally, not just bad as run or presented or envisioned by an opponent, but unable to serve its stakeholders at an acceptable cost. While federal-level politicians have been able to blithely suggest that government is bad and still provide largely the same kind of government, urban elected officials face a tougher set of issues.

Garbage collection, sewer and water, local schooling, public parks, social service programs, police and fire, and local roads are more present, more real, and more costly to the average local person that the National Oceanic and Atmospheric Administration, the United States Department of Commerce, or the Immigration and Naturalization

Service. The genie may be released from the bottle in Washington, but mayors have to deal with the fact that city-dwellers in their millions continue to want a full range of municipal services and think they are paying too much for them.

The assertion is blandly made and simply accepted: Government should run like a business. It is easy to understand where this idea comes from. Take the belief that businesses are efficient and well-run that packs the media day after day, sprinkle in generously the idea doggedly marketed year after year that governments daily victimize local citizens with their incompetence. *et voila!* The next question never gets asked. What do businesses do to obtain their celebrated efficiencies? They get out of low profit businesses. They leave territories where low-income customers are unlikely to bring high levels of profit. Businesses routinely target each other to eventually control markets and achieve unhindered price-setting power. If we take the stories printed daily in the business sections of major American newspapers and transfer them to the Metro Sections, what would we conclude. Do we want government to run like a business? Would we expect city services to be provided the way many private sector services are?

Maybe we do. But the elected leaders who have made this assertion in recent decades have rarely engaged their people in the lengthy, nuanced, and revelatory conversations that would result in a city that is ready to embark on experiments that seek to fundamentally change the DNA of government. Granted, the often-heard riposte that if businesses ran like governments they would go out of business is probably true. It is also true that a hawk is not a turkey, and a skyscraper is not a mansion. We give businesses and governments totally different assignments in our lives, so it should not be a surprise that they behave differently. But, in a way, that recent love affair with the idea of the work of government is part of the alchemy of our common lives. It is difficult to compare mayors and administrations and records of success in straightforward ways in which 2+2 always equals 4.

Along with the examinations of indebtedness, tax bases, and the complex marriage of county and city functions, there are also important assessments of political considerations to deliberate. This bifurcated lens is, in my view, one of the hardest things about any comparison between Mayor Lugar in 1975 and Mayor Goldsmith 20 years later. All the conventional yardsticks are important: revenue, spending, borrowing, social indicators, capital spending, the needs of downtown versus the needs of the neighborhoods. But what did the polis make of it all?

I talked to hundreds of people for hundreds of hours about a handful of American cities in preparation for a book about postwar urban America. I expected some difference in perspective depending on age, race, life situation. But I wasn't prepared for just how different memories of similar times in similar places could be. As a journalist, I fell back on the tools and folkways of my own craft—talk to people who lived through the time, ask people what they remember about the times—but scholars must do more. Here, they do. The alchemy of human sentiment is presented, along with the nuts and bolts of municipal housekeeping. But the team of writers understands that these two categories do not operate in discrete, and hermetically sealed realms.

Mayors and their mayor mayoralties get ideas, auras, odors, successes and failures attached to them that often have little to do with the individual politicians strengths and weaknesses. Just as often a mayor's failures are a telling illustration of their human strengths and weaknesses. to accept blame and criticism, to share the glory, to cede power, to compromise and cajole. Watching the interplay of the personal, and the black and white letter of the law and policy, is what makes this part of our shared life so interesting. More than ever, mayors must live by their own cunning, and can no longer rely on the kindness of strangers.

The last 20 years have brought along an outstanding class of urban leaders, including Wellington Webb in Denver, Vera Katz in Portland, Brett Schundler in Jersey City, Michael Menino in Boston, Rudolph Giuliani in New York, Richard Daley in Chicago, Emanuel Cleaver in Kansas City, Susan Golding in San Diego, John Norquist in Milwaukee, Ed Rendell in Philadelphia, Michael White in Cleveland, Jerry Brown in Oakland, Richard Riordan in Los Angeles, and many, many others. Assessing mayors, even when executive talent is in strong supply, is an important task. The book you are about to read is an important addition to the urbanist's toolbox.

Ray Suarez

September 2000

Preface

Performance: Fact or Fiction?

The national preoccupation with efforts to "reinvent" government, and to privatize service delivery must be implemented in the "real world" environment of local government, where the application of a market approach carries both promises and risks. In Indianapolis, Mayor Stephen Goldsmith spent his two terms as chief executive creating an urban laboratory for programs designed to bring market efficiencies to municipal government—to make government smaller and more effective, and to remove regulatory burdens on business.

During the eight years of the Goldsmith Administration, citizens of Indianapolis experienced a form of cognitive dissonance: as national media outlets waxed more and more enthusiastic over Goldsmith's programs, local citizens became increasingly disenchanted and cynical, shrugging off the national accolades as evidence of a masterful public relations machine. For those of us who study issues of governance, the discrepancy suggested the need for a closer look at the realities of the Indianapolis experiment. Did the Goldsmith years herald new approaches to be emulated elsewhere? Or did the national coverage simply demonstrate the importance of "spin" in the treatment of urban initiatives? What really worked, what did not, and why?

The major thesis of the Goldsmith administration was that "marketized" public services could be delivered at lower cost, without a corresponding decline in the quality or quantity of those services. A subsidiary, but important, theme was that economic growth could be encouraged and the tax base increased by eliminating duplicative and unnecessary regulation. In his book, *The Twenty-First Century City*, Goldsmith claims to have made massive investments in infrastructure, to have effected significant reductions to the city payroll, and to have provided dramatically increased funding for neighborhoods and public safety, all while achieving an overall savings of $230 million dollars. During the 1999 mayoral campaign, the figure (as cited by Newsweek) had grown to $400 million[1] (Brant 2000).

Can those claims be substantiated? Critics say they cannot, and level a number of serious charges: 1) that operating costs were shifted to the capital budget, keeping the operating budget artificially low and causing the municipal debt to skyrocket; 2) that existing debt was refinanced in order to minimize payments due during Goldsmith's tenure, costing taxpayers hundreds of millions more due to capitalized interest and unreasonably extended repayment terms; 3) that problems Goldsmith inherited—unfunded police and fire pensions, obligations to United Airlines, deferred maintenance of city sewers—have not been addressed, and remain for successors to resolve; 4) that the reason the claimed "savings" did not result in tax relief was because savings were computed by subtracting actual expenditures from the administration's own estimates of what programs would. otherwise have cost, and that such "calculations" were political rather than fiscal in origin.

In this book, a variety of academic experts and public figures examine available data in an effort to determine which picture is accurate.

The first part of this book, *Setting the Stage*, provides context. In Chapter 1, Professor of Law Ellen Dannin provides an overview of the legal and procedural issues that have been identified in privatization initiatives around the country. Historian and Republican Party operative George Geib details the history and politics of Indianapolis' Unified Government (Unigov) in Chapter 2. In Chapter 3, Sheila Suess Kennedy, Professor of Law and Public Policy and one of this book's editors, compares Mayor Goldsmith to his two predecessors, also Republicans.

Part Two, *Doing the City's Business, Balancing the Books*, considers management issues in Indianapolis in relationship to the privatization experiments. Political Science Professor William Blomquist discusses change as a management tool in Chapter 4. Urban Policy Professor Samuel Nunn looks at the city's books in Chapter 5. And in Chapter 6, Sheila Suess Kennedy examines the impact of "marketization" on political, civic and fiscal accountability.

Part Three examines *Service Delivery in the Privatized City*. Chapter 7, by Paul Annee, a former Indianapolis Police Chief, looks at public safety under Goldsmith. In Chapters 8 and 9, LaMonte Hulse, Executive Director of the Indianapolis Neighborhood Resource Center, examines Goldsmith's claims that he empowered and reinvigorated the city's neighborhoods. Chapter 10, by Professor Robert Lehnen, discusses Goldsmith's education reform efforts and why they failed. Kelly Bentley, a member of the Indianapolis Board of School Commissioners, provides a Board member's perspective on Goldsmith's war on the Indianapolis public schools in Chapter 11. And in chapters 12 and 13, Ingrid Ritchie, Professor of Environmental and Public Policy and one of this book's editors, addresses how the Goldsmith administration met the opportunities and challenges of local environmental issues and how it attempted to reinvent environmental health regulations.

Part Four, *"Marketizing" Public Assets*, looks at some of the specific problems encountered in Goldsmith's privatization efforts. Jack Miller, Coordinator of the Indiana Alliance for Democracy, explores the impact of privatization in various city departments in Chapters 14 through 16. Dennis Rosebrough, Public Information Officer for the Indianapolis Airport Authority, discusses the effects of private management at the airport in Chapter 17.

In the afterword, *Summing Up*, we do just that.

For each chapter, the editors asked authors to assess objectively the claims made for programs Goldsmith instituted. Those claims have been quite expansive, as readers of *The Twenty-First Century City*, the *Indianapolis Star*, and the national press will appreciate. At the conclusion of his second term, for example, Goldsmith gave an interview to the *Indianapolis Star* in which he claimed, among other things, that he had invested an additional one *billion* dollars in neighborhoods, and had reduced the city's operating budget by eighteen million dollars (*Indianapolis Star* 1999). We were unable to reconcile those numbers with the Comprehensive Annual Financial Reports issued by the City of Indianapolis. Other questions about the numbers arose: did the billion dollars cited as neighborhood revitalization include the five hundred million or more (numbers varied) that he claimed was invested in "infrastructure"? What was included in the category of infrastructure? If the billion dollars was "additional," what was it in addition *to*? Expenditures of his predecessor? Projected outlays?

Was Indianapolis under Goldsmith the great fiscal success the former Mayor claims? Or was it, in the words of Democratic City-County Counselors Rozelle Boyd, Susan Williams, Monroe Gray and Jeff Golc, "the worst sham that has been visited upon a citizenry that one can possibly imagine . . .We have seen a 63% increase in spending over the Hudnut years, and it has been deficit spending to boot" (Boyd et al. 1996).

Were Indianapolis' efforts to achieve smaller and more effective government hobbled by unreasonable regulatory red tape as Goldsmith claims repeatedly in his book? Or was the *Indianapolis News* correct when it editorialized about one privatization initiative:

> To contract with WREP without understanding how state laws apply was irresponsible. The Goldsmith administration should have slowed down the process, opened it up to the public sooner and paid more attention to the legal aspects of the deal. Unfortunately, this kind of carelessness isn't new. It happened with the privatization of the city's golf courses. (*Indianapolis News* 1994)

Was the reduction of supervisory personnel and the weeding out of middle management an important step in reducing bureaucratic bloat as Goldsmith asserts? Or did it create a costly loss of institutional memory and justify the use of well-placed, high-cost consultants, as critics allege?

Did neighborhood-based efforts lead to increased participation and empowerment of neighborhood residents as has been claimed? Or was the empowerment rhetoric a euphemism for shirking responsibility that belonged to City Hall, as critics complained?

In short, the editors decided to ask the famous question, "Where's the beef?" We realized it would not be easy, and that our efforts were unlikely to be comprehensive. As Brian Howey, a local political columnist, has aptly put it, separating the hype from the facts about Goldsmith's performance would be a lot like peeling an onion (Howey 1999). In fact, it proved to be extremely difficult to get certain fiscal information, because accounting categories were changed, quasi-municipal agencies like the Indianapolis Bond Bank were used to expedite financing and in several instances documentation was simply nonexistent. We felt, however, that the effort was important, because Indianapolis is a good case study for the "reinventing government" movement that has been the subject of so much governmental and academic attention. Public policy should be informed by facts, not by press releases issued by partisans on either side of the debate.

The attempt here is to be accurate, to set the record straight when necessary and to acknowledge successes when and where they occurred. While *The Twenty-First Century City* was filled with undocumented claims, we instructed authors that they were not to make statements of fact for which there was not objective evidence. Every political figure has enemies, and Stephen Goldsmith clearly has more than his share; we did not want this book not become a vehicle for unsubstantiated accusations or political gamesmanship. We wanted, instead, a case study that could be a reliable and valuable tool to inform urban policy.

We believe that the chapters to follow will provide insight into the political and administrative processes that characterized municipal government under Mayor Goldsmith's privatization experiment. The Indianapolis story is not adequately captured by either the spin-doctors or the bomb-throwers; as our authors demonstrate, reality is more complex than ideology, and that was certainly true for the eight years that Stephen Goldsmith was mayor of Indianapolis.

Sheila Suess Kennedy & *Ingrid Ritchie*

August, 2000

Notes

[1] This was also the number used by Mitch Daniels, Jr., a close political advisor to Goldsmith, in a campaign video used to support the candidacy of Sue Ann Gilroy, Goldsmith's choice to succeed him as Mayor. Gilroy campaigned on the promise of continuing Goldsmith's policies. Her loss gave Indianapolis its first Democratic Mayor in 32 years.

Acknowledgements

The authors gratefully acknowledge the large number of colleagues in the academy and local government who contributed valuable insights and hard-to-find information in order to help us produce an accurate analysis of the Indianapolis experiment under Stephen Goldsmith.

Part One

Setting the Stage

Chapter 1

To Market, To Market: Caveat Emptor[1]

Ellen Dannin[2]

Introduction

One rainy November day on a visit to Washington, DC, I stumbled into the nearest refuge, which turned out to be the Museum of the Building. No doubt, this is one of the more obscure of the Smithsonian museums and probably least likely to be on anyone's must-visit list. However, inside is a magnificent hall with soaring ceilings, floor and ceiling connected by enormous faux marble columns. On that first visit, the building was in the midst of renovations after years of neglect. Yet, even then, its dignity shone through. The Museum of the Building was built to house workers who processed payments to Civil War veterans, former members of the Grand Army of the Republic. In other words, it was built for public workers who were providing services for former public workers.

So enervated is our opinion of public service today, it is a shock to conceive of building such an edifice for mere government workers—bean counters and paymasters at that. At one time, though, and not so long ago, public buildings were important symbols of the might and majesty of our government and, by close connection, of the people. They embodied this country's image of itself as a shining city on a hill. Government service was a calling, and a noble one. A drive through county seats such as those in Ohio's rural areas will recapture the type of buildings once conceived as appropriate for housing government.

Government buildings still symbolize how Americans view government. Today's government buildings are unaesthetic, bland, even depressing places, built on the cheap. They are demoralizing places to transact the public's business. But, no doubt, if polled, most would agree they are good enough for government workers. Public workers and government work are more likely to be the butt of jokes today than to be held in high esteem. Is it any wonder there is a strong popular movement to shed government work and move it to the private sector? Today the private sector seems to embody our aspirations and is seen as the engine of our nation's prosperity and the best way to improve public services (Wessel 1995; Sclar 2000; Holloway 1997; U.S. Newswire 1997; Shays 1997).

But there is another side to the story of privatization. On February 20, 1998, the lights went out in Auckland, New Zealand's largest city. It was months before it again had a reliable supply of power. Auckland businesses lost millions of dollars. Businesses tried to stay open by using noisy generators. Diesel smoke filled the air of fashionable downtown streets. Hundreds of companies said they would sue Mercury Energy, the private company that had recently contracted to supply Auckland's electricity. The cause of the blackout and Mercury's lethargic response to it appear to be the price for that company's drive for increased profits. Once disaster struck, it came to light that Mercury had cut many corners. It failed to do cable maintenance and to have cables in reserve. It allowed cables to remain in place months past their normal life. It had no staff who could do the repairs because Mercury had disbanded its local squads of cable-jointers who then had left the country in search of work. As a result, Mercury had to locate people with the necessary skills and then fly them from Australia into New Zealand to make repairs because no one in New Zealand had the necessary skills. (Hutton 1998; Reid 1998; McNabb & Martin 1998; Gray 1998a; Gray 1998b; Cohen 1998)

Just a few months earlier, Californians greeted 1998 with the news that a contractor had left the state park reservation system in shambles and absconded with $1 million of public money (*Los Angeles Times* 1998a, 1998b; Stienstra 1998; Ellis 1997). It left no record of reservations and new reservations could not be made. This was a disaster for a state that depends on tourism. Even when the company was making reservations, its workers were unable to provide callers with information about parks, because it was located outside California, and the reservation clerks had never been in the state.[3]

A few months earlier, the California Supreme Court had found that the Department of Transportation was illegally contracting out engineering work. The court noted the contracted out work cost twice as much as having the work done by public employees. The decision affirms the potential for poorly conceived subcontracting decisions to save no money and to harm the public. Even worse, the circumstances under which the subcontracting decisions were made raise concern that some degree of corruption might have been involved—that the contracts were let in return for campaign donations or on the basis of cronyism.[4] Whether these rumors could ever be substantiated, as the Court observed, the cost of subcontracting the work to a private consultant was double that of having the work done by state employees.[5]

States may suffer from errors involving privatization in other ways (Shays 1997). For example, Missouri taxpayers faced liability for the beating of Missouri inmates by the employees of a private prison company in Texas and for costs and fees to defend suits (Rudd 1997; GAO 1996, 2).[6] More can be lost than just money. Residents of Ellijay, Georgia learned that three years worth of water quality records were falsified by the private company operating their sewer system (Rudd 1997). The British suffered even more: illness and death followed problems linked to subcontracting. In fact, Britain's private water companies put public health at risk on more than 500 occasions over six years (Poulter 1999; *London Observer* 1997).

These stories have been repeated across the country and around the world. They are mentioned here, not to condemn privatization as inherently bad, but rather, to raise the need for caution and circumspection when decisions are made to subcontract. Serious—even deadly—consequences hang on these decisions. Privatization has been taking place for a sufficiently long period of time that one would expect the process to be well regulated. The shocking truth is that it is not regulated in the overwhelming majority of states and barely regulated in the rest. Only Alaska, Colorado, the District of Columbia, Kansas, Kentucky, Louisiana, Massachusetts, Montana and Utah provide legislation approaching comprehensive regulation of government subcontracting. Other states have piecemeal legislation or legislation directed only to specific programs. This is imprudent at best and is a disaster waiting to happen at worst. Despite this, since at least the 1980s there has been a massive movement to privatize public services of all kinds (GAO 1997, 2) without the benefit of uniform and well thought through regulation.

The claims made for the benefits of privatization are many and portentous. Privatization is supposed to have all the virtues attributed to the market and competition: to provide the best service at the lowest price. So strongly held are these assumptions by some that several years ago, and even now, it is possible to claim, and face no demand for proof, that the public sector is always inefficient and more costly and that the private sector always provides superior services. It is astounding that for such an important area, there have been few useful, comprehensive and nonpartisan studies. Even studies that find lower costs for privatization have, upon investigation, been found to provide no guidance on privatization decisions. The General Accounting Office (GAO), for example, found that studies concerning prison privatization offered "little generalizable guidance for other jurisdictions about what to expect regarding comparative operational costs and quality of service . . ." (GAO 1996, 3). It found that some focused only on specialized inmate populations; others had serious methodological weaknesses, such as using hypothetical facilities or nonrandom samples; contexts differed so greatly they might not apply outside that context; and other factors, such as the age of the system, had an impact (GAO 1996, 3).

Ideas that privatization is always better and can foster any goal have even been incorporated into or at least shaped legislation in some state statutes. For example, the goals to be achieved by privatizing the Arizona works program for welfare recipients are:

1) Fostering the development of responsible and productive citizens through program administration that provides participants with incentives to achieve self-sufficiency;

2) Making certain administrative processes more efficient and cost-effective;

3) Encouraging innovative partnerships with organizations that enhance the Arizona works program;

4) Providing an opportunity for a system that is heavily dependent on human interaction and subjective determinations to offer performance incentives for employees and the flexibility to hire and promote successful individuals;

5) Ensuring that applicants who are qualified for benefits in the department of economic security empower redesign program, including any income disregards, are automatically qualified for the Arizona works program. (Ariz. Rev. Stat. § 46-342 (1999))

While some of these may be reasonable goals for such a program, there is nothing about privatizing the program that necessarily would lead to achieving them or to achieving them more successfully than would public administration—especially for goals 1, 4 and 5.

Logic and a more realistic assessment of market processes suggest that privatization is likely to have the type of flaws all human institutions do. Indeed, greater experience with privatization has already provided the opportunity for a better, more realistic understanding of public services and contracting out to which an overly simplified theory should long ago have given way. Spectacular privatization failures have occurred, costing taxpayers money and lost services, leading to cost overruns and flouting environmental and other laws (Shenk 1995, 16). The question is how to use this knowledge to prevent failures and, where failure nonetheless happens, how to soften its impact.

Even those strongly committed to the market should not be opposed to creating safeguards for subcontracting. Certainly, this is an area in which ideological lines are drawn. However, blind ideological commitment to privatization creates an obvious danger of victimization. Much is at stake when public work is subcontracted, so it should be easy to accept that it is wise to be cautious.

On the other side, rigid opposition is not appropriate. Government has always contracted with the private sector for some services and goods it would rather buy than make, such as paper, computers, pens, and many other items readily available on the market. The problem is ascertaining which the market can best provide, and those it cannot.

Recent experiences with privatization have given us the ability to generate a more realistic—hence, more complex—understanding of the nature of government services. Economist Elliott Sclar points out that the debate on how to provide public services offers "a valuable opportunity to meaningfully improve public service. The debate . . . presents us with a rare chance to move the issue of improving the efficiency and effectiveness of public service provision from the policy back burner to the front" (Sclar 2000, 5).

Using What We Know—Guidelines for Policymakers

Privatization is a blanket term that includes different ways of shifting from publicly to privately produced goods and services: 1) the cessation of public programs and disengagement of government from specific kinds of responsibilities; 2) sales of public assets, including public lands, public infrastructure and public enterprises; 3) financing private provision of services—for example, through contracting out or vouchers—instead of directly producing them; and 4) deregulating entry into activities that were previously treated as a public monopoly.

(Starr n.d.; see also GAO 1997, 1)

In the following discussion, the focus will be almost solely on the third—contracting out or subcontracting—and, to some degree, on the first, cessation of programs and governmental disengagement.

Beyond soliciting bids and awarding contracts to the lowest bidder, is there anything more that should be considered in subcontracting and, if so, what and why? To answer that question, it is first helpful to step back for a quick overview of some of the economic issues involved in public versus private provision of goods and services. All too often an appealing but overly simplistic model of the market is used as a basis for explaining privatization, one that stops at competition and never goes on to take into account the well-known problems that occur when markets do not work. For anyone who doubts there are such problems, just consider jokes about the military's purchases of toilet seats and screwdrivers. In fact, defense department purchases can be thought of as a massive privatization scheme where the government tries to get private companies to meet specifications as to quantity, quality and price and where there have been constant failures to achieve these. These failures warn us that having the private sector provide goods and services will not automatically solve all problems of quality and cost.

Privately provided services are nothing new. In fact, historically in the United States and elsewhere, there has always been a tension over whether the government or the private sector can best buy or make a service or product. In other words, privatization is not a new innovative concept that will remake the world.

Economists and others conclude that many services can only be provided effectively by government; for example, where continuity of service is essential, where no profits are generated, and where no competition exists or can exist. Many government services are natural monopolies, where there is naturally no competition and, thus, no market impetus to provide improved service at lower cost. In addition, in some situations bigger does mean cheaper, so that the first big provider can drive all competitors out of business because it can undercut their prices and still make a profit. Once it has a monopoly, it can then charge whatever price it wishes. In this situation, the public cannot rely on the market but, rather, needs government to run or regulate the natural monopoly.

Indeed, it is for these reasons that many services came to be provided by the government. Welfare, child protective services, roads, public health, education and many others began as private services, but problems of corruption, predatory pricing and poor quality eventually led government to take them over in an effort to promote the public welfare. Other related problems led to establishing the Civil Service and its rules that attempt to prevent corruption and thus a failure to serve the public interest.

It is always a mistake to assume that the past cannot provide important lessons. Before engaging in a single-minded pursuit of privatization, it is worth considering whether these problems existed only under very different circumstances. Government and others need to ask: When markets are not competitive can the private sector improve on public sector performance even as it falls short of the competitive ideal (Richards 1996, 141; Sclar 2000, 69-93)? Although it is possible to attempt to create a market by dividing a public service into smaller units, this may lead to greater inefficiency, lack of coordination, duplication and thus greater expense (Sclar 1989, 18, 27). Indeed, competition may not be possible in all parts of the country and may be a particular problem in rural areas and where technical expertise is needed. Privatization of many types of services may suffer from cherry-picking; that is, when private companies are allowed to operate only the profitable parts of a service, leaving government with those that are most expensive to serve.

Many public services are public goods. In economists' terms they generate positive externalities; that is, they have positive side effects that cannot be confined only to those who pay for them (Heilbroner and Thurow 1994, 186-93). Vaccination, for example, protects both the one vaccinated and others who are at lower risk of contracting the disease because the pool of potential carriers is smaller. Street lighting is a classic example. Education benefits not only the one who receives it but also those who gain by having a more educated populace. Public goods create a temptation to become a free rider, to get the benefits without paying. Under these circumstances, soon no one will be willing to pay for the service or good so government must provide it, if it is to be provided at all.[7]

In many cases, government services are ones for which price competition is not as important as assuring guaranteed results. Society wants the Center for Disease Control (CDC) to track down and prevent threats to the public health far more than it wants the CDC to operate cheaply or at a profit. A private vendor may not have as much interest in controlling disease as increasing the price of its stock and returning value to the shareholders.

Finally, a subcontractor's need to add profit and its higher cost of borrowing (Sclar 2000, 105) create a hurdle that make it harder for the private sector to deliver projects and services at lower cost.[8] Indeed, a March 1994 GAO report found government could save millions of dollars by performing certain functions directly, rather than by subcontracting the work to private contractors (Hannah 1997).

All this is not to say that all work that is currently performed by government must stay with government. Rather, it must be recognized that, just as there are things the private sector does well, there are rational reasons why government has come to perform many services. An objective examination of these reasons may lead to the logical conclusion that the service in question should remain in the public domain. The question is how to provide that objective scrutiny.

Subcontracting decisions must take into account both substantive concerns (What are the benchmarks and standards to be applied to measure performance?) and procedural concerns (What is a fair, honest and reasonable way to make decisions as to subcontracting?). Most fundamentally, better decisions will be made by establishing standards and procedures in advance rather than through ad hoc decision-making.

Uniform substantive criteria that establish benchmarks for subcontracting must be available to assist the decision-maker that would otherwise lack guidance in making important decisions. Such criteria will ensure that reasoned decisions are made; ensure that oversight can be and is exercised; and protect the public welfare if problems arise and a contract must be terminated.[9] Indeed, in terminating a contract, as elsewhere with privatization, simple remedies may not be effective. Educational Alternatives, Incorporated (EAI) actually preferred that the Baltimore school district terminate its contract to having to meet its requirements. As a result, terminating the contract—a common remedy for a breach—was not a useful remedy (Richards 1996, 154). Procedural safeguards provide a reasonable process that ensures decision-making is transparent, due process is given, and the public interest is furthered.

Substantive criteria and procedural safeguards foster uniform procedures within a state or city (GAO 1997, 10-11) and allow decision-makers to capitalize on an administration that is trained and experienced. Freeing decision-makers from having to invent standards in each instance frees them from worries they might have overlooked relevant criteria. As a result, articulated standards make the process of subcontracting more streamlined, less cumbersome, more accurate and less costly. The processes embodied in state legislation and experience provide a useful starting point for exploring what should be included in subcontracting decision-making and why it should be there. The next two sections provide an in-depth discussion of the substantive and administrative criteria that can help ensure uniform procedures for privatization efforts.

Substantive Criteria

Substantive criteria must address problems that experience with subcontracting have revealed. States that have legislated subcontracting standards also provide useful insights into the range of requirements to be included. Once these substantive criteria are developed, they can be inserted throughout the process of making privatization decisions wherever the decision-maker feels they are relevant.

Determining Policy Goals

States that advocate privatization—rather than taking a more balanced approach—implicitly assume that privatization will always and automatically achieve improved public service at lower cost. Arizona, for example, requires that the administration of its welfare program be contracted out (Ariz. Rev. Stat. §§ 46-300.01, 46-342, 46-343 (1999)). This demonstrates a strong faith in the value of privatization but offers no opportunity to test that faith.

Furthermore, it fails to recognize that the goals of public service have always been larger than merely providing a service at the lowest cost. Public education, for example, is intended to do more than merely teach reading and writing or simply prepare students to join the workforce. It is intended to support our democracy by ensuring all citizens can take on the task of self-governance and to transmit a sense of shared identity. The Postal Service delivers mail, but more important is its role in helping knit a very large country together and in promoting productivity and democratic engagement by ensuring all residents in every area, no matter how remote, can communicate. A highway gets a traveler from point A to point B, but a network of public highways that reaches even remote, less traveled areas unites the country and promotes commerce. It is important then to bear in mind that, although discrete parts of these goals can be run at a profit, the whole may not be profitable, because some parts cannot be made profitable.

Furthermore, achieving larger goals vital to us as a nation may be priceless but cannot always be done at a profit. While it is possible to educate people, deliver mail, and operate tollways at a profit, it is not necessarily possible to educate all people, deliver all mail and provide a network of highways and make a profit. Indeed, for many of these services, the value of having the whole system is far greater than the sum of its parts—particularly, of its profitable parts. Although value for money is important, there is no reason to think that these traditional social goals of government are no longer important. Thus, where they conflict, a decision must be made as to which "trumps" and how all are to be accommodated.

Some states have taken a more holistic view of privatization and its goals than has Arizona. The District of Columbia, for example, requires a demonstration that privatization involving services essential to health or safety will not adversely affect the recipients (D.C. Code § 1-1181.5b(a)(9) (1999); see also D.C. Code § 1-1191.3(b)(6) (1999)). Massachusetts expresses a particularly wide range of goals in its privatization policy:

> The general court hereby finds and declares that using private contractors to provide public services formerly provided by state employees does not always promote the public interest. To ensure that citizens of the commonwealth receive high quality public services at low cost, with due regard for the taxpayers of the commonwealth and the needs of public and private workers, the general court finds it necessary to regulate such privatization contracts . . . . (Mass. Ann. Laws ch. 7, § 52 (1996))

Massachusetts is not at the opposite end of Arizona—it does not forbid subcontracting. But it is at the opposite end in looking at privatization with open eyes rather than blind faith. Taken together, the values that these states articulate provide a good starting point for policymakers to establish their own goals.

Preventing Fraud, Criminal Activities and the Spoils System Redux

Government agencies face a number of risks when fraud, criminal activities and neo-spoils systems arise in connection with privatization. They mean services are not being provided, value is not being received or revenues are being siphoned off. In addition, if care is not taken, the agency may find itself legally liable for the contractor's misdeeds and practically liable when it must make up any shortfall. These problems must be addressed before contracting out; remedies and other protections must be in place beforehand should problems arise during the term of the contract.

Most fundamentally, subcontracting decision-making must be pro-active. It must bar individuals and companies who have engaged in past criminal activities.[10] The vehicle repair contractor Los Angeles fired for costing $1 million more than the contract amount and for poor performance was being investigated at the time the contract was entered into for criminal activity (including a 26 percent overcharge) in the management of a $250-million service contract at Redstone

Arsenal, the Army's missile headquarters in Huntsville, Alabama. Despite this knowledge, ardently pro-privatization city council members decided to enter into the contract (*Los Angeles Times* 1991; Merina 1998).

Studies and reports have disclosed instances in which services contracted for have not been performed or outright theft and misfeasance have occurred. Other contractors have violated state and federal wage and safety requirements. Some have been repeat violators. Considering the essential nature of most government services and the sensitive content of others, those entrusted with performing them must not use their positions as an opportunity to loot the public coffers or put the public health and welfare at risk. Government cannot turn a blind eye to problems such as corruption and illegality no matter how enticing a low bid may appear. (Sclar 2000, 151-155)

Other actions, while not crimes, may verge on the fraudulent and thus subvert the intent of subcontracting. Before awarding a contract, an investigation should be made to determine whether a subcontracting situation involving managed competition—that is, an attempt to create a market by dividing a service and offering those parts for bid— involves real competition rather than private employers dividing up jobs in a way so they do not actually compete with one another. This is easy to do when contracts are offered for different routes or geographic regions. Although the service is provided in parts and by apparently different providers, they do not really compete with one another under these circumstances. Ostensibly independent bidders on bus service in Denver actually had an interdependent relationship at the national level. As a result, bus lines run by differently named companies were a de facto monopoly. (Sclar 2000, 87-88)

Another recognized problem has been that of patronage. Colorado declares its policy concerning privatization to be encouraging the use of private contractors to achieve increased efficiency, however, "without undermining the principles of the state personnel system requiring competence in state government and the avoidance of political patronage." It bases this policy on a recognition "that the ultimate beneficiaries of all government services are the citizens of the state of Colorado" and therefore declares its intent "that privatization of government services not result in diminished quality in order to save money" (Colo. Rev. Stat. § 24-50-501 (1998); Colo. Rev. Stat. § 24-50-503(f)(III) (1998)).

This issue can affect subcontracting in many ways. When contractors employ former government officials, they effectively create a vested interest in having contractors, and this can affect whether decisions are made in the public interest (Richards 1996, 174). Subcontracting standards must thus address whether members of a subcontracting decision-making or oversight body are to be barred from or limited in accepting employment with a contractor (Ok. Stat. § 595.4 (1999)). They need to consider whether others might be improperly affected if they are allowed to accept employment with a contractor, even though they do not serve on an oversight or decision-making body. An example would be high public officials and administrators of an agency when less than the entire workforce is subcontracted.

Those who continue to administer the part of the agency not privatized should perhaps also be barred from accepting employment with a contractor (*Cf.* Ky. Rev. Stat. Ann. § 11A.130 (1998); Mass. Ann. Laws ch. 268A, § 5 (1996)). A decision must be made about setting limits on whether any of these administrators, board members, or officials may work for lobbyists who represent current or potential subcontractors or bodies advocating positions on privatization. Finally, if there are to be bars, details must be worked out as to their geographic reach, subject matter and time limits.

Even with the best prior investigation, it is possible to have missed a problem in this area or to have one arise with no predecessor evidence. That vulnerability can take two forms. One is having to intervene quickly to ensure continuity of service. The second is limiting government liability for the contractor's misdeeds. Government should not leave itself vulnerable to these occurrences.

One obvious method of preventing the first problem is to require contractors to meet requirements that are similar to those contractors face on a large building project. These can include posting bonds and securing insurance. Other methods of being pro-active about these problems are implicit in the other protections discussed throughout this chapter.

Whenever illegalities or tortuous actions take place during the term of a contract, or serious disbarring activity is discovered, the government should have the right to terminate the contract immediately and step in (Rudd 1997). This may need to be negotiated in the contract, but the law should also provide it.

Taxpayers must be protected from liability for the actions of subcontractors. Colorado, for example, provides that the contractor bears the liability for its actions and may not plead sovereign or governmental immunity as affirmative defenses for any acts arising from the performance of its contract (Putnam 2000). This is not as simple as it may appear. While taxpayers should not be liable, it may be impossible to avoid paying extra—at least in the short run—to ensure other taxpayers do not suffer a loss when the contractor proves unreliable. In addition to tort or tort-like liability, a state may find itself ultimately liable for unpaid bills. The State of Michigan terminated a contract with its private prison health care provider but then found itself liable to pay 40 percent more for the contract of the successor who had paid off $12 million of its predecessor's unpaid bills (Putnam 2000).

Apples and Oranges: Making Costs Comparable

Any shopper knows that sale prices, markdowns and discounts cannot be taken at face value. The "original" price may be exaggerated, or the item offered may not be of the same quality or offer the full range of features as the discounted item. The same ideas apply to subcontracting.

It goes without saying that it is impossible to know if money will be saved without reliable comparative information about the cost and quality of the existing service and the subcontracted service. This means there must be a two-step process. A crucial first step is deciding which costs are properly included. Experience has shown that obtaining precise and complete cost data is no simple matter; as a result, most government agencies have used only estimated cost and performance data in subcontracting (GAO 1997, 5, 12, 13-14). This is unacceptable. Without accurate data, it is impossible to be certain subcontracting benefits the taxpayers. Discussing accounting issues with private firms as part of the process of assessing costs can be helpful in gaining a better understanding of cost and quality issues (GAO 1997, 13).

Assuming that accurate and complete cost data for the public service is obtained, it is then essential that comparable costs be used in assessing both the public and private provision of the service. Unfortunately, experience has also shown this second step does not always happen. Problems of comparability can occur when only part of a service is subcontracted—and especially when that part is less expensive, leaving the government to provide the more expensive part. For example, it would be inappropriate to compare the costs of running private prisons with government prisons if private prisons are all low security and government runs high security prisons (Shenk 1995, 16). Thus, government must take measures to determine price and quality in the same way that individual consumers comparison shop for goods and services.[11]

One common problem is that overhead costs are included in the public service's costs because they are imbedded in the department's budget, but they are not included in the contracted-out service's costs, even though those same overhead and oversight costs continue. This means that services could be privatized even though public sector workers were actually doing them more economically. Indeed, failing to have comparable cost accounting makes it impossible to know true costs. Thus, overhead and other costs must be included in the cost of providing the privatized service if they would continue with a contractor.

Omitting these costs is more than avoiding mere "bean counting." If they are not included, no oversight may take place, and, as a result services may be improperly performed or not performed at all. For example, in February 2000 the Michigan Auditor General reported that the state had paid $26 million to United Correctional Managed Care of Anaheim, California, but the company had spent only $17 million on inmate health care, leaving $9 million unaccounted for. The contract was terminated and the successor company had to pay $12 million to cover its predecessor's unpaid bills. It then negotiated a 40 percent increase in its contract to reimburse it for these unforeseen costs (Putnam 2000). It cannot be said too often that unless there is specific provision for them, oversight costs are easily overlooked. Once the service is subcontracted, they might be omitted from the agency's budget. If there is no money to fund oversight, it will not be done.

Privatization proponents might argue that no oversight is necessary, that the market will ensure performance. Albany's experience with subcontracted vehicle maintenance demonstrated that oversight was necessary and that the associated costs were substantial. They included spending money to re-engineer its voucher and data-processing system, buying additional computers, and employing additional auditors and expert mechanics (Sclar 2000,104-105, 116-117).

Proper oversight in the right—or, wrong—circumstances may make the difference between life and death. This is not only a problem in public sector subcontracting but, rather, is imbedded as a problem when different organizations or even departments must coordinate their activities. There is always a danger of things falling through the cracks, and subcontracting creates cracks in the structure of an enterprise. A major cause of the 1996 ValuJet crash was found to be a subcontracting arrangement that failed to provide definitively for oversight of critical functions (Sclar 2000, 16-18). Oversight was omitted because it appeared to save money; however, in hindsight it is clear that costs avoided were far less than the financial and human costs of the crash.

Unless oversight costs are included in the budget, this essential function is likely to be overlooked. On the other hand, when it is included at an appropriate level, people can be hired whose work is dedicated to oversight and those paying the bill are more likely to take steps to ensure they are receiving value for money.

Another easily overlooked cost, but a real one nonetheless, is the cost of converting or transferring the service to the private sector. Someone must bear those costs, and they have the potential to be large enough to consume any apparent cost advantage. Arizona includes costs of "conversion, transaction, disruption, contract monitoring costs, and revenue increases and decreases related to a privatization" (Ariz. Rev. Stat. § 41-2773(6)(a) (1999); see also Colo. Rev. Stat. § 24-50-503(1)(a)(II), (III) (1998)). Arizona further defines "total costs" as "all costs borne by an agency to provide a state function including all indirect costs and applicable allocated costs" (Ariz. Rev. Stat. § 41-2771(9) (1999)). However, it does not require a preliminary study to ascertain these costs, although such a study may be undertaken (Ariz. Rev. Stat. § 41-2773(4) (1999)).

The issue of proper cost allocation is complex and, for that reason alone, can easily be mishandled. Each agency and state must undertake a study to identify and accommodate its idiosyncratic needs. In addition to overhead costs and transfer costs, agencies should include training or retraining costs which will be incurred in any transfer to ensure that the contracted-for level of services is provided (Ky. Rev. Stat. Ann. § 45A.551(2)(e) (1998)).

Special Problems in Setting Financial Criteria

Privatizing government services is founded on the idea that markets set the proper price, and where there is no market, as when government provides a service or where there is a monopoly, the price will be too high (Heilbroner and Thurow 1994, 173-205). However, there are a number of reasons why this may not happen. Most fundamentally, there may be no market to provide the types of services government does, because many government services are public goods (Heilbroner and Thurow 1994, 186-93). Even where analogous services are provided privately—the "yellow pages" test—they may not be fully comparable (Sclar 2000, 28-32). Ostensibly similar services may in fact be different because government may have different goals than a private business. With no market for the services to be subcontracted, it becomes difficult to feel assured that a proper price has been set.

Testimony by Geraldine Jensen, President of the Association for Children for Enforcement of Support, Inc. (ACES), exemplifies this uneasiness. Jensen testified that "private vendors appear to vary prices charged for the same services provided. PSI charged Ohio, $22,130, PA

- $34,190, WV - $20,082, SD - $11,800, AR - $10,000 and RI - $7,000 to review and update their child support guidelines. States seem to be unaware of the usual market price for services rendered. This information is needed to negotiate contracts" (Jensen 1997). In fact, the differing prices could be the result of truly different services contracted for in these states and different conditions in which the contracts must be performed. On the other hand, price differences of over 50 percent in adjacent states and as much as 500 percent from the lowest to highest price could be, as Jensen fears, an artifact of factors other than value provided or cost of rendering the service. With no market to set the price, it is reasonable to feel uneasy.

Special Problems in Setting Nonfinancial Objective Criteria

Government services are often spoken of as essential services—in fact, so essential that most public employees are not allowed to strike (Wollett 1993, 252-87). Whatever the merits of the right to strike, its ban implicitly recognizes that people depend on public services and on their being of high quality. For example, although trash pickup may seem to be mundane, undesirable work, everyone knows that failure to pick up and dispose of trash properly creates serious health risks. Water is another example. Americans depend on access to uncontaminated water supplied in sufficient amounts. It would be absurd to think that people would support privatization, no matter how much money it saved, if it meant receiving contaminated water and inadequate supplies, a problem that occurred with privatizing water in England (Poulter 1999; Private Water, 1997).

Continuity of service must certainly be included among important nonfinancial considerations. Public agencies must consider how this can be assured when work is performed by a private contractor whose workers have the right to organize, bargain collectively and strike. Indeed, the right of private sector workers to strike was cited by the Justice Department as a reason not to privatize certain prison facilities (GAO 1996, 1). For those states where public sectors do not currently have the right to bargain collectively or to strike this will entail a major change in relationships.

If public work is indeed essential, this also means subcontracting cannot be done solely or primarily on cost while ignoring qualitative benchmarks. An important step prior to advertising for bids is setting measurable quantitative and quality standards. These can be developed as part of setting a baseline as discussed below. As difficult as it can be to account for all costs, setting qualitative standards is much more

difficult. The GAO's discussion of quality standards applied in studies
of prison privatization provides some good examples of the problems
that must be deal with:

> The concept of "quality" is neither easily defined nor measured. For
> example, although the American Correctional Association (ACA) sets
> accreditation standards for prisons, accredited facilities can vary widely in
> terms of overall quality. According to ACA officials, such variances occur
> because ACA accreditation means that a facility has met minimum
> standards.
>
> Generally, however, assessments of quality can take several approaches.
> For example, one is a compliance approach, that is, assessing whether or
> to what extent the prisons being compared are in compliance with
> applicable ACA standards and/or court orders and consent decrees.
> Another approach is to assess performance measures. For example,
> measures of safety could include assault statistics, safety inspections
> results, and accidental injury reports. (GAO 1996, 4-5)

For example, one GAO study reviewed surveys of correctional staff
and inmates at one institution concerning the quality of services there.
The results directly contradicted one another (GAO 1996, 9). This
demonstrates both the difficulty of trying to make quality assessments
of complex services objective and comparable, and it also demonstrates
the importance of relying on multiple sources to attain a full assessment
(GAO 1996, 13).

Qualitative measures may also be difficult because professional
judgment involves applying conflicting values based on complex,
shifting and unpredictable situations. GAO's Mark Nadel observed that

> . . . . setting clear goals and measuring performance can be difficult. For
> example, programs may face competing or conflicting goals. In child
> welfare, program managers and workers must reconcile the competing
> goals of ensuring the safety of a child, which may argue for removing a
> child from his or her home, with the goal of preserving the family. As a
> result, measuring success may be difficult in some cases. (Nadel 1997)

Furthermore, a decision must be made whether quality should be
measured based on inputs or outputs (Richards 1996, 145). It may be
argued that public services have functioned without such detailed
criteria; therefore, a private provider should also be able to. However, a
private provider may not have a clear stake in the service's success but,
rather, in its stock's success and in projecting an appearance of success

in enriching its shareholders (Richards 1996, 76).

These difficulties do not mean that quality benchmarks should not be set. While it may be impossible to set perfect standards, it would clearly be an abdication of responsibility to set none and thus to make compliance oversight impossible. The proper standard would be to set quality benchmarks to the best degree humanly possible. Where setting qualitative benchmarks is not possible, this may suggest that privatization should not take place. Indeed, some government agencies have decided not to subcontract certain services precisely because it was too difficult to define and measure performance and then to express those standards in a contract (GAO 1997, 17).

Once qualitative standards have been set, bidders must be required to demonstrate they could meet or exceed these criteria. National Association of Government Employees legislative director, Christopher M. Donnellan told a congressional panel:

> Contractors are able to present the agency with a seductive package of cost reductions by reducing the level of services. Inadequate investigations of the statement of work by the agency allow the contractor to achieve this result. In the interwoven environment of a federal installation, any reduction in support or related services will have a domino effect on the agency's capacity to perform. (Hanna 1997)

Guarantees, not mere assurances, must be required. Documentation, not mere statements of good will, is necessary to prevent lowball bids[12] or awarding contracts to those unable to perform the work—either because they do not have the expertise or have submitted such low bids they will lack the means to operate (Sclar 2000, 88). This means bidders would need to provide sufficient detail as to their sources of financing, how they plan to meet the requirements and to back this up with objective evidence that they could meet them. Necessary evidence includes the bidder's past track record in performing similar work and compliance with government environmental and labor regulations.[13] Agencies may want to be pro-active by sharing information as to price, performance and vendor qualifications to ensure competitive prices and to guard against subcontracting to poor performers.[14]

Massachusetts is a model in this area. It demands supporting evidence and requires the head of the agency and the commissioner of administration to certify in writing to the state auditor that:

- the quality of the services to be provided by the bidder is likely to satisfy the established quality requirements;
- the quality is likely "to equal or exceed the quality of services

that could be provided by regular agency employees"

- the quality is provided in the most cost efficient manner;
- the contract cost will be less than the estimated cost based on best practice;
- the contract takes into account compliance with all relevant statutes concerning labor relations, occupational safety and health, nondiscrimination and affirmative action, environmental protection and conflicts of interest; and
- the proposed contract is in the public interest. (Mass. Ann. Laws ch. 7, § 54(7) (1996))

Essential information includes details about the number of workers who will be performing the work. Only in this way can there be an assurance that the bidder is not low-balling the bid and can actually perform the work. Experience has shown that assurances about staffing levels cannot be left to the subcontractor on the assumption that the market will discipline it.[15] The market is more likely to discipline the public who will face losing vital services if the subcontractor cannot perform. In other circumstances, the contractor may provide poor services, but this may go undetected if the client population is incompetent or a despised and powerless group. If information nonetheless leaks out, the government agency will be in the unpleasant situation of being forced to decide whether to terminate the contract or step in and whether it has the ability to resume operation quickly. Wackenhut, for example, was forced to provide more training for guards and recruit additional employees after a local Michigan newspaper reported dangerous conditions in the youth correctional facility it was running, and the state was forced to route youth offenders to other facilities until the problems were resolved[16] (Kolker 2000b). When Educational Alternatives, Incorporated was unable to meet educational qualitative criteria, Baltimore was forced to decide among difficult courses of action to prevent the collapse of the school system (Palast 2000; Green 1997; Thompson 1995).

Establishing uniform and reliable standards and procedures for cost accounting can assure good decision-making, avoid repeating efforts, and avoid the risk of omitting necessary considerations for each bid decision. Establishing uniform standards for ascertaining desired levels of service can provide the same benefits. To the extent possible, these guaranteed levels of service should specify objective and measurable standards and consequences for failing to achieve them. Contracts with performance criteria linked to rewards and penalties provide an incentive for the contractor to do a good job. Contracts also mean that the contractor cannot later claim that it misunderstood what it agreed to (Richards 1996, 145). When a subcontractor can determine the level of services it is to provide and must also pay for additional services it finds necessary, it is given an incentive to find them unnecessary (Putnam 2000).

Some current subcontracting laws require a subcontractor to demonstrate it can guarantee specified savings and higher levels of quality. For example, the District of Columbia requires evidence of a five percent savings (D.C. Code Ann. § 1-1181.5b(a)(1)(3) (1999)). Florida requires a savings of at least 7 percent (Fla. Stat. Ann. § 957.07 (1996)). Arizona does not set a benchmark level but, rather, requires the office in charge of privatization to "develop minimum savings criteria for governing the award of contracts resulting from the competitive government process" (Ariz. Rev. Stat. § 41-2773(5) (1999)).

Mandating specific savings and requiring the subcontractor to demonstrate its ability to achieve them and the means by which it plans to do so is a prudent and reasonable requirement. There is no reason to subcontract unless there is strong evidence better work can be done at less cost. Subcontracting comes with a cost in terms of upheaval, risk and unforeseen consequences. Therefore, there should be a good reason to do it—demonstrably lower cost and guaranteed better service—unless a legislature has decided that privatization must take place for purely ideological reasons without regard to the public welfare. The factors to be considered in subcontracting are complex and cannot be fully accounted for or reduced to objective criteria; thus, even under the best of circumstances, relevant factors may be overlooked. Mandating a margin of demonstrated improvement is a way of taking these problems into account and is, in reality, a way of ensuring that the service is not worse and costs are not higher than before subcontracting. Otherwise, what appear to be cost savings in a bid may turn out to be cost overruns in reality.

Accounting for Public Property

Public assets can take many forms, including structures, buildings, machinery, systems, land, water rights, easements and rights-of-way, improvements, utilities, landscaping, sidewalks, roads, curbs and gutters, equipment, furnishings, information, paying clientele, money and employee knowledge and skills. It will increasingly take the form of intangible property.

Property connected with privatization can take many forms and be affected in a variety of ways. In some cases, subcontractors have been given or lent materials, equipment, buildings or money, either directly or in the form of subsidies. Others may acquire, improve or control public assets. Each of these situations creates problems. Some subsidies to subcontractors are direct and obvious. For example, New Orleans would have incurred more than $526,000 in additional annual costs in its contract to operate certain privatized bus routes had the federal government not awarded a grant to subsidize the subcontractor $1,467,000 each year (Sclar 1989, 26-27). But subsidies can also take less obvious forms. Allowing a contractor to have public property or the benefit of its use, acts as a subsidy to the subcontractor and means the contractor has not submitted a competitive bid, unless it is taken into account in a fair manner. If the subcontract involves the subcontractor's building or acquiring property to perform the service, there needs to be a means of returning the property to the public at a fair price based on the contract expectations. Sclar describes one county that paid 30 percent over the costs of construction to acquire a privatized parking facility (Sclar 200, 104-105). Entrusting assets to a subcontractor may mean the government has made itself unable to take over the services when there is evidence of nonperformance or unsatisfactory performance.

However property comes into a contractor's hands, prudence demands protecting assets the public has purchased. Good practice would require accounting for such items at many points in the process. They must be included in cost accounting, protected from injury or waste, and returned to the public in good condition at fair cost at the end of the contract or upon default or breach and in a condition that does not diminish their value. Otherwise, if no provision for their return is made, a contractor may appropriate, sell, transform or waste assets (Sclar 2000, 114-115).

Before any public assets are entrusted to a subcontractor, they need to be identified, assessed and properly valued. Montana, for example, requires listing all public assets and their intended disposition under a privatization plan (Mont. Code Ann. § 2-8-303(1)(d) (1998); see also Utah Code Ann. § 63-95-104(1)(a)(ii), (b)(ii) (1999)). Depending on the asset, valuation may either be simple or very complex. Many public assets are unique, and this may be true even of buildings. Thus, there may be no comparable properties to use in setting the fair market value (Sclar 2000, 18-19). Some public assets currently generate revenues or may be privatized in order to generate revenues. Privatizing a revenue-generating asset could mean depriving the public of income; in some cases those revenues mean an asset has greater value to the public if it remains in the public sector.

If managing a public asset requires or entails some investment by the subcontractor, the contract must state how those investments will be treated at the contract's end. Depending on the circumstances, the investment could be removed by the contractor or remain with the asset and be returned to the public (and potentially to a later contractor). If the latter occurs, there must be some consideration as to whether the government must reimburse the contractor for the investment and, if so, how to value them, or whether the investment was included in the contract price. All investments will be paid for with public funds, but in some cases they might be seen as more appropriately being treated as the government's investment and in others as the contractor's. In some cases, investments may represent real value added, while in others they may have been useful to the contractor but to no one else. Sometimes improvements or investments cannot easily be separated from the asset. Certainly, parties will act differently during the term of the contract depending on how assets will be treated at its end. Failing to consider and agree how these assets and investments will be treated at the contract's end ensures a complex and costly dispute that may negate cost savings gained from privatization.

A state considering privatization should also decide whether and how to tax the assets and operations of the subcontractor. A failure to tax when private property or businesses normally would be taxed is a hidden subsidy to a private business (*Cf.* Kan. Stat. Ann. § 12-5509 (1995)).

If the contractor invests in the asset, the government should decide whether it will lend the money to the contractor and at what rate, or if it will assist the contractor in achieving favorable rates (*Cf.* Kan. Stat. Ann. § 12-5503 (1995)). If the contractor is allowed to charge the public in connection with the use of the asset, a decision must be made about the use of the money collected and who will be entitled to what portion of it. In addition, will the contractor be able to set the rates unilaterally, or will the rates be controlled, approved or set by the government? If the government pays a service fee to the contractor or becomes obligated financially in other ways as a result of the contract, how will that fee or other money be paid: by a bond, taxes, or otherwise (*Cf.* Kan. Stat. Ann. § 12-5505 (1995))?

Assets that may be entrusted to the subcontractor include not only tangible items such as buildings and equipment but also fees or other money that the subcontractor collects and is supposed to forward to the public treasury. Money is fungible and easily misappropriated. Californians learned this lesson the hard way when in 1997, a contractor left the state park reservation system in shambles as it absconded with $1 million of public money (*Los Angeles Times*, 1998a, 1998b; Steinstra 1998; Ellis 1997). This was a disaster for a state that depends on tourism, and it also forced the state to decide whether to spend resources tracking down the money to recoup it or to write it off as a loss.

When the assets the subcontractor will acquire include information, even more difficult problems arise. Government collects and maintains detailed, personal and confidential information. Considering the sensitive nature of much information government agencies collect, it seems unlikely the public wants it to be marketed to increase a subcontractor's profits. But contractors may feel tempted to use information as the valuable resource it is and sell or rent it. Information, just as with other types of property that has been paid for by tax dollars, should not just be given away to subcontractors. In addition, as with other assets, a decision must be made about its ownership at the contract's end.[17]

While it is easy to know if a tangible asset, such as a building or vehicle, has been returned, ensuring the return of information, and especially electronic information, is more complex. When it is in electronic form, it can also be easily transferred and even broadcast. Unlike most forms of property it can both be returned to the government while being retained by the contractor. Thus, it is not sufficient only to demand its return at the contract's end; the contractor must also be required to divest itself of all copies.

Government may also want to retain physical property and human capital so it is can respond quickly to a crisis. It is easy to see that government may need to keep reserves of oil because it is in the national interest to protect the public from price and supply shocks (Shenk 1995, 16). But more than this, contracting out can mean diminished government expertise in key areas leading to reduced ability to address future problems (Hanna 1997). Maintaining in-house expertise helps set competitive prices, particularly when there is no market; it can be used to test whether a private company can beat the government's price (Shenk 1995). Richard Boris, Virginia Private Prison Administrator observed:

> If you privatized everything, you would have within about 10 years no expertise left within your department of corrections because they hadn't been running. You learn about running prisons by running prisons. That's one of the reasons.

If you ever had to take over a facility—now, this is a jail down in Texas, but I think it's Brazzio (ph) [sic] or whatever where we heard about the inmates from Missouri being beaten and there were videotapes shown on TV nationwide and all—where would you get correctional officers to move in quickly if you weren't running some of your own? (Corley 1997)

It can be just as important for government to have ready access to expertise and even to develop and foster expertise that has no use in the private market or that might even be seen as leading to an inefficient market. A democratic government has a special obligation to serve the poor and disenfranchised who are least able to protect themselves or to use dollars to have an impact on the market. A private market might find it advantageous not to provide services to these populations. Jocelyn Frye, of the Women's Legal Defense Fund, argues that certain tasks, such as setting eligibility requirements, are not appropriate functions for the private sector (Fernandez 1997). These miscellaneous services, expertise and means of providing services can be seen as assets or forms of property which government needs to retain in order to perform its functions.

Worker Protections

Government as employer has always played an important role in modeling employer behavior by providing disadvantaged groups secure jobs at good pay and making it possible for them to do work vital to the social fabric of this country. The impact of these actions goes far beyond the pay packet of an individual worker who might not otherwise have had a job or as good a job or received a living wage or been able to play an important role in promoting public policy. It has also helped secure a more equitable distribution of government services to all members of the community. Workers who receive pay sufficient to support a family will pay taxes, not require government services, and raise children in an environment more likely to lead them to be contributing members of society. Minority workers may have greater understanding or sensitivity to their communities' needs and may literally be able to talk the language of disadvantaged parts of the community. They help make a government for the people.

An overly zealous cost-cutter might not see this larger picture and might focus only on costs directly under its control, ignoring those that can be shifted to other parts of the government. Costs may be lowered and profits generated by cutting wages, lowering benefits, using more part time workers or eliminating health insurance. In its 1984 study of privatization in the Los Angeles area, HUD found that the lower costs of private contractors' were explained in part by greater use of part-time workers who were paid no benefits, shorter vacations, less experienced workers, lower-skilled workers, and non-unionized workers (HUD 1984, 16-17, 25, 27, 39, 41-42; Wessel 1995). But can it be said that the lower costs are due to the virtues of competition such as greater efficiency as opposed to being able to do what government may not be able to do—cut wages and benefits? Is achieving cheapness under these circumstances desirable?

To the extent decisions about subcontracting ignore factors other than the discrete cost of a job, they may end up costing government as a whole more. If, for example, a contractor cuts costs by eliminating health insurance, government on some level is likely to have to assume those costs. This can occur through subsidies to public hospitals, in welfare payments, through the loss of workers who must care for persons made more seriously ill because they delayed seeking treatment, in increased levels of disease in the population, or through other remediation made necessary by a lack of adequate health care.

It is in the government and the public's self-interest that the standard set by government as employer should continue to be the standard even when the private employer is delivering a public service. Colorado includes this as part of its privatization policy (Colo. Rev. Stat. § 24-50-501 (1998); Colo. Rev. Stat. § 24-50-503(1)(d) (1998)). It reinforces this by providing that, in comparing costs, any savings attributable to lower health insurance benefits provided by the contractor shall not be included (Colo. Rev. Stat. § 24-50-503(1)(a)(IV) (1998)). This, then, fixes attention on the question whether a better, more efficient service is being provided or just a cheaper one.

Although taxpayers might initially feel pleased to get value for money, in the sense of getting the service at a lower wage cost, workers willing to work for lower wages may not provide the value more highly paid workers would. Low-waged work is the type of work most prone to frequent turnover (Sclar 1989, 29-30), but many public services need long-term workers with historical knowledge of clients, methods and services (Sclar 2000, 110-111). Wage levels affect and reflect the quality of worker an employer can attract. Wages set too low will cause that quality to deteriorate.

Several states' privatization statutes have attempted to address these concerns. Massachusetts requires that every contract must contain a statement that the subcontractor will comply with anti-discrimination laws and will take affirmative steps to comply with equal employment opportunity (Mass. Ann. Laws ch. 7, § 54(3) (1996)). It further requires a bidder to provide detailed information about the wages that a contractor proposes to pay for each job (Mass. Ann. Laws ch. 7, § 54(2) (1996)). Montana requires privatization plans to include a list of all employees employed in a program and the estimated effect of privatization on them (Mont. Code Anno., § 2-8-303(1)(c) (1998)). This ensures comparable services will be provided. In other words, if a subcontractor were to offer a bid based on an average wage, that wage might be based on lower-paid job classifications than those who would actually be capable of doing that type of work. To remain within the contract price, the employer would have to raise the offered wages but then have too few workers to provide a comparable level of service. Requiring this information reveals whether a service is likely to be provided at the contract price only by relying on too few workers to deliver the service or on unqualified workers.

Some might argue that cutting wages is permissible as an exercise of the market. That is, if an employer can attract workers at lower wages, then that is the appropriate wage and any other is a waste of assets. However, if a contractor is allowed to eliminate health insurance for its employees, and taxpayers have to subsidize the contractor's profits by bearing the cost of health care for uninsured workers, this means that taxpayers are subsidizing an uncompetitive private sector employer. To avoid subsidizing the employer and to ensure it is competitive, the cost of the subsidy would have to be included in the bid so it accounts for all costs of contracting and to make it fully comparable with public sector costs. Making such an assessment, however, would be very difficult. It is simpler to require a continuation of comparable working conditions; thus no subsidy is needed.

Government also needs to consider whether it will permit subcontractors to terminate and replace current workers. Allowing this raises a number of complex issues, including obligations owed to those employees and ensuring continuity of services.

States that have addressed this issue have taken different approaches. Colorado forbids permitting this as part of privatization (Colo. Rev. Stat. § 24-50-503(2) (1998); Colo. Rev. Stat. § 24-50-504 (1998)). Massachusetts requires the contractor to offer employment to qualified public employees displaced by subcontracting, thus discouraging the practice (Mass. Ann. Laws ch. 7, § 54(3) (1996); see also V.I. Code Ann. § 73 (1996)). The District of Columbia requires that any subcontractor who displaces government employees must offer the employees a right-of-first-refusal to employment in "a comparable available position for which the employee is qualified" for at least six months and, during that time, the employee cannot be discharged without cause. If the employee's performance during the six-month transition is satisfactory, the new contractor must offer the employee employment under the contractor's terms and conditions (D.C. Code § 1-1181.5b(a)(3), (5) (1999)). Employees who are to be displaced must be given at least thirty days notice (D.C. Code § 1-1181.5b(a)(8) (1999)). Florida provides that as part of a privatization project public workers may be leased to the contractor. Those employees are entitled to continue as part of the public employees retirement system (Fla. Stat. Ann. § 288.901 (1996)). Montana requires notice be given to an employee and the employee's collective bargaining unit as soon as possible prior to privatization. When twenty-five or more employees are affected, the notice must be given at least sixty days prior to the privatization, and when fewer than twenty-five employees are affected they must be notified at least fourteen days prior to the privatization (Mont. Code Anno., § 2-18-1206 (1998); *cf.* N.J. Stat. § 30, 1-7.4 (1999)). Arkansas requires agencies that intend to lay off employees as a result of privatization to report those impending layoffs to the Legislative Council and the Office of Personnel Management of the Division of Management Services of the Department of Finance and Administration. The report must include details about the number and grade of employees laid off and how the decision was made. Those positions are then removed from the agency's budget for the next two years (1999 Ark. Acts 17).

Many public sector workers are represented by unions, and their right to join a union is protected by state law and sanctioned by federal law and policy. It is therefore inappropriate for government to enter into a subcontracting arrangement that subverts workers' legal rights and de-unionizes the workplace. This means the legislature should provide for the continuation of union representation of those employees if they taken on by the subcontractor. In fact, the National Labor Relations Act achieves just this result under the successorship doctrine (Lincoln Park Zoological Soc'y v. NLRB).

There are many terms of employment in addition to wages, hours, and benefits that are set by regulations or public sector rules. A determination needs to be made whether and how these will apply to the contract. Furthermore, if they do not apply to the contract, is there any reason they should apply to the work when done in the public sector? Is there a reason to free a private contractor from regulations that might impede doing the work more efficiently in the public sector? Doing so is a subsidy to the subcontractor, means the work is not comparable, and subverts legislative judgment that those regulations are necessary.

One concern that might arise as a result of subcontracting is how to ensure that a subcontractor, particularly if it is an out-of-town corporation, is responsive to the community's needs and concerns. Traditionally, city governments have tried to ensure this by imposing residency requirements on public employees. When a service is privatized, those concerns still exist. Consideration should be given to whether the contract should impose residency requirements and, if so, whether they should also apply to all or a percentage of officers and stockholders in the private company (Rudd 1997).

In short, in subcontracting it is important not to subsidize uncompetitive employers, and this end can be promoted by requiring contractors be bound by the same laws as government agencies, such as providing a nondiscriminatory workplace and fair working conditions. Assurances with regard to employees' working conditions may mean requiring the posting of bonds, incentives for meeting and exceeding certain benchmarks, and assessing penalties for failure to meet requirements.

Procedural Criteria—Steps in Making Prudent Subcontracting Decisions

The need to have a special procedure for making decisions about contracting out government services may not be obvious. After all, government at all levels has long purchased private services and goods. However, there are important differences between the types of contracting out done in the past and today. Special interest groups are lobbying vigorously in its favor. There appears to be public support for it, and a wide range of institutions is being considered for some degree of marketization. Certainly, there is a qualitative difference between buying toilet paper from the lowest bidder and providing health care and disease control services. In the former, decisions are much simpler. Price is likely to be the most important consideration, and it is easy to set quality criteria. In the latter, while no one would want waste or overspending, quality and continuity of the service will be far more important and the criteria to be considered are much more complex. It is far easier to assess whether toilet paper meets specifications and to find another supplier if problems with the contractor arise than is the case for health care and disease control. Furthermore, finding a substitute provider for disease control is much more difficult—and the consequences to public welfare more dire—if the subcontractor fails to perform satisfactorily.

Establishing specialized procedures for each step of subcontracting, from soliciting bids to assessing bids to oversight, becomes far more important as requests to subcontract become more common, the criteria more complex, and the consequences of mistakes more serious. Only experienced, sophisticated, and qualified decision-makers can meet these needs. Centralized, established processes can provide accountability and ensure the integrity of the process.

There are a number of necessary steps involved in deciding whether to subcontract. How they are divided is a matter each governmental unit must decide based on its own needs. They could be assigned to one entity that would have complete responsibility for subcontracting, or they could be subdivided among different bodies. The decision to subcontract should consider whether the organization's goals are more efficiently achieved in one body or by distributing them to more narrowly specialized bodies. Other considerations are whether oversight of the decision-making process is more effective with one body or by having separate agencies acting as checks on one another and whether quasi-legislative or quasi-executive roles are better kept separate or integrated. Finally, the entities need to conform to the existing state governmental structures.

Alaska provides an example of a privatization body with a very broad agenda. Its Commission on Privatization and Delivery of Government Services has an extensive, sophisticated and flexible mandate (1999 Alaska Sess. Laws 62; see also Ga. Code. Ann. §§ 36-86-4, 45-12-178 (1996); GAO 1997:2). It requires addressing the question of how to most appropriately deliver a service: to study existing services and determine whether they are more suitably delivered by federal or state government, the public or private sector, or consolidated public agencies. To achieve these ends, the Commission is to review and evaluate other states' policies and recommendations; solicit public comment; review Alaska's policies and procedures and identify whether state functions could be more efficiently and effectively provided by other means. Other means of providing services that must be considered include transferring them to the private sector, local government, regional service organizations or the federal government; retaining them at the state level; eliminating them; agency consolidation or other efficiency changes; or a combination of these (1999 Alaska Sess. Laws 62).

The basic functions of a privatization body, regardless of where such a body is located, should include: 1) proposing regulations, 2) identifying potential functions to subcontract, 3) collecting information,

4) assisting an agency in instituting best practices to establish a baseline, 5) drawing up bid specifications, 6) receiving bids, 7) taking evidence and testimony relevant to the decision, 8) deciding whether to subcontract and, if so, which bid to accept, 9) negotiating the contract, 10) exercising oversight, 11) terminating or renewing contracts, 12) prosecuting breaches and other misfeasance, and 13) reporting periodically to the legislative oversight committee.

Proposing Regulations

If there are to be detailed substantive guidelines, some entity will have to promulgate them. It might be that the legislature would enact highly detailed statutes, specifically spelling out those guidelines after hearings. On the other hand, it is not unusual for a legislative body to enact more general statutes, delegating the duty to be more specific to an agency. In other words, this responsibility could be part of a privatization body's duty. This decision will depend on the degree to which it is desired to subject these decisions to more or less politicized decision-making and whether there is a desire to delegate responsibility to an expert body. Deciding whether delegation is even appropriate will, of course, depend on each state's administrative agency laws and state constitution. Even if the body does not have the power to regulate, it might provide useful expertise in advising the legislature on future enactments.

Arizona, for example, charges its office of management and budget to design standardized methodology for how the state identifies and evaluates state functions to subcontract (Ariz. Rev. Stat. § 41-2771(1) (1999)). It also charges this office with determining if future competitive contracting with the private sector and other state agencies is in the best interest of the state. Thus, the legislature has ceded to this office responsibility not only for identifying services to privatize and to make the decision but also to establish the procedures and guidelines. The same office also reviews petitions forwarded to it by the private enterprise review board (Ariz. Rev. Stat. § 41-2773(6)(d) (1999)).

Identifying Potential Functions to Subcontract

Government agencies can take either an active or passive role in initiating potential privatization. A body can play a relatively passive, almost judicial role that involves only weighing whether to consider subcontracting based on requests by others and on the record others have created. It takes an active role if the body is charged with itself initiating an evaluation of functions to be privatized. The Kansas Board plays a passive role. It initiates a study of the government function and whether it should be or remain in the private only sector after it receives a request from the public or from government employees to do so (Kan. Stat. Ann. § 75-3739(4)(a) (1996)). In contrast, Arizona is an example of a body that plays a highly active role. However, it does this with a strong tilt towards promoting privatization. For example, its legislation declares: "the state's fiduciary responsibility to taxpayers [is to encourage] value in the provision and delivery of state services by identifying and pursuing opportunities for increasing the use of market forces in the delivery of state services, while preventing unfair competition between state agencies and the private sector" (Ariz. Rev. Stat. § 41-2772(A) (1999); Ariz. Rev. Stat. § 41-2773(1) (1999); see also Utah Code Ann. § 63-55a-3(1)(b) (1999)).

Most states that take an active role assume a more neutral stance than does Arizona. They focus less ideologically on identifying potential functions to subcontract by using criteria based on cost and quality. For example, Mississippi's Joint Legislative Committee on Performance Evaluation and Expenditure Review prepares a report on the privatization after analyzing all areas of state government to identify programs and services that could be performed by the private sector at lower cost or greater efficiency. It is charged to consider a wide range of outcomes, including contracting out, competitive bidding and the sale of state assets (Miss. Code Ann. § 27-103-209(2) (1998)). In contrast, Montana uses a two-way process. The legislative auditor is required to identify subcontracted programs that could be administered more cost-effectively directly by the public agency as well as the reverse (Mont. Code Anno., § 2-8-304(1) (1998)). In addition, "[m]embers of the public, elected bargaining agents or employee representatives, elected officials, legislators, and agency directors may submit to the legislative audit committee a request to review programs being conducted under contract by an agency that may be administered more cost-effectively directly by the agency" (Mont. Code Anno., § 2-8-304(2) (1998)).

The role a body is to play should affect its the structure. The more active a body is in seeking out functions to subcontract, the better it is to have a separate body decide whether to subcontract. A body that both seeks out bids and decides whether to subcontract faces either a conflict of interest or the appearance of a conflict. It cannot credibly decide whether to subcontract in instances in which it has initiated the process for fear of capture and actual or perceived lack of impartiality. Even the appearance of bias can have a negative effect on the body's performance and public acceptance of its decisions.

Collecting Information

A more in-depth analysis of the existing functions needs to be made both as part of the process of initiating the decision to consider functions for subcontracting and as a vital part of actions once that decision is made. This ensures information is gathered that permits assessing qualitative and cost criteria. Information plays a vital role at multiple steps in the process.

Louisiana provides an example of the kinds of information sources to be sought and also provided during the privatization process. Its legislative auditor is required to:

1) Evaluate the basic assumptions underlying any and all state agencies and the programs and services provided by the state to assist the legislature in identifying those that are vital to the best interests of the people of the state of Louisiana and those that no longer meet that goal.

2) Evaluate the programs, policies, services, and activities administered by the agencies of state government and identify overlapping functions, outmoded programs or methodologies, areas needing improvement, and/or programs amenable to privatization.

3) Evaluate the impact, effectiveness, and cost-effectiveness of all state agencies and of their programs, services, and activities.

4) Evaluate the efficiency with which state agencies operate the programs under their jurisdictions and fulfill their duties.

5) Evaluate methods agencies use to maximize the amount of federal and private funds received by the state for its programs in order to ensure that the people of Louisiana receive a fair share of the taxes which they pay to the United States government and to provide for the effective efficient use of private resources.

6) Evaluate the management of state debt.

7) Evaluate the assessment, collection, and application of user fees.

8) Make recommendations each year relative to the programs and services the various state agencies provide as well as recommendations for elimination of or reduction in funding for agencies, programs, or services based on the results of performance audits. Such recommendations shall be submitted in a report to each member of the legislature no later than February fifteenth each year.

9) Make annual recommendations to the appropriate oversight committees of the legislature and the Legislative Audit Advisory Council as to amendments to statutory and constitutional provisions that will improve the efficiency of state government, including, if appropriate, recommendations concerning the reorganization or

consolidation of state agencies.

10) Evaluate the methods used by each agency in the estimation, calculation, and reporting of its performance, and evaluate the actual outcomes of each agency's performance with regard to its performance indicators as defined in R.S. 39:2. (La. Rev. Stat. § 24:522(C) (1999))

The state auditor is to be assisted in this task by state agencies charged with developing measurable performance criteria, including program goals and objectives (La. Rev. Stat. § 24:522(D) (1999)).

Public policymakers might want to emphasize other sources of information to be considered at this preliminary step, but Louisiana provides a useful look at the range of informants that can be used, the information to be collected, and the types of reporting to be generated for the purposes of assessing whether privatization is being properly pursued.

Assisting an Agency in Instituting Best Practices to Establish a Baseline

When Joni Mitchell observed, "You don't know what you've got 'til it's gone," she was not advocating this as good practice. It cannot be known whether contracting out will improve public services without first establishing a baseline understanding of the existing service. This needs to take place early in the process, before bids are requested. Therefore, privatization should not be consummated until an agency knows what it has, what it costs, and how it operates.

As discussed earlier, determining existing cost is not easy. It must include computing all costs connected with providing the service and assessing current workload and performance standards. It must consider the target population and the service's role in and for that community. Under the best circumstances, undertaking this process can have highly beneficial effects. Self-analysis is essential to determining how to reorganize in order to provide the most efficient, economical service (Sclar 2000, 71). This step alone, even before and without subcontracting, will take the agency towards the twin goals of improving service and saving money.

Some might argue that self-analysis is unnecessary, that an inefficient service does not deserve a chance to lift its game and that, in any case, contracting out by itself will bring market forces to bear and result in improved service. Indeed, some state legislatures do not require such a process, and they essentially forbid it by mandating privatization instead (*See* Ariz. Rev. Stat. §§ 46-300.01, 46-342, 46-343 (1999)).

Such an inflexible mandate, however, is not in the public's interest. If this step is skipped, it will never be known whether subcontracting saved any money or provided better service because there will be no comparison with the highest level achievable by the public sector. When a self-analysis and reorganization occurs, any bid that outperforms that best practice will clearly be an improvement.[18] Oklahoma recognizes that the current employees are essential to the process and provides that before state services can be privatized the agency must allow its employees the opportunity to submit proposals to improve the agency's operations and efficiency (OK. Stat. § 595.3 (1999)).

Although the public agency's management and employees will have valuable information about its functions, they will almost certainly need help in rethinking the organization. An expert body which has experience in reorganization and which takes a facilitative role can perform a particularly valuable role. Thus, the process of study and reorganization should not simply be left to the agency that performs the work; rather, it should be done under the guidance and assistance of an expert body, in particular by a centralized privatization body. On the other hand, such a body cannot perform a reorganization without the help of the public workers who understand the nuances of their jobs. In other words, the best reorganization is a two-way process.

Drawing Up Bid Specifications

Once a reorganization has taken place and cost, quantity and quality standards have been ascertained, the bid specifications can be drawn up. Massachusetts, for example, requires the preparation of a specific written statement of the services proposed to be the subject of the privatization contract (Mass. Ann. Laws ch. 7, § 54(1) (1996)). The statement must specify the quantity and standard of quality of the services, and it is then used as a basis for soliciting competitive sealed bids. The statement, which is a public record, is also transmitted to the state auditor for review. Bids are solicited from any and all parties. This means that public workers are allowed to bid on continuing to perform the work.

Although it should not be controversial, some argue that state workers should not be allowed to bid on performing their own work[19] because they have an advantage as a result of being familiar with the work. Another potential advantage that is frequently cited is that government works are inherently cheaper because government does not pay taxes. Gary D. Eugebretson, President Contract Services Association of America, testified:

> For the private sector, the playing field is not, and likely never will be, entirely level. This is primarily due to the fact that, despite several recent laws, the government does not have cost accounting systems in place to provide accurate or reliable financial data on workloads, does not have to pay taxes, and the methods by which it computes its overhead rates are not comparable with those of industry, nor does the government "pay" for infrastructure (e.g. buildings and land). In addition, the government does not face, either qualitatively or quantitatively, the same risks as a commercial contractor (e.g., on issues relating to termination for default, absorption of cost overruns or potential Civil False Claims penalties). (Eugebretson 2000)

The better reasoned view is that the public welfare depends on public workers' being allowed to bid. This is the only way to ensure the bidding is truly competitive and that the taxpayers' interests are protected (GAO 1997). Privatization proponents are not the only ones aggrieved by the processes undertaken at this step. American Federation of State, County and Municipal Employees Vice-President Joe Flynn complains that in fact much work that should be competitively bid under Office of Management and Budget (OMB) Circular A-76 is privatized with no competition. He argues:

> Currently, most work is contracted out without public-private competition by even DOD—the agency often held out as the champion of OMB Circular A-76. Although DOD contracts out in excess of $60 billion annually, public employees have no chance of competing for almost all of that work even with the Pentagon's increased reliance on the circular. For example, according to an Army study, only 16,000 contractor jobs out of the service's entire contractor workforce of 269,000 were competed through OMB Circular A-76. (Flynn 2000)

If the market is the force that improves service, then it is essential to ensure a market exists. The optimum situation to promote competition and better service cannot be subcontracting to one bidder but, wherever possible, finding as many bona fide bidders as possible. The difference between promoting real competition as opposed to transforming a public monopoly into a private monopoly appears to have been overlooked by many (see, Kan. Stat. Ann. § 12-5508 (1995)). There is nothing about a monopoly, including a private one, which is likely to involve competition and thus promote the improvements sought.

However, the reality is there may not be many bidders. In many cases, the service may not be one provided by private contractors. Allowing the current workers to bid on their own work helps create the best semblance of a market in this situation. If competition is supposed to ensure that services are provided in the most efficient way, it makes no sense to exclude government workers or any group which otherwise meets the substantive criteria from bidding. Furthermore, excluding the workers who have been providing the service stacks the deck and all but ensures that the work must be contracted out, even if no one could do the work better or at lower cost. It seems unlikely most taxpayers would favor contracting out a service if this means higher cost, but this may well happen if current workers are barred from bidding.

There is one other way in which allowing public workers to bid on their work is essential to promoting the public interest. If workers know they are unable to bid and that the work will be contracted out, they are unlikely to be willing participants in efforts to rationalize and improve their agency's function. In contrast, if they know they have a period of time in which to make their agency the best possible and that if they do so they could retain the work, they have a strong incentive to put every effort into the process. The beneficiary will be the public.

Indeed, this is already recognized by some jurisdictions. The District of Columbia requires that any solicitation for proposed contracts must include information concerning a procedure by which the current government employees may bid on the contract (D.C. Code § 1-1181.5b(a)(6) (1999)). Massachusetts has a detailed process of which workers' bidding is a part (Mass. Ann. Laws ch. 7, § 54(4)-(5) (1996)).

Receiving Bids

Once bid specifications are released, an agent must be designated to receive the bids and process them. Their processing should be a multi-step process. Later steps are considered below, but preliminary functions should include basics such as checking that all requirements have been complied with and initial investigation and assessment of the undertakings set out in the bid to prepare the bid for the decision-making process.

Taking Evidence and Testimony Relevant to the Decision and Deciding whether to Subcontract and, if so, Which Bid to Accept

Although different steps, these two share many common procedural concerns, making it more economical to consider them together. It goes without saying that decisions to contract out government services should not be made lightly to ensure there is no interruption of service or poor quality. Despite this, many legislatures stack the deck by limiting the information to be sought or which is allowed to come before the decision-maker; by limiting those included on the decision-making body to less than all interested parties—or even to limit it only to privatization partisans; and by limiting those to be consulted. Taking any of these actions will prevent optimum decisions from being made.

How open should the process of subcontracting be? On the one hand, decisions could all be made out of the public's sight. On the other, the process could be an open one complete with notice and an opportunity for all interested parties to be heard. Montana, for example, provides that before privatizing a program, a privatization body is to prepare a privatization plan and release it to the public, any affected employee organizations and the legislative audit committee at least ninety days before the proposed implementation date. Thirty days later, the legislative audit committee must conduct an open hearing at which public comments and testimony must be received. Fifteen days later, the legislative audit committee is to make public a summary of the hearing results and the committee's recommendations (Mont. Code Anno., § 2-8-302 (1998)).

Certainly providing for sufficient notice, a timely public hearing or other public input in a manner that allows a meaningful opportunity to be heard will help ensure prudent decision-making that takes into account a wide range of needs and issues. To some degree, though, the question of how to receive information (by public comment, hearing, or otherwise) will depend on the nature of the service being considered for privatization and practice within the geographical area.

Information

Some states limit information to be considered to that in favor of privatizing. Utah's privatization board, for example, is charged with the responsibility of maintaining communication with and access to information from entities promoting privatization, but it is not charged to seek out information and maintain access to those opposing or neutral on privatization (Utah Code Ann. § 63-55a-3(1)(e) (1999); see also Va. Code Ann. § 9-342 (1996)). The better practice is to require considering a wider range of evidence, including evidence that does not support privatizing. Montana, for example, requires a privatization plan to include "a narrative explanation and justification for the proposed privatization" and:

1) an estimate of cost savings or additional costs resulting from privatizing the program, compared to the costs of the existing, nonprivatized program, including cost of inspection, supervision, and monitoring of the contract and costs incurred in discontinuing a contract.

2) estimated economic impacts of privatization on other state programs, including public assistance programs, unemployment insurance programs, retirement programs, and agency personal services budgets used to pay vacation and sick leave benefits.

3) increases or decreases in costs and quality of goods or public services.

4) changes in workers' wages and benefits. (Mont. Code Anno., § 2-8-303(1)(e)-(i) (1998))

Colorado specifically requires considering "the consequences and potential mitigation of improper or failed performance by the contractor" (Colo. Rev. Stat. § 24-50-503(1)(f)(I) (1998)). It also requires considering whether privatizing a particular service would mean the improper delegation of a state function (Colo. Rev. Stat. § 24-50-503(1)(f)(II) (1998)).[20]

These kinds of information should certainly be included, as well as anything relevant from any interested parties.

The Decision-Maker's Qualifications

If a state or other governmental entity is considering a program of contracting out government services, it is essential that it establish an expert body whose job it is to assess bids and ensure that all procedural and substantive requirements have been met and to create a uniform process. The officer of that entity must have sufficient skills and access to information to be able to assess complex financial and technical specifications and bids. Finally, the decision-maker must also be impartial and be seen as impartial. Alaska's chief procurement officer, for example, is part of the partially exempt service and must have "at least five years of prior experience in public procurement, including large scale procurement of supplies, services, or professional services, and must be a person with demonstrated executive and organizational ability" (Alaska Stat. § 36.30.010 (1999)).

Again, the legislative body should consider at which points such an office would become involved in the process. If the functions are divided among different entities, these would appear to be relevant basic qualifications for each of them. States with existing programs vest this function in a number of different offices. Alaska, for example, vests the power in a commissioner of administration and chief procurement officer who is given power over procurement of supplies, services, and professional services (Alaska Stat. § 36.30.005 (1999)). To some extent, these reflect political or practical views and the variety of duties vested in the body. The wider the range of responsibilities vested in the agency, the harder it will be to find people competent to perform them all. On the other hand, if they are divided among different agencies, some means of ensuring coordination must be established.

The Membership of the Decision-Maker

One way to ensure access to the best information possible is to include a wide range of interests among members of the body which makes the decision to privatize. The interests represented should include those for and against privatization, public employees, public employee unions, agency clients, the community at large and business interests. Almost as important as which interests are included is the appointment process.

Utah's Privatization Policy Board, for example, is composed of thirteen members who serve staggered four-year terms. The governor is directed to appoint: 1) two senators and two representatives, one each from each political party; 2) two members to represent public employees whose names are to be recommended by the largest public employees' association; 3) one member from state management; 4) five members from the private business community; and 5) one member representing education. (Utah Code Ann. § 63-55a-2 (1999))

In contrast, Arizona's legislative mandate to privatize the administration of its welfare program is reflected in its "works agency procurement board." Its membership makes it unlikely to have anything other than a pro-privatization bias. The statute states that it is "established to receive proposals and award a contract by January 1, 1999 with a private entity for implementation of the Arizona works program." The board, whose members are appointed by the governor, is to be made up of nine members who will be: "1. The director of the department of economic security; 2. Two people from the private sector who have procurement experience; 3. Two representatives of a major employer in this state; 4. Two representatives from community based organizations; and 5. Two representatives from small businesses in this state" (Ariz. Rev. Stat. § 46-343).

Mississippi charges the body, which is to review government

functions for privatization, to consult with representatives from the private sector (Miss. Code Ann. § 27-103-209(2) (1998)). This is a highly skewed and limited directive. Missing from both Arizona's and Mississippi's boards are important interested parties, including representatives of employees, unions and welfare recipients.

Alaska's eleven-member commission not only has a far more representative composition than does Arizona's, its members are more likely to represent the interests they are appointed to serve. Rather than being appointed by the governor, they are selected by the interest group. The Commission includes: 1) one member of the senate appointed by the president of the senate who serves as co-chair; 2) one member of the house appointed by the speaker of the house who serves as co-chair; 3) one member appointed by the Alaska Municipal League; 4) two public members appointed by the president of the senate, one of whom shall be a representative of a Native corporation; 5) two public members appointed by the speaker of the house, one of whom shall be a representative of a Native corporation; 6) one member appointed by the Alaska State Chamber of Commerce; 7) one member appointed by the American Federation of Labor-Congress of Industrial Organizations; 8) one member from the minority caucus of the house appointed by the speaker of the house; and 9) one member from the minority caucus of the senate appointed by the president of the senate. It further expands the input it receives by appointing an advisory council to assist it in carrying out its duties. (1999 Alaska Sess. Laws 62)

Compare this with Kansas. Its five-member performance review board must include at least one member with cost accounting experience, and no more than three members may be from the same political party. The governor appoints them to a term of four years, subject to confirmation by the senate (Kan. Stat. Ann. § 75-3759(2)(a) (1996)).

It might be argued that there is no point in including public employees on such a board because they will only be obstructionists. However, Representative John L. Mica (R-Fla), chairman of the House Government Reform and Oversight Subcommittee on Civil Service, contends that federal employees should have the chance to challenge cost-saving claims (Hanna 1997). Challenging claims in such a context and forcing claimants to upgrade information is a vital way to protect the public interest, as important as providing the information initially.

Indeed, it needs to be recognized, admitted, and taken into consideration that the process of subcontracting is a very political one, with strong feelings on all sides of the spectrum. And, public employees eager to save their jobs are not the only ones whose position might have some elements of predictability. This means that, while it is important to have the involvement of partisans who will actively advance their views, if the process is to be free from charges of corruption, incompetence or favoritism, it is vital that the office and officer charged with making the decision be isolated from political pressures and be seen as impartial. Alaska attempts to do this, in part, by providing that its chief procurement officer is appointed for a term of six years and may be removed by the commissioner of administration only for cause (Alaska Stat. § 36.30.010 (1999)).

The importance of these firewalls was demonstrated by experience in Massachusetts after it passed a subcontracting law in 1993 designed to save the taxpayers money, ensure continuity of service, and prevent graft and corruption. The "Pacheco law" requires that the state can only contract out government services if it is given written evidence that demonstrates subcontracting will save money and improve the quality of service (Wallin 1997).

In 1997, Massachusetts State Auditor Joe DeNucci, the individual charged with administering the law, refused to approve a plan to privatize transit routes because there was no evidence that privatizing them would save any money or improve service. DeNucci explained that the private bidders had had "significant performance problems" in other cities, that the plan called for giving them heavy subsidies, that the bid had failed to include important information concerning how the work would be performed and that it distorted other information. DeNucci's decision was bitterly attacked by those who argue that public services should be contracted out despite evidence that contracting out would cost more and provide less. Before the Pacheco law was passed countless public services had been contracted out without any requirement to prove this was in the public interest. DeNucci's critics wanted to return to those earlier practices. (Jordan 1997; DeNucci 1996)

Utah has taken the initiative to avoid these problems by forbidding certain interactions (Utah Code Ann. § 63-95-102(7) (1999)). These include forbidding certain individuals, such as officials of the quasi-governmental entity, lobbyists, and entities in which those individuals hold business interests, from receiving specified benefits under privatization contracts. The forbidden benefits include compensation from a quasi-governmental entity if it is conditioned in whole or in part on legislative or executive action related to privatization; assets of the quasi-governmental entity or its successor; and certain forms of compensation related to privatization (Utah Code Ann. § 63-95-103

(1999)). Violations can result in felony, misdemeanor and civil penalties (Utah Code Ann. § 63-95-105 (1999)).

Thus, avoiding real conflicts of interest and the appearance of partiality by the actual decision-maker must be made a priority. Decision-makers must be protected from undue pressure or temptation. Given the very nature of the undertaking, there are enormous opportunities for corruption, insider dealing, and the like—all of which mean the decision-making process is corrupted and the public welfare is compromised for someone else's benefit. (Sclar 2000, 105-106)

Negotiating the Contract

Once a decision is made to award a contract, someone must undertake the negotiations. Many of the concerns involved at other steps also apply here, including ensuring expertise, avoiding partiality, specifying standards, providing oversight, and including details as to terminating the contract. Virtually all elements discussed above concerning substantive issues come into play in negotiating the contract.

One point that should be emphasized is that contract negotiation involves highly specialized skills. This is particularly the case in subcontracting. The negotiators must be pessimists in the sense of trying to predict and provide for all potential errors, defaults and misfeasance. These special skills are the type that should lead the legislative body to consider who best can perform this critical role. Although the public agency would have expertise in the nature of its work, it would not necessarily have expertise in negotiating and preparing contracts. In addition, it is likely to be seen as biased. Thus, while it certainly should be available for consultation on technical matters, care should be taken as to just what role it plays in the negotiation process. This, again, is a job that may better be carried on by a centralized body, but not necessarily the same people who made the decision to subcontract. Making the decision to subcontract and assessing the information require different skills than negotiation.

By the time this stage has been reached, and especially if layoffs are contemplated, the affected employees' union must become part of the process. Failure to do so is a breach of the duty to bargain and may result in the state's liability for back pay, benefits and reinstatement of the workers. (Brenner 1997)

Exercising Oversight

A recent GAO study found oversight to be the weakest part of privatization (Nadel 1997). Joshua Wolf Shenk reports that the Department of Energy (DOE), which relies more heavily on the private sector than any other agency, has a miserable record. Eighty to ninety percent of its budget is paid to private companies, but the agency has only 20,000 civil servants and anywhere from 7 to 10 times that number of employees on private contract. At the Rocky Flats plutonium plant, Rockwell International poured toxic and radioactive waste into the ground, and stored more in leaky metal drums, leaving 108 separate waste dumps and toxic solvents in the earth at 1,000 times the acceptable concentration. DOE officials gave Rockwell $27 million to clean up five "ponds" of radioactive and hazardous waste it had helped create. Rockwell bungled the procedure and the GAO estimated cleaning the pond would take until 2009, at a cost exceeding $170 million. Astonishingly, Rockwell received a rating of 90 out of 100 and $26.8 million in bonuses. The DOE's management is so thin and the burden of oversight so heavy that there is virtually no accountability. "[W]hen government contracts out, the lack of qualified managers—or sheer incompetence—often leads to a surrender of authority to the shadow government. With time, as contractors make the crucial decisions and develop expertise and authority, the government starts working for the contractor instead of the other way around. Decisions that should be the province of elected officials fall into the hands of hired guns" (Shenk 1995).

One committed to the marketplace as a fully self-regulatory mechanism might argue that there need be no oversight of subcontracted work. However, the ideal market conditions of competition with many small buyers and sellers and complete information are unlikely to exist for most types of governmental functions. Therefore, some method of ensuring compliance with contract terms is necessary. Some entity must be charged with ensuring that subcontracted work meets the agreed-upon criteria during the term of the contract as well as assessing whether the express performance benchmarks are adequate or need improvement (GAO 1997, 16-18). Oversight must take place on a regular and frequent basis to ensure work is done, quality is maintained, and an early warning systems is in place in order to prevent a subcontractor's absconding or engaging in financial improprieties. If oversight is not frequent and regular, problems that could have been prevented may become serious and even irreparable.

The skills needed by such an oversight body include contract auditing and performance monitoring. Contract auditing ensures that payment is made only as provided in the contract, while performance monitoring ensures services meet quality standards (GAO 1997, 17). The oversight body can take many forms, depending on the situation. It can, for example, be lodged within the department whose work was subcontracted, if that is appropriate and can best assure proper performance.[21] The department has the advantage of expertise and can thus more accurately assess whether the contract terms are being carried out and also make recommendations for improvement. Another oversight candidate would be the same body that decides whether or not to subcontract. Both will understand most fully the context in which the subcontracting is taking place. Certainly, in all but the simplest contracting out situations, the assessment criteria are many and complicated and often cannot be understood outside their context.

However, there are important reasons why neither should be the overseer and certainly not the sole overseer (GAO 1997, 18). Most fundamentally, the overseer must be able to assess fairly whether the contract terms have been met. Agency capture, cronyism, and even conflicts of interest between an agency, the entity which decided to subcontract, and a subcontractor must play no part in the oversight process. Sclar describes the many ways in which Massachusetts' decision to subcontract road maintenance suffered from assessment by an interested party (Sclar 2000, 28-46, 119-121). Massachusetts wanted to prove the program was a success. As a result, it allowed costs to be deferred to later years and shifted to inappropriate accounts, public sector workers to be pressed into service to perform the subcontractor's work, public assets to be lent to the subcontractor, supervision costs to be understated, and important parts of maintenance left undone. In addition, many tasks did not meet the requirements of the contract, no benchmarks or baselines were created, and, worst of all, the oversight body set up by the executive branch was not motivated to find any fault with the subcontractor's performance.

An oversight body should have distance from individual contractors so it is not tempted to slant its findings. The public has to rely on the probity of the oversight body because, unfortunately, it is easy for it to slant its findings as to whether the complex criteria are met and to escape detection. It is important for the oversight agency and the body deciding whether to subcontract not to be ideologically motivated, the captive of ideologues with rigid positions on privatization, or have other motives not to perform oversight solely in the public's interest. One example of this is hiring contractors to monitor each other's performance. While it may appear that their natural competitiveness and expertise would make them especially good critics of each other's performance, in fact they may extend "professional courtesy" to one another, hoping a kind eye will later examine their own operations. ACES President Geraldine Jensen testified:

> Another expensive and worrisome practice is when states hire one vendor to monitor another vendor's performance. For example: Massachusetts paid Lockheed Martin IMS $13.2 million for a computer system and paid Maximus $1.9 million to monitor the Lockheed Martin IMS contract. Oklahoma paid PSI $1 million for work on the computer and then paid Maximus $102,000 to monitor PSI's contract. We are concerned that having one vendor monitoring contracts of another, gives both vendors an incentive not to complete the contract on budget and on time. Cost overruns and not meeting deadlines has been a repetitive problem found with vendors on state automated child support enforcement systems. (Jensen 1997)

The oversight process must give the public easy access to lodge complaints, ask questions and get responses. Jensen further testified:

> ACES members in all of the states utilizing private companies for child support enforcement report problems identifying that a private company was responsible for action on their case. They also experienced the inability to find the government agency responsible to monitor the private company to voice a complaint of problems with the contractor. Attached to my testimony is a list of states who have contracts with PSI, Maximus and Lockheed Martin IMS. Families who report little or no action or incorrect action on their cases by private vendors cannot determine who to hold accountable. If the family is lucky enough to be able to determine which government agency hired the vendor, the state agency often tells them there is nothing they can do because the case has been turned over to a private company. (Jensen 1997)

If the public cannot find someone to whom problems can be reported, then no one can be held accountable and subcontracting may fail to provide a superior service or even the same level of service.

Terminating or Renewing Contracts

Contracts may terminate either when the contract's end date is reached or when there is a breach. Some states mandate a term limit. Massachusetts, for example, limits the term of privatization contracts to five years (Mass. Ann. Laws ch. 7, § 54(1) (1996)). There are both advantages and disadvantages to such a scheme. On the one hand, it may be disruptive to have a periodic reassessment of the initial decision to subcontract and change in provider. On the other, a fixed date means all parties know there is a chance of nonrenewal. Most affected would be the subcontractor who will be unable to feel it has gained a sinecure and will be impelled to perform at a level it feels will make renewal likely. A specific termination date requires the government to assess whether the subcontracting met the goals set for privatization. In addition, having a specific date lets the government be ready for a graceful transition to another contractor or to recapture the work.

Some privatization experiments do fail, and when they fail, the government must be prepared to intervene, preferably through well thought out contract processes. Disastrous results can occur when there has been no forethought given to handling failures. When Educational Alternatives, Incorporated failed to meet its contractual undertakings, the City of Baltimore was suddenly faced with the prospect of having to step in to ensure public education would still be provided. (Palast 2000; Green 1997; Thompson 1995)

Prosecuting Breaches and Other Misfeasance

An enforcement mechanism must be part of the contract negotiations, and it might include an array of litigation or para-litigation devices, including mediation. Failures to comply may also be dealt with through a combination of existing criminal or civil penalties and contract remedies built into the subcontracting arrangement. Deciding what to include in the contract and what remedies to seek in the case of a breach or misfeasance means assessing what range of existing statutory remedies are sufficient and whether additional ones specific to subcontracting this service are necessary.

Periodic Reporting

Oversight requires regular reporting to the legislature, executive and public. Reporting should be on at least an annual basis—or more frequently if necessary. More frequent reporting is advisable where sensitive matters are handled, large sums of money are involved, or the interruption or degradation of service would be especially serious. The Arizona welfare privatization program requires bimonthly reporting with a comprehensive report at the end of the first year which includes: 1) whether the vendor has met the contract's requirements, the goals of the program, and the requirements of its performance bond; 2) the fiscal impact of Arizona works implementation; and 3) the impact of Arizona works on placement of recipients in paid employment, reduction of caseloads, and development of community partnerships (Ariz. Rev. Stat. § 46-344 (1999)). A more comprehensive report is required in the fourth year of the program. In addition to the type of information in the annual report, it includes a survey of client satisfaction (Ariz. Rev. Stat. § 46-345 (1999)).

Conclusion

Must privatization take place with none of the guidance that experience and common sense can provide? Must people be victimized by scams, failures, and cost overruns in the name of privatization? The answer is no. Government can protect a community's assets and services, save taxpayers millions of dollars, and prevent graft and corruption if political leaders only have the wisdom and courage to learn from privatization mistakes and successes. This is a case in which being wise requires hard work and the courage to stand up for what is right in the face of true believers who preach a simple and seductive message: the market will provide. Political leaders need to remember that most taxpayers are not true believers. What they want is good quality, stable public services at reasonable cost—not subcontracting to satisfy an ideology or to help a subcontractor make a profit.

Hard-line ideology, simplistic theories and slogans make it easy to draw lines and make decisions, but not necessarily good ones. A politician may believe she can better advance her career by making an unsupported claim to have saved the taxpayers money by contracting out public services than by explaining the nuances of market theory—and she would probably be right. News stories announcing subcontracting and projected savings are more likely to be trumpeted and to make front page news while reports of subsequent problems are more likely to be hushed up and buried. An agency that privatizes may be able to cut costs but only by quietly and less visibly shifting them to another agency or to the public. As tempting as it is to avoid the complex decisions necessary to decide whether a specific service is best provided by the public or private sector, public officials know they have a responsibility not to waste public money, and they certainly do not want to be accused of causing waste by making ill-advised, poorly considered decisions.

Notes

[1] An earlier version of this article was delivered at the Law and Society Conference, Miami Beach, Florida, May 26, 2000.

[2] The author gratefully acknowledges Neil Buchanan for his thoughts, Max Sawicky for early suggestions on approaching this issue and research assistant, Shawn Arend, for his assistance.

[3] The author speaks from personal experience. During a transaction, the author discovered that the reservation worker who was assisting the author had never even been to California. This individual was unable to answer any questions about the parks and their facilities. The services provided were only the most basic, that of making reservations, and on this occasion the business was unable to satisfy the needs of park visitors.

[4] The decision in *Professional Engineers* gives the details of a campaign to contract out this work in defiance of law— not only once but also again and again.

[5] These problems are not isolated. The privatized Denver bus costs increased 100 percent in same period publicly run lines increased 11 percent (Sclar, 2000, 87). In 1991, for example, Los Angeles canceled a five-year vehicle-repair contract after an audit showed it had cost $1 million more than expected and had not performed up to the contract's standards (County Cancels, 1991; Pasternak, 1989b; Pasternak, 1989a).

[6] Illinois has banned privatizing prisons: Sec. 2. Legislative findings. The General Assembly hereby finds and declares that the management and operation of a correctional facility or institution involves functions that are inherently governmental. The imposition of punishment on errant citizens through incarceration requires the State to exercise its coercive police powers over individuals and is thus distinguishable from privatization in other areas of government. It is further found that issues of liability, accountability and cost warrant a prohibition of the ownership, operation or management of correctional facilities by for-profit private contractors.

[7] Elliott Sclar provides a different breakdown differentiating public services from private markets (Sclar, 2000, 23-28).

[8] Indeed, the Freedom from Government Competition Act (S 314, HR 716) which was introduced in 1997 implicitly recognized this. It required federal agencies to procure all goods and services from the private sector except for those which are inherently governmental functions or deemed critical to national security, as well as those where the private sector fails to meet government needs or where the government provide the best value. (Flynn, 1997).

[9] Terminating a contract may not be a useful remedy if the contractor would prefer that to having to meet the contract's requirements, as was the case with EAI. Craig Richards, et al. *Risky Business: Private Management of Public Schools* 154 (1996).

[10] The State of Michigan awarded a contract to Correctional Medical

Services Inc. of St. Louis, a company that was under indictment for causing the death of an inmate in North Carolina. The company hired a doctor, who lost his license to practice in Michigan for having sex with his patients, to run statewide psychiatric services in Alabama. An opinion from an Idaho judge stated that care provided by the company had been more like "physical torture than incarceration" in the case of one inmate. (Putnam 2000)

[11] A similar problem can occur when comparing costs from one state to another. Geraldine Jensen, President of the ACES, contended that Lockheed Martin IMS was receiving seven times as much money in Maryland as Virginia for doing exactly the same type of work. She asked: "Who is responsible for monitoring contracts states have with private vendors" (Jensen 1997). Jensen may be correct in her concern, but different states, even adjacent ones, may have different legislative, economic and other considerations that mean the work is not exactly the same.

[12] *See* Colo. Rev. Stat. § 24-50-503(1)(a) (1998). Initial bidding on privatized Denver bus lines involved lowball bids which quickly doubled (Sclar 2000, 86, 109-113).

[13] Wackenhut has received contracts to run prisons, despite having compiled a troubled record (Kolker 2000b).

[14] see note 11 above

[15] When asked about including this information, OMB's acting director for management, G. Edward DeSeve, responded that it was too expensive to collect this information and, in addition, there was no need to. He said that he was not willing to "assume that the competitive process required under the current federal acquisition regulations is insufficient to establish appropriate prices and quality levels." (Hanna 1997)

[16] One additional problem was that the facility was housing inmates older than seventeen in violation of state law. However, Michigan's contract with Wackenhut guaranteed an occupancy level that was apparently difficult to meet with available offenders below that age (Kolker 2000b); see also (Kolker 2000a).

[17] If, for example, a private company is contracted with to publish statutes and judicial decisions and then claims it owns copyright in the material, the government may find itself embroiled in litigation to establish its ownership rights.

[18] For a detailed analysis of such a process, see (Sclar, 2000, 130-150).

[19] The Freedom From Government Competition Act S.314, introduced in 1997, and S.1724, introduced in 1996, required federal agencies to procure all goods and services from the private sector with limited exceptions, including where goods or services were inherently governmental functions or critical to national security, where private sector practices failed to meet government needs, or where the government could provide the best value to the taxpayer. It thus virtually mandated contracting out. (Flynn 1997; Stevens 1997; Stevens 1996).

[20] "Asked by Senator David Pryor (D-Arkansas) if other government

contractors were performing 'inherently governmental functions'—deciding
where and how to spend taxpayer money and exercising judgment on matters of
due process—a GAO report responded with a resounding yes. In just a few
agencies it found dozens of examples" (Shenk, 1995).

[21] Arkansas requires that when state functions of the Division of Youth
Services are privatized the contract must include a performance evaluation
outlining a method for evaluating services provided and identifying the
contracts goals and performance indicators and how the state agency intends to
evaluate the services. In addition, the Department of Human Services must
make an annual report to the legislature concerning the subcontractor's
performance. (1999 Ark. Acts 525)

Chapter 2

Political Context: The Republican Party and the Unigov Experiment

George W. Geib

Any interpretation of the Goldsmith years in Indianapolis/Marion County must take into account the decline in voter turnout support he encountered in his second mayoral elections. In his first race for mayor, Goldsmith matched some of the best of the totals posted by his predecessors, winning the 1991 election with 110,545 votes. But from there the decay in support became apparent. In his 1995 re-election race his turnout was only 65,868 votes. Something had clearly caused a loss of support among base Republican voters of the county. Several factors undoubtedly contributed to this decline. This chapter explores one of them: Goldsmith's failure to work effectively with the leadership of the local Republican Party organization, the Marion County Republican Central Committee [MCRCC]. In several ways he failed to conform to a set of political expectations developed a quarter century earlier by MCRCC leaders in the formative years of the Unigov Era. An understanding of that earlier period can thus contribute to an understanding of Goldsmith's later, troubled relations with his party.

One path to understanding MCRCC participation in local affairs is the recognition that it was one of the few functioning, effective party machines remaining in the United States. Long after most areas had shifted to a politics based upon candidate mobilization of interest groups, MCRCC was capable of recruiting approximately 5,000 to 6,000 party volunteers to staff precinct election boards, phone and greet registered voters, and conduct other aspects of grass-roots campaigning.

Any review of the published literature on Indianapolis government since the late 1960s will demonstrate the central role that Unigov played. That label is commonly used to describe the partial consolidation of city and county government responsibilities that was adopted and implemented under Mayor Richard Lugar. Under Unigov a number of functions previously performed by county officials, such as roads and drainage, were joined to the city under a mayor and council elected countywide. Because certain other functions, such as public safety and schools, maintained their older jurisdictions, the Unigov experiment is usually studied in the context of economic development—where the new system's effects were most clearly felt.

Although less studied, a similar analysis could be applied to party affairs. Those who participated in the Unigov years were in substantial agreement that Lugar's actions and accomplishments were made possible in part by a remarkable series of partisan political changes within the Republican Party between 1964 and 1967. As C. J. Owen and York Willbern observe in their 1985 study, *Governing Metropolitan Indianapolis*, "the extent and intensity of Indiana's political partisanship facilitated the Unigov reorganization."

Unlike many other cities of comparable size, Indianapolis had both a history and a practice of strong party organization. The Unigov laws had arisen out of a context that included a strong focus upon building both a volunteer organization and a voter base that would sustain the Republican Party as it gave direction to the new Unigov systems.

Several elements marked that partisanship. There was a strong factional component that had surfaced in a highly publicized struggle for party control in 1966, and it lent a status approaching folk legend to the successful Republican Action Committee of that year. There was a heavy emphasis upon team building that included a number of active Republican townships and ward clubs that were regular venues for GOP public officials. And there was a strong element of patronage that extended not only to salaried and hourly wage jobs in government offices, but also to board and commission appointments and to vendor contracts.

As a result, concerns of the party were often included in decisions of the elected leaders of Unigov. Striving to maintain a sense of "mandate," a term they often used, they routinely asked the electoral implications of policy and depended upon patronage sources to assist in mobilizing wavering portions of that electorate. Using modern polling techniques, it was common for GOP leaders to present their case in ways that reflected and reinforced public opinion. The GOP leaders concluded that the conservatism characteristic of many party activists was not a central voter concern—because the Indianapolis community as a whole and the majority faction in the local Democratic Party were perceived as also being conservative. Republican voters, if anything, disliked much of that conservative image. They identified it with a generation of World War II veterans whose leaders had developed an embarrassing record of corruption when they ruled the state in the 1950s. Many voters thought it stodgy, or saw it as an impediment to economic growth and social progress in their community. The phrase "empowering boosterism" can be used to describe this resultant mind set, which sought to attract voters by pledging a local government that would mobilize economic growth, seek innovative funding for public projects and bring youthful and honest leaders to power for the purpose of making the community a success.

In the process, the GOP avoided several alternatives that their surveys suggested enjoyed potential electoral appeal. The emotional hot buttons of the period were found in the public schools, then headed for court-ordered desegregation or what many outside critics called "forced busing." But the GOP judgment was that schools, whose boards were elected on a non-partisan basis, fell outside the responsibility of party politicians—and, they should remain there because they posed problems for which there were few local solutions. The GOP had nothing bad to say about the most visible member of the school board, Richard Lugar, as he wrestled with options plans in the high schools. But the GOP put such issues aside to be used only if needed in emergency.

That spirit best manifested itself in the subsequent reorganization of Indianapolis city/county government in 1969-1970. It is well to keep in mind that the party reformers' early victories in 1966 and 1967 did not themselves produce Unigov. Instead those early victories brought individuals to power (in both party and government circles) who moved on to create Unigov. For Unigov to be adopted, several additional steps needed to be implemented.

First, the Indianapolis Republicans needed party control of state government. Indiana is a state with little tradition of "home rule" for counties and municipalities; most significant changes require state legislation passed by the General Assembly and signed by the

Governor. That required the GOP to await the results of the 1968 election when their party captured the Governorship and a Republican majority in both houses of the legislature.

Second, the Republicans needed to capitalize upon the strong role of the Marion County delegation in that legislature. Here they were helped by the complexities of reapportionment in the 1960s. Indiana had resisted reapportionment between the 1920s and the early 1960s, producing a marked imbalance toward rural areas of declining population. When this situation ended in 1962, the ensuing struggle over reapportionment had resulted in the decision to allow the Marion County delegation (8 senators and 15 representatives) to be elected at-large within the county. This winner-take-all situation, assured a very strong voice for the Republican county delegations chosen in 1966 and 1968, and allowed them to trade off their support on other issues for a controlling voice in local affairs.

Third, the GOP needed to create the sense of broadly based support for its proposed legislation. The first proposals for city-county government appeared quietly in the press, but they were soon followed by the creation of a series of citizen committees, which provided both advice and legitimacy for the emerging Unigov law that was passed in 1969 for implementation in 1970. As one leader put it, "We sold Unigov the way we sold the Action Committee."

Fourth, the GOP needed to demonstrate public support for their initiative. The GOP treated the 1971 election as the test vote, running Lugar (who had won in the old city in 1967) county-wide against Democrat challenger John Neff for mayor, scoring a victory of almost two to one and capturing two-thirds of the new City-County Council. Critics would later object that no separate referendum was held on Unigov, but the lopsided nature of the 1971 vote makes it hard to believe that such a referendum could have been defeated.

It also invites us to look at that formative period between 1966 to 1971 and inquire if we can draw insight into the Unigov era from the people who served as its principal creators. Unigov's formative years have produced a number of interpretations—some designed to illuminate the events of the era, others to advance partisan agendas that appeared later. Several deserve comment.

One viewpoint holds that the people who created Unigov were reacting, chiefly if not exclusively, to the issue of race. This is a common theme of critics, often set forth in lawsuits over apportionment that appeared after 1980. It has the appeal of raising an issue that is often in public consciousness, but the disadvantage of confusing public perceptions with leadership motives. Unigov operated at several levels, and race was generally a peripheral issue at each. It was a peripheral issue for several reasons. First, it was not clearly linked to the problems of urban image and urban growth that drove most Unigov thinking. The images that drove the Unigov visions were those created between 1930 and 1960 by an earlier generation of civic leaders who failed to manage or improve the physical form of the city. Such a view could incorporate minority community problems, but, as one commentator has put it, referring to such items as the appearance of local housing and businesses, "Indianapolis is a city that masks its poverty well."

Without a major race riot or boycott to draw attention to racial tensions, the issue appeared primarily in the debates over school desegregation. Those debates failed, in turn, to conform to partisan alliances. If anything, the debate was driven by the agenda of the Indianapolis Chamber of Commerce. The Chamber was consistently a champion of open housing (arguing that any person should be free to sell property to whomever they chose) and of improved schools for all (arguing that urban growth required better work force training for all citizens). Such a viewpoint caused those within the Chamber connection to resist the circle of individuals that had formed around Judge John Niblack to control the school board. When critics of the Niblack circle appeared, as they did with Richard Lugar, the Chamber was generally supportive of the alternative, not the status quo. Such considerations helped to mute the question of race, and to make it difficult to argue it was, in fact, a driving force behind the Unigov initiative.

A second viewpoint approaches the Unigov debates by arguing that the rivalry of city and suburbs was a central feature. In its usual form, the argument portrays the Unigov creators as suburban politicians eager to annex the city for the economic benefits that would accrue. Race is involved mainly because the minority population concentrated in the pre-Unigov city; however, the dominant theme is the tax base. This viewpoint has more going for it. Unigov was the product of astute politicians who were highly attentive to voting behavior. As astute men and women, they knew that the conventional wisdom of American politics placed the Republican vote among the more educated and affluent, and those voters were located in the suburban areas. The Unigov act had the effect of freezing the boundaries of the old city as they were in 1969; this made it easy to watch changing demographics and voter behavior both inside and outside those fixed boundaries. The record is instructive. It shows that Republicans carried the suburban areas in each Unigov election, and they drew the bulk of their district council members from those areas. But it also shows that, with the exception of 1975, the GOP also carried the old city for mayor and won enough council seats within the old city area to control the police and fire service district.

A more interesting feature of this suburban/urban confrontation was the way it impelled each of the parties to rethink their traditional political bases. Aware that they needed an urban vote base, the GOP concentrated upon several strategies to win support within the old city. Some, as might be expected, were traditional appeals to patronage, offering city/county employment to political supporters.   Largely abandoned only in the 1980s, the "two percent club" was an early manifestation of this style.   Other initiatives were more innovative, often tied to appeals to young professional interests: downtown housing, initiatives for new construction, historic preservation and downtown entertainment venues (from festivals to nightclub districts).

The most interesting of the outreach appeals, however, is often forgotten. It was the attempt to reach out to the older elites who were in danger of losing power to the young men of the Unigov movement. These groups are often overlooked in the story, if only because they had often shunned publicity and avoided holding the formal reins of political power. This "old money" Indianapolis represented a coalition of interests drawn from the business and the social realms, whose venues were the genteel clubs and societies of the older city.

Influenced strongly by the events of Depression and World War II, they looked with disfavor upon most types of reform that appeared to threaten an established order. Many had reached the conclusion that Indianapolis, as a community, was unable to achieve its booster expectations. Some were advocating alternatives in which they engaged in various types of withdrawal from the process of community. Forgotten today, their most important initiative in the 1960s was the proposal for an Acropolitan Center. This was to be a cultural and residential district, generally along the northern banks of White River from 30th to 56th Streets, to which the cultured minority of Indianapolis would withdraw to achieve among themselves what was unachievable in a larger community.

The sense of withdrawal and failure that permeated the Acropolitan ideal goes far to explain why the Unigov group rejected its proposals. Yet, as cultured and involved individuals, the Unigov leaders knew they would ultimately need the support of this older elite if they were to govern. Much of the Unigov experiment is really a story of relocating the Acropolitan center downtown (as they would do with many institutions such as the Indianapolis Symphony) and of winning the children of that older elite to the causes of downtown.

To do so involved a potentially important realignment. Many of those older leaders were active Democrats, albeit practicing a style of Bourbon democracy that was becoming increasingly unfashionable in the era of the Great Society. If they were won to the cause of a renewed Indianapolis, they might be lost to the Democrat party they had often dominated in the past. It was the battle for this group that was probably the most important that would be fought out in the 1970s.

Such struggles, remembered or forgotten, were an important part of the background of the Goldsmith era. Like most politicians of his generation, Goldsmith rose to power in a city governed by Unigov and colored by its myths and legends. Given the youth of many of the Unigov founders, one might expect a substantial portion to remain active in the Goldsmith years. Some certainly did, witness City-Council President Beurt SerVaas or State Senator Lawrence Borst. But beyond a few visible leaders, the turnover in both office holders and party leaders was considerable, producing an overwhelmingly post-Unigov generation under Goldsmith. A 1991 survey of Republican Party precinct and ward leaders showed that over 75 percent of such activists had first registered to vote after the implementation of Unigov, and that the ages of party activists were an average of three years younger than the age distribution of the county's voters. If the founding years of Unigov played a role in the Goldsmith years, they did so more by example than by memory. Certainly the emphasis upon effective forms of economic development continued.

But interesting differences appeared in the party realm. The bottom line is that Goldsmith's break with his organizational party base was not something that could easily have been predicted. He had first worked in the GOP in an organizational capacity, organizing volunteers in the mid-1970s to conduct apartment house canvassing and voter registration. In 1978 he had sought his first elective office when he ran for Prosecutor against Andrew Jacobs, Sr., father of the long-time Democrat Congressman. The elder Jacobs had served in Congress in the 1950s, and he was currently completing a term as Superior Court Judge during which he had built a no-nonsense, law-and-order reputation. In early polling Goldsmith trailed nearly three to one. But he enjoyed several advantages, including active GOP organization support, as he focused upon the administrative problems of the Judge's court, and eventually won by a narrow margin.

Goldsmith remained in the good graces of the party for the next decade. He was easily re-elected Prosecutor in 1982, a year that saw his party lose the Sheriff's race for a second straight time. By 1986, the party's urgent desire to recapture the Sheriff's post led many to urge Goldsmith to run for a third term and thus provide stability and support for the ticket. He probably would have done so anyway, keeping his name in the public eye as he waited, first in line, to replace Mayor William Hudnut III. But appearing to respond to a draft made for good press, and Goldsmith accepted the party endorsement.

Similarly, in 1988, Goldsmith found himself in a position where he could easily present himself as a champion of an embattled GOP. Here the problem was a disastrously mismanaged campaign for Governor. The Democrats were running Evan Bayh, then Indiana Secretary of State; the Republicans were offering John Mutz, then Lieutenant Governor. In searching for a campaign issue, the Mutz advisers fastened upon residency requirements when they discovered that Bayh had long resided with his father, a former United States Senator, in Washington. A lengthy and highly publicized court fight ensued as the GOP sought to disqualify Bayh. The attempt failed, and the effect upon public opinion was devastating. Massive numbers of voters perceived the issue as one of fairness, and Mutz's support numbers dropped by half—at one point falling to 25 percent of the electorate. At that point the party convention assembled to name a Lieutenant Governor candidate (the two officers are elected together on a single ballot in Indiana), and needed a visible office holder with an image of honesty.

The choice fell upon Goldsmith, and the party's electoral support numbers began to rebound. The rebound was not great enough to win Governor, but it was enough to suggest that Goldsmith enjoyed positive voter support. Goldsmith, moreover, built a significant portion of his campaign around visits to county party leaders around the state. His detractors would later note that he might have been positioning himself to be considered for appointment to the United States Senate seat being vacated by Dan Quayle (running successfully for Vice President with George Bush). The seat later went to Dan Coates, but Goldsmith emerged with no serious negatives and remained positioned to succeed Hudnut as Mayor in 1991. In 1991 the party organization continued to find no serious public fault with Goldsmith, and he was easily elected with a vote total similar to those enjoyed by his predecessor in the 1980s. Then the changes came. In 1992 and 1993 the new Mayor and his party's leaders had a serious and permanent falling out. It came suddenly, and for many it was very unexpected.

To understand the break between the Mayor and party leaders, it is necessary to look at the sources of possible friction. They come down to two main elements: personal management style and patronage decisions. The former probably drove the latter. In style, Goldsmith preferred to concentrate power in his own office rather than disperse it, as his predecessor had often done, in the hands of department directors. In substance, he preferred to privatize functions and thus eliminate public positions of power. There was less and less room in such a world for an alternative source of power such as the GOP organization. For a time, Goldsmith toyed with the approach of setting up a parallel structure that would eventually replace the party's precinct structure, and then he considered simply replacing the key party figures. Condemnations of party leaders for lack of support began to appear in the local press, and a quest began for a replacement county chairman.

The battleground of this quest would be the 1993 Republican county convention held every four years, as the law required, to choose the officers of the county Republican committee. The law required that the vote for chairman be cast by the precinct committeemen elected in 1990 (and by their appointed vice committeemen); the law also allowed the county chairman to fill vacancies in those precinct positions. The county chairman whom Goldsmith targeted was John Sweezy, who had held the position since 1972. Sweezy was a manager by both education and experience, a quiet team builder with a wide circle of supporters, and a firm believer in the importance of the continuity that effective party structures can provide. He took pride in his success record, which included almost 99 percent of all primary elections and 83 percent of all general election races in the county under his tenure. Sweezy took umbrage that Goldsmith chose to forget the support that the local party had provided during the nearly two decades of his leadership, and he chose to seek another term.

It created a challenge that Goldsmith could not master. Sweezy, with his appointive power in the county convention, could name loyal supporters to vacant positions. Many local elected officials, appreciative for support in past primary and general elections, rallied to their chairman. Richard Lugar, in whose mayoral administration Sweezy had served as a department director, endorsed his ally at a key moment. Sweezy was eventually re-elected without convention opposition.

In the process, however, Goldsmith had made Sweezy's ability to provide future support more difficult. Goldsmith later acknowledged one aspect of this when he began to discuss the ways in which the elimination of middle managers in city government had made it more difficult for the party to recruit middle managers for election campaigns. The number of such individuals, however, was actually rather small, perhaps no more than a dozen. The real problems came in two other areas: board appointments and fund raising. Much of the work of Unigov was done by a host of boards and commissions, many of them appointed by the Mayor. Traditionally, the members of these bodies had been drawn heavily from the ranks of the GOP volunteer base. But in 1992, Goldsmith began making appointments mainly from outside the party base, severing a key linkage of party and government.

At the same time Goldsmith moved to reduce the fund raising capability of the county party. It was not a new development. During the 1980s, growing criticism of several traditional bases of party financial support had caused other Republican officials to eliminate two important sources of funds: the control of the county license branches by county chairmen and the collection of political donations (the "two percent club") by state workers. Goldsmith built upon this by largely eliminating contributions by city workers and then holding a series of one-on-one meetings with leading donors in an effort to shift their contributions to him. By 1995, the funding of the county party was barely two-thirds of what it had been in 1991.

Whether all this served Goldsmith well is debatable. The main argument for advantage is negative: the absence of campaign issues related to mayoral association with party leaders. The main argument for disadvantage is electoral: the dramatic decline in voter turnout in 1995 and 1996. One thing is certain—the desire to empower the Republican Party as a tool for empowering government had ceased to resonate on the 25th floor of the City-County Building.

Chapter 3

Governing a City: Thirty-Two Years

Sheila Suess Kennedy

Introduction

As Mayor of Indianapolis, Stephen Goldsmith followed two widely acclaimed public managers: Richard Lugar and William H. Hudnut III. Any assessment of Goldsmith's tenure must be made in the context of the city they bequeathed him. Some historical background on Indianapolis is necessary to understand the significance of Unigov, and accomplishments of the Lugar and Hudnut administrations subsequent to its enactment.

As William Blomquist (1994) has noted, municipal reform movements throughout the United States during the last decade of the 19th century and first decade of the 20th focused on removing, or at the very least separating, politics from public administration. The stated goal (which sounds eerily familiar) was to make government more "businesslike." In Indianapolis, this led to the creation of a number of separate municipal departments, each governed by a board of individuals who were appointed, rather than elected. The theory was that appointive boards would be insulated from political influences.

If citizens were unhappy with the action of a department, it was virtually impossible to know whom to blame. It was even difficult to know whether a given department had jurisdiction over any particular neighborhood, since some of the commissions that were established were county-wide, some were limited to the boundaries of the city, and others presided over separately drawn "districts" that coincided with neither. The problem was exacerbated by the proliferation of separate municipal corporations that also had varying jurisdictions. Each of these entities determined its own policies, levied its own taxes and issued its own bonds. As Blomquist has observed:

> Voters did not elect these board members, and no elected government official or body could appoint a majority of them. Board members served staggered terms with vague or no provision for removal, so local voters could replace their city council members, mayor, county council members, and county commissioners without necessarily changing the governance of important local government services. (Blomquist 1994, 92)

In 1959, when the League of Women Voters published a pamphlet with the telling title, *Who's in Charge Here?*—the only honest answer would have been "no one."

Richard G. Lugar

In 1967, Richard G. Lugar, who would serve two terms as mayor before becoming Indiana's longest-serving United States Senator, defeated the Democratic incumbent, Mayor John J. Barton. Lugar and his political mentor, L. Keith Bulen, proceeded to lay the foundation for the modern city called Indianapolis. Their most significant accomplishment was the passage of Unigov, which largely consolidated the dizzying patchwork of overlapping and separate departments and brought most of the municipal corporations under the control of a strong mayor and a combined City-County Council.

Unigov has been criticized on a number of counts: as a political, rather than a governmental, coup;[1] as incomplete (schools and public safety were two of the most notable exclusions); and as a way of giving suburban voters "representation without taxation" (Grunwald 1998). Blomquist has suggested that the city's undeniable successes since 1968 may owe more to the "extraordinary leadership" of Lugar and Hudnut than to Unigov's structural changes. It is incontrovertible, however, that Unigov ushered in an era of vastly improved accountability and cohesion, and gave the Mayor both an expanded tax base and far more control over the management of the city than had previously been the case. The efficiencies realized simply by eliminating duplication—consolidating separate legal departments, purchasing departments, buying insurance and the like—allowed Lugar to reduce the civil city tax rate in each of seven consecutive years following passage of Unigov (Lugar 1974), while actually expanding city services.[2]

If presiding over the creation and political passage of Unigov must count as Lugar's most important accomplishment as Mayor, it was by no means his only one. Lugar's administration marked the emergence of a modern mayoralty for Indianapolis (Walls 1994). Lugar reversed the city's previous antipathy to federal grants and ushered in a far more activist role for the city's administration. Construction projects were initiated: not just improvements to infrastructure, but public works that began the downtown renaissance that would play so large a part in the Indianapolis story. Under Lugar, Indianapolis saw the renovation and rededication of the historic City Market and the development of Market Square Arena and Merchants Plaza. City partnerships also enabled construction of a Hilton Hotel on Monument Circle, in the heart of downtown.

Despite these projects, Lugar could not fairly be characterized as a "bricks and mortar" administrator. His prior political experience had been as a school board member, and he retained a lively interest in education issues along with a due respect for the prerogatives of the elected Board of School Commissioners. Lugar was an early supporter of the women's movement and an increased political role for women; he also had significant personal relationships with the city's African-American leadership. Those relationships contributed to the relative calm enjoyed by Indianapolis during the major civil rights disturbances in other American cities during the late nineteen-sixties and early nineteen-seventies. However, it would be misleading to conclude from the absence of civil strife in the form of riots and similar eruptions that Indianapolis did not have race relations problems. It did, and it does.[3] Lugar acknowledged their depth in a speech given April 9, 1968, shortly after the assassination of Martin Luther King. In that speech, he spoke out strongly against racism, and pledged the city to a broad array of ameliorative measures (Lugar 1968).

Like Hudnut and Goldsmith after him (all three were Phi Beta Kappa), Lugar took a highly cerebral approach to the task of governing. A former Rhodes Scholar, he was widely viewed by his peers and media commentators as an authority on municipal issues. In 1970, he was elected president of the National League of Cities, a post that Hudnut would also occupy.

In Lugar's Second Inaugural Address, he outlined his belief in the efficacy of government and his goals for Indianapolis:

> Four years ago, we inaugurated an administration dedicated to
> governmental reform and renewal of the human spirit in our city . . . . The
> basic domestic issue in the United States is the definition of the "real city,"
> a living and vital group of people and physical resources which make
> sense in terms of political structure, economic progress, environmental
> quality, and transportation and communications, and a shared sense of
> community idealism and values . . . . As individual human beings, we are
> meant to find our spiritual destiny in community, in living, achieving, and
> suffering together with other men and women . . . black and white people,
> rich and poor people, people of all ages and lifestyles must have a voice,
> must meet together with the privileges and resources of the real city of
> Indianapolis and not various geographical fragments, must elect a Mayor
> and Council who are responsible and accountable, and who must produce
> constructive results or be removed by the voters. (Lugar 1972)

During his second term, Lugar increased his emphasis on urban
redevelopment, and worked diligently to establish Indiana University
Purdue University at Indianapolis (IUPUI) as a major university for the
city. When the privately owned bus company went out of business, he
created Metro, the public transportation agency, to insure the
availability of public transportation for those who relied upon it. In
1971, well before such commissions were commonplace, he created a
municipal Task Force on Women.

When Lugar left office, the National Council on Municipal
Performance had named Indianapolis "The City with the Healthiest
Economy in the Nation." The city's bond rating was triple-A (a rating it
would maintain throughout the Hudnut and Goldsmith administrations).
In 1974, the city ranked sixth in the nation in the total value of new
building permits issued (Walls 1994). Less tangible, but no less
important, there was an emerging sense of city momentum and civic
pride.

William H. Hudnut III

It fell to William H. Hudnut III to build a major city on the new
possibilities Lugar had created, and in an unprecedented four terms as
mayor, he did so. Hudnut was a Presbyterian Minister turned
Congressman.[4] His administration was shaped in large measure by his
personality and by his conviction that the mayor should formulate
policy and then delegate and monitor its implementation. Hudnut's

tenure has been called, aptly, "entrepreneurial," and was characterized by collaboration, conciliation and inclusion (Hudnut 1995).

Hudnut was not afraid to raise taxes or to issue bonds for projects he felt to be important, and he was tireless in his efforts to explain, promote and "sell" those projects to the public. He was, however, a careful fiscal manager. Indianapolis maintained its triple-A bond rating, and he took a "pay as you go" approach to fiscal management (see Chapter 6). Sinking funds were employed to insure timely payment of debt, and deficit financing was not considered an option. Hudnut had two ironclad fiscal rules: 1) never allow the aggregate of the sinking funds to exceed 10 percent of the total budget; and 2) never allow indebtedness in any of the taxing districts to exceed 50 percent of the allowable maximum (Hudnut 1999).

Despite Goldsmith's later claim that there was a twenty million dollar budget deficit when he assumed office, the "deficit" was evidently calculated without taking separate, earmarked funds, notably the sinking funds, into account. When those funds are included, the city actually had a *surplus* of $300 million (Armstrong 1999). During Hudnut's tenure, city employees were given training in public administration, and strict fiscal review policies were put in place for all city departments, supervised by deputy controllers working in the various departments and reporting to the City Controller. An Ethics Board was established and yearly disclosure forms required of city employees, in an attempt to avoid conflicts of interests.

Hudnut created the Indianapolis Economic Development Corporation and the Indianapolis Project to build national recognition for the city and to engage in partnerships with national economic development organizations. His "penchant for coalition building" (Hale 1994, 718) was displayed in the numerous public-private partnerships that characterized his time as mayor. One of the most influential of those partnerships was with an entity called the Corporate Community Council, comprised of chief executive officers of major companies who served as sounding boards and financial advisors, and who were sometimes enlisted to help promote civic projects.

Hudnut also expanded the Greater Indianapolis Progress Committee, which had been created by Barton and adopted by Lugar, using it to interact with and reach out to additional members of the business and civic leadership of the city. Economic and community development—especially the revitalization of the urban core—was the highest priority of his administration. An oft-repeated and favorite line from many of his speeches was the admonition that Indianapolis must not become a "doughnut" with a hole at its center, but should instead be a cookie, "solid all the way through" (Hudnut, 1999).

To encourage downtown development, the Hudnut administration devised a variety of incentive packages, job training programs and infrastructure improvements. These policies succeeded; during Hudnut's four terms, downtown was the site of at least 30 major building and beautification projects (Hale 1994, 719). Monument Circle (arguably one of the finest civic spaces in the country) was paved with bricks and received new plantings and lights; Union Station was restored as a festival marketplace (a national fad that was no more successful in Indianapolis than elsewhere, but did save a magnificent historic structure that was so badly deteriorated it might not have been salvageable had more time passed); IUPUI was expanded; and additions were made to the Convention Center. The Hoosier Dome (now the RCA Dome) was built adjacent to the Convention Center, where it doubled as additional exhibition space. A number of new, major buildings altered the Indianapolis skyline. Architecture, planning, land acquisition and financing were begun for the Circle Centre Mall, an enormously complex development that took seventeen years from conception to opening. Hudnut left office just after excavation had begun, and the mall was completed during Goldsmith's first term.

Again, despite the enormity of the physical change to the city, it would be a mistake to describe the Hudnut years in terms of brick and mortar. His concern was for the human ecology, the *livability* of urban centers (Hudnut 1998). Hudnut placed high priority on environmental issues, including beautification of the city. In 1978, Indianapolis became the first city in the country to establish a full-time Environmental Court. He created a Clean City Committee (early ads for proper trash disposal featured the "Hudnut Hook"—a picture of the mayor tossing his trash in basketball-player fashion into a city receptacle) and began an extensive beautification program. In 1984, the city built a state of the art waste-to-energy incinerator. The city also built a sludge handling facility and a wastewater treatment plant, and implemented a sewer maintenance program. By 1992, when Hudnut left office, the city had decreased air and water pollution levels significantly—in several cases, doing better than federal standards required.

Hudnut was a gifted orator and an enormously popular mayor, re-elected three times by very large margins. Much of his appeal was to voters who did not normally vote Republican, but who responded to his highly inclusive approach to municipal governance. His undeniable commitment to the advancement of women and minorities could be misplaced, as with his ill-fated support of an ordinance equating pornography with sex discrimination,[5] but it was best characterized by his defense of affirmative action and his commitment to racial justice.[6]

Hudnut was sometimes referred to as a "cheerleader," in recognition of his consistent ability to engage and motivate a crowd—to make ordinary citizens feel that they were part of the great "adventure" of building a better Indianapolis. One gets a sense of what is meant by a paragraph from his most recent book, *Cities on the Rebound*, which also conveys the essence of his approach to governance.

> The successful city will be led not just by political and business leaders but by a host of concerned citizens who believe in the value of civic involvement. The developer, the planner, the architect; the lawyer, the preacher, the doctor; the banker, the broker, the baker; the seniors, the boomers and the X-ers will all practice the art of "cityship," that is, the art of city-building. Those who answer the call that went out as long ago as the story of the Tower of Babel—"Come, let us build ourselves a city"— will hold the city in their hearts and hands. They will see themselves as partners in building it up rather than tearing it down, responsible stewards of its resources, constructive citizens who believe in civic involvement, leaders who are willing to take risks in order to create positive change . . . The successful city of the future will nurture a cadre of citizen leaders who recognize the peril to democracy of disengagement and who are prepared to walk a second mile for their community's well-being. (Hudnut 1998, 3)

Stephen Goldsmith

Goldsmith represented a significant break with the philosophies of his two immediate predecessors. Political analysts have suggested that his background as a prosecutor may have predisposed him to see issues more in terms of right and wrong, black or white. It is also likely that his policies reflected the rightward drift of the Republican Party (Lugar is far more conservative today, as a senator, than he was as mayor) (Geib 1999). As George Geib, a history professor at Butler University in Indianapolis and long-time Republican Party operative, has noted:

> Goldsmith's [1991] campaign reflected much of the new political emphasis on technology and television, and hinted at an independence from traditional party structures—characteristics of many high-visibility local candidates throughout the country. His campaign spoke to social issues of concern to an increasingly active body of evangelical Christian groups. Goldsmith was also keenly aware of a growing anti-taxation sentiment in the electorate, and campaigned on a platform that emphasized

cost-cutting initiatives using such labels as privatizing and downsizing. Some commentators predicted his administration might represent as important a break with political precedent as Lugar's had in the 1960s. (Geib 1994, 169)

Other chapters in this book address the philosophy and various programmatic initiatives of the Goldsmith administration, and it would be repetitive to engage in extended analysis here. What may be illuminating, however, is to contrast the more salient features of the Goldsmith approach to governing with those of his two predecessors.

Contrasting Approaches to Governing

Governing Visions

Lugar and Hudnut were both highly pragmatic mayors; they articulated substantive goals they wanted the city to reach, and (within the fiscal restraints they set for themselves) were flexible in their choice of strategies for achieving those goals. Goldsmith, in contrast, was highly ideological, focusing his energies primarily on issues of privatization and "marketization." Thus, where Lugar and Hudnut repeatedly spoke of building a city, Goldsmith talked primarily of "holding the line on taxes," "reinventing government" and saving money (Goldsmith 1997).

Political Styles

Hudnut was extraordinarily people-oriented. While Lugar has had a more reserved public demeanor, personal relationships and loyalties have nevertheless defined much of his political career. Both men devoted a great deal of time and effort to party building—raising money for the Republican organization, actively engaging in party activities. Hudnut met one Saturday each month with small groups of precinct committeemen, and he had an aide in the mayor's office whose sole job it was to handle citizen and committeeman complaints about potholes, snow removal or other city services. Goldsmith, on the other hand, resolutely distanced himself from the party organization. He did most of his fundraising in a manner separate from (and, party officials complained, in competition with) the organization (Sweezy 1999). His distaste for socializing is legendary; where Hudnut loved nothing better than working a crowd, Goldsmith made it clear that he considered his attendance at functions obligatory rather than enjoyable. To his credit, he freely admitted the problem. At a race-relations meeting attended by the author in 1998, a vice-president of the local Urban League suggested that some of the problems the group had been discussing might be ameliorated if Goldsmith did not always come to community events, make his scheduled appearance, then immediately leave. "Stay awhile, get to know folks," was the suggestion. Goldsmith smiled and responded, "You might be interested to know that that isn't a complaint exclusive to the black community." The remark elicited appreciative laughter because everyone in the room recognized its accuracy.

Management Styles

Both Lugar and Hudnut believed that the mayor's job was to set policy, then delegate. In the Goldsmith administration, very little was delegated. The mayor's office insisted upon signing off on virtually everything, even minor change-orders on construction projects. This insured control, but critics argued that it did little to build institutional capacity or foster efficiency (Gilmer 1999; Annee 1999).

Policy Implementation

Lugar and Hudnut placed great emphasis on collaboration and consensus building. In contrast, the Goldsmith administration was widely criticized for being technocratic and "top down." Goldsmith disputed this characterization and cited "customer surveys" his administration conducted (Goldsmith 1999). Lugar and Hudnut did not refer to citizens as "customers." Their term was "stakeholder" or "shareholder." The difference in language is subtle, but telling; customers are certainly important, but shareholders own the store.[7]

More significantly, when his "customers" held views contrary to those Goldsmith believed to be correct, those views were simply ignored. In *The Twenty-First Century City*, Goldsmith (1997) details his efforts to prevent the Indianapolis-Marion County Public Library from issuing bonds to build new branches and bring existing facilities into compliance with the Americans with Disabilities Act. What he did not mention were the numerous public meetings the library board held during the year preceding that decision. The meetings were extremely well attended, and not a *single person* testified against the bond issue or the expansion. When the bond petition was filed, there was no remonstrance. The public, the media, the school systems, even the Chamber of Commerce publicly supported the library proposal. Despite this overwhelming evidence of "customer" opinion, Goldsmith fought tooth and nail against the project, arguing in his book that "customers" who want the movie "Die Hard" should buy it in a store and not expect libraries to make it available at taxpayer expense (Goldsmith 1997, 81).[8]

Responsiveness

Lugar and Hudnut presided over administrations notable for their inclusiveness: there was outreach not only to women and minorities, but also to the primarily Democratic constituencies of the disadvantaged, neighborhood organizations and labor unions. (For example, cabinet members in the Hudnut administration were expected to attend the monthly meetings of the Mayor's Neighborhood Advisory Council and the Mayor's Labor Advisory Council, where they were to be prepared to respond to questions or complaints.) There was even a police liaison to the gay community during Hudnut's last term—a significant outreach for a Christian minister at that time. In contrast, Goldsmith's initiatives were largely tailored to the concerns and priorities of the religious conservatives who were so important a part of his political base. So where Hudnut established a Campaign for Healthy Babies to educate poor pregnant women and teens about nutrition and child care (Hale 1994; Sawyers 1999), Goldsmith embarked on a campaign to "re-stigmatize" unwed motherhood (Goldsmith 1997, 175).

Philosophy of Governance

Perhaps the most obvious difference between Goldsmith and his predecessors can be found in their rhetoric about the role of government. Lugar and Hudnut both articulated a confidence that government could make people's lives better. As Republicans, they promised fiscal restraint and a limited role for government. But both were willing to use government as a tool to collective ends; both would fairly be characterized as activist mayors. Goldsmith's philosophy was sharply in contrast with that confidence in the ability of government. A sample of quotes from his book is illustrative:

Not only are cities on skids, but in most cases government itself has been the grease that hastened the pace of decay (Goldsmith 1997, 5).

Because government simply confiscates dollars rather than competing for them, government managers do not get good information about their customers' needs and wants" (Goldsmith 1997, 67).

Welfare as a social program must cease to exist (Goldsmith 1997, 96).

Welfare subsidizes bad behavior (Goldsmith 1997, 100).

Fiscal Stewardship

Lugar and Hudnut talked about solving people's problems. Lugar extolled "practical political unity and brotherhood" (1972, 12) and one of Hudnut's favorite metaphors was building the "city on the hill" (Hudnut 1999). Goldsmith talked primarily about efficiency, fiscal management and saving money. It is thus ironic that both Lugar and Hudnut left Indianapolis in excellent fiscal health, while Goldsmith increased bonded indebtedness, exhausted the balances that were in the tax increment financing accounts when Hudnut left office and pledged the next ten years of wheel tax receipts, which are the major source of street resurfacing funds (Armstrong 1999).

Toward the end of Goldsmith's tenure as Mayor, Amos Brown, a local political reporter, wrote:

> The true condition of the city's finances is the Achilles Heel of Mayor Stephen Goldsmith's eight years in office. Though Indianapolis has a "perfect Triple-A" credit rating, the amount of indebtedness Indianapolis has incurred has increased exponentially during Goldsmith's eight year reign . . . The city's profligate use of the municipal credit card could be the issue that runs Republicans out of the City-County Building on a rail! (Brown 1999)

For some observers, the increasingly regressive distribution of the tax burden was even more troubling than the increase in debt. Unigov was originally seen as a method of expanding the Indianapolis tax base beyond the center city and spreading the costs of urban revitalization. During the Lugar and Hudnut years, a substantial portion of debt was general obligation, making use of the new access to bond markets afforded by the greatly expanded assessed value under Unigov. In contrast, Goldsmith used bond financing to shift more of the tax burden to those residents of the center city—primarily poor African-American Democrats—whose properties were neither abated nor located within tax increment areas (Rosentraub 2000).

Summary

Several of Goldsmith's programs and initiatives were successful, as other chapters in this book document. Others have been less so, and those failures are also documented. Any evaluation of his tenure in office, however, must take into account the fact that he did not begin with a blank slate and the effect that his highly authoritarian management style had on his ability to make programmatic changes.

While politicians are notoriously reluctant to give credit to their predecessors (unless it is "credit" for a problem or bad decision), every city administration begins where the prior one left off. Both credit and blame must be awarded within that historical framework.

Notes

[1] Republicans have controlled the mayor's office and the City-County Council for 32 years following Unigov.

[2] The city resurfaced 689 miles of street during Lugar's first term, compared to 86 miles the prior four years. Lugar also expanded garbage collection and began a curbside, heavy trash pickup service.

[3] A major component in that tense relationship was, and is, the Indianapolis Police Department, which has defied attempts by all three mayors to improve it. Charges of corruption, cronyism and racism have plagued the department since well before Unigov; if anything, the situation worsened during the Goldsmith administration. Many political observers attributed Goldsmith's decisive defeat in his campaign for Governor to a widely publicized police "brawl" during which a group of drunken officers shouted sexist and racist epithets at passersby, and beat an African-American who responded in kind.

[4] In 1972, Hudnut defeated the incumbent, Andrew Jacobs, Jr., and represented Indiana's 11th District in the United States Congress. Two years later, Jacobs reclaimed the seat. The campaigns were marked by their mutual respect and civility, and the two remain close friends to this day.

[5] That case, *American Booksellers et al v. Hudnut*, involved a city ordinance that equated "pornography," as defined by the Ordinance, with sex discrimination and proposed to make it actionable under anti-discrimination laws. The Ordinance was held to be unconstitutional by the United States District Court, the 7th Circuit Court of Appeals and the United States Supreme Court. The author acted as local counsel for American Booksellers in that litigation.

[6] Hudnut's belief in affirmative action remedies for women and minorities was legendary, and it frequently came at a political cost. For an excellent discussion of his defense of affirmative action in hiring police and firefighters even after the Supreme Court questioned such measures in *Firefighters Local*

Union No.1784 v. Stotts (1984), see the chapter on policing written by David Bodenhamer and William Doherty in *The Hudnut Years* published by Indiana University Press in 1995.

[7] As Christine Reed noted in a Book Review essay, "In the new order, citizens are customers, and competition insures consumer choice; public spending on social services is an unproductive cost rather than a social investment in the public interest; consequently, bureaucratic neutrality and professional judgment are barriers to entrepreneurial government" (Reed 1999, 264).

[8] *NUVO Newsweekly*, an Indianapolis alternative newspaper and frequent critic of the Goldsmith administration, referred to the library controversy in a column by Harrison Ullmann, its editor. Ullmann wrote: "Our world has had an entire century of revolutions—big ones, like those in Russian and the rest of the former Evil Empire, and little ones, like those that get their paragraphs in the New York Times. In all those revolutions—all but one—it has been the people who have revolted against their governments. That last revolution, the peculiar one, is the revolution happening right here, right now in Indianapolis. In our city, the government wants to overthrow the people" (Ullmann 1999, 5).

Part Two

Doing the City's Business, Balancing the Books

Chapter 4

Organizational Change as a Management Tool: Mayor Goldsmith's Approach

William Blomquist

Introduction

Some leaders come into executive positions viewing their role and the challenges before them through the lenses of the organizational or institutional milieu from which they came—governing even in the executive branch as a "man of the Senate," a loyal party person, a career officer, and so on. Their approaches to problems and solutions are often formulated with the assumption that these institutions existed before one's administration and will continue afterward, and changes in policy are accomplished through them.

Other leaders come into executive positions guided by an ideological or academic perspective that sees and thinks in terms of goals and solutions, values and purposes, hypotheses and experiments. For them, institutions and organizations are malleable things—means rather than ends. What already exists has no particular claim upon their allegiance; everything should be re-thought and re-evaluated in light of their goals and values. Creating organizational and institutional change is a method in the service of one's vision.

Stephen Goldsmith's eight years as mayor of Indianapolis—and his review of those years in his book, *The Twenty-First Century City*—make clear that he was of the latter type. Merely cataloguing the organizational and institutional changes he wrought or attempted would exceed the permissible length of one chapter in a book. Many stories of organizational change are told elsewhere in this volume. Here, then, are a few cases—most of them not among the recollections Mayor Goldsmith shared in his book—representing his approach to organizational change and his relationships with institutions within and outside city-county government.

Find Your Street Department!

When Stephen Goldsmith took office as mayor of Indianapolis in January 1992, the basic structure of city-county government had been set by the 1969 state law that had created Indianapolis-Marion County's Unigov structure. That state law organized the executive branch of city government into the office of the mayor and six departments under the direction of mayoral appointees—Administration, Metropolitan Development, Parks and Recreation, Public Safety, Public Works and Transportation. Each of the six departments was also advised on policy matters by a board appointed (in various combinations, depending upon the board) by the Mayor, City-County Council, and County Commissioners.

The day before he took office, Mayor-elect Goldsmith reportedly waved at an organization chart showing the six departments and their respective divisions, and said, "This ought to go away, and what you really ought to see is a city that's set up: this is a deputy mayor of the Southside, this is a deputy mayor of the Northside, this is a deputy mayor of the Westside, this is a deputy mayor of the Eastside." Each of those individuals would be responsible for providing and obtaining public services for that part of the city. Asked whether he could implement that sort of revision, Goldsmith conceded, "It's a fairly substantial change of government" (Lanosga 1992a).

In that interview Goldsmith stated his intention to go to the Indiana General Assembly and ask for revisions to the state law, to allow the city to do away with at least two of the six statutorily established departments: Administration and Metropolitan Development.[1] In the meantime, he planned to shift several of their functions under deputy mayors in the Office of the Mayor and contract some administrative services out to county officials.[2] He was also considering having the Senior Deputy Mayor serve ex officio as director of the Department of

Administration, and a new Deputy Mayor for Neighborhoods serve ex officio as director of the Department of Metropolitan Development, thereby eliminating two department director positions. (Lanosga 1992a)

Although the formal elimination of departments would have to gain legislative approval, substantial changes in staffing levels were planned in all six departments. Eight days after taking office, Mayor Goldsmith announced plans to save $170,000 per year through streamlining of the Indianapolis Police Department, largely through the implementation of a geographical district structure and elimination of several middle-management positions in the central police administration (Schuckel 1992a).

On January 30, 1992, the Mayor announced his plans to form a private-sector commission—which came to be known as the Service, Efficiency, and Lower Taxes for Indianapolis Commission (SELTIC)—with the charge to review every function performed and service provided by city-county government. SELTIC was to make three determination with respect to each service or function: first, whether it ought to be performed by government at all; second, the "real cost" (as Goldsmith always described it) of current governmental provision of the service; and third, if the service were still to be provided by government, how it might be done more efficiently.

As he announced his plans to establish SELTIC that day, Goldsmith reportedly said, "My goal is not to lay off city workers" (Lanosga 1992c). Five days later, the headline on the front page of the *Indianapolis News'* "Local" section read, "90 City Employees to Lose Jobs" (Lanosga 1992c). The reductions would occur in the Department of Transportation, where the Mayor and the new transportation director, E. Mitchell Roob, Jr. were eliminating several supervisor positions. Although few Indianapolis residents knew (or know) of the Department of Administration's existence, the initial round of layoffs spawned controversies on several fronts. Several of the laid-off employees throughout the department were party loyalists, some of whom reported having worked for Goldsmith's election the year before, which stirred some dissatisfaction within the local party organization. The layoffs included fourteen of the twenty-one positions in the department's Equal Opportunity Division, which triggered concern about whether the city's commitment to compliance with equal opportunity laws and regulations could be sustained with one-third the number of staff. The microfilm and archives division director (himself a layoff target) publicly questioned the information base on which the decisions had been made—Goldsmith had characterized the archive division as an "Alice in Wonderland" operation, but the director said that Goldsmith had never been to the division and his staff members who claimed to have reviewed it had visited the wrong rooms (Lanosga and Schuckel 1992). Members of the City-County Council expressed reservations about a lack of consultation when the Mayor eliminated positions (Lanosga 1992f), and challenged Goldsmith's claim that the city faced a $20 million budget deficit that necessitated the drastic measures (Schuckel 1992e).

The next month another 100 layoffs were announced, coming from the Department of Public Works and the Department of Metropolitan Development. Both sets of layoffs accompanied major reorganizations of those departments. At that point, the city's workforce had shrunk by nearly 800 through a combination of position eliminations and hiring freezes on vacant positions (Schuckel 1992f). The elimination of positions and reorganization of departments continued. Toward the end of his second term, Goldsmith, who had entered office with a stated goal of a 25 percent reduction in the size of city government, was able to claim a 40 percent reduction in the number of non-public safety employees (Goldsmith 1998).

But staffing reductions and efficiency improvements were not the only managerial changes Mayor Goldsmith sought while in office. Through the mechanism of organizational change, Goldsmith tried to implement his philosophy of governmental administration, disrupt existing modes of operation and foster new combinations of alliances among residents and the mayor's office. At times, it became apparent that these goals were even more important than some of the stated goals of making government more accessible and customer-oriented.

The changes in the departments of Public Works and Transportation provide a case in point. Although Mayor-elect Goldsmith talked on the eve of his inauguration about eliminating the departments of Administration and Metropolitan Development, some of the biggest changes were in store for these departments.

In his book, *The Twenty-First Century City*, Mayor Goldsmith lauds the management and staff of the Department of Transportation, crediting them with achieving 25 percent savings and a 68 percent productivity increase in the first two years of his administration (Goldsmith 1997, 21). Their reward? Transportation was eliminated as a separate department. It was replaced in 1994 with something called the Department of Capital Asset Management (DCAM).

An institutional manifestation of Mayor Goldsmith's philosophy that city governments should manage the provision of services rather than produce services, the idea of a Department of Capital Asset Management was to create an agency responsible for the management of city facilities such as wastewater treatment and solid-waste recycling plants, storm-water drainage and sewage collection systems, and streets. The initiation of the Department of Capital Asset Management drew favorable attention from think tanks and conservative publications as a prime example of Mayor Goldsmith's innovative approach to city administration. The unique department name alone was undoubtedly worth a few column-inches of print.

Initially, many of the day-to-day service delivery functions that had previously been performed by the Department of Transportation—snow and ice removal, traffic control, grass and weed control—were transferred to the Department of Public Works. Thus, Public Works, which had previously been responsible for operating the city's solid and liquid waste sanitation services, storm water and flood control facilities and air pollution control programs, gained additional responsibilities that included maintaining streets, buildings and grounds, and controlling traffic, grass and weeds (City of Indianapolis 1994). But the transfer of services came after Public Works had experienced a combination of staffing reductions and voluntary resignations. City employees, City-County Councilors, and neighborhood association leaders criticized the Mayor for having triggered an exodus of experienced Public Works personnel in 1992 and 1993. Director Barry Baer, Executive Assistant Director Michael Sweeney (who had been with the department for eleven years) and Tom Quinn (who had administered the city's wastewater treatment plants) all resigned between mid-1992 and mid-1993. Engineers and other managerial personnel left Public Works in such numbers that even the Mayor lamented the losses (Schuckel 1992i). Thus, in 1994, transportation operations migrated to a Public Works department that had lost many of its experienced administrators and engineers.

Over the next few years, service responsibilities were reshuffled between the Department of Capital Asset Management and the Department of Public Works. By the end of Goldsmith's second term, parking services had shifted from Capital Asset Management to Public Works, but street construction, wastewater and sewers, storm water control and flood control had shifted from Public Works to Capital Asset Management. Both departments listed street maintenance and wastewater treatment among their responsibilities (City of Indianapolis 1997).

Although a Department of Capital Asset Management may have represented an institutional innovation—or at least an innovation in the naming of government departments—it did have the undesirable effect of hiding from ordinary city residents the identity of their street department. Prior to the reorganization and renaming, residents searching in vain through the blue pages of the Indianapolis telephone directory for "Streets, Department of" might eventually have tried "Transportation, Department of" and found what they were looking for. It does not seem likely that a resident with an inquiry about streets would look for "Capital Asset Management, Department of," nor is it likely that residents would have any idea what the newly-stenciled "DCAM" on the flashing barricades around a street maintenance project stood for.   And even if residents knew that Capital Asset Management was the successor to the old Department of Transportation, they still would have been rerouted to the Department of Public Works, depending on which year it was and which department was in charge of street maintenance that year.   Whatever merits this institutional innovation and organizational change may have had, making city government services more accessible to citizens was not among them.

A final note regarding personnel turnover: the churning of top positions at Public Works was not limited to that department or to the early days of the Goldsmith administration.   Even by the middle of the Mayor's second term, the office of department director apparently featured a revolving door.   Two of the six department directors serving in 1997 had held those positions for three years.   The other four had held their positions for one year or less.[3]

A Department of Metropolitan Dishevelment

The Department of Metropolitan Development set the standard for turnover, with four department directors in the first four years of the Goldsmith administration.   Mayor Goldsmith initially implemented his plan to make the Deputy Mayor for Neighborhoods ex officio director of the Department of Metropolitan Development.   After one year, that idea was dropped and the separate position of director reinstated, with three individuals cycled through the director's position between 1993 and 1995.

The department was also reorganized internally. Divisions in this department (and others) were created, combined, renamed, done away with and reestablished over Goldsmith's eight years in office.

Goldsmith's transition team had clearly taken a dim view of the department, and the briefing books he received from them "roundly criticized" it (Lanosga 1992d). To the transition team members, and probably to the new mayor himself, Metropolitan Development contained and represented some of the worst aspects of government. They were planners and regulators—the folks who issued permits, researched requests for zoning variances, inspected buildings and issued citations. They were rich targets for the metaphor manufacturers—quintessential bureaucrats, a bunch of meddlesome do-gooder types whose principal aim and effect appeared to be to make the lives of property owners and developers miserable, hamstringing change with millions of Lilliputian ropes of red tape.

Of course, as the old saying in politics goes, where you stand depends on where you sit. The transition team Mayor-elect Goldsmith assigned to review Metropolitan Development contained fifteen individuals from the development and real estate community—to whom the department represented paperwork, fees, permits and inspections—but only four representatives of the neighborhood associations who valued the department's role in zoning and code enforcement. Questioned about the composition of the panel, Mayor Goldsmith justified it as representing "the customers of government services"—in other words, since the development community was on the receiving end of the department's permit, zoning, inspection, and enforcement functions, they should be the one with the primary input on the department's reorganization (Lanosga 1992e). He acknowledged that neighborhood associations may have been underrepresented, but pledged to compensate by consulting with them before making any changes (Lanosga 1992e).

The city's more than 200 neighborhood organizations held a different view of Metropolitan Development. To them, it was the department that stood between them and uncontrolled development, the department they called about abandoned or dilapidated buildings, the department that maintained the city's comprehensive land use plan, reviewed requests for variances and notified potentially affected neighborhoods. When neighborhood association officials or members had questions about zoning, housing or historic preservation issues, it was the Metropolitan Development staff they called.

This is not to say that neighborhood groups all thought they were receiving excellent service from Metropolitan Development. Many of them complained about slow response and insufficient building code enforcement activity, and they lobbied for increased staffing and attention to meet their concerns.

Instead, in his first four months in office and with the assistance of his new Deputy Mayor for Neighborhoods, Mayor Goldsmith announced a reorganization of Metropolitan Development and the layoffs of fifty-five employees. Combined with frozen vacant positions, the layoffs dropped Metropolitan Development's staffing from more than 400 down to 341.

Neighborhood association leaders complained that, despite public statements from both the Mayor and Deputy Mayor that they would be consulted before any changes were made, no such consultation had occurred (Morgan 1992). Pressed by reporters, Deputy Mayor Nancy Silvers acknowledged that the restructuring of the department "had to be done by fiat," and that now there would be "ample time for input" (Schuckel 1992g).

Neighborhood groups also criticized the changes for reducing the number of zoning inspectors and code enforcement personnel—the very positions they felt were understaffed previously. The newly established Marion County Alliance of Neighborhood Associations (McANA)—a countywide assembly of neighborhood groups—had requested an *increase* in code-enforcement staff. There were nine enforcement personnel when Mayor Goldsmith took office, according to Steve Johnes, President of McANA. Now there would be five (Morgan 1992). City-County Council members joined in, criticizing both the extent and abruptness of the changes. One Council member, noting that the layoffs were announced to the public, the Council and the affected employees all on the same day, referred to it as "a massacre" (Schuckel 1992g).

Goldsmith and Silvers defended the changes as part of an effort to create a more neighborhood-oriented and responsive Department of Metropolitan Development. The reorganization's key feature, in their view, was the replacement of the larger number of specialized staff with a smaller number of geographically assigned "generalists" (Schuckel and Lanosga 1992). Metropolitan Development would contain "township teams" and "township team leaders" for each of the county's nine townships. Those staff would interact regularly with the neighborhood groups in their part of the county—attending neighborhood association meetings, and being the point of contact for any question or request for service, regardless whether it was about zoning or code enforcement or something else. The overall concept was analogous to that behind communities policing—get the line personnel out of the City-County Building and into the neighborhoods, and try to establish relationships between neighborhood activists and their township team leaders.

The McANA met on April 4, 1992, just days after the reorganization of Metropolitan Development was announced. The comments made at that meeting included the following:[4]

This mayor surrounds himself with developers, not representatives of neighborhoods, environmental groups, or City-County Council members.

We knew there would be changes with a new administration, but we assumed nothing irredeemable would happen without our consultation. Instead, the "heart and soul" are being cut out of city services.

We wanted zoning enforcement beefed up; instead, half of the zoning inspectors are being fired. Why demand conditions from developers if you're not going to follow up and enforce them?

The city makes permit errors. Now, the zoning technicians who check permits are being fired.

The remaining zoning enforcers/inspectors are being reorganized into "township team leaders." We have professional planners with master's degrees working the counters and answering the phones at DMD. We want specialists, not generalists.

The DMD division that regulates land use and growth is now being headed by a microbiologist who specializes in fertility problems.[5]

Zoning violations threaten all neighborhoods; we need to get the attention of the people on the 25th floor [the location of the mayor's office at the City-County Building].

Later that month, Deputy Mayor Silvers attended a series of meetings at various locations around the county to get the neighborhood associations' "input" on the already announced reorganization. She heard comments such as the following:[6]

Who are the township team leaders and how were they chosen?

Who is this Elizabeth [Williams, Pike Township team leader]?

If she's a team leader, who else will be on the team?

How do we get our voices heard? And if our township team leader is supposed to be our point of contact in the administration, how can we make sure she will be heard?

What do these team leaders do, other than wait for the phone to ring? Are these new positions?

From a Pike Township perspective, the previous system under the previous administration wasn't broke, so why are you fixing it? You've laid off good people, who were experienced and responsive and knew how to get things done.

What will the township teams be doing, besides zoning and code enforcement? And will this add to the duties of the employees?

We need to be able to count on the comprehensive plan. Zoning boards and the Metropolitan Development Commission (all appointed) seem to make capricious decisions, allowing all kinds of developments to occur that are not consistent with the comprehensive plan.

Our real concern in this part of the county is with land use decisions. It's the amateurs versus the professionals—not a level playing field.

If you're going to have fewer staff to respond to neighborhood complaints and concerns, then you'd better implement a more restrictive policy toward variances and rezoning requests; otherwise, we'll be completely outgunned.

The input did not change the outcome. The reorganization remained, although the reaction prompted Deputy Mayor Silvers to concede by the end of the month that the administration "might want to rethink" some of the layoffs (Franklin 1992).

Township team leaders (later renamed township administrators) were assigned, and that aspect of Metropolitan Development's organization remained in place through the remainder of the Goldsmith administration. Here too, however, staffing turnover bedeviled the effort to establish the kinds of relationships the Mayor and Deputy Mayor might have hoped for between the neighborhoods and their assigned staffers. Within two years, most of the nine townships had seen their township administrator change at least once. And as had occurred in Public Works, dozens of other experienced Metropolitan Development personnel departed voluntarily during that first two years. Over his entire time in office, Mayor Goldsmith notes in *The Twenty-First Century City*, Metropolitan Development was downsized by one-third (Goldsmith 1997, 161).

Mr. Goldsmith's Neighborhoods

One measurable, lasting effect of the Goldsmith administration's early months in office was a sizable increase in the number of neighborhood organizations that joined McANA. Before Goldsmith took office in January 1992, McANA had been established by just six neighborhood associations from four townships. By April 1993, the alliance had 43 member associations, including members in all nine townships (McANA 1993). The Alliance's expansion was due in part to the role it assumed of trying to present a more united neighborhood-level response to the changes occurring in city government—not only at Metropolitan Development but in the Police Department and at Public Works and Transportation.

Mayor Goldsmith, on the other hand, had campaigned on a neighborhood-empowerment theme, and Goldsmith perceived himself and his administration (including even the changes at DMD) to be pro-neighborhood. The disjuncture between the Mayor's perception of himself and the perception of his early administration by neighborhood organizations was fostered by several interrelated causes.

The first and most obvious cause of the difficulties that emerged between this self-styled pro-neighborhood mayor and individuals who represented the neighborhoods was the scale and pace of organizational change during his first hundred days in office. Between January 1 and April 1, 1992, Mayor Goldsmith reorganized the Metropolitan Development and Police departments and laid off a combined total of hundreds of employees in Administration, Metropolitan Development, Public Works and Transportation, almost entirely without consultation with the City-County Council or the neighborhood organizations. Whether the Council members and neighborhood groups, upon sober reflection, would have agreed with the changes Mayor Goldsmith was making or not, they were taken aback and alienated by the sheer extent and speed of the transformations and the lack of communication about them.

At a minimum, the disruptions created by the reorganizations and the staffing reductions took a toll on the established neighborhood organizations and City-County Councilors. They had known how to "work" the old system, and within less than a year they found themselves confronting a new one. Experienced Republican City-County Council members and savvy suburban neighborhood association officers had been quite effective at reaching into the catacombs of city-county bureaucracy and procuring services and benefits. Suddenly, they no longer knew whom to call, or whether a new person would still be around another month or two later. The Mayor had not just shifted around some boxes on an organizational chart. He had disrupted a system of relationships built on a web of geographical and political alliances, some of which were very long standing. In its place he had created a swirl of change.

The second major cause of the disparity between Goldsmith's perception of himself and many neighborhood leaders' perceptions of him was the meaning he attached to being "pro-neighborhood." Mayor Goldsmith's downsize-privatize-decentralize philosophy undergirded nearly everything he did in his first year in office, from staffing reductions to community-based policing. His approach to the relationship between the city and the neighborhoods reflected his views that city government ought to get out of the business of being a centralized producer of services and that, wherever and whenever possible, the individuals and groups most immediately affected ought to make the decisions about what to do and how to do it.

Making his initial "State of the City" address in three installments in January 1992, Mayor Goldsmith devoted the middle installment to the topic of the relationship between the city and the neighborhoods. "My hope is city government won't do anything *for* you," he reportedly said. "It will do a lot of things *with* you. It won't deliver services to you; it will structure partnerships with you" (Schuckel 1992c). In the Mayor's view, being "pro-neighborhood" combined a reduction in the role of city government as the provider of services and guarantor of quality-of-life in the neighborhoods with an "empowerment" of the neighborhoods themselves. Neighborhood institutions—not only neighborhood organizations per se, but churches, schools and community development corporations—would become centers of community decision-making and partners in the provision and production of public services.

During the election of 1991, many people may have heard candidate Goldsmith espouse these views without recognizing two important things. One, he actually believed them. Two, the basic change he was advocating was enormous and fundamental—nothing less than a re-configuration of the underlying political dynamic of the city. The existing and long-standing political dynamic of the city of Indianapolis (and most other medium- and large-sized cities in the United States) posited city government as both the policymaking body and the producer of goods and services, and neighborhood institutions as interest groups. The proper role of neighborhood organizations as interest groups—as in the basic pluralist conception of American politics that dominated political science throughout the 20th century—was to lobby from outside the formal governmental structure for more and better goods and services from government. Effectiveness of a neighborhood organization was measured by how much it was able to procure in attention, staff and expenditures from city government.

This conception of a city's basic political dynamic also contained a role for the city's legislators, the City-County Council members. Representing district-based constituencies throughout the city, council members are "brokers" who play a mediating role between the executive branch (where the service-producing bureaucracy is housed and functions) and the neighborhood organizations and other interest groups who want services from the city bureaucracy. The effectiveness of a city legislator is measured in terms of his or her perceived efficacy at cutting through red tape, getting the attention of city administrators and even rattling the occasional cage or two on behalf of the groups that comprise his or her constituency.

Republican cities work this way; Democratic cities work this way. Indianapolis had worked this way, under Democrats and under Republicans, before Unigov and since Unigov.

Fundamentally, Mayor Goldsmith did not see this as the way a city was supposed to work. In his conception, neighborhoods ought to figure out for themselves not only what they wanted but where and how to get it—including producing and procuring goods and services themselves. The city government administration ought to provide information, advice and a little bit of coordination, serving as a facilitating resource helping neighborhood institutions connect with the private- or public-sector organizations that could produce those services that neighborhoods needed or wanted, but were not going to produce for themselves.

After his inauguration, Mayor Goldsmith's vision began to become clearer to people who had not heard it or had not grasped it during the campaign. At that "State of the City" address the month he took office, Goldsmith paid as much attention to the need for citizens to make personal and organizational commitments to work with government in their neighborhoods as he did to the city's ability to serve the neighborhoods. And he encouraged neighborhood institutions to develop suggestions of how *they* could provide services in their neighborhoods more efficiently or more effectively than city government could. He even revealed that he was working on a plan whereby the city government would pay neighborhoods for doing the work themselves (Schuckel 1992c).

The Mayor's SELTIC commission clearly shared his vision, and later in 1992 it began recommending that certain city government activities be contracted out to neighborhood organizations. Mayor Goldsmith further suggested that neighborhood organizations actually submit bids to the city for those services they were going to assume, in order to document and quantify the comparative costs and potential savings (Schuckel 1992d). The SELTIC recommendation that captured the greatest attention—probably because it was simple to communicate and understand—was that the city contract with neighborhoods for the mowing and maintenance of the small, neighborhood-scale parks that dot the county. While SELTIC was suggesting that these kinds of nuts-and-bolts services be devolved to neighborhood organizations, the Mayor was suggesting that neighborhood churches take a similar role with respect to social services (Fahy 1992).

Here, then, was a mayor and his allies who were not promising neighborhoods more and better park maintenance and equipment or more multi-service centers staffed to provide referrals to welfare and public health agencies. But neither were they merely preaching a message of fiscal austerity, for example, that some service levels would have to be reduced in order to save money. They were suggesting that the institutions that existed at the neighborhood level ought to actually function as something other than interest groups lobbying the city for services.

Also throughout 1992, Mayor Goldsmith discussed and received from a team of Indiana University academics (including the author) a proposal for shifting the authority for decision-making to elected neighborhood councils for a selected number of neighborhood-scale policy matters. The proposal, titled "municipal federalism" and published at the beginning of 1993 by the newly established Center for Urban Policy and the Environment at Indiana University Purdue University Indianapolis (IUPUI), called for the establishment or reactivation of elected community councils and town boards throughout Indianapolis.[7] These publicly accountable neighborhood-scale bodies could decide whether to exercise, in lieu of city-county government, decisions regarding neighborhood parks (programming and equipment acquisitions as well as maintenance), traffic control on secondary- and tertiary-level streets within their neighborhoods and community development activities. They would also constitute the first level of review for zoning variance requests. They would receive funding from city-county government to support their activities; their decisions could not be inconsistent with city-county ordinances; and city-county government would retain governance and administration of all other public services—hence the "federalism" aspect of the concept.

Each of these pronouncements and proposals brought into focus the Mayor's vision of neighborhood empowerment, and also how completely different his vision was from the underlying political dynamic by which the city had operated for as long as anyone could remember. Goldsmith's vision was broadly criticized and rejected. His vision entailed a shift in neighborhoods and their institutions from the role of interest groups—supplicants and advocates—to becoming service providers, service producers and more nearly self-governing communities. His vision also contained no clear role for the twenty-nine City-County Councilors—if neighborhoods were going to elect their own councils and potentially take over decision-making about some key neighborhood-level concerns, and if district-level deputy chiefs and township administrators were going to be neighborhoods' points of contact regarding policing, land use and other services—what, if anything, would replace the "broker" role played by city legislators? There was no clear answer.

When the "municipal federalism" concept was presented at a McANA meeting on March 20, 1993, both City-County Councilors and some key neighborhood organization leaders spoke in strong opposition to it.[8] One City-County Councilor expressed her view that "people probably don't want to come home from work at the end of the day and have to climb into a street-paving machine to work on their own streets." (There had been no suggestion that neighborhoods would become responsible for street maintenance, but it made for a vivid metaphor that prompted a lot of heads in the room to nod in agreement.) The neighborhood association leaders said that the neighborhood residents did not want to provide city services for themselves—that was why they paid taxes and voted for city officials! The roles of interest group and broker were the roles these folks knew how to play and wanted to keep playing.

Mayor Goldsmith's vision of being "pro-neighborhood" came to be seen by many neighborhood leaders and City-County Councilors instead as an assault on the neighborhoods. He had laid off their employees in Metropolitan Development and Public Works, his SELTIC group wanted them to mow their own parks[9] and these nutty professors wanted them to take responsibility for traffic, parks, and community development policies within their neighborhoods. The Mayor's relationship with McANA and with several City-County Councilors remained largely adversarial for the duration of his administration.

But there were notable exceptions. A few neighborhood leaders did not object to "municipal federalism," or even to the SELTIC ideas of the city compensating the neighborhoods for providing certain services to themselves (Schuckel 1992d). The neighborhood leaders who did not object (and in one notable case, even embraced) the Mayor's vision of a different political dynamic for the city generally shared two characteristics. First, they and their neighborhood associations were either not members of, or not key players within, McANA. Second, they represented neighborhoods that had not worked the old system particularly well. Several of them represented predominantly nonwhite, inner city or near-downtown neighborhoods. Their past success at the interest-group, lobbying role had been limited. Their City-County Councilors were marginalized Democrats who were at times outnumbered by two- and three-to-one ratios by Council Republicans, and who had found playing the "broker" role on behalf of their constituents somewhat more difficult.

While these residents and organizations had not previously been supporters of Goldsmith (to put it mildly), they were more receptive to his proposals about neighborhoods. Perceiving themselves as having very little to lose by abandoning the status quo, they were intrigued by the notion of getting some of the decision-making power out of the City-County Building, electing their own governing bodies and obtaining funding from the city to provide and produce some services in their own neighborhoods.

Mayor Goldsmith and Deputy Mayor Silvers quickly noticed the more positive reception their ideas were getting from these neighborhood leaders, and they began differentiating their treatment of neighborhoods accordingly as early as the end of Goldsmith's first year in office. Even as neighborhoods around the county were attempting in 1992 and early 1993 to develop and strengthen their countywide alliance, Goldsmith began selecting some for particular attention and assistance.

During 1992, Mayor Goldsmith and Nancy Silvers, the Deputy Mayor for Neighborhoods, planned and announced the identification of seven "targeted neighborhoods." These targeted neighborhoods would become the focus of the city's redevelopment, crime reduction and social service efforts.

The neighborhoods—the Near Westside-Haughville, Near North, United Northwest/Riverside, Citizens, Martindale-Brightwood, Near East and Fountain Square—all surrounded the downtown area. The targets did not, however, include gentrified or gentrifying downtown neighborhoods such as Lockerbie Square, Chatham Arch, St. Joseph and the Old Northside, or two downtown neighborhoods (Babe Denny and the canal area) that were expected to be redeveloped soon from primarily residential to commercial uses.

Targeting certain neighborhoods for massive and coordinated governmental intervention represented a significant change of approach in a very short time for the Goldsmith administration. There is no way of saying for certain that the administration would not have come around to that approach anyway, but the negative reaction the Mayor's "neighborhood empowerment" vision received from the better-established and more influential suburban neighborhoods, from McANA and from certain City-County Councilors, certainly did not impede the transformation.

The most outspoken advocate of the Mayor's neighborhood-empowerment ideas had been Rev. Olgen Williams of the Near-Westside/Haughville neighborhood and the Westside Community Organization (WESCO). Williams, a black pastor from a low-income and crime-troubled inner-city neighborhood, became a vocal proponent of everything from privatization to municipal federalism. When the Goldsmith administration switched to the targeted-neighborhoods strategy late in 1992, no neighborhood was "targeted" more than Haughville and no neighborhood organization was cultivated like WESCO. United States Justice Department "Weed and Seed" funding for crime reduction and redevelopment were directed to Haughville. The city obtained a grant from the Annie E. Casey Foundation to support social services and supplemental educational opportunities for children and youth, and it too was focused upon Haughville.

While Olgen Williams and some other leaders in the targeted neighborhoods were receptive to the notion of neighborhood empowerment, they were also quick to point out to Mayor Goldsmith and Deputy Mayor Silvers that even the most active residents in their communities often had less formal schooling and fewer organizational skills than their counterparts in other neighborhoods. Bolstering the leadership and institutional capacity of neighborhood organizations in the inner city, providing staffing and other means of organizational support and establishing a center for neighborhood development were all quickly added to the Goldsmith administration's neighborhood agenda (Goldsmith 1997, 160).

Mayor Goldsmith sounded the theme of building organizational and human capital in the targeted neighborhoods at a December 1992 meeting. He suggested that the city use public and private funding to establish a "neighborhood academy" to provide training to neighborhood leaders in "the kind of skills they need to promote community and economic development, crime prevention programs, social services and an array of other programs neighborhoods may identify" (Penner 1992). In September 1993, he contracted with Robert Woodson's National Center for Neighborhood Enterprises to come up with a plan for such an academy by spring 1994.

In September 1994, the Indianapolis Neighborhood Resource Center (INRC) opened its doors.   Not a city government agency but a nonprofit entity funded with a combination of public and private monies, the INRC has provided information and training for individuals becoming involved in neighborhood issues or programs. Its workshops cover topics from establishing a crime-reduction program to handling zoning issues and applying for foundation or government funding. Although the INRC provides its services to any neighborhood organization in the county, its outreach efforts have been extended especially to the targeted neighborhoods.

Two other institutional creations during the Goldsmith administration have not been targeted-neighborhood initiatives per se but have concentrated on those parts of the city. In his first term, the Mayor established the Community Enhancement Fund to provide financial support to neighborhood institutions with improvement projects. In his second term, Goldsmith had taken great pride in the Front Porch Alliance. In a variation on the INRC concept but for church leaders, the Front Porch Alliance sponsors workshops for inner-city pastors and other church and neighborhood leaders, "helping them learn more about the resources available from the community organizations and local government" (Lathrop 1998).

To characterize the targeted-neighborhoods approach as a "divide-and-conquer" strategy would exaggerate the case and make unsupportable claims about the mindset of its inventors. But the shift in approach clearly accompanied the very negative reaction Mayor Goldsmith's neighborhood-empowerment agenda received from the more affluent parts of the city, and it gave Goldsmith a new set of alliances upon which to establish the pro-neighborhood legacy he proclaims in *The Twenty-First Century City.*

In at least one instance, however, a Goldsmith administration initiative clearly did divide neighborhoods, even members of McANA. The development of a cluster of high-priced condominiums on what had been public property along the White River split two neighborhoods that had been leading organizations within McANA—the United Northwest Association (UNWA) and the Nora-Northside Community Council.   UNWA activists supported the development, which would take place within their neighborhood. Coincidentally or not, UNWA was one of the Goldsmith administration's seven targeted neighborhoods. Nora-Northside and other neighborhood associations that were much farther away from the site opposed it vigorously. Coincidentally or not, Nora-Northside had been among the Mayor's most vocal critics on everything from the Department of Metropolitan Development reorganization to municipal federalism. The UNWA-Nora split kept McANA from effectively taking sides on the issue.

But Why Not the Buses?

Throughout his first term, Mayor Goldsmith busily established other new organizations and institutions. In addition to SELTIC's review of city service delivery, he created a Regulatory Study Commission to review existing city government regulations and propose elimination or revision of unnecessary or excessively burdensome ones. With business and governmental leaders from neighboring counties, he established the Metropolitan Association of Greater Indianapolis Communities (MAGIC), to discuss regional economic development. A Central Indiana Regional Citizens League (CIRCL) provided a forum for discussion of other regional issues such as transportation planning and urban sprawl. In concert with the Greater Indianapolis Progress Committee, the Mayor established Visioning Indianapolis Tomorrow, a group of individuals representing a multitude of constituencies within Marion County to identify future directions for improving education, neighborhoods, culture and public safety. The White River Environmental Partnership was created to take over the operation of the city's wastewater treatment plants. Mayor Goldsmith and others who supported his views on K-12 schooling reform founded the Alliance for Quality Schools, a political group intended to identify, recruit and elect pro-reform candidates to the Board of Indianapolis Public School Commissioners. (Goldsmith 1997)

Combining these with all of the other initiatives mentioned earlier in this chapter and elsewhere in this book, it is clear that Mayor Goldsmith embraced and implemented a strategy of management through organizational creation and change. But here too, there is an exception.

The Indianapolis Public Transportation Corporation (once nicknamed Metro, now nicknamed IndyGo), the city's public transportation system, plays a prominent role in Mayor Goldsmith's 1997 book, *The Twenty-First Century City*. He opens the book with a boldly stated indictment of the city's transit system and the story of his effort to improve bus service in Indianapolis. With a mixture of earnestness and frustration, he acknowledges and describes at length how (and, in his view, why) the effort failed.

In retrospect, his discussion is interesting for what it does not say as well as for what it does. First, there is no acknowledgement that the operation of some bus routes was, in fact, given over to private contractors. Goldsmith details his efforts to bring competitive bidding to the city's bus service, and the political opposition those efforts generated. But he leaves out the fact that bus routes were indeed privatized. In a book filled with examples of successful privatization, there is somehow no mention of the privatization experiment that occurred with the city's bus system.

Second, Metro seems to have been an exception to Mayor Goldsmith's approach of creating a new organizational or governance structure (or reorganizing existing ones) in order to accomplish change. Among the statements in his litany of complaints about Metro is this: "The transit authority, commonly called Metro, is governed by an appointed five-member board, further insulating it from political accountability" (Goldsmith 1997, 2). But in his own discussion of his experience with the bus system, as elsewhere in the public record, there is no indication that Mayor Goldsmith attempted to reorganize the governance of Metro—for instance, by increasing its public accountability. The Indianapolis Public Transportation Corporation remained at the end of the Goldsmith years as it was in the beginning— a separate municipal corporation governed by a board of directors appointed by the Mayor and the City-County Council.

Mayor Goldsmith instead shaped transportation policy through two other principal means. First, he made his own appointments to the transit system's governing board—claiming credit in his book for appointing "new members . . . who shared a commitment to low taxes and smaller government" (Goldsmith 1997, 3). With two new appointees in place in January 1992, the Metro board on a 3-2 vote demoted the man who had been general manager of the bus system since 1984 and began the search for his replacement. According to a newspaper account, that vote "came despite warnings from the board's current lawyer, William K. Byrum, that the move could be illegal and lead to the withdrawal of state and federal support for the bus system" (Schuckel 1992b). The board then voted, 3-0 with two abstentions, to replace Byrum as Metro's attorney with David Brooks, who was also a member of the City-County Council. Additional appointments later in his administration solidified Goldsmith's control of the board's membership.

Second, Goldsmith seized the opportunity of the 1995 state legislative session—the only state budget session during his two terms as mayor when Republicans controlled both chambers of the Indiana General Assembly—to obtain approval of a bill re-directing state transit funds from the Indianapolis Public Transportation Corporation to the city itself. Goldsmith reports the move in his book as follows:

> The city persuaded the Indiana General Assembly to move $5.6 million of the state's support for public transportation from Metro's budget to the city's budget, where federal rules governing transit authorities would not apply. Free from the constraints of federal regulations, the city could use the money to purchase services in the competitive marketplace in ways that Metro could not. (Goldsmith 1997, 4)

The combination of these moves raises some challenging questions about the approach to governance and institutional arrangements at work here. Although Mayor Goldsmith lamented the lack of accountability in the transit system's governance structure, he did not attempt to change it. Rather, he used the appointment system to gain control of the transit system board and to change administrative personnel. The January 1992 changes, for example, "made it clear that Mayor Stephen Goldsmith's administration . . . will play a critical role in the selection of the two administrators" (Schuckel 1992b).

It is quite understandable that a mayor may disapprove of the governance structure of a city service and yet decide not to spend the political capital to alter it. But when we add the 1995 legislation redirecting state public transportation funds from Metro to the city, it does not seem that simple. Based on his description of the event and its motivation, Mayor Goldsmith clearly believed the city administration could make better decisions about what was in the best interests of the "poor" bus riders if the administration were freed both from those burdensome federal regulations *and* from the transit system board's own control of state public transit dollars (which are mostly passed-through federal funds).

Instead of fixing the lack of accountability of Indianapolis' public transit system, Mayor Goldsmith retained the insulated position of the transit board while capturing control of part of its funding. This might not make the transit system more accountable to the public, but it would certainly make the transit system more accountable to *him*. Later in the book, in a discussion of privatization but not in the context of bus service, Mayor Goldsmith resolves the apparent dilemma by equating mayoral control with city control and thus public accountability. Rejecting criticism that privatization would produce some loss of accountability or responsiveness, Goldsmith cites the contractual provisions that allowed him to reward, sanction, or get rid of a producer. He writes, "In each of our competitive initiatives, *the city* (emphasis mine) retained and even enhanced its control over services. In all too many American cities, mayors and city managers operating in monopolistic governments have very little control" (Goldsmith 1997, 71). *L'urb, c'est moi!*

The other challenging aspect of Mayor Goldsmith's approach to the bus system problem is how to square it with his fervent criticisms of the paternalistic attitudes of "big government." In his description of the transit system experience, it is clear that Mayor Goldsmith's firm conviction that privatization and competitive bidding would improve bus service forged his belief that *he* knew what the system's customers wanted and needed, and *he* knew how to provide it for them (Goldsmith 1997, 8).[10] One might ask how this approach differs from the one he decries just a few pages later when discussing the War on Poverty? It, he writes, "was rooted in the notion that government knows better than people what is in their best interest" (Goldsmith 1997, 8). He contrasts that with his approach, which is based on a few principles, among the first of which is, "People know better than government what is in their best interest" (Goldsmith 1997, 9). His handling of the Metro situation appears to have had as much in common with the War on Poverty assumption he disdains as with the principles he espouses.

There is a similar disjuncture between his handling of the Metro situation and his comments about public employees. Much of the Mayor's description of the bus service experience is devoted to criticism of the system employees and their union leadership. All of the arguments they raised at the time in opposition to privatization are derided by the Mayor as classic bureaucratic obstructionism and public-employee union featherbedding. Only in the next chapter, where Mayor Goldsmith is praising the willingness of street maintenance employees to bid for their own jobs, do we find this statement from the Mayor: "Contrary to their poor public image, most civil servants are hardworking and talented—and they know a lot more than their mayors do about how to do their jobs well" (Goldsmith 1997, 22). Perhaps bus drivers are the exception. The juxtaposition of chapters one and two of *The Twenty-First Century City* leaves a strong impression that city employees who responded to the Mayor's competition initiatives in the *right* way demonstrated what wonderful things can happen when employees are "freed," while city employees who rejected or criticized his initiatives were and are troublemakers and bureaucrats.

Before concluding this section, it is worthwhile to anticipate the response that the bus system was in crisis and something radical had to be done. This city's bus system is not good; it was not in 1991 and it is not today. Comparatively few residents, despite rising automobile traffic and lengthening commute times, use the bus system. But perceptions of a crisis were not universal when Goldsmith took office in 1992. Less than ten years earlier, the city's bus service had been highlighted in a Harvard Business School case study as one of Indianapolis' assets. In its reference to the city's "excellent bus-based municipal transportation system," the 1983 case study noted that Indianapolis ranked 67th among the 267 U.S. metropolitan areas in quality of public transit systems (Harvard Business School 1983). On the other hand, Mayor Goldsmith's transportation director E. Mitchell Roob Jr. observed that from 1983 to 1992, ridership had declined from 15 million to 10 million persons per year and local tax support for the bus system had shot up from $1.7 million to $5.3 million (Schuckel 1992b). Still, even the hyper-conservative *Indianapolis News* editorialized seven weeks before Goldsmith's election as mayor, "Metro's condition brings home a reality that this city has yet to face. If Indianapolis is to have a comprehensive system of public transportation, taxpayers are going to have to cover more of the cost" (*Indianapolis News* 1991). Clearly, the city's once-praised bus service was not functioning as well and needed to improve, but just as clearly, whether the improvements required private operation or the diversion of bus system funds to the city government were matters over which people other than Mayor Goldsmith disagreed.

The biggest improvement to the city's bus service in the last decade, as Mayor Goldsmith notes, has been the addition of some cross-town routes that have eliminated the need for every transit rider to come all the way downtown and then ride all the way back out in order to get from one corner of the city to another. These route improvements came relatively late, however—after all the hubbub over privatization had died down—and it is not clear why simpler improvements such as these could not have been made without the privatization effort and all of the difficulties that attended it.

Summary

Stephen Goldsmith was not the first executive to practice "management by stirring things up," and he will not be the last. But there are probably few large-city mayors in the United States who have adopted and implemented the strategy as aggressively and thoroughly as he, and there is little question that Indianapolis has not seen his equal in this regard.

The Twenty-First Century City is filled with his stories of the successes the approach yielded, and it clearly gained him a national reputation. But it misfired on occasion too,—occasions that receive scant attention in his book.

In some instances, his organizational-change approach appears to have been oriented toward enhancing control over public services by the mayor's office. While Goldsmith or any mayor can justify such moves as "enhancing accountability," in the case of the bus system or street maintenance in Indianapolis, it is far from clear that the accountability of these services to the general public or the City-County Council was enhanced by the changes.

It was also clear that Mayor Goldsmith's approach exacted a price from some of the employees and organizations that had worked for and with the city before. In some instances, it took a toll on the Mayor's own reputation locally.

The managerial record is more mixed than the Mayor presented in his book. Before future executives decide to take their cues from his account of his achievements, they would do well to take a wider perspective.

Notes

[1] The Department of Administration handles some cross-departmental and citywide services such as human resources and equal opportunity compliance, insurance and risk management, microfilm and document archives, and vehicle maintenance. The Department of Metropolitan Development administers planning and zoning services, construction permits and code enforcement, housing development and historic preservation.

[2] For example, he was reviewing a staff recommendation to have the offices of county auditor and county treasurer take over payroll, investment and cash management services for the city (Lanosga 1992a).

[3] One deputy mayor had held the position for three years, the other for one year. The city controller had held that position for one year.

[4] Author's notes.

[5] Leslie R. Rubin, a 36-year-old health-care researcher at the Hudson Institute who had previously served as laboratory director of andrology (male fertility research) in the Department of Obstetrics and Gynecology at the Indiana University Medical School, was hired by Goldsmith and Silvers as the new administrator of planning in Metropolitan Development. The process of hiring is illustrated in this quotation from the newspaper: "She sent her credentials to Goldsmith's transition office after he was elected," Goldsmith

said. None of the fifty-five Metropolitan Development employees laid off by the Mayor was interviewed for the post, and the position was not advertised. "Goldsmith has stressed he's not looking for people with municipal government expertise, he's looking for good managers." (Shuckel 1992h)

[6] Author's notes, April 20, 1992 meeting with neighborhood leaders at Traders Point Christian Church in Pike Township; April 21, 1992 meeting with neighborhood leaders at Southport Baptist Church in Perry Township; and April 22, 1992 meeting with neighborhood leaders at Franklin Township Middle School in Franklin Township.

[7] This concept resurrected a proposal known as "Minigov" that had accompanied the consideration of the Unigov legislation passed by the Indiana General Assembly in 1969.

[8] Author's notes.

[9] Even the city's weekly business publication reviewed SELTIC's parks proposal as "one of its greatest flops," noting that, a year after the recommendation had been floated, "not one of the city's 135 parks came under neighborhood control, which prompted SELTIC members and city staffers to retreat and regroup" (Heikens 1993).

[10] Much as Goldsmith knew, perhaps, what the neighborhoods wanted and how to give it to them.

Chapter 5

A Tale of Two Mayors: Indianapolis Municipal Finances, 1986 to 1998

Samuel Nunn[1]

Mayors have been able to make policy decisions with a view toward issues of fiscal stability only when they are protected from the vagaries of electoral politics and the demands of special interest groups. *The need to win reelection forces the city's chief executive to devote too much attention to short-term problem solving which delivers a tangible political return on his investment. For most mayors, the long-term costs of maintaining and administering programs and projects they initiate are simply never considered* (Fuchs 1992, 279; emphasis mine).

Municipal administration has its share of challenges, but perhaps its greatest is the ongoing need to practice effective and efficient financial management. The reasons for this are numerous. Since at least the 1970s, an anti-tax, neoliberal aura has surrounded the administration of government at all levels. At the local level, in particular, anti-tax referenda such as California's Proposition 13 and others like it have placed actual or political ceilings on the amount and types of revenues available to city government administrators (Levine 1980). Within a short time of his election in 1981, President Reagan eliminated federal revenue sharing, which had over the previous thirteen years provided a cushion of 'surplus' revenues for local governments (Judd 1988, 340-

344). Local governments were encouraged to become more competitive with other municipalities by offering lucrative supply-side economic incentives to business firms—cities should become more attractive places to do business as the major way of combating physical and financial decline (Bartik 1991). The real estate crash and the savings and loan banking crisis of the mid-1980s further eroded the fiscal capacity of urban land to support existing property tax burdens, let alone new assessments (Logan 1993). By the time this hollowing-out of local property values had begun to run its course, the "re-inventing government" movement emerged, with a newly energized conservative emphasis on efficiency as the prime directive of local government administrators and politicians (Osborne and Gaebler 1992). Government re-invention spawned urban entrepreneurialism by city administrators engaged in public-private partnerships built on the use of public funds to leverage private investment (Sharp 1990). The next millennium's cast of city politicians, managers and administrators will be required, as they generally have in the past, to strike a sometimes precarious balance among city spending, city revenues, city services and economic growth and development. How the public stewards of municipal governments strike this balance is often the major determinant of their perceived success or failure as they occupy their "watch" over city government. The measure taken of this balance is often the financial health of city government.

As the government re-invention movement began in 1992, Stephen Goldsmith, a former Marion County prosecutor, became the 46th mayor of the city of Indianapolis, but just the *third* mayor of the *consolidated city-county government* of Indianapolis-Marion County, known as Unigov, the only first-class city so defined by the state of Indiana (Henn 1992; Bodenhamer and Barrows 1994). The Goldsmith administration followed that of William H. Hudnut III, who had been the consolidated city's mayor from 1976 to 1992. Hudnut's popularity had been high enough that in 1983 the two-term limit that had shackled previous mayors was lifted, allowing a four-term stay for the former Presbyterian minister. When Goldsmith assumed office after the 1992 election, he continued a political regime of Republican mayors that went back to the putative architect of the 1970 creation of Unigov, Richard Lugar, who held office from 1968 to 1976. Prior to Unigov, Indianapolis mayors had been split about equally between Democrats and Republicans.

Since 1969, the consolidated city-county of Indianapolis has been managed under three Republican mayoral regimes because, according to conventional wisdom, the Unigov consolidation internalized the wealthier, and predominantly Republican, inner ring suburbs within Marion County, allowing a conservative Republican voting majority there to overwhelm the smaller numbers of inner city Democrats. As a result, variation in municipal fiscal policy in the city during the last thirty years has not reflected the potential for substantial political differences that might otherwise exist when changes in mayoral administrations are also changes in the ruling political party. At this writing, Indianapolis acquired its first Democratic mayor in three decades, so fiscal policies could clearly change. Nonetheless, within the broad neoliberal political context that had affected nearly all cities since the Reagan presidential years, succeeding Indianapolis mayors have typically attempted to demonstrate their administrative and fiscal superiority over their predecessors. This was particularly true for Goldsmith, who "campaigned on a platform that emphasized cost-cutting initiatives using such labels as privatization and downsizing" (Geib 1994, 169). The mantra of the Goldsmith administration was *competition*. This doctrine was derived from several different sources. One was the re-invention movement championed by Osborne and Gaebler (1992). Another was from information generated by conservative think tanks such as the Reason Foundation and the Manhattan Institute. The other local source was a major advisory group utilized by Goldsmith before and after his election, SELTIC—the Service, Efficiency, and Lower Taxes for Indianapolis Commission. Goldsmith referred to SELTIC as a competitiveness council (Goldsmith 1992). Competitiveness was to be instilled into the delivery of city services, the administration of city government, and the very civic fabric of the region.

This competitiveness ideology was considered to be the hallmark of Goldsmith's administration, its vehicle to cost savings and more efficient municipal management, and thus a way of differentiating it from the previous Hudnut administrations—it was to be the distinction that made a difference. But, *was* this a distinction that made a difference? After twenty-three years of Republican mayoral regimes running Unigov, how much change would another Republican mayor bring? For example, Hudnut had also emphasized competition, utilizing since 1990 his own competitiveness council, called PEPPER—the Public Entrepreneurship, Privatization, Productivity, Efficiency and Restructuring committee—which was described as a source of "workable solutions for reducing government costs while maintaining optimum service" (City of Indianapolis 1990). Analysts who conducted a review of two different systems of municipal reform (in Indianapolis and Charlotte, North Carolina) concluded that Goldsmith had "inherited a city government with a history of professionalism and innovation," rather than one marked by inefficiency and sloth (Potapchuk, Crocker and Schechter 1998). In his own book on Indianapolis, Goldsmith noted that when he came into office in 1992, "Indianapolis's finances were sound: taxes were relatively low, our public workforce seemed lean, and the city boasted a healthy bond rating" (Goldsmith 1997, 9). Nonetheless, five years before his book and before his first full year in office was completed, Goldsmith was reported to have ". . . cut millions out of the City's operating budgets and eliminated chronic deficit spending" (Anderson 1993). This prompted a heated letter from Hudnut to KPMG-Peat Marwick (the consulting firm that published the Anderson newsletter article) in which he characterized *that* characterization as "unfair, unwarranted and untruthful" (Hudnut 1993). As discussed below, Goldsmith's claim about eliminating deficit spending was short-lived.

From this brief exchange emerges a standard and widely regarded measure of how one municipal politician would attempt to differentiate his administration from preceding ones: fiscal prudence and efficiency. Goldsmith's 1997 book and his frequent exposure in municipal trade magazines, journals and national media that described him as an innovative financial and operational manager, all combined to create at least an implicit impression that Goldsmith somehow *improved* the consolidated city-county government of Indianapolis-Marion County beyond its performance during the Hudnut administration. That is, in the netherworld of political code, to constantly seek and publicize improved productivity and efficiency, as Goldsmith did on a regular basis, was to sully indirectly the preceding performance of the municipal project under Hudnut. Even Harvard College seemingly underscored the "superior" nature of Goldsmith's approach by publishing a case study of Indianapolis's move to competition, subtitling its case study, interestingly enough, as "the quest for lower costs" (Husock 1995). By the time Goldsmith announced he would not run for a third term in 1999, the organizational and managerial changes in Indianapolis city government wrought by his nearly eight years in office were considered to be a substantial and significant departure from the Hudnut years, if not from empirical observation then certainly via his press releases and media machinations. How did these two mayors differ, if at all, in terms of their financial management performance while in office? How did the financial health of the Indianapolis municipal project vary during selected years of two mayors who belonged to the same party but vowed that they had major differences in the style and substance of municipal management?

Municipal Finances and Mayoral Regimes

All municipal governments are ongoing legal entities that routinely outlive their human administrators. That is, the municipal *corpus* is always managed, but only temporarily by a given set of elected and appointed officials, with the regular and inevitable changes in the composition of these sets dictated by electoral cycles and political appointment. Different legal forms are used to organize the administration of the municipality (for example, a strong mayor, a council manager, or a commission form of city government), and these forms tend to dictate the nature and frequency of changes in the mix of human actors charged with administering the municipal project at any particular time. After elections, new mayors are installed; when city councils are reconstituted, new city managers are appointed; with new political appointments, new department heads are hired; and so on. Under the watch of each new set of actors, decisions are made to allocate the municipal organization's resources in particular ways. These decisions, of course, alter the condition of the municipal project by creating more or fewer city employees, greater or lesser levels of municipal services, higher or lower revenues and expenditures, with both short- and long-term repercussions. And, more significantly, each set of actors makes decisions that have both short- and long-term financial repercussions for the municipal organization. So, over time, the cast of municipal managers changes, the municipal organization stays roughly the same, *but the general operating and financial conditions of the municipal organization may change radically based on the actions of each new set of actors charged with administrative responsibility.*

As political regimes in control of city governments change, conflicts emerge around the existing state of the city, the extant financial conditions within which the reins of power are transferred, and the challenges that are faced by the new political and administrative controllers to continue a positive, or alter a negative, course of affairs. This is particularly the case in large, strong mayor cities. Under this model, the mayor serves as both the chief political and administrative officer, and there is no formal separation of the policy and administrative spheres of city management. Because mayors must be elected to obtain and retain office, they must call attention to their accomplishments or condemn the misdeeds of previous mayors in ways that non-elected professional city administrators do not. Mayors must differentiate themselves from their predecessors; otherwise, voters see little reason to "throw the rascals out" or to even go to the trouble of voting. Mayors also must demonstrate their 'distinctiveness' if they have higher political aspirations.

The City of Indianapolis is organized as a strong mayor form of government. In the Indianapolis political model of city administration, as in other strong mayor municipalities and as shown earlier, elected politicians vie for credit for the good things and shift blame for the bad things that happen within the city, especially those regarding the financial health of the city. But in Indianapolis, one of the problems with any of its various mayors capturing credit and shifting blame is the highly fragmented nature of the municipal project. Despite the legend and rhetoric of municipal government consolidation embedded in the Unigov concept (from its 1970 inception), the "City" of city government fame is not one but several distinct and interrelated organizations, all of which have certain circumscribed, but not closely interlinked, responsibilities for the delivery of a full-range of municipal services. The eleven "component units" that comprise the total municipal project within Indianapolis are:

The "City"
   1)   Consolidated City of Indianapolis
Five other independent municipal corporations:
   2)   Indianapolis Airport Authority
   3)   Health and Hospital Corporation of Marion County
   4)   Indianapolis-Marion County Building Authority
   5)   Indianapolis Public Transportation Corporation
   6)   Indianapolis-Marion County Public Library
Five special taxing districts:
   Three with Marion County boundaries:
   7)   Metropolitan Thoroughfare District
   8)   Flood Control District
   9)   Public Safety Communications and Computer Facilities District
   Two with Indianapolis Center Township boundaries:
   10)Indianapolis Redevelopment District
   11) Solid Waste Disposal District

The "City" of Indianapolis, then, is not a strictly consolidated, unified municipal corporation under the control of a single executive authority. To the contrary, by a formal organizational reckoning, it is comprised of eleven component units, most of which possess their own executive and administrative staffs!

In a fragmented system like this, it is legitimate to ask who has responsibility for the financial health of the city. Indeed, who *is* responsible? In part, the answer depends on *which component* is the object of analysis. The connection between the mayor's executive (and political) authority for the *consolidated city* and the executive and administrative authority for the other ten component units is based almost exclusively on appointment powers. Obviously, the financial health of the consolidated City of Indianapolis is the direct responsibility of the mayor. But the day-to-day operating decisions for the airport, the public hospital, the transportation utility and the library are all vested in other executives and other administrative staffs (some of whom are appointed by the mayor, while others are hired by those appointees) not directly under the mayor of Indianapolis. It is reasonable to argue from this perspective that the mayor should be evaluated on the basis of the consolidated city's financial health primarily, not the financial health of *all* the fragmented components of Indianapolis city government. On the other hand, cost shifting among these fragmented components *could* occur, whereupon a complete evaluation would require an analysis of each set of books maintained by the eleven fragmented components. This is beyond the scope of the analysis presented in this chapter.

In 1992 Stephen Goldsmith, like all elected politicians, inherited a set of financial conditions and obligations from the actions taken by previous mayoral regimes, in this case primarily the Hudnut administration. These conditions and obligations are, of course, contested terrain over which the political parties bicker and internecine warfare occurs. In the case of the Hudnut-to-Goldsmith mayoral transition, even though both were Republicans, Goldsmith campaigned on the need to make city government more business-like and efficient and, at least implicitly, was critical of the operating and financial performance of his predecessor. It is reasonable, then, to seek some indication of improved financial conditions if he were successful in implementing campaign promises. To measure whether this took place—that is, resolving questions about how the financial health of the Indianapolis municipal project might have changed during the tenure of different mayors—analysis should be based on standardized and fundamentally accepted measures of financial performance and solvency. Such measures can be built from various combinations of standard accounts that are reported annually in city financial reports. These accounts include the following:

1) Assets, liabilities, and retained earnings (equity)
2) Revenues and expenditures
3) Capital outlays
4) Debt and debt service

Furthermore, given the complexity of the consolidated city's financial status *only*, there are at least six vectors of financial performance that ought to be drawn from several different funds in order to paint a complete picture of the city's financial condition. For Indianapolis, these include the following funds:

1)	General	6)	Internal Service
2)	Special revenue	7)	Trust and agency
3)	Debt service	8)	General fixed assets
4)	Capital projects	9)	General long-term debt
5)	Enterprise		

From this perspective, basic questions can be asked about the financial performance in these fund areas, similar to those that might be posed to business executives in charge of a private company. How much did assets and liabilities grow or decline? To what extent did revenues exceed expenditures, by how much and during what years? What is the relationship of capital and operating expenditures? How does the rate of capital investment compare to the growth in property values in Indianapolis generally? How much debt has the city accrued, and how much debt service must be paid each year to amortize that debt? By examining the annual answers to these questions during a time series that covers both the Goldsmith period and an (equal) earlier period during the Hudnut administration, an overview of the respective mayors' impacts on the financial health of the City of Indianapolis can be produced.

Methods and Data

The primary analysis reported here comes from an examination of thirteen years of consolidated city-county of Indianapolis component unit financial reports (CUPR), covering the period 1986 through 1998. This allows a comparison of the last six years of the Hudnut administration to the six years of the Goldsmith administration for which data are available, with 1992 considered a transition year marked by the Goldsmith election. Thus, 1992 becomes the *last* year benchmark for Hudnut and the *starting* benchmark for Goldsmith. The issue of mayoral transition somewhat complicates the assignment of 1992. Goldsmith was elected in November 1991, and took office in

January 1992, so Hudnut effectively does not serve at all in 1992. However, the 1992 budget is largely the creation of the last months of the Hudnut regime, since a new operating budget had to be in place in January 1992 as Goldsmith took office. Even if Hudnut and Goldsmith cooperated in crafting a fiscal year 1992 budget, its "obligations" largely reflect what is in place *while Hudnut is in office but before Goldsmith assumes office.* Thus, the most reasonable approach is to assign 1992 to *both* mayors. In rough fashion, the examination of data in this way becomes an interrupted time series analysis. The basic idea is to expose a variety of financial measurements and ratios classified into the 1986-1991 period (the Hudnut administration), an election (transition) year (1992, assigned to both mayors), and the last six years of the Goldsmith mayoral regime (1993 to 1998). In most cases, tabular presentations and line graphs are used to compare the two periods, using standardized measures such as per capita or proportional ratios. Unless otherwise noted, the sources of the data are the CUPRs for each of the years from 1986 through 1998 and, as noted, most measures are taken in constant 1992 dollars in order to eliminate the effects of inflation during the period.

In the Indianapolis financial reporting system, the most interesting action occurs in three funds: the general fund, the debt service fund and the capital projects fund. This is because these funds house the major operating departments and track the major capital improvement activities of the city. There is less activity, and far lower fund balances reported in the special revenue, trust and agency, fiduciary, and enterprise funds. The general fixed assets fund is largely an accounting entity that tracks the city's physical plant (for example, streets, buildings and facilities) in various ways, and the general long-term debt fund essentially reports on outstanding debt.

An Analysis of Indianapolis City Finances, 1986-1998

Assets and Liabilities

Assets and liabilities are the basic building blocks of the city's financial system. In the traditional fund accounting model, assets minus liabilities equals the fund balance (equity), and the fund balance is further subdivided into reserved and unreserved equity. Each separate fund in the city (for example, general, special revenue, debt service and so forth) has a set of assets, liabilities and fund balances. A normative perspective for city governments suggests that, overall, it is "good" when assets increase, liabilities decrease and (therefore) equity increases, in particular *unreserved* equity. As noted earlier, Indianapolis has nine different funds with separate balance sheets. In the following analysis, these funds are consolidated to track the overall changes from 1986 to 1998.

The general model can be applied in the case of Indianapolis, but there is a minor twist: the city recognizes and lists (like many other municipalities) a category of liabilities known as *unfunded pensions*. Typically, this refers to the block of money that would be needed if the accounting entity (the City of Indianapolis, in this case) had to pay *all* of its employees for their retirement benefits (primarily salaries) if they *all* retired at one time (Reed and Swain 1990). That is, most city governments fund pension payments on a "pay-as-you-go" basis, paying only for the current year pension liability out of current revenues *each year*. Technically, subsequent years' pension payments thereby become unfunded liabilities, although by prudent financial standards they would be funded each year out of *that* year's current revenues.

Changes in the structure of assets, liabilities, and equity spanning the 1986 to 1998 period are shown in Table 1. Overall, the three categories of assets, liabilities and total equity grew more during the Hudnut period than during the mayoral regime of Goldsmith. From the normative perspective mentioned above, only Goldsmith's annual rate of growth in liabilities (3.9 percent) compared favorably to Hudnut (for example, Goldsmith's liabilities increased at a higher average rate than Hudnut's). Furthermore, unfunded pension liabilities grew much larger (32 percent versus 7.2 percent) and at a much faster annual rate (5 percent versus 1.6 percent) during the Goldsmith administration. As a result, the growth in equity was actually negative during Goldsmith's watch (fund balance declined on average 1.1 percent each year). However, the *unreserved* portion of equity increased substantially after Hudnut left office, although it has been declining steadily since then, from $360.5 million when Goldsmith took office, to $176.3 million at the end of fiscal year 1998. If examined in terms of the unreserved fund balance as a percentage of assets (a rough parallel to *return on assets* in a private sector context), the unreserved portion peaked during Goldsmith's election year at 14 percent, but it has declined gradually to 6.1 percent in 1998. The trend lines in per capita assets, liabilities, unreserved equity, and unfunded pensions are shown Figure 1. Assets per capita have climbed from $3,000 in 1986 to nearly $4,000 in 1998, although in both the Hudnut and Goldsmith periods there were relatively steep increases followed by declines. A similar pattern is evident for liabilities, which have increased from about $1,000 per capita in the Hudnut years to around $1,500 during the Goldsmith era. Unfunded pensions have remained generally stable on a per capita basis, while unreserved equity per capita (for example, cash reserves) has been declining since 1992, from $483 to approximately $238 in 1998.

Table 1: Assets, liabilities, unfunded pensions and equity ($000, 1992 constant dollars)

	Assets	Liabilities	Pensions	Unfunded Equity	Liabilities	Unreserved as percent of assets
Hudnut						
1986	$2,156,616	$681,365	$528,203	$947,047	$49,647	2.3%
1987	$2,213,956	$699,350	$489,626	$1,024,980	$48,752	2.2%
1988	$2,734,406	$817,771	$565,086	$1,351,548	$62,549	2.3%
1989	$2,937,249	$917,481	$640,547	$1,379,221	-$16,846	-0.6%
1990	$2,401,604	$728,154	$622,938	$1,050,512	-$2,649	-0.1%
1991	$2,362,349	$722,610	$579,514	$1,060,226	$308,376	13.1%
Goldsmith						
1992	$2,573,083	$875,356	$566,092	$1,131,635	$360,496	14.0%
1993	$2,870,600	$1,077,152	$581,252	$1,212,196	$380,680	13.3%
1994	$2,756,896	$1,043,166	$571,007	$1,142,722	$258,741	9.4%
1995	$2,645,664	$997,398	$548,648	$1,099,617	$229,951	8.7%
1996	$2,601,308	$991,646	$564,360	$1,045,301	$183,918	7.1%
1997	$2,745,901	$1,063,175	$665,607	$1,017,118	$167,924	6.1%
1998	$2,874,064	$1,076,257	$747,367	$1,050,440	$176,274	6.1%

Total growth				
Hudnut, 86-92	19.3%	28.5%	7.2%	19.5%
Goldsmith, 92-98	11.7%	23.0%	32.0%	-7.2%

Annual growth				
Hudnut				
86-87	2.7%	2.6%	-7.3%	8.2%
87-88	23.5%	16.9%	15.4%	31.9%
88-89	7.4%	12.2%	13.4%	2.0%
89-90	-18.2%	-20.6%	-2.7%	-23.8%
90-91	-1.6%	-0.8%	-7.0%	0.9%
91-92	8.9%	21.1%	-2.3%	6.7%
Average	3.8%	5.3%	1.6%	4.3%
Goldsmith				
92-93	11.6%	23.1%	2.7%	7.1%
93-94	-4.0%	-3.2%	-1.8%	-5.7%
94-95	-4.0%	-4.4%	-3.9%	-3.8%
95-96	-1.7%	-0.6%	2.9%	-4.9%
96-97	5.6%	7.2%	17.9%	-2.7%
97-98	4.7%	1.2%	12.3%	3.3%
Average	2.0%	3.9%	5.0%	-1.1%

Figure 1: Per capita balance sheet measures (1992 constant dollars)

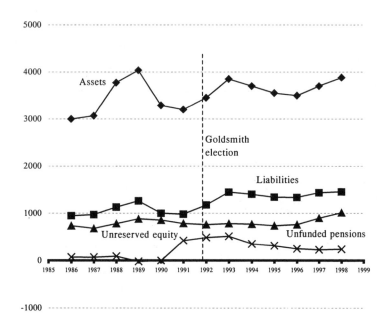

Operating Expenditures

The City of Indianapolis traditionally classifies its routine municipal operating expenditures into several general categories, summarized as follows: public safety, culture and recreation, community development and welfare, public works, and general government. However, assessing the city's general performance within these categories during the 1986-1998 period is made somewhat difficult by changes in financial reporting practices. For example, regarding operating expenditures, the city CUPRs set out broad categories of expenditures for city services that were consistent from 1986 to 1995. Thereafter, the categories changed, which makes it more difficult to track precisely the changes in the composition of city expenditures for basic services. The following chart shows how the categories were combined in this analysis for consistency after 1995:

Expenditure Categories Used In This Analysis	From CUPRs Covering 1986-1995	From CUPRs Covering 1996-1998
Public safety	Protection of people and property	Public safety
Community cultural and recreation	Community cultural and recreation	Culture and recreation
Community development and welfare	Community development and welfare	Community development and welfare Economic development and assistance Urban redevelopment and housing Health and welfare
Public works	Transportation and related services Environmental services	Public works
General government	Executive/legislative affairs Administrative services	General government

Furthermore, the departmental composition of each of these broad categories has varied during the 1986-1998 period. Although this makes it difficult to precisely decompose each one into the exact departments responsible for the activity, the current departmental arrangement provides a general picture of the city's municipal organization. In 1998, public safety included emergency management, police, fire, weights and measures, and animal control. Public works included solid waste, environmental resource management and a large contract compliance operation that monitored the private management contract for the wastewater treatment plants. Community development and welfare consisted largely of the Department of Metropolitan Development, and the Department of Parks and Recreation comprised the culture and recreation function.

Total operating expenditures for these functions are depicted in Table 2, and they reveal several contrasts between the Hudnut and Goldsmith eras. If annual average expenditures are examined, Goldsmith spent *on average* more (in constant 1992 dollars) than Hudnut each year in all functions except public works. However, annual changes reflect a different picture. Total operating expenditures (all functions) under Hudnut grew by nearly 22 percent, but declined by more than 12 percent under Goldsmith. During the Goldsmith period from 1992 to 1998, only public safety expenditures increased (4.6 percent overall; less than 1 percent annually), while all other functional categories declined, some by more than one-fourth (for example, public works and general government). In terms of average annual growth, all the broad municipal functions grew during the 1986-92 Hudnut regime, led by general government (19 percent annually) and public works (4.8 percent annually). In contrast, the 1992-1998 Goldsmith regime showed an average annual decrease in every function except public safety (which all but stayed the same, at 0.8 percent annual growth), with the steepest declines in public works and general government, a reversal of the high growth functions under Hudnut. Similar trends appear in an examination of per capita operating expenditures spanning the 1986 to 1998 period (Figure 2). Public safety has been generally increasing, from $139 to $164 per capita, with only slight differences between the two mayors. Conversely, per capita public works expenditures climbed during the 1986 to 1992 Hudnut administration, peaking at $178, but these have declined sharply during the Goldsmith regime to $132. Most of this decline is no doubt linked to the much-heralded privatization of wastewater management initiated by Goldsmith in 1993 (Montgomery and Nunn 1996). Per capita spending on culture and recreation has remained essentially stable around $22 through both mayoral administrations.

Operating Revenues

To pay for municipal operations, Indianapolis mayors must rely on an array of revenue sources. The revenue categories used in this analysis and their specific sources of funding were:

Revenue categories used in this analysis	Specific sources of revenue
Taxes	Property taxes; wheel taxes; motor vehicle taxes; local option income taxes; financial institution taxes; other local taxes
Charges, licenses, fees and so forth	Licenses and permits; charges for service; traffic violations and municipal court fees
Intergovernmental	Federal government revenues; Indiana state government revenues; revenues from other governmental units
Other sources	Other financing sources (for example, bond proceeds)

Table 2: **Indianapolis operating expenditures, 1986-1998 ($000, 1992 constant dollars)**

		Public safety	Culture recreation	Community development & welfare	Public works	General govt.	Total
Hudnut	1986	$100,343	$16,113	$35,823	$101,099	$8,445	$261,824
	1987	$104,866	$17,172	$26,087	$96,310	$7,565	$252,001
	1988	$106,186	$15,216	$34,975	$97,726	$13,983	$268,086
	1989	$110,125	$15,182	$35,641	$109,129	$16,901	$286,978
	1990	$114,477	$16,307	$32,176	$113,225	$23,116	$299,300
	1991	$118,323	$15,813	$32,167	$118,258	$25,759	$310,321
Goldsmith	1992	$116,293	$18,228	$33,914	$132,649	$18,138	$319,222
	1993	$111,595	$16,783	$36,548	$114,020	$18,803	$297,749
	1994	$112,818	$15,465	$38,805	$102,774	$23,045	$292,908
	1995	$111,341	$15,478	$46,529	$109,568	$24,988	$307,904
	1996	$121,147	$16,357	$42,834	$98,244	$16,964	$295,546
	1997	$119,425	$16,856	$39,383	$98,540	$14,388	$288,592
	1998	$121,598	$17,053	$29,608	$97,601	$13,585	$279,444
Averages							
Hudnut, 86-92		$110,088	$16,290	$32,969	$109,771	$16,272	$285,390
Goldsmith, 92-98		$116,317	$16,603	$38,232	$107,628	$18,559	$297,338
Total growth							
Hudnut, 86-92		15.9%	13.1%	-5.3%	31.2%	114.8%	21.9%
Goldsmith, 92-98		4.6%	-6.4%	-12.7%	-26.4%	-25.1%	-12.5%
Annual growth							
Hudnut							
86-87		4.5%	6.6%	-27.2%	-4.7%	-10.4%	-3.8%
87-88		1.3%	-11.4%	34.1%	1.5%	84.8%	6.4%
88-89		3.7%	-0.2%	1.9%	11.7%	20.9%	7.0%
89-90		4.0%	7.4%	-9.7%	3.8%	36.8%	4.3%
90-91		3.4%	-3.0%	0.0%	4.4%	11.4%	3.7%
91-92		<u>-1.7%</u>	<u>15.3%</u>	<u>5.4%</u>	<u>12.2%</u>	<u>-29.6%</u>	<u>2.9%</u>
Average		2.5%	2.4%	0.7%	4.8%	19.0%	3.4%
Goldsmith							
92-93		-4.0%	-7.9%	7.8%	-14.0%	3.7%	-6.7%
93-94		1.1%	-7.9%	6.2%	-9.9%	22.6%	-1.6%
94-95		-1.3%	0.1%	19.9%	6.6%	8.4%	5.1%
95-96		8.8%	5.7%	-7.9%	-10.3%	-32.1%	-4.0%
96-97		-1.4%	3.1%	-8.1%	0.3%	-15.2%	-2.4%
97-98		<u>1.8%</u>	<u>1.2%</u>	<u>-24.8%</u>	<u>-1.0%</u>	<u>-5.6%</u>	<u>-3.2%</u>
Average		0.8%	-1.0%	-1.2%	-4.7%	-3.0%	-2.1%

The 'other' category is the least straightforward of the group and by far the most volatile, as in the analysis that follows. Generally, this volatility is linked to the use of the 'other' category to include revenues generated via bond proceeds, bond re-funding or special transfers. For example, in the 1992 transition year from Hudnut to Goldsmith, the 'other financing sources' category jumped from $98 million (constant $1992) in 1991 to $809 million and included transfers for bond refundings and capital lease financing for the United Airlines maintenance operating center (MOC) (City of Indianapolis 1993). To control for this regular variation in the 'other' category throughout the entire 1986 to 1998 period, Table 3 documents the changes in each of the four summary revenue categories, as well as a 'total' and 'total excluding other sources' category.

Figure 2:   Per capita expenditures, by function (1992 constant dollars)

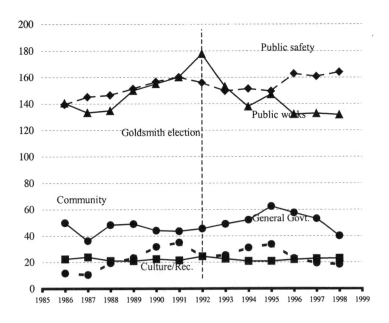

Table 3: Indianapolis operating revenues, 1986-1998 ($000, 1992 constant dollars)

		Taxes	Charges, licenses, fees	Inter-govt.	Other sources	Total	Total (excl.other sources)
Hudnut	1986	$175,697	$67,088	$130,020	$109,078	$481,883	$372,804
	1987	$198,442	$68,538	$121,610	$95,248	$483,838	$388,590
	1988	$201,565	$70,043	$131,493	$389,518	$792,620	$403,102
	1989	$210,320	$78,213	$129,054	$32,828	$450,417	$417,588
	1990	$220,890	$91,549	$110,810	$55,325	$478,574	$423,249
	1991	$221,414	$90,812	$102,069	$98,135	$512,431	$414,296
Goldsmith	1992	$224,259	$88,665	$101,356	$808,572	$1,222,852	$414,280
	1993	$220,740	$98,785	$98,124	$264,218	$681,867	$417,649
	1994	$218,526	$82,411	$110,354	$96,273	$507,564	$411,291
	1995	$234,563	$89,092	$117,114	$110,681	$551,451	$440,770
	1996	$224,900	$80,003	$121,661	$38,835	$465,399	$426,564
	1997	$223,526	$80,328	$128,903	$28,638	$461,394	$432,757
	1998	$223,907	$80,785	$114,339	$139,744	$558,775	$419,031
Total growth							
Hudnut, 86-92		27.6%	32.2%	-22.0%	641.3%	153.8%	11.1%
Goldsmith, 92-98		-0.2%	-8.9%	12.8%	-82.7%	-54.3%	1.1%
Annual growth							
Hudnut							
86-87		12.9%	2.2%	-6.5%	-12.7%	0.4%	4.2%
87-88		1.6%	2.2%	8.1%	309.0%	63.8%	3.7%
88-89		4.3%	11.7%	-1.9%	-91.6%	-43.2%	3.6%
89-90		5.0%	17.0%	-14.1%	68.5%	6.3%	1.4%
90-91		0.2%	-0.8%	-7.9%	77.4%	7.1%	-2.1%
91-92		1.3%	-2.4%	-0.7%	723.9%	138.6%	0.0%
Average		4.2%	5.0%	-3.8%	179.1%	28.8%	1.8%
Goldsmith							
92-93		-1.6%	11.4%	-3.2%	-67.3%	-44.2%	0.8%
93-94		-1.0%	-16.6%	12.5%	-63.6%	-25.6%	-1.5%
94-95		7.3%	8.1%	6.1%	15.0%	8.6%	7.2%
95-96		-4.1%	-10.2%	3.9%	-64.9%	-15.6%	-3.2%
96-97		-0.6%	0.4%	6.0%	-26.3%	-0.9%	1.5%
97-98		0.2%	0.6%	-11.3%	388.0%	21.1%	-3.2%
Average		0.0%	-1.0%	2.3%	30.1%	-9.4%	0.3%

Goldsmith administration, there was a 0.2 percent decrease overall in tax revenue—in other words, essentially no change.

Charges/licenses/fee revenues also declined by nearly 9 percent during the 1992 to 1998 Goldsmith period. Only intergovernmental revenue increased for Goldsmith (by 12.8 percent, or 2.3 percent annually). As suggested above, the 'other' category is misleading for both mayoral regimes, particularly during the Hudnut period, because of the odd 1992 injection of bond refunding revenue and UAL lease revenues. Even so, the 'other' category generally was declining from 1992 to 1997, although bond proceeds increased the total in 1998 as in several previous years. Per capita revenues suggest fewer differences between the two periods, but there are consistent trends in each category (Figure 3). Taxes per capita climbed steadily under Hudnut from $244 in 1986 to $300 in 1990, but they have remained steady at around $300 per capita through 1998. Conversely, per capita intergovernmental revenues had declined from 1986 to 1993, but they began to increase slightly until 1997. Other per capita fees and charges did not vary greatly from one mayoral regime to the other.

Figure 3: Per capita revenues (constant $1992)

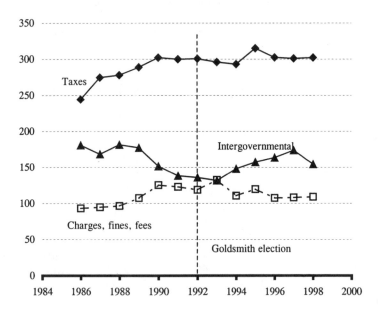

Net Revenues and Operating Margins

Like any other organization, the City of Indianapolis must bring in more revenues than expenditures if it is to be a viable municipal government. Two measures can capture the sometimes-volatile relationship between revenues and expenditures. First, the *operating margin* gauges the relationship between operating revenues and operating expenditures—that is, only those financial flows that are used to pay for and provide basic municipal services. Thus, the revenues and expenditures used to estimate the operating margin *exclude* bond proceeds, other revenues, debt service, capital expenditures and other expenditures. A higher operating margin gives city administrators more leeway in meeting bond payments, capital outlays and other extraordinary spending than does a lower margin. Low operating margins mean the municipality is "barely" generating enough revenues to fund their basic statutory service requirements. The second measure, *net revenues*, is more straightforward: it is simply the difference between *all* revenues and *all* expenditures, in this case *including* debt service, bond proceeds, capital outlays and all the rest. Again, high net revenues are typically superior to low net revenues and reflect, at least indirectly, the city's overall handling of financial flows.

Both of these measures demonstrate interesting trends during the thirteen years of analysis indicated here (Table 4). The Goldsmith administration has demonstrated operating margins that are similar to those in the last six years of the Hudnut regime, although these margins have generally grown from year to year under Goldsmith, in contrast to a consistent annual decline during the Hudnut years that were examined. Hudnut's operating margin grew from 1986 to 1987, but declined annually until the 1992 election year, after which the margin generally climbed under Goldsmith's direction. Even so, one year's margin declined from the previous year in three of the six Goldsmith years (compared to five of six Hudnut years). Goldsmith did, however, build the operating margin back to its previously highest level under Hudnut in 1987. Examining these data from another perspective, if the operating margin measure is standardized as a percentage of operating revenues (shown in Figure 4), then a pattern of decline during the six Hudnut years, followed by a steady increase in the Goldsmith years, is quite clear. In part, this is not surprising, given Goldsmith's explicit political platform to increase the efficiency of the city (for example, decrease its operating costs)—that is, to implement the SELTIC competitiveness credo that accompanied his election to office.

Table 4: Indianapolis operating margin and net revenues, 1986-1998 ($000, constant dollars)

		Operating margin	Net revenues Total	Cumulative
Hudnut	1986	$110,981	$82,374	$82,374
	1987	$136,589	$79,394	$161,768
	1988	$135,016	$217,431	$379,200
	1989	$130,610	-$44,486	$334,714
	1990	$123,949	-$3,842	$330,873
	1991	$103,975	$11,606	$342,479
Goldsmith	1992	$95,058	$49,990	$392,469
	1993	$119,900	$103,183	$495,652
	1994	$118,383	-$118,797	$376,854
	1995	$132,866	-$77,546	$299,309
	1996	$131,018	-$42,888	$256,420
	1997	$144,164	-$30,760	$225,661
	1998	$139,587	$13,655	$239,316

Annual growth

Hudnut

86-87	23.1%	-3.6%	96.4%
87-88	-1.2%	173.9%	134.4%
88-89	-3.3%	-120.5%	-11.7%
89-90	-5.1%	91.4%	-1.1%
90-91	-16.1%	402.1%	3.5%
91-92	-8.6%	330.7%	14.6%
Average	-1.9%	145.7%	39.3%

Goldsmith

92-93	26.1%	106.4%	26.3%
93-94	-1.3%	-215.1%	-24.0%
94-95	12.2%	34.7%	-20.6%
95-96	-1.4%	44.7%	-14.3%
96-97	10.0%	28.3%	-12.0%
97-98	-3.2%	144.4%	6.1%
Average	7.1%	23.9%	-6.4%

NOTE: *Operating margin* = Operating revenues - operating expenditures, which excludes bond proceeds, other revenues, debt service, capital outlays, and other expenditures.
Net revenues = Total revenues - total expenditures

But operating margins only approximate the narrowest fiscal environment of basic municipal services, the difference between *operating* revenues and expenditures. The broader environment includes revenues and expenditures for *all* activities, especially sporadic major capital projects. The second measure used here, net revenues, suggests a very different pattern that reflects the volatility of capital expenditures, debt issues, debt service and 'other' extraordinary revenue injections into and expenditure extractions from the city's financial flows. In this context, both mayors experienced substantial variation in annual net revenues. A nutshell summary suggests that Hudnut created large net revenue figures from 1986 to 1988, followed by two years of *negative* net revenues and then began to recreate a positive net revenue basis for the city. Of course, in order to sustain operations and projects in a negative net revenue position in any given year, the city had to have accumulated a "bank" of revenues, which the 'cumulative net revenue' column reflects. Thus, Hudnut built-up cumulative revenues in the mid-1980s that permitted a few years of negative net revenues that closed-out the decade. On an annual growth basis, Hudnut's net revenue positions were not "bad" in a normative sense: in only two years did he fail to produce an *improvement* over the net revenues of the previous year (1987 and 1989). Patterns in the Goldsmith years were generally similar.

Figure 4: Margins and net revenues

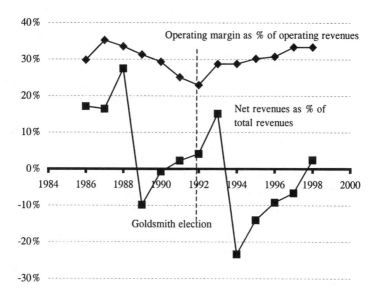

Goldsmith's net revenue positions were positive in only three of the seven years these data depict. As a result, the sizeable cumulative net revenue figure that had accumulated by 1993 declined substantially from 1994 to 1997, recovering only slightly in 1998. But, as with Hudnut, annual changes in net revenues were more positive: despite the use of accumulated revenues to cover each year's net revenue deficit, Goldsmith was still improving the previous year's net revenue position in all years but one (1994). When considered in normalized terms of net revenues as a percentage of total revenues (Figure 4), it seems clear that Goldsmith and Hudnut experienced a precipitous—and remarkably symmetrical—decline in net revenues, which was followed by several years of gradually improved annual positions. By 1998, Goldsmith had regained a positive net revenue status.

Capital Outlays

In parallel with the day-to-day operating expenditures for police and fire service, public works, recreation and other routine functions, municipal governments also spend substantial annual sums on capital facilities and infrastructure systems. Known as *capital outlays*, these expenditures for new roads, parks, wastewater treatment facilities, new municipal buildings and municipal rolling stock (for example, police cars, fire trucks and city vehicles) typically are paid for through current revenues, bond fund proceeds, intergovernmental grants or some combination of the three. Together, these expenditures make up the physical assets of city government that are in turn major components of the urban service delivery system. Obviously, Indianapolis mayors regularly face crucial decisions on what combination of revenue sources to use for the extraordinary capital outlays required from year-to-year for both ongoing operations (for example, a new police facility) and special projects such as Circle Centre Mall. Capital outlays are critical because, in many ways, they pay for acquisition of the assets needed to create and maintain the physical infrastructure (for example, roads, bridges, sewer lines, storm sewers and sports and recreational facilities) that forms the landscape for economic growth and development of the city. Further, capital outlays create a high level of volatility in city expenditure patterns as noted above.

Assessing the annual capital outlays of any city is complicated for several reasons—and the City of Indianapolis is certainly no exception. First, city governments differ in their classification of capital expenditures. To be considered a capital outlay, an expenditure must be for an asset that costs a certain minimum amount (for example, $10,000) and has a useful life exceeding a certain period (for example, five years). These classification rules can change from year-to-year, so that capital outlays in one year might be considered operating expenditures in another year. Second, city governments differ in their capital outlay reporting practices. Some partition capital outlays into a separate fund (for example, a capital projects account), while other include capital outlays as a specific line item in the general, special revenue and other funds. The City of Indianapolis does both. Third, cities differ in how they account for capital expenditures for major infrastructure systems such as streets. For instance, Indianapolis indicates in its CUPRs that "public domain (infrastructure) general fixed assets, consisting of certain improvements other than building (for example, streets, sewers and bridges) are not capitalized." Thus, these expenditures appear in funds as "capital outlays," but not necessarily as "fixed assets" in other accounting reports. Thus, getting a handle on the capital outlays of Indianapolis requires an examination of several different measures that can cope with the differences in reporting practices inherent in an analysis using thirteen different years of financial reports in a complex municipal operation.

Indianapolis capital outlays during the 1986 to 1998 period are described in several measures shown in Table 5. Total capital expenditures in the city are composed of two sets of spending: money spent on physical assets that are capitalized into the "fixed asset" account (for example, 'additions to fixed assets'), and money spent on physical assets that are not capitalized into fixed assets ('outlays not capitalized'). During the 1986 to 1991 Hudnut period, the 'additions to fixed assets' category always exceeded 'capital outlays not capitalized,' but during the 1992-1998 Goldsmith period, the situation was reversed—'capital outlays not capitalized' always exceeded 'additions to fixed assets.' During both periods, Indianapolis CUPRs report that streets and bridges are included in the 'capital outlays not capitalized' category. Moreover, capital spending is typically a "lumpy" affair in that city governments might spend a great deal one year, followed by much lower expenditures the following year. The City of Indianapolis has followed this pattern with high variation in spending levels annually during both the Hudnut and Goldsmith periods shown in Table 5. Furthermore, it should be noted that the 1989-90 fiscal year under Hudnut was clearly unusual for three reasons: the large decreases in capital spending *and* in total fixed assets and the large increase in Indianapolis property values (which was partly the result of property tax reassessments performed during the year).

Table 5: Indianapolis capital outlays, 1986-1998 ($000, 1992 constant dollars)

		Capital spending			General		Prop. value per	Capital expend.
		Additions to fixed assets	Capital outlays not capitalized	Total capital expend.	municipal fixed assets	Indianapolis property value	$ of fixed assets	as % of operating expend.
Hudnut	1986	$58,700	$21,320	$80,020	$650,667	$15,395,313	$23.66	30.6%
	1987	$75,890	$33,439	$109,330	$687,596	$15,259,567	$22.19	43.4%
	1988	$95,226	$46,985	$142,210	$816,829	$15,318,625	$18.75	53.0%
	1989	$112,873	$43,085	$155,957	$888,175	$15,255,494	$17.18	54.3%
	1990	$44,830	$23,733	$68,563	$684,818	$21,216,021	$30.98	22.9%
	1991	$46,856	$18,273	$65,129	$691,767	$20,918,994	$30.24	21.0%
Goldsmith	1992	$35,905	$99,201	$135,106	$697,589	$20,870,747	$29.92	42.3%
	1993	$35,127	$100,188	$135,316	$695,528	$20,918,983	$30.08	45.4%
	1994	$77,189	$121,856	$199,045	$741,991	$20,800,476	$28.03	68.0%
	1995	$68,311	$87,793	$156,103	$775,276	$20,713,682	$26.72	50.7%
	1996	$14,423	$111,593	$126,016	$761,815	$22,767,368	$29.89	42.6%
	1997	$41,636	$79,358	$120,994	$762,332	$23,146,786	$30.36	41.9%
	1998	$31,600	$56,984	$88,584	$780,421	$23,195,101	$29.72	31.7%
Averages								
Hudnut, 96-92		$67,183	$40,862	$108,045	$731,063	$17,747,823	$24.70	38.2%
Goldsmith, 92-98		$43,456	$93,853	$137,309	$744,993	$21,773,306	$29.25	46.1%
Total growth								
Hudnut, 86-92		-38.8%	365.3%	68.8%	7.2%	35.6%	26.4%	
Goldsmith, 92-98		-12.0%	-42.6%	-34.4%	11.9%	11.1%	-0.7%	
Annual growth								
Hudnut								
86-87		29.3%	56.8%	36.6%	5.7%	-0.9%	-6.2%	
87-88		25.5%	40.5%	30.1%	18.8%	0.4%	-15.5%	
88-89		18.5%	-8.3%	9.7%	8.7%	-0.4%	-8.4%	
89-90		-60.3%	-44.9%	-56.0%	-22.9%	39.1%	80.4%	
90-91		4.5%	-23.0%	-5.0%	1.0%	-1.4%	-2.4%	
91-92		-23.4%	442.9%	107.4%	0.8%	-0.2%	-1.1%	
Average		-1.0%	77.3%	20.5%	2.0%	6.1%	7.8%	
Goldsmith								
92-93		-2.2%	1.0%	0.2%	-0.3%	0.2%	0.5%	
92-94		119.7%	21.6%	47.1%	6.7%	-0.6%	-6.8%	
94-95		-11.5%	-28.0%	-21.6%	4.5%	-0.4%	-4.7%	
95-96		-78.9%	27.1%	-19.3%	-1.7%	9.9%	11.9%	
96-97		188.7%	-28.9%	-4.0%	0.1%	1.7%	1.6%	
97-98		-24.1%	-28.2%	-26.8%	2.4%	0.2%	-2.1%	
Average		32.0%	-5.9%	-4.1%	1.9%	1.8%	0.1%	

As a consequence, total growth and annual rates of growth in capital outlays are highly variable, and somewhat misleading. Both mayors show evidence of reductions in total additions to fixed assets, but this is an artifact of the beginning and ending totals for each period. On an annual basis, Hudnut averaged about a one percent reduction each year in fixed asset additions, while Goldsmith averaged a 32 percent annual increase. This pattern was reversed for capital outlays not capitalized, suggesting differences between the two regimes in their financial reporting policy of which assets were capitalized or not. Because of these very different patterns, the *total capital expenditures* measure is probably a more valid comparison, and it shows an increasing level of expenditures under Hudnut (total growth of nearly 69 percent, or 20.5 percent annually), and a decline under Goldsmith (total decline of more than one-third, or 4.1 percent annually). However, Goldsmith spent more on average each year for capital expenditures ($137 million versus $108 million annually by Hudnut). Another measure that indirectly compares the capital spending patterns during the two regimes is the relative growth of the general fixed asset account group. Overall, the Hudnut administration increased the value of fixed assets from $650.7 million to $697.6 million —a total growth of 7.2 percent, or 2 percent annually. Goldsmith's addition to municipal fixed assets increased at approximately the same annual rate, but overall, it grew more (11.9 percent). The average value of municipal fixed assets under Hudnut was $731 million compared to Goldsmith's average of nearly $745 million. This difference is also reflected in the average capital-to-operating ratios during each mayor's tenures analyzed here: 38 percent for Hudnut and 46 percent for Goldsmith.

Another indirect indicator of city infrastructure spending is property values, which for any city are typically aided and abetted by capital projects executed by city government. Indianapolis assessed property values increased by more than one-third under Hudnut, but this was boosted greatly by a major increase caused by statewide property value reassessments in 1989-1990. Property values increased by 11.1 percent during the 1992-1998 Goldsmith period. Combining the two measures of municipal fixed assets and city property values can give a rough indication of property value per unit of fixed assets. In this context, property value per $1 of fixed assets has remained virtually unchanged during Goldsmith's terms, hovering around $30 each year. During the 1986 to 1992 Hudnut period, property value per $1 of fixed assets was declining until the 1989-1990 reassessment, after which it was "artificially" increased by the reassessment.

On a per capita basis, no clear trend characterizes either of the mayoral regimes (Figure 5). Total capital outlays under Hudnut climbed from 1986 to 1989, dropped until 1991, then climbed again—before and during Goldsmith's first term—until 1994, only to have continued dropping through 1998. Per capita fixed assets and property values were both affected by the 1989-90 reassessment, but since then have remained generally steady. Since the property value reassessment in 1989-90, property value per capita has only increased from $29,012 to $31,290, a jump of 7.8 percent over the eight-year period. This is somewhat puzzling for the Goldsmith years, because fixed assets per capita climbed slightly and then remained stable while per capita capital outlays declined from $267 to $119 after 1994; this suggests some evidently unremarked changes in financial reporting practices that underpin the CUPRs.

Outstanding debt and debt service

Expenditures for infrastructure facilities and other capital outlays typically require revenue generated via bond sales, which in turn generate annual debt service requirements and, in effect, encumber future revenues for future debt service payments. Thus, the picture of the city's financial health is incomplete without assessing the structure of annual debt service payments and the projected future payments required to amortize total outstanding debt due in upcoming years. It is in the area of debt and debt service that the commitments of city staff and politicians in one period have longstanding repercussions into the future. Municipal debt is routinely a long-term affair, with general obligation and revenue bonds stretched-out over 20-year periods or longer. In the case of Indianapolis, for example, debt issues made in the six-year Hudnut period under examination would become layered into debt decisions made during the six-year Goldsmith period under evaluation. Indianapolis also classifies long-term leases as a part of outstanding debt, and it has used lease arrangements in several cases as incentives to close major economic development deals such as the United Airlines MOC at the airport. Like standard debt issues, these leases also create long-term financial commitments that span different mayoral generations.

The 1986 to 1998 debt picture for Indianapolis shows several major increases rooted in the use of tax increment financing (TIF) bonds and growth in long-term lease commitments (Table 6). Under Hudnut, total TIF debt increased by a factor of eight from 1987 to 1988 in order to begin financing Circle Centre Mall in the downtown TIF district, known official as the "Consolidated Tax Allocation Area." As a result, although outstanding serial bonds actually decreased by 40 percent during the Hudnut regime, the massive increase in TIF debt meant total debt increased by nearly 58 percent from 1986 to 1992. Outstanding TIF bonds during the Goldsmith period have been declining slightly, increasing only from 1996 to 1997. Another significant economic development project, the United Airlines MOC, created a major increase in long-term leases payable from 1991 to 1992, Hudnut's last year in office. Once ratcheted-up to pay for the United Airlines MOC facility, leases payable remained high during Goldsmith's administration. As might be expected from the periodic and abrupt changes in outstanding debt, annual debt service requirements varied considerably under both mayors' regimes. While generally stable for Hudnut from 1986 to 1991, the 1992 debt service payment jumped

Figure 5: Per capita (1992 constant dollars)

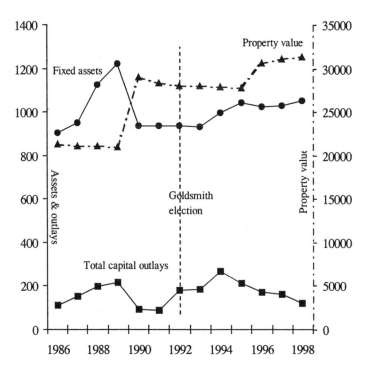

Table 6: **Indianapolis outstanding debt and debt service, 1986-1998 ($000, 1992 constant dollars)**

		\multicolumn{3}{}{Outstanding long-term debt}			
		Serial bonds	TIF bonds	Other debt	Total standard debt	Leases payable	Debt service
Hudnut	1986	$320,430	$36,052	$31,242	$387,724	$52,427	$64,166
	1987	$352,602	$34,021	$23,651	$410,274	$43,877	$54,960
	1988	$379,024	$289,077	$29,199	$697,300	$6,864	$59,986
	1989	$341,970	$283,570	$32,213	$657,753	$9,891	$67,980
	1990	$241,212	$282,939	$16,194	$540,345	$9,223	$79,825
	1991	$214,718	$312,522	$15,425	$542,665	$7,816	$66,660
Goldsmith	1992	$192,320	$356,541	$62,385	$611,246	$127,320	$346,608
	1993	$383,335	$349,449	$55,687	$788,471	$133,493	$125,393
	1994	$334,083	$346,226	$53,065	$733,374	$144,856	$74,810
	1995	$316,494	$330,298	$46,314	$693,106	$142,417	$105,695
	1996	$301,076	$320,457	$59,146	$680,680	$137,334	$73,243
	1997	$284,088	$324,884	$58,294	$667,266	$131,965	$67,261
	1998	$267,711	$275,249	$130,034	$672,994	$135,708	$150,939

Averages

		Serial bonds	TIF bonds	Other debt	Total standard debt	Leases payable	Debt service
Hudnut, 86-92		$291,754	$227,817	$30,044	$549,615	$36,774	$105,741
Goldsmith, 92-98		$297,015	$329,015	$66,418	$692,448	$136,156	$134,850

Total growth

		Serial bonds	TIF bonds	Other debt	Total standard debt	Leases payable	Debt service
Hudnut, 86-92		-40.0%	889.0%	99.7%	57.6%	142.9%	440.2%
Goldsmith, 92-98		39.2%	-22.8%	108.4%	10.1%	6.6%	-56.5%

Annual growth

Hudnut

		Serial bonds	TIF bonds	Other debt	Total standard debt	Leases payable	Debt service
86-87		10.0%	-5.6%	-24.3%	5.8%	-16.3%	-14.3%
87-88		7.5%	749.7%	23.5%	70.0%	-84.4%	9.1%
88-89		-9.8%	-1.9%	10.3%	-5.7%	44.1%	13.3%
89-90		-29.5%	-0.2%	-49.7%	-17.8%	-6.7%	17.4%
90-91		-11.0%	10.5%	-4.7%	0.4%	-15.3%	-16.5%
91-92		-10.4%	14.1%	304.4%	12.6%	1528.9%	420.0%
Average		-7.2%	127.7%	43.2%	10.9%	241.7%	71.5%

Goldsmith

		Serial bonds	TIF bonds	Other debt	Total standard debt	Leases payable	Debt service
92-93		99.3%	-2.0%	-10.7%	29.0%	4.8%	-63.8%
93-94		-12.8%	-0.9%	-4.7%	-7.0%	8.5%	-40.3%
94-95		-5.3%	-4.6%	-12.7%	-5.5%	-1.7%	41.3%
95-96		-4.9%	-3.0%	27.7%	-1.8%	-3.6%	-30.7%
96-97		-5.6%	1.4%	-1.4%	-2.0%	-3.9%	-8.2%
97-98		-5.8%	-15.3%	123.1%	0.9%	2.8%	124.4%
Average		10.8%	-4.1%	20.2%	2.3%	1.2%	3.8%

more than 400 percent, due primarily to the redemption of TIF bonds. Debt service payments under Goldsmith fluctuated up and down, with average annual growth of just less than four percent between 1992 and 1998.

The varying levels of debt and debt service are also evident on a per capita basis, as shown in Figure 6. The big TIF bond increase from 1987 to 1988, the increase in debt service from 1991 to 1992, the increase in other debt from 1991 to 1992 and the large bump in serial bonds are all depicted in the graph. Only the latter occurred during the Goldsmith regime, although the development decisions that led to these changes were all taken during Hudnut's administration when the deals on Circle Centre Mall and the United Airlines MOC were closed. Since 1993, Goldsmith's first full year in office, there have been steady declines in per capita TIF and serial bonds, while other debt per capita has been generally flat until the 1997 to 1998 period, when it doubled. Under Goldsmith, debt service too has been generally declining, except for a 1997 to 1998 increase.

Figure 6: Outstanding debt and debt service per capita

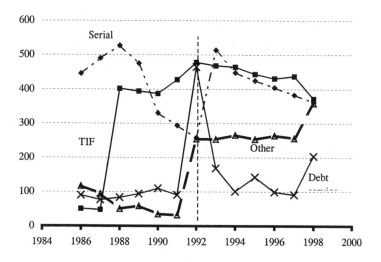

One final picture of Indianapolis municipal debt is needed. This is the anticipated future annual debt service that the city faces at various points in time. Figure 7 shows the total projected debt service that was in place in 1990 under Hudnut toward the end of his regime, in 1992 at the start of the Goldsmith administration and in 1998 as the Goldsmith administration was winding down. The most significant finding here is the major spike in debt service scheduled to occur from 2000 to 2001 that can be attributed to tax increment debt decisions made during Goldsmith's tenure. This is due to a jump of nearly $30 million in debt service on outstanding TIF bonds, issued during the Goldsmith administration, that are due in 2001. Thereafter, debt service payments shrink, but remain high, especially in comparison to the projected debt service from previous years. Overall, the first twenty years of the next millennium reflect a level of outstanding debt service that has shifted considerably beyond what was in place when Goldsmith took office in 1992. As of the end of 1998, outstanding debt payments are approximately $20 million more each year between 2002 and 2018 than they were in 1992

Desperately Seeking Differences: Hudnut, Goldsmith, and Indianapolis Finances

No mayor ever performs the tasks of municipal finance and administration exactly as those who occupied the office before. By the same token, the challenges of providing and paying for city services and municipal infrastructure are curiously similar year in and year out, regardless of whom serves as mayor. Services must be delivered, facilities must be built and maintained, and the path for economic development should be smoothed. In the case of Indianapolis city finances during the 1986 to 1998 period, this combination of different mayors facing similar challenges has created an interesting tableau of assets and liabilities, operating expenditures and revenues, debt and debt service. Differences are evident under the regimes of the two mayors, but there are also similarities.

With respect to the changes in the relationship between assets and liabilities, Hudnut, in raw amounts, had built-up a large unreserved equity balance by the time he left office, which was reduced by half during the Goldsmith years examined here. However, in standardized terms, Goldsmith has managed the proportional relationship between unreserved equity and assets fairly effectively, maintaining rates of return generally higher than during the Hudnut years that were examined. Overall, Hudnut generally had more favorable rates of growth in assets, liabilities and equity. But in per capita terms, Goldsmith had maintained relatively stable trends in these balance sheet measures, although unreserved equity per capita definitely has been declining. On balance, the differences between these two mayors in their management of assets and liabilities are not large.

Figure 7: Total projected debt service at the end of 1990, 1992, and 1998

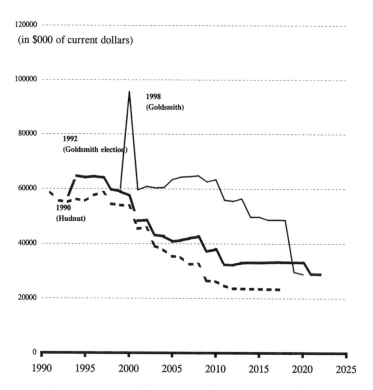

While there are some differences between the two mayors in their management of operating expenditures, inarguable characterizations of cost savings and efficiencies are less clear. Because efficiency was the main thrust of Goldsmith's mayoral platform, and because the identification of operational cost centers was a major administrative mission of the mayor's staff, it is perhaps surprising that the differences in operating expenditures under the two mayors were not greater. This, of course, is subject to some qualification. Under Hudnut, annual change or average annual increases in spending for all functions usually *increased* during the 1986 to 1992 period, while annual changes typically decreased on average or the increases that occurred were smaller under Goldsmith from 1992 to 1998. Some of the difference here is linked to the fact that by 1992, Hudnut had built total operating expenditures up to its peak (a high of $319 million for the entire 1986 through 1998 period), which thereafter generally declined. In large part it is only in the area of public works that Goldsmith can claim a major departure—that is, a decline in spending—from the half-dozen Hudnut years preceding him. But this, too, was a decrease from a 1992 high point. Otherwise, Goldsmith's *average annual* expenditure in all other functions was higher than Hudnut's. An alternative question—and one that is unanswerable using financial data such as these—has to do with the quality of services and the changing regulatory environment of services such as public works. Even if expenditures were reduced, the consolidated City of Indianapolis has generated little systematic information about the perceived or actual quality of municipal services delivered to and consumed by its citizens, and without such information a normative assessment of decreases or increases in spending is hard to obtain. Reducing some operating expenditures can lead to poorer services. For example, a reduction in public works spending may simply reflect a "penny-wise and pound-foolish" approach to municipal wastewater management.

In late 1999, during the waning days of the Goldsmith administration, substantial political and regulatory pressure was applied by the Indiana Department of Environmental Management to the city in an effort to persuade the city to invest substantially in improving the combined sewage-storm water collection system that has contributed to numerous permit violations by the Indianapolis wastewater treatment plants. Presumably, such investments could have begun earlier in order to avoid the current problems. However, such spending would not be on the radar screen of a mayoral administration committed to cost-cutting initiatives. Thus, without other more systematic assessments of the *quality* of Indianapolis' municipal services, all the expenditure data can suggest is that Goldsmith, when compared to Hudnut, reduced spending in public works, increased spending in other areas and generally stabilized or reduced *per capita* spending. From this analysis, it is difficult to depict substantive differences between these two mayors.

As for operating revenues, one clear difference between the two mayors, at least on per capita basis, was that intergovernmental revenues under Goldsmith increased after a constant decline under Hudnut. Per capita taxes under Hudnut had been increasing and then generally stabilized under Goldsmith, similar to the pattern of charges and fines. Thus, Goldsmith appears (at least on a per capita basis) to have captured what is politically perhaps the best of all possible revenues sources, intergovernmental funds—in effect importing other governmental dollars from "outside" Indianapolis city government. However, examining operating revenues in terms of raw dollars, there are fewer differences in the total revenues available to either mayor throughout the thirteen years analyzed. Total revenues (excluding the volatile 'other' category) grew annually by just less than two percent under Hudnut, but remained largely unchanged during the Goldsmith years. From this perspective, Goldsmith's cost cutting could simply be a response to a constant or declining body of operating revenues, which was clearly unlikely to grow because any tax increases would be decisions *non grata* if exposed within the context of campaign commitments and political promises to reduce costs and not increase taxes.

When the combined revenue-expenditure relationship was examined in terms of operating margins and net revenues, both contrasts and similarities between the two mayors again became evident. As for raw dollar amounts, Hudnut and Goldsmith typically maintained operating margins of more than $100 million during most of the years examined. However, Goldsmith clearly began using the "savings account" that had accumulated by the 1992 and 1993 fiscal years, insofar as cumulative net revenues (which reflected *all* income and spending) declined steadily from 1993 through 1997. Again, this kind of financial performance could be consistent with a cost-cutting mentality that focuses on minimizing spending but not increasing taxes or routine operating revenues.

The volatility borne of bond proceeds, economic development projects and capital expenditures required to meet public-private dealmaking commitments may in part have driven the decline in cumulative net revenues under Goldsmith, which even though occurring under Goldsmith's watch actually had roots in the Hudnut administration. For example, financial commitments made by Hudnut for Circle Centre Mall and the United Airlines MOC facility demanded cash outlays that would not become due until fiscal years during Goldsmith's regime. When those commitments come due, if a mayor is unwilling to raise *new* income via increased operating revenues (for example, taxes), the cash requirements must still be met from someplace, and the savings accumulated from past 'surpluses' is a key candidate. Thus, in this context, Goldsmith appeared to be more effective than Hudnut in maintaining a growing proportional relationship between *operating* income and spending, but the periodic cash crises associated with economic development commitments put heavy pressure on the net balance of *all* income and expenditures. It is also interesting that both mayors experienced precipitous declines in net revenue as a percent of total revenues, followed by several years of recovery (Hudnut in 1988 and Goldsmith in 1993). This suggests that any mayor who is forced or decides to spend a large part of previous surpluses accumulated in other years must then rebuild the financial balance, if not the political capital, during subsequent years.

Capital outlays present an apparently clear area of difference between these two mayors. Annual capital outlays under both Hudnut and Goldsmith have been highly variable, but typically large, ranging from a low of 30.6 percent of operating expenditures (under Hudnut) to a high of 68 percent (under Goldsmith). The preponderance of capital outlay measures, however, suggests that Goldsmith generally spent more money on capital outlays, which makes some sense given the role of the "Building Better Neighborhoods" capital spending campaign in the latter half of the 1990s. But the true impact of capital outlays on the financial health of Indianapolis is perhaps better conveyed by the differences in debt service and outstanding debt linked to the two mayors. In constant dollar terms, Goldsmith can be associated with higher serial and TIF bond debt, other debt and debt service. This is perhaps most clear in looking at average annual debt and debt service, which in all cases is higher during the Goldsmith years. Evidently, Goldsmith spent more on capital outlays, which in large part were financed by debt, rather than operating expenditures, which were financed with taxes and other non-debt revenue. The former was paid for in installments, the latter on a pay-as-you-go basis. Here perhaps is the crucial difference between Hudnut and Goldsmith.

Thus, if a mayor were seeking a method by which large sums of money could be spent, spread around the city like fertilizer without necessarily having a commensurate *instantaneous* impact on current revenues, then just such a method might be invoked. A mayor could minimize operating expenditures, preserve operating revenues (without raising taxes) and issue debt with favorable repayment terms. Considerable sums could be (and were) spent on capital projects, while less would be spent on day-to-day operating activities. It is this profile, this theory, that perhaps best fits the data describing the half-dozen Goldsmith years in comparison to the last six years of the Hudnut regime. The problem with such a reading, however, is that some of the outstanding debt and debt service amounts that pushed Goldsmith's annual tallies higher than Hudnut's were actually generated by financing decisions made during Hudnut's administration. The two big hits, of course, were linked to Circle Centre Mall and the United Airlines MOC, commitments made by Hudnut. Of course, by the end of the year 2001, Goldsmith will have returned the favor to the next Indianapolis mayor (Bart Peterson, elected on November 2, 1999, the first Democrat to occupy the mayor's post since 1968), when outstanding debt service will jump from $60 million to nearly $95 million. Peterson will be left with dealing with Goldsmith's debt, in much the same way that Goldsmith had to find ways to amortize Hudnut's debt. This theme is proverbial in municipal administration.

Summary

The financial health of any city government is an ongoing drama, involving a changing cast of characters but the same stage and the same props with which to produce their version of the municipal play. The comparison of two of these players in Indianapolis, Stephen Goldsmith and William H. Hudnut III, suggests that both operated from similar financial scripts, even though the plot details may have varied from year to year. If there were significant differences between the two mayors in their fiscal impacts on the city of Indianapolis, the differences were perhaps explained most by their respective styles, in the ways each mayor went about making and spending city dollars. Yet at the conclusion of each mayor's reign, the city's fiscal house was generally in order. When Hudnut left office, the financial health of Indianapolis was fairly sound, characterized as such not only by the data contained in this analysis but by Goldsmith as well. As Goldsmith leaves office, the financial health of the city is also fairly sound. The new mayor, Bart Peterson, will face periodic future increases in debt service that are attributable to Goldsmith just as Goldsmith faced those linked to Hudnut. Goldsmith consumed some of the total revenue surpluses that both he and Hudnut had built, but he also maintained a sizeable operating margin in support of daily municipal services. Spending for municipal operations followed similar patterns in the periods analyzed for both mayors' administrations (with the exception of public works under Goldsmith). But overall, within the lens of the data examined here, a conclusive declaration of which mayor was the better financial manager would at best present a blurry image. For Indianapolis as for most large cities, new mayoral regimes are discrete events inserted into the otherwise continuous process of municipal financing. While financial changes clearly occur, the momentum of municipal operations, its revenue sources, its spending pattern and its borrowing practices carries mayors along by virtue of a whole current of past and present decisions made under different regimes. As the next millennium opens, the play and its process will begin again with Bart Peterson in a starring role, facing many of the same challenges that his predecessors faced.

Notes

[1] The editors gratefully acknowledge Julia C. Abedian for her review and comment on this chapter.

Chapter 6

Accountability: The Achilles Heel

Sheila Suess Kennedy

Introduction

Calls to "reinvent government" and achieve efficiencies through "privatization" raise issues that have engrossed political scientists and public administrators for years. At the heart of the conversation is the question, recently articulated by Elkin and Soltan (1993): How does society combine its concerns for economic efficiency and democratic control? In other words, what is the best way to govern? The answer to that question is almost entirely political, because the administrative methods that are used reflect the most fundamental convictions about the nature of the democratic state and the role of government officials.

Michael Spicer (1995) provides a very useful characterization of the various answers that have been proposed. Spicer has surveyed the literature of public administration and has identified two contradictory visions: "discretionist" and "instrumentalist." The discretionist sees public officials as akin to independent agents; citizens elect or hire certain individuals, presumed to be qualified by training or experience, to decide for citizens what is in their interest and citizens expect them to use their best judgments to effectuate that interest. If they go too far astray, citizens can "fire" them at the next election, but while they occupy the elected position they exercise autonomy of action. This might call this the "father knows best" approach to public management. The instrumentalist, on the other hand, sees public administration as an exercise in effectuating the political will of the community. In this view, the elected official has an obligation to act almost entirely in accordance with the desires of his constituents. This might be called the "I didn't elect you to think" approach.

Most public administrators and political scientists would agree that effective management requires a judicious blend of the two approaches. But it seems fair to place advocates of privatization well toward the discretionist end of the spectrum.[1] Privatization is thus one aspect of the so-called "scientific" or "rationalist" theory of public administration which views government primarily as a provider of services (Kirlin 1996) and constitutional checks and balances as impediments to efficiency rather than essential safeguards against overreaching and arrogance (Spicer 1995).

Contracting out for government services is neither new nor inherently ominous. As Kettl suggests, however, "The constellation of issues generated by growth of government contracting spill over onto the most basic questions of American governance" (Kettl 1993, 211). The growth Kettl alludes to is largely due to current disenchantment with government and the belief of some theorists and politicians that privatization is the "magic bullet" that can produce efficient and responsive government (Goldsmith 1992; Boaz 1997; Epstein 1995). This more extreme reliance on the benefits of "marketization" might be called "privatization ideology" to distinguish it from the longstanding use of contracting as one useful tool among many available to the urban manager. That ideology rests largely on a view of government as primarily a provider of services for "customers" rather than a shared enterprise of citizens (Kirlin 1996, 161). However, if government is more than a service provider, if it is an important generator of social capital (Romine 1997; Hudnut 1998) and an instrument of collective choice (Kirlin 1996), then efforts at privatization will be measured against a different set of criteria.

From 1992 until 1999, Stephen Goldsmith, Mayor of Indianapolis, was a leading proponent of privatization, which he prefers to call "marketization." His efforts have been widely reported, in glowing terms by the national media (Washington Post 1993; Stern 1994) and in somewhat less glowing terms by local commentators (Miller 2000, Howey 1998,1999). Other public officials are being urged to emulate his programs, and George W. Bush, at this writing the Republican candidate for President, looks to him for domestic policy advice (Brant

2000). In light of the reception Goldsmith's ideas have received, it seems a particularly appropriate time to evaluate the extensive changes he instituted in Indianapolis.

One caveat to this inquiry should be noted. The character and personality of a government official is always pertinent to the success or failure of programs. Citizens do not elect robots and simply program them to manage their civic affairs in accordance with this or that political theory. In Indianapolis, advocates for privatization insist that certain obvious failures of the Goldsmith administration were not due to the inadequacy of the underlying theory, but are instead a product of this particular Mayor's temperament and personality. The thesis of this chapter, however, is that many of the problems that have been blamed on Goldsmith's character flaws or management style really *are* inherent in privatization as the term has been understood and applied in the Indianapolis experiment, and would have manifested themselves under any mayor who pursued "marketization" so single-mindedly.[2] As Kettl has noted, there is a tendency by privatization advocates to see problems that emerge as isolated instances of mismanagement rather than as "a generic thread that winds its way through contracting relationships"(Kettl 1993, 207). It is thus important to examine the political implications of privatization in Indianapolis apart from criticisms that might be leveled at this particular privatizer.

This chapter will examine: 1) the effect of privatization (while Goldsmith prefers the term "marketization," this chapter will use the more familiar terminology) on citizen participation and local party politics; 2) potential conflicts between privatization and American constitutional principles; and 3) policy implications of the Indianapolis approach, most notably the effect upon public accountability.

Citizen Participation and Party Politics

Citizens participate in their government in a number of ways beyond campaigns and elections. They serve on Boards and Commissions and ad hoc committees. They attend public hearings. They call City Hall to complain about potholes, or to demand installation of a traffic signal. They obtain permits. They work for government as employees, consultants or contractors. They are vendors to government agencies. In the process, they partake of a civic and political culture.

Culture has been defined in terms of shared meanings and expectations—patterns of belief, symbols, rituals and myths that evolve over time and function as the glue that holds associations of all kinds together (Hennessey 1998, 525). Any significant change in the way government does things upsets those expectations, and it requires a corresponding change in the political culture if it is to be sustainable (Blomquist, 2000; Gregory 1999).

Available literature on "reinventing government" suggests that effecting such change is anything but easy, and the way change is managed has important public policy implications. Privatization, if pursued too aggressively, minimizes the contacts that citizens have with their government. When functions that were previously handled by government are contracted out to private companies, fewer committees and boards are needed. Fewer public hearings are held, because "experts" rather than citizens are driving the decision-making processes (Montgomery and Nunn 1996; Yankelovich 1991). Government agencies are doing less and so buy fewer goods. In Indianapolis, Goldsmith even hired private firms to dispense drainage permits. Contracting thus substantially reduces the points of contact between citizen and city (Smith and Lipsky 1993, 118) and with that reduction comes an attenuation of civic ownership, the sense of shared enterprise that characterizes a workable and working *polis*.

As Robert Gregory (1999, 67) has recently noted, social trust arises out of networks of civic engagement and norms of reciprocity. At a time when so much national attention is focused on the fragmentation of the polity and the dominance of special interests, privatization has increased the perception that most important decisions are being made by technocrats and their allies (and potential contractors) in the business community (Yankelovich 1991, 241). In Indianapolis, the civic leaders who used to play an important role in our public life, whose motives for participation were founded on a sense of duty rather than a potential for profit, have all but disappeared. There are many reasons for that phenomenon; but privatization has been identified as one culprit. An article in *NUVO Newsweekly*, an Indianapolis weekly paper, noted:

> .... the city has lost a class of leaders that built domes and plazas, brought in pro football and international sports. They don't make 'em like Tom Binford [a local business and civic leader] any more. Those days of community good work were replaced by Goldsmith's revolutionary urban governance that was authoritarian, cynical and sneering, with significant doses of fear and blackballing. (Ullmann 1998)

When "discretionists" hire "experts" and eschew public participation (Montgomery and Nunn 1996), the sense of connectedness, of "ownership" essential to the building of community, suffers. Political capital dwindles (Gregory 1999, 65). Such sentiments are difficult to measure, but their political significance is very real. Goldsmith himself attributed his decisive loss of the 1996 Indiana governor's race partly to backlash over privatization (Hasse 1996).

Enthusiasm for privatization is one consequence of our current lack of enthusiasm for government. Proponents of contracting out base their arguments largely on the presumed incapacities of government. Recommendations to privatize are thus generally accompanied by a good deal of bureaucrat-bashing and antigovernment rhetoric; certainly that has been true in Indianapolis. The early days of the Goldsmith administration were marked by a procession of press releases reporting efforts to cut middle management (almost invariably referred to as "fat") and replace "bloated bureaucracy" with "more efficient" private providers of goods and services (Remondini 1991).

Such rhetoric tends to devalue government employment. What is less obvious, perhaps, is that the constant denigration of government also tends to dampen enthusiasm for politics. Once one's party has elected someone to dismantle the bureaucracy, what is left to keep the political party worker engaged and interested? Political parties, after all, are about electing people to government. When government work has been demonized, it should not be surprising that participation in party politics declines as well.

Privatization has more direct implications for party politics, as *The Howey Political Report*, an Indiana political newsletter, has detailed. In a piece published just after the November 1998 elections, Howey and contributor Schoeff wrote:

> When Goldsmith sacked the mid-level bureaucracy that had accumulated during the Republican Lugar and Hudnut administrations, he essentially disemboweled one of the most prolific and successful political machines of modern Midwest history.... Since then, the beleaguered Marion County GOP has compiled an excruciating record of failure. (Howey and Schoeff 1998)

Howey and Schoeff go on to report on the effects of that party bloodletting: inability to get out the vote, lack of enthusiasm and lack of manpower. They conclude:

> Why? Because the Republican patronage is gone. The bureaucrats Goldsmith sacked don't bother to get out the vote. Unions can reward their activists, so they turn out the vote. There are no rewards for Republican partisans in Indianapolis. (Howey and Schoeff 1998)

This lack of rewards for grass roots political activity was a key element in the politics of Indianapolis during Goldsmith's administration. While some people participate in the political process for the sheer love of it, most party workers of the past knew that victory would bring them *something:* maybe a city job, a paved street or just improved access to the powers that be. In the privatized city, political contributions are rewarded, not party activities such as polling and registration and phone banks. With the award of significant contracts to manage operations previously handled by municipal employees have come persistent allegations that political contributors are being rewarded with lucrative city business, that privatization is simply a less desirable form of patronage. A July 1996 article in the *Indianapolis Star* reported:

> Seventeen days after getting a lucrative city contract, executives of the [privately owned] Indianapolis Water Company and its development partner will throw a fundraiser for Mayor Stephen Goldsmith.
>
> The $250-per-person dinner planned for Wednesday would not be the first fundraiser for Goldsmith, the Republican nominee for Governor, to come on the heels of a privatization contract.
>
> Shortly after privatization of parts of Metro Bus and the municipal golf courses, contractors held similar events for Goldsmith. (Johnston 1996)

While the influence of money on American politics is a national and systemic problem, in Indianapolis privatization exacerbated this problem because it made more government business available to the right people. Yesterday, blue-collar workers polled their neighborhoods hoping for a job; today, business owners contribute $5000 hoping for a contract. And nobody polls the neighborhood.

Constitutional Issues

As Spicer has pointed out, many public administrators see the Constitution as a problem rather than as a basis for legitimacy of government action. The Founders devised a system of checks and balances intended to impede the efficiency of the state in order to protect individual liberty. When public administrators are concentrating on making the trains run on time, those checks can seem onerous.

> Constitutional checks on power . . . provide a system of multiple veto

points in the political process. These veto points limit the ability of any particular group of political leaders to simply impose its will on others in the political process. As a result, constitutional checks on power force political leaders to take account of information and opinions held by others about the effects of public policies. (Spicer 1995, 51)

Some of the most consistent public criticisms of Goldsmith's re-invention efforts have focused upon the widespread perception that public decisions were made without the benefit of this constitutionally required deliberative process. This perception created an atmosphere of political cynicism that was largely absent during prior Republican administrations, and which made it more difficult for Goldsmith to achieve his policy objectives. In his book, he complains that efforts at redeveloping a portion of the riverfront were met with accusations of cronyism and hidden agendas (Goldsmith 1997). Such suspicions are an inevitable outgrowth of the "government by expert" privatization model, which gives high priority to *product* and short shrift to *process*. The problem is intimately connected to the issues of political and fiscal accountability addressed below.

Legally, privatization raises troubling issues of state action (Smith and Lipsky 1993). Civil libertarians have questioned whether independent contractors, even those operating under government contracts, are exercising state action so as to be bound by the Bill of Rights. Only the government can violate one's civil liberties. Can a city avoid compliance with due process or intentionally infringe citizens' First Amendment rights by the simple expedient of contracting with a private company? Are records maintained by such private contractors subject to Freedom of Information inquiry? Emerging law in this area is unclear. If city governments can avoid compliance with the Bill of Rights by engaging private contractors to manage selected pieces of the civic enterprise, the constitutional and political implications will be profound.

In "The End of the Republican Era," Theodore Lowi (1995) reminds us that we are in danger of losing the constituency for the rule of law, preferring *authority* to *rules*. While privatization is almost always defended as a method for producing smaller and more responsive government, in fact it simply empowers—*authorizes*—private interests to act under government's imprimatur, shifting the locus but not the magnitude of the task at hand. It privileges authority over the rule of law. For example, when the private managers of the Indianapolis wastewater treatment plant were charged with various improprieties, including evasion of Indiana bid laws, Goldsmith defended the noncompliance and criticized the laws as inadequate to the governance of a twenty-first century city (*Indianapolis Star* 1994).

Policy Implications

Management by Change

It is a truism that change is a constant. One of the challenges public administrators face is the management of change so that citizens experience continuity rather than dislocation. James Madison observed that "it poisons the blessings of liberty itself [if the laws] undergo such incessant changes that no man who knows what the law is today can guess what it will be tomorrow" (Spicer 1995, 47). It is not only laws that can be amended; executive branch discretion for administration is broad, and permits substantial opportunities for institutional change. Stability and predictability are widely supposed to be important elements of governmental legitimacy. By its very nature, privatization, with its emphasis on finding a better deal, a cheaper supplier or a different or more efficient way of delivering services, invites—indeed celebrates—constant change. Change becomes a positive goal, an end in itself, rather than a side effect of necessary improvements. William Blomquist, a political science professor at Indiana University Purdue University, Indianapolis, has noted:

> What Indianapolis had evolved by 1991 was an "interest-group" culture of politics. With a 29-member City-County Council and nearly two hundred neighborhood organizations, a principal *modus operandi* of citizen participation was for neighborhood organizations to wrestle with the city bureaucracies over some desired service (parks, streets, drainage, etc.) and call in their City-County Councilor to intervene if the neighborhood wasn't getting the response it wanted.

From January, 1992 on, Goldsmith's ceaseless reorganizing, renaming, reshuffling and out-sourcing disrupted that organizational culture so completely that neither the neighborhood leaders (even long-serving, savvy, suburban ones) nor the City-County Councilors (even long-serving Republican ones) knew how to make the system work any more (Blomquist 1999).

In a recent article in *Public Administration Review*, J. Thomas Hennessey, Jr. looked at the management of change in several agencies during "reinvention" initiatives. He reported the following comments by middle managers in agencies that were not successful in their reinvention efforts. "There are constant changes and no one tells us why. One day we are doing this, the next day that. I am not sure anyone knows what is going on" (Hennessy 1998, 522). Hennessey's analysis suggests that when change is experienced in this way, the new methods—good or bad—are not sustainable.

The Indianapolis model is a case in point. From his first day in the office, Goldsmith kept his promise that it would not be business as usual. Department names were changed; the Department of Public Works became the Department of Capital Asset Management. Personnel changes were frequent—many employees were fired, many others were reassigned (Miller, 2000). Functions were relocated or contracted out with virtually no prior notice to the agencies affected. For example, in many courtrooms during the early days of the administration, court records piled up in boxes for months, awaiting the choice of a new, private microfilm company (Zore, 1992). Change was a mantra. Not long after Goldsmith's election, his Deputy Mayor told Goldsmith's predecessor, William Hudnut, that the motto of the new administration was "If it ain't broke, break it and then fix it" (Hudnut 1999).

Not surprisingly, city workers took these changes as a repudiation of everything they had done up to that point. Political party workers loyal to prior administrations were similarly offended. At the first Republican county convention held after Goldsmith's election, the political reaction was marked. Goldsmith spoke first, focusing on his commitment to change and enumerating why his approach to privatization was superior to prior methods of administration. The County Chairman spoke next, and during his remarks tactfully reminded the Mayor that change simply for the sake of change was not the goal, and that upheaval also imposes costs. Following the County Chairman to the rostrum was a longtime local political figure, Tom Schneider, Mayor of one of the four "excluded cities" within the Indianapolis Unigov system.[3] He began his remarks by saying, "Frankly, if I hear the word *change* one more time, I'm going to puke." He received a standing ovation.

Morale among city workers was a persistent problem during the Goldsmith administration, as was employee turnover (O'Laughlin 2000). Both problems contributed significantly to the political party difficulties described above. While it is easy to blame this state of affairs on Mayor Goldsmith—and certainly his management style was responsible for part of it—privatization ideology requires change to be a goal. How else do we understand the concept of "reinvention"?

Minority Employment and Race Relations

Government has often been the employer of "first resort" for women and minorities, easing their transition into the workforce and offering an avenue to gain management experience. Under Goldsmith, the city workforce was trimmed by 629 employees,[4] whose functions were largely contracted out (Morgan 1993). The impression in the Indianapolis African-American community is that this process resulted in significantly diminished opportunity for blacks. Employment figures do show a more substantial decline in the number of African-Americans employed by the civil city (employment exclusive of police and fire uniformed personnel). At the beginning of 1992, there were 690 African-Americans employed by the City of Indianapolis; at the end of 1998, there were 460, which represented a reduction of 230 jobs or 33 percent. During that same period, total city employment decreased by 27 percent.

While the city gave major contracts to at least one black-owned business, Oscar Robertson Smoot, based in Ohio, the local black community viewed privatization as a method of rewarding mostly white political contributors at the expense of the blacks who had been well represented in city hall during the Hudnut administration. This perception, coupled with persistent community-relations problems in the Indianapolis Police Department, had a significant negative effect on race relations in Indianapolis. Rozelle Boyd, minority leader of the City-County Council, observed:

> To its own detriment, the administration was very slow to respond to the broadly publicized "Meridian Street Brawl." The Brawl was a downtown police-initiated confrontation with citizens, characterized by racial slurs, that has come to be viewed as a kind of index to the administration's general responsiveness to the minority community. This obtains in both civil and economic arenas, especially the so-called 'privatization' process.

> There is a fairly widely held perception that response to the need for minority involvement and participation is minimal and that even then it comes only after determining that there are broader implications that need to be considered. (Boyd 1999)

Accountability

Government reliance on private contractors raises accountability issues different from those involved when government is providing services directly (Kettl 1993, 174; Smith and Lipsky 1993). As noted above, much of what passes for bureaucratic and governmental inefficiency is really what Russell Hardin (1998, 12) has tactfully called "institutional design that encapsulates the self-interest of government officials" and what others call precautions against corruption. If, as many social scientists assert, trust in government requires accountability, lack of accountability contributes to distrust and even cynicism about government and those who are engaged in it (Hardin 1998).

In the private sector, the market can provide very effective checks and balances, as anyone who has ever gone out of business can attest. The checks and balances applied to government, however, address fundamentally different concerns. The political system requires structural safeguards that recognize the differences between government and private enterprise and that compensate for deficiencies in leadership and protect against abuse. One of the problems with the political rhetoric accompanying privatization is its failure to acknowledge that government is fundamentally different from the private sector. As Gregory has noted:

> [W]hen core public services are increasingly enjoined by government to operate as if they were businesses (as distinct from being required to work in a business-like manner), [political] commitment is weakly signaled. Genuine and forceful commitment to standards of ethical probity in public service rests on political recognition of those factors that make public administration essentially different from corporate management and that demand an appreciation of the idea of the public interest. (Gregory 1999, 66)

The differences are so fundamental that Jane Jacobs has identified different "moral syndromes" applicable to government and commerce (Jacobs 1992). The checks and balances built into our system were intended to address that insight, and to require political, legal and fiscal accountability by officeholders to those they serve.

In Indianapolis, privatization has undercut accountability in several important ways. As Spicer (1995) has documented, good government administrators and middle managers provide an internal check on the excesses of elected officials. Privatization can be an "end run" around that safeguard (Rosenbloom, 2000). Private companies do not have a history or ethic of public service, nor can they provide the institutional memory that citizens have a right to expect, and that frequently keeps newly elected officials from costly or embarrassing errors. As Gregory has written, "There is no clear evidence that corporate business has any unequivocal commitment to [the concept of public interest] and considerable room for valid debate as to whether it should have"(Gregory 1999, 66).

Externally, at least in the Indianapolis experiment, privatization has had a marked and troubling effect on public criticism of the administration. Reporters investigating allegations of misfeasance tell similar stories of sources unwilling to be quoted or even to talk to the media (Krull 1999; Ullmann 1999). When a contract is important to a company, its owners and employees will take great pains to keep it. The implicit (and sometimes explicit) threat of losing business quiets the companies involved, and it exerts a discernable "chilling effect" on relatives, business associates, and those who may want to do business with the city in the future. Furthermore, when criticism does arise, it is often imputed to "sour grapes." This was the case with a lawsuit brought by a city worker, George Tomanovich, alleging improprieties by the Oscar Robertson Smoot (ORS) company. Tomanovich had been a city engineer displaced by the contract to ORS. When he charged that the company was receiving payments far in excess of the market and performing negligently, the administration dismissed the charges as the complaints of a disgruntled bureaucrat. It eventually settled the case for $300,000 after local media were able to confirm Tomanovich's allegations; however, it remains unclear whether ORS ever made restitution, and it continued to do business with the city for several years afterward. That episode, together with an investigation by the *Indianapolis Star* that led to a prolonged expose involving privatization of the city's golf courses, "golfgate," and reports over irregularities involving the wastewater treatment plant, left many citizens uneasy and raised questions about the adequacy of the city's capacity to monitor contractors' performance (Howey 1998; Howey 1999).

Open books and records, regular audits and other proofs of financial regularity are an essential element of accountability. Privatization can make it difficult to get a complete picture of city expenditures. As Kettl (1993) points out, a company doing business with the city does not thereby bargain to open its books to the world. If onerous reporting restrictions are imposed, the costs of complying with those restrictions will become part of the overhead charged against the contract—reducing the very cost benefits privatization is supposed to provide. On the other hand, when public money is being spent, the public has a right to ensure that it is being spent in accordance with the contract and the law.

The issue of auditing those doing business with the city has been raised in several contexts. Midway through the Goldsmith administration, it took legislation to the Indiana General Assembly that was intended to expedite the contracting out process. One of the changes proposed to existing law by H.B. 1398 would have removed from the definition of "public money" sums paid to a private contractor pursuant to a legally binding and enforceable contract. Had that provision of the bill been passed, no public audit of the contract could occur once payment to the private contractor had been made. Even without that provision, H.B. 1398 made accountability for privatized activities far more difficult (Miller 2000).

There has been no comprehensive public audit, and few performance or management audits, during the Goldsmith administration, either by the State Board of Accounts or by a private auditor. *NUVO Newsweekly*, a persistent critic of the administration, editorialized:

> One problem is that the State Board of Accounts has not been auditing the books of Unigov, leaving it to Unigov's mayors to hire their own auditors. While the State's watchdog slept, the foxes in city government have been shuffling funds without regard for law on the management of public funds and without regard to budgets passed by the Unigov council and appropriations passed by the General Assembly. Federal grants for specific purposes have been mixed with the money from state and local taxes in the city's general fund. Costs have been deferred, checks have been kited, floats have been lengthened and funds have been juggled. (Howey 1999)

Similar accusations were leveled by City-County Councilors Rozelle Boyd, Jeff Golc, Monroe Gray and Susan Williams (Boyd et al. 1996). The administration countered these allegations by pointing out that Indianapolis was extremely active in the bond markets,[5] and bond underwriters require audits and assurances. But one of the changes instituted by the Goldsmith administration was a change in budget categories that made year-to-year spending comparisons extremely difficult, while most financial reports available to rebut charges of impropriety came from other private contractors who faced questions about their own independence. The city's financial statements were produced by a large accounting firm, Coopers and Lybrand (now PriceWaterhouse-Coopers). The firm was paid $1,166,800 between 1993 and 1999, and it contributed over $30,000 to Goldsmith's political campaigns during that same time period, raising conflict of interest charges (Howey 1999).

Under Goldsmith, the city did not retain the internal bookkeeping and audit capacities developed by the prior controller—many of those functions were "contracted out," leaving the city without the management depth needed for good internal documentation and fiscal controls. The current controller estimates that as many as 30 percent of the contracts inherited by the Peterson Administration are legally inadequate; that is, contracts had not been properly bid or lacked required documentation (Davis 2000).

The Goldsmith administration made much of the fact that the limited audits that were performed by the State Board of Accounts, initiated by taxpayer petition in 1999, found no evidence of intentional criminal activity. Those reports documented a pattern of rampant and pervasive noncompliance with statutory requirements including: lack of required documentation; acceptance of bids without statutorily required engineering estimates; incorrect cost codes; awards made to nonresponsive bidders; notices to proceed issued 100 days after the expiration of the allowable statutory period; change orders executed after the issuance of a certificate of substantial completion; contracts awarded despite the fact that fewer than the required three bids were received; and even mathematical errors in the computation of city payments due (State Board of Accounts 1999).

By the end of Goldsmith's administration, questions about fiscal management and financial accountability were constant (Howey 1999, *Indianapolis Star* 1999, Williams 1999). Despite repeated claims that privatization saved money, tax revenues climbed from $224,258,758 in 1992 to $283,175,302 in 1999 (CAFR 1999). Much more significant was damaging evidence that expenses that had previously been paid from the city's operating budget had simply been shifted to the capital budget and deferred, so that tax rate increases could be avoided in the short term (Howey 1999; Nunn 2000; Miller 2000). Streams of revenue due in the future were pledged to bond repayment, effectively "borrowing" from future administrations. A case in point was wheel tax revenues due from the state. The wheel tax is the largest source of street resurfacing money. The city received $6,754,770 from the wheel tax in 1997, $7,197,090 in 1998 and $6,996,500 in 1999 (Nytes 2000). In 1999, the *Indianapolis Star* reported that Goldsmith had pledged $4,500,000 of the amount due for each year through 2010, thus reducing by over half the funds available to his successors for street repaving until 2010 (*Indianapolis Star* 1999).

Another pledge of future revenues was accomplished through the "relinquishment" of state highways to municipal control. In one such transaction, Goldsmith negotiated relinquishment of U.S. 40, which runs through downtown Indianapolis as Washington Street. The state paid the city $20 million dollars to cover estimated maintenance costs for the succeeding twenty years, in return for Indianapolis' assumption of all further financial liability for maintenance. However, according to news reports, the state payment was not placed in an account and earmarked for street maintenance. Instead, it was spent on Goldsmith's Building Better Neighborhoods programs. The financial obligation has been shifted from state government to the city, but the money is gone. Estimates are that such relinquishment agreements brought $70 million dollars into the budget that was spent on current programs, leaving future administrations without the revenues necessary to meet the added obligations Goldsmith assumed on behalf of the city. (Howey 1999)

Rather than reinventing city government, critics were suggesting that what Goldsmith had really "reinvented" were two decidedly old-fashioned political behaviors: patronage and the art of concealing or postponing costs until subsequent administrations took office. Rather than saving money, constant refinancing of municipal debt simply stretched out payment while accruing additional interest (Howey, 1999). As Brian Williams charged, in an article in the *Indianapolis Business Journal*,

> Under the current administration, the city's general-obligation debt policy was restructured, resulting in reduced principal payments in the near term, level principal and interest payments over the term of the bonds and a stable tax rate. Unfortunately, this action also resulted in increased costs to the taxpayers. The city's property taxpayers will pay an additional $193 million over the term of the [general obligation] bonds [and] an additional $336 million over the term of the Circle Centre bonds, which were originally issued in 1986 and now mature in 2028. (Williams 1999)

Williams also noted the precipitous rise in debt service as a percentage of the City budget. Between 1992 and 1998, debt service grew by $7,000,000 annually to absorb 31 percent of the total city budget. Williams quoted Moody's Investor Service to the effect that the city's debt "will become increasingly difficult to sustain" (Williams 1999).

The campaign to succeed Goldsmith was fought substantially over these issues of fiscal and managerial accountability, with Democrat Bart Peterson charging that Goldsmith had "mortgaged the future" and Republican Sue Ann Gilroy insisting that Indianapolis was "the best-run city in America" (*Indianapolis Star* 1999).

Summary

As Kettl (1993) has noted, the choice for public sector managers is not between government and market, it is how to strike the best balance between them. Prior administrations in Indianapolis contracted for services with private companies for many years. It is when privatization or "marketization" becomes more than simply another tool in the manager's arsenal, when it becomes an end in itself, that it subverts the political and organizational cultures that sustain and legitimate governmental activity. In Indianapolis, it ultimately became more important to prove that "marketization" was the one-size-fits-all answer to urban problems than it was to be fiscally prudent and politically accountable.

Government is an essentially political enterprise. The Indianapolis experiment under Goldsmith was an attempt to remake government in the image of private business, where competitiveness and the ability to accommodate constant change are necessary to survival, technical expertise drives decision-making and management is decisively top-down. The Indianapolis experiment suggests that such an approach threatens public accountability, discourages political participation, breeds cynicism, and it undermines the public trust necessary for effective governance.

Notes

[1] Montgomery and Nunn (1996, 43) noted, "Current efforts to restructure local government service delivery through privatization and contracting-out potentially privilege the public management model over the participatory model."

[2] It should be noted that Indianapolis is a strong mayor city, where the chief executive enjoys substantial autonomy. The political constraints of a city manager or strong council system would be likely to force a number of compromises that would produce different results.

[3] When city and county governments were consolidated in 1971, four small cities within the borders of the new entity were "excluded" from the new system, retaining their own mayors and city councils. As a practical matter, those communities remain subject to a wide number of countywide authorities and are closely integrated into the fabric of Unigov.

[4] The figure used by Goldsmith in his press releases is 800; however, figures provided by Mayoral Assistant Sally Spiers during the latter days of the Goldsmith administration put the number at 629. Attempts to verify employment numbers by reference to required EEOC filings were inconclusive,

since the city would include uniformed public safety officers in some reports but exclude them from others, and the breakouts were not sufficiently detailed to allow correction for that fact.

[5] Bonded indebtedness grew dramatically during the Goldsmith administration. Figures taken from the city's Comprehensive Annual Financial Reports show that, as of December 31, 1991, total bonded debt was $328,678,745. By December 31, 1998, it was $521,722,195, an increase of $193,043,450.

Part Three

Service Delivery in the Privatized City

Chapter 7

Policing the 21st Century City

Paul Annee

Introduction

I joined the Indianapolis Police Department (IPD) in September of 1965 and remained until 1999. During my years on the force, I had the opportunity to work in a variety of assignments including serving as Chief of Police between August 1986 and December 1991. On January 1, 1992, Steve Goldsmith appointed James Toler to replace me, and I reverted back to my merit rank of Captain. In 1999, I retired and took a position in the private sector. While I have discovered that there is a rewarding and enjoyable life after IPD, the fortunes of the department in which I served for so many years, and the problems faced by my fellow officers who are still there, will always be important to me. I am not an unbiased observer of the Goldsmith Administration, but I believe I am a knowledgeable and fair one.

When Goldsmith appointed Toler, he said Goldsmith told him, "I am going to turn the police department inside out and shake it." Shake it he did. The IPD's 1992 Annual Report begins with the statement "The year 1992 brought unprecedented change to the Indianapolis Police Department." Change has, in fact, been the story of Goldsmith's eight years in office. In many respects, it was the only constant.

The Goldsmith Agenda

Like most newly elected mayors, Goldsmith came into office with an agenda. For the IPD, a division of the Department of Public Safety, that agenda had two major elements: community policing and fiscal restraint (Goldsmith 1997). (The latter was to be achieved through his emphasis on privatization or "marketization.") Both goals are worthwhile, but they require thoughtful implementation and the cooperation of the officers in the IPD for successful outcomes. Community policing theory emerged in the early 1980s as a "new" form of policing. Unlike the traditional emphasis on response to calls, community policing has a strong preventive element. Police officers get out of their patrol cars and onto the beat in order to be closer to the citizens they serve. Ideally, they will interact with the neighborhood, become familiar with the residents and learn first-hand what makes them feel secure. Officers may remove the drunk sleeping on the stoop who is obstructing foot traffic, intercede with the noisy kids on the corner and watch for suspicious visitors who may later commit crimes. Eventually, they will come to be seen as a part of the community, rather than occasional intruders whose arrival signals a problem. This greater and more natural day-to-day involvement should increase the cooperation between residents and the officers who serve them. It should make citizens safer and officers more effective.

By 1990, most cities were in the process of implementing some form of community policing, and Indianapolis was no exception. Toward the end of William H. Hudnut III's term as Mayor, Indianapolis had taken the first steps under a plan for the gradual implementation of community policing.[1] The IPD had established neighborhood facilities at Washington Park, 42d and College, Madison Avenue and Michigan and King Street; and my deputy chiefs and I had begun regular discussions with the line officers and supervisors whose cooperation would be needed if we were to be successful. We had also begun internal analysis of functions that we could decentralize without jeopardizing effectiveness or economies of scale, and had begun placing civilians in some office positions in order to put more sworn officers on the street. To learn more about community policing, I had attended conferences at Harvard University (I went to one of them, "Policing in America" with then-Prosecutor Stephen Goldsmith). As we became more knowledgeable about community policing, Hudnut and I began to appreciate that proper implementation would affect not just deployment but also recruitment and training. We would be recruiting for *service*, not for war. A genuine culture change would be required, with all that would entail.

Goldsmith, however, told us that community policing would be implemented immediately. Among his first steps was the hiring of consultants who were well-known advocates of the theory. Robert Wasserman was a former research fellow with the Program in Criminal Justice Policy and Management at Harvard. George Kelling, together with James Q. Wilson, had developed a variation on community policing known as the "broken windows" theory. Wilson and Kelling believe that lack of attention to relatively low-level neighborhood deterioration—broken windows, abandoned cars and littered vacant lots—creates an environment where residents conclude that no one cares. Broken windows lead to petty crimes like public drunkenness and vagrancy, and their presence can snowball into more serious crime. The community policing approach begins by "saturating" neighborhoods with police officers who are trained to identify problems before they escalate. Wilson and Kelling had published a study demonstrating that this form of policing can make residents feel safer and improves police morale (Wilson and Kelling 1982). While some studies have disputed the "broken windows" theory, most police officers believe that when community policing has merit when it is properly understood and implemented.

Wasserman and Kelling eventually cost the city significant sums in consulting fees for advice that was largely ignored (Campbell et al. 1999). As an article in the *Indianapolis Star* said at the time, Goldsmith himself was the driving force behind the decision-making, and it was his interpretation of community policing that was implemented (Shramm 1993). Goldsmith's interpretation of community policing was very "bottom up;" that is, he equated it with getting rid of the "brass." Decisions were to be pushed to the patrolman level. As he says in his book, "[A]uthority and discretion [should] be given to those in the front lines, to the street officers" (Goldsmith 1997, 134). This view required him to ignore several of the experts he himself hired and to overlook deep differences of opinion between those experts, an experience that was to be repeated with a long line of subsequent consultants.

For example, while Robert Wasserman and George Kelling were both experts in the academic study of policing, they had very different priorities and approaches. Wasserman was a management wizard with very strong opinions about organization and strategy. He believed that management structure, lines of authority and interdepartmental communication were very important. A proponent of community policing as an evolutionary process, Wasserman believed that structure would be a vehicle for implementation (Wasserman 1973). Kelling, on the other hand, believed that departmental structure was an obstacle to implementation. He saw himself as the advocate of the patrol officer, and he constantly emphasized empowerment for the patrolman on the beat. Wasserman guided the top management team, while Kelling coached line officers on the finer points of "beat" policing.

The major flaw in this division of labor was the lack of philosophical compatibility between the two consultants. Organizational confusion was rampant throughout the IPD. Kelling was coaching patrol officers to assume more responsibility and exercise more discretion, but Wasserman was instructing top management in the importance of a more traditional organization that would develop a policing strategy and communicate it to the patrol officers. No one in the IPD, including the Police Chief, knew "the plan" (*Indianapolis Star* 1992d). From the perspective of those of us in the IPD, at least, the Mayor and Public Safety Director appeared to be equally confused. The term "Harvard Consultant" became a point of irritation within the IPD, and ultimately a joke. Rather than assisting in a smooth transition to a well-considered community policing plan, Kelling and Wasserman left a department that was divided, confused, frustrated and overwhelmed.

While I think Goldsmith knew that his first effort using national consultants had been a failure, he never seemed to lose his zest for outside "experts." Many more passed through Indianapolis, collecting substantial sums before moving on. Among them were Lawrence Sherman, Robert Trojanowicz, Reuben Greenberg, the Police Executive Research Team (or PERF), the Hudson Institute and the National Institutes of Justice (NIJ) (Office of the Controller 2000). It is anyone's guess what the total bill was for these services.[2] One of several contracts with Lawrence Sherman of the University of Maryland, for example, was for $50,000 to conduct a gun seizure project that the *Indianapolis Star* later called "grossly ineffective." In six months, the project confiscated twenty-one guns for a cost of $2,381 *per gun* (Lanosga and Johnston 1995). The *Star* editorialized that the "losses may be worthwhile if they cause the administration to re-examine its unbridled enthusiasm for consultants"(*Indianapolis Star* 1995). Unfortunately, the enthusiasm was never re-examined, and since there was very little coordination among the consultants or consistency to their advice, it is highly debatable how much value taxpayers got for the dollars that were spent.

The Devil in the Details

One reason experts on community policing advise going slowly with implementation is because careful planning is needed in order to avoid unanticipated or negative consequences (Rosenbaum 1994; Goldsmith 1997, 134). The speed with which new programs were introduced, and the rapidity with which they were changed meant that the IPD experienced a number of unintended consequences.

Responsibility Without Power

"Broken windows" policing gives police, as Goldsmith says in his book, "responsibility for identifying and solving neighborhood problems."[3] The problem, as critics have observed, is that police are not community development officers or code enforcement specialists. Police have a different area of expertise. In Indianapolis, the program imposed responsibility on people who did not have any real power or capacity to do anything about the problems they encountered. An officer who spotted a fallen tree, for example, was "responsible" for its removal, but he could only contact the appropriate city department and report the need. Unfortunately, as one officer remarked (Campbell et al. 1999), other city departments were experiencing the same turmoil that the Police Department was, so follow-up was undependable. The neighborhood then blamed the city's lack of response on the IPD.

Supervision and Accountability

"Broken windows" was not the only Kelling theory that Goldsmith adopted. Much more consequential was his advice to "flatten" the organizational structure of the IPD (*Indianapolis Star* 1992c; Campbell et al. 1999). Kelling believed that middle management was unnecessary in policing, so an entire level of supervision was simply ignored, or—worse, for morale at the IPD—blamed for "obstructing" the Goldsmith reforms. In his book, he says

> Mayors can choose the police chief and the deputy chiefs, but they cannot hire, fire, demote, or promote any individual officers. In Indianapolis, if a chief comes from inside the IPD, when he or she is replaced he or she stays with the rank of captain and remains part of the culture. Management and beat officers all belong to the same union, forging virtually impenetrable solidarity (Goldsmith 1997, 134).[4]

This is a reference to the statutory merit system. In fact, early in his tenure, Goldsmith floated a plan to "hire, fire, demote and promote" in defiance of those laws and to substitute for the merit system an idea of his own. His plan would also reward performance in a manner he had identified as more in line with his approach and rid the department of management-level supervisors whom he felt were obstructing his goals. A group of captains raised $3,000 from their personal funds, and they sent Goldsmith notice threatening suit if he went forward. Presumably, he conferred with city lawyers because the plan went no further.[5]

In these efforts to get rid of layers of supervision, like so many of the radical shifts that occurred during the Goldsmith years, no effort was made to understand why prior administrations had believed such supervision was important. It was assumed that the existing structure was just the result of happenstance, rather than an intelligent response to past *experience*. So supervisors were described as being "bureaucratic bloat," and Goldsmith similarly criticized the Police Department for being "top heavy" with appointed ranks. (Given this criticism, it is interesting to point out that there were eleven appointed positions, including the position of Chief, when Goldsmith took office; but there were *seventeen* by January of 1999. This 50 percent increase does not seem very consistent with Kelling's advice to "flatten" the organization.) (IPD 1992-1999b).

There are many different management philosophies, but all of them require some way of seeing to it that employees' actions are consistent with the mission of the organization. Supervision becomes critical when the employees in question are armed and legally empowered to kill. The need for supervision is greater in the IPD than, for example, in the Parks Department. Money saved by eliminating supervisors can easily be lost to plaintiffs in successful liability lawsuits. Much more than money is at stake when patrolmen are not adequately directed and supervised. Law enforcement becomes less effective as the statistics later in this chapter demonstrate. Police corruption also becomes much more difficult to detect and weed out. It was partly in response to scandals during the 1970s that the IPD increased supervision and centralized several departmental functions. Beginning in February of 1974, the *Indianapolis Star* had run a series of Pulitzer-Prize winning articles alleging that promotions were being bought and sold. There were charges of influence peddling and a number of accusations revolving around a business—Morty Dock's Pawn Shop—where kickbacks were said to have been traded for "looking the other way" when stolen merchandise was involved. Inadequate supervision was identified as one reason such behaviors occurred. More recently, the scandals in Los Angeles and the shooting of Amadou Diallo in New York have shown how important credible, professional supervision is. As William Bratton, the former NYC police commissioner, said in a *Time* "Viewpoint" about those tragedies, "Only constant supervision and training can prevent abuses and mistakes" (Bratton 2000).

Decentralization

Closely connected to the supervision problem was the issue of departmental decentralization. Again, the goal was a good one—get the police out into the community. According to the Mayor, having to report downtown for roll call and report writing was a waste of time better spent patrolling the neighborhoods. So Goldsmith decided that all functions should be handled directly in their respective districts rather than in a central office. During the Hudnut administration, patrol officers reported to these district offices, but each district was the responsibility of a major who reported to a Deputy Chief of Operations who worked downtown. The Deputy Chief coordinated the districts for consistency and made sure that each district was following the same procedures and rules. Goldsmith gave autonomy to each district. Each district had its own Deputy Chief, and no one was in charge of coordinating. The effect was to turn a single department into five smaller, virtually independent departments. Consequently, many functions were duplicated. For example, prior to decentralization, the IPD had one hit and run section to serve the whole city. Under decentralization, hit and run incidents became just one more item on the list of district duties. When hit and run incidents are competing for attention with rapes, aggravated assaults, burglaries and similar crimes, they are understandably low on the priority list. Detectives were overwhelmed with more significant crimes, and they lacked the specialized experience that would have made them more efficient at investigating hit and runs. While results varied from district to district, hit and run incidents were often simply never investigated. Under decentralization, each district was expected to handle all aspects of policing without any corresponding increase in manpower. Police officers were not only to "walk the beat" but also were to investigate and solve a wide variety of cases, all during their regular beat time.

Hit and run investigations were only one example of the practical difficulties the IPD faced as a result. Several other types of crimes had also previously been investigated by specialized task forces, units having experience with, and training in, that particular type of crime. In 1991, before decentralization, the number of aggravated assault cases solved (the "clearance rate") was 78.8 percent (IPD 1992a). After decentralization, aggravated assault crimes were handled by a general detective who was also expected to handle larcenies, burglaries, auto thefts, missing persons and a number of other crimes (IPD 1992a). By 1997, the clearance rate for aggravated assaults had fallen to 55.5 percent (IPD 1997a). Much of the same problem occurred with missing persons investigations. Before decentralization, the IPD's missing persons section had a national reputation as one of the nation's best; I often got calls from other departments around the country asking for our procedures and policies. When it was eliminated, and that duty given to the districts, each district had the final say on how the investigation would be handled by its personnel. Response time went from a virtually immediate investigation in 1992 to as much as three months lag in some cases. In the latter part of the Goldsmith administration, a missing persons unit was reassembled, but in 1997 it was still taking an average of thirty days before the case was even assigned to the unit (Campbell et al 1999).

By the time Goldsmith left office, special task force units had been quietly reestablished not only for missing persons but also for fraud, auto theft and organized crime. These are activities best handled by specialized task forces with institutional memory and expertise in solving that particular type of crime (U.S. Advisory Commission 1971).

Personnel

The statutory merit system was originally implemented to protect police officers and departments from political interference and corruption, and its existence limits a mayor's ability to fire and demote without cause. However, the mayor has the authority to appoint—and fire—the Chief of Police who has legal responsibility to run the Police Department. The Chief is accountable to the mayor, who is accountable to the public. This allows a mayor who wants to implement change, who wants to "shake" the department, to be involved with nearly every departmental decision, including personnel decisions. During the last eight Hudnut years, there were six changes in the senior management of the IPD, and two of those were retirements (IPD 1984-1992b). During the first seven years of the Goldsmith administration, when the mayor's office either dictated or was consulted about every transfer and every promotion (*Indianapolis Star* 1994), there were 67 changes within the appointed ranks—Majors, Assistant Chiefs, Deputy Chiefs and Chief, a total of 12 positions. The twenty-three people holding the rank of Captain were moved 111 times just *within* that rank (IPD 1992-1999b). Those ranks account for the entire senior management of the police force. That rate of change made consistency and accountability almost impossible.

"Street Hours"

At the end of 1991, there were 980 officers on the force. At the end of Goldsmith's term, the number stood at 1050 (IPD 1992-1999b). Goldsmith claimed, however, that he increased the "street hours" spent by IPD officers, and that he was able to do so without increasing costs (Goldsmith 1997, 134-135). Even if his computation of "street time" did not include Park Rangers and civilian public safety officers, which it does (IPD 1992-1999b), the claim is misleading at best.

Before Goldsmith's term, 25 percent of police officers were off duty at any given time, except for Sundays, when 50 percent were off duty. Officers worked 8-hour shifts, and they worked 20 days in each 28-day pay period. Goldsmith agreed to demands by the Fraternal Order of Police that the schedule be changed. (These demands were not new, but management had not previously given in.) Shifts were extended by one-half hour each day, and in exchange for the additional half-hour, 33 percent of all officers are now off at any given time. The change gave every uniformed officer an additional *17 days off every year,* in return for a daily half-hour that is meaningless, in my opinion, in terms of coverage and manpower. The statement that there has been "no cost" involved is difficult to understand. Taxpayers are paying the same amount of money they were before, but receiving seventeen fewer days per police officer. As a result of this change, each district has lost an average of two to three people *per shift per day*, and the IPD has gone from 75 percent available to work to 66.7 percent available to work.

Manpower and Staffing

The most serious personnel problem, however, grew out of the fact that community policing is personnel-intensive, and the IPD just did not have enough manpower to implement community policing properly. As State Representative Glenn Howard pointed out in 1993, when criticism of the disorder within the IPD was generating headlines, Milwaukee—a city the same size as Indianapolis—had 1950 officers on the force. This was approximately 900 more than Indianapolis. "Steve Goldsmith is off track if he thinks he can get community policing with 900 policemen," Howard said at the time (Shramm 1993). Howard's criticism was later taken up by the current mayor, Bart Peterson, who made hiring 200 additional officers and the "proper implementation of Community Policing" a major issue in his successful campaign (Peterson 1999).

Rapid Response Policing

Goldsmith begins the Crime and the Community chapter in his book with a criticism of the IPD's commitment to "rapid response policing," saying that it did not "promote public confidence" in the Police Department (Goldsmith 1997). He gives no documentation or reason why he believes that rapid response affected public confidence one way or another. "Rapid Response Policing" is just a name given to the procedure of sending an officer out to the scene of reported incidents to investigate and take witness statements. Soon after he took office, Goldsmith designated Public Assistance Officers (civilians and limited-duty officers) and had them accept reports of larcenies, vandalism and similar crimes over the telephone. Most officers liked the new system, which saved them the trouble of a run, but the citizens who were victims of these crimes did not (Patterson 1992). Complaints multiplied: victims felt (justifiably, in my opinion) that those whose taxes support the Police Department have a right to expect police to respond in person when they have been the victims of a crime. The program was discontinued for a time, then later re-instituted. It continues to get complaints (Campbell et al. 1999).

The theory behind this change was that officers would be freed up to interact with neighborhood residents under the new community policing initiative. Goldsmith believed that "rapid response" was diverting officers from more important duties. However, policing studies document that much duty time is spent "in service." This means that the officer is on the job and patrolling, which is certainly important, but not engaged in specific crime-fighting activity (Wilson and Kelling 1982; Richardson 1974). There is no reason a police officer cannot interact with neighborhood residents *and* respond to calls, and a good deal of evidence that the personal response improves, rather than diminishes, police-community relations. Like so many of the initiatives of the Goldsmith administration, the approach was "either-or." The Police Department could respond to calls, *or* it could interact with neighborhoods. In reality, the IPD can and should do both.

Fiscal Management

In his book, Goldsmith says that savings from his privatization programs allowed him to add $100 million to the IPD's crime-fighting efforts during his first five years in office (Goldsmith 1997, 134). According to the city's 1998 Comprehensive Annual Financial Report, spending for all of Public Safety went from $116,299,858 in 1992 to $139,278,315 in 1998 (CAFR 1998). The IPD's share of the Public Safety budget grew by a total of $17,624,225 during Goldsmith's first five years (IPD 1992-1997a). The whereabouts of the additional $82,300,000 or so remains a mystery to those of us who worked in the IPD during that period of time. Extra dollars certainly were not reflected in salaries, many of which (including Chief Toler's and four Deputy Chiefs) were cut (*Indianapolis Star* 1992c).

The discrepancies between claims made to the public and what we in the Police Department saw were not limited to spending. The Mayor talked constantly about bringing better business practices to the city, but in the IPD, at least, there were many business management decisions that were hard to understand. When Goldsmith was first elected, for example, the Police Department was in the middle of building a horse barn, to stable the horses that were used in downtown patrols. The barn was well over 50 percent complete, and $300,000 had already been paid to the contractor for work the city had accepted. We had a contract for the whole project, so the portion of the barn's $729,131 construction cost that had not yet been paid was legally encumbered (*Indianapolis Star* 1992). It did not seem to matter. Goldsmith ordered the barn torn down and we paid additional damages to the builder. Toward the end of his second term, Goldsmith was shopping for a site to build a horse barn (Campbell et al. 1999). The action seemed irrational to me then and it still does.

The city also paid over half a million dollars for a personnel software program called "PeopleSoft" that was never used. Beth O'Laughlin, Administrator of Human Resources, had put together a team of people from city departments that relied upon the city's Information Services Agency (ISA) to decide what to do about the antiquated mainframe and software that had outlived their usefulness. After several months of review, the team decided to purchase PeopleSoft. The IPD was a major part of the team, and it agreed with the choice. When O'Laughlin reported back to the mayor's office, she was told there was no money available for the upgrade. Rather than give up, she came back to the departments that would use the system, and each department signed a contract to pay a share out of its departmental budget, just as we were then paying ISA. The Indianapolis Bond Bank funded the purchase was using the contracts as collateral for the loan. But after the software was installed, Goldsmith decided to privatize ISA, and an exodus from the agency began. Turnover was constant and manpower insufficient for even the basic needs of city departments, and PeopleSoft required specialized training. O'Laughlin kept training technical support people, who would then leave, and there was no money for outside consultants, because her initial budget was based on using ISA personnel, whose hourly rates were much lower than rates of private providers. She tried to make the administration understand that we had significant "sunk costs" for software and training that would be wasted if we could not fund proper implementation. She was never able to get the resources to implement the system, and she finally quit in frustration (O'Laughlin 2000).

Efforts at privatizing support services had mixed results. The outsourcing of computer management produced complaints of a steep decline in the quality and timeliness of service (Campbell et al.1999). Other contracts yielded better results. Officers were given credit cards to purchase gasoline at Speedway stations, saving time that had been wasted under the prior system, which required them to go to a central location for refills. And combining support functions such as the property room, identification and records with the Marion County Sheriff's Department eliminated wasteful duplications. In a single county, there is no point in having two property rooms or two sets of criminal records, and two different sets of people in charge of them.

Crime—The Real Bottom Line

In *The Twenty-First Century City,* Goldsmith discusses a number of the new programs that he started, several of which are discussed above. What he does not discuss is their effect on the Police Department's ability to fight crime in Indianapolis. The IPD Annual Reports tell that story: a steady decline in city safety rankings. In 1992, the major crime rate comparison, compiled from the FBI Uniform Crime Reports, showed that Indianapolis ranked 46th in the incidence of major crime (FBI 1992). We were safer than 21 cities that were smaller than we were. By 1995, thanks to a soaring crime rate, we ranked 21st in the incidence of major crime (FBI 1995).

Furthermore, the rates for most major crimes climbed between 1991 and 1997. That is, the number of such crimes per thousand residents increased: murder went from 0.2 to 0.3 (a 50 percent increase);

robberies went from 4.1 to 7.3 (a 78 percent increase); burglaries went from 18.1 to 21 (a 16 percent increase); larceny from 31 to 39.4 (a 27 percent increase) and motor vehicle theft from 10.8 to 15 (a 39 percent increase). Only the incidence of rape declined, from 1.2 to 1.0, a 17 percent decrease (IPD 1992-1997a). There are many reasons that crime rates escalate, but in my opinion as a police officer with thirty-four years of experience, the turmoil in the Police Department was responsible for much of it.

The worst part of the disorganization and confusion caused by the constant change was the affect on the IPD's ability to fight crack cocaine. Indianapolis had an overwhelming crack epidemic midway through the first year of the Goldsmith administration. That epidemic could have begun anywhere; however, the IPD's ability to respond was undermined by Goldsmith's unending and inconsistent directives. He told Jim Toler he planned to "turn the department inside out and shake it" and that is just what he did. The core narcotics squad was broken up and their responsibility given to the quadrant detectives. For at least three months, and probably longer, everyone was confused about who was responsible for what. Morale was at an all-time low. It appeared that no one was attending to narcotics business. And at this critical time, the Captain of the narcotics branch was told that he could not use overtime with his detectives (Campbell et al.1999). The rest is Indianapolis history. A level of violence began in our city that we had never seen before. Every year until mid-1999, the city set new records for murder and aggravated assault (Grunwald 1998b).

Knowledgeable police officers compare crack cocaine in a city to cancer in a human body: if you do not detect it and root it out early, it spreads and becomes almost impossible to stop. The timing of the shakeup of the IPD certainly must be considered a major contributor to our difficulty in countering an aggressive crack problem and the violent crime it caused.

If the media attention to our crime problem complicated community relations, other controversies only made matters worse. The worst public relations debacle during the Goldsmith administration was the "Meridian Street Brawl." By 1997, Jim Toler had been replaced by Donald Christ, thought to be a close ally of the Mayor (*Indianapolis Star* 1994), as Chief of Police. Christ and several of his close friends on the force had the use of Goldsmith's suite at Indianapolis' new baseball park. It was later reported that Christ, who was in uniform, was seen drinking in the suite with the other officers, but that he decided to leave early (Gelarden 1996). After the game, several officers left the suite and began walking to their cars in the downtown area.

Several of them were evidently drunk and abusive to people they passed on the sidewalks. Racial and sexual insults were made, and a series of fights broke out (Gelarden 1996). In the aftermath, Don Christ resigned, and Goldsmith attempted damage control, but only after the media criticism became impossible to ignore. Goldsmith tried to distance himself from the events, but he was the one who had given permission for use of the city's suite, and he was the one who ultimately controlled the IPD. The brawl came in the middle of his campaign for governor; the worst possible time for any politician. It allowed the Democrats to point to the deterioration of police community relations and to publicize the complaints of the minority communities.

Despite the administration's rhetoric about concern for community relations, resources devoted to the IPD's programs that actually improved those relations had declined under Goldsmith. The IPD no longer partnered with the Indianapolis Public Schools—"Officer Friendly" was retired and "Say No To Drugs" was scaled back. Most damaging, in my opinion, was the cutback in recruitment efforts. The IPD has been criticized in the minority communities for a long time because of lack of racial balance within the department. Under Hudnut, Indianapolis tried hard to recruit minority officers, although we were not as successful as we would have liked. Typical efforts while I was Chief included trips to largely minority universities, attendance at job fairs and targeted mailings. In 1998, Goldsmith's budget for all recruiting efforts was $1,500. You cannot do very much with $1,500. If you are going to do community policing, it helps if police officers look like the community they are policing. Under Hudnut, African-Americans had gone from 9.8 percent of the police force to 17.8 percent and female representation had increased from 6.9 percent to 14.7 percent (Bodenhamer and Doherty 1995). At the end of 1999, those percentages were 16.5 percent African-American and 14.1 percent female (IPD 1999b).

Summary

The IPD is filled with good officers who want to do a good job. The Police Department certainly has its problems, as any department does, but effective supervision, clear lines of authority and consistent enforcement of the rules will minimize them.

When there is no continuity, when organizational structure and personnel are constantly shifting, when new programs are started with each visit by a new consultant or "expert," and just as abruptly abandoned, it should not come as a surprise that departmental performance suffers.[6] Chaos is not a workable management method, and chaos is what the IPD has experienced during the past eight years. The new mayor has his job cut out for him; I wish him well.

Notes

[1] For a fuller discussion of our progress and philosophy, see the chapter on "The Police Department" in The Hudnut Years, written by David Bodenhamer and William Doherty.

[2] Even the Controller of the City of Indianapolis has been unable to produce an estimate of the amount spent on consultants. This is because a large number of them were paid by "direct voucher" and not through the normal purchasing procedures. The only way to fully document the expenses, according to the Controller's office, would be to review cancelled checks. Since the city's accounting software was changed about mid-way through the Goldsmith years, there is no easy access to the check records (White 2000).

[3] While the book is vague about the nature of "neighborhood problems," he later refers to looking for "dangerous buildings" and "abandoned garages where assaults might occur" (Goldsmith 1997, 137).

[4] In fact, this is inaccurate. Chiefs revert back to whatever merit rank they held before becoming chief.

[5] I was one of those captains.

[6] In 1998, in The American Prospect, Michael Grunwald summed up the police experience during the Goldsmith Administration: "Goldsmith and his police brass have banged away at the reactive culture of the Indianapolis Police Department ever since [his election]. They tried cracking down on quality-of-life crimes like public drunkenness and speeding, the "Broken Windows" strategy devised by Kelling and James Q. Wilson. They tried copying New York City's vaunted crime-mapping program and Boston's model gun-tracing program. They expanded bike patrols, foot patrols, canine patrols. They moved officers from desks to streets. They launched a seemingly endless array of community policing initiatives: IMPACT. Safe Streets. Directed Patrols. SCAT. The Violent Offenders Program. Project Saturation. Graffiti Busters. Zero Tolerance. Metro Homicide Response Teams." (Grunwald 1998a)

Chapter 8

Targeting Neighborhoods

Lamont J. Hulse

Introduction

On January 1, 1992, citizens gathered at Pan Am Plaza, one of the landmarks of the city's downtown development in the 1980s, for the inauguration of Stephen Goldsmith as Mayor of Indianapolis. Despite the surroundings, the new mayor's comments centered on the theme of neighborhoods. "The soul of our city is in its neighborhoods. The government needs to remake itself around those neighborhoods." The inaugural speech paired neighborhoods with the other prominent theme from Goldsmith's campaign, his desire to reshape government for efficiency and frugality. "We need to break up large government. We need to look at more efficient ways to deliver services. We need to help citizens take back their neighborhoods, take back their government, take back their own responsibilities" (Remondini 1992).

Goldsmith's inaugural address signaled his intentions for change, first, in the way that Indianapolis government operated. Sandwiched between the Reagan presidency of the 1980s and the 1994 congressional Republican "Contract with America," Stephen Goldsmith's emphasis on reinventing government echoed familiar themes played on a national stage. Much of the national attention towards the Goldsmith administration since 1992 has focused on privatization, the transfer of services from government to private sector vendors. But Goldsmith also called for a major shift of priorities in Indianapolis, away from downtown to the city's neighborhoods. Although not without national significance, the Goldsmith administration's attention to neighborhoods resonated most strongly on the local level.

It remains unclear whether Goldsmith permanently implemented his inaugural promise of remaking city government in Indianapolis. But the city's expectations of its neighborhoods have changed. The extent of change has been constrained by an ongoing tension between his initiatives to remake government on one side, and the needs and aspirations of neighborhood residents on the other. This tension, influenced by the personality of Stephen Goldsmith, shaped the neighborhood policy of the Goldsmith administration. However, Goldsmith also introduced new strategies of neighborhood redevelopment and the focus of his administration on them made neighborhoods more important in Indianapolis. It is clear that Goldsmith's two terms have changed the attitudes of Indianapolis citizens about their neighborhoods. Neighborhood organizations and the citizens who make them up have assumed new roles in the way that Indianapolis operates.

The Local Context

In the local politics of the 1991 mayoral election, Goldsmith called for the transformation of the direction and operations of city government established during nearly twenty-five years of Republican mayoral rule in Indianapolis, first under Richard Lugar (1968-1976) and then William H. Hudnut III (1976-1992). Goldsmith's reorientation from downtown to neighborhood in Indianapolis is best understood in the context of what neighborhoods meant during the terms of Goldsmith's two Republican predecessors.

Mayor Richard Lugar's accomplishments in Indianapolis included capital improvements, made possible largely through an unprecedented reliance on federal funds, but his greatest impact on neighborhoods came through the consolidation of the Indianapolis city government with that of Marion County. The creation of Unigov, as the consolidated city-county government was called, in 1990 increased the population of Indianapolis from 476,258 to 744,624, an increase of approximately 56 percent. Since Center Township, which included the older, urban neighborhoods of Indianapolis, actually lost about 60,000 people during the decade 1960-1970, the Lugar era population increase came with the inclusion of suburban neighborhoods under the jurisdiction of the combined governments. Although the legislation that created Unigov contained a provision for "mini-gov," a form of neighborhood level governance, little official recognition was given to neighborhoods (Walls 1994, 935-37; Hulse 1994, 139).

Many critics saw Unigov as less an improvement of governmental systems and more a partisan coup by suburban Republicans. By bringing thousands of suburban voters into the election for consolidated city-county political offices, the creators of Unigov threw the balance of power in Indianapolis to the Republican Party from 1970 until the election of Democrat Bart Peterson as mayor in 1999. Critics, particularly African-Americans in the older, more urban sections of the city saw the motives of city-county consolidation as insidious attempts to disenfranchise black citizens just as their population growth and the social changes from the 1960s promised them greater power (Blomquist 1994, 1352; Hudnut 1995, 256).

For much of the post World War II era, both public and private civic leaders rejected any federal aid for urban renewal in Indianapolis. John Barton, Lugar's predecessor cautiously began to reverse this trend. Under Lugar, Richard Nixon's favorite mayor, Indianapolis leaped into federal programs such as Model Cities and actively sought federal funding for urban renewal projects such as extensions of the Interstate highways I-65 and I-70 into downtown Indianapolis. These projects facilitated travel from the suburbs to downtown jobs and attractions, but also displaced thousands of homeowners, many of them African-Americans, in Center Township neighborhoods. The other major urban renewal project of the early 1970s was the creation of a campus for the combined Indiana University Purdue University Indianapolis (IUPUI). The IUPUI project displaced many African-Americans from the historically black Midtown neighborhood adjacent to downtown, along Indiana Avenue. Like those people uprooted by the I-65/I-70 "Inner Loop," the exiles from Midtown carried a long-standing resentment against city government.

During four terms lasting from 1976 through 1991, Mayor Hudnut applied his considerable skills as a consensus builder and cheerleader to downtown development. However, the Hudnut administration did not neglect the city's neighborhoods, either suburban or urban. As was his administrative style, Mayor Hudnut delegated neighborhood issues to the Department of Metropolitan Development (DMD). Procedurally, leaders of neighborhood organizations dealt with the DMD about issues such as code enforcement, zoning, land use and planning (Swindell and Parks 1995, 153-163).

Hudnut also extended authority over economic development to the DMD, including responsibility for implementing many of the projects that comprised downtown's boom during the 1980s. By the 1990s, the DMD had achieved great authority, while also earning the resentment that often goes with power. However, sixteen years of familiarity had taught many neighborhood leaders, especially Hudnut's constituents in the Republican suburbs, how DMD worked and how to work with the Department and its staff.

During Hudnut's last term, the administration increased attention to housing redevelopment in urban neighborhoods that had suffered from physical decline and economic disinvestment. Hudnut's DMD planners initiated housing plans for several neighborhoods, including some that would later be targeted for special attention by Stephen Goldsmith (Cunningham 1999). Related to these housing efforts, Hudnut quietly began informal monthly meetings with leaders from those neighborhoods (Porter 1999). Central to Hudnut's housing policy were cooperative efforts with philanthropic and civic leaders to create the Indianapolis Neighborhood Housing Partnership in 1988 (Ehret 1994, 793-794).

By 1991, over 200 neighborhood organizations had registered with DMD. Both Lugar's and Hudnut's policies influenced the types of organizations that developed and the dynamics under which they operated. Several different varieties of organizations occupy the neighborhood landscape of Indianapolis. Mayor Hudnut's interest in housing directed special attention to one type of community-based organization, Community Development Corporations (CDC). CDCs are not-for-profit organizations with an emphasis in Indianapolis on housing development. Their mission mandates an orientation towards the market, as well as emphasis on technical skills such as construction, property management and financing. CDCs are governed by boards of directors that may include neighborhood residents, but also representatives of banks and large businesses with expertise and financial resources to apply toward building market-valued housing in vulnerable neighborhoods (West 1995, 261-262).

In contrast to CDCs, neighborhood associations are composed of community residents. While CDCs are concentrated in areas of vulnerability, neighborhood associations are located throughout Marion County. The associations that are registered with the city represent a range of demographic, socio-economic and geographic variables, and they vary widely in the issues that they address. Neighborhood organizations include homeowners associations for affluent suburban subdivisions and community-based organizations in older, urban neighborhoods.

Leadership in neighborhood associations is rarely elected from the neighborhood as a whole, but rather by members of the association. Few neighborhoods are able to boast of more than a small minority of residents as members. Both members and leaders volunteer their time for association activities. Thus, neighborhood associations are more voluntary than democratic. Many neighborhood associations are representative and inclusive, striving to reflect the citizens of that area. Usually representation is difficult. Homeowners are more likely to participate in neighborhood associations than are renters. All associations find organizing their community by recruiting residents as members to be challenging. Few of these voluntary associations find the combination of motivation, skill and sustained efforts necessary to build a stable, inclusive neighborhood organization. A few leaders of neighborhood associations are accused of jealously guarding their power by resisting greater neighborhood involvement.

Particularly in urban neighborhoods where the issues are difficult and resources are scarce, the conflicting interests of different stakeholders make relationships within and between neighborhood associations contentious. In neighborhoods, issues such as property maintenance, trash, parking, pets, children and noisy parties feed disputes between homeowners and renters, tenants and landlords and residents and businesses. Adjacent neighborhoods clash over zoning decisions, traffic patterns, and law enforcement while also competing for scarce resources.

Relationships between neighborhood associations and community development corporations are often strained. Conflicts between the two types of community-based organizations are rooted in the differences in mission and culture between the market-oriented, economic rationality of professionally staffed CDCs and the community-focused, social informality of voluntary neighborhood associations. Because they are involved in the physical redevelopment of neighborhoods, CDCs act in ways that can affect land use patterns and property values. These market-oriented organizations build new housing that alter the neighborhood streetscape, create rental projects that may offend home-owning neighbors, and, based on economic criteria, award development resources to some stakeholders while denying resources to others. The CDCs often see neighborhood associations as obstructive to their efforts and unrealistic about the demands and constraints of the real estate market under which development corporations must operate. As voluntary organizations, neighborhood associations operate on a long-term timeframe, and, to CDCs, they appear slow to respond to both opportunities and threats.

Umbrella organizations represent yet another variety of community organization. The people who form voluntary neighborhood associations tend to see their communities as areas that are geographically confined to, at most, just a few blocks, with some coherence in terms of resident demographics. The small size tends to promote relationships and communication between leaders and residents. However, the size that makes community building feasible is inefficient for more comprehensive efforts, such as those initiated by governments. As a result, umbrella organizations in Indianapolis have usually been promoted by agencies outside the community.

Beginning with the Model Cities program of the 1960s, city government frequently fostered the creation of umbrellas in urban Indianapolis. The umbrella organization represents a hybrid that groups several adjacent, smaller voluntary associations into a confederation. Umbrellas offered the administrative efficiencies associated with relatively large catchment areas while also fulfilling the requirements for federal mandates for maximum local participation. Although imposed from outside the neighborhoods, some umbrella organizations have been effective in serving citizen needs. For instance, the Near East Side Community Organization (NESCO) relied on a combination of Model Cities funding and locally based Alinsky-style organizers to build a coherent network of associations. Although the strength of NESCO has ebbed and flowed since its creation, the umbrella has remained an important organization since the 1960s. The United Northwest Area (UNWA) umbrella organization has persisted despite the geographic partition of the area by interstate highway construction in the 1970s (Crawford et al. 1994, 83).

Other umbrella organizations have foundered over the past thirty years. Many neighborhoods, jealous of local control, resist outside pressures to form umbrellas. Their leaders recognize little advantage in the confederated form and see umbrellas as efforts by outside entities, referred to generically and specifically as "the city," to supersede local organizations.

During 1991, Hudnut's last year in office, the Lilly Endowment, along with United Way and city officials convened a conference on Indianapolis neighborhoods. This gathering foreshadowed a major reorientation about how such things as social services and economic development would operate in Indianapolis. Their interest in neighborhoods anticipated the "comprehensive community initiatives" that would soon gain such favor among other national philanthropic organizations. Many of the specific suggestions coming out of the conference were practices that Stephen Goldsmith would later emulate. These outcomes included recommendations to appoint individuals to coordinate planning, help organize residents and encourage inter-organizational collaboration in urban neighborhoods. The conference also proposed the establishment of a resource and training center for neighborhood organizations and leaders.

Despite these hints of reorientation to neighborhoods, activities in the city's center eclipsed Hudnut's neighborhood programs. The sixteen years of the Hudnut administration saw wholesale redevelopment of the downtown. Hudnut himself acknowledged that the downtown stadium, the Hoosier Dome, would probably provide a "fitting signature on the Hudnut years" (Hudnut 1995, 279). Inescapably, his four terms (1976 to 1992) focused on the downtown.

Redevelopment of the downtown, known locally as the "Mile Square," did not come without resentment from the urban neighborhoods that surrounded the city's center. Neighborhoods on the suburban periphery of Marion County also expressed frustration about the city's perceived lack of attention. The same national articles that lauded the "rebirth" of downtown Indianapolis noted the discontent of many neighborhood leaders. One national reporter relayed the comment from two unidentified older citizens that the downtown revival of the 1980s was "nice, but for the rich." Fay Williams, an African-American attorney, criticized the imbalanced attention paid to downtown development versus human needs in the neighborhoods, calling for a "renaissance in human development." Williams noted that for many vulnerable residents of urban Indianapolis, "civic pride is a luxury," while also criticizing the small circle of civic leaders who made decisions isolated from the voices of neighborhoods and their citizens. "Development here is a game only a few can play," said Williams.

"They draw the covered wagons around them" (Jackson 1987, 78).

The Idea Man

In the context of the downtown development of the 1980s, many voters welcomed a reorientation from "downtown" to "neighborhood." Both mayoral candidates in 1991, Republican Stephen Goldsmith and Democrat Louis Mahern, featured the theme of neighborhoods in their campaigns. Candidate Goldsmith claimed that his proposed policies were informed through small group meetings in about 85 to 150 neighborhoods (Stackhouse 1991; O'Neil 1991). Most of these gatherings took place in the suburbs, where Republicans like Ruth Hayes gathered party loyalists for Goldsmith. Hayes, who led the suburban Nora/Northside neighborhood association, recalls Goldsmith's meeting at her house. She was impressed with the candidate's attentive listening. "He brought one of those yellow legal pads and wrote down what everyone was saying," remembers Hayes (Hayes 1999).

"I didn't talk to any of them, they talked to me," said Goldsmith in describing the meetings. Because neighborhoods interacted with DMD often and frequently, Hayes, her neighbors, and others who met with Goldsmith offered commentary about how DMD addressed neighborhood issues, stressing the need for aggressive zoning enforcement to combat sprawl. The candidate interpreted these comments as a confirmation of his other campaign theme, the need to downsize government. When recalling their interactions with DMD and other city agencies, "They were pretty critical," he recalled (O'Neil 1991a).

The few specifics of Goldsmith's neighborhood platform responded directly to issues raised in the neighborhood meetings. After hearing citizens complain about difficulty in securing information from city government, Goldsmith promised that all calls to the mayor's office would be returned in 48 hours and that city employees would improve telephone manners with callers. He also suggested the creation of neighborhood "advocates," ombudsmen to "cut red tape" in city hall. More substantively, Goldsmith proposed opening "family investment centers" in neighborhoods, "one stop shops" where low-income families could access private and public services. In response to concerns about gangs and youth crime, Goldsmith endorsed "community policing," as did his opponent Mahern (Traub 1991a).

Some of the biggest criticisms from Goldsmith's neighborhood discussions dealt with maintenance and repair of sewers, streets, bridges and parks, issues to which Stephen Goldsmith was much more hesitant to respond. The Democrat and the Republican candidates differed significantly in their reactions to a study by the Indianapolis Chamber of Commerce that called for an estimated billion dollars in infrastructure repair. These recommendations had been assembled by a broad-based bi-partisan group of business and civic leaders. Louis Mahern endorsed the Chamber's report, called it the "blueprint for my administration," and offered a financing plan of increased sewer tax, as well as new storm runoff and commuter taxes. Goldsmith found a tax increase anathema, offering instead to consider increasing "user fees" after the election. Goldsmith also rejected the Chamber report's recommendations on parks, curbs and public housing, although he did say that as mayor, he would use the report as a "guide" (O'Neil 1991a).

Goldsmith's campaign themes proved popular enough for the Marion County electorate. In post-Unigov Indianapolis, the election of any Republican candidate was virtually assured. After winning against Mahern by a 30,000-vote margin, Stephen Goldsmith was finally able to fulfill his long-standing ambition to become Mayor of Indianapolis.

Goldsmith had considered his agenda for the mayor's office for many years. As Marion County Prosecutor from 1979 to 1990, he established his reputation as intelligent and aggressive, with an extraordinary work ethic reflected in working 70 hours on a weekly basis. Foes and friends alike acknowledged Goldsmith's uncanny ability to build name recognition through astute use of print and electronic outlets. Acknowledging his political ambitions, Goldsmith found his career path blocked by other, older Republican office-holders, particularly William Hudnut (Gelarden 1986).

After Hudnut opted to seek an unprecedented third term as mayor in 1984, Stephen Goldsmith invested his professional energies into a third term as prosecutor. Goldsmith then attempted a 1988 run for Lieutenant Governor, teamed with John Mutz as the gubernatorial candidate. Throughout this period, he also directed his intellectual intensity into an association with the Kennedy School of Government and into teaching at Indiana University Purdue University Indianapolis, carrying new ideas from academe into city government. As a result, Goldsmith earned respect, sometimes grudging, for the intellectual vigor that he brought to his office. He revealed his love for ideas on how to remake government, ideas that he found he could not contain in the

Prosecutor's office. In 1986, one unnamed city official remarked that Goldsmith, "has an insatiable appetite for other people's business. He is always coming up with ideas on how to run their shops" (Gelarden 1986).

Goldsmith's personality as well as his ideas was an issue in the 1991 mayoral election. John Mutz lauded Goldsmith for "an almost unimaginable amount of energy" and for his "knack of sorting out ideas that people bring to him." Democratic Councilperson Susan Williams acknowledged Goldsmith's intellectual power, saying, "there's no question that he's very bright." But Williams carefully noted an observation about Stephen Goldsmith heard from both Republicans and Democrats. "But he's also—I'm trying to think of the right word. He has a superior attitude with people. I think he's a very detached person. He has said himself he does not work well in large groups. That's a problem in my view . . . . The mayor needs to get people whipped up" (Traub 1991b).

People often perceived Goldsmith's personal detachment as arrogance. The candidate and later the Mayor's discomfort with large groups hampered his abilities to work in the rough and tumble atmosphere that characterizes neighborhood interactions. Goldsmith lacked experience and inclination towards consensus building, the painstaking construction of win-win situations with many stakeholders. Instead, Goldsmith's professional career had been in the courtroom, an arena where winners and losers were clearly differentiated. John Mutz acknowledged that, "If you are talking about the deal in which everyone has to come out smelling good, he has not done many of those" (Traub 1991b).

If Stephen Goldsmith was sometimes faulted on interpersonal skills, he was credited with a "media mastery" in service to his ambition, an instinctive ability to focus attention on himself in the midst of his accomplishments as prosecutor. As candidate and later as Mayor, Goldsmith found it difficult to share the public stage with others. His public communications always featured an "element of self-promotion" that allowed little room for anyone, be they city-county council members, governmental employees, or citizens (Harris 1984; Gelarden 1986).

One interaction during the transition illustrates how Goldsmith's affinity for new ideas and disdain of process often ran afoul of relations with neighborhood leaders. Jerry King, a leader in the NESCO neighborhood was also active in a coalition of urban neighborhoods that had studied the concept of community policing and considered the complexities of that new philosophy in Indianapolis. At a "Meet the Mayor" session in December, King hoped to offer the coalition's assistance to Goldsmith in implementing the new policing approach. Ushered into his private session with Mayor-elect Goldsmith, King began to describe the proposal. "About thirty seconds into what I was saying, I saw Goldsmith's eyes begin to glaze over and he interrupted me, saying, 'I plan to institute community policing in my first ninety days in office. Next question?'" (King 1999).

In a post-inaugural interview, Goldsmith recalled how his campaign experience raised many questions as to the specifics of running city government. He maintained that he wanted citizens to suggest the answers to those questions. But in his interactions with individuals and in public settings, Goldsmith's intellectual energies, his interpersonal detachment and his constant quest to appear as the city's ultimate problem-solver appeared much like arrogance. As he began the transition into the mayor's office, Stephen Goldsmith was increasingly presenting himself to neighborhoods not just as the man with ideas, but as a man who believed that he had the answers (O'Neil 1991).

Managing by Chaos

Within days after the election, Goldsmith provided a detailed agenda for his administration. The Mayor-elect convened a transition team of 150 "ambassadors" including business and civic leaders, as well as neighborhood representatives largely drawn from the Republican suburbs (Schuckel 1991; Johnston 1991). Goldsmith made clear his commitment to change, demanding that the transition team "think outside the box," a phrase that became a mantra during the first months of the administration. The Mayor-elect refused to let his plans to remake government be constrained by existing legal restrictions. Goldsmith said that laws and ordinances could be changed, a statement that alarmed members of the transition team, particularly long-time Republicans (Schuckel 1991; Hayes 1999).

Goldsmith gave the transition team a detailed agenda centered on a mandate to reduce city government by 25 percent. Many of these savings could come from the elimination of "non-essential services," specifically targeting services provided by DMD. With these statements about DMD, Goldsmith reinforced his intentions to contrast his administration with William Hudnut's (Schuckel 1991; Johnston 1991).

Goldsmith strongly suggested that significant additional cost savings would be accomplished through privatization, transferring city services to private groups, including neighborhoods. As an example of privatization, Goldsmith suggested that neighborhood groups could assume responsibility for maintenance of parks in their community (Schuckel 1991; Johnston 1991). For neighborhoods, the full implication of "privatization" became clear. Goldsmith expected these voluntary groups to take responsibility for city services (Hayes 1999).

Members of the transition team drawn from neighborhoods found their hopes for the new administration challenged. Traditional Republicans heard Goldsmith's disregard of existing statutes as a call to radical change. Despite their occasional frustrations with DMD, many neighborhood leaders interpreted the plans to strip the agency as a proposal to do away with services to neighborhoods. Neighborhood associations, staffed by volunteers, ridiculed Goldsmith's plans to privatize city services through neighborhoods.

"People in Nora started a joke about how we would park all the neighborhood's snowplows in my driveway," said Ruth Hayes. Hayes and other leaders had shared their desires for increased and more responsive services with candidate Goldsmith—but not because they thought their neighborhood associations could perform those services better than the city. While they were willing to take an active role in their neighborhoods, they had no illusions that some services—for example, street cleaning, parks maintenance and snow removal, as well as zoning enforcement, public safety and comprehensive planning—were better performed by professionals (Hayes 1999).

After taking office, Goldsmith continued to press his privatization strategy on neighborhoods. "Just as reformers in Washington, DC, would soon embark on efforts to devolve authority to states and cities, we were trying to devolve power from City Hall to dozens of neighborhood-level organizations," remembers Goldsmith in his book (Goldsmith 1997). A few neighborhoods expressed guarded curiosity about Goldsmith's plans for devolution of city services. For instance, a Franklin Township neighborhood leader said that, "If it's something we don't already have, there may be interest. But if it's a service we take for granted, it would be tough to generate the interest" (Schuckel 1992a).

When they hesitated to accept the mantle of privatization and expressed doubt about Goldsmith's approach, neighborhood leaders perceived that the administration excluded them from decision-making.

"There hasn't been any questioning. Nothing. We're not involved. I don't think we have a voice at all," said the president of one neighborhood association (Schuckel 1992b). "I think there's a vast resource of talented individuals who have been overlooked by the new administration," offered Steve Johnes, who chaired a new group, the Marion County Alliance of Neighborhood Associations (McANA) formed primarily from suburban neighborhoods. Increasingly, this group began to stand in opposition to Goldsmith's policies (Schuckel 1992b; Morgan and Morrison 1992a, 1992b).

Even as he compelled privatization in neighborhoods, much of Goldsmith's attention during his first weeks in office was focused internally on the details of remaking government. Like all new mayors, Goldsmith exercised the option of placing his own people in key positions of authority in the administration. Many of his senior department heads reflected Goldsmith's belief in private sector solutions. These private sector appointees included E. Mitchell Roob, Jr. a young Master's in Business Administration graduate from Notre Dame who came to the administration from the consulting firm, Crowe Chizek. Roob was tapped to head the Department of Transportation (which became the Department of Capital Asset Management), and later he moved to head the Health and Hospital Corporation of Marion County, the County's public health department and hospital. Michael Wells moved from Browning Investments, a development company, to serve as the head of the Mayor's kitchen cabinet, and Wells eventually headed the Airport Authority. Other officials came from government posts elsewhere, such as Leon Younger, who left Cleveland to direct IndyParks and Nancy Silvers, recruited from the Housing and Urban Development offices in Washington to assume the new position as Deputy Mayor of Neighborhoods (Schuckel and Lanosga 1993). The new administration also made conspicuous use of consultants from outside Indianapolis, some with established reputations and others who were not so well known. One former public employee criticized Goldsmith's extensive use of consultants saying, "Who's running the show? Everybody talks in terms of hiring consultants, but I think you have to have staff familiar with the issues" (Morgan and Morrison 1992a).

Goldsmith attracted a number of bright, younger people to the 25th floor of the City-County Building. "I've recruited wonderful people who are absolutely brilliant and, in the end, will contribute great value to the people of Indianapolis," said the Mayor. "Young intellectuals, technocrats, people not plugged into the political system. You have a lot of young people who want to save the world. Convinced every day counts" (Morgan and Morrison 1992a). Margaret Goldsmith, the Mayor's wife, honed in even closer to how many long-time city employees, as well as many citizens, saw the people of her husband's administration. "They're young, and they're not arrogant but they're a little smug" (Morgan 1992).

These articulate, creative, enthusiastic and energetic young professionals brought great ambition, not only for themselves, but also ambitions for Goldsmith's new administration. All of the new people surrounding the Mayor, whether outside expert or new convert, shared a mission to reinvent government by "thinking outside of the box." Most importantly, the new people shared an absolute conviction in their cause, complete confidence in their beliefs, and unqualified loyalty to Stephen Goldsmith. "Steve Goldsmith has the clearest vision of any politician I've ever met," said Mitchell Roob (Annala 1999; Morgan and Morrison 1992a).

Following the Mayor's own schedule, staff extended their workdays far into evenings and weekends. "Just mind-boggling commitment on the part of everybody," is how Special Counsel Robert Swhier described the people surrounding Goldsmith. Anne Shane, former campaign manager and special assistant echoed Swhier's assessment. "You have people that, every day, come to work and the intensity level is so incredible, and Steve engenders a lot of that." But Shane went on to identify a problem of perception in the community. "The problem is, when you're so busy and you're so intent on dealing with the day-to-day business that you don't have time to go out an cultivate a lot of community contacts" (Morgan and Morrison 1992a). John Thomas, after resigning as Director of Youth and Family services complained that, "We spent a lot of time in meetings, a lot of time looking at the effect of policies and not a lot of time rubbing elbows with the folks being affected by this" (Schuckel and Lanosga 1993).

Goldsmith advocated a "flat" organization, with people reporting directly to him. Michael Wells, a close associate of the Mayor commented that, "Goldsmith is not a big fan of structure. It's one of his management philosophies that structure sometimes kills good ideas. So there's no structure at all" (Morgan and Morrison 1992a). According to Nancy Silvers Rogers, who served as Deputy Mayor for Neighborhoods in the administration's early years, Goldsmith saw value in creating professional tensions between his staff through competition. Sometimes staff didn't know they were competing. The Mayor independently gave projects to more than one person. Only after they had invested weeks of work did staff find out about the duplicated assignments. The Mayor also rewarded staff who took initiative on projects, even in areas not functionally assigned to those employees (Rogers 1999).

"We're for change for change's sake," said Goldsmith. "The point was, a lot of people spend an awful lot of time designing programs and getting legislative mandates and carefully thinking through the changes, and some other people say, 'Here is what we are trying to do and let's just start it and keep changing it as you go.' We are doing more of the latter; we have some guiding principles, but we are trying to encourage people to make their own mistakes" (Gelarden 1992).

Goldsmith said that employees should experiment in new programs, even if the experimentation would "drive managers crazy" (Schuckel and Lanosga 1993). Nancy Silvers Rogers recalls a certain "flavor of the month" tone to the early months of the Goldsmith administration, where the Mayor's interest in new ideas promoted a constant turnover of new, experimental programs (Rogers 1999).

"Managing by chaos," laughs Rogers, recalling the heady but confusing early days of the Goldsmith administration (Rogers 1999). This chaos consisted of one part intentional disorder in his staff, designed to promote creative competition. But the second chaotic element of the Goldsmith administration centered on the intentional destruction of existing governmental systems, particularly the DMD.

In the months following the election, the city's DMD bore a heavy burden from Goldsmith's schemes to downsize government. Working with outside consultants, the new administration undertook a comprehensive review of the DMD's staffing and operations, which led to dismissal of large numbers of people. The DMD was especially hard hit at the senior levels, in its Division of Administration as well as the Division of Housing and Economic Development, which oversaw project implementation. Among the projects halted were the housing initiatives planned with urban neighborhoods during Hudnut's last four years (Neal 1999; Alley 1999).

The DMD staff and neighborhood leaders had difficulty reconciling the downsizing with Goldsmith's stated interest in neighborhoods. As many as 60 percent of the neighborhood planners, the DMD staff who worked most closely with neighborhoods and were most knowledgeable about their needs, were dismissed. Reflecting the mayor's philosophy about the evils of government regulations, code and building inspectors were also fired. Both urban and suburban neighborhood leaders had emphasized the importance of code enforcement to candidate Goldsmith. By dismissing inspectors, Goldsmith stripped away the city's capacity to enforce regulations. Neighborhoods were aghast and vocal in their criticisms of the Goldsmith (Hayes 1999; Cunningham 1999).

The rapid dismantling of the DMD also disrupted the lines of communication between established neighborhoods and the city's government (Gelarden 1992). In addition to the other problems at the DMD, Goldsmith was also particularly slow in naming a Director for the agency. For more than a year, the DMD was only one of the many functions reporting to the Deputy Mayor for Neighborhoods. In April 1993, Goldsmith hired Dan Kozlowski, a real estate developer, as Director, and he stayed until July 1994. When financial consultant Elaine Bedel became the Director in August 1994, the *Indianapolis Business Journal* began to refer to the position as the "DMD revolving door." In November 1995, Moira Carlstedt, a property manager and leasing agent for a development company, took over from Bedel. Already understaffed and with plummeting morale, the lack of consistent leadership further eroded the DMD's ability to hold its own in the intra-administration politics of Goldsmith's first term (Heikens 1994; Lanosga and Johnson 1994; Johnston 1995).

In turn, Stephen Goldsmith's concerted attack on the DMD deprived his administration of a group of city employees equipped with experience and expertise about the city's neighborhoods and the people who led them. His dismissal of experienced staff such as inspectors and neighborhood planners also deprived his administration of a knowledge source essential to building effective neighborhood policy and practice. Goldsmith's assault on the DMD also proved the final breach between his administration and several suburban neighborhoods. If the Mayor valued change above all else, established neighborhoods appreciate continuity. During the election, suburbanites had asked the candidate for more neighborhood services. Not only had Stephen Goldsmith disregarded that request, his dismantling of the DMD, his disregard of their opinions and his continued insistence on privatization sent a message to established neighborhoods that their interests did not matter to his administration.

Deprived of the counsel of experienced neighborhood hands and disregarding the input of established neighborhoods, the administration committed several actions that ran afoul of neighborhood concerns.

One came in the fall of 1992. In mid-September, just as the autumn leaves began to fall, Goldsmith announced that city sanitation trucks would no longer pick up leaves in plastic bags. Instead, Goldsmith said that leaves must be placed in biodegradable paper bags. Unfortunately, the brown bags were expensive and in short supply. Irate homeowners by the thousands phoned the Mayor's Action Line, while other citizens dumped plastic bags full of leaves in city parks. Faced with a clear message of opposition on their leaf bag policy, the administration backed down (Morgan 1993).

Neighborhoods saw another more serious breach of faith with the Downtown Canal Redevelopment Project, an effort by the city and the Indianapolis Water Company to build 600 market-price homes along downtown's Central Canal. To make way for the development, the city proposed to evict several long-time homeowners in an African-American neighborhood that had already lost thousands of residents as a result of urban renewal in the 1970s. The Mayor attempted to argue for canal redevelopment from the perspective of economics, arguing that the project made business sense. "The basic problem is that the city has an economic development project worth $20 million in this canal," said Goldsmith in a newspaper interview. "There are 15 remaining houses versus the potential for several hundred million dollars in investment" (Gelarden 1992).

Although Goldsmith promised to reimburse homeowners with payments above the market value of the older houses, homeowners and community leaders remained adamantly opposed to canal redevelopment. The symbolism of the proposed evictions was unmistakable. The proposed redevelopment was located just south of the I-65/I-70 highway inner loop and just east of the IUPUI campus, the two urban redevelopment projects that had displaced thousands of African-Americans in the 1960s and 1970s. Long-time neighborhood activists, many of them African-Americans, pointed to the plight of the "Canal People," as evidence that Goldsmith's verbal commitment to urban neighborhoods would not stand against the interests of downtown businesses. Many urban neighborhoods saw the actions against the Canal People as evidence that this administration would continue to treat them as fodder for urban redevelopment.

The cause of the Canal People provided a rallying point for McANA. This body was only a loosely organized coalition when Goldsmith took office, but by the fall of 1992, McANA had formally incorporated and counted fifty neighborhood associations as active members (Schuckel

1992b; Morgan 1993). Throughout the Goldsmith administration, McANA maintained a vigilant eye on the Mayor's neighborhood policies and was especially critical of his privatization of IndyParks.

Within a few months of Goldsmith's taking office, members of the City-County Council also became vocal, as well as bi-partisan, in their frustration with the Mayor. "Did the mayor's modus operandi make the council's job more difficult? I would say it did," said Republican President of the Council Dr. Beurt SerVaas. Goldsmith exchanged accusatory letters with council member Beulah Coughenour, after the Republican released information about the Mayor's "selling" of wastewater treatment plants. Coughenour argued for the public's right to the information. In turn, Goldsmith called Coughenour "adversarial" and accused her of "intentionally misleading" citizens. Worst of all, Goldsmith charged the Republican council member of being against change and "categorically against privatization" (Schuckel and Lanosga 1993).

Faced with this opposition, Goldsmith's first reaction was to isolate himself, particularly from the suburban neighborhoods that had elected him (Schuckel and Lanosga 1993). Goldsmith's attitude towards the suburban neighborhoods sometimes took a personal turn. Ruth Hayes, recognized by media as a forceful advocate for her suburban neighborhood, was sought by reporters for her comments on Goldsmith's neighborhood policies, and she shared her concerns for publication (Schuckel 1992a, b). Hayes is still surprised at the new administration's reactions against her and other neighborhood leaders who went public with their criticism. "I had no idea how quickly the situation would deteriorate. Within months, I had a senior aide tell me that Goldsmith considered me an enemy of the state" (Schuckel 1992a, b).

Targeting Neighborhoods

By June 1992, Mayor Goldsmith acknowledged that the radical changes he had proposed for city government had stalled (Gelarden 1992). The administration responded to rebuild credibility. Quietly, they began to hire back code inspectors, acknowledging the validity of zoning code issues in neighborhoods.

Goldsmith also created new positions for Township Administrators, who were to act much like the ombudsmen he proposed during the campaign. The Township Administrators would serve as contacts for all township residents with a question or concern for city government. As first presented, one Township Administrator was assigned to each of the nine townships in the county. Careful observers wondered about the equity of the job assignments, with one Administrator assigned to each of the townships, regardless of the population disparity. How much easier was it for the Franklin Township Administrator (population about 21,000) versus the workload of the Center Township Administrator (estimated population, 182,000) (Cunningham 1999; Neal 1999)?

Experienced neighborhood leaders, knowledgeable about city government and with their own contacts in the DMD and other agencies, initially found the concept useless. Those who knew city government continued to contact remaining acquaintances at DMD. Urban neighborhoods saw the Township Administrator as just another makeshift strategy from city government, one that appeared decentralized without actually having to be so (Haerle 2000).

As time passed, leaders from suburban and urban neighborhoods began to see the Township Administrator as positive. Much of this success is due to the people who have filled those positions. Administrators were drawn largely from the DMD staff who had experience in neighborhood issues. In contrast to the frequent turnover elsewhere in city government, several of the Township Administrators retained their positions over time. Continuity fostered familiarity as neighborhoods developed relationships with Administrators (Haerle 2000; Goldsmith 1997, 161). The influence of the Township Administrators extended also through their efforts to form new neighborhood associations, a measurable activity strongly encouraged by the mayor's office (Cunningham 1999).

Several processes implemented by Administrators facilitated communication between neighborhoods and the city. For instance, they regularly provided neighborhood organizations with lists of capital improvements in their neighborhoods. The Mayor encouraged administrators to provide quantifiable measures of performance, such as numbers of meetings attended. Administrators also facilitated monthly code compliance committees, where citizens and city officials, including police, met to identify various types of violations and monitor enforcement. These committees proved to be effective and popular, constituting one of the lasting achievements of the Goldsmith administration (Cunningham 1999; Goldsmith 1997, 161).

Other tactics implemented in late 1992 focused on improved public relations. The Mayor made himself and his staff available for a series of newspaper interviews to acknowledge the problems with neighborhoods and attempted a defense. Goldsmith and Deputy Mayor Nancy Silvers pressed the administration's case in a series of neighborhood forums. Citizens brought to the forums their concerns about disrepair of streets, sidewalks, and curbs. In response, Goldsmith focused not just on ideas, but on targeting tangible activity in the neighborhoods (Crawford 1994).

During the summer of 1992, the mayor's office sent an urgent request to remaining staff in the Information Resources Office at the DMD, asking for a list of those Center Township neighborhoods with the greatest needs. Analysts quickly returned a list of potential census tracts based on information from the 1980 and 1990 United States Census (1990 data on income and education had not yet been released by the Census Bureau). In response to a second request from the Mayor, Information Resources reconciled these census tracts with areas claimed by seven existing neighborhood associations. Only later did the staff realize that their efforts had targeted the seven Center Township neighborhoods that would occupy so much attention during Goldsmith's eight years in office (Neal 1999; Alley 1999).

Goldsmith's first announcement of this initiative paired the "Seven Targeted Neighborhoods" with his intentions of "Building Better Neighborhoods." This pairing allowed the Mayor to provide tangible activity in the neighborhoods while also addressing the long-neglected Chamber of Commerce recommendations for infrastructure repair in the city. Although Goldsmith had expressed ambivalence about the Chamber's report during the election, he found it difficult to disregard when the needs were confirmed at neighborhood forums.

In September 1992, Goldsmith presented his $519 million capital improvement plan to the City-County Council. Publicity emphasized the portion of the request, as much as $60 million that would fund improvement in Center Township neighborhoods. Although the announcement made no mention of the Chamber's report, the administration's capital improvements plan accommodated some of the Chamber of Commerce recommendations. At the same time, the new administration put money behind its commitment to neighborhoods. Very soon, visible repair projects on streets and sidewalks appeared throughout the city, always coupled with the soon familiar blue and white "Building Better Neighborhoods" logo (Schuckel 1992 c).

The repairs to sidewalks and streets were distributed throughout the city, not just in the older, urban neighborhoods of Center Township.

But "Building Better Neighborhoods" answered those critics in urban neighborhoods who challenged the administration to make the first moves in neighborhood redevelopment. Since 1992, the city's investment in long-neglected infrastructure repairs proved to be popular in both urban and suburban neighborhoods. Throughout his two terms, Goldsmith built on the "Building Better Neighborhoods" policy base to implement changes, especially in the seven targeted neighborhoods.

Even as the targeted neighborhood initiative was announced, the targeting process itself came under criticism. The concentration on Center Township ruled out suburban neighborhoods established after World War II, neighborhoods that by the 1990s were a generation old with emerging problems of their own. Other areas adjacent to the targeted neighborhoods saw little rationale in their exclusion from redevelopment efforts. The administration's failure to communicate clear rationales for their selection process exacerbated the resentments of non-targeted neighborhoods. The targeting process polarized neighborhoods. Goldsmith's concerted and public focus on the targeted neighborhoods, combined with his perceived snubs of McANA, polarized urban from suburban neighborhoods.

As Goldsmith and his staff attempted to implement their initiative, they encountered antagonism in the targeted neighborhoods. Several of their early actions, including their approach to the "canal people," indicate the extent of the ignorance that the administration brought to this complex, often contentious landscape. Without the benefit of the experienced people that the city had lost through remaking government, the administration faced a steep learning curve about the city's neighborhoods and the various types of organizations that served them. In his rhetoric, Goldsmith credited neighborhoods with the abilities to take on any number of functions normally performed by government. In reality, Goldsmith and members of his staff often displayed great naivete about existing neighborhoods, a lack of understanding about neighborhood realities and impatience with the deliberate pace by which communities, including neighborhood associations, operate.

The seven targeted neighborhoods presented great complexity to Stephen Goldsmith and his staff. Within those neighborhoods, the administration found seven different organizational climates and seven distinct community cultures (see Table 1). While all of the seven neighborhoods had large numbers of low-income people, the specific circumstances of the different communities differed markedly.

Several of these urban neighborhoods, such as NESCO and UNWA, but also Mapleton-Fall Creek, Martindale-Brightwood and the Citizens neighborhood boasted existing neighborhood organizations dating back at least to the 1960s. The organizational pictures in the near westside neighborhoods of Haughville, Hawthorne and Stringtown, as well as on the southeast side were more complex, with a mix of neighborhood associations, community development corporations, community centers and umbrella organizations. These different types of organizations sometimes cooperated, but often competed with each other.

The definition of some of the targeted neighborhoods evolved over time. In some cases, the redefinition came because of the administration's initial ignorance of neighborhood realities. For instance, the targeting scheme initially paired the Near North area with Mapleton-Fall Creek, a neighborhood with an unusually strong organization and well-defined boundaries. The two areas were physically separated by a major waterway, Fall Creek, and by one of the city's major thoroughfares, Meridian Street. The area defined by the administration as Near North was served by two different organizations, UNWA and a fledgling Near North association. There was no particular enmity between Mapleton-Fall Creek and Near North. Rather, the extent of physical and organizational separation was such that the two neighborhoods had few dealings with each other. Administration efforts to pair the two different areas as one targeted neighborhood came to naught. During Goldsmith's second term, Near North became a separate target for redevelopment, the eighth of the seven targeted neighborhoods (Crawford 1994).

Similarly, targeting initially paired two southeast side neighborhoods, Fountain Square and Fletcher Place. In reality, the two areas were separated by the I-65 inner loop highway and by less visible differences of history and culture. In this case, existing housing development efforts involved both neighborhoods. Southeast Neighborhood Development (SEND), the CDC in that area, had incurred significant opposition from the Fountain Square Neighborhood Association, as the Mayor's staff would find to their chagrin.

In *Twenty-First Century City*, Goldsmith claims his first encounter with the often-contentious Fountain Square Neighborhood Association led to a victory for him and for the neighborhood. He recalls his plans to announce plans for "Building Better Neighborhoods" efforts at a press event in the neighborhood. Instead of the 'warm welcome' he expected, Goldsmith was surprised by a demonstration of children and mothers. Estelle Perkins, who was President of the Fountain Square

Neighborhood Association, presented demands for a new park, and
Goldsmith recalls how he overcame bureaucracy to create a playground
within ninety days (Goldsmith 1997, 159).

Table 1: Targeted neighborhoods[a]

Neighborhood	Population	Median Household Income	Families Below Poverty	Owner Occupied Houses	Median Housing Value
Citizen's	9,062	$ 15,691	40%	26%	$34,200
Mapleton Fall Creek[b]	11,402	$ 18,605	30%	35%	$42,500
Martindale-Brightwood	12,934	$ 14,213	31%	61%	$26,500
NESCO	25,647	$ 17,687	28%	44%	$27,900
Southeastern[c]	25903	$ 17,877	23%	55%	$25,100
UNWA	16,378	$ 14,733	24%	48%	$29,000
WESCO	15,810	$ 16,303	26%	50%	$25,600
Indianapolis	797,159	$ 29,152	9%	52%	$60,600

[a] Data primarily drawn from the User-Defined Areas Program of the United
States Census (1990) as shown in Indianapolis Department of Metropolitan
Development for each of the neighborhoods. Geographies of the Defined Areas
may differ from boundaries used by the neighborhood associations.
[b] Estimate of data provided by The Polis Center at Indiana University Purdue
University Indianapolis from United States Census (1990).
[c] United States Census

The enmity that Goldsmith found in Fountain Square had deep roots.
The Fountain Square Neighborhood Association had a particularly
long memory, recalling a history of grievances against the city dating
back as far as the first announcement of interstate highway construction
through the neighborhood in the 1960s. By the time Goldsmith arrived
for his press conference, a deep cynicism and abiding distrust of local
government had permeated the neighborhood's psyche (Wilson 1993,
577-594).

Fountain Square was also internally divided by conflicts between the
neighborhood association and SEND. The neighborhood association,

primarily reflecting homeowners, objected to SEND's redevelopment plans, many of which focused on rental housing for low-income people. Perkins also counted personality conflicts between SEND staff and Fountain Square residents as contributing to the rift between the two organizations (Perkins 1995).

The Fountain Square Neighborhood is named for the urban landmark at its core, a commercial center at the confluence of Virginia Avenue, Shelby and Prospect Streets. The Goldsmith administration was committed to work with SEND to complete a high profile redevelopment of the historic Fountain Square Theater Building as well as other visible projects in this heavily traveled transportation node (Goldsmith 1997, 163-164). By associating with the CDC, the city guaranteed the enmity of the Fountain Square Neighborhood Association. The relationship with Fountain Square proved to be so combative that the administration eventually chose to bypass that Association in order to implement Targeted Neighborhood projects. The newly developed Southeast Community Organization (SECO), which focused on public safety issues in areas adjacent to Fountain Square, proved more amenable to the city's efforts, as did historic preservation groups such as the Fletcher Place Association. Under the aegis of these organizations and SEND, the mayor's staff promoted the creation of a new umbrella, the Southeast Umbrella Organization (SUMO) to serve as the designated partner in the targeted neighborhoods initiative. SUMO administered the funding channeled by the city to this targeted neighborhood and became the last of the seven neighborhoods to fully implement the targeted neighborhoods initiative by appointing a neighborhood coordinator in October 1994 (Crawford 1994, 76-77).

Goldsmith's initial approaches to the near Westside suggested that similar problems might arise in this area immediately west of the downtown and including the neighborhoods of Haughville, Stringtown and Hawthorne. Urban geography divided these neighborhoods, with Haughville on the north side of the railroad tracks and Hawthorne and Stringtown on the south. The three neighborhoods were also divided by race. The two southern neighborhoods were primarily European-American including many people of Appalachian heritage. To the north, Haughville was historically one of the few ethnic neighborhoods in Indianapolis. But in the post World War II era, the descendants of Slovenian immigrants moved to the suburbs to be replaced in Haughville by African-Americans, many of them displaced by the interstate highway and IUPUI projects in the 1960s and 1970s. Their memories of urban renewal brought Haughville's new citizens a special bitterness to their dealings with "the city" (Amerson 1996, 19).

At the time of the announcement of Targeted Neighborhoods, only Haughville was represented by an active neighborhood organization. The Haughville Community Council, reflecting the attitude of many citizens on the Near Westside, was openly skeptical of the mayor's plans for the targeted neighborhoods. In *Twenty-First Century City* Goldsmith personalizes this cynicism in a challenge from Olgen Williams to "Face up to your responsibilities, then we will respond" (Goldsmith 1997, 158).

The administration found the organizational framework for efforts on the near westside under the umbrella of the Westside Cooperative Organization (WESCO). The fortunes of WESCO had ebbed and flowed since it was first established in 1974. Staffed and active in the 1980s, WESCO had waned in the 1990s until resuscitated by Goldsmith's targeted neighborhood initiative (Porter 1999). The WESCO umbrella provided the administration with mechanisms for involving Hawthorne and Stringtown while finessing the skepticism of the Haughville Community Council. Under the auspices of WESCO, Goldsmith turned his administration's energies toward what would become the most targeted of the targeted neighborhoods in Indianapolis.

Chapter 9

Empowering Neighborhoods

Lamont J. Hulse

The Neighborhood Empowerment Initiative

During the 1990s, the concept of "empowerment" was a central component in the intellectual milieu for urban policy. That milieu included philanthropic organizations, such as the Ford Foundation and the Annie E. Casey Foundation. Think tanks and consulting groups such as Robert Woodson's Neighborhood Enterprise Institute in Washington DC and the Aspen Roundtable (Stephen Goldsmith was a member) offered the concept of neighborhood empowerment as a central principle in the new approaches to urban problems that developed early in the decade. These strategies came to be known as "Comprehensive Community Initiatives" (CCI) (Smock 1997).[1]

The definition of comprehensive community initiatives includes several components. First, it comprehensively encompasses economic and physical development, but it also bridges to human services while working to build social capital, the network of human relationships that holds community together. Rather than different systems operating in parallel lines, CCIs approach economic, human and social development holistically. Second, the comprehensive approach demands the commitment of multiple organizational partners, including a mix of public agencies and private organizations, all bringing distinct resources for the benefit of the community. Collaboration between the many different organizations requires consensual decision-making, a negotiated approach that allows all the partnering organizations to gain by their participation in the initiative. The comprehensive approach is applied to a specific neighborhood, a coherent geographic entity recognized by the people who live there and the communities that surround it. Finally, CCIs emphasize the centrality of citizen participation, empowering residents of the neighborhood to assume leadership in the direction of the community initiative (Smock 1997).

Although Stephen Goldsmith has never explicitly described his administration's approach on the near westside of Indianapolis in the context of a comprehensive community initiative, all of the elements are there. The earliest recorded use of the word 'empowerment' in the Goldsmith administration probably came in a July 1992 letter from the Mayor to leaders in the Near Westside. Goldsmith's letter invited them to participate in a planning process to develop an "empowerment model based on assets rather than problems" (Crawford 1994). The process was funded by a planning grant from Baltimore's Annie E. Casey Foundation, a name that soon became familiar in the westside neighborhoods. The Casey Foundation's commitment to strengthening families and its experiences in Baltimore's neighborhoods encouraged them to develop a national strategy on bolstering the urban environment in which so many vulnerable families lived. Extensive conversations between Goldsmith and Casey Foundation staff, including a visit by Goldsmith to Baltimore early in 1992, led to the award of a planning grant.

The Annie E. Casey process ran concurrently with another planning process supported by the federal Department of Justice through its "Weed and Seed" program. Although plans for the application were underway even prior to the 1991 election, United States Attorney Deborah Daniels, who had worked for Goldsmith in the Prosecutor's office, sponsored the application to the Department of Justice early in 1992. On April 30 of that year, the selection of the near westside as a pilot site for Weed and Seed was announced. The Weed and Seed program worked in partnership with the West District of the Indianapolis Police Department. This pilot program attracted the participation of neighborhood leaders because of its focus on their most immediate and visible problem, crime, especially the rapidly growing crack cocaine trade. In addition to "weeding" out crime, the program also offered significant federal funds to "seed" the westside with a variety of programs, a concept that proved of great interest to neighborhood leaders (Crawford 1994).

The award of these two grants marked the beginning of the Goldsmith administrations' concentrated initiative on the near westside. In his book, Goldsmith criticized previous efforts that diffused resources over many neighborhoods, resulting in little apparent progress. Goldsmith described his 'revised strategy' to "cluster private and public investments to show dramatic turnaround in an entire neighborhood and encourage a ripple effect from a revitalized core" (Goldsmith 1997).

In addition to the investment of significant financial resources, the administration's efforts on the near westside differed from other neighborhood efforts in its patient attention to the processes of governance and leadership development. Beginning in late 1992, Nancy Silvers Rogers devoted much of her remaining three years as Deputy Mayor for Neighborhoods to the painstaking process of building commitment and brokering relationships with existing and emerging leaders in Haughville, Hawthorne and Stringtown. Particularly with the Weed and Seed effort, the commanders and officers in the Indianapolis Police Department West District also invested considerable time building trust with residents who had many past experiences to prevent their trust of police. Officials from the Department of Metropolitan Development and other city agencies also joined in training and development efforts on the near westside.

Early planning for both Weed and Seed and the Annie Casey initiatives began during the summer of 1992 and extended into early 1994. Initially, the planning group was convened and led by governmental officials, including Nancy Silvers Rogers, Deborah Daniels and Prosecutor Jeffrey Modisett. By early 1993, a combination of pressure from neighborhood representatives on the committee and realization by city officials of the need for resident ownership of the process led to the election of Olgen Williams to chair the planning committee (Crawford 1994).

Both Stephen Goldsmith and Nancy Silvers Rogers personified neighborhood leadership in the character of refinery worker Olgen Williams. William's contributions to discussions at Tate's Barber Shop (sic) on West 16th Street led older leaders to encourage his involvement in community activities in Haughville. Because of his outspoken participation at the administration's westside community forums, Goldsmith and Rogers picked Williams for a leadership role in the Westside Cooperative Organization (WESCO). Olgen Williams brought street credentials, community dedication and political expertise to the tasks of rebuilding an effective umbrella organization on the near westside. But Williams was only the most visible of a large number of existing neighborhood leaders in the three westside neighborhoods. Leaders in Hawthorne and Stringtown such as Claude Parker, Harvey Knox, Dan Ragan and Daniel Fugate responded to the opportunities presented by the administration by reviving inactive neighborhood associations and setting aside old animosities with Haughville. The Haughville Community Council, including Rev. Jimmie Harrington and Patrice Abdullah, also provided long-standing leadership in the neighborhood. In addition to the formal organizations, clergy from a few socially active churches supported neighborhood activities, including Rev. Roosevelt Sanders, Rev. Mel Jackson, Rev. Douglas Tate and Rev. John Neece. The Hawthorne Community Center and Christamore House in Haughville provided Diane Arnold and Cindy Clements, leaders with ties to the neighborhoods as well as expertise in the city's social service and governmental networks.

Despite their motto, "Working Together Works," the coalition that developed around WESCO was not without problems. For instance, the Haughville Community Council, well established when Goldsmith first came to the westside, often expressed its resentment about the increasing power that the administration's support brought to WESCO. Stringtown, the smallest of the three neighborhoods, felt that their interests were neglected both by the administration and WESCO. Specifically, Stringtown was unable to get support to establish its own community center. Like many other neighborhoods, lack of communication and low-level conflicts plagued the relationship between the neighborhood associations and the Westside Community Development Corporation (WCDC). These and other organizational tensions, combined with interpersonal clashes, challenged the planning of Goldsmith's initiative on the near westside and often placed a strain on WESCO as those efforts continued throughout the 1990s. However, the months of effort spent in building the coalition during 1992-1994 have helped WESCO to weather internal tensions and external pressures.

The early efforts in bringing WESCO together encouraged Goldsmith to think that the westside could fulfill his ambition to transfer government services to neighborhoods. In early 1993, several Indiana University professors presented a concept for privatization of services to the neighborhood level, a program that they called "Municipal Federalism." Their proposal detailed the privatization sketched earlier by Goldsmith, including how government services might be transferred to neighborhood organizations (Blomquist 1993). Goldsmith endorsed the proposal and presented it to the WESCO coalition in February of 1993. Although WESCO had many questions about Municipal Federalism, they did express their interest in implementing the proposal on the near westside. However, after the city-county councilor for the area made clear his opposition to municipal federalism in his district, further consideration of the plan was halted (Crawford 1994; Amerson 1995, 29-30).

Municipal Federalism was the last major attempt of the Goldsmith administration to privatize governmental services to neighborhood organizations. Disappointed by this failure, Goldsmith began to seek privatization partners other than neighborhoods, particularly religious organizations. However, the experience in WESCO and other neighborhoods had suggested to Goldsmith an alternate vision, a new idea that combined his goal of remaking government with a new goal of fighting poverty. If the obstacles of government could be removed, citizens of urban neighborhoods would have the freedom to pull themselves up by their bootstraps. As he wrote in a 1992 guest editorial in the *Wall Street Journal*, "By liberating our urban citizens from the shackles of bureaucracy, we can empower local institutions fighting for the responsibility, values and economic development needed to turn our urban neighborhoods into the centers of peace, opportunity and hope we all want them to become" (Goldsmith 1992).

Particularly in WESCO, citizens that the administration sponsored and mentored as new leaders responded favorably to the concept of neighborhood empowerment. One key person in defining the meaning of empowerment was Robert Woodson Sr., President of the National Center for Neighborhood Enterprise (NCNE). The Washington-based NCNE emphasized free-market strategies for community development, a philosophical approach consistent with Goldsmith's market-based approach for remaking government. Woodson in turn referred to Indianapolis as a "laboratory" for the types of urban reform he advocated (Penner 1994).

Robert Woodson and the NCNE proved extremely influential in shaping the Neighborhood Empowerment Initiative (NEI) and developing leaders in WESCO and other targeted neighborhoods. In December of 1992, Goldsmith convened a roundtable meeting of leaders from the seven targeted neighborhoods to introduce Woodson and his philosophy. After a series of visits to the city throughout 1993 the city contracted with Robert Woodson and the NCNE to conduct training. The first session of the Indianapolis Training Development Institute (INDI) convened in October of 1993; city officials chose participating neighborhood leaders (Amerson 1995, 5-6).

Neighborhood participants criticized some aspects of the NCNE training, particularly Woodson's emphasis on Community

Development Corporations (CDCs). He urged neighborhood leaders in Indianapolis to take on housing and economic development projects, an approach that neighborhoods felt confused the separate roles of what in Indianapolis were two very different types of organizations, CDCs and neighborhood associations. Although the NCNE revealed a profound misunderstanding of neighborhood realities in Indianapolis, Woodson and his staff did provide an important inspirational function, encouraging leaders that they could assume power for neighborhood change (Amerson 1995, 8).

After a second training session in December of 1993, which focused on organizational development for neighborhood organizations, Robert Woodson raised the stakes in a proposal to provide each of the targeted neighborhoods with a $50,000 project grant. He argued that these grants would allow neighborhoods trained by NCNE to implement projects to demonstrate their empowerment. Mayor Goldsmith accepted the challenge, but sought funding for the program from foundation sources. When foundations other than Annie Casey initially proved uninterested, the Mayor instead began the process with funding through federal Community Development Block Grants (CDBG) (Amerson 1995, 6).

Ironically, increased funding for CDBG came because of support from the administration of Democratic President Bill Clinton for this program. In *The Twenty-First Century City*, Stephen Goldsmith described federal funding as "greased skids" that led America's cities to decay and ruin. However, like other American mayors before him, Goldsmith proved eager to acquire federal funds for his purposes. By feeding from the federal trough, he avoided the allocation of city funds and possible local tax increases. However, his reliance on outside funding delayed implementation of NEI and burdened neighborhoods with the kinds of regulations and restrictions of which the Goldsmith was so critical.

CDBG funding carried complex guidelines and requirements. The city employed NCNE to assist three of the seven neighborhoods (WESCO, United Northwest Area (UNWA), and Martindale-Brightwood) in translating neighborhood plans and priorities into CDBG eligible projects. NCNE also worked with neighborhood leaders to develop their understanding of the complexities of CDBG funding, and also of governmental systems (Goldsmith 1995, 19-20).

Targeted neighborhoods complained about the lack of technical assistance following NCNE's initial training. Without funding, the Washington-based organization was unable to provide the ongoing advice, counsel, and support that emerging leaders needed as they attempted to move into a more "empowered" mode of operation. In his book, Goldsmith claims that his response was to create the Indianapolis Neighborhood Resource Center (INRC) (Amerson 1995, 160). In fact, plans for the INRC grew out of the 1991 Lilly Endowment conference on neighborhoods. The concept had been shepherded by the United Way of Central Indiana, which in 1993 issued a request for proposals. A combined proposal by the Indianapolis Neighborhood Housing Partnership, the Community Organizations Legal Assistance Project, and three other organizations was chosen and those founding bodies spun off the INRC as a not-for-profit organization (Annala 1999).

Concurrent with the 1994 opening of the INRC, the administration invited Robert Woodson to address the city's prestigious Economic Club and touted Woodson as a consultant to the new center (Penner 1994). In actuality, the relations between NCNE and the INRC were often strained during early years. Leadership at INRC came from the city's human services professional community, many members of which resented Goldsmith's attacks on social services organizations such as Community Centers of Indianapolis. The relatively low level of funding offered to INRC also contrasted with the fees paid to out-of-town consultants from NCNE. The targeted neighborhoods, equipped with CDBG and other funds, often opted for training and assistance by Woodson and other nationally recognized consultants. Other neighborhoods without those resources did rely on the INRC for free or low-cost training and development of technical and organizational skills.

As Woodson had less direct involvement in Indianapolis during Goldsmith's second term, INRC and NCNE established better relations, with the Washington consultant offering assistance to the Indianapolis organization. However there remained a perception of two parallel neighborhood training tracks in Indianapolis, one national-level for the targeted neighborhoods and a separate track for the several hundred other neighborhoods that relied on the INRC. Because they associated Stephen Goldsmith with the INRC, neighborhoods affiliated with the Marion County Alliance of Neighborhood Associations[2] (McANA) were leery of the INRC. Despite these tensions, the INRC has been an important development in the city, one that promotes the formation of new neighborhood organizations and trains leaders in organizational and technical skills necessary to nurture those organizations (Malone 1999).

Even as the INRC was finding its footing in 1994, the administration and selected neighborhood leaders detailed the plans inspired by Woodson's project grant suggestion. Early in this process, it became clear that the complexities of grant application and reporting, as well as management of the projects demanded that a person be hired to coordinate the efforts in each of the neighborhoods. Sometime in 1994, the administration began to apply the phrase "Neighborhood Empowerment Initiative" (NEI) to encompass several activities in the seven targeted neighborhoods, including the project grant process, the various neighborhood projects and the coordinator positions.

The concept of a paid staff person serving neighborhood purposes was not original to the NEI. The 1991 Lilly Endowment Indianapolis Neighborhoods Conference recommended the creation of this type of position for vulnerable communities. Despite Goldsmith's seeming acceptance of the concept, his definition of a role for the neighborhood staff person was slow to form. In a 1993 application to the Ford Foundation, the Mayor referred to a "neighborhood planner," employed by the neighborhoods (Amerson 1995, 15-16). In the *Twenty-First Century City*, Stephen Goldsmith describes the appointment of an individual in each of the targeted neighborhoods to serve as what he calls an "advocate." As Goldsmith describes in his book, the advocate/coordinator was to serve as an organizer, involving residents in the neighborhood umbrella organization (Goldsmith 1997, 120).

In reality, the neighborhood coordinators served in a variety of roles, administrator, office manager, information conduit, fundraiser and manager of the projects allocated to neighborhoods under NEI. The press of these duties, estimated at 60 to 90 percent of the coordinator's time, left little opportunity for the coordinator/advocates to perform extensive community organizing activities (Amerson 1995, 19-22).

One neighborhood, Near Eastside Community Organization (NESCO), which had one of the more experienced neighborhood organizations, did budget part of their project grant towards an effort to organize block clubs. NESCO leaders also attempted organizing efforts to identify, survey and recruit renters into a tenant-landlord organization as part of the NESCO umbrella (Crawford 1994, 69). Few of the other targeted neighborhoods expended NEI funding on organizing efforts. Neighborhood organizing, particularly in the early stages, is an activity with few immediate results that are tangible and visible. Organizing involves extensive communication with citizens, listening to their interests and building trust, often on an individual basis. Effective organizers seek out people where they congregate, including door-to-door contacts if necessary. Building an effective neighborhood organization can require years of effort (Tom 1999).

Elected officials tend to be impatient with the long time frames required for community building and this was especially true of the results oriented, performance measuring Goldsmith administration. The neighborhood projects were intended to allow neighborhoods a "quick win," the opportunity to achieve some outcome that would be immediately visible to people inside and outside the neighborhood. Short-term, deliverable results also benefited the Mayor's political interests. Goldsmith's market orientation and constant search for new ideas reinforced his desires to seek measurable positive results in very short time frames. On the other hand, the challenges faced by the targeted neighborhoods had developed over generations. Not only were the problems long-term, but communities also operate on much longer time cycles than businesses or politics. The variance between community and political time frames and the differing expectations between city and neighborhoods discouraged organizing activity (Amerson 1995, 19-22).

Goldsmith also writes that his city government avoided direct funding of the advocate/coordinators in order to preserve their autonomy. However, the impetus for creating the positions in the targeted neighborhoods came from the mayor's office, and city officials oversaw the funding flow that supported neighborhood coordinators. Strictly speaking, the seven coordinators were employed by umbrella organizations and much of their funding did come from private foundation money, supplemented by CDBG dollars (Goldsmith 1997, 169; Amerson 1995, 20-21). The result was to burden the new neighborhood coordinators with financial reporting and project management responsibilities (Amerson 1995, 20-21). The City of Indianapolis served as the intermediary for this funding and it was clear to neighborhood coordinators that they were accountable to the city (Tom 1999; Polin 1999; Amerson 1995, 19-20). Knowledge that city government controlled their funding placed coordinators in a difficult situation, pressured to respond to city initiatives, while also being responsive to the neighborhoods they served (Amerson 1995, 20-21).

Observers of comprehensive community initiatives in other cities have identified two sets of dynamic tensions inherent in neighborhood efforts. One tension is between process and product. On the one hand, stakeholders need to see some tangible results early in the initiative to reward their efforts. The urgency of human need in vulnerable neighborhoods gives special weight to the demands for immediate results. On the other hand, people and agencies working in community initiatives must also understand that much of their effort needs to be directed towards long-term investments in the capacities of individuals, organizations and communities. Change at this level takes time, especially given the magnitude of the challenges faced by urban neighborhoods (Aspen Institute 1999). An example of a process-product tension were the choices that Indianapolis neighborhoods made between organizing a membership infrastructure over the alternative of a project that produced a short-term deliverable such as a youth program, a playground or a roof repair on the neighborhood center.

A second dynamic in comprehensive community initiatives is around questions of power and authority. CCIs demand local empowerment of the neighborhood and its residents. At the same time, the spark that ignites an initiative and the financial resources that fuel neighborhood efforts come from agencies outside of the community. Community initiatives must seek a balance that allows power and authority to be shared between those actors inside the neighborhood and interested stakeholders from outside the community. Forming the complex relationships necessary to resolve the "inside-outside" tensions is difficult and requires both sides to examine their own expectations critically and to put aside accustomed behaviors. Foundations or governments must learn to respect their neighborhood partners, while community leaders must develop trust for outside agencies with whom they may have troubled histories.

The dilemma of balancing the "inside-outside" tensions is complicated by the fact that the formula for shared power may change over the life of a community initiative, with funders often exercising more authority at the outset. As a comprehensive initiative progresses, the neighborhoods should assert increasing authority over efforts to build their communities (Aspen Institute 1999). The NEI saw considerable inside-outside conflicts, particularly around the conflicting demands on neighborhood coordinators between the city and the neighborhood associations.

The tensions inherent in a comprehensive community initiative can never be fully resolved. Rather they need to be navigated by a process of ongoing communication and negotiation. Stephen Goldsmith found these extended processes difficult to maneuver. "The amount of time necessary to stay in touch with people and for them to feel like they're in touch exceeds the amount of time available," said the Mayor in a 1993 interview (Schuckel and Lanosga 1993).

However, some observers believe that Goldsmith learned much about the process of community building during the first years of his term, especially about the importance of relationships and trust. "Steve's not a 'touchy-feely' person," said Nancy Silvers Rogers, "and he had so much he wanted to get done (Rogers 1999). But he did learn how to encourage and complement people, those on his staff and in the neighborhoods."

"He tells more jokes now," Olgen Williams recalled, making the point that Goldsmith has 'loosened up' through his experience with WESCO and other neighborhoods. "In eight years, Goldsmith has learned that he doesn't have to be in control—people can make the decisions in low-income neighborhoods" (Williams 1999).

Nancy Silvers Rogers also devoted considerable efforts towards guiding WESCO and other neighborhoods through the transition from 'Building Better Neighborhoods' to the 'Neighborhood Empowerment Initiative' and beyond. Rogers, the most visible representative of the "outside" in the formation of the various comprehensive initiatives taking place, contributed patient consistency with insistent pressure that the NEI efforts continue despite internal conflicts and external obstacles. Some of her authority was philosophical. One observer commented that her contributions to NEI were from "the classic Republican perspective that citizens need to be informed and empowered" (King 1999).

One factor that hampered the abilities of the targeted neighborhoods to balance the process-product and inside-outside tensions and fully realize the vision for NEI was the crack cocaine epidemic in Indianapolis. This drug arrived in Indianapolis somewhat later than in other cities, and the Indianapolis Police Department officially noted its arrival around 1992. But the drug trade in the city's urban neighborhoods boomed, as did the violent crime that accompanied that trade. The homicide rate in Indianapolis reached record levels in 1994, 1996, 1997, and 1998, dubious records that carried the city to national media attention (Goldsmith 1997, 130).

In the targeted neighborhoods crack cocaine and murder represented not merely disturbing statistics, but rather human misery that counteracted citizen efforts to rebuild their communities. In those neighborhoods where the development of community policing was going well, particularly on the south and west sides, leaders and citizens redoubled their efforts to assist police. Many neighborhoods began "drug marches," direct action demonstrations against the locations from which drug dealers were suspected to operate.

Still the drug trade continued to boom. Drug dealers, driven from one neighborhood by effective policing or public scrutiny, simply moved to another neighborhood and opened up again. In early 1997, the seven targeted neighborhoods, increasingly frustrated with individual efforts, began to discuss a comprehensive, cross-neighborhood strategy. Meeting independently of governmental representatives, neighborhood representatives drafted a Memorandum of Understanding that detailed their intentions to curb the drug trade. The Memorandum listed the tactical objectives, an anti-drug work plan, and it defined the roles and responsibilities of the neighborhood organizations, as well as the police, the prosecutor, the Health and Hospital Corporation, and the mayor's office (Indianapolis Police Department et al. 1997).

In *Twenty-First Century City,* Goldsmith highlights this action by the combined neighborhoods as a culmination of his administration's efforts to establish community policing and to empower neighborhoods. "For five years we had struggled to build community leadership in the fight against crime, and to convince the police that they needed the support of strong citizens to succeed, especially in tough areas. To us, this contract was clear evidence that the new approach had taken root" (Goldsmith 1997, 150).

Neighborhood representatives were enthused about implementing the Memorandum of Understanding. By fulfilling their responsibilities detailed in the Memorandum, participating neighborhoods intended to solve the most immediate problem their communities faced. They had considered the actions needed to drive drug markets out of their neighborhoods. They deemed this work plan their top priority. But they found out that, although the city supported their efforts, neighborhood leaders and coordinators were still expected to participate in the many activities that were part of NEI. The annual CDBG application and reports had to be filed and the projects funded by CDBG had to be managed. Meetings at the city-county building had to be attended. New programs were announced that demanded neighborhood participation. All of the new programs offered possible benefits to the neighborhoods. The Front Porch Alliance (discussed later in this chapter), for example, held potential for establishing religious organizations as community assets. Some new programs, such as the Indianapolis Police Department's No Tolerance Zones, and the extension of Weed and Seed into additional neighborhoods could have direct impact on neighborhood crimes.

But all of the new programs demanded time from neighborhood leaders—time they would rather have given to their own initiative to eliminate drugs from their communities. The many demands from the administration distracted neighborhoods from the plan outlined in the Memorandum of Understanding.

Still, neighborhoods were heartened when Mayor Goldsmith contacted them early in 1999 and offered to sign a renewal of the Memorandum. The seven targeted neighborhoods arranged a conference for Saturday, October 9. They planned to review conditions in their neighborhoods and how those conditions might have changed in the two years since the original memorandum. They planned to consider new tactics to respond to changing conditions in making their neighborhoods safer places to live.

Unfortunately the conference was not held, but was instead postponed indefinitely. It seems that aides to the Mayor had planned a citywide neighborhood fair at the Indianapolis Zoo for that same Saturday. Leaders of the targeted neighborhoods were especially urged to attend in order to celebrate their achievements during the years of the Goldsmith administration (Polin 1999; Malone 1999).

Accounting for Community

Stephen Goldsmith prizes the notion of accountability, the bottom line by which government can measure effectiveness. In *Twenty-First Century City*, he cites performance measures as one of the five "strategic tools" his administration applied to remaking government. "Measuring and rewarding performance are indispensable, requiring us to pay close attention to what we actually produce, and not simply the amount of money we spend on a given service" (Goldsmith 1997, 58). His ideological bias towards the private sector gave special credence to Goldsmith's search for metrics used by businesses, especially those that could be expressed in financial terms.

Goldsmith's fondness for market-oriented measures meant that community development corporations received special recognition from the administration. CDCs, with their efforts on physical redevelopment, provided tangible results useful as visible evidence of success in neighborhood efforts. For instance, in the *Twenty-First Century City*, Goldsmith proudly claims "remarkable results" in his administration's housing program, with "hundreds more new houses built . . . tripling previous efforts" (Goldsmith 1997, 161).

Urban housing construction and reconstruction boomed in Indianapolis during the 1990s. A number of factors contributed to this boom, including momentum from housing policies implemented during the last term of Goldsmith's predecessor, William H. Hudnut III. The Indianapolis Neighborhood Housing Partnership, established in 1988, played a major role in urban housing development. A partnership between Citizen's Gas Company and Methodist Hospital (now Clarian Health Systems) also expended significant funds and great efforts in housing development in the Near North and UNWA neighborhoods.

Elsewhere in his book, Goldsmith noted a basic dilemma about urban housing development, the difficulty in finding buyers for houses in neighborhoods that were been abandoned by the real estate markets. CDCs exist because of those market failures but they are expected to succeed in market terms. Yet, it can be difficult to sell new and rehabilitated houses in urban neighborhoods when equivalent structures at competitive prices can be found in suburban neighborhoods without problems such as crime and perceived lack of schools. As Goldsmith noted in *Twenty-First Century City*, "government dollars cannot make a retail project successful without customers who are willing to pay for the product" (Goldsmith 1997, 170). Many community development professionals have struggled with an excess of products, rehabilitated and new urban houses, without buyers.

In his book, Goldsmith brings up the "Rivers Edge" in UNWA as a successful marketplace development in one of the targeted neighborhoods. He alludes to the troubled history of this site, adjacent to the Naval Armory and at the north end of Riverside Park, once the location for a segregated amusement park. He neglects to mention how the city closed Riverside Amusement Park in the 1960s with charges of histoplasmosis contamination. Goldsmith also avoids discussion of the transfer by the last private owner of the property to the city of Indianapolis with the legal stipulation that it always remain as part of the park system (Goldsmith 1997, 167-168).

The city's apparent disregard of this stipulation sparked the opposition of McANA to the River's Edge development. In his book, Goldsmith specifically describes the Nora Community Council, a founding member of McANA, as the villain in this story when they "rose up to wage war on the neighborhood and me." McANA did publicly challenge the River's Edge plans on legal grounds, arguing that the terms of the original property transfer to the city were irrevocable. According to McANA leaders, the city had violated the transfer contract by transferring the 23-acres to a private developer in a land swap. They also raised the concern about histoplasmosis as a long-term health threat connected to the site. But rather than a challenge to the residents of the Riverside neighborhood and UNWA umbrella, McANA saw its opposition to the private development in the context of ongoing concerns about parks privatization (Smith 1995; Lanosga 1995).

When one drives by the development in 1999, it is difficult to see River's Edge as an integral part of the Riverside neighborhood. A sign at the entrance announces "Houses from $110,000." Platted with curvilinear streets like a suburban subdivision, the appearance of the area contrasts greatly with the older neighborhood that is laid out on a rectangular grid pattern. The new vinyl-sided houses face inward, away from the existing neighborhood, and access is limited to only one entrance. The iron fence that surrounds the development might be merely decorative in the suburbs, but provides both a physical and symbolic barrier to the neighbors who already live in Riverside. Many of the new houses appear to be occupied and these new residents will certainly enrich the tax base and may, over time, bring other contributions to the communities of UNWA. Nevertheless, Goldsmith's attempt to paint River's Edge as a victory of a grass roots urban neighborhood rings hollow.

In contrast to his enthusiasm for community economic development, Goldsmith often targeted the human service system for criticism. In one instance, Stephen Goldsmith's drive to enforce market-based measures imposed an artificial emergency that threatened an important service provider in the city's urban neighborhoods.

Community Centers of Indianapolis (CCI) represents a network of fourteen neighborhood-based, multi-service centers. In many ways the city's community centers resemble Goldsmith's campaign promise for "family investment centers." Many of the community centers serve residents of the same neighborhoods targeted by the Goldsmith administration, providing "one stop shops" that give access to basic human services as well as entry points into the social services network. Community centers also provided emergency assistance while families awaited entry to other services, helping an estimated 20,000 people in 1993. Many of these centers, such as Christamore House in Haughville, Flanner House in UNWA and the Hawthorne Community Center have served their neighborhoods for decades.

As the 1995 city budget was assembled in 1994, the Mayor publicly threatened the non-renewal of city funding to CCI. His argument focused on a familiar issue for the administration, accountability. Goldsmith argued that the community centers operated without clear measures of program success and that the only significant outcome measure was job placement. He demanded the immediate adoption of a singular measure, successful employment, when the operations of community centers encompassed multiple services, not just employment counseling. Community centers countered the Mayor's threats by asserting that their mission as multi-service centers was broader and that abrupt cessation of government funding threatened the system of service provision at the neighborhood level. The director of the Flanner House estimated that the costs of an effective job placement program ($5,000 per client) far exceeded the $700,000 under contention (Horne 1994).

Earline Moore, Executive Director of CCI, challenged the timing of the demands. There had been a few general discussions about the Mayor's interests in job training, talks that intensified during the summer of 1994. Staff of CCI thought they had accepted a plan to move more intensively into job placement in 1996, using 1995 as a preparation year. The budget offered in September made it clear that Goldsmith wanted change to happen sooner. Fortunately, the City-County Council stood on the side of the network of centers and voted to give the $700,000 to CCI (Morgan 1994a; Morgan 1994b; Penner 1994; Penner 1995, *Indianapolis Star* 1994).

Goldsmith accepted the Council's vote. But he also continued to press CCI to adopt job placement as the primary outcome for performance measures. In 1999, publicly and candidly, CCI staff acknowledged value in wider adoption of outcome measures. But long-time employees remember the Mayor's abrupt and arbitrary demands for CCI "accountability" as an unnecessary attack that has left traumatic effects on the agencies (Arnold 1999; Annala 1999).

Stephen Goldsmith's political ambitions gave special emphasis to his interest in performance measures. By the time of the announcement of NEI in 1994, Goldsmith was already preparing for his mayoral campaign the next year. Even during the mayoral campaign, he and his aides were planning for the 1996 gubernatorial election. Both campaigns demanded achievements that were easily communicated in sound-bites and stump speeches. The campaigns commanded Goldsmith's time, as did other needs in Indianapolis, such as the completion of Circle Centre Mall and construction of a new fieldhouse for the Indiana Pacers.

Goldsmith's stated interest in the development of the seven targeted neighborhoods never waned throughout his second term. Even after he lost the governor's election in 1996—including a defeat by Democrat Frank O'Bannon in Marion County—the Mayor responded that the loss would provide him time "to go to neighborhood meetings" (Lanosga and Johnston 1996). The Mayor also renewed his interest in Building Better Neighborhoods with the proposal of an additional $326 million for repair of streets, parks, and sewers in 1996 (Lanosga 1996).

However, Goldsmith could not resist the allure of new ideas, including attempting reforms in two areas over which he had no statutory authority, the welfare system and Indianapolis Public Schools. As his second term progressed, he grew increasingly involved in encouraging religious organizations to provide community services. That all of these issues—welfare to work, educational choice, and 'faith-based' human services—were receiving increased attention on a national stage seemed to encourage Goldsmith's concentration on them rather than to the ongoing, incremental work of neighborhood development in Indianapolis. It was during the period following Goldsmith's defeat for governor as he pondered his political future after 1999, that Goldsmith completed and published *Twenty-First Century City*. The book won his standing in the forefront of the 'new breed' of mayors, which attracted reporters from a number of national newspapers, and booked Goldsmith on such national electronic media outlets as the National Press Club and the NewsHour with Jim Lehrer.

While the issues of welfare, public schools, and churches as assets touched Indianapolis urban neighborhoods in significant ways, they were tangential to the NEI efforts. Oversight of the neighborhood coordinators fell to the able Deputy Mayors who succeeded Nancy Silvers Rogers, first Irma Neale and then John Hall. By the second term, certain expectations had become established between the city and the targeted neighborhoods about how NEI procedures would operate. The management by chaos of the Goldsmith administration never disappeared. The new programs announced from the city-county building demanded the time of neighborhood coordinators and leaders, more time than they had to give. Yet, there was also certain regularity to the relationships between city and neighborhoods. Neighborhoods knew which city staff was assigned to work with them and understood the procedures for such important tasks as annual funding requests and reporting requirements. If this were an administration that would allow such a thing, the system began to look much like a bureaucracy.

Valuing Civil Society

Efforts with the targeted neighborhoods continued after 1995, but Goldsmith had less direct involvement. Instead, staff from the mayor's office and other city agencies assumed more responsibility in working with neighborhoods. During his second term, Stephen Goldsmith turned increasing attention to the idea that "mediating institutions" should reestablish civil society in the neighborhoods and introducing positive values to residents afflicted with the moral decay that comes with over-reliance on welfare. Goldsmith began to argue that religious organizations were the key to this process.

Some observers date Goldsmith's interest in religious organizations to his realization that neighborhoods would not or could not assume responsibility for services formerly provided by government. When neighborhoods rejected the wisdom of privatization, these critics say,

Goldsmith began to look to the city's 1200 churches, synagogues and mosques as potential service providers.

As Goldsmith recalls in *Twenty-First Century City*, some of the administration's first partnerships with the religious community came when ten churches in urban neighborhoods received contracts for maintenance of city parks. Of course, parks maintenance had been Goldsmith's classic campaign example for community privatization. Despite extensive efforts, Goldsmith was never able to recruit neighborhoods or other community-based groups to accept privatized responsibility for park maintenance. When he was able to convince religious organizations to step up to this task, it suggested new possibilities to the Mayor.

Although only a few churches participated in Goldsmith's initial park maintenance experiments, the Mayor claimed victory for his experiment in religious-public partnership. Soon he would launch more ambitious efforts to recruit religious organizations to join in his administration's social service policies. One such program, described in *Twenty-First Century City*, attempted to use religious organizations in the forefront of welfare reform. In 1996, Goldsmith announced that Indianapolis would initiate a program named Faith and Families. Modeled after an effort in Mississippi, Faith and Families proposed to pair families on welfare with a religious organization. The concept calls for a congregation to assume a mentoring role as single parents undertook the transition from welfare to work (*Indianapolis Star* 1996; Higgins 1996).

One of the advantages of Faith and Families is that it is largely staffed by volunteers from the participating organizations and coordinated with extraordinary dedication by Dick Wiehe, a retired professor from the University of Indianapolis. The program deserves the credit given to it by Goldsmith, both for assisting families in need and also for involving more affluent congregations in direct assistance. However, Goldsmith himself defines the limitations of Faith and Families in his book by acknowledging that in the first year the program involved only 23 congregations in service to 50 families. Faith and Families has grown modestly since 1995, yet the issue of capacity remains real. Even if every one of the 1200 congregations in Indianapolis participated, they would make only modest impact towards helping families move off welfare (Goldsmith 1997, 181-182).

Another program conceived since the publication of *Twenty-First Century City* aimed to make religious organizations active builders of community at the neighborhood level. In September 1997, the Mayor addressed the Indianapolis Downtown Rotary Club to announce what he described as the second major neighborhood policy step after Building Better Neighborhoods. Goldsmith evoked a homey symbol as he previewed the new initiative, saying that; "The front porch is the meeting place on every block, the ideal location for child recreation and supervision, and the ultimate outpost for crime detection and prevention." This symbol provided the name for the Front Porch Alliance, a program that sealed Goldsmith's national reputation among Republican policy-makers (Bell 1997).

As originally presented, the goal of the Front Porch Alliance was to encourage neighborhood organizations and families, as well as congregations, to take more active roles in translating values into community action. The image of the Front Porch recalls homes rather than churches, porches being vantage points from which family members and community elders monitor neighborhood activities, especially those of children. However, from the very outset, the Front Porch Alliance concentrated its efforts on religious organizations.

Much of the concept for the Front Porch Alliance was inspired by a former aide to Indiana Senator Dan Coats, Bill Stanczykiewicz, who brought his vision of an expanded social role for churches to Indianapolis in 1997. Not only did Stanczykiewicz share Goldsmith's political and social philosophy, he also provided energetic leadership to the first year of the Alliance's efforts. A young, enthusiastic, and committed staff, including Kim Didier and Issac Randolph, effectively connected with networks of religious leaders, particularly to a few African-American clergy who were seeking more active social roles in their neighborhoods. Goldsmith himself brought his own contacts to bear on building relationships between suburban and urban churches. For instance, the Mayor was instrumental in convincing the suburban evangelical congregation, East 91st Street Christian Church, to partner with the urban, African-American Oasis of Hope Baptist Church to create the Jireh Sports Center and provide recreation to young people in Martindale-Brightwood (Farnsley 2000).

The Front Porch Alliance provided a catalyst, aggressively encouraging a few clergy and congregations to present programs in the neighborhoods that surround them. In a random survey of 33 congregations involved in its efforts, 63 percent of the congregations were recruited for community involvement by the Alliance. Only 37 percent of the respondents were already involved in community outreach prior to their contact with the Alliance (Polis 1999, 10).

The Front Porch Alliance's greatest claim for success came after it arranged a visit from Rev. Eugene Rivers, nationally recognized for his community activism in Boston. Alliance staff capitalized on the visit of

Rev. Rivers to encourage a group of ministers to form their own "Ten Point Coalition" to combat the drug trade in the UNWA area. The Coalition has continued the practice of direct action against drug dealers introduced earlier by administration staff.

The Alliance staff served effectively as ombudsmen, running interference to help religious organizations navigate governmental regulations, while also helping them access resources. The Mayor provided the Front Porch Alliance a small pool of funds to allow the award of very modest grants of a few thousand dollars from the city. The Porch Light grants program awarded funds to churches totaling $58,000 in 1998 and $71,000 in 1999. In addition, the Alliance encouraged religious organizations to apply for available CDBG funds. In 1998, of the 21 CDBG grants awarded, three of those, totaling $98,000 went to religious organizations. The following year, 1999, the number of CDBG grants awarded to religious organizations increased to four of the 53 grants awarded overall. However, the amount awarded to churches grew to $250,000 in 1999. Alliance staff has also helped churches identify other funding sources, encouraging funders to consider religious organizations for awards and even writing grant applications for churches (Polis 1999 7, 11). As a result of its efforts to bring religious organizations into community work, the United States Department of Housing and Urban Development (HUD) recognized the Front Porch Alliance with a John J. Gunther award in 1998 (U.S. HUD 1998).

But these successes did not come without criticism. The Front Porch Alliance tended to focus on congregations new to community-service efforts, ignoring existing faith-based programs. For instance the Mid-North Church Council and its member churches have worked in community building and human service to Mapleton-Fall Creek for more than thirty years. Although HUD Secretary Henry Cisneros recognized the Mid-North Church Council as a national model of church-community partnership in 1995 (Cisneros 1996), this organization benefited little from Front Porch Alliance support. Similarly, Catholic Social Services provides assistance to youth and families in parishes throughout Indianapolis without support or recognition from the Front Porch Alliance (Polis 1999, 15).

Fundamental issues may also hamper the long-term viability of the types of efforts promoted by the Front Porch Alliance. One such issue is capacity. The philosophy behind the Alliance is that the hundreds of small congregations occupying space in urban neighborhoods represent a resource for those neighborhoods. The reality is that many, if not most, of these small "store front" or "house" churches have very few resources to extend programs outside the church walls. Led by bi-vocational pastors, supporting their ministries with day jobs, these churches are largely unoccupied except for Sunday services and Wednesday prayer meetings. Small churches such as these simply have limited ability to take on case management (Farnsley 2000).

The Front Porch Alliance philosophy also holds that urban congregations are somehow closer to the neighborhoods in which they are located, and thus better able to judge the needs of those neighborhoods. In Indianapolis, closer analysis of congregational membership suggests the impact of population mobility. Many and often a majority of members travel from outside the neighborhood to attend these churches. Congregants may once have had ties to the neighborhood, but have moved elsewhere, returning only for worship. Thus the clergy and the people in the pews have little relationship with neighborhood residents and little knowledge of community dynamics and needs (Farnsley 2000).

This information deficit may help explain another criticism leveled at the Front Porch Alliance. With few ties to the neighborhoods that surround them, clergy and congregations have often displayed ignorance of the community-based organizations and programs already in service. The few efforts by the Front Porch Alliance to coordinate between faith-based activities and neighborhood associations have met with little success. Only on the near westside have the WESCO ties to activist clergy helped to maintain communications between religious and secular organizations in that neighborhood. Elsewhere in the city, churches launched service programs with little knowledge of existing activities offered by the neighborhoods or human-service organizations. The newcomers enjoy the support and publicity engendered by Alliance mentorship, causing resentment among those organizations that have labored in service for years and decades (Polis 1999, 13).

These faith-based "newcomers" to community service compete with existing agencies and programs for scarce resources. For instance the increase in CDBG funding provided to churches from 1998 to 1999 (from $98,000 to $250,000) came largely through the redirection of existing funds from secular to religious organizations. Goldsmith and the Front Porch Alliance argued that faith-based efforts were potentially more effective in community building than existing service providers, but that contention remains unproved. What was clear to those secular agencies was that churches had been recruited by the Goldsmith administration to compete for limited funds (Polis 1999, 15).

In fact, the Front Porch Alliance has drawn only a relatively small number of churches into community outreach. Alliance publicity claims 400 faith-based partners, an estimate that probably includes representatives at public events sponsored by the Alliance. Attempts to count active congregational partners—those receiving funds or actively involved in Alliance Programs—suggest a much smaller number. For instance, in a survey of 33 congregations with the names supplied by the Front Porch Alliance, only about a third of all respondents reported that the Alliance provided direct support through funding, program assistance, or referral. About 20 percent of the respondents reported dissatisfaction from their contact with the Front Porch Alliance (Polis 1999, 11).

While local efforts are underway to sustain certain elements of Goldsmith's neighborhood policy past 1999, the future of the Front Porch Alliance remains uncertain. The new mayoral administration of Bart Peterson has continued the Front Porch Alliance, but the program has moved from the Office of the Mayor to the Department of Metropolitan Development. Many observers question the abilities of congregations to continue outreach without the direct assistance of the type formerly offered by Alliance staff. Those same observers also doubt whether that assistance can be effective without the power of the mayor's office behind it (Sword 2000). Other programs at the state and federal level advocate for continued support for faith-based programs. The outcome of the 2000 presidential election may provide additional encouragement and put additional resources behind community and social efforts by congregations. However, many questions about the efficacy and capacity of these experimental faith-based programs remain unanswered.

The Goldsmith Legacy

In the waning days of his administration, Stephen Goldsmith found occasion to be reflective about his work with neighborhoods. Asked about what he considered the successes of his two terms, the Mayor looked out the windows of his office on the 25th floor of the City-County Building. "Fountain Square, Haughville, UNWA. I could literally walk around this building and show you a neighborhood in an awful state of decline where they are now confident the future is better than the past. To me the successes have the faces of the people in these toughest neighborhoods" (Neal 1999).

Olgen Williams, now the Executive Director of Haughville's Christamore House, often played point man for Stephen Goldsmith's neighborhood policies. Williams speaks highly of Goldsmith the man and the mayor. "I'm not ashamed to say that he's a friend. Stephen Goldsmith is one of the ten most influential people in my life. He allowed me to grow and mature in my life. His aspirations and desires are consistent with building central city Indianapolis. By allowing neighborhoods to build themselves up, he has helped us to make a difference. He didn't have to do that for us" (Williams 1999).

Williams was right, Stephen Goldsmith did not have to choose to focus on urban neighborhoods and the many challenges they face. In fact, Goldsmith's commitment to the seven targeted neighborhoods represents a political paradox. Within months of assuming office in 1992, Mayor Goldsmith had alienated significant and powerful portions of the Republican suburban constituency. The formation of McANA marks the opposition that continued throughout the Mayor's two terms. Few of the citizens in the seven urban neighborhoods targeted by the administration had voted for Republican Goldsmith in 1991. Center Township remained a Democratic stronghold despite the attention paid to the seven targeted neighborhoods by the Goldsmith administration.

Why did Stephen Goldsmith abandon the Republican suburbs while targeting his attentions—and significant financial investment—on the Democratic central city? Given the animosity that many powerful suburban neighborhood groups express towards Goldsmith, it is difficult to imagine what the administration could have done to build bridges to the suburbs. Perhaps Goldsmith assumed that Republican suburbanites would continue to support him despite the opposition of their neighborhood associations. Urban activists maintain that by investing in cosmetic improvements in the neighborhoods around downtown, Goldsmith preserved the pace of downtown development, an issue of more importance to the Republican power base than the complaints of a few suburban homeowner groups (Tom 1999).

There remains the possibility that Goldsmith's efforts targeted neighborhoods on principle. Nancy Silvers Rogers notes the power differential between suburban and urban neighborhoods before Goldsmith took office. "The suburban neighborhoods were always listened to. Historically that wasn't the case with these (targeted) neighborhoods and attention had to be spent on their needs. I'm not a hero, Steve's not a hero, it just makes good sense. We fix it now for the future" (Rogers 1999).

The $800 million of funds that Goldsmith claimed were invested in needed infrastructure development, including repairs on streets and sidewalks, have certainly had an impact on the future of Indianapolis, in urban and suburban neighborhoods as well as downtown. But the very popularity of these capital improvements masks an irony of Goldsmith's neighborhood policy. During his campaign and throughout his term, Stephen Goldsmith decried his predecessors in Indianapolis and elsewhere for throwing money at urban problems. He has contrasted his approach with "big government policies," emphasizing the devolution of government responsibilities to the private sector and citizens, as well as his abilities to maintain lean and thrifty government operations. Despite outstanding questions about how this program was funded, Goldsmith's greatest victory in neighborhood policy, Building Better Neighborhoods, was clearly a spending program. In the context of Indianapolis, the $800 million spent on Building Better Neighborhoods would qualify as a fairly large spending program.

Goldsmith invested fewer dollars in the development of social infrastructure. The money that he put into people, projects and organizations in the targeted neighborhoods came from CDBGs or foundation support. Yet, the few hundred thousand dollars that he has spent each year on people capacity in neighborhoods began a process that, if continually nurtured, may lead the city's neighborhoods to increasing empowerment in the years ahead. Goldsmith's supporters laud the doubling in the number of neighborhood organizations that have formed during his two terms, from 200 to more than 400. Not to deprive the Mayor of due credit, but this increase came largely as a result of a process begun before 1992, although the creation of new neighborhood associations was certainly spurred by city officials such as township administrators, and nurtured by the INRC.

Equally important to the numerical increase in neighborhood associations has been the personal growth in the people who lead neighborhoods. During Goldsmith's two terms a few leaders in neighborhoods rose up to address challenges, accepted responsibility, and recorded accomplishments in their neighborhoods. Some of these leaders came forward at the Mayor's invitation and some assumed leadership in reaction to Stephen Goldsmith's personality and actions. But all of the new leaders hold potential to give increasingly empowered neighborhoods a greater voice in the years ahead.

Some of those new leaders in the targeted communities credit Goldsmith for having shifted the ground to allow neighborhoods more influence over their future. But their acknowledgments of his contributions are clouded by frustrations over how personality and politics worked against his stated intentions for neighborhood empowerment. The Mayor's enthusiasm for radical change, embracing the newest idea and program concept, ran counter to the incremental processes of community building at the neighborhood level.

Goldsmith's impatience with process and his emphasis on short-term, measurable achievements interfered with neighborhood interests in organizing themselves to address their own priorities. For instance, in drafting the Memorandum of Understanding, urban neighborhoods stated their intentions of applying a comprehensive strategy to combat what they saw as their greatest challenge, drug related crime. But neighborhood leaders felt pressures to remain responsive to the many demands that city officials placed on their time. These demands included the necessity to participate in the "flavor of the month" program initiatives arising from the mayor's office and city agencies, often developed by young, motivated staffers "thinking outside the box." These outside distractions prevented neighborhood leaders from what they saw as their real agendas inside their neighborhoods.

Neighborhood empowerment remains an incomplete process and governance of neighborhoods is imperfect. Neighborhood leadership is still exercised by only a few people and citizen participation in neighborhood activities is abysmally low. Even more new leaders must come forward to support and relieve leaders who have exhausted themselves in years and decades of community efforts. The challenges facing many Indianapolis neighborhoods, and not just those targeted by the Goldsmith administration, are significant. If neighborhood empowerment is to continue, attention must be paid to the processes of community organization and community building. Political, civic, and philanthropic leadership in Indianapolis must learn patience with the time-consuming, largely invisible, and often painstaking work that builds the capacities of people, organizations and communities.

Additional money must also be invested in the city's neighborhoods. The financial investments of the Goldsmith administration, while significant, seem small against the results of decades of disinvestment in older urban and suburban neighborhoods. But the city's leaders should not let their natural desires for short-term accomplishments overshadow the need for neighborhoods to reestablish social capital free from the glare of political attention.

Goldsmith closed his chapter on "Neighborhoods" in *Twenty-First Century City* with his own balanced judgment about his administration. "Many of our neighborhoods are now on the way back, but not without fits, and starts, and mistakes made by all of us" (Goldsmith 1997, 170). During his two terms, the politics and the personality of the Goldsmith administration often obstructed the empowerment process in the targeted neighborhoods. The Mayor's ambitions as expressed in *Twenty-First Century City* and elsewhere may have claimed more success than citizens and observers may actually find in the neighborhoods of Indianapolis. Stephen Goldsmith, like all politicians, claimed credit for things accomplished during his term, if not by his hand. There is little evidence that privatization, either of government or of human services, holds much value for neighborhoods. The Mayor's brash and arrogant handling of suburban neighborhoods has fostered a division, a Balkanization between the city and the suburbs that must be mended for the sake of neighborhood development citywide.

"A change agent is not necessarily a good collaborator. He can be very impatient if things are changing too slowly, and citizen processes can by very slow," said Ellen Annala, who observed and participated in Goldsmith's programs from the human service perspective of the United Way. "But Steve and his administration has refocused Indianapolis on its neighborhoods" (Annala 1999).

Certainly Stephen Goldsmith engineered a dramatic shift in the ways power is exercised in Indianapolis. Goldsmith said that he would measure his success by the level of challenge coming from citizens. This has been forthcoming, reflected in part by the 1999 election of Democrat Bart Peterson as mayor. But the "Peterson Plan," the detailed platform on which Bart Peterson was elected, maintains the city's dedication to neighborhoods.

Stephen Goldsmith did not invent neighborhood revitalization, nor was his the only effort that has furthered those impulses through the 1990s.[3] But as mayor, he represented and promoted a process that has begun to reshape Indianapolis around its neighborhoods. There is much to be done to further this process and those involved in that process can learn much from both the mistakes and the successes of the Goldsmith administration.

Notes

[1] See also Prudence Brown, "Comprehensive Neighborhood-Based Initiatives," *Cityscape,* Vol. 2, #2; May 1996), 161-176. Anne Kubuusch, "Comprehensive Community Initiatives: Lessons in Neighborhood Transformation," *Shelterforce Online,* January/February 1996, [cited 15 October 1999]; available at www.nhi.org/online/issues/85/compcominit.html>; *Voices from the Field: Learning from the Early Work of Comprehensive Community Initiatives,* (Washington DC; Aspen Institute, 1999), [cited 15 October 1999]; available at <www.aspenroundtable.org/voices>. Robert Halperin, *Rebuilding the Inner City,* (New York, Columbia University Press; 1995), 193-214.

[2] McANA is an umbrella organization of neighborhood associations throughout Marion County.

[3] For instance, collaboration between the Pew Charitable Trust and the Indianapolis Foundation through the Neighborhood Preservation Initiative invested funds and efforts in community building on the Indianapolis Far Eastside. Beginning in 1994, the three-year effort engaged several outside agencies in partnership with residents to organize this suburban neighborhood, recruiting and training volunteer leadership, encouraging them in strategic planning and launching the new community organization towards implementation. Among the outcomes of this process was an innovative merger of the CDC with the community center, under community governance. "The Pew Charitable Trusts' Neighborhood Preservation Initiative: Sustaining Neighborhood Capacity-Conference Report," (Unpublished Report, August 1997).

Chapter 10

Ideology Versus Patronage Politics: Why Indiana School Reforms Fail

Robert G. Lehnen

Introduction

Public education in Indiana rarely receives much attention from its city and town mayors, so Mayor Stephen Goldsmith's efforts to reform public education in the city of Indianapolis generated considerable attention and commentary. During his eight-year tenure as mayor, Goldsmith used his office to promote a set of initiatives directed at reforming education in the Indianapolis Public Schools (IPS), Indiana's largest school district. His reforms, shaped by the ideology of economic conservatism, focused on efforts to raise test scores, establish an accountability system, and recruit candidates for the IPS school board who were favorable to his views on education.

Depending on one's perspective Goldsmith's reforms, which were based on a conservative ideology, either attempted to improve a troubled, urban school district or represented a thinly disguised partisan effort to destroy the power base of the Marion County Democratic Party and the Indianapolis Education Association (IEA), the National Education Association's teacher bargaining unit in IPS. Goldsmith's education policies were viewed in black and white terms. This polarization of views and analyzes what happened to efforts of a conservative Republican mayor to reform an urban school district controlled by a mostly Democratic constituency.

Education Politics: Indiana Style

Historically, Indiana has had a patronage system of government in which the incumbent political party reaps the spoils of office for victory at the ballot box, including jobs, contracts, and public tax monies. Political parties have had strong organizations in Indiana because the patronage system provided many benefits to party regulars, including jobs and contracts. A contrasting form of government is one based on merit and performance, where decisions are driven by observable results or "outcomes."

One example of past patronage practice in Indiana state and local government was a vehicle license registration system in which the party winning the governor's office operated the motor vehicles license branches at the county level. This system, which lasted until the 1980s, helped fund local party organizations through revenues derived from the operation of these county-based offices. Employment at the license branches was a party affair that created a large number of patronage positions in addition to the revenues derived from the licensing process. Indiana political parties also maintain a closed primary system where participants must declare a party and a public record of participation exists. These primary voting records are an important part of the patronage system, since opportunities for employment in most state departments, including the Indiana Department of Education, are enhanced by a recommendation from one's precinct committee person. In some departments patronage appointments comprised over two-thirds of all employees, reaching well below the policy level positions to entry-level administrative jobs, such as secretary. One consequence of this patronage system is that it created strong and well-financed political parties at the state and local levels. Although this strict patronage system is slowly changing to a merit-based system, the political culture of patronage continues today.

The culture of patronage shaped the opportunities for education reform available to Mayor Goldsmith. Public education is a large employer in most counties that provides many well-paying jobs, contracts for service, and capital improvements projects. Every school board election, while raising policy issues about how best to educate children, also generates, and potentially risks, patronage benefits distributed by the incumbents.

Thus, local politics, including elections for school boards, are shaped not only by education philosophy but also by practical concerns to protect these material benefits. Because IPS is the largest school district in the City, school board elections place a large amount of patronage at risk.

The political culture of public education that Goldsmith encountered was shaped in the 1970s by the passage of Unigov under the administration of Mayor Richard Lugar, now the senior U.S. senator from Indiana. Unigov successfully integrated most public services into a countywide system of government, which were previously administered by independent towns, the (old) city of Indianapolis, county and township governments, and special purpose governmental units. The city of Indianapolis (Marion County) now has one mayor acting as the chief executive and one city-county council serving the legislative function. Two areas of local government services—public safety and education—were excluded from the Unigov structure because they posed insuperable political issues for the Unigov reformers.

Marion County has 11 public school corporations. Two of these are conterminous with the separate towns of Beech Grove and Speedway, Indiana, which also have separately elected mayors and city councils. These two school districts are excluded from the discussion that follows because Goldsmith had no administrative authority over these areas (see Figure 1). The reference to "public schools in Indianapolis" includes Indianapolis Public Schools and the eight township-based school districts.

Table 1 lists the enrollments, the percent of households living in poverty, the per capita income, the assessed valuation per pupil, and the total expenditures per pupil for these nine school districts. IPS is the state's largest school district with an enrollment of over 41,000 students. It also has the largest number and percent (26 percent) of children in or near poverty and the lowest per capita income ($11,009) in the city, indicators that often characterize children "at-risk" for obtaining a good education. IPS also has one of the smallest property tax bases, as indicated by its assessed valuation per pupil ($56,728). Finally, its expenditure per pupil ($7,872) is one of the lowest in the county.

The township school districts, mostly "urban" in character, cover the old suburbs of the city. The percent of at-risk children in these districts is less than half that found in IPS, and the residents of these districts have substantially higher per capita incomes. These school districts also have generally higher assessed valuations per pupil and expenditures per pupil. Thus, IPS and the township schools face some of the same problems because they are "urban" schools, but IPS differs significantly from the township schools in the scale and size of its educationally at-risk student population and its smaller financial resources.

Another factor affecting Goldsmith's education reform efforts was the political geography of the county. When the Lugar administration implemented Unigov in the 1970s, it achieved noteworthy success in streamlining city government, but the reform also broke the back of the Marion County Democratic Party in city elections. Prior to Lugar's administration the old city of Indianapolis voted Democratic, while the townships were mostly Republican. By implementing a countywide system of voting for mayor and city council, Republicans controlled both the mayor's office and the city council since the 1970s. Stephen Goldsmith's replacement, Bart Peterson, was the first Democratic mayor in nearly three decades.

Figure 1: Marion County School Corporations

Marion County, Indiana

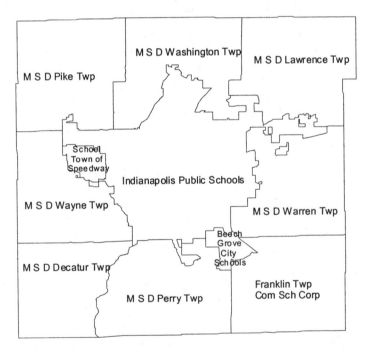

The IPS school district boundaries today closely follow the old city of Indianapolis, a traditionally strong Democratic area and the power base of the Marion County Democratic Party. At the federal level, the 10th congressional district of Indiana mostly covers the old city area. It has voted Democratic during the entire period covered by this analysis and is considered a safe seat for the Democrats. At the state level several legislators represent districts based in part or wholly in the old city limits, and these legislators also are Democrats and often minorities. Thus, IPS is a Democratic area of long standing.

Table 1: Indicators of size, social economic conditions, and public funding for public school corporations in the City of Indianapolis[a]

District	Students	Percent families in poverty	Per capita income	Assessed valuation per pupil	Expend. per pupil
Franklin Township Com Sch Corp	5,468	2	$16,349	$53,255	$6,845
Indianapolis Public Schools	41,359	26	$11,009	$56,728	$7,872
M S D Decatur Township	5,481	10	$12,080	$46,504	$7,264
M S D Lawrence Township	15,214	6	$19,423	$71,923	$8,311
M S D Perry Township	11,816	5	$15,355	$68,358	$8,110
M S D Pike Township	9,260	4	$21,239	$134,400	$8,612
M S D Warren Township	10,587	6	$14,042	$88,087	$8,104
M S D Washington Township	9,996	5	$23,135	$113,914	$8,063
M S D Wayne Township	13,071	10	$13,823	$78,892	$7,866

[a]   Source: Indiana   Department   of   Education   website: <http://ideanet.doe.state.in.us/htmls/education.html> (May through July 2000).

The Marion County Republican Party organization is well organized in the townships surrounding the old city of Indianapolis. It has two competing factions representing the economic and religious conservative wings of the national party. Goldsmith also faced an added dimension of conflict in reforming education in Indianapolis from the partisan split between the Democratic education stakeholders in IPS versus the Republican stakeholders in the townships.

To summarize, Goldsmith confronted a long standing political culture based on patronage supported by both political parties, a fragmented political system of public education left over from the Unigov reforms of the 1970s and a partisan split between a mostly Democratic area served by IPS and a predominantly Republican one served by the eight township school corporations.

Education Reform: An Economic Conservative's View

Stephen Goldsmith's views on reforming public education are firmly rooted in the ideology of economic conservatism. He acknowledges the theories of Professor Milton Friedman, a conservative economist at the University of Chicago, as a guiding force in his thinking about education reform (Goldsmith 1997, 115-116). To quote Goldsmith,

For me, the best crystallization of the need to inject competition came, perhaps not surprisingly, from Milton Friedman. I had the pleasure of spending some time with the Nobel Laureate economist and asked him what we could do to improve our public schools. When I began, 'Dr. Friedman, I would like to talk about public schools,' he politely stopped me. 'They are not *public* schools,' he said quickly. 'They are *government* schools.' Public, he explained, meant open to anyone. The schools to which I referred were government schools.

Not yet grasping the magnitude of what Friedman was saying, I continued as if he had made a semantic point, interesting but hardly of paramount importance in the general discussion. But he persevered. 'Quit trying to reform the government schools,' he said, 'they are a monopoly. The only thing that will reform a monopoly is competition.'

'Innovation,' he went on, 'derives from markets, and markets come from customers. If you do not have customers, you do not have markets. And if you do not have markets, you cannot have innovation.' Because the school system is a monopoly, the customers—parents who want the best for their children—have little impact. We will not see any improvement in the nation's woefully inadequate system of government schools until parents become customers (Goldsmith 1997, 115-116).

Economic conservatives, then, are reformers who use an economic paradigm as the foundation for their beliefs about improving public education. The economic paradigm assumes that a free market better allocates resources—such as money, personnel, and capital assets—to produce better products and services.[1] According to economic conservatives, government exists to provide a product or service *only in situations where markets cannot or do not operate.* Government is necessary where there is "market failure," and economic conservatives call the products of government under conditions of market failure "public goods."

The classic example of a public good is national defense because everyone shares its benefits. Unlike gasoline or food, individuals cannot choose to buy more or less national defense, and the government is the only supplier of national defense. Economic conservatives believe that education is a service that should be treated more like gasoline or food than like national defense. Citizens (customers) should have the opportunity to choose the supplier of education for their children under a free market system just as they would choose which kind and how much gasoline or food to purchase.

Economic conservatism, *as applied to education,* is an ideology because it represents a theory and a set of assumptions mostly untested by the policy sciences (Chubb and Moe 1990). Much of the opposition to the economic conservative approach to education reform is that it is untested in "the real world," and children should not be the objects of a grand social experiment.

Outlining the ideology of economic conservatism provides the reader some insight into the ideology shaping Goldsmith's views on education, and why he approached education reform in Indianapolis in a specific manner. Economic conservatives in Indiana have applied their ideology to education by advocating reforms such as education choice, vouchers, and charter schools. Goldsmith was also a strong proponent of these reforms, as discussed in his chapter on education in *The Twenty-First Century City* (Goldsmith 1997, Chapter 8).

Accountability in Public Education

Stephen Goldsmith's major education reform initiatives centered on the pursuit of accountability in public education and the passage of state law P.L. 340. His views on accountability were mostly shaped by his economic conservatism, but his implementation of his ideas was influenced largely by his Republican partisanship. Economic conservatives define accountability in education in two primary ways. On the input side, they focus on expenditures of public monies, referred to here as "fiscal accountability." On the output side, they are concerned about school performance, usually measured by test scores and referred to here as "performance accountability." Goldsmith endorsed both views of accountability in public education, and he attempted to incorporate these views into his IPS reform proposals.

Fiscal Accountability

School finance policy in Indiana and the related notion of fiscal responsibility has been shaped by a Republican coalition consisting largely of business and farming interests. Organized through their lobbying organizations—the Indiana Chamber of Commerce, the Indiana Farm Bureau, and the Indiana Association of Manufacturers—these education stakeholders have had a major impact on education policy in Indiana. As early as 1973, under the administration of Republican Governor Otis Bowen, the General Assembly passed "school reform" legislation, actually a property tax reduction measure, that sought to reduce the reliance on property taxes to fund local government.[2] Indiana school corporations, the local governmental units most reliant on the property tax, experienced the greatest disruption in the flow of revenues. Throughout the 1970s and 1980s the General Assembly passed school finance formulas that shifted school funding in Indiana away from the property tax and more toward state general revenues. This resulted in a shift in the property tax/general revenue ratio from about 67:33 percent in the 1970s to about 33:67 percent today. The General Assembly has effectively eliminated local control of school revenues by deciding where two-thirds of the revenues for public education comes from and closely regulating the property tax levies at the local level for the remaining one-third.

Not only did Goldsmith support this long standing business-farmer property tax coalition to reduce or eliminate the property taxes as a source of support for public education in Indiana, he also linked taxes in general, and property taxes in particular, to education performance. He characterized his pressuring of local school districts to maintain or reduce property tax levies as "education reform," but his position on holding the line on taxes appeared to be more inspired by long standing Republican views on taxation than by the theories of Milton Friedman.

Goldsmith criticized parents for fighting tax reductions and wanting more money for education. He argued that the:

. . . numbers consistently belie that assumption [that more tax money improves education]. Every year urban school budgets go up. Every year, urban enrollment goes down. It does not take a math major to figure out that per pupil expenditures are going through the roof. (Goldsmith 1997, 122)

Economic conservatives and Republicans in Indiana are greatly influenced by the "money doesn't make a difference" debate initiated by the research of Professor Eric Hanushek of the University of Rochester (Hanushek 1981). Hanushek conducted a review of more than 100 research studies in the education policy literature dating mostly from the 1960s and 1970s. He found that many studies did not find a significant positive statistical correlation between the level of spending and some measure of achievement. In other words, a large number of the research studies could not demonstrate a positive link between spending (input) and achievement scores (output).

It is important to understand the statistical language used in these studies and in the work of Hanushek because the science behind these studies has been interpreted erroneously, partially based on a misunderstanding of the statistical tests that are the basis of this body of literature. When scientists conduct statistical tests, they begin their study by assuming that a hypothesis of "no association" is true. This hypothesis is called the "null" hypothesis—null meaning "none" or "no association." Scientists will then conduct a scientific study by collecting data to determine whether or not there is evidence of an association. For example, the researchers in the studies reviewed by Hanushek collected data on funding levels and test scores and used statistical tests to determine if there was an association between higher education funding and improved test scores.

If the evidence demonstrated an association between these two variables, the scientist would decide to reject the null hypothesis of no association in favor of the alternative that an association existed between the two variables. If the evidence from the study demonstrated a lack of association, the scientist would "fail to reject" the null hypothesis. Notice that in all statistical tests, scientists begin by assuming the lack of an association and then look for evidence from their study to the contrary. Failing to reject the null hypothesis does not mean that there is no association between the two variables under study; rather, it means that the study did not provide any evidence to cause us to doubt the assumption of no association. Most scientific studies fail to reject the null hypotheses; this situation is a normal and expected part of scientific inquiry. Since scientists around the world are doing studies on the very same question (hypothesis), a large number of contradictory findings are produced with some studies "failing to reject" the null hypothesis and others "rejecting" it. After scientists complete a large number of independent studies, a pattern appears that either supports the truth or falseness of the assumption of no association.

Most of the studies reviewed by Hanushek failed to reject the null hypothesis; a smaller number of research studies were able to show a *positive* correlation—that is, as spending increased, achievement test scores improved. A few of the studies actually found a *negative* correlation—meaning that spending more money on education was associated with a *decline* in test scores. This pattern of conflicting results is not unusual in the policy science field.

The arguments used by conservative Republicans in Indiana, unfortunately, are based on a misunderstanding of the meaning and interpretation of the "fail to reject" decision for statistical tests of significance. Policy scientists understand that failure to reject a null hypothesis in a statistical test means simply that more research is needed, because the existing study is inconclusive about the association between expenditure levels and achievement. The possible reasons for the "failure to reject the null hypothesis" decision are many, including such explanations as insufficient sample size, measurement error, or an invalid statistical model, as well as the possibility that no association between the variables, in fact, exists in the "real world." In other words, more study is needed to determine why a particular study did not find a statistically significant result.[3] By failing to reject, the scientist had no evidence to cause doubt about the *assumption* of no association—assuming something is true does not make it so.

Hanushek's literature review found that among the statistically significant research studies, those with a positive association far exceeded the number of studies with a negative association, suggesting that higher expenditures probably did improve test scores under some circumstances, but the nature of this relationship is not fully understood. Some Republicans have misunderstood the meaning of Hanushek's initial research, and they have used the large number of studies that "failed to reject" the null hypothesis as evidence that no association exists. They have used this mistaken "fact" to justify restricting spending for public education in Indiana. They repeat the mantra, "money doesn't make any difference" and cite Hanushek as justification.[4]

Another closely related argument used by Republicans in Indiana is the belief that public schools "waste" money by spending a disproportionate amount of revenues on school administration and not enough "in the classroom." Goldsmith called for an activity-based accounting system, similar to that proposed by Bruce Cooper, Professor of Education at Fordham University, and the U.S. Chamber of Commerce (U.S. Chamber of Commerce n.d.) so that " . . . principals would see where every dollar was being spent within the school" (Goldsmith 1997, 122). Goldsmith's recommendation on giving principals this kind of financial information assumes, quite incorrectly, that they could use the information to make meaningful changes and that they also have the time and ability to implement such changes. It is not obvious how Goldsmith's activity-based cost accounting system gets dollars into the classroom.

Performance Accountability

The second area of accountability championed by economic conservatives and articulated by Goldsmith is the improvement of achievement test scores. They argue that public education is not preparing high school students for the workforce. In his book, Goldsmith justifies his view that public education is a failure by such anecdotal evidence as a conversation with members of the Indianapolis Private Industry Council:

> I talk with executives each month who complain about the shortage of qualified labor, and I know that many businesses resort to recruiting workers from Mexico and beyond. Yet thousands of Indianapolis residents remain unemployed. (Goldsmith 1997, 113)

He maintains that the public schools—specifically in IPS—were substantially failing the children of Indianapolis, yet he did not address similar issues faced in some of the township schools (Goldsmith 1997; 2000). He also championed the "superior" quality of Catholic schools in Indianapolis and his belief that public monies should flow via vouchers, choice programs and/or charter schools to religious schools and private organizations. All of these issues are very controversial positions in Indiana (Goldsmith 1997, 112-113).

The quality of Catholic schools in Indianapolis, the separation of church and state under the First Amendment, and maintaining accountability over the spending of public monies are "hot button" issues in Indianapolis. Goldsmith, by advocating the more extreme positions on these issues, magnified the divisions among education stakeholders.[5] As will be demonstrated below, these positions contributed to the failure of Goldsmith's education reforms in Indianapolis.

One area of continued public debate in Indiana is the interpretation of test scores from the state-mandated achievement test ISTEP+. This test is a general achievement test covering the areas of mathematics and English/language arts. It is administered statewide annually to the third, sixth, eighth, and tenth grades. The tenth grade test involves "high stakes" testing since it is now used to determine whether a student receives a high school diploma or simply a certificate of completion. ISTEP+ is controversial in Indiana not only because it determines who graduates, but also because of how test scores are used to evaluate the quality of public education in Indiana in general, and about IPS in particular.

There is no question that IPS students consistently average below their township peers on both parts of the ISTEP+ test. Table 2 shows the percent of students in Marion County school corporations that pass the ISTEP+ essential skills portion. The percent passing the essential skills portion (28 percent) among IPS students is substantially lower than the percent of students in the township schools.[6] Though this finding is not in dispute among the opposing sides of the education debate, the interpretation of it is. There is no consensus among the opposing groups about why IPS is "failing to educate" its students. According to economic conservatives, such as Goldsmith, the reason for the substandard performance of IPS students is the lack of competition among schools in Marion County to motivate teachers and school officials to adequately carry out their responsibilities as educators. He notes that we do not have bad public employee/teachers and administrators, we have "good people in bad systems" (Goldsmith 2000, A6).

Democrats, the teachers union (IEA) affiliated with the Indiana State Teachers Association, school board members, and school officials argue that teachers are overwhelmed in the classroom with overcrowded classes and the lack of funds to buy essential teaching materials and computers. They also believe there is inadequate training and professional development for the certified staff, to help address the unique problems of urban school districts. The public debates about poor IPS student performance were intense, as illustrated by the columns of Harrison Ullmann, editor of the alternative newspaper *NUVO Newsweekly*.

Ullmann attacked the conservative Republican arguments with a comprehensive analysis of state ISTEP+ test scores in Indianapolis (Ullmann 1999a; 1999b; 1999c; 1999d; 2000). In one piece Ullmann demonstrated that IPS's consistently lower test scores were more the result of the mobility and selection of housing by families in Marion County than from anything happening in the school buildings. Using ISTEP+ data at the school level, Ullmann showed that the mean Cognitive Skills Index (CSI), more a measure of the ability to learn than a measure of the mastery of content, for IPS students (measured as part of the ISTEP+) was substantially below that of the township schools. He also observed that the academic ability of the average IPS student was substantially below that of students in township schools. Ullmann explained this difference in abilities among the student populations as a product of the flight of the middle class, both black and white, to the townships and beyond.

Table 2: Average results of Cognitive Skills Index and ISTEP+ Essential Skills testing[a]

District	Cognitive Skills Index	% Passing ISTEP+ Essential Skills
Franklin Township Community School Corporation	104	62
Indianapolis Public Schools	93	28
M S D Decatur Township	101	55
M S D Lawrence Township	107	63
M S D Perry Township	104	57
M S D Pike Township	103	54
M S D Warren Township	104	55
M S D Washington Township	105	61
M S D Wayne Township	101	52

[a] Source: Indiana Department of Education website (May through July 2000): <http://ideanet.doe.state.in.us/htmls/education.html>

Ullmann further noted that once one adjusted for these differences in aptitude, IPS students actually performed better on ISTEP+ scores than many of the township school districts and also performed *equal to or better than the inner city Catholic schools*. Ullmann's comparison of IPS and Catholic schools was especially noteworthy because conservative Republicans had actively promoted public-private voucher programs based on the assumption that IPS parents would use the state tuition money (education vouchers) to enroll children in the (better performing) inner city Catholic schools and the township systems.

An analysis of the data in Table 2 undertaken by the author produced equivalent findings.[7] A regression analysis of the CSI scores and the percent of children passing the essential skills portion of ISTEP+ for the nine school districts in Indianapolis explains 93 percent ($r = 0.928$) of the variation in achievement test scores. This finding means that the CSI accounts for practically all of the differences observed in average test scores among the school districts in Indianapolis. The importance of this finding is that one need not introduce social-economic explanations, such as poverty levels, percent minority enrollments, or per capita income, to explain achievement score outcomes. The differences in achievement scores among school districts in Indianapolis result from differences in the makeup of the student populations, as measured by the CSI in the nine school districts. This analysis of the CSI scores shows that IPS students are not as likely to have the essential skills—basic knowledge about math and language—to succeed academically.

Explanations of test score differences among the Indianapolis school districts should focus on the social and economic forces that have caused families, particularly those from the middle class, to leave the inner city for the townships and outer suburbs. As Ullmann noted, the quality of the public schools is only one, and probably not the most important reason, that middle class families leave the inner city. "Push" factors such as old and deteriorating buildings, health risks like lead exposure, crime, lack of convenient retail services, and the general blight of the inner city encourage families to seek housing elsewhere. At the same time, the suburbs offer such "pull" factors as job opportunities, a perception of superior public education, lower crime, new and better housing, superior retail opportunities, and good public services as inducements to move out of the inner city.

The analyses of Ullmann and the data in Table 2 suggest that where a family chooses to live has more to do with average test scores than factors associated with the school and the classroom, but Goldsmith did not believe the findings. He attempted to discredit the findings by asserting that those who oppose his reforms assume " . . . that the quite difficult circumstances of these children mean they won't or can't learn (Goldsmith 2000, A6). As Goldsmith explains, "These lower expectations lead to social promotion, and insufficiently educated young adults" (Goldsmith 2000, A6). However, his interpretation of the opposition's arguments is misleading. He seems unwilling to acknowledge that children vary in their ability to learn and educating each child to his or her full potential, the stated goal of the Education Commission of the States, still will not make every child above average.

Children are born with different capabilities to learn, but they also grow up in families that offer different kinds of learning environments. Some environments are highly conducive to learning, allowing the child to learn to his or her full potential; others are not as supportive of learning. The social-economic data in Table 1 suggests that IPS children do not have environments providing the same opportunities to learn at home as children in the townships. In addition to lower incomes, IPS families are not as likely to have two parents at home, or a parent with a college education. These families also do not have sufficient disposable income to provide the "extras" that contribute to learning at home, a personal computer and a connection to the Internet, educational games and toys and vacations to new and different places.

Public schools in Indiana, including IPS, do not have the resources to fill this learning gap left by the family and created mostly in the pre-school years. Spending more on daycare education, preschool, and full-day kindergarten would make a substantial difference in getting inner city children "ready to learn" when they enter IPS. These programs can help all children, regardless of their economic status, with an equal opportunity to learn and achieve their potential.

Goldsmith involved himself in an area of local public policy where viewpoints and interpretations of the evidence were highly polarized. Rather than bring a new perspective or evidence to the discussion, he simply allied himself with existing conservative Republican positions and further alienated education stakeholders already hostile to these well-known views.

P.L. 340 and Accountability

Undoubtedly, the most controversial education policy initiative during Goldsmith's administration was the passage of P.L. 340.[8] Using the Republican majority in the House and Senate of the General Assembly, Goldsmith crafted school accountability legislation that established new requirements for teachers, school administrators, school buildings and the school corporation. Though P.L. 340 was controversial for its approach to education reform, it became especially so because it applied only to IPS and not to any other of the nearly 300 school districts in the state, including any of the township school corporations in Marion County. Yet several of the township school districts, as illustrated by the Ullmann analysis, had performance issues at least as serious as those faced in IPS. Furthermore, Indiana has other urban school districts, though not as large as IPS, with similar student profiles and performance outcomes.[9]

This legislation's extensive and detailed requirements placed a substantial new administrative load on already stressed IPS teachers, building administrators, and central administration. The legislation required all teachers to be evaluated twice each school year. The practice prior to P.L. 340 was to evaluate untenured teaching personnel each year until tenured and tenured teachers every three years. At the building level, the requirement for administrators to evaluate each teacher two times each school year would absorb an estimated minimum of 13 to 14 days of each building level administrator's time. This means that 4 to 6 weeks of the administrative staff time (based on a typical number of 3 administrators per building) would be consumed in teacher evaluation. The author knows of no cost-benefit analysis that would answer the question of whether sufficient educational benefits would justify this substantial investment of time and effort. The accountability law also specified the criteria by which the teacher would be evaluated. These criteria included the development and maintenance of parental involvement, student achievement on assessment testing and teacher attendance rates.[10]

Building administrators were to be evaluated annually on the number and percent of students meeting or exceeding ISTEP+ test standards and the improvement of ISTEP+ scores for each class grade and the school building as a whole. The law also added criteria for improvement in graduation rates for high school administrators.   Performance measures for central administrators included the management of the General Fund, improvement of teacher attendance rates for each school, the number of teachers per student and the number of certified administrators per student. P.L. 340 also established a detailed list of administrative requirements, including the preparation of an improvement plan for each building (to be developed by teachers and administrators).

Another highly controversial provision of P.L. 340 included the removal of collective bargaining authority for the Indianapolis Education Association by restricting its authority only to matters of salary and benefits. Working conditions, disciplinary measures, and due process issues in the workplace were placed beyond the collective bargaining process. These provisions effectively removed the teachers' union from the decision-making process of school improvement, even though teachers as individuals are included in the school improvement committees required under P.L. 340.

The accountability legislation eliminates decision-making by building level personnel through a provision that states, "no decision by an education group in a building may supersede any statute, regulation, or district policy" (IPS 1997). Thus, teachers and their union, and to a lesser extent building administrators, have little power to direct the course of reform, but they are held responsible for failure to achieve the mandated goals.

The Education Legacy of an Economic Conservative

Stephen Goldsmith's foray into local education policy set up classic confrontations between ideology-based and patronage-based politics. In these situations, reformers are put into office by people who want to improve the existing system. Initially, the reformers make dramatic statements and sometimes produce significant results, but over time, the enthusiasm for reform wanes. Supporters realize that the problems, as defined in the election campaign, may not be quite what they expected. Often they are co-opted by the interests they had displaced by forming a coalition with the supporters of the *status quo*. Reform movements usually run their course after several years, and the political system reverts to the *status quo* that existed before the reformers assumed power. But things are never exactly as they were before, so the assessment of the reform initiatives must focus on the legacies left by their efforts.

This classic pattern of reform movements generally explains what happened to public education policy during the Goldsmith administration, but it also accounts for what has happened to education reforms attempted by many others over the past decades. Some refer to this process as the "revolving door of education reform" where each set of reformers, inspired by new ideas, assumes power and attempts to implement reforms, but ultimately most of what they sought to do is either implemented or overturned by the next set of reformers.

An iron rule of politics says that one must assume that the *status quo* serves the interests of some powerful constituencies. The task of aspiring reformers is to understand the core values and interests of those being challenged and, ideally, to convert potential opponents into allies through consensus building.

Goldsmith's approach to education reform was guaranteed to create powerful opponents, not allies. In *The Twenty-First Century City* Goldsmith asserts that he formed a bipartisan political action committee, the Alliance for Quality Schools, and met with representatives of the IPS teachers' union (IEA) to propose state legislation for IPS. Although Goldsmith may have viewed his efforts as consensus building, the education stakeholders' perception was very different. From their point of view, Goldsmith failed to listen and did not seek alternatives that incorporated the ideas and values of the contesting side. His deal-making approach, which did not recognize the substantial benefits derived from maintaining at least part of the *status quo,* did nothing to prevent further polarization.

Consensus building is difficult for someone driven by ideology because it is viewed as a sacrifice of fundamental values. All parties in these discussions want to improve education outcomes, yet they intensely disagree about the means to achieve these mutually endorsed goals.

Goldsmith mixed unconventional ideology, economic conservatism and traditional Republican positions to conduct "politics as usual." His dramatic actions and confrontational style created even greater divisions and heightened suspicions among the stakeholders about each other's motives.

The passage of P.L. 340 early in his term sent a powerful message about Goldsmith's approach to "reform," and as a result he framed perceptions about his fairness and objectivity, mostly to his own disadvantage. Many education stakeholders wondered why the General Assembly, under Goldsmith's leadership, singled out IPS when other school districts in Indiana had similar problems, and why the metropolitan township schools were excluded. They also felt that P.L. 340 was punitive toward IPS, especially the teachers' union, and they questioned whether educational reform was really the goal. David Young, President of the Indiana State Teachers Association, believed otherwise, "I consider P.L. 340 a terrible travesty and a union busting scheme . . . ." (Young 2000)

Reforming a human resource intensive service such as education requires positive human resource policies that secure the willing cooperation and active support from teachers. P.L. 340 instead removed most of the bargaining rights of IPS teachers, especially in critical areas such as workplace disagreements. P.L. 340 restricted teachers only to bargaining for salaries and benefits, but then teachers were criticized as being interested only in money and not children. Such posturing greatly diminished the possibility of meaningful education reform.

Goldsmith intended to place the primary responsibility for low test scores on teachers and school administrators. P.L. 340 held teachers and administrators responsible both for parental involvement and the behavior of students in improving achievement test scores. Unfortunately, there are parents in Indianapolis, as elsewhere, who have little interest in their children or in the education they receive, or whose circumstances leave little time for involvement. For these parents no amount of "parental outreach" efforts, community involvement programs or Parent-Teacher Organization initiatives will make them or enable them to participate in their children's learning. But economic conservatives assume that the public schools "monopoly" is what prevents parents from being involved in their children's education.

Goldsmith's ideology caused him to ignore or discount data and the explanations of others that disagreed with his views on education. His inability to work with education policy leaders such as the State

Superintendent of Public Instruction, Suellen Reed (also an elected Republican), led him to reject alternatives that might have worked in Indianapolis. Had he been more attentive to the ongoing and substantial discussions of key education officials, he would have acknowledged that reforming urban education was much more complicated than his economic theories allowed. Choice, vouchers, and charter schools do not address the fundamental issues underlying education reform in Indiana.

The Mayor's education reforms also produced several unintended and undesirable consequences. While achievement test scores in IPS remain essentially the same after five years of P.L. 340, the legacy of P.L. 340 is entrenched. Instead of deregulating IPS, the legislation imposed a burdensome oversight system, especially on IPS building-level personnel, that actually increased regulatory oversight by the State Department of Education. This is an ironic legacy for someone who champions deregulation and market forces to reform education (Goldsmith 1997, 119-125).

Goldsmith's constant efforts to improve ISTEP+ scores in IPS also have created counterproductive results. Rather than improving test scores, his efforts have contributed to the very forces that keep the IPS students' scores so low in comparison to the township schools. To understand this contradiction, one needs to consider why the average Cognitive Skills Index is so much lower among IPS students than for township students. Families make decisions about where to live based on a complex set of criteria, and the perceived quality of public schools is only one of several considerations. Goldsmith's criticisms of IPS could not help but affect *perceptions* of the quality of an IPS education.

He acknowledged the decline of IPS enrollments and the movement of families away from the inner city since he graduated from high school in 1964, but he always placed the primary blame on poor public school education in the inner city. This social process is too complex to use a "one cause" (poor public education) explanation to account for the exodus of white and black middle class families to the suburbs. However, to the extent that perceptions of public schools affect family decisions, Goldsmith only exacerbated the situation through his continual public criticisms of IPS.

Over the long term, other Goldsmith policies—including his efforts to maintain, improve, or develop the quality of life of inner city neighborhoods; reduce crime; and improve housing opportunities—could have had a profound impact on the quality of education in IPS, and Marion County, by slowing, if not stopping, the movement of middle class families out of the inner city. Goldsmith seems never to have made the connection among neighborhood improvement, crime reduction, economic development strategies and education improvement strategies (Goldsmith 1997, Chapter 8). He never promoted these policies as providing one more good reason to live in the city and educate one's children at IPS. By failing to promote this positive message, he missed a key opportunity to link his education and other quality of life policies in a truly innovative way.

In the end, Stephen Goldsmith's economic conservative ideology created the conditions for his own failure in the education area. Although he made education reform a priority, like most reformers before him, he had little positive impact on education in the Indianapolis Public School system.

Notes

[1] For an excellent summary of the economic paradigm used by economic conservatives, see Wolf (1994).

[2] See Lehnen and Johnson (1989) for a complete discussion of property tax reform in Indiana and its impact on public education.

[3] Statisticians know that if 20 independent studies are conducted with a 95 percent level of confidence, even where the null hypothesis is true, the expectation is that one of the studies will fail to reject the null hypothesis. Thus, the seeming inconsistency in statistical tests is simply an artifact of the level of confidence selected by the researchers.

[4] See the work of William Styring III, once the chief education lobbyist for the Indiana State Chamber of Commerce and later researcher at the Hudson Institute in Indianapolis (Garber et al. 2000).

[5] For example, less controversial forms of choice, such as statewide public school choice, have been adopted in the state of Minnesota, and charter school legislation elsewhere often limits charters to public, non-religious organizations, thereby excluding religious and private schools from qualifying and avoiding the First Amendment issues.

[6] Other groups, such as the Hudson Institute, also use combined SAT scores of high school seniors intending to enroll in college to judge the performance of Indiana school corporations. As with the ISTEP+ scores, the combined SAT scores of IPS seniors falls substantially below those of the township schools. Thus, IPS students perform worse than their peers in the township schools on both the state-mandated achievement test and the combined SAT scores. For a discussion of the issues surrounding the use of SAT scores as measures of school performance, see Lehnen (1992).

[7] The analysis presented in Table 2 is based on district level data, whereas Ullmann's analysis used school-level information.

[8] Indiana Code 20-3.1.

[9] See Lehnen and Johnson (1989) for a statewide analysis of performance. See also Garber et al. (2000).

[10] All facts about the application of P.L. 340 to IPS come from Indianapolis Public Schools (1997).

Chapter 11

Education and Politics in the 21st Century City: A View from the School Board

Kelly Bentley

Introduction

There are few issues more contentious than public education. The issues facing America's public schools are complex and all too often the discussions addressing education reform are handled in sound bites rather than with careful deliberation and analysis. Parents want good, safe schools for their children, the business community wants a better-prepared workforce and lower taxes for businesses, taxpayers want educated citizens and level property taxes and teachers want competitive salaries and better workplaces. Reform efforts must not ignore any of these constituencies if they are to be productive.

In 1969, Indiana passed legislation that allowed consolidation of the City of Indianapolis with the surrounding suburbs of Marion County, and Unigov emerged as the consolidated city and county government). However, school systems were left out of Unigov and today the consolidated City of Indianapolis boasts eleven school corporations (with eleven central administrations, eleven superintendents, and eleven school boards). Indianapolis Public Schools (IPS) continues to be the largest school corporation in Indianapolis (and the largest in Indiana).

With an enrollment of over 40,000 students, it is about three times the size of the largest township system. (Indiana Department of Education 1999). While the boundaries of IPS are by and large the old city limits, the majority of the district is located in Center Township, home to the central business district and many of the county's poorest residents.

Prior to the enactment of Unigov much of the new development in the township areas was annexed into Indianapolis. This meant that the children living in all those developments attended IPS. Annexation of new developments ceased during the late 1960s and the boundaries for IPS were frozen (Rosentraub 2000).

In 1968, individual plaintiffs and the United States Department of Justice sued IPS for racial segregation. IPS, along with the City of Indianapolis and the State of Indiana, eventually lost the suit. IPS tried to integrate its schools through system-wide busing, however in 1981 Federal Judge S. Hugh Dillon ordered one-way busing of minority students from IPS to several of the township school districts (IPS Planning Department 1991).

In 1968, enrollment peaked in IPS at 108,611 students (IPS Business Office, 1999). The district's enrollment since that time has declined steadily. Ironically, the total enrollment today for all of Marion County schools combined is only about 15 percent higher than the enrollment of IPS in 1968, indicating a slowdown in total population growth (Indiana Department of Education 1999). Former Mayor Stephen Goldsmith contends that "enrollment declined because parents exercised school choice the old-fashioned way: they moved" (Goldsmith 1997, 111). That is true, but it is also generally acknowledged that families with school age children did not move because their children were receiving an inferior education. "White flight" occurred because of plain old-fashioned racism and people's fear that their children would not receive a good education sitting next to a person of color.

People continue to move out of the old city limits of Indianapolis for a variety of reasons, including high crime rates, deteriorating neighborhoods, gang activity and because of the perception that the schools in the suburbs will be better and safer. Families also leave because of the lure of new developments with the latest in home design. The white flight of the 1970s has been replaced by middle class flight of the 1980s and 1990s, leaving economically disadvantaged people, both black and white, isolated in the neighborhoods and the schools within the old city limits. Segregation by race has been replaced by segregation by class in Indianapolis. There are still many middle class families, both black and white, which continue to live in many of the neighborhoods within the old city limits. Many of these families continue to send their children to schools in IPS and continue to be satisfied with the quality of the education that their children are receiving (Maher et al. 1999).

The schools are undoubtedly an important element of the economic development plan of Indianapolis and negative perceptions of them hinder redevelopment efforts within the old city limits. It is difficult to understand, therefore, why Goldsmith deliberately exacerbated the negative perceptions of IPS. During his two terms in office, Goldsmith was an unremitting critic of IPS. Some of the headlines from the *Indianapolis Star* reinforce this point:

> Mayor defends lower taxation for the mall: Circle Centre can't be solely blamed for IPS' cash crunch, Goldsmith says (1993b); Mayor wants big changes in IPS (1994h); Mayor calls IPS tax hike 'disaster': School board blames state for the increase (1994d); Mayor says he'll fight plan to hike school tax (1994e); Mayor rips into Schools (1994c); Mayor to push for reforms (1994b); Board president fights splitting up IPS: Opposition pits her against Goldsmith, a past supporter (1994a); Mayor poised to reinvent IPS (1995); Bill seeks to split IPS: If schools fail, Mayor wants drastic action (1995i); Mayor to push for 'charter' schools, vouchers (1995b); Mayor, IPS again at odds (1995a); Mayor touts reforming IPS as way to solve city's woes (1997a); Mayor lobbies legislators to overhaul IPS board (1997b).

In 1999, a development of new and rehabilitated owner-occupied homes was announced in an area north of downtown called Fall Creek Proper. At the news conference, Goldsmith praised the neighborhood for its diversity and ease of access to downtown jobs but admitted the drawbacks to home ownership included crime and the troubled IPS school system. He said, "I can fix the crime through neighborhood involvement and aggressive police activity, but the schools are still a problem" (*Indianapolis Star* 1999). In reference to the constant IPS bashing by Goldsmith and others, Harrison Ullmann, editor of *NUVO Newsweekly* wrote, "With the constant alarms about the failures of IPS, it is surprising there are any parents left in the city who would keep their children in the city schools" (Ullmann 1998).

Robbing Peter to Pay Paul: The Issue of Property Taxes

In his book, Goldsmith cites skyrocketing property taxes as the reason people are fleeing the urban areas of Indianapolis. He states that, "more than any other service, education drives the growth of big-city taxes" and goes on to say "Residents of Indianapolis are usually shocked when they learn that approximately 44 percent of their property tax dollars goes to fund the schools" (Goldsmith 1997, 112). However, one only needs to look at the property tax bill for anyone living inside any of the eleven school corporations in Marion County to see that the percentage of property tax dollars going to fund education is about the same. This percentage is roughly the same throughout Marion County (and throughout Indiana). Since this is not a new phenomenon, it is difficult to understand why Indianapolis taxpayers would be "shocked" by these rates.

The tax rates for all education funds do differ from one school corporation to the next. There are five property tax funds for education and all Indiana school corporations have them: the General Fund, the Transportation Fund, the Capital Projects Fund, the Debt Service Fund and the Pre-School Special Education Fund. The only exception would be school corporations, such as Speedway City School Corporation, that do not provide transportation.

In Marion County in 1999, Speedway City School Corporation had the lowest total tax rate at $3.57 per $100 of assessed valuation, and Franklin Township Community Schools had the highest rate at $5.99. Indianapolis Public Schools had a total rate of $5.85 (IPS 1999). There are three important contributing factors to the high tax rates in IPS; the high number of business development incentives granted, such as tax-exempt, tax abated and TIFed properties (those properties located in tax increment financing districts); the annual shortfall in property tax collection; and drops in the assessed value of property within the school corporation's boundaries.

The tax rates for the property tax funds for education are set by local school boards; however, the tax rate for the largest fund—the General Fund (used primarily for salaries and benefits, but also for classroom supplies, magnet/option programs, school police, English-as-a-Second Language programs and so forth)—is controlled by the state tuition funding formula, not by the local school board. In IPS, about 40 percent of the General Fund revenue are generated by local property taxes; 60 percent comes from the state (IPS 1999). The tax rate for the Capital Projects Fund (property tax revenue used for new construction, facility upgrades and renovations, facility maintenance, furniture and equipment) is controlled by the local school board but capped by the state. The same is true for the tax rate for the Pre-School Special Education Fund (property tax revenue used to provide services to pre-school aged children with special needs). The tax rates for the Transportation Fund (property tax revenue used for transportation needs) and the Debt Service Fund (property tax revenue used to pay back debts) are controlled by the local elected school board and are seriously affected by abated, exempt and TIFed properties (Rosentraub 1994, 2000). Decreased or flat rates of assessed valuation and uncollected property tax revenue affect all funds (IPS 1999).

The large number of tax exempt, tax abated or TIFed properties in Center Township and the effect of those development incentives on tax rates are troubling. It is estimated that over 30 percent of the property in the IPS taxing district is exempt, abated or TIFed (Rosentraub and Nunn 1994). The net result is to shift the burden to other taxpayers in the taxing district, and that is what causes tax rates to increase.

Since 1988, IPS has experienced a consistent annual shortfall in property tax collections of approximately 2.5 percent ($14,253,000 collectively during 1988-1996). In 1997, the shortfall was 4.64 percent ($6,290,000) and in 1998 it was 3.89 percent ($5,388,000). Overall, IPS has lost $25,931,000 of approved property tax levy revenue due to collection shortfalls since 1988. There are a variety of reasons why taxes are not collected, but in 1997 and 1998, 93 percent of the shortfall in property tax collections, or a total of $10,862,481 (including $1,671,991 in interest), was due to property tax appeals granted by the State Board of Tax Commissioners (IPS 1999). This is revenue that IPS never sees, but because of the complicated way schools are funded, the State assumes that 100 percent of the property tax is collected, and it calculates financial support based on that assumption.

Assessed valuation (AV) within the IPS taxing district has stayed relatively flat since 1988. The most recent three-year average shows an increase of approximately 2 percent per year. The AV for 1999, however, decreased by 1.5 percent. This translated to a drop in assessed valuation in 1999 of approximately $40 million dollars. The irony is that the assessed value for all of Marion County went up in 1999.

Goldsmith failed to discuss the annual shortfall in property tax collections, and the continued drop in assessed value of property within the IPS taxing district and the effect both these realities have on education funding. He consistently blamed IPS for driving up the tax rates for property owners in Center Township. Those accusations made for good politics, but obscured the real problem, namely, development incentives (abatements and tax increment financing), which the mayor controls, together with property tax appeals, reductions in assessed valuation, uncollected property taxes, tax exempt properties and serious flaws in the property tax assessment system. These are the real causes of escalating Center Township tax rates (Rosentraub 1994, 1999). Despite these problems, IPS has been able to hold the line on property tax rates. The total property tax rate for IPS has increased by only 5.06 percent since 1988 (IPS 1999).

The Realities and Politics of Spending

Goldsmith also regularly criticized IPS for increasing expenditures while enrollment in the school system was dropping steadily. During each of the last several years, enrollment in IPS has decreased by approximately 700 students—this translates into one student per grade per school. The enrollment decline does not occur at one or two schools but occurs across all 75 schools (IPS 1999). This means IPS would have to redraw its boundaries every year in order to realize any savings, but this would cause serious instability for children and families. The IPS Board has made a decision not to engage in constant juggling of boundaries; however, other steps have been taken to achieve savings. During the 1996-1997 school year, the decision was made to close 10 elementary schools and to cut staff and programs. During the 1998-1999 school year the Board again decided to cut staff, a decision that decreased expenditures by $5,000,000 for the 1999-2000 school year.

Decisions to reduce staffing levels have repercussions for students. After the 1996 reductions, there was an outcry from the community because of the fear that most of the cuts would come in art, music and physical education. One parent told the board, "The next Van Gogh, or Chopin, or even another Michael Jordan may be in the IPS school district. Don't deprive our children of adequate exposure to these subjects because you deem them to be less important than math and English" (*Indianapolis Star* 1996). These concerns are valid. Decisions about reductions in force are made at the building level, and the reality is that principals and teachers are being held accountable for test scores in math and language arts—not in art, music and physical education.

Goldsmith's argument that school systems, including IPS, should privatize non-instructional services such as transportation, janitorial services and food services (Goldsmith 1997, 123) to save money would be compelling, but only if money can be saved without decreasing the level of service. The IPS food service, for instance, is self-supporting—there are no local or state tax dollars supporting it. Revenue to cover these costs is generated by the actual purchase of the meals by the students and by reimbursement from the federal government for those students who qualify for free or reduced-price lunches. IPS not only provides this service to its own schools, but also to any non-public school in the area that chooses to participate in the federal school lunch program (IPS 1999).

The percentage of dollars that are spent in the classroom has been the focus of an ongoing debate. Goldsmith acknowledged that a political argument exists over the percentage of dollars that are spent for direct instruction. He estimated that about thirty cents of every dollar goes into the classroom (Goldsmith 1997, 123). That estimate ignores an inconvenient bookkeeping reality. Many of the costs properly allocated to an individual school are actually accounted for at the central level because of the complicated way school systems across the state are required to account for their expenditures. For example, all employee benefits and indirect costs (social security taxes, state retirement fund payments and so forth) are shown as central office expenses. The expense of desegregation (money that flows into IPS and is then paid out to the township school systems) is also included in the total for the school system. When the desegregation costs are removed and the employee benefit costs are properly classified as building expenses, the percent of dollars allocable to the classroom jumps to about 66 percent—sixty-six cents on the dollar—a percentage on par with state and national averages for direct instructional costs (IPS 1999).

These facts about IPS expenditures are easily obtainable, and verifiable, by anyone genuinely interested in an accurate picture of the school system's budget.

The Goldsmith Plan: Competition, Competition, Competition

In his book, Goldsmith talks extensively about school choice—public school choice, state supported vouchers, charter schools, private for-profit education providers and privately funded scholarship programs. He speaks of "breaking the monopoly" of public education and deregulating supply (Goldsmith 1997, 117-125). This argument assumes that competition increases student achievement. But in the cities where school choice exists (Milwaukee and Cleveland), studies have failed to show such improvement in student achievement. In a 1998 report of the Cleveland, Ohio voucher program by Indiana University researchers led by Kim Metcalf, students using a voucher to attend an established private school performed about the same as public school students in reading, math and social studies, and they only slightly outperformed the public school students in language arts and science (Metcalf, et al. 1999, 25). Students using a voucher to attend one of the new schools that opened specifically to serve the voucher program performed significantly lower than the students in the public schools in all subjects tested (Metcalf 1998). In Milwaukee, the data also fail to show any measurable difference in academic achievement between students in the public schools and students in the choice schools. John Witte, who was hired by the state of Wisconsin to evaluate the Milwaukee voucher program states, " . . . there were no differences in achievement gains in either reading or math between choice and Milwaukee Public School students" (Witte 2000, 150).

In 1994, IPS began a "Select Schools" program that allowed parents the choice of sending their children to any school in the IPS system so long as the court-ordered racial balance of 85 percent to 15 percent per school was achieved. At the time, Goldsmith was a big proponent of the Select Schools, a school choice plan (*Indianapolis Star* 1992). However, after just three years the program had to be scrapped because of the high costs of transportation, the large percentage of families who never made any choices and the large percentage of families who chose schools near to their homes. Today, in response to the clear preference of a majority of IPS families, the school system has gone back to a boundary system and most students are assigned to their neighborhood school. In 1998, IPS was granted unitary status from court-ordered desegregation, and the court ordered the return of bused students to IPS over an 18-year period. Part of the agreement calls for IPS to continue to balance its schools racially. Because most neighborhoods in Indianapolis are not integrated and because of the requirement that IPS racially balance all schools, some students do continue to be bused to schools outside their neighborhoods (*United States vs. Board of School Commissioners* 1972, 1998).

Even without the Select School program, however, IPS still boasts more school choice than any other public school system in the state of Indiana. Roughly 28 percent of the students are enrolled in one of over thirty magnet programs. Of those enrolled, approximately 68 percent are minority and 32 percent are non-minority. These programs reflect differing educational philosophies, variations in teaching and learning styles and variations in the content of what is being taught. IPS has three Montessori schools, plus the Center of Inquiry, Cold Spring Academy and Key Learning Community, all of which have been expanded to kindergarten through eighth grade. The Key Learning Community has also added a high school. At the elementary level, IPS also offers three magnets in communication arts, one in performing arts and the 21st Century School.

At the middle school level there are two academies in environmental studies, two in math/science/technology, one in life science and wellness, and one in international studies. The middle school program also includes the Crispus Attucks Academy and the School for Visual and Performing Arts.

At the high school level, there are the Center for Visual and Performing Arts, Center for Humanities, Star (Science and Technology of Agriculture and Its Resources) Academy, and Academy of Success. The high school program also includes magnets for math/science, business and finance, telecommunications and the Health Professions Center. IPS offers an extensive vocational education program, adult education programs, the Learning Center program for pregnant middle and high school girls and New Beginnings High School and New Horizons Middle School (both for students in need of an alternative learning environment). IPS also has a program at Arsenal Technical High School that allows high school students to take college level courses offered by Indiana University Purdue University at Indianapolis.

In 1991, Pat Rooney, founder of Golden Rule Insurance Company, created The Choice Charitable Trust, a private voucher program that provides an $800 tuition voucher to students who qualify. The voucher can be used at any participating private or religious school (state accredited or non-accredited) that accepts the student. Goldsmith, a member of the Trust's board of directors, asserted that students who receive Choice grants consistently outperform their counterparts in IPS. He cited St. Phillip Neri as an example to prove his point (Goldsmith 1997, 112-113). Based on data from the Indiana Department of Education in 1997, 59 percent of St. Phillip Neri's third graders, 76 percent of its sixth graders, and 94 percent of its eighth graders scored above the state standard on the ISTEP exam in language arts. In math 56 percent of third graders, 57 percent of sixth graders, and 94 percent of eighth graders scored above the state standard. In 1998 and 1999 the number of third grade students scoring above the state standard increased, but it decreased significantly in sixth and eighth grades. At the same time, the number of students taking the exam decreased as enrollment at the school declined. In 1999-2000 only seventeen students were tested in the 8th grade. Two years earlier, when these same students would have been 6th graders, twenty-one students had been tested.

There are eight inner city Catholic schools in Indianapolis. St. Phillip Neri and Central Catholic have the most students meeting state standards among the eight schools. St. Rita had the lowest among the eight schools. In 1997-98, the percentage of students meeting the state standard in language arts was 46 percent of third graders, 25 percent of sixth graders, and 42 percent of eighth graders. In math, 42 percent of third graders, 10 percent of sixth graders, and 8 percent of eighth graders met the standard. In 1999-2000, the percent meeting standard dropped in every grade and the number of students taking the exam again decreased as enrollment declined. In 1999-2000 thirteen students were tested in the eighth grade. In 1998-1999, when the same students would have been sixth graders, twenty were tested (Indiana Department of Education 1999).

Goldsmith states that the academic performance of IPS students and those in other urban districts is intolerably poor (Goldsmith 1997, 112). This is absolutely true and very troublesome to all involved in education. In Milwaukee, the first city in the United States to provide tax-supported vouchers to private schools, data indicate that the private schools are struggling against the same types of forces affecting public schools (Witte 2000). In Indianapolis, the test data demonstrate that, like Milwaukee, inner-city parochial schools are not doing any better than their public school counterparts on standardized tests. The systems achieve similar results with similar populations; *despite* the fact that public schools must accept everyone and non-public schools can pick and choose among applicants. Goldsmith also argues that the longer students are in a Catholic School, the better they do (Goldsmith 1997, 113). However, he does not mention the significant declines in enrollment those schools experience. It is the author's belief that declining parochial school enrollments in the upper grades occur because many students, due to lack of funds, discipline problems, special education needs and/or low academic performance, are being asked to leave the non-public schools and are returning to IPS.

Goldsmith and the Indianapolis Public Schools: The Reality

Goldsmith has said that he has "probably notched more unsuccessful attempts to improve education than any other mayor in America." Among his attempts at improving education, he lists pressuring districts not to raise taxes (Goldsmith 1997, 114). Given the complicated way schools are funded in Indiana, it is not clear how this strategy would improve education. Certainly local school boards must be fiscally responsible with tax dollars, but that responsibility must be balanced against the need for the district to provide necessary educational services.

Another initiative to "improve education" cited in his book is his effort to motivate the Indiana legislature to fund private school vouchers with tax dollars (Goldsmith 1997, 114). Again, it is not clear how this strategy improves education, since available data clearly show that urban non-public schools are not performing better than urban public schools (Witte 2000; Metcalf 1999; Indiana Department of Education 1999).

Goldsmith also cites the creation of the Alliance for Quality Schools in 1994 to support reform candidates as another important effort to improve education. This was probably his best idea—a partnership with several other officeholders, the Chamber of Commerce and other business leaders and parents to slate school board candidates who were committed to reforms. Unfortunately, rather than uniting the community behind an attempt to elect quality school board members, the Alliance caused serious polarization among public education stakeholders. Goldsmith's inability to work collaboratively with all stakeholders caused fear that the public would be shut out, and some began to question the motives of the group. There was also a concern the group would politicize the school board elections (*Indianapolis Star* 1994o). For example, the Indianapolis Education Association, the union representing IPS teachers, was not part of the group, and it endorsed its own candidates. Only two parents were included and neither represented any existing parent organization within the school system, causing many of the most involved parents to feel left out of the process. Another group that was excluded from the Alliance was Concerned Clergy, a coalition of African American ministers who also chose to endorse candidates for school board.

In 1994, the Alliance endorsed three candidates for the IPS school board and two won. In 1996, the group endorsed all four incumbents, and three won. In 1998, the last year the Alliance participated in board elections, there were four seats up for election. The group endorsed candidates in three of the four races, but only one of their candidates won. A newly formed political action committee made up of IPS parents, called the Parents PAC, endorsed the other three winners. The evening of the election, the Mayor said the Board was "badly fractured" (*Indianapolis Star* 1998), a clear indication he would be unwilling to work collaboratively with the newly elected school board members.

When his attempts at "improving public education" failed (Goldsmith 1997, 114), Goldsmith authored reform legislation giving IPS broad powers to hold schools more accountable. The Indiana General Assembly passed the bill in 1995, and it became known as Public Law 340. The law charges IPS with responsibility for developing and implementing a plan to increase student performance and achievement. Under the IPS Academic Achievement Plan, each school, through its School Based Decision-Making Committee, creates a school improvement plan based on standards set by the school system. These standards include student achievement, student attendance and teacher attendance. Each school is then measured, or held accountable, by its progress toward achieving its goals. The law also gave IPS the authority to provide performance awards to certified staff in those schools that have shown the most improvement in academic performance and attendance. IPS has established a three tier award system-Tier I ($300 per certified staff member), Tier II ($600 per certified staff member), and Tier III ($900 per certified staff member).

In 1995, prior to the passage of P.L. 340, Goldsmith's legislative proposals for IPS had caused polarization among public education stakeholders, again because of his failure to work collaboratively with all constituencies affected. The locally elected school board, including the two members he had helped elect, and the administration of IPS were not consulted about his legislative proposal (*Indianapolis Star* 1995k). That proposal included provisions to return to neighborhood schools and to divide the system into mini-districts, each with its own administration. This provision ignored the fact that IPS was still under court-ordered desegregation and the IPS School Board was legally unable to make such changes even if it wanted to. Other provisions of the Goldsmith proposal included providing tax supported vouchers to private schools, charter schools, greater accountability for teachers and administrators, merit pay and changes to the collective bargaining laws. The teacher's union was staunchly opposed to the legislative proposal and many other stakeholders were angry about being left out. Even some of his allies from the Alliance for Quality Schools were angry and Goldsmith was accused of being on a "power trip" (*Indianapolis Star* 1995m). Still others accused him of over-stepping his authority (*Indianapolis Star* 1995n).

In his book, Goldsmith says that since the adoption of P.L. 340 in 1995 the "results have been slow in coming" (Goldsmith 1997, 114). During the 1996-97 school year, the first year in which the IPS Academic Achievement Plan was implemented and the year

Goldsmith's book was published, only one school earned a performance award. By the end of the 1997-1998 school year, the number of schools receiving awards jumped to twenty-one. During the 1998-1999 school year, there were thirty-one schools that qualified for an award—almost half of the schools in the district (IPS 1999). The goal of greater accountability, which was clearly the intent of the law (a concept embraced by the current school board and administration), has come with a cost. For example, teachers in IPS do not have full collective bargaining rights, and the implementation of the law has created an additional administrative burden on building principals and teachers. There is also the challenge of differing interpretations of the law and whether or not IPS has fully implemented all of its provisions. The state legislature also failed to appropriate any additional resources for implementation of the law or for the performance awards, so IPS must draw the money out of its General Education Fund. The experience with P.L. 340 has been mixed, but since its adoption and the adoption of other reform policies, IPS has shown steady improvement in student achievement.[1]

In 1997, after publication of his book, Goldsmith sponsored a series of "Mayor's Forums" to discuss the state of education in Indianapolis. Huge crowds turned out, but rather than echoing Goldsmith's call for vouchers and mayoral control of the schools, as he had clearly anticipated, citizens told the mayor to stop his constant bashing of IPS, and demanded added support for the public schools. "The negative talk about IPS needs to stop" was one parent's mandate to the Mayor, "how can you expect them to succeed when all they hear is how bad they are?" People spoke about taxes and the serious inequities of education funding. They spoke about children's health issues, poverty, violence in the neighborhoods and gang activity and the effect all these issues have on a student's ability to succeed (*Indianapolis Star* 1997c).

Where Do We Go from Here? A Mayor's Role in Education

As a school board member, the author believes the single most important action a mayor can take to support public education is to respect the jurisdictional boundary between the mayor's job, which is to run the city, and the elected school board's job, which is to run the schools. Recognition of the limits of mayoral authority does not mean that mayors cannot have a substantial impact on education; it means that a mayor's efforts should be consistent with his job description.

This does not mean the mayor should not be involved, but it does call for a collaborative approach to common concerns.

Indianapolis has eleven school corporations, with eleven school boards and eleven superintendents; the mayor should work with each of those systems on issues such as public safety (neighborhood crime, gang activity), children's health concerns, poverty, mobility, school readiness and parental involvement. Mayors can make sure there are safe after-school and weekend activities available for children through the city's parks department. Mayors can also help facilitate collaborations between the schools and the city's policing agencies, youth serving agencies, healthcare providers, churches and other religious institutions, service organizations and businesses.

The safety of children in IPS is a priority. Many of our schools are located in high crime areas where drugs are routinely sold on the streets, gang activity is great, alcohol abuse is common and prostitution is an everyday fact of life. More often than not, the problems in the neighborhood spill over into the schools, creating a serious financial drain on the school system. In recent years, IPS has spent close to $4 million annually on school security, and its police force is the third largest in Marion County (IPS 1999). The funding for school police must come from the general education fund, dollars meant for educating children. If Goldsmith had really wanted a greater percentage of education dollars to reach the classroom, providing public safety would have been a very good place to start. During his first campaign for mayor, Goldsmith, as a part of his "safe schools plan" pledged to put a police officer on the beat around every city school (*Indianapolis Star* 1991). That promise was made in 1991, and as far as the author is aware, the police officers never materialized.

Another issue that dramatically affects a child's academic performance is mobility, which is defined as the number of times a student moves and must change schools. School 14, located on the near-east side of Indianapolis, has a mobility factor of over 90 percent. This means that there will be transfers in and out of the building equal to over 90 percent of the total enrollment in a given year. Mobility has a profound impact on student achievement (Rose 1999) and makes teacher accountability much more difficult. How can teacher effectiveness be assessed when the children tested at the end of the year are not the same children who were tested at the beginning of the year?

Poverty has a significant impact on children, and IPS has a high percentage of children who live in poverty. Two out of every three children in IPS are eligible for the federal free lunch program (IPS 1999), which is based on family income. More than half of the children living in the IPS district come from single parent households and almost one-third of adults living in the district lack a high school diploma, according to the 1990 census. All these statistics are used by the state to determine a school system's "at-risk" index because they are recognized as factors that place children at a higher risk of not successfully completing their education (Indiana Department of Education 1999).

Children who live in poverty are significantly more likely to drop out of school, repeat a grade, be suspended or be expelled than children from families with high incomes. Poor children have more health problems, learning disabilities and emotional and behavioral problems than children from more affluent families (Brooks-Gunn and Duncan 1997). Studies have shown that poor children who enter kindergarten are more likely to be developmentally delayed, sometimes by as much as two years (Brooks-Gunn and Duncan 1997). The percentage of children suffering from asthma is significantly higher among the urban poor, and children who suffer from this disease miss school more often (Brooks-Gunn and Duncan 1997). Head lice are easily treated, but they keep more children out of school than any other reason. Health problems and the lack of access to health services are a fact of life for the many children who live in poverty in Indianapolis.

   Poor children are more likely to suffer from lead poisoning, which has been linked to ADHD (attention deficit hyperactivity disorder), speech and hearing problems, motor impairments and brain damage leading to learning disabilities. Poisoning from exposure to lead in paint, water and soil is one of the most serious environmental and health problems that the children of Indianapolis must face. In Indianapolis, the majority of children with high levels of lead in their blood live inside the boundaries of IPS (Ullmann 1998). Most of their exposure comes from lead-based paint in their homes, but high levels of lead have also been found in the soil in some of these areas. The solution to this problem will require a significant expenditure of resources to remediate or replace lead-contaminated housing and soil.

The children of the IPS district also face additional environmental issues, including exposure to sewage from combined sewer overflows. Many creeks and streams running through the poorer neighborhoods in Indianapolis become open sewers full of human excrement during even a light rain. One such creek, Pogues Run, flows through the property of two IPS schools, where hundreds of children are exposed to this filth on a regular basis. The combined sewer overflow issue is another that will require significant resources to solve.

In his book, Goldsmith states that he is proud of his attempts to improve education, yet not a single one of his ideas for education address the social, environment and health problems facing poor children in Indianapolis—poverty, homelessness, inadequate health care, drugs, violence, gangs and teen pregnancy. These are problems that directly and dramatically affect a child's ability to do well in school (Lewit 1997), and they are issues that were within the Mayor's jurisdiction and control. When educators and parents raised these issues in public forums or letters to the editor, he accused them of making excuses for poor performance—an allegation he repeated in his book (Goldsmith 1997, 112). The reality is that deficiencies in parenting, nutrition, health care, as well as problems in the wider community such as drug dealing and gang violence are not excuses but social barriers that require additional resources if learning is to occur. Ironically, when the playing field is leveled by taking poverty and other factors into consideration, many IPS schools outperform their counterparts in wealthier township school systems (Ullmann 1998). Doug Williams, Perry Township Schools' Superintendent has said "IPS may indeed do the best job with the kids they get of any school district in the state of Indiana" (Carpenter 1995).

There is absolutely no credible evidence that Goldsmith's goal of "breaking the monopoly" of public education by diverting tax dollars to private and parochial schools will improve the education of poor children. Holding educators accountable for student achievement, along with improving the conditions under which many poor children live, will improve the chances of these children to achieve their potential. A mayor who sincerely wants to improve education will help poor children overcome social and environmental barriers, so each of these children can enter school able to learn.

Notes

[1] Editorial Note: The author's statement regarding improvements in student achievement are based on her inspection of several indicators including district mean norm-referenced scores from ISTP+, percentage of students meeting state criterion-referenced "academic standards" and the number of schools qualifying for awards under the District's "AAA Plan" mandated by P.L. 340.

The statistical analysis of ISTEP+ scores presented in Chapter 10 shows that there was no statistically significant difference in performance among the IPS District's schools. The author of Chapter 10 conducted a statistical evaluation in which the effect of the performance of all schools is considered as a group. A school that achieves an award in one year may not receive an award in the next.

The net effect is that the District's average performance on standardized tests may not necessarily improve over time because some schools' gains are offset by other schools' losses. In other words, the District's performance as a whole may not have improved, but individual schools may have improved, in some instances dramatically.

Chapter 12

"Reinventing" a City's Environmental Programs

Ingrid Ritchie

Introduction

Members of the environmental community have described Mayor Goldsmith's performance on environmental issues as marked by a lack of vision, lost opportunities, indifference, arrogance, exclusion and a strident anti-regulatory, pro-market posture. Tim Maloney, Executive Director of the Hoosier Environmental Council (HEC)[1] commented "Goldsmith's philosophy towards the environment ranged from neglect to outright hostility" (Maloney 2000). The business community, on the other hand, appeared to see Goldsmith as someone who understood their frustrations with environmental regulation and who was committed to easing burdensome requirements that stifled productivity and economic growth.

Over his eight years as mayor, Goldsmith had many opportunities to improve the environmental conditions for citizens in Indianapolis. He also had an opportunity to position Indianapolis as a twenty-first century city by promoting municipal initiatives that would integrate sustainable development into the city's governance structures and municipal operations. Was he successful? The discussion that follows highlights some, but not all, of the environmental problems and opportunities that faced Indianapolis during the Goldsmith tenure, and how his administration reacted to these challenges.

Tree Preservation—An Initial Test

Goldsmith's initial test began early in his administration in February 1992. A citizen initiative to preserve trees in the community was nearing completion at the end of Mayor William H. Hudnut's administration. Hudnut's Tree Preservation Task Force, which included builders, landscapers and environmentalists, had reached consensus on the principles for a model ordinance to preserve trees from destruction by developers. After Goldsmith took office, this initiative was stopped. This was an important issue because of the dramatic decline of trees on privately owned land in Marion County, primarily as a result of urban sprawl and development. Determining exact estimates of tree decline is difficult because of data limitations, but there has been no question that a decline has occurred. In 1820, about 99 percent of the county's 2,567,281 acres were forested (Miller 2000). Today, less than 2 percent of the county has high quality wood lots (five acres or more, public and privately owned) (Miller 2000). In 1966, the U.S. Forest Service estimated there were 1,300 acres of privately owned forested land and by 1986 only 900 acres remained (Niederpruem 1994a). (This estimate is based upon marketable timber, a more narrow definition that excludes smaller sized trees).

The level of frustration with Goldsmith's termination of the Tree Preservation Task Force and Ordinance is palpable in an early letter from one Task Force participant to the Mayor. David Lakin of Groups Advocating Urban Greenspace Environments (GAUGE) wrote to Goldsmith on January 23, 1992 shortly after he learned of the Mayor's decision to stop work on the ordinance. Lakin urged the Mayor to proceed proceed with the Tree Ordinance Task Force and the ordinance writing process, and he argued that failing to do so would have "far reaching consequences for the environmental health of our city" (Lakin 1992). Lakin also argued that if development practices that disregard tree preservation were not changed, "neighborhoods will decline, quality of life will diminish and we will have lost forever a chance to preserve our natural heritage." Lakin's final comments were:

> Much volunteer effort has been devoted to this essential ordinance . . . .
> The clear mandate from a task force composed of all segments of our city
> . . . deserves to continue and be brought before the City-County Council . .

. . The future face of this city now is in your hands. (Lakin 1992)

Mayor Goldsmith, who responded to the letter from Lakin on March 24 wrote, "I am committed to urban forestry and pursuing a tree preservation ordinance" (Goldsmith 1992). Goldsmith claimed that the reason that the tree ordinance was put on hold was the reorganization of city staff and "Once all of the (reorganization) is in place, I feel that the development of a tree ordinance will continue at a faster pace" (Goldsmith 1992).

Leaders of the HEC met with Goldsmith on June 24, 1992 to discuss the Mayor's environmental policy plans, including tree preservation. Among those present was Tim Maloney, who at the time was HEC's natural heritage director and also served on Hudnut's Tree Preservation Task Force. According to Maloney, Goldsmith "made a commitment to us . . . that he was going to reenergize that (tree preservation) task force" (Maloney 2000).

In 1994 the press resurrected this issue when City-County Councilman Gordon Gilmer, a Republican, was surprised by a denuded acreage in his district. Gilmer, who compared the loss of trees to a bombing site, was now convinced that the city needed a tree preservation ordinance. He commented, "I'm not one of those wild-eyed environmentalists, but this just hit me the wrong way." Although Goldsmith was quoted as saying it would be helpful to again "jawbone" the issue, his comments at the time ("I have some reservations whenever government interferes with private property") and lack of action were perceived to be anti-regulatory toward tree preservation. In this same article, Lakin was interviewed and asked about the Mayor's action on the tree preservation issue. Lakin commented, "I've seen no significant movement" . . . "I don't see any sense of urgency on his part at all. He doesn't want to regulate, pure and simple." (Niederpruem 1994a)

Despite promises to GAUGE and the HEC, neither the task force nor the tree ordinance was revived by Goldsmith. Clarke Kahlo, program director for Protect Our Rivers Now, voiced the preservationists' continuing frustration in a letter to the editor in 1998, "Mayor Steve Goldsmith, . . . has had two terms to do anything meaningful to protect Indianapolis greenspace and open space resources. Instead, he has rejected every conservationist's plea for a better system of protection while decimating and privatizing what little remained of the city's forestry section" (Kahlo 1998).

Creating A Vision for Environmental Problems and Prospects—A Lost Opportunity

Environmental Policy Work Group

The environmental community's hopes were raised in the fall of 1992, when Goldsmith established the Environmental Policy Work Group to identify environmental issues of concern in Indianapolis (Harris 1994a). With this action, Goldsmith could have demonstrated initiative and a positive vision for the environment. However, discussions with a number of environmental leaders indicate he did otherwise, and many, in retrospect, believe this exercise was "a scam to create the illusion of interest and progress" (Kahlo 2000). The 90-member work group[2] that was convened had a diverse membership including environmentalists and business representatives, and they developed draft policy papers[3] on the following issues:

- regional environmental problems,
- surface water contamination,
- loss of wetland/open space/critical land habitat,
- groundwater and soil contamination,
- indoor air pollution,
- illegal dumping/littering,
- energy efficiency in land use,
- lack of sanitary sewers in populated areas, and
- loss of trees (Environmental Policy Work Group 1993).

Each of these issues was developed according to a standard format that included a statement of the problem, purpose of policy development, data and background, current/past efforts, policy options, cost/benefit summary, recommendations and priorities, limitations of action, and action plan evaluation methods. After nearly a year of effort, the Work Group made close to one-hundred recommendations, including:

- develop a comprehensive environmental planning process that is regional in nature,
- develop plans to extend sewer service into areas using septic systems,
- provide tax abatement to encourage re-use of urban land,
- develop a wellhead protection program,
- establish minimum operation and maintenance provisions for building ventilation systems,

- require all law enforcement officers to respond appropriately to illegal dumping in progress,
- encourage traditional neighborhood developments,
- create a forest trust, and
- develop a tree preservation/conservation ordinance that promotes incentives for the protection and establishment of vegetative areas. (Environmental Policy Work Group 1993)

These recommendations, and the others in the draft report, reflect a deliberate and thoughtful approach to addressing complex issues facing the community. One of the work groups noted that it was not able to consider, due to time constraints, additional issues that should be studied, including air, light, noise and signboard pollution. Many of the recommendations (for example, regional planning, encouraging traditional neighborhood developments to save petroleum resources and reduce pollution, creating a forest trust, tree preservation and tree planting) were exactly the type of "vision" projects that would help move Indianapolis in the direction of creating a community based on sustainable development.

The completed draft report went to the Mayor's office in the fall of 1993. It was DOA (dead on arrival). Repeated efforts to find out what happened and what the Mayor's plans were for the proposed policy initiatives were also DOA. In April 1997, after Goldsmith was soundly defeated in his bid for governor, the *Indianapolis Star/News* reported that Goldsmith acknowledged that the draft report had been shelved, but that he would ask his recently hired environmental policy advisor, Mary Euler, "to dust that off" (Niederpruem 1997). The *Star/News* also reported,

> Goldsmith admits that he hasn't done a good job of reaching out on environmental issues. So he's proclaiming a new "inclusiveness" for those he previously ignored. "Historically these groups have opposed me in every election," he said. "We need a group of committed environmentalists to express their concerns that lead to more balanced policies." (Niederpruem 1997)

The 90-member Environmental Policy Work Group had already done this—in 1993. On January 30, 1998, the Mayor's office sent a memorandum to some of the "Environmental Action Survey Participants" in which his office characterized the 1992 recommendations as dated and " . . . developed without any clear problem definitions. Consequently, the next step will be to work to develop clear goals, identify work that has been done and what remains to be done" (Euler 1998). This communication was worded in such a way that "blame for the Mayor's inaction" was placed back on the participants rather than in the Mayor's office where it belonged.[4] The tone and content of the letter reinforced for many in the environmental community their view that Goldsmith was not serious about environment and public health. The Mayor did not "dust off" the environmental policy papers and recommendations contained in them; however, the new administration of Mayor Bart Peterson has indicated a willingness to reinstitute this visioning effort (Kahlo 2000).

A Second Chance to Create a Vision: The Peirce Report

Neil Peirce, author and urban expert, and Curtis Johnson came to Indianapolis during 1996 to assess the strengths and weaknesses of Indianapolis and offer solutions for the region. The Indianapolis Newspapers Inc., Indianapolis Foundation and the Metropolitan Association of Greater Indianapolis Communities (MAGIC) sponsored their work. Peirce's report was based on wide-ranging discussions with community representatives from business, environmental organizations, and other interests.[5] He believed that communities such as Indianapolis needed to focus on a regional approach to sharing of resources and responsibility for problem solving. The Peirce Report begins, "Coming to modern, businesslike, heavily promoted Indianapolis, visitors are shocked to find . . . "

- one of the largest concentrations of septic-served homes of any large city in the country;
- poor air quality in the central Indiana region;
- highly developed areas surrounding reservoirs built to ensure water supply and control flooding;
- no controls on digging wells;
- an antiquated sewer system that leaks and contaminates water;
- the distinction of being the largest metropolitan area with a combined piping system to carry sewage and storm water;
- the lowest rates of recycling anywhere in America;
- no strategy to protect regional watersheds from contamination;
- no strategy for land conservation to control sprawl; and
- no strategy for transportation planning to reduce energy consumption and air pollution. (Peirce and Johnson 1996)

These problems were certainly not of Mayor Goldsmith's making; they had been a part of the Indianapolis landscape for many years. However, Goldsmith did have the benefit of many opinions dating to

1990 that characterized the problems and identified solutions that would help meet the enormous financial challenges they posed.

In 1990, toward the end of his term, Mayor Hudnut challenged the Chamber of Commerce to examine the city's infrastructure. In response, the Chamber, through the efforts of more than 200 business and community professionals, developed GIFT (Get Indianapolis Fit for Tomorrow). GIFT was a detailed set of recommendations for the city's sewers, storm water system, solid waste disposal, parks and other infrastructure and a plan to finance each one. The estimated price tag for all areas was staggering ($1.1 billion). Goldsmith initiated infrastructure improvements, but not for sewers and storm water facilities. Peirce and Johnson noted, "Yet despite Goldsmith's moves (on infrastructure), one's still hard-pressed to find evidence that any department of any government in the Indianapolis region has any get-it-all together formula for environmental stability. You'd get better odds on finding a mountain in Marion County." (Peirce and Johnson 1996)

In 1993, Goldsmith had the benefit of the Environmental Policy Work Group's Environmental Papers and its nearly one hundred recommendations that included regional planning and infrastructure investment. During 1995 Goldsmith had the benefit of the Chamber of Commerce's *Business Agenda 1996-1999* which advocated a variety of initiatives including long-range regional planning, regional infrastructure maintenance and expansion and a single-multi-county mass transportation system (Indianapolis Chamber of Commerce n.d.). In 1996 Goldsmith had the benefit of the Peirce Report recommendations which reflected a broad cross-section of community input. The first recommendation of the Peirce Report was for the Indianapolis region to make a "commitment to serious, integrated planning" for environment. The report states, "Determine that your regional environment challenge is as important as getting a professional football team. It's not rocket science. It matters a lot. Do it" (Peirce and Johnson 1996). The second recommendation was to "think and act regionally."

Not surprisingly all of these voices—GIFT, the Environmental Policy Papers, the Chamber's *Business Agenda*, and the Peirce Report—were giving the Mayor the same message—environmental issues are important to the community, take some positive actions today and plan for the future.

In 1997, the *Indianapolis Star/News* reaffirmed the environmental community's view of Goldsmith's poor record on environment:

His administration is marked by mostly exclusion and often indifference on environmental issues, say people who represent a wide group of interests. That consensus comes from those who work for him to the most strident outside critics. From preserving trees to promoting recycling, he is not a mayor given credit for listening. (Niederpruem 1997)

A Sampling of the Goldsmith Administration's Performance on Environmental Issues

The Goldsmith administration failed to create a vision, ignored the environmental and public health communities in planning for the future and favored short-term business interests over environmental and public health interests. Chapter 13 discusses the Mayor's attack on environmental health regulations and how citizens rallied to fight his efforts to eliminate or weaken these regulations. A few additional examples are provided to give a broader picture of the Mayor's "environmental agenda."

Air Pollution

Refined Metals

The perception that Goldsmith favored industry over the environment and public health was present even when he attempted to bring an enforcement action against a major air polluter. Such was the case in late 1994 and early 1995 in an action against Refined Metals, Inc., a secondary lead smelting company on the southeast side of Indianapolis. This company had a history of problems dating back to the late 1980s. In the most recent actions, the company was cited for excess emissions of sulfur dioxide, failure to file timely test reports, tampering with a lead monitoring device and violating visible emission standards (Niederpruem 1994b). During 1994, neighbors of the plant filed 339 complaints with the city over chronic odor problems coming from the facility (Francis 1994). The odor problems (which included a choking odor, rotten egg odor and odor of plastic burning) were so severe that it was impossible for residents to use their yards or allow their children to play outdoors.[6] An additional concern for the residents was the potential health effects from exposure to the pollution coming from the facility (lead particles and unknown contaminants in the pollution cloud from the facility). Carbon disulfide and carbonyl sulfide, both toxic chemicals, were eventually identified as the likely source of the rotten egg odor (Niederpruem 1996a).

The city proposed a fine of $1.185 million to bring Refined Metals into compliance with air pollution regulations. The penalty was negotiated down to $200,000, still the largest air pollution fine levied in Indianapolis, and the settlement required the company to install $800,000 worth of pollution control equipment (Zogg 1995). However, much to the chagrin of neighborhood activists, Refined Metals was allowed to continue operating before the pollution controls were installed, including some controls that would take up to a year to install.

Mary Davis, a resident who lived ten blocks from the plant and who led citizen efforts to clean up the plant said, "What they've gotten is another extension . . . A temporary shutdown until all the (pollution control) equipment was installed—that would have made us happy. Now we have to wait another year." (Morgan 1995)

City-County Councilor David Smith agreed, saying that residents should be better protected. Smith said, "I feel it really lets the neighborhood down . . . Asking those folks to live another summer there is just intolerable" (Zogg 1995).

A year earlier another resident, Catherine Burton, president of the Franklin Township Civic League commented, "I do not understand how any business that has a long history of violations can continue to be given chance after chance after chance" (Francis 1994).

Mayor Goldsmith's response to the neighborhood concerns was typical of what many environmental activists point to as a philosophy that favored industry over environment. Goldsmith said, "It's (Refined Metals) a company that employs people and contributes to the tax base . . . and who also contributed to the deterioration of the environment" (Morgan 1995). In speaking of the settlement, Goldsmith said, "This extraordinary agreement with the company will protect the neighbors and allow them (Refined Metals) to stay in business" (Morgan 1995).

Mary Davis was not convinced, "While the city collects its money . . we'll still be sitting here. Our property values will go down" (Morgan 1995).

The pollution from Refined Metals, that Goldsmith allowed exacted a price on the neighborhood. Residents were burdened with concerns about their health and properties that they could not sell because of their proximity to the smelting facility. As a consequence 268 homeowners received a thirty-percent property tax break from the Warren Township tax assessor because of their proximity to the Refined Metals facility. The tax break applied for a five-year period or until the problem was corrected. Refined Metals operated for a period of time, but then shut down without implementing the required controls.[7]

Asbestos

The only environmental issue mentioned in Goldsmith's book, *The Twenty-First Century City*, was his effort to deregulate asbestos abatement in Indianapolis using his Regulatory Study Commission (RSC) as the vehicle for the deregulation effort. The RSC, which is discussed in Chapter 13, was established to examine existing regulations and "to eliminate outdated, unneeded, and often counterproductive rules" (Goldsmith 1997, 87-88). Goldsmith identifies the asbestos regulatory review as "one of the RSC's most important battles" (Goldsmith 1997, 88). Goldsmith achieved a small victory with the asbestos deregulation effort. However, he lost the most important battle for deregulation which was the attempt to eliminate or reduce the city's environmental health regulations at the Health and Hospital Corporation of Marion County (see Chapter 13 for this discussion).

At the time of this review, Indianapolis had an existing asbestos regulation that was more stringent than the federal or Indiana state air pollution rules. The Air Pollution Control Board had passed this asbestos regulation in 1988, but the rule was outdated because both the federal and state rules had been revised since that time (in 1990 and 1991, respectively). The existing rule also had some provisions that were viewed as overlapping with the Indiana Occupational Safety and Health Administration (OSHA) enforcement program. The Air Pollution Control Board began its deliberations to revise the asbestos regulation in 1991.[8] The revisions ultimately resulted in strengthening the 1988 rule, and the RSC objected to the revised rule based on duplication of federal and state rules, lack of health basis for stronger provisions and duplication with occupational safety and health regulations enforced by another agency.

The Board Adopts the Asbestos Regulation. The Board preliminarily adopted its asbestos regulation (Regulation XIII, Asbestos Abatement) on June 11, 1992 (Indianapolis Air Pollution Control Section 1992). The preliminary adoption had been preceded by about eighteen months of study and discussion among the Board members in meetings of the whole and in subcommittee meetings. The Board also heard from the public, asbestos contractors, and other interested parties. The preliminarily adopted regulation was more stringent that the federal or state regulations in a number of areas. Some of its provisions included:

- a requirement for an Indiana accredited project supervisor to be on-site at all demolitions (XIII D.2.b); the state had less protection and only required the use of Indiana accredited contractors and workers;
- a requirement for workers to wear protective clothing during work on all projects (XIII F.5); this requirement was not in the state or federal regulations, but it was part of OSHA regulations;
- a requirement for all friable asbestos containing material to be removed prior to demolition or renovation of a space or building at all sites (XIII F.2); the state and federal regulations also required removal, but only for larger projects;
- a requirement to adequately wet friable asbestos containing materials (XIII F.8); the state and federal regulations also required wetting of asbestos materials, but only for larger projects;
- a requirement to use a special procedure (glove bag procedure) for certain sized projects (XIII F.15.b); this was not contained in the state or federal regulations; and
- a requirement for asbestos abatement projects to pass personal air monitoring requirements and abatement projects to pass aggressive air clearance monitoring requirements (XIII F.11 and Appendix A); these were not contained in the state or federal regulations, but they were required in OSHA regulations. (Indianapolis Air Pollution Control Section 1992)

The inclusion of these and other provisions into the Board's rule were based on extensive technical data, cost/benefit analyses and staff experience with asbestos demolition and renovation projects that identified the need for stronger, not weaker, regulation. The proposed provisions were intended to prevent asbestos fibers from becoming airborne during renovations and demolitions involving asbestos-containing materials. The Board and its staff strongly believed that existing federal and state regulations were not adequate to protect the *public health and safety*. Both the federal and state regulations provide local jurisdictions with the flexibility of adopting more stringent regulations in order to respond to local needs.

The staff prepared a detailed technical support document that included health risk assessments and cost/benefit analysis. The staff analysis demonstrated that the Indianapolis regulation would increase the costs of compliance by about 16 percent when compared to the federal regulation. However, when compared to the existing industry practices at the time, the Indianapolis regulation would not increase costs of compliance except for large demolition projects (Indianapolis Air Pollution Control Section n.d., 4). The staff also determined that asbestos emissions and health risks from a project regulated by the proposed local regulation would be reduced by 99.98 percent compared to a reduction of only 60 to 70 percent under the federal rules (Indianapolis Air Pollution Control Section n.d., 5). Furthermore, the proposed regulation was actually less costly (by 41.4 percent) per kilogram of asbestos reduced than the federal regulation.

On April 8, 1993 after more months of study, discussion and testimony the Board adopted Regulation XIII, Asbestos Abatement, which was essentially unchanged from the preliminary adoption. The preliminary adoption of this regulation was a strong statement by the Board. The Board and the staff of the Air Pollution Control Division were under considerable pressure from the Mayor's office and the RSC not to pass the regulation. The RSC Chairman, James Sommer, sent a letter to the Board's Chairman, Dr. Robert Daly, shortly after this vote. In the letter, Sommer states:

> . . . . As you know, the RSC is not opposed to appropriate asbestos regulation. As you also know, however, there already exists extensive federal and state regulations governing asbestos. Regulation XIII proposes to add an additional local layer to such regulations, a layer which our analysis indicates can not be justified on a cost/benefit basis. (Sommer 1993a)

The RSC Responds. While the Board's process was open and invited all points of view, the RSC conducted its review of the asbestos regulation in a closed and inaccessible process. On December 30, 1992 the RSC produced an Information and Analysis Statement (IAS) that was vague, misleading and without foundation. Two weeks later on January 14, 1993 the RSC had adopted its recommendations on the regulation (Sommer 1993b). Members of the public could have submitted comment on the RSC's recommendations from December 30, 1992 to January 10, 1993, providing that they knew the RSC's IAS was located in the adult reference section at certain public libraries under the title "Indianapolis Regulatory Review" (Lausch and Rose 1992).

On the issue of enforceability, the RSC said that "regulations promulgated at local jurisdictions should conform to and not exceed regulations at the state and federal level barring extraordinary or unusual circumstances." The RSC concluded that the regulation would be burdensome "while greatly increasing the pro-rata cost." Another conclusion was that the regulation has "proven only marginal due to subjective enforcement, lack of sufficient professional training, lack of accountability, staff turnover and regulatory language open to the subjective interpretation of staff personnel." It characterized the revisions to Regulation XIII as "without merit" and offering "almost no public benefit." Finally, the RSC recommended that any language in the proposed regulation that was more stringent than the federal or state standards be eliminated, effectively removing from the Board its authority to regulate air pollution activities so as to protect the public health and safety. (RSC n.d.)

None of the RSC's assertions was backed by factual data. The IAS did not quantify costs, risks or benefits of its position. The IAS assertions were qualitative and lacked scientific support.

In early 1993 David Jordan, Assistant Administrator of the Air Pollution Control Section, had sent a candid letter to Barry Baer, Director of the Department of Public Works, in which he expressed concerns shared by the Board about the RSC review. Jordan and most of the Board had been concerned about the RSC's lack of technical competence to handle a thorough analysis of a regulation as complex as the asbestos and other air pollution regulations. This concern was justified. None of the RSC staff had expertise in this area, and conversations between some of the Board members and the RSC staff revealed a significant lack of understanding on the part of the RSC about the technical basis for the asbestos regulation.

Jordan expressed concern that Bruce Wallace, a Board member and owner of Alliance Environmental, Inc. (a company that consulted on asbestos issues), was unduly influencing the process.[9] Jordan stated, "I am concerned with a single individual's apparent ability to influence a powerful advisory body behind closed doors. That does not seem to be in keeping with the concept of 'open' government as I have tried to practice it for the last several years" (Jordan 1993). His comment regarding Wallace was based on the RSC's acknowledgement that it had met with two "experts"—Jordan and Bruce Wallace. Jordan cautioned, "It will be difficult to convince the Board to follow the RSC's recommendation where the RSC provides no support for their statements" (Jordan 1993). Jordan also challenged the RSC's blanket statements about the Air Section's asbestos program, which implied that the program was seriously flawed and that personnel were incompetent. Jordan[10] was highly regarded by the regulated community, and the Air Section's programs (including asbestos) enjoyed considerable support from the regulated community.

It should be noted that the RSC staff's selection of certain "experts" (those who espoused deregulation) was to be repeated in the review of the environmental health regulations at the Health and Hospital Corporation of Marion County (see Chapter 13). Similarly, its charges that the public program was incompetent would also be repeated in the Health and Hospital regulatory review.

The RSC's Expert. Wallace's appointment to the Board in June 1993 was a surprise to the Board because the position that he was appointed to was designed to represent the public-at-large.[11] This gave the appearance of a conflict of interest, which Wallace confirmed in his public statements. For example, Wallace stated, "The industries I represent on the board have voiced strong concern, both through my office and the Indianapolis Chamber of Commerce, that local regulations more stringent than either the federal or state regulations . . . are not required and will not be supported by the community at large" (Niederpruem 1994c). In this same article Wallace said, "All of industry wants less regulations . . . ." Several members of the Board expressed concern and directed the Assistant Administrator (Jordan) to bring this matter to the attention of the Mayor, but Goldsmith was nonresponsive to these concerns.

Wallace subsequently became the subject of two complaints to the Indiana Department of Environmental Management (IDEM). In one case Wallace's company was the consultant involved in overseeing an asbestos removal project at a high school in the Indianapolis Public School system. In this case, inspectors identified multiple occasions of dry asbestos removal (all removals must be done with asbestos-containing materials wetted to prevent the fibers from becoming airborne) (IDEM 1999). The total penalty in the case was $43,200; Wallace and the removal contractor each paid portions of the penalty (IDEM 1999). In another referral Wallace represented his company as having "project designer" credentials when in fact the company did not have this designation. Wallace, who "is not accredited in Indiana as a management planner" was identified "in each . . . report as the management planner" (IDEM 1998). This referral, which includes signed statements attesting to the allegations, is pending with the agency.

Final Note. The need for a stronger asbestos regulation that would be protective of the public's health and safety was underscored by a newspaper report in 1993. This article reported that the state's environmental agency was aggressively focusing on asbestos companies and workers for using forged certification cards (Niederpruem 1993). This article noted that four of the agency's five criminal investigators had asbestos cases pending from around the state. The State of Indiana requires all phases of asbestos work to be performed by workers who had been trained, tested and certified to do the work. Although this system is not perfect, it does ensure a minimum level of competence for this type of work.

While the Board produced a regulation that was carefully studied, deliberated and substantiated in an open, public process, the RSC produced a vague, unsubstantiated analysis statement in a closed process that demonstrated a lack of understanding of the regulation and the science behind it. Further, the RSC's deliberations and conclusions were heavily influenced by an asbestos contractor, who was appointed to the regulating authority by Goldsmith, and who subsequently was found in violation of the asbestos regulations.

The City-County Council, which had been heavily lobbied by the Goldsmith administration, rejected the Board's revised asbestos regulation in May 1993. There was essentially no deliberation on the regulation's merits. Two years later, the City-County Council passed another revision of the asbestos regulation. This regulation, which is currently in effect, is nearly identical to the weak state and federal regulations.

Overflows of the Sewer System

Indianapolis Dumps Sewage into Its Rivers and Creeks

As previously noted, Indianapolis has an antiquated sewage system that also collects rainwater (storm water) in the central portion of the city. The combination of sewage, industrial discharges and rainwater are transported to the city's wastewater treatment plants through an aging and leaking piping system (about 100 years old and made of bricks in some parts of the city). In the newer parts of the city, the sewage and rainwater systems are separated.

The city's combined sewer systems pose serious health and environmental problems because disease-causing pathogens routinely are discharged into the area's creeks and rivers, even during light rains. The area's residents and downstream users are exposed to raw untreated sewage and industrial discharges (some of which are not fully treated) on a regular basis. The combined sewer overflows (CSOs) also kill fish and cause other damage to the receiving waters because the sewage and chemical-laden water depletes oxygen and increases the toxic chemicals in the water.

Indianapolis has 130 combined storm-sanitary sewers that dump four to five billion gallons of combined sewage each year into the White River and its tributaries (Fall Creek, Eagle Creek, Pleasant Run and Pogue's Run) (Kaplan 1999a). There are about two dozen parks and recreation facilities and three schools located on the White River and its tributaries (Kaplan 1999a). The stench of sewage in these areas can be overpowering. In addition, one of the city's two wastewater treatment facilities routinely overflows 30 to 40 times each year (McClaren 1999a).

Rather than address the basic problem—crumbling 19th century sewers—Goldsmith lobbied the State Legislature to relax water quality standards so that Indianapolis could continue to pollute legally. This 1996 Goldsmith bill failed by a close margin. One Republican state senator noted, "I have cities that have spent lots of money to meet these requirements, and we didn't get any reprieve" (McIntyre 1996).

The Mayor Sues the State to Block a New Permit

The city's existing wastewater permit, which expired in 1990, had been the subject of protracted negotiations with the Indiana Department of Environmental Management. The environmental community complained that city officials had "dragged their feet for years on the problems, which could have been solved a decade ago for $200 million" (McClaren 1999). Goldsmith, who had the benefit of Hudnut's commissioned GIFT report, was fully aware of the problem, and he could have acted aggressively to begin to solve the infrastructure problems. However, he decided on a different tactic.

When the IDEM told the city that a new permit was going into effect, Goldsmith filed a lawsuit against the state. The lawsuit blocked the state from adopting the permit pending public input. The IDEM, however, pointed out that it had already held three public meetings on the permit and had gathered extensive comment from the public and environmental groups. Nevertheless, Marion County Judge William Lawrence granted a temporary restraining order against the state, thereby ensuring that the matter would be put off until after the mayoral election in November (McClaren 1999a).

Goldsmith then began a "grass roots" appeal telling citizens that the IDEM's permit would cost ratepayers between $8 billion and $23 billion. He attempted to alarm homeowners by stating that the cost of clean water would bankrupt them, force them out of their homes and raise their sewer bills to over $150 each month (McClaren 1999a). In a letter to the editor, he predicted that the monthly bills would shatter forever the "dreams of future home ownership" of "our poorest residents" (Goldsmith 1999). In another exaggeration he asserted that the IDEM was requiring the city to make the river waters "swimmable" immediately and the city could not afford a $7 billion beach (Strauss 1999).[12]

Goldsmith also spent $17,000 in public money to buy radio time for an ad campaign against the new clean water permit. Amos Brown, a spokesman for two of the radio stations that aired the ad, observed, "I've been in this market 25 years, and I don't recall any unit of government buying ads to blast another unit of government" (Sword 1999).

During the fall of 1999, two environmental groups charged the Goldsmith administration with environmental racism for blocking the clean-up of the city waterways, especially in the poor districts of Indianapolis (McClaren 1999b). Goldsmith countered by charging that the environmental groups were "tormenting our poorest residents" (McClaren 1999b).

In response to the Goldsmith propaganda, the IDEM's Commissioner Lori Kaplan published an opinion in which she reiterated, "The permit IDEM proposed for Indianapolis has the same water-quality standards that the agency has issued to 82 other Hoosier cities and towns with combined sewer overflow problems" (Kaplan 1999a). Kaplan further noted that Goldsmith's cost estimates were not applicable because " . . . in his own variance (to the permit), the mayor says the city isn't thinking about implementing these costly options, which are not required by IDEM's permit" (Kaplan 1999a).

Goldsmith's successor, Mayor Bart Peterson, has proposed a twenty-year program of improvements that would cost in the range of $840 million to $1.3 billion, depending on which options were selected. This program would increase user fees by 17.8 percent. The monthly sewer bill would increase from $10.91 to $12.85 for an average residence using 7,000 gallons of water per month. These estimates are an order of magnitude below Goldsmith's assertions. Mayor Peterson has stated he could guarantee the rate for five years, through 2005. After that, another rate hike would be likely. (*Indianapolis Star* 2000)

Goldsmith compounded the problem of paying for the sewer system and wastewater facility infrastructure improvements because he had diverted nearly forty percent of the savings from the privatized wastewater treatment facilities to other areas. He used these savings to pay down the United Airline maintenance center debt and to cover deficits in the underfunded public safety pension system. In discussing these diversions, Mullins and Zorn state, "these activities have no direct relationship to wastewater treatment consumption and are inconsistent with the intended purpose of the fee system; they violate the integrity of the enterprise account . . . Using wastewater fees to subsidize general fund activities requires a rate structure which charges excessive prices for wastewater treatment, creating inefficient pricing signals" (Mullins and Zorn 1996, 17). The diversion of these funds will cause problems for Goldsmith's successor because money that was available to fund upgrades to the existing treatment facilities no longer exists.

The *Indianapolis Star* subsequently editorialized on the subject of sewers, "It's just not acceptable, at the start of the 21st century, that Indianapolis is still relying on 19th century methods for disposing of sewage" (*Indianapolis Star* 2000). It will be expensive for Indianapolis to upgrade its sewer system infrastructure, and Goldsmith's policies and actions have increased the bill for the citizens of Indianapolis.

Septic Systems

GIFT, the Environmental Policy Work Group and The Peirce Report all identified the high percentage of septic systems in Indianapolis as a significant problem. The Indianapolis metropolitan area ranked second among the nation's cities in the percentage (11.33 percent) of septic systems per occupied home[13] based on 1990 census data (Peirce and Johnson 1996).   Marion County had been estimated to have about 35,000 homes with septic systems (Environmental Policy Work Group 1993). It has been estimated that Indianapolis has 18,000 houses on septic systems (Rohn 2000a). More recent numbers will be forthcoming when new census data are published, but regardless of the exact number, Indianapolis has a serious problem.

The Indianapolis metropolitan area has a high water table, flat topography and clay soils, which makes most of the area unsuitable for septic systems. Many of the aging lateral systems are failing. The laterals (also called finger systems) are the pipes that carry the sewage from the septic tank to the soil in the yard so the sewage can be filtered by the soil. When it rains, the clay soils in these areas are unable to filter the sewage and rainwater, and the incompletely treated sewage (called gray water) rises to the surface and pools in homeowners' yards. The gray water exposes residents, especially children, to the sewage and potential disease-causing organisms. In these areas, the rainwater runoff, which contains sewage-laden water, can also contaminant streams and unprotected wells. Measurements of *E. coli* (bacteria associated with fecal matter) in some area backyards have more than 10,000 times the level of environmental standards for these bacteria.

Mayor Goldsmith once proposed eliminating all septic tanks by 2004, but by the time he left office that date had been revised to 2044. The average cost to a homeowner to bring new sewers into a neighborhood is $5,000 to $15,000. Hooking up to the system can add another $500 to $1,500. These costs can be spread out over 10 years at a seven- percent interest rate, but that cost is still too high for many homeowners. (Rohn 2000a).

Glenn Pratt, an environmental consultant, activist and former EPA official said, "Since these septic systems never should have been approved and never been installed in the first place, we as a city have an obligation to help solve the problem, instead of leaving people with this huge payment . . ." (Rohn 2000a). Goldsmith's successor has pledged to address the problem of septic systems, but the resources to do so have been spent elsewhere during Goldsmith's tenure. It remains to be seen whether or not the new administration can succeed.

White River Environmental Partnership (WREP)

Goldsmith Decides to Privatize the City's Wastewater Treatment Facilities

Privatization of the city's wastewater treatment facilities was a cornerstone of the Goldsmith reinvention agenda, but the privatization was controversial and questioned by many observers. The existing facilities had been cited as model facilities that were efficiently operated. Many observers were not convinced that that privatization was needed. In the spring of 1993, Goldsmith established a "bipartisan review committee to examine the city's options for the wastewater treatment plant" (Goldsmith 1997, 202). The composition of the committee and the lack of public participation in the privatization decision were widely criticized. As an article from an academic public works journal noted,

> At no time between September 1992 and November 1993 did the mayor or his administration hold public hearings on the plans to contract out plant operations and management. Fundamentally, beyond the mayor's expressed intention to shrink the Indianapolis public sector, primary input in the most formative stages of the effort came from SELTIC, which not

only made the initial recommendation to privatize the wastewater treatment plants, but also recommended consultants to perform the necessary studies. (Montgomery and Nunn 1996)

The Director of the Department of Public Works defended the lack of public input by suggesting that the potential for savings would have been compromised had the city been required to open the process (Morgan 1994a). Susan Williams, a City-County Council member, retorted that, if the deal were so good, it could stand the test of public hearings (Gelarden 1993).

The Contract is Awarded to WREP

The contract to manage the advanced wastewater treatment (AWT) facilities was eventually awarded to the White River Environmental Partnership, a consortium composed of three companies: IWC Resources, Inc. (parent firm of the Indianapolis Water Company); Lyonnaise des Eaux-Dumez, a French firm; and JMM Operational Services, Inc. (a subsidiary of GWC Corp, which in turn was owned by Lyonnaise and the engineering firm of Montgomery-Watson). The partnership proposed to effect its savings by "slashing personnel, supply and professional service costs" and through "advanced technology" (Gelarden 1993).

Goldsmith described the partners' environmental records in glowing terms, citing in particular JMM's "impeccable reputation for environmental safety" (Goldsmith 1997, 205). Other observers were less impressed. Glenn Pratt, an environmental consultant, charged that the water company, WREP's controlling partner, had repeatedly violated clean water permits, a charge confirmed by Marion County health officials (Morgan 1994b). The *Wall Street Journal*—no foe of privatization initiatives—reported scandals involving Lyonnaise, including allegations of substantial corruption in water and public works contracts (Truell 1994) and large political contributions to local officials who have authority to award treatment contracts (Browning 1994). A plant managed by JMM (and praised by Goldsmith) had dumped "tons of raw sludge into the Delaware River" prior to the award of the Indianapolis contract (Morgan 1993). Documents from the Marion County Health Department obtained by local media provided evidence that the Water Company had violated clean water permits in Marion County for fifteen years (Harris 1994b), and it had persistently lobbied against environmental reforms (Mason 1993). Even the local NAACP voiced concerns about the partnership's commitment to environmental standards (*Indianapolis News* 1993b).

Indianapolis entered into the original five-year contract with WREP on December 20, 1993. Section 6.15 of the contract specifically allowed WREP to institute a "Process Change," defined as "adjustments to major components of the AWT Facilities, such as land application of sludge and use of chlorination" (AWT 1993). Staffing levels were left to the discretion of the contractor. Routine maintenance was to be WREP's responsibility, but—as Goldsmith acknowledged (Goldsmith 1997, 205)—all capital costs, including vehicles, would continue to be paid for by the city (AWT 1993), significantly reducing contractor risk.

The contract was inadequate in a number of areas, including oversight. While the contract called for the submission of various reports to the city, no other monitoring or oversight provisions[14] were included. The Director of the Department of Public Works explained that the city had "no special procedures in place to monitor WREP's compliance with its contract" (Lanosga and Johnston 1994). It is unclear what recourse the city might have in the event reports were not made or if they were unsatisfactory. In the event of an uncured breach of contract, the city's only remedies were recovery of money damages or termination of the agreement; however, the contract did not address the very significant practical realities of a termination. For example, all plant workers would now be employees of WREP, not the city. Under the termination provision of the contract, the city has the right to "utilize" WREP employees at such time as it assumes control and the corresponding obligation to reimburse WREP for their use, but no time period is referenced. Would those workers "revert" to the city at the end of some specified time? If the skilled workers chose not to remain, what recourse would the city have? Would there be a hiatus in water treatment? Who would own management materials and records that WREP had prepared? How would logistics of the transition be handled? None of these questions was addressed.

Whatever the merits or deficiencies of the contract, a virtually identical contract was signed between the parties in 1998. There have been cost savings under WREP management, as Goldsmith claimed. However, the precise savings are difficult to determine since the $65 million dollar "savings" figure was determined against Goldsmith's "projected" costs, and those projections have been subject to dispute (Schramm 1994). The savings that have been realized, however, have more to do with the water treatment choice made by the operator than with private management efficiencies. This source of savings was foretold in an article in the *Indianapolis News* after the contract was awarded to WREP, "Much of the savings will be realized through changes in wastewater treatment processes . . . " (Harris 1993a).[15]

Environmental Issues Under Privatization

Before privatization, Montgomery and Nunn noted that the city's wastewater treatment plants were among the most advanced in the country "because they used ozonation, rather than chlorination, for disinfection in their treatment process. Ozonation is more expensive, because it requires more energy and labor, but it may be environmentally safer: the chlorination process creates by-products thought to be carcinogenic." (Montgomery and Nunn 1996, 47)

Environmentalists claimed that chlorine treatment was "outdated and hazardous" (Schramm 1994), and considerable concern was voiced about the proposed change in treatment technology. Glenn Pratt, environmental consultant, warned that river oxygen levels would decrease and toxic contaminants would result in dead fish and water quality violations (Harris 1993b). The *Indianapolis News* editorialized:

> The most persuasive argument against current proposals for city wastewater treatment has to do with keeping White River clean and safe. Will private management maintain the high environmental standards that the city's workers have implemented at the treatment plants?
>
> WREP plans to eliminate the present treatment process, which consists of ozone and cryogenic oxygen generation.
>
> This process costs more than other treatment methods but is considered among the safest, most effective and most environmentally sound.
>
> WREP would replace that method with a chlorine-based process, which is a less expensive means of treatment, but one that critics say is dangerous to workers and potentially harmful to the environment. High levels of chlorine, for instance, can kill a river's fish and other aquatic life. (*Indianapolis News* 1993)

A researcher from the American Federation of State and county Municipal Employees charged that the city, in its zeal to privatize the wastewater facilities, had ignored environmental concerns voiced by its own consultants (Harris 1993c). Those concerns led William Beranek, Jr., the highly respected president of the Indiana Environmental Institute, to propose the formation of a bipartisan committee to provide technical oversight and environmental monitoring. "There may be permit conditions which are in the best interest of the management company but would not be in the best interests of the city . . . It is critical that the city maintain an independent oversight function" (Harris 1993d). However, Beranek's proposal was "summarily dismissed" by the administration (Harris 1993d).

Whatever the relative merits of the two systems, it is true that the less-expensive chlorination process complied with existing EPA standards, as the city insisted. It is equally true that the city could have achieved the same cost savings by opting for the less expensive treatment itself. The previous administration had made a policy decision favoring the more expensive treatment on environmental grounds. The Goldsmith administration could have made a decision that the added water quality was not worth the added cost, rather than hiring private management to effect the change.

There have been a number of highly publicized fish kills since WREP assumed control of the wastewater treatment facilities despite the administration's insistence that chlorination posed no environmental threat and the claims made for the environmental safeguards the new partnership would observe. For example, state conservation officials reported that raw and partially treated sewage polluted the White River for about ten hours during the weekend of September 22 and 23, 1994. The spill led to an investigation by then-prosecutor Jeffrey Modisett into the operation of the plants and allegations of an attempted cover-up (Morgan 1994c). Five hundred thousand fish were killed in that incident. The Indiana Department of Natural Resources (DNR) blamed the operation of the Belmont wastewater treatment plant, and assessed a fine against the city. Goldsmith initially refused to pay, insisting that WREP was not responsible, but the city and the State later negotiated a settlement (*NUVO Newsweekly* 1995). The DNR report concluded that WREP had dumped water with too much chlorine and too little oxygen into the river (*NUVO Newsweekly 1995*).

In February of 1996, after additional problems, the Goldsmith administration asked the state legislature to force the Indiana Department of Environmental Management to relax water quality standards applicable to the city's sewage treatment facilities. The bill was rejected in the Senate by a vote of 26-24 (McIntyre 1996). Sen. Glenn L. Howard, a former member of the City-County Council for 17 years and a Democrat from Indianapolis, had pointed words about the Goldsmith initiative. Howard charged that the city was "leading the way in not being responsive" to its water pollution problems (Niederpruem 1996b).

By July of 1996 there had been three fish kills, and a group of environmental activists picketed a fundraiser given for Goldsmith by the Water Company's James Morris. The *Indianapolis Star* reported "The event came just 17 days after the White River Environmental Partnership—a consortium known as WREP that includes IWC Resources, the Indianapolis Water Co.'s corporate parent of which Morris is President—won a $23 million city contract." One of the protesters, Stephen Gibson, said, "We want to raise public awareness about what's going on in the environment" (Ignarski 1996b).

Public awareness did increase. One of the most effective campaign ads during Goldsmith's bid for governor was a spot that highlighted dead fish and proclaimed "Steve Goldsmith. Bad for fish, bad for Indiana."

More Prevailing Wage Problems

The switch to chlorination provided a large share of the savings under privatization. The other significant saving realized by WREP came at the expense of the city's workers, 132 of which were displaced (AWT Update 1994). The author was not able to determine how much, if any, of that downsizing was attributable to the difference in manpower requirements between the two treatment processes.

In addition to the ongoing debate about environmental impact, privatization of the AWT plants ran into some of the same problems that had bedeviled other Goldsmith privatization efforts. Shortly after assuming control of the wastewater facilities, the *Indianapolis News* reported that approximately $715,000 of corrective maintenance work had been done in violation of the state bid and prevailing wage laws (Lanosga and Johnston 1994). Goldsmith's response was first to contend that state laws were "outmoded," "hopelessly confusing" and "too antiquated for sophisticated modern government," and to complain that benefits of privatization would be lost if WREP had to pay the prevailing wage. In a later letter to the *Indianapolis News,* he tried a different approach, suggesting that "whatever WREP pays is the prevailing wage because the treatment plant operation is the largest in the state." As a deputy attorney general pointed out, size is not the legal criterion for determining the prevailing wage (Lanosga and Johnston 1994). The *Indianapolis News* offered its own perspective in an editorial:

> Unfortunately, this kind of carelessness isn't new. It happened with the privatization of the city's golf courses. And it could happen again with the

Airport Authority, if the Goldsmith administration isn't more careful. To argue, as the mayor has, that Indiana's prevailing wage law is outdated is beside the point. We agree that the law works against the forces of the free market, driving up the cost of public projects. We agree that it should be abolished.

But it is the law, and until it is changed, the city of Indianapolis and its contractors are obliged to obey it—even if that slows down or adds to the cost of privatization. (*Indianapolis News* 1994)

Where Are We Now?

In *The Twenty-First Century City*, Goldsmith acknowledged that the existing city plants had "won numerous accolades for innovation, safety and overall outstanding performance" and that the city's problem was with the "wastewater collection system," that is, the city's sewers (Goldsmith 1997, 200). Originally, the privatization of the sewage treatment plants was supposed to generate savings that would be used to repair those sewers. An article in the *Indianapolis News* quoted Goldsmith as saying that the anticipated $65 million dollar savings over the five-year contract "will allow the city to avoid a hefty sewer rate increase to pay for the repair of deteriorating sewers" (Lanosga 1994).

In January, 2000, the *Indianapolis Star* ran an article by David Rohn, detailing the problems with White River and fish kills throughout the state. Rohn wrote, "The major problem with treatment plant failures and combined sewer overflows is the discharge of ammonia into the river. It depletes oxygen, harming aquatic life . . . replacement of combined sewers will eliminate most of those problems" (Rohn 2000b).

The sewage treatment plants were privatized, substantial savings were claimed, and Goldsmith said these savings would be used to replace the combined sewers. However, by 1999 the worsening condition of the city's sewers had become a major issue (Kaplan 1999a, 1999b). The WREP savings had been used elsewhere. Goldsmith's lack of aggressive action on sewer repair has left the new administration and citizens to cope with a significant environmental health hazard and an enormously expensive fix to those problems.

Despite the problems that have been identified, the City of Indianapolis entered into a $39 million dollar contract with WREP in July 1996 to privatize the sewer maintenance system. Rather than give the sewer maintenance to a separate firm, which would arguably have been more consistent with a goal of ensuring competition, WREP was effectively given a private monopoly over the entire Indianapolis wastewater system (Ignarski 1996a). The performance of WREP under this contract has not had the benefit of a formal audit by the Department of Capital Asset Management (DCAM).[16]

Wellhead Protection, Recycling, Greenspace Preservation . . .

The number of environmental issues facing Indianapolis and how the Goldsmith responded to those challenges is far more extensive than can be covered in a single chapter. However, a brief overview of a few additional problems is illustrative. For example, Indianapolis does have a wellhead protection program, but it relies on education and voluntary registration to protect groundwater resources. Leadership and support from Goldsmith might have produced a model program that included greater citizen involvement, lowered threshold quantities for exempt businesses, reduced opportunities for waivers to requirements, placement of the program review responsibilities within the Health and Hospital Corporation and other more protective measures. Recycling does occur in Indianapolis, but the city does not have a free citywide curbside recycling program (one of Goldsmith's campaign vows). Greenspace is at a premium in Indianapolis and, under the Goldsmith administration, opportunities to gain and maintain public greenspace were lost to private developers. Like other older American cities, Indianapolis has a large number of homes that are contaminated with lead-based paint. Identifying children with lead poisoning, treating them, and remediating the homes in which they live is expensive and challenging. The Health and Hospital Corporation of Marion County has a small, but effective program. However, the program, which is largely funded by federal dollars, is substantially underfunded. Leadership and support from the Mayor's office in the form of increased staffing and money for testing would have increased the likelihood that many more children will achieve their full potential. The Mayor, who worked hard to pass anti-clean water regulations, might better have used his energy to lobby for legislation to reduce childhood lead poisoning. The list goes on . . .

Summary

The story of Stephen Goldsmith's reinvention of environmental programs in Indianapolis includes an absence of positive vision for environment, poor stewardship and missed opportunities. Whatever positive accomplishments were made during his eight years as mayor can largely be attributed to a motivated group of front-line professionals who attempted to advance the public's interest in environment, despite a leadership deficit from the Mayor's office. Goldsmith has saddled the new administration with serious environmental and infrastructure problems, and it will be expensive to begin solving them.

Most citizens do not expect any single mayor to solve long-standing and difficult problems overnight, and the same was true of Goldsmith. However, they do expect problems to be recognized and tackled in a forthright manner. On environment, and many other issues, Goldsmith and his administration were defined by an arrogance that prevented them from addressing pressing issues effectively and governing in a democratic manner.

Notes

[1] The HEC is the state's largest environmental advocacy group. Its membership includes representatives of other environmental advocacy groups and concerned citizens.

[2] The author served on the indoor air pollution work group.

[3] Members of the Environmental Policy Work Group are listed in "Environmental Policy Papers" (1993).

[4] This communication also informed recipients that members of the original group (it is not known how many) plus "a series of environmental and business organizations were asked to review the draft and name their top 10 action items at this time" (Euler 1998). This poll was then collated into a spreadsheet that gave a numerical score to the action items in terms of benefits to human health, resources, potential for public assistance, and ease of implementation.

[5] The author participated in these discussions.

[6] Author's notes. The author served on the Air Pollution Control Board during this case, attended neighborhood meetings and met with neighbors to experience first hand their situation. As a Board member, the author argued for stiff penalties, stringent corrective actions and the shutdown of the facility. The Indiana Department of Environmental Management was also involved in the settlement of the case.

[7] Author's notes.

[8] The author had been a member of the Indianapolis Air Pollution Control Board since 1984 by the appointment of Mayor Hudnut. The author served on the Board until 1995.

[9] During the course of the struggle over the asbestos regulation, the author asked Wallace to recuse himself from a vote on the regulation because of a potential conflict of interest. The author believed that Wallace, who sought contracts to remove or renovate asbestos-containing materials, could have benefited from a weakening of the asbestos regulation. The author requested an

opinion from the Board's counsel who was hired by Goldsmith. Counsel found that Wallace did not have a conflict of interest.

[10] Jordan subsequently resigned from his position. The author speculates his resignation was arguably due to the Mayor's handling of the regulatory review and micro-management of the Section.

[11] The Air Pollution Control Board is a nine-member board that primarily represents various aspects of industrial concerns. Two of the positions, however, represent the interests of the public. The Mayor appointed Wallace to fill one of these positions. Goldsmith filled another "public representative" position in 1995. His choice was Blake Jeffery, a manufacturing lobbyist. The *Indianapolis Star/News* reported, "there was a small public outcry, but the appointment stuck."(Niederpruem 1997).

It is interesting to note that Wallace, in a resume furnished to the Mayor's office in his connection with the appointment to the Air Board, claimed he was a Professional Engineer (PE) and a Certified Safety Professional (CPS), and he signed his name on contracts with school corporations for Americans with Disabilities Act work using these designations. In a lawsuit involving Wallace, he claimed that "PE" meant "plant engineer" and "CSP" meant "competent safety professional." Wallace had an associate degree in applied mechanical engineering technology. (Marion Superior Court Cause Number 49D109410C) 0048, Marion County, Indiana).

Under Indiana law, offering to engage in the practice of professional engineering without certification is a Class B misdemeanor. It appears that the Goldsmith administration was aware of these fabrications, but Wallace remained on the Air Board.

[12] The idea of people splashing around in a pristine river, idyllic though it is, was not what the regulators had in mind. The goal was simply that a person who experienced "full body contact" with the river water would not get sick (an example of full body contact would be falling into the water). Many portions of the White River are limited to fishing and wading; other areas have signage that warns against any contact whatsoever with the water.

[13] The first-ranked city was Jacksonville, Florida with 26.70 percent of its homes served by septic systems. For comparison, the third-ranked city, Phoenix, had 2.96 percent of its homes on septic systems.

[14] No formal audits had been completed on the facility's performance as recently as May 2000. The Department of Capital Asset Management (DCAM), however, does prepare a monthly report on the facility. Author's notes from meeting with DCAM staff on May 12, 2000.

[15] DCAM staff confirmed that the initial cost savings were primarily due to the switch from ozonation to chlorination. Author's notes from May 12, 2000 meeting with DCAM staff.

[16] Author's notes on meeting with DCAM Staff, May 12, 2000.

Chapter 13

Removing Regulatory Burdens: Citizens Take Control

Ingrid Ritchie[1]

Introduction

Mayor Goldsmith believed that government regulation created serious barriers to investment and economic development. In *The Twenty-First Century City* he states: "Regulation kills the economy with a thousand pinpricks. Excessive regulation increases the cost of doing business, which drives existing businesses out of cities and discourages others from moving in" (Goldsmith 1997, 86-87).

Goldsmith goes on to comment that his administration " . . . did not want to eliminate regulations that really did protect public health and safety. But we did want to adopt the philosophy that government interference is a last resort for solving problems." (Goldsmith 1997, 88)

The public health and environmental communities viewed this philosophy with alarm because it ran counter to a fundamental principle of protecting the public's environmental health. Prevention and wellness promotion, not solving problems after the fact, are the primary goals of these regulatory programs. Many believed that the Mayor intended to gut regulations that protected public health and safety. Others and that portion of the business community that was intimately involved in setting the Mayor's agenda strongly supported the review of all local regulations and anticipated that it would reduce regulatory burdens, freeing the market to perform "efficiently and effectively."

On November 16, 1995 the Board of Trustees of the Health and Hospital Corporation of Marion County took the unprecedented action of sunsetting its environmental health regulations (Health and Hospital 1995a). The Board gave itself until December 31, 1997 to accept, reject or modify the regulations by re-codification of the ordinances. If the Board failed to act on a regulation by that date, the regulation would expire.[2]

This chapter explores the Health and Hospital regulatory review process as it evolved and examines the outcomes of the review, using the housing regulations as the case example. Goldsmith's themes of efficiency and effectiveness provide a context for drawing conclusions about this effort to "reinvent" and deregulate local government.

The City—County Framework for Environmental Health Programs

The management of environmental health issues in Indianapolis and Marion County is carried out by a combination of city and county agencies, primarily the Department of Public Works and the Marion County Health Department, a division of the Health and Hospital Corporation. Another component of environmental regulation in Marion County is the Environmental Court, a superior court established in 1978 during the administration of former Mayor Hudnut to address violations of city/county environmental regulations that cannot be resolved through the administrative process.

The Department of Public Works

The Department of Public Works maintains the city's infrastructure, including sewers, manages municipal solid waste collection, and houses the city's agency for environmental programs, the Environmental Resources Management Division (ERMD). The ERMD was established in 1992 after Mayor Goldsmith took office, during a citywide reorganization that was intended to reduce bureaucratic inefficiencies.

Prior to the Goldsmith administration, the Department of Public Works housed the Air Pollution Control Division (dating back to the 1950s) and the Water and Land Protection Division (established in the mid-1980s). Under Goldsmith, these divisions were reduced in status to sections and combined with an enforcement program to form the ERMD. The ERMD currently has forty-two employees, and their program responsibilities include the following:

- Air Quality Management Section—planning, air quality monitoring, issuing air permits and stationary source compliance
- Water and Land Management Section—surface water quality monitoring, emergency response for sewer systems, household hazardous waste collection, environmental remediation contract oversight and other environmental contractual services
- Enforcement—industrial pretreatment, asbestos compliance, mobile source compliance and illegal dumping.

The Health and Hospital Corporation of Marion County

The Health and Hospital Corporation of Marion County, a municipal corporation created in 1951 by the Indiana legislature,[3] operates Wishard Hospital, the county's primary health care resource for indigent care, and the Marion County Health Department, the Corporation's division of public health (Indiana 1951).[4] A seven-member Board of Trustees, appointed by the Mayor of Indianapolis, City-County Council, and the County Commissioners, governs the Corporation.[5] The Board appoints the Executive Director and President, a position that also serves as Executive Secretary of the Board. It also appoints a medical director to direct the activities of Wishard Hospital and a Public Health Director (also a licensed physician) to lead the Marion County Health Department. Both appointments are renewable four-year terms.

The Public Health Director is responsible for the public health department's two bureaus: population health and environmental health. The Bureau of Environmental Health, currently staffed by 200 employees, is responsible for the county's environmental health programs including:

- retail food establishments
- housing code enforcement and neighborhood health
- private sewage disposal and wells for potable water
- swimming pools
- child care facilities
- mosquito and rodent control
- water quality
- solid waste and refuse containers

- indoor air pollution
- childhood lead prevention
- occupational health
- hazardous materials management and emergency response

Over the years, the Bureau of Environmental Health has been responsive to emerging problems such as indoor air pollution and childhood lead poisoning, and it has developed model programs in these areas.

Prior to the Goldsmith administration, the Public Health Director wielded considerable power over public health issues and functions and was largely independent of the mayor's office, reporting directly to the Board of Trustees. In the area of environmental health regulation, the Public Health Department was viewed, by some in the regulated community, as a powerful, independent agency that was not politicized compared to the agencies that were more directly under the control of the mayor's office. Hiring, except at the highest executive level, was not governed by political affiliation and public health issues were primarily decided on their merits, not on political considerations. The Public Health Director had a working relationship with the mayor's office, but the Public Health Director, not the mayor's office, was in charge of the agency and public health policy-making. This independence was not by accident. Warren Moberly, a lifelong Republican and long-time attorney for Health and Hospital, helped craft the Corporation's enabling legislation. In 1975 he provided a history of Health and Hospital in which he stated that one of the two reasons for creating the Corporation was to "take the professional services of the hospitals and of public health functions away from direct political control" (Health and Hospital 1975, 7).

With the advent of the Goldsmith administration, the independence of Health and Hospital's Public Health Department on environmental health issues was viewed by some (especially landlords and the food industry) as problematic. It was difficult to apply political pressure to reverse decisions made by staff as a consequence of inspections of restaurants, grocery stores, housing units, septic systems, wells, and other areas regulated by Health and Hospital. Historically and even today, only a small proportion of environmental health cases are referred to the county's Environmental Court, but a majority of these are housing code and sanitation problems, perhaps leading to a perception that Health and Hospital's staff was "overly aggressive" and "out of control" on enforcement issues. Other city agencies including the ERMD also refer cases to Environmental Court, albeit in smaller numbers.

Health and Hospital's Housing Code Enforcement Program

Health and Hospital adopted the county's first housing ordinance in 1954. The ordinance[6] (and subsequent revisions), which is based on the American Public Health Association's (APHA) model code, takes a multi-pronged approach to preventing and correcting problems that affect public health and safety. Under this approach, owners and occupants are each responsible for ensuring a safe and decent home environment. The ordinance regulates the physical structure of the dwelling (and its condition and maintenance) and the sanitary condition in which people live.

The physical structure is important because housing that is in poor condition and poorly maintained can contribute to disease and accidents (Salvato 1992; Ritchie and Martin 1994). For example, toilets, sinks, and septic systems that are not operating properly can expose residents and the community to sewage and water-borne diseases. Plumbing without proper traps can allow sewage and dirty water to flow back into the living space. Poorly maintained roofs, windows, and exterior walls, sewage back-ups, and leaking toilets and water fixtures cause structural damage from moisture. Water damage, from whatever source, encourages the growth of mold, which causes respiratory illness in susceptible individuals. Disease-transmitting mice and rats can enter homes through holes in foundations and the exterior structure. Poorly maintained flooring and broken stairs can cause injuries due to falls. Worn-out or overloaded wiring and electrical fixtures can result in shocks, burns and death from fire and shock hazards. Fire hazards and indoor air pollution, including carbon monoxide poisoning, result when furnaces, hot water heaters, and other combustion appliances are poorly maintained. In some housing, the building materials pose hazards. For example, asbestos is a known cause of lung cancer and lead-based paint causes a variety of effects including learning disabilities, brain and kidney damage, and hearing problems.

The ordinance also prevents the spread of disease and contributes to wellness by regulating the sanitary conditions in which people live. Examples of these areas include basic cleanliness inside the dwelling, especially kitchens and bathrooms; the storage of trash inside and outside the dwelling; requirements for space, lighting, ventilation; and the control of rats, mice, cockroaches, and other pests.

The ordinance specifies the minimum standards to be achieved in each of the regulated areas. As evidenced by articles in the local press, there was a view by the media and some in the business community that some standards were arbitrary, picayune, or arcane; however, each of the areas regulated has an established public health principle as its foundation. For example, Article 4: Sec. 10-401(c)) of the code specified that refrigerators must be capable of storing food at temperatures less than 45°F but more than 32°F under ordinary summer conditions. This measure prevents the illnesses that result from consuming spoiled food. Another example: Article 5: Sec. 10-501 specifies that every habitable room must have a least one window or skylight facing directly outdoors, which can be opened easily or other device to provide adequate ventilation conditions. The public health basis for adequate lighting is to prevent accidents, and ventilation is needed to prevent the buildup of odors and indoor air pollutants from the use of pesticides, combustion sources, hobbies, and building materials. Adequate ventilation also helps reduce heat-related health problems by moderating the buildup of extremely hot temperatures indoors.

In addition to these benefits, housing code enforcement prevents neighborhood deterioration, which has other economic and social benefits:

- Creates a beneficial impact on property tax revenues—individual properties and neighborhoods in good condition have a more positive influence on property tax revenues compared to those in poor condition
- Creates a beneficial impact on insurance rates and availability
- Removes potential sources of drug and other illegal activities by slowing the increase of abandoned properties and creation of vacant lots
- Helps avoid costs of other public programs/services, including: demolition and boarding of vacant buildings, removal of trash and debris from abandoned properties, crime control in vacant structures, fire protection services, rat and mosquito control
- Provides support to other governmental units including: Indianapolis and Marion County Police and Fire Departments; Marion County Prosecutor's Office; Child Protective Services and Adult Protective Services; Animal Control; Department of Public Works; Department of Metropolitan Development; Mayor's Action Center (Health and Hospital n.d.a).

The quality of the inspection staff is at the core of any enforcement program. Health and Hospital's housing code inspectors were required to have a bachelor's degree in a related area (this requirement has since changed). Upon hiring they participate in a three-week training and mentoring program, as well as a longer period of on-the-job training. Each inspector develops competencies in the following areas:

- basic public health principles, including factors that contribute to infectious illness, chronic disease, and preventable injuries
- housing construction and operation of internal systems, including heating and ventilation, plumbing, electrical, water supply, and sewage disposal
- sanitation and vector control (rodents, flies, mosquitoes, and other carriers of disease)
- principles of public health law, administrative law, enforcement policies and procedures, court procedures, and expert witness testimony
- understanding the responsibilities and procedures of other public agencies and working cooperatively with their programs
- communicating with the public, applying both health education techniques and dispute resolution skills
- working cooperatively with community organizations, civic groups, business representatives, elected and appointed officials
- knowledge of community resources that can provide human support services, especially neighborhood-based associations, churches, housing agencies, economic development corporations, and health clinics (Marion County Health Department 1996).

A Businessman Is Hired to Run Health and Hospital

The Goldsmith administration, through the Health and Hospital Corporation's Board of Trustees, replaced Lawrence Buell, a former Republican legislator who had been Executive Director for 10 years, with E. Mitchell Roob, Jr., director of the city's transportation department and top advisor to Goldsmith.[7] Roob's appointment began on February 1, 1994, eighteen months before the official call for the review of Health and Hospital's regulations. John M. Whelan, Chairman of the Board for Health and Hospital, commented: "We did not go after Mitch to privatize the thing. We sought Mitch for his skills as a businessman, for his ability to look at a complex organization and develop a vision, for his effectiveness in developing an organization . . . " (Schoch 1994a, B7).

Roob's resume included experience working as an aide to Illinois Governor Jim Thompson and United States Senator Charles Percy after graduating from DePauw University with a bachelor's degree. After receiving a master's degree in business administration from Notre Dame in 1989, Roob accepted a position with Crow Chizek and Co., an Indianapolis accounting firm, where he worked as a consultant to local governments. In 1991, he volunteered for Goldsmith's mayoral campaign, where he impressed Goldsmith with his analytical capabilities: "Mitch analyzed several organizations, including health and hospital," Goldsmith recalled. "His insights were extremely impressive, to say the least." Roob's service to Goldsmith led to his appointment as Director of the city's Department of Transportation, a position he held for about two years. (Price 1994a, A1)

With his appointment as Executive Director of Health and Hospital, Roob would be responsible for 3,750 employees and Health and Hospital's $190 million budget (Price 1994a, A1). Wishard Hospital accounted for most of these resources—the Public Health Department, responsible for environmental health and public health programs, had 505 employees and a budget of $23.5 million (Fahy 1994, B1).

The environmental health community viewed the appointment with concern and uncertainty for two reasons: Roob's lack of experience and his role as "one of the architects of Mayor Stephen Goldsmith's reorganizations that resulted in layoffs in several city departments . . . " (Schoch 1994b, B1). Roob, age 32 at the time of his appointment, had no prior experience in public health or health care administration, and Goldsmith, the Board, and Roob did not appear to believe that experience and knowledge in the field were needed to run the organization. The *Indianapolis Star* reported, "Regarded by some as Mayor Stephen Goldsmith's 'fair-haired' boy, Roob cheerfully concedes he had no health care experience before he began overseeing about 3,750 employees at Wishard and the Marion County Health Department" (Price 1994a, A1).

Reacting to a question about Roob's lack of health experience, Goldsmith responded, "He didn't have road experience before he went to the transportation department . . . It's far more important to have extremely capable generalists who are committed to serving the customer. They can learn the technical aspects" (Price 1994a, A1). Some viewed this attitude as naïve and not consistent with Goldsmith's intention of "running government like a business"—would a major health care organization in the private sector hire a generalist, with limited management experience and no understanding of its core business, to manage the organization?

The second major concern about Roob's appointment was his intention to bring competition with the private sector to Health and

Hospital (Schoch 1994a, B7). Roob identified only one government service that would be off limits to privatization: national defense (Morgan 1994, D1). "You don't ever stop competing the work . . . The only way is to measure yourself in the marketplace every day. Constantly focusing on the customer—that's the only way we'll do it." (Morgan 1994, D1). But who was the customer?

One unidentified Health and Hospital employee captured the mood of the organization given Roob's history of orchestrating layoffs at the city—"a lot of people are paranoid about it" (Schoch 1994b, B1). Staff fears were confirmed on "Black Thursday," (May 19, 1994) when Roob announced the layoff of 41 employees to cover an operating deficit of $750,000 at the Health Department (Fahy 1994).

Under the Goldsmith administration, the relative independence that Health and Hospital had enjoyed under the previous mayor changed. Roob espoused Goldsmith's theme of "reducing government control by turning the public's business over to private interests" (Goldsmith 1997, 70). This sentiment played well to much of the business sector, especially among those who were dissatisfied with Health and Hospital's actions on public and environmental health and safety issues.

It was clear from the beginning that Roob would be a hands-on executive director. In one example, Roob did not like *Indianapolis Star* reporting about the possibility of histoplasmosis at a controversial public-private land swap[8] supported by the Goldsmith administration. Roob insisted the site was not a "confirmed location of any histoplasmosis concerns" and he opposed precautions that were favored by physicians. (He also placed a moratorium on staff discussions with the reporter who broke the story.) (*Indianapolis Star* 1996a). The previous executive directors left the handling of these issues with the medical director, and Roob's intervention was unprecedented.

Over time, it appeared that the Public Health Director, and consequently the Public Health Department, was losing its independence as Roob became more directly involved in setting policy for the Health Department and in its day-to-day operation. Under Roob, political considerations appeared to play a more active role in the public health policy-making process, and greater emphasis was placed on political dimensions rather than on public health and safety.[9]

The Process for Reinventing Local Government Regulations

The Regulatory Study Commission

The review of Health and Hospital's environmental health regulations had its roots in the Regulatory Study Commission (RSC) that was established by Mayor Goldsmith shortly after he took office. According to Goldsmith, the purpose of the RSC was to "create a balance" between regulators and the regulated community:

> We established the Regulatory Study Commission (RSC) to act as a counterweight to the good intentions of bureaucrats and other well-meaning regulators by examining existing regulations and helping to eliminate outdated, unneeded, and often counterproductive rules. (Goldsmith 1997, 87-88)

The chairman of the RSC was James Sommer, of Sommer & Barnard, a legal firm in Indianapolis; other members were drawn from the business community.[10] The RSC developed a set of eight principles that would guide each review and a standardized format for reporting on the findings of the reviews. The eight review principles were:

1) Regulations should reflect values for which there is a substantial community consensus.
2) Regulations must have legal authorization and not violate the Indiana or Federal Constitution.
3) Regulations must not impose costs (on regulated parties and on consumers of goods and services provided by regulated parties) that exceed the benefits conferred on the community.
4) Regulations should be enforceable. A regulation that cannot be practically enforced will create an unfair result: citizens who comply with the regulation will bear burdens that those who should, but do not comply, do not bear.
5) Regulations should not be replicative. Where Federal or State laws or regulations are in effect in a subject matter area, the RSC will make an initial assumption that the area should not be further regulated by local government. A very strong showing must be made to justify adoption of local regulations in such an instance. If local government has a choice about whether to enforce Federal or State laws or regulations through adoption of a local regulation, a "clear benefit to the community" standard should be applied in making that decision.
6) Regulations should impose the minimum constraints needed to achieve the regulatory goal.

7) Regulations should be simple. A complex regulation reduces the level of public understanding and increases the difficulty of complying with it.

8) Regulations should be clearly expressed and written in a manner to facilitate compliance. (Regulatory Study Commission 1996)

These principles, which were at the heart of Goldsmith's deregulatory "reinvention" philosophy, are, on their face, eminently reasonable. But the way in which they were defined was hostile to any true regulatory review and placed the proponents of local regulation at a significant disadvantage. The idea that regulations should be "practically enforceable" (Principle 4) provided an important platform for the argument to deregulate. Practically enforceable meant "that the enforcing agency would be able to enforce according to its terms, relative to all situations regulated, with a substantial degree of success, and within a reasonable time frame" (RRC 1996a, 16). Showing that a regulation would not meet this test would be relatively easy, and, as discussed below, the Mayor's staff attempted to argue that the housing code was not practically enforceable under this definition.

The imposition of the strictly worded cost benefit analysis in Principal 3 imposed a heavy burden on citizens in favor of regulation. The costs of regulation are relatively easy to define, but quantifying the benefits can be challenging, not because they do not exist, but because of the complexity of the task.

Principle 5 addresses the concern of the regulatory burden imposed by multiple authorities regulating the same areas. Multiple or differing regulations at the federal, state, and local levels do increase the complexity and expense of compliance for the regulated community. Balancing the public health and safety needs of the community with the economic interests of business has become an increasingly difficult and challenging task. Nevertheless, communities must have the flexibility and ability to address the needs of their communities, which may not be reflected in minimum federal or state standards.

Principle 6 is difficult to argue against. Of course, regulations should not be overly burdensome. However, the interpretation of what constitutes minimum constraints can pose serious difficulties, especially if the real goal is to diminish or remove local government oversight.

Even the first principle proved to be problematic because the deregulators initially intended to conduct the review deliberations behind closed doors and with only representatives of the business community—an action that would make it impossible to reflect the values of the community or even to know if a community consensus existed on particular regulations.

The Indianapolis Chamber of Commerce Singles Out Health and Hospital

In 1995 the Indianapolis Chamber of Commerce had developed an agenda for the city in a report, *Business Agenda 1996 - 1999 Strategies for a Successful Community*, which was addressed to candidates for Indianapolis mayor (Goldsmith was running for a second term) and City-County Council. This report, which detailed strategies to improve the business and economic environment of Indianapolis, singled out Health and Hospital and called for a complete audit of its activities that regulated business (Indianapolis Chamber of Commerce n.d., 1).

Goldsmith and the Chamber of Commerce had developed close ties. In his letter to Roob, calling for the regulatory review of Health and Hospital, Goldsmith states:

> The Chamber and I agree that economic prosperity depends upon limiting government regulation of business to that which is justified, cost effective and streamlined. Duplicative, over-reaching and unjustified regulation of business, is logically, a detriment to business growth and economic prosperity. (Goldsmith 1995a)

Interestingly, of the twenty-three initiatives advocated by the Chamber in the *Business Agenda*, only one singled out a city-county agency for special treatment:

> Increased Accountability for Health and Hospital Corporation
> A complete audit of Health & Hospital's activities which regulate business should be undertaken in order to assess similarity or duplication with other units of government, and overlapping functions should be transferred to appropriate city agencies. (Indianapolis Chamber of Commerce n.d., 2)

There was some overlap between the city's environmental and the County's environmental health programs—for example, Health and Hospital and the Department of Public Works both had program responsibilities in water quality control and hazardous materials. However, over the years, the agencies had been able to effectively integrate their activities, and working relationships among the staff generally were free from inter-agency rivalries. If environmental programs were to be consolidated, it arguably would have been more logical to move the Department of Public Works' programs to Health and Hospital and integrate them into the Bureau of Environmental Health. Health and Hospital had a larger program, both in number of staff and breadth of responsibilities. There was also concern that "the fox was guarding the hen house" because the city's wastewater treatment facilities were located in the same agency that also regulated air and water pollution from the facilities. From the public health and environmental community perspective, another important reason for locating these programs in Health and Hospital, not Public Works, was the relatively greater independence of Health and Hospital from the influence of the mayor's office. However, this was probably the very reason the Chamber wanted to transfer Health and Hospital's programs to the city.

Under the area of business regulation, the Chamber called for additional initiatives including:

- a one-year regulatory moratorium,
- review of all regulatory ordinances and regulations over a three-year period,
- expiration of all regulatory ordinances and regulations after five years unless reenacted, and
- elimination of local ordinances and regulations which were more stringent than state or federal counterparts, unless an overwhelming need could be justified through a cost-benefit analysis.

Goldsmith Announces Regulatory Review for Health and Hospital

On January 17, 1995 Goldsmith initiated the regulatory review of the Health and Hospital Corporation by asking Eugene (Gene) Lausch, a city official and RSC staff member, to get someone "to look at high-cost regulations at Health and Hospital" (Goldsmith 1995a). Information gathering about Health and Hospital's environmental health programs actually had started soon after the RSC was formed, but early in 1995 this process became more formalized when the RSC assigned a staff member to "monitor H&H full time" (Ashley 1995, 13). Goldsmith issued the formal request for the review of Health and Hospital's environmental health programs on October 25, 1995 (Goldsmith 1995b). The stakeholders that were listed for the review process included the Chamber, public health officials and neighborhood leaders, but Goldsmith forecast the prominence of the business community in the process:

The Chamber has offered to participate actively in thoughtful analysis and review of environmental policy and resultant environmental regulation or other means of protecting the public health. I would like this process to ensure that truly verifiable health and safety hazards are subject to Health and Hospital regulation only after other alternative methods, including market-based environmental protection, are sufficiently explored. Such a review can not (sic) be complete without the involvement and participation of public health officials and neighborhood leaders.

I believe that some of the regulations of Health and Hospital needlessly drive economic development across the county line and reduce small minority and women ownded (sic) business opportunities. Further, they increase the cost on urban residents who can least afford it by driving costs higher than necessary to secure the health and safety required. (Goldsmith 1995b)

This letter set the stage for the battles that were to follow. Goldsmith's emphasis on "truly verifiable health and safety hazards" and "regulation only after alternative methods, including market-based environmental protection, are sufficiently explored" pitted the public health community's philosophy of "preventing disease and injury and promoting wellness" against the Mayor and those in the business community who wanted to deregulate and privatize governmental services. Goldsmith's plan called for the sunsetting, or termination, of all "unnecessary regulations and providing a sharper focus to justifiable regulation" at Health and Hospital by the end of 1996 (Goldsmith 1995a). In response, the Board of Trustees passed the previously discussed ordinances to review and sunset regulations in Chapters 8 through 22 of its regulatory code. These chapters encompassed the following topics:

- Food Establishments and Food Vending (Chapters 8 and 9)
- Solid Waste and Refuse Containers (Chapters 12 and 13)
- Hazardous Materials (Chapter 20)
- Housing and Unwholesome Substances (Chapters 10 and 17)
- Commercial Premises (Chapter 19)
- Child Facilities (Chapter 11)
- Private Sewage Disposal, Swimming Pools and Wells (Chapters 14, 16 and 18)
- Administrative Hearings and Violations Bureau/Administrative Fees

The Board directed the review to include, but not be limited to, an "analysis of the rationale and costs of regulating under such Chapters" (Health and Hospital 1995a). The Board found that these Chapters "have not, historically, been subject to periodic review to determine the effectiveness of or the continuing need for such ordinances" (Health and Hospital 1995a, Sec. 1). This statement, which also appears in the parallel review process for the city, is somewhat misleading and gives the impression that the ordinances (and by association, the organization) were stagnant, frozen in time. In fact, the ordinances had been amended over time on an as needed basis, but they had not been subjected to a formal outside review process that considered all of the ordinances in their entirety and as a group.

The Board directed Roob, with Board approval, to appoint a panel (the Regulatory Review Commission) to review Chapters 8 through 22 to:

- improve regulation,
- avoid the maintenance of obsolete or ineffective regulations,
- eliminate unnecessary duplication, and
- ensure that regulation is efficiently conducted and to further the mission of Health and Hospital and the health, welfare, and best interests of the residents of Marion County. (Health and Hospital 1995a, Sec. 1 and 3)

Allan Hubbard, an Indianapolis businessman and past director of former Vice President Dan Quayle's Council on Competitiveness, was selected by Goldsmith to chair the Regulatory Review Commission. Eight work groups would conduct the reviews; each had a moderator who was to be linked to the Commission through a Commission member. The role of the Commission member was to bring oversight to the work group and advise it during its deliberations.

As the process was outlined, the moderators were responsible for "compiling all data and information presented to the work group in the course of its deliberations into a report . . . " (Uhl 1995). The original framework for conducting the reviews outlined a process in which each work group would formulate a study outline that called for developing an understanding of the regulated areas, conducting an analysis and making recommendations (Health and Hospital 1996a; RRC 1996c). At the end of the review process each work group would develop a report of its findings, which could include recommendations to remove or revise ordinances. The Commission's representative to each of the work groups would be responsible for presenting the report to the Commission, which, in turn, would deliberate and make recommendations to the Health and Hospital Board of Trustees. The Board retained the right to adopt or reject any of the recommended changes.

Based on the Mayor's call for the review and the Board's directive and ordinance requiring the review, it could be surmised that the process would be inclusive and embody the principle of public participation and a democratic process. Unfortunately, as events unfolded, many neighborhood stakeholders and other observers believed that the process was stacked against them from the beginning.

Some Opinions about the Review

At the time, there were differing opinions about the true intention of the review. The print media, including two business publications, welcomed and applauded the project. One of the editorials opined that regulatory review was a cure for the "overreg-it is" malady that the Health and Hospital suffered from (*Indianapolis News* 1995a). Additional editorial comments included:

The project is an extension of the Goldsmith administration's push to eliminate unnecessary government regulation and red tape (*Indianapolis Star* 1995a).

The goal is to eliminate duplicate or unnecessary regulations that levy excessive costs on businesses, whose owners should welcome the opportunity—and be prepared—to give their input to these review groups (*Indianapolis Star* 1995a).

What the Goldsmith administration wants is for the HHC environmental health regulations to be examined for possible elimination or replacement (*Indianapolis Business Journal*, 1995).

Regulatory review is good government (*Indianapolis Business Journal*, 1995).

Some of these regulations were written as many as four decades ago and have not been systematically reviewed since. This is what happens so often with government. Old rules develop lives of their own, resistant to change and common sense. Times change, but regulations don't. (*Indianapolis Business Journal*, 1995)

This is what we see as the most significant aspect of the proposed changes. Unless regulations are reviewed periodically, they can pile up on each other, creating massive bureaucracies . . . . But government must also be willing to eliminate regulations that no longer serve a purpose. For that reason, the HHC review is a good step toward greater government efficiency. (*Indianapolis Business Journal*, 1995)

An article that appeared in *Indianapolis C.E.O.* just after the sunsetting action of the Board was particularly troubling to staff, neutral observers, and supporters of the Health Department. One of the headlines on the front page of the magazine stated: "Pulling the Plug on a County Tyrant. Health and Hospital's regulation reign of terror ends?" (Ashley, 1995). The anti-government and anti-Health and Hospital posture was amply represented by the article's heavy-handed and biased rhetoric:

> Hated. Feared. Reviled. Those are just a few of the adjectives that describe the relationship between Indianapolis' health department—Health and Hospital Corp.—and Realtors, builders, restaurant owners, grocers and myriad others who fall under H&H's thousands of regulations. (Ashley 1995, 12)

> One of central Indiana's most unpopular governmental agencies has finally cried, "Uncle!" to pressure from the mayor's office, the Indianapolis Chamber of Commerce and thousands of businesses. But although Health and Hospital Corp. has sunsetted all its rules and regulations effective Jan. 1, 1997, the fight to redefine its power has just begun. (Ashley 1995, 12)

In this article, all of the quotes, except one, from businesses about Health and Hospital's performance were negative toward the agency. Some in the public health and environmental community took a wait-and-see attitude. However, neighborhood organizations throughout Indianapolis and Marion County believed the Goldsmith administration's interest in environment, public health and safety was largely political rhetoric, a smoke screen for accomplishing the ideological goal of freeing the marketplace of "misguided government interference" (Goldsmith 1997, 87). As discussed previously, this view was bolstered by Goldsmith's anti-regulatory rhetoric and actions, his lack of interest in environmental issues and his unwillingness to involve environmental stakeholders in decision-making (see also Chapter 12).

The cautious attitude by the environmental community and staff was heightened by some of the public comments of Goldsmith and his administration:

> Goldsmith . . . expects the H&H Sunset ordinance to substantially change the regulatory climate of Indianapolis. "We should be able to make a pretty substantial dent in some of the irrational regulations, the mayor adds. " (Ashley 1995, 13)

The whole Sunset direction could end up being a big *el floppo*, but it has intriguing possibilities, says Bill Styring, chairman of Goldsmith's regulatory study commission [sic]. You may find the H&H board inclined to take a skeptical view of some of their regulations when their noses are rubbed in them. (Ashley 1995, 13)

The perception that Roob was an extension of Goldsmith was fueled by Roob's comments, including: "I technically don't work for the mayor anymore, but frankly, I still morally work for him. I am one of his lieutenants." Roob's view of the Bureau of Environmental Health and its staff appeared to be ambiguous—in one quote, Roob commented that environmental health "operates pretty efficiently," but his subsequent remarks about Health and Hospital's regulations and staff gave mixed messages. For example, "H&H doesn't have to do that stuff. It has just evolved that way over the years." (Ashley 1995, 13)

"Are there isolated instances where H&H has been arbitrary and vindictive?" Roob repeats, "Yes, there are. Is it pervasive in the organization? I don't think so. The vast majority of our employees are dedicated." (Ashley 1995, 17)

Another View—Citizens Protest a Closed and Flawed Process

The initial meeting of the Regulatory Review Commission was in December 1995. At this meeting, Allan Hubbard, the Chairman, began the session with the comment, "we want to encourage an environment that does not have a negative impact on health" (Schoch 1995, B-2). In response, Phillip D. Pecar, both a commissioner and member of the Health and Hospital Corporation's Board of Trustees, suggested the group "turn that around and make it: have a positive impact on health" (Schoch, 1995a, B-2). At first glance this may appear to be a trivial clarification, but it represented fundamental differences—among the players—on the goal of Health and Hospital's environmental health programs and what regulatory review should accomplish. The deregulators—as represented by the Mayor and his administration, the Regulatory Study and Review commissioners, the moderators and work groups, and some in the business community—were intent on a controlled process. They wanted a process that would ensure the outcome that the Mayor and the Indianapolis Chamber of Commerce were anticipating: deregulation and transfer of environmental health programs away from the "rogue" agency. The public health and environmental communities, primarily neighborhood organizations and professionals in the field, initially expected to work in collaboration with the administration. They quickly realized this would not be possible. They realized that they would have to fight to keep programs that were working from being decimated by the deregulators (Walker, 2000).

Should the Meetings be Open? Should Everyone be Represented in the Deliberations?

Conflicts over meetings and who would participate started almost immediately. According to *The Indianapolis Star* (Niederpruem 1995), neighborhood groups, and apparently Health and Hospital staff, were surprised to learn that the study groups' meetings would be closed. The neighborhoods vigorously protested this secrecy. The Marion County Alliance of Neighborhood Associations, Inc. (McANA), an umbrella organization that encompassed other neighborhood organizations took a lead role in protesting the closed door meetings and lack of non-business citizen representation on the work groups. The Butler Tarkington Neighborhood Association (BTNA), a founding member of McANA, distributed a flyer in which it stated:

> As originally designed, the de-regulators' plan called for only the de-regulators to do the reviewing of the ordinances—with no public oversight or input. McANA protested the lack of public participation to the Mayor and was ignored. McANA took the issue to the media. (BTNA n. d.)

The decision to close work group meetings was confirmed in the media by Indianapolis Deputy Mayor Skip Stitt and Sue Uhl, Deputy Corporation Counsel and Counsel to the Regulatory Review Commission. Both were strong proponents of closed meetings. Work would be done in private and only the recommendations would be made public. The decision to keep the meetings closed appeared to be a deliberate attempt to circumvent meaningful public participation. Steve Key, government affairs director for the Hoosier State Press Association, commented: "They're within the rules. They did their homework" (Neiderpruem 1995)

Deputy Mayor Stitt attempted to rationalize the need for secrecy by stressing that the short timetable for the work "would make it almost impossible to notify the public" and that many members "would be meeting informally and at the spur of the moment." According to Stitt group members might also " . . . meet in a library and pore over a journal. Consultations could occur daily, if not more often, ... "

(Niederpruem 1995)

In this same article, Harold Anderson, President of McANA, expressed his group's concerns:

> The mentality of this group is going to be less than acceptable . . . . We've only been told that there are too many ordinances, that state law and city ordinances may be in conflict and overlap, that the business community has too many hoops to jump through. . . . If it is , so what? That's the cost of doing business. (Niederpruem 1995)

The *Indianapolis Star*, which initially had been supportive of the review, echoed the community's concerns in one of its editorials:

> The process set up to review Marion County's health and environmental code hasn't quite begun yet, but it is already proving to be seriously flawed. . . . This is a case in which the public interest requires more than the law.
>
> Any secrecy casts doubt on whether the stated goal is the real goal, or whether a hidden agenda could be at work.
>
> Anderson is right. Meetings of the study groups should be opened up to public scrutiny. For public input to be meaningful, it must occur during the research phase of the overhaul, not at the end.
>
> Otherwise, any final recommendations will lack credibility, which is an essential part of the regulatory review process. (*Indianapolis Star* 1995b)

The public furor and unfavorable media coverage were instrumental in opening the meetings to the public. Dr. Henry Bock, a member of Health and Hospital's Board of Trustees, raised concerns at the December Board meeting. He suggested that Commission change its policy "so there would be an opportunity for the public to provide input" and to provide "some public forum where the public would be invited to comment on any changes that would occur to the regulations." Although a formal vote was not taken, the Board of Trustees, which felt strongly that meetings should be open, made its wishes known to the Commission. (Niederpruem 1996)

About three weeks after the Board of Trustees meeting, the Regulatory Review Commission responded to the Board, and opened the process, but not entirely:

- work groups were to include neighborhood representatives and staff[11] in addition to persons or businesses subject to the regulations;
- all work group and Commission meetings would be open to the public (Board meetings were already open to the public);
- each Commission and Board meeting would be the subject of published notice; and
- at least two work group meetings would be subject to published notice. (Health and Hospital 1996a)

The issue of participation and open meetings continued to be controversial, even to the end of the process. Although the neighborhoods were now able to join in the work group deliberations, their interests were still at a significant disadvantage for three reasons. First, the eight work groups had a total of 46 members (including eight Health and Hospital staff). However, there were only eight neighborhood representatives, one in each of the work groups. There were two members from Health and Hospital's Board of Trustees and the remaining members were drawn from the business community. Second, the neighborhoods did not have a representative on the Regulatory Review Commission, the group that would make final recommendations to Health and Hospital's Board of Trustees. Third, the leadership of the work groups (moderators and the commission representatives) did not include the neighborhoods (Health and Hospital 1996b).

Another sore point was the fact that William Styring, well known for his anti-regulatory views, would play a leading role in the process. Not only was he a member of the Mayor's RSC, but he was also hired to chair two of the work groups (foods and childcare) and he provided testimony to the work groups, which seemed to be a conflict of interest to some observers. Three other moderators were all deregulators: Sue Uhl (commercial premises and sewage disposal/swimming pools/wells) wielded considerable power as attorney to the Commission and she was also Health and Hospital's counsel. Tom Rose (administrative hearings and fees) and Gene Lausch (housing) were members of the Mayor's RSC staff. In addition, John Myrland, President of the Indianapolis Chamber of Commerce, (and Chairman of the Mayor's RSC) also served on the administrative work group (this group considered hearings and fees).

The fact that most of the work group meetings, at which the recommendations were to be developed, would still be held without published notice was also a concern. Interested parties would have to call the hotline (which seldom worked) if they wanted to be aware of the meeting dates, times, and locations.

Sue Uhl, the Commission's attorney, was among the administration's representatives who continued to state that formal postings of meetings were not required under Indiana's Open Door law because the work groups were appointed by Health and Hospital's staff, not by the Commission or the Commission's Chairperson. The *Indianapolis News* criticized this continuing attempt to circumvent public participation:

> While the creation of these groups may somehow keep them from falling under the Open Door Law, there is little question that the work they will be doing is public business. . . . According to the Open Door Law, a group does not have to make final decisions to be taking official action. The law defines "official action" as any of the following:
> * Receive information
> * Deliberate
> * Make recommendations
> * Establish policy
> * Make decisions
> * Take final action (*Indianapolis News* 1996, A06)

The editorial went on to note that the work groups and the Commission would in fact be doing all of these activities and would be taking official action. A final quotation summarizes the feelings of many: "Each step is a link in the chain of doing the public's business, and the public deserves to know about and input at each step, regardless of how the work groups came to be" (*Indianapolis News* 1996, A06).

This rough beginning reinforced for many citizens the suspicion that the Goldsmith administration wanted to limit public involvement in order to achieve its predetermined goal of deregulation. The process, as revealed by available documentation, continued to be flawed and anti-democratic. The deregulators attempted to 1) change and manipulate the Board's charge to the work groups, 2) misrepresent or ignore work group deliberations with which they disagreed and 3) submit reports for review without the approval of the work groups. All of these efforts were intended to enhance the likelihood of deregulation.

Trying to Get a Second Bite at the Apple

In June 1996, nearly at the end of the review process, the *Indianapolis Star* reported that some of the work group reports were being written to reflect the opinions of the administration, not those of the work group members (Fahy 1996). This report was disturbing, but not unexpected because the struggle between the administration's deregulators and the neighborhood pro-regulatory forces had never stopped. Mary Walker, the neighborhood representative who kept detailed notes and recorded each meeting she attended, recollected that the process "got ugly" when it became clear the work groups were supporting (and in some instances strengthening) the existing regulations instead of the efforts to deregulate (Walker, 2000). She believed that the role of the moderator in almost all of the work groups, except those that had a member of Health and Hospital's Board of Trustees as the link to the Commission, had devolved into that of a strongman, who often acted independently of the work group in formulating issues and reports in an effort to keep deregulation alive. Her recollection is supported by documentation involving both sides of the debate.

One of the strategies used by the deregulators to manipulate the outcome was to replace work group recommendations with "discussion items." For example, the *Indianapolis Star* reported that the Food WorkGroup approved a report on April 30 that stated that thrift stores, variety stores, and produce stands should continue to be licensed. However, the administration, as represented by the moderator of the work group, prepared a May 14 report in which the regulation of these types of stores was called a "discussion issue." In other words, the recommendation approved by the work group was ignored and the deregulators had a second chance to provide the Commission with an opportunity to vote on deregulation.[12] (Fahy 1996)

In a second example, members of the Housing WorkGroup agreed that Health and Hospital should keep rules requiring gutters, exterior door locks, exterior paint, and handrails on stairways. However, the moderator drafted a report on behalf of the work group that also called the elimination of these requirements a "discussion issue," and "suggested they may not be closely related to public health and safety" (Fahy 1996). This position was diametrically opposed to the actual conclusions reached in the work group.[13]

The moderator of the Housing WorkGroup prepared at least seven drafts for the members to review (RRC, 1996 a, c-m). These reports show the progression from recommendations (in the first three drafts) to recommendations and discussion issues (fourth draft) and only discussion issues (drafts five through seven). The distinction between recommendations and discussion issues was significant: "Recommendations are suggestions for action on which members of the Workgroup agreed . . . Discussion issues are possible actions that at least some members thought should be presented for informed consideration by the Commission" (RRC, 1996f). This meant the rules of the game had changed. The decisions of the work group, which were reached through a deliberative process that took place over months of study and discussion, could be circumvented by a moderator or any unknown or unnamed member who was not satisfied with the outcome.

Citizens and work group members protested this action through the press and in written communications to the work group and commission members (Fahy 1996; Horseman 1996a; King, et al. 1996; Walker 1996a,b, c). These comments were made by representatives of the neighborhoods about one of the Moderator's drafts of the Housing WorkGroup report:

> . . . six of the recommendations adopted by the workgroup were not presented as recommendations but instead were presented in Part II as issues to be additionally discussed and ultimately decided by the full Commission, affording advocates against the workgroup's recommendations a "second bite at the apple" after being unsuccessful at swaying the workgroup's opinion. The format of Part II does not reflect the consensus of a majority of the workgroup which adopted actual recommendations regarding the discussion issues. (King et al. 1996)

The Housing WorkGroup protested, but the Moderator refused to change the report to reflect the group's recommendations. In response, the Housing WorkGroup required the Moderator to identify his report titles with the language, "drafted by the Moderator" (RRC 1996a, l). Ultimately, when the Moderator's final Housing WorkGroup report to the Commission did not reflect the consensus of the work group, an alternative report, which was framed in recommendations reached by the work group, was submitted to the Regulatory Review Commission (Walker, 1996a).

In a third example, members of the Child Care Facilities WorkGroup also submitted an alternative report to the Regulatory Review Commission in which it was charged that the moderator did not "accurately reflect the testimony presented during the public hearings . . . this report does not represent the consensus of the Workgroup as to the value and significance of the Ordinance" (Burton et al. 1996).

In a fourth example, the author of the report on public swimming pool, spa and beaches regulation acknowledged that there were issues not discussed by the work group members. But, the author "preserved" these issues by listing them and providing alternatives to the existing regulatory framework (RRC 1996o, 8).

Representatives of the Goldsmith administration attempted to defend their actions of "baiting and switching" at the end of the process. Sue Uhl, attorney to the Commission, acknowledged that officials modified proposals approved by the work groups "to preserve issues for the review commission to discuss" (Fahy 1996). Allan Hubbard, the Chairman of the Commission, wrote, "It is not necessary for the work group to reach a consensus" (Fahy 1996).

Although the Chairman and the Commission may have decided that they could ignore the deliberations of the work groups, it is clear that the work groups did not share this opinion, and debate over this point continued until the end of the Commission's review. One week prior to the Commission's discussion of the Housing WorkGroup Report, Gene Lausch (moderator of the Housing WorkGroup) in a memorandum to Chairman Hubbard stated that the neighborhood groups "acceded on the issue of the authority of the Commission to ask that issues be preserved for Commission discussion and action" (Lausch, 1996). However, the alternative report, which includes recommendations but no discussion items, indicates that this was not the case:

> The Moderator's "report" contains language that the Workgroup had voted to change or delete, does not contain information that the Workgroup voted to include, contains significant omissions and insertions that the Workgroup did not approve, misrepresents positions held by Workgroup members, misstates the ordinance and the facts, and continues to assert a negative tone that the Workgroup does not share. (Walker 1996a, 1)

The fact that the reports were changed to reflect a deregulation agenda, which was not part of the work groups' findings, reinforces the conclusion that the Goldsmith administration was ideologically driven and willing to circumvent the democratic process to achieve its ends:

> This handling of the work group recommendations has raised concerns that the panels are being sidestepped by aides to Mayor Stephen Goldsmith, who are overseeing the review process. The mayor, a candidate for governor, has made more-efficient government a priority. (Fahy 1996)

Arguments to Deregulate Housing Code Enforcement

The issues discussed by the Housing WorkGroup are too numerous to detail in this chapter, but a few examples are discussed below to illustrate the Goldsmith administration's "deregulate at all costs" philosophy. Most of the arguments made by the administration in favor of deregulation were the result of a flawed logic at best, or, at worst, little or no understanding of and regard for the public health and safety issues being considered. Even when it became abundantly clear that citizens of the neighborhoods throughout Marion County strongly supported the existing housing code enforcement ordinance and Health and Hospital's housing enforcement staff, the Goldsmith administration continued its efforts to deregulate, even to the point of attempting to misrepresent findings, as noted in the previous section.

The arguments for housing code deregulation were centered on key questions:

- Is there an empirically demonstrable relationship between Chapter 10 provisions and health and safety risks?
- What is the effect of Chapter 10 enforcement on housing in different neighborhoods?
- Are the provisions of Chapter 10 practically enforceable?
- Do Chapter 10 provisions inappropriately alter the pattern of rights and responsibilities to landlords and tenants?
- Do the benefits of enforcing Chapter 10 provisions outweigh the costs of such enforcement?

Before each of these questions is discussed, a brief history of the development of housing codes provides a context for understanding the Health and Hospital regulations.

Historical Perspective on Housing Codes[14]

Housing code enforcement is not new to this century—its roots date to the Colonial era in American history. In the early to mid-1600s, there were housing regulations to prohibit the construction of wooden chimneys and thatched roofs that resulted in frequent fires; prohibitions against throwing rubbish and filth into streets or canals; and residents were required to keep the streets clean and orderly. As America grew, large cities with serious housing problems emerged. Immigrants, who were crammed into unhealthy and unsafe tenements, provided the impetus for housing code enforcement in New York City and the first comprehensive legislation to address the problems of substandard housing—the Tenement Housing Act of 1867. The provisions of this act were intended to reduce crowding (and the diseases spread by crowding) and to improve sewage disposal, lighting and ventilation.[15]

The Tenement Housing Act of 1867 was beneficial, but had gaps and inadequacies that were addressed in 1879 by a second act and subsequent amendments. Efforts to enforce these occupancy standards were ineffective, and slumlords failed to remedy identified problems. In a pivotal case, Trinity Church, the largest owner of tenements in New York City, challenged the constitutionality of the Act in 1892. In this case, the City of New York accused Trinity Church of violating the provisions of the Act of 1882, by failing to provide running water on every floor of its buildings. A district court levied a fine of $200 against the Church, which in turn appealed to the Court of Common Pleas. The Court set the law as aside as unconstitutional,[16] but eventually the law was upheld. Living conditions in New York City continued to improve with the Tenement House Act of 1901, and the basic principles and methods embodied in this law still provide the foundation for housing code legislation in today's American cities.[17]

An important step toward defining minimum standards of acceptable housing that could be applied nationwide occurred in 1939 when a national committee of experts in the American Public Health Association (APHA) published *Basic Principles of Healthful Housing*. This document was used by local governing bodies as a basis for more comprehensive standards for occupied housing. A decade later, the federal Housing Act of 1949 defined a national policy for housing that included "a decent home and suitable living environment for every American family" (Mood 1986, 76). The basis of this policy was "general agreement among public health officials that the quality of housing and the residential environment have great influence upon the physical and mental health and the social well-being of each individual, and in turn, upon the economic, political, and social conditions of every community" (Mood 1986, 1).

This early action fell short, however, and today there are no federally defined minimum standards for "decent home" and "suitable living environment," and it is up to local jurisdictions to define these terms. To fill this gap and provide guidance for eliminating the serious health hazards associated with substandard housing, the American Public Health Association's expert committee published *A Proposed Housing Ordinance* in 1952. This model code, which is now called the *APHA–CDC Recommended Minimum Housing Standards*, has been revised over the years and serves as a model for state and city housing codes (including the Marion County code) throughout the nation. It is against this history of housing code enforcement that the deregulation efforts were framed.

Is there an empirically demonstrable relationship between Chapter 10 provisions and health and safety risks?

Is there a direct relationship between housing code provisions and public health and safety? According to public health officials throughout the United States and the world, the answer is an unequivocal "yes" both historically and today. During the regulatory review process the following individuals and organizations also answered "yes" as they gave resounding support to Health and Hospital's housing program and its enforcement of the housing code:

- citizens represented by over 70 neighborhood organizations throughout Marion County,[18, 19]
- the Indianapolis Fire Department,[20]
- the Indiana Coalition on Housing and Homeless Issues, Inc.,[21]
- the Citizens Neighborhood Coalition, Inc.,[22]
- the Indianapolis Police Department,[23]
- Indianapolis Downtown, Inc.,[24] and
- the Marion County Prosecutor's Office[25]

In a May 11 draft report of the Housing WorkGroup, the deregulators, as represented by the Goldsmith administration's Moderator of the Housing WorkGroup, agreed that better housing had historically contributed to improved human health and longevity, but . .

While adequate housing appears to contribute to improved health and safety, it is difficult to establish a direct relationship between many housing code provisions and public health and safety. Empirical data is not generally available to show that adherence to one standard will promote health while allowing a somewhat less restrictive standard will degrade it.[26] (RRC 1996c, 11)

While the empirical relationship between the public health and safety provisions of Chapter 10 is difficult to establish, there would appear to be some situations where the relationship is clear . . . (RRC 1996c, 11).[27]

The May 11 draft report included an additional sentence, which was dropped from subsequent drafts because of vigorous protests from the neighborhood representatives:

And accepting the assumption that better housing has a direct and positive effect on human health, it is doubtful if housing codes have more than a marginal overall influence in causing housing to be improved or well maintained (RRC 1996c, 11).

The Moderator identified two situations as presenting a clear relationship to health and safety: lead-based paint and squalid housing. The regulation of lead-based paint in housing and remediation of houses with deteriorated lead-based paint was justified because there was "an increasing body of scientific evidence that shows that lead is harmful to humans, especially children" (RRC 1996b, 19). Squalid housing—"housing in which residents live in filth and perhaps without heat, water, or toilet facilities"—was the second issue that passed the health effects test (RRC 1996b, 19). In this case, the rationale was that squalid housing presents conditions that pose health risks to the person causing the squalid conditions, harms the innocent such as children and negatively affects the quality of life of neighbors and the values of nearby housing units. Health and Hospital estimated that there were about 50 to 80 houses each year that met this definition of squalid housing.

This line of logic provided support for the deregulators' recommendation to "pare back" the code to only the "core concept" provisions that directly related to health and safety (RRC 1996c, 19). The core concept argument was to identify minimum regulatory constraints (Regulatory Review Commission Principle 4) that should be imposed by a housing code, and thereby lessen the regulatory burden on the community so the market could do its work. Under the core concept argument, the only housing code provisions that should be regulated were those supported by scientific evidence or extreme cases of problems. Implicit in these examples is the notion that only certain empirical data or scientific evidence (proof meeting a very high standard such as study designs based on random sampling and tests of statistical significance) would be acceptable for supporting the housing code provisions. A question that begs to be answered is who would decide what evidence is acceptable?

As interpreted by the Moderator on behalf of the deregulators, other parts of the code did not meet the core provision test.[28] For example, there was a proposal to eliminate requirements for gutters, leaders and downspouts because these are not "closely related to health and safety" (RRC 1996l, 11). However, the staff provided the public health reasons why gutters, leaders and downspouts are needed (see endnote 13). Support for the "empirical data" argument came from two dated quotations from the public health field, which were applicable in their day. A 1969 quotation attributed to Dr. Eric Mood was:

Housing legislation usually implies the existence of criteria of acceptability. It suggests that data are available which separate with precision unfit, unsanitary, unsafe, and inadequate housing from that which is decent, clean, safe and sanitary. Unfortunately, such a bank of data does not exist. . . The state of art today is such that there is no single comprehensive evaluation procedure available that will clearly and concisely delineate the presence or absence of a relationship between the quality of housing and health. (RRC 1996b, 18)[29]

The neighborhood groups hotly contested the use of such outdated arguments, which were provided without context.[30] Nearly twenty years after his earlier statement, Dr. Mood, a noted authority on public health and housing, was the Chairman of the Committee on Housing and Health that revised the model housing code. Appendix II of the model code included the following statements by Chester Tate Jr. in 1986:[31]

The relationship between an adequate housing environment and the health status of individual and the community has been clearly demonstrated. Direct effects of the housing environment on health are the most obvious and the easiest to study. Instances of lead poisoning, accidents, contact infections, and enteric diseases resulting from grossly unsanitary methods of waste disposal and/or contaminated water supplies are all directly correlated with residential environmental conditions.

However, numerous studies indicate that housing acts more often as an indirect or passive contributor to adverse resident health, as when overcrowding contributes to the spread of tuberculosis and other respiratory diseases, the lack of home maintenance contributing to rodent infestation, or the lack of adequate ventilation exacerbates existing respiratory diseases. (Mood 1986, 79)

During the next decade, knowledge continued to accrue, and now it is clearly established that overcrowding, lack of home maintenance and poor ventilation all contribute, directly and indirectly, to adverse health and safety effects. In any case whether the effect is direct or indirect is not important from a public health perspective. The salient point is that the relationship exists, and the model housing code, upon which Health and Hospital's code is based, represents the "best thinking of health and housing experts as to what constitutes reasonable minimum public health standards that are attainable, enforceable, and practicable" (Mood 1986, 2). These minimum housing standards are used as a worldwide guideline for determining the acceptability of housing (Salvato 1992, 1176).

As noted in the beginning of this section, the community, including the Mayor's police[32] and fire departments and the Marion County

Prosecutor, provided strong and unequivocal support for the relationship between housing code enforcement and public health and safety (see endnotes 18-25). The deregulators attempted to manipulate science and the debate by structuring the question of health evidence in such a restrictive manner that it would be difficult for citizens (or busy staff) to provide supporting scientific data to justify each provision of the code. This strategy failed.

What is the Effect of Chapter 10 Enforcement on Housing in Different Neighborhoods?

This question developed into one of the most controversial issues raised during the Housing WorkGroup meetings. At the heart of the controversy was a draft report in which the deregulators recommended cutting back housing inspections in the poorest neighborhoods because the code was "not practically enforceable in many inner city and mid city areas in Marion County" (RRC 1996c, 15). Under this deregulation scheme, Health and Hospital would focus its inspection and enforcement on areas where it would be most effective: areas that were basically stable but are showing some signs of distress (RRC 1996c, 21). Overall, this policy would give slumlords relatively free rein.

This recommendation also included a kinder, gentler approach to housing code enforcement that would change the culture of the neighborhood. Under this proposal, Health and Hospital's involvement would be initiated only if a neighborhood requested it. The approach would emphasize establishing informal standards of neighborliness, education, the signing of contracts to fix properties, and using expectations, not legal action to correct problems. (RRC 1996c, 20)

The reaction from the neighborhoods was swift and emphatic. They were not interested in being responsible for correcting code violations, nor did they want poor neighborhoods to receive less code enforcement attention. In fact, they supported Health and Hospital's enforcement program and wanted more of it. Newspaper articles and letters of protest demonstrated a sharp and critical reaction from the public:

"Saying we shouldn't enforce housing codes uniformly is a form of legal apartheid," said Karen Horseman, an attorney who has represented several neighborhood groups. She said recommendations in the report would hasten the decline of poor neighborhoods. (Fahy 1996)

Last night I learned that today May 21 there is a hearing where a recommendation will be made that H&H inspections will not be expected to give citations to folks violating codes in "poor" neighborhoods because it doesn't do any good. This news was quite shocking since I had just left a Citizen's Neighborhood Code Enforcement meeting where we think it does do some good. (Pontious 1996)

The neighborhoods objected strenuously to the attitude of "socio-economic apartheid" apparently espoused by the author(s). . . .The neighborhoods let it be known that all areas and neighborhoods need to receive equal enforcement. (Walker 1996c)

The administration, however, stood behind the deregulation analysis: Deputy Mayor Skip Stitt acknowledged that the "statistics were somewhat in debate," but he called the report "well-researched, thoughtful and inclusive" (Fahy 1996). He further commented that the proposals would allow limited resources to be used efficiently by targeting inspections to "factors that impact health and safety."

The "scientific" underpinning for these and other recommendations was a study, conducted by the Moderator's staff,[33] which attempted to examine the compliance characteristics of five neighborhoods during 1994 and 1995. Each neighborhood had varying rates of poverty (from 6 percent in the most affluent area to roughly a fourth to a third in the least affluent areas), incomes (median income ranged from about $14,000 to $40,000), and home ownership (26 percent to 61 percent). Six performance measures from sampling orders issued during this period were tabulated and the performance of each individual area was compared to the aggregate (averages for each of the measures were compared to one another). This analysis found that total compliance was not achieved on all orders and when compliance was achieved it took a long time. In 1994, the average compliance rate was 47 percent with an average of 290.48 days to comply and in 1995 the compliance rate was 29 percent with an average of 128.76 days to comply (RRC 1996c, 10). Another finding was that the highest rate of compliance was found in the study area with high income, high home ownership. The other study areas "had relatively low compliance rates" (RRC 1996c, 10).

Available documents show that the Health and Hospital's staff were asked to provide data to the Moderator, but the staff were not asked to participate in the original study design and interpretation of the data (Health and Hospital 1996c). As a consequence, the deregulation analysis was highly flawed from start to finish: the methodology was inappropriate and the data were selectively and inappropriately interpreted. Citizens and the Health and Hospital's staff repeatedly criticized the methodology and findings and asked for the removal of this section, but the Moderator continued to include the analysis in his reports (Lausch 1996).[34]

Health and Hospital's staff presented an alternative analysis to the work group in which they demonstrated an overall compliance rate of 79 percent for the five-year period from 1991 through 1995. Compliance ranged from a low of 68 percent in 1994 to a high of 99 percent in 1991. The staff analysis, however, did not appear in any of the Moderator's reports. (Health and Hospital 1996c, d)

Overall, the record reflects that the Goldsmith administration continued to push the deregulation argument that enforcement was not effective despite: 1) a highly flawed analysis, 2) strong protests from neighborhoods, 3) a work group vote to exclude the report in which the material appeared, and 4) an alternative analysis that showed that housing code enforcement was effective. These facts support the neighborhoods' contention that the administration's primary aim was deregulation to reduce costs for landlords, not community improvement.

Are the provisions of Chapter 10 practically enforceable?

One of the principles for the Regulatory Study Commission's review of regulations was that a regulation must be practically enforceable. Under the Goldsmith administration's approach, a regulation that was not practically enforceable was unfair: Those who complied with the regulation would bear the burden of compliance while those who did not comply would not bear these costs. This thinking was consistent with the administration's goals of deregulation. In the absence of regulations, empowered citizens could express their displeasure through market forces and/or use the civil justice system to seek redress.

A few examples may illustrate the logic. Roob believed strongly that Health and Hospital should not regulate public swimming pools, because these regulations were not practically enforceable and in his view there was no clear relationship between code enforcement and health. [35] Under this logic, anyone who swam in a public pool would do so at his or her own risk—a parent in the inner city could sue a pool owner if a child were injured in the pool. A similar logic applied to childcare centers. Rather than regulate childcare centers, a parent could sue the center when their child became ill as a result of poor hygiene or they could take their business elsewhere. As applied to housing, citizens could move out of substandard housing, take a landlord to court, or neighborhoods could assume the responsibility for solving problems themselves. One problem with this logic is that citizens are not equally able to pursue these remedies.

The Moderator of the Housing WorkGroup concluded that the housing code was not practically enforceable in Marion County for three reasons. First, the ordinance was not enforced according to "its own terms" because there were "numerous" code provisions that Health and Hospital decided not to enforce. It is not possible to say exactly what the Moderator intended because the basis for this assertion was never clearly articulated. However, one may assume that this reason refers to items in the code that are not used on a regular basis. For example, Article 8 of the code addresses maximum density and minimum space requirements for each dwelling unit. Unless a complaint was lodged specifically on this issue, an inspector would not be able to know if the space requirements were being violated. If the inspector did not know how many people were using the space, it would be impossible to cite this section of the code. In this instance, Health and Hospital made a policy decision not to "seek and search" for additional occupants, unless there were complaints or evidence to suggest that overcrowding was an issue.

Even so, it would still be important for Health and Hospital to retain the requirement in the code so it could serve as a legal basis for remedying situations in which overcrowding was occurring. In any case, the term "numerous" appears to exaggerate the number of instances when this situation applied. Based on a review of the findings of the Housing WorkGroup, there were only three items in the housing code that were not used on a regular basis, and a related chapter on unwholesome substances was no longer needed because it was covered under other parts of the code.[36]

Second, the Moderator concluded that enforcement "tended to not be uniform" in areas that had many notices of violations because violation notices were issued primarily on a complaint basis. This reason identifies a problem with staffing and resources, rather than a problem with code enforcement. It would be reasonable to assume that if more inspectors were available, more attention could be given to conducting inspections on a basis other than complaint generated inspections.

Third, compliance rates were very low in some areas of the county, especially in poor "weak" areas compared to more affluent areas. As discussed previously, the third reason, lower code enforcement in poor areas compared to more affluent areas, was based on faulty logic and not supported by data. Lower code enforcement in these areas identifies a need for additional resources to assist less affluent citizen so they can live healthy and safe lives, as noted in the Housing WorkGroup recommendations (Walker 1996, 29).

Taken all together, the argument that the housing code was not practically enforceable was another weak attempt by the Goldsmith administration to provide a rationale for deregulation. The neighborhoods and the Housing WorkGroup rejected this rationale, but the Moderator, on behalf of the deregulators, continued to preserve this issue as a discussion item for the Commission.

Do Chapter 10 provisions inappropriately alter the pattern of rights and responsibilities relating to landlords and tenants?

An important charge levied at Health and Hospital by the business community was that the agency was too aggressive, even vindictive, in its inspection efforts. Quotations from the *Indianapolis C.E.O.* article echoed this view. For example, the Government Affairs Director of the Metropolitan Board of Realtors remarked, "One landlord told me that once you get into H&H's bad graces, it will pull your ownership records and go after every single property that you own . . . " (Ashley 1995, 15). A landlord, with more than a dozen citations against his properties, complained about an inspector, "The inspector said she needed to make her quota. . . . If H&H goes into any building, it will come out with citations. There's no doubt about it" (Ashley 1995, 15). Another quote from an unidentified realtor warned that inspectors who did septic inspections should not be allowed into the home, "If an inspector gets inside, . . . he will begin writing citations for other things . . . ; things that have nothing to do with the septic inspection" (Ashley 1995, 13).

These accusations, which range from rogue inspectors to an institutionalized conspiracy against landlords, do not appear to be consistent with an objective review of Health and Hospital's enforcement process. If an inspector exercised bad judgment or engaged in inappropriate behavior, a landlord would have ample opportunity to work within the system to correct a problem.

The enforcement process, which is defined in Article 12 of Chapter 10, begins when an inspector believes there, is a violation of the ordinance that "affects the health of the occupants of any dwelling, dwelling unit or rooming unit or health of the general public."[37] A written notice of the alleged violation must be provided to the responsible person(s), and it must include a statement of why it is being issued, allow a reasonable time for the correction of the problem, provide an outline of remedial action that will achieve compliance, and be properly served.

The housing code enforcement program had (and still has) a system of checks and balances in place to provide quality service. These elements included hiring qualified staff, adequately training staff, checking the quality of inspections through the use of quality control checks by supervisory staff, Health and Hospital's enforcement policies and procedures, ordinance requirements regarding notice and appeal rights, and constitutional and due process requirements.

This enforcement system, which is based on the APHA-CDC model code, has a number of formal and informal opportunities if a recipient of a violation notice did not understand the notice or believed it to be incorrect or unfair. Citizens could discuss the notice of violation with the inspector who issued the notice, the inspector's supervisor, the housing administrator, or the Chief of the Bureau of Environmental Health. The vast majority of cases were resolved within Health and Hospital, but alternative avenues were available to citizens. They could involve the Director of Public Health, Health and Hospital's President or Board of Trustees, the City-County Council, the mayor's office, state legislators, congressional representatives, the courts, and the news media. This program remains unchanged. (Health and Hospital n.d.b)

As previously noted, the APHA-CDC model code has served as a model for numerous state and city housing codes: "Numerous court decisions have been rendered concerning the reasonableness and the validity of the minimum housing standards suggested in this code" (Mood 1986, Appendix I, 73). Furthermore, the Environmental Court in Marion County has upheld these cases since the Court's inception in 1978.

The issue of rights and responsibilities relating to landlords and tenants in the Moderator's initial report did not appear in subsequent versions, but some of the recommendations in these versions were intended to give landlords greater power in controlling Health and Hospital's housing code enforcement program. For example, the Moderator suggested establishing a Citizen's Advisory Committee for Chapter 10 enforcement. This committee would consist of landlord, tenant and neighborhood representatives, and it would address policy and process issues such as tenant-landlord conflicts and Health and Hospital's role in such disputes. The Advisory Committee would meet with Health and Hospital's management and make recommendations to the Board of Trustees for action (RRC 1996c, 19). The Housing WorkGroup did approve an advisory committee to assist Health and Hospital in the design and implementation of programs to address citizens' housing concerns, but it specifically voted against the advisory committee becoming involved in tenant-landlord disputes (Walker 1996a, 28).

Do the benefits of enforcing Chapter 10 provisions outweigh the costs of such enforcement?

Determining the costs of providing services is a much easier task than computing the benefits of those services. Salaries, office supplies, equipment, and other tangible costs of program delivery can be tabulated with comparative ease. The health, economic, and intangible benefits to individuals and the community can be identified, but it is difficult, if not impossible, to assign a dollar value to them with certainty. The cost-benefit analysis in the Moderator's reports included a general discussion of costs and benefits that was supported by limited data. The cost-benefit test was considered in four questions in the Moderator's reports; the answers to these questions were the same in each of the reports (RRC 1996c, 12).[38] They are rephrased slightly for clarity.

What are the benefits? Benefits are protection against health and safety risks, improvements in quality of life, increase in value of property, preservation of neighborhood property values, provision of work for contractors and increases in the tax base.

What is the magnitude of the benefits? Benefits are difficult to quantify.

What are the costs? Costs include the administration and enforcement of Chapter 10, compliance costs, inability of the person who received the order to spend the money in other ways, paperwork response costs, interference with privacy interests, increased cost of housing because of the reduction of low cost housing and a greater likelihood the urban area will suffer from a more severe homelessness problem.[39]

What is the magnitude of the costs? The amount budgeted for the administration and enforcement of Chapter 10, well over two million dollars.[40] Other costs are difficult to quantify.

Although the staff of Health and Hospital provided information to the Work Group on health benefits, albeit in a limited way, and more detailed information on the benefits of the enforcement program, the Moderator elected to use only a portion of the information provided by the staff (and this was included in two footnotes).

Investment in the Housing Stock

During 1995, a staff of 28 housing inspectors conducted 64,175 housing code enforcement and sanitation inspections (Walker 1996a, 4). These staffing and inspection levels reflect typical annual efforts before and since regulatory review. It should be noted that reports of noncompliance do not result from each all inspection.

Health and Hospital's staff developed an estimate of the investment in housing stock that resulted from bringing properties into compliance during 1995 (see Table 1). This estimate was based on a sample of 20 representative cases and the repair costs needed to bring those units into compliance[41] (Health and Hospital 1996e). Based on this analysis, Health and Hospital estimated that $10.60 of repair dollars was invested in the housing stock for each inspection dollar spent, and the total investment in the housing stock attributed to bringing units into compliance was nearly $7 million in 1995 alone.

Table 1: Community costs/benefits of housing code compliance in Marion County in 1995

Costs and Benefits	Dollars
Total Health and Hospital Program Costs (includes 1,535 units brought into compliance)	$ 57,430
Cost per Unit Compliance	$ 428
Total Repair Costs for 20 Units	$ 90,823
Average Repair Cost	$ 4,541
Investment in Housing Stock As a Result of Repairs (average repair cost x number of units repaired)	$6,970,665
Repair dollars invested in housing stock for each inspection dollar spent	$ 10.60

The staff also determined that during the period 1991 through 1995, there were 12,482 cases of voluntary compliance with the housing code (sanitation cases were not included), representing tens of thousands of individual housing code violations. The estimated value of the repairs to these units was about $57,680,000 (Health and Hospital 1996c, 1). The value of the repairs to the community, the health and safety benefits to the occupants, and the avoided public health service costs are not included in this estimate.

Based on the program costs and benefits that derived to the community in terms of reinvestments in the housing stock, it would appear that a leveraging of $10.60 investment in housing stock for every dollar spent on inspections should be considered an excellent cost-benefit ratio.

Cost vs. Benefit to the Community

Bringing housing units into compliance delays the ultimate removal of the unit from the housing stock, and this saving is significant and far below the cost of replacement of the units. For example, in 1996, a project to build 22 new housing units in the downtown areas was estimated to cost about $68,000 per unit (Nancrede 1996, B-3). For the price of a single unit at $68,000, roughly 14 units could be repaired and brought into compliance (based on an average 1995 repair cost of $4,541 plus $428, the per unit cost of the compliance program). This, coupled with Health and Hospital's estimates that every inspection dollar spent in 1995 resulted in a $10.60 investment in the community's housing stock, would indicate that the program was successful. Of course, there were additional benefits to the community that were not calculated. These include cost savings that derived from prevented injuries, illnesses and deaths caused by falls, fires, electrical injuries, carbon monoxide poisoning, exposure to molds, asthma, rat bites, and so forth.

During the Housing WorkGroup hearings, community leaders such as Dixie Ray (President of the Near Eastside Community Organization (NESCO)) provided strong testimony in favor of housing code enforcement and Health and Hospital's staff. In response to efforts to weaken the housing code and its enforcement, Ray commented:

> NESCO supports stronger enforcement of the current code. . . .H&H housing code enforcement provides invaluable support to neighborhoods like the near eastside in our efforts to improve and enhance the living conditions in the neighborhood. (Ray 1996)

The deregulators' efforts to inflate the costs of housing code enforcement and minimize the benefits failed. The strength of the community's support for the housing code enforcement program was so overwhelming, that it was ultimately recognized, albeit in a more muted tone, in the Executive Summary of the Housing WorkGroup Report to the Regulatory Review Commission:

- There is strong support among neighborhood leaders in the entire county for the continued existence and enforcement of a housing code.
- There is strong public support for enforcement efforts that deal with rubbish and trash throughout the county. (RRC 1996m, 1)

Summary

Was the regulatory review process efficient, cost effective, and democratic? Was the time and energy invested in the process by the various stakeholders worthwhile? Not surprisingly, the answers to those questions vary.

The regulatory review process originally was to last six months, but it took over a year to complete. From the beginning, the Goldsmith administration set the rules according to its own interests, chose the people who would decide and excluded those who might disagree. When citizens protested such blatant manipulation, the administration still controlled the notice of meetings, decided on the agenda, selected those who would offer testimony and wrote the work group reports for the Commission.

However, citizen protests enlarged the circle of participants and opened the process to the public.[42] At the end of the deliberations, the administration changed citizen recommendations to "discussion items" in order to keep alive the possibility of deregulation, even when work groups voted otherwise. In other words, some of the moderators wrote "work group" reports that misrepresented and changed the consensus reached in the deliberations and gave only the most grudging acknowledgement of the effectiveness of Health and Hospital's programs.

Although one might be tempted to argue that the problems that emerged were the result of a poorly managed process, that explanation, while true, is not sufficient. It is clear that the philosophical commitment to deregulation was driving the regulatory review, and it is equally clear that the Goldsmith administration's goal was to deregulate, whatever it took. This single-minded adherence to ideology over fact drove the attempt to evade and thwart the democratic process. It would have succeeded if it were not for the efforts of the many citizens who made their voices heard. There were also certain members of Health and Hospital's Board of Trustees (from both political parties) who influenced the outcome. Dr. Henry Bock, Phil Pecar, Stephen West and Lula Journey provided crucial support to the public health and environmental communities at critical stages of the process.

Even the business community—responsible builders, child care facilities, food establishments, swimming pool installers, hazardous materials facilities, environmental consultants and other business interests—provided crucial support by giving testimony that the regulations and enforcement programs protected their interests as well as the health and safety of the community.

The deregulators claimed victory, saying that the environmental health enforcement program in Marion County was more efficient and there were fewer regulations. These statements were bolstered by a comparison of the number of pages and section numbers in the codes before and after regulatory review (a claim was made that the reduction in each was about half) (RRC 1996o). But was it really true? Overwhelmingly, the answer is no.

A fairer comparison is to look directly at the provisions of the various codes and evaluate the status before and after review. The housing code provides a typical example. Some sections of the code were strengthened,[43] some sections were relaxed,[44] and three parts were deleted.[45] But, the substance of Health and Hospital's housing and other codes and its enforcement capability were not diminished.

So, what was the substance of the deregulators' claims? Again, the housing code provides an example. There were wording changes (it is not clear that they made the code clearer), some definitions were moved, and a few definitions were deleted. For some of the chapters, but not housing, many of the existing regulations were adopted by incorporating references to the state code. This makes the local codes appear smaller because there are fewer pages, but the codes are actually larger because the state codes are much longer than the original codes of Health and Hospital. In addition, users now have to go to two sources and cross-reference the two codes to be sure they will be in compliance. The end result is that many users of the codes now have a more cumbersome and burdensome process than before.

The neighborhoods claimed victory, saying they took a closed process, with no accountability or checks and balances, opened it up to public scrutiny, and they added a layer of accountability to the deregulation effort. They felt, however, that more could have been accomplished for the community if the Goldsmith administration's true intention had been regulatory review rather than a predetermined reduction of government responsibility. As Mary Walker reflected back on the process, she commented,

We had to insist that the purpose of the review was to make our community a healthier and safer place in which to live (and do business). It was worth all the time and energy we invested. The deregulators didn't get to dismantle Health and Hospital. The environmental health program continues to be a professional organization with regulatory tools needed to protect the community.[46]

Ironically, in his book Goldsmith stated, "People know better than government what is in their best interest" (Goldsmith 1997, 9). In this instance the people of the community spoke, and let the Mayor know that strong environmental health regulations and enforcement were in their best interests.

Notes

[1]The author gratefully acknowledges Mary Walker for providing access to the repository of materials she gathered throughout the regulatory review process. Walker attended and taped all of the work group, Commission and Board meetings and collated work group materials. Her repository is especially valued because the Regulatory Review Commission did not provide a recording secretary for the work group deliberations. The author also gratefully acknowledges Eric Larmore for his assistance in researching background information.

[2]Because the review process took longer than anticipated, the sunsetting ordinance was subsequently amended (General Ordinance No. 9-1996(A)) to give the Review Panel and the Board more time to complete its work. A subsequent proposed ordinance, General Ordinance No. 15-1996, which was not passed, would have required each of the Corporation's ordinances to be reviewed in public hearings at ten-year intervals.

[3]Indiana Code, Chapter 287. H. 82, approved March 7, 1951 created a municipal health and hospital corporation in counties having a population of more than 500,000.

[4]In the remainder of this chapter, the terms Health and Hospital and Corporation will be used interchangeably with the Marion County Health Department.

[5]The membership of the Board of Trustees has expanded from five members in the enabling legislation to seven members. Three of the members are appointed by the mayor, two by the Board of County Commissioners, and two by the City-County Council. The four-year terms are staggered and no more than four of the members may be from the same political party.

[6]Housing and Environmental Standards Ordinance, Chapter 10 was the subject of the regulatory review (Health and Hospital Corporation of Marion County 1980)

[7]Buell did not leave the Corporation, but was appointed treasurer, a position he held prior to becoming Executive Director. Buell's salary at the time was $68,515. Roob was appointed with a salary of $90,000.

[8]The site was the former Riverside Amusement Park that was slated for a major housing development. In 1978-1979, there was an outbreak of histoplasmosis in this areas and the site was implicated as a source of the outbreak. Mary Walker, who lived in the neighborhood at the time recalled that many residents developed histoplasmosis at the time. The neighborhood viewed the "swap" as a trading of public land for private benefit (Walker 2000c).

[9]Roob resigned from his position as Executive Director in 1998, but was then appointed by Goldsmith to serve on the Board of Trustees, where he continued to be influential in directing the Corporation's policies. He was not reappointed to the Board in 2000 when his term expired.

[10]Other members included Robert P. Thomas, Capital City Ford; Otto Frenzel IV, Merchants National Bank; Gene McFadden, Freight Masters, Inc.; Yvonne Perkins, Citizens Gas and Coke Utility; Tom Kincannon, Imperial Coatings, Inc.; William Styring, Indiana Chamber of Commerce; Dr. Henry Bock, Methodist Hospital, Hon. Tobin McClamroch, City County Council; Roger Schmelzer, Assistant to Representative Paul Mannweiller; Todd Stuart, Stuart Moving and Storage, Inc.; Tom Crouch, 38th & Shadeland Improvement Association; and Blair Vandiver, Benchmark Products, Inc.

[11]The Health and Hospital staff was included in the process at the initiation of the Corporation's Board, but the degree of staff participation was determined by the moderator of each work group. In general terms, the moderator looked to the staff only for information about the Corporation's programs. The neighborhood representatives believed that the staff restrained during the work groups and were "walking on eggs" (Walker 2000).

[12]In this example, an argument for the continued regulation was that some believe the "potential for harm exists" if produce stands are not regulated. The argument in favor of eliminating the regulation was "consumers can view the produce themselves to determine whether it is spoiled." The deregulation argument is weak and contrary to the principles of food protection. While a consumer can detect gross spoilage, it is not possible to determine spoilage in its initial stages or to identify disease-causing organisms that are not visible to the naked eye. Knowledgeable trained inspectors are needed to make these determinations.

[13]The work group concluded that the gutters are needed to ensure proper drainage and prevent breeding grounds for mosquitoes. Mosquitoes can spread mosquito-borne viral encephalitis and other diseases. Gutters also prevent water and moisture from entering the foundation and dwelling, which prevents structural deterioration. Water and moisture indoors can degrade air quality and lead to mold growth that causes respiratory problems. Exterior locks protect the occupants from intruders who may injury them, and they protect small children who might be injured or harmed if they leave the dwelling unnoticed. Exterior

paint is needed to prevent moisture from entering the dwelling. Handrails prevent injuries.

[14]The primary source for the historical review in this section is *Basic Housing Inspection*, a publication of the United States Department of Health Education and Welfare (1976). This document can be accessed at <http://www.cdc.gov/nceh>.

[15]The Act requirements included: ventilation for occupied sleeping rooms; proper fire escapes; banisters on stairs; water closets or privies at a rate of one to twenty occupants; roofs in good repair; cleansing of lodging houses to the satisfaction of the Board of Health.

[16] Interestingly, the Court's thinking at the time mirrored issues raised by efforts to reinvent environmental health services in Indianapolis. In its ruling, the Court stated there is no evidence, nor could the court know, that the presence of water on every floor would improve the health of the occupants. The Court unanimously believed there was no legislative compulsion on a landlord to provide water to every floor, since if the tenants required it, their self-interest and market competition would secure it. Further, the Court wondered "at what point must this police power pause" if this expense were imposed on the landlord, and the Court believed that a decision in favor of the tenants would lead to socialism, the disappearance of individual responsibility, and ultimately, the death of liberty.

[17]The Act of 1901 strengthened requirements for fire protection, privacy, lighting and ventilation.

[18]Brookside Neighborhood Association et al. (1996). This memorandum addressed the Housing WorkGroup recommendations and provided strong support for the housing code, stronger enforcement of the code, and the performance of the Corporation's housing program.

[19]Ray (1996). This memorandum on behalf of the Near Eastside Community Organization spoke against efforts to deregulate, and addressed inaccuracies in the Moderator's report regarding the relationship between health and housing. It also called for stronger code enforcement.

[20]Smith (1996). The Chief of the Indianapolis Fire Department supported the existing regulation on prohibiting dumpsters in alleyways because the regulation allowed the Department to have access to homes in the event of fires: "Maintaining the current regulation is in the interest of public protection and provides at least a policy that can correct a problem."

[21]Williams (1996). This letter from the Public Policy Director, Indiana Coalition on Housing and Homeless Issues, Inc. expressed concerns about the accuracy of the Housing WorkGroup draft reports and strongly supported all of the structural code provisions.

[22]Pontious (1996). The Board Member and Treasurer of the Citizens Neighborhood Coalition, Inc. expressed support for housing code enforcement in poor areas.

[23]Nanavaty (1996). The City of Indianapolis Police Department expressed support for the existing requirement for door locks on rental units and

strengthening the code to include window locks: "I feel that without these safety measures many members of our community would become victims of crime . . . We believe that crimes against individuals is (sic) not only a police issue, but also a public safety and health concern."

[24]Zahn (1996). The President of Indianapolis Downtown, Inc. recommended continuing the Health and Hospital Corporation's existing regulation of refuse containers/dumpsters.

[25]Spillane (1996). The Marion County Prosecutor's office was highly supportive of the Corporation's inspection staff and strongly supported the existing nuisance abatement provisions of the housing code: "Nuisance abatement projects definitely demonstrate the connection between living conditions, crime and increased neighborhood problems in addition to criminal activity."

[26]The words "appears to contribute" are changed to "contributes to" in drafts after May 11. See subsequent drafts: 1996e (12); 1996h (13), 1996b (18).

[27]The words "there would appear to be" are changed to "there are some" in the June 19 version (1996b, 19)

[28]The core concept test and lack of relationship to health and safety are used as reasons to deregulate in the Moderator's reports from May 29 drafts to the end of the Commission's hearings.

[29]The source for Dr. Mood's quotation was listed as: E. Mood, n.d. "The Development, Objectives, and Adequacy of Current Housing Standards." In: *Housing Code Standards: Three Critical Studies*, (13, 18).

[30]Dixie Ray, NESCO President was one of the neighborhood leaders who objected: "In your argument against the relationship of health and housing you cite a 1969 article that states it is difficult to establish this relationship. Using a single old article is a ploy I would expect from a freshman student desperate to support his position." (Ray 1996, 2)

[31] The author was also a member of the APHA Committee on Housing and Health, which was chaired by Dr. Mood.

[32]It should be noted that the effort to eliminate the housing regulations was inconsistent with Goldsmith's philosophy of community policing, which emphasized the importance of "mending broken windows." (see Chapter 7)

[33]Alison Cole, Principal Planner for the Indianapolis Department of Metropolitan Development was the assistant selected by the Moderator to assist the Housing WorkGroup on this and other issues.

[34]One week before the Commission was to vote on the Housing WorkGroup Report, the Moderator sent a briefing memorandum to the Chairman of the Commission. In this memorandum, he highlighted the analysis prepared by Alison Cole as "useful" and attached a summary of it to the memorandum. In addition, he described the neighborhood leaders as "hyper sensitive" about the issues, but he failed to report that the WorkGroup voted to delete that material (and his report containing it) from the materials to be sent to the Commission.

[35] After regulatory review, Roob was quoted, "I was the only person who felt swimmers should swim at their own risk" (*Indianapolis Star/News* 1997). In an

ironic twist, this article also reported that Roob, who did not want government to inspect and regulate swimming pools, called the Health and Hospital swimming pool inspectors, not private inspector, to investigate cloudy water in a pool he was using at the Indianapolis Athletic Club.

[36]The sections of the Chapter 10 Housing Code that were listed as not being used or used only infrequently included:

Section 10-317 that makes it unlawful for vacating occupants to leave garbage and rubbish behind.

Section 10-326 that requires owners who are selling a property subject to Chapter 10 to notify the Corporation of the name and address of the new owner and to notify the new owner of the Chapter 10 orders.

Article 10 that allows the Corporation to condemn a dwelling unit as unfit for human habitation.

In addition, a related chapter on unwholesome substances was no longer used as a legal basis for dealing with unsafe buildings

[37]Marion County Health Department, Housing and Environmental Standards Ordinance, Chapter 10, Article 12:Sec. 10-1201.

[38]also in May 17 draft (pg 13-14); May 30 draft Part I (pg 14-16); June 19 draft Part B (pg 20-21)

[39]The inclusion of the last two costs were apparently motivated by a 1978 article by William Tucker in which he argues that rent control, growth control and tight zoning contributed to homelessness in the 1980s. In addition, he argues that the single-room occupancy hotels in Chicago disappeared as the result of being targeted by urban renewal programs and municipal campaigns to clean up downtown areas. Building code enforcement and condemnation were listed as reasons for their disappearance and zoning laws for preventing their replacement. Tucker did not discuss housing code enforcement.

[40]The costs of the housing code administration and enforcement were substantially less than two million dollars. The Moderator may have intended to include all housing program costs.

[41]Some of the assumptions included: a 45 ft. x 26 ft. two story house; repair costs were estimated based on cost figures provided by contractors and the 1995 *Home Tech Remodeling and Renovation Estimator Manual*. The deregulators criticized these estimates because they were not based on randomly selected cases, actual houses and actual dollars spent on repairs.

[42]The Housing WorkGroup, one of eight work groups, evaluated an enormous body of information and heard testimony from 30 individuals who represented various interests. They met fourteen times, for an average of more than three hours each time. Ten professionals from the Corporation provided information and support to the WorkGroup; the total amount of time that staff spent on the regulatory review process is not known, but a review of materials that staff developed would suggest that the time spent was considerable. The number of citizens who donated their time and expertise to the process is not known.

[43]Sections that were strengthened include Sec. 10-206 (redefined lead); Sec. 10-307 (clarified residential hazardous materials); Sec. 10-408 (added a requirement for window locks for rental units); Sec. 10-501 (allowed an exemption from window and skylight requirements if the dwelling unit meets the requirements of the Indiana One and Two Family Dwelling Code); Sec. 10-505 (upgraded electrical requirements); Sec. 10-602 (allowed the use of specified kinds of permanently installed unvented fuel-burning room heaters in accordance with the Indiana One and Two Family Dwelling Code; this ordinance specifically mentions carbon monoxide); Sec. 10-703 (established the Corporation's authority to deal with drainage on private property)

[44]Sec. 10-303 was modified to require usable wood to be stored eighteen inches above the ground, but only in areas where rat infestations occur rather than countywide; Sec. 10-701 was modified to allow carpeting in bathrooms and kitchens, providing certain conditions are met; Sec. 10-704 was modified to eliminate requirement for gutters, leaders, and downspouts on accessory units if these were not part of the original installation; Sec. 10-707 was modified to eliminate requirement for fences to be painted; Sec. 10-804 was modified to allow an exemption for access to bedrooms and nurseries in "shotgun homes."

[45]Sec. 10-326, the requirement for notification of code violations upon property transfers, was deleted because it was not used; Article 10 allowed condemnation of units unfit for human habitation, and it was deleted because it was not used); Chapter 17, (unwholesome substances, was deleted because it was addressed in other parts of the code).

[46] Author's Note. It remains to be seen, however, if the agency's Public Health Department, which was highly politicized under Goldsmith, and its Public Health Director can fully recover their former independence.

Part Four

"Marketizing" Public Assets

Chapter 14

Privatization in Indianapolis: Problems, "Proximity Issues" and Oscar Robertson Smoot

Jack Miller

Introduction

Privatization has been touted as a marvelous success in Indianapolis, but a closer look will show otherwise. One problem is that privatization was justified only in economic terms with no attention paid to the potential for negative impacts on values other than money, such as democracy, citizenship and shared community. Even judged by its own strictly economic standards, however, the privatization effort in Indianapolis was a failure. What was not well understood during the Goldsmith administration was that privatization appeared to be economically successful in Indianapolis because the Mayor himself defined costs and savings. Also, much of what was reported in the media (especially out-of-town media) was taken, generally uncritically, from Goldsmith's own speeches and press releases, which consistently laudatory. Examples from *Time* and *Forbes*, respectively, illustrate this coverage. "A pioneer in privatization, he has put more than 70 city services up for competitive bids; mayors across the country are learning from his success" (Cohen 1997, 21). "Indianapolis Mayor Stephen Goldsmith may not be reinventing government, but he sure is making it efficient—and mayors from New York to Los Angeles are soliciting his advice" (Stern 1994).

Goldsmith viewed government as the cause of problems facing urban cities and privatization as the answer to those problems. This view appeared to be black and white. Government was inherently bad, business was inherently good. In his book, *The Twenty-First Century City*, he states: "Not only are the cities on the skids, but in most cases government itself has been the grease that hastened the pace of decay" (Goldsmith 1997, 5) and Because government simply confiscates dollars rather than competing for them, government managers do not get good information about their customers' needs and wants" (Goldsmith 1997, 67). In contrast, business is described as the " . . . lean, mean private sector" (Goldsmith 1997, 20).

Goldsmith's view of privatization was enveloped in a nostalgic, highly selective and thus inaccurate view of the past. He states, "Privatization is an attempt to reverse much of the history of the twentieth century . . . ." He goes on to praise privatized city suburbs, "These edge cities, born well after World War II, never had a progressive era to overcome . . . . " (Goldsmith 1997, 17). He made similar points in a speech to the Allegheny Institute for Public Policy, assuring listeners, "Cities in the 21st Century can be just as exciting and vibrant as they were in the early part of the 20th Century . . . the 19th Century . . . if we follow these basic principles, we can again see cities as wonderful places in the 21st Century as they were before" (Goldsmith 1998). These are truly astounding statements considering the history of the cities of that era—cities that provided a life for most people that was filthy, brutish and short. Mullins and Zorn have noted, " . . . the Goldsmith administration is not paying enough attention to United States urban history. As early as the mid-1800s, excesses in the private provision of municipal services led to a backlash against contracting out and privatization" (Mullins and Zorn 1996, 19).

His view of privatization and business as the salvation of urban decay produced a single-minded dedication to dismantling governmental systems that were working, in many cases very efficiently and effectively. In their stead, Goldsmith installed private contractors who often produced shoddy work and engaged in illegal and unethical practices. His tacit and actual approval of these situations has left an imprint on Indianapolis that is both financial and emotional, one that will not be easily removed. Many in the community believe that

Goldsmith's "take no prisoner" attitude about privatization produced a significant backlash that ultimately resulted in his decisive defeat in the 1996 governor's race.

The first part of this chapter provides an overview of issues important to an understanding of the privatization process in Indianapolis, including deciding what to privatize, the use and accountability of consultants and contractors and the troubling influence of campaign contributions on the award of contracts. The second part of this chapter is a case study of the privatization of construction management in Indianapolis. Chapters 15 and 16 continue with case studies of the privatization of public golf courses and swimming pools. These "case studies" and examples illustrate a number of problems associated with privatization in Indianapolis, including:

- Lack of accountability and oversight.
- Pervasive influence of campaign contributions.
- Institutionalization of secrecy in city government.
- Increases in user fees to the public.
- Shifting of contract costs from the City of Indianapolis operating budget to the capital budget.

Deciding What to Privatize

Advisory Groups Set the Agenda

A few weeks after his election in 1991, Goldsmith delivered a speech to his transition team, in which he promised that with their help, he would produce a smaller, more responsive city government run by 25 percent fewer employees. Addressing the impending layoffs, he assured listeners, "The good people have nothing to fear" (Remondini 1991). The official transition team of 172 members was drawn primarily from the business, banking and legal communities. One hundred ten of those "team" members had been responsible for $180,000 or 11 percent of the $1.6 million Goldsmith had raised for his winning campaign (Lanosga 1992a). The team was charged with scrutinizing city government with the goal of injecting competition through privatization. In a remark that was prophetic, Goldsmith told team members, "Just figure out the best way to do it. Then we'll assign someone to change the law, change the ordinance, change the statute" (Remondini 1991).

Foremost among the advisory groups was the Services, Efficiency and Lower Taxes for Indianapolis Commission (SELTIC), a ten-member advisory board of powerful business executives led by former Reagan administration official and Eli Lilly & Co. executive, Mitch Daniels, Jr. The members of SELTIC, their families and their companies were important supporters of Mayor Goldsmith. According to one newspaper report they had contributed at least $50,332.50 to the Mayor's 1991 campaign (Lanosga 1992b). City-County Councilor Susan Williams referred to SELTIC as "another spooky little committee" (Lanosga 1992b). However, this "spooky little committee" was to have far-reaching power over the future institutional memory and capacity of local government. SELTIC's goal was to find opportunities for privatization. Its conclusions, as demonstrated by the swimming pool privatization (see Chapter 16), were often based upon faulty or partial analysis. These and other problems could have been avoided if the composition of SELTIC had been more inclusive, with representatives from neighborhood groups and even city employees.

In his report on the criminal investigations into the 1993 golf scandal, Prosecutor Jeff Modisett stated: "The discussion and preparation for golf privatization was done too quickly and did not include sufficient consultation with individuals having valuable, specific knowledge about the city's golf operations." The prosecutor went on to say: "The two individuals who had the best working knowledge of the practical and legal ramifications of the city's management of golf facilities before privatization . . . apparently were not included in SELTIC committee and other high administration discussions concerning the implementation of privatization." He concluded by pointing out that it is "dangerous and ill-advised for upper management and outside commissions to make sweeping policy change" without sufficient consultation with the people who must carry them out. (Modisett 1994, 8) Also in that first year a more informal "advisory" group, the Mayor's "Gold Team," was formed. The Gold Team consisted of 458 people who had given a minimum of $1,000 each to his 1991 campaign. These individuals had a monthly opportunity to meet with the Mayor and "offer advice and have questions answered about reform efforts" (Schuckel 1992a). To remain in good standing on the "Gold Team," Goldsmith asked each member to donate another $1,000 at the end of 1992, calling it "no big deal" (Schuckel 1992a). The extent to which the Gold Team had influence is not known. However, the issue of campaign contributions in return for influence and contracts was one that remained with Goldsmith throughout his administration.

Activity-Based Cost Accounting—A Tool to Identify Inefficiency

Activity-based cost (ABC) accounting was one of the management tools (along with performance measures, customer surveys, popular budgets and employee empowerment) that Goldsmith called the "strategic tools initiative" (Goldsmith 1997, 58). Goldsmith believed these tools, which he described as "simply common sense procedure in the private sector," were essential to his ability "to pull the Indianapolis bureaucracy into the competitive market-place" (Goldsmith 1997, 58). An important use of ABC was to show that city-provided services were not as efficient as those provided by private contractors. However, there were a number of problems associated with using ABC to make this case.

In a memo to department directors in January, 1993, Mayor Goldsmith explained that ABC would provide information "to be used to move municipal services into the competitive marketplace to maximize efficiency" (Goldsmith 1993). KPMG Peat Marwick was the private contractor selected to implement the ABC system in all but two departments. The initial contract was signed in December 1992 for $40,000 and a subsequent contract for $137,000 was signed in 1993. The company was paid an additional $219,000 in 1993 to set up the related "Popular Budget" (City of Indianapolis 1992-1993).

The ABC system was a way to put a price tag on every city service and is, according to Indiana University researchers David Mullins and Kurt Zorn, "quite subjective and imprecise." (Mullins and Zorn 1996). One of the problems that they identified was the fact that the administration identified savings as the difference between the activity-based cost of a city service and the contract bid amount for the service by the vendor (Mullins and Zorn 1996, 11). Identifying savings in this way obscures the true cost of the activity because the city did not consider all costs in the ABC system, and because of inherent difficulties in determining the activity-based cost. An internal audit by the city released in December 1995 confirms this evaluation. The report states that: "controls ensuring that the information is complete, accurate and appropriately applied are very weak. The volume and diversity of discrepancies/inconsistencies were many . . . " (Internal Audit Agency 1995). As the audit demonstrated, it was virtually impossible to calculate the direct cost of an activity in which the same workers and equipment were used for several different activities. For example, it is difficult to apportion the time and equipment for a truck crew that fills potholes, plows snow and hauls gravel. The direct costs in this case could be exaggerated by multiple counting, making government services seem far more expensive than they really were. Indirect costs are even harder to figure. Overhead and administrative costs involved in the previous example require very creative guesswork. If there is a political bias against public workers, this "guess work" is likely to inflate the government "cost" of the service and consequently the "savings" attributed to privatization.

In 1995, when ABC was to be implemented in the remaining departments, Kathleen Jones of the Department of Administration wrote a cautionary memo to Deputy Mayor Skip Stitt: "I believe that using these models will set us up for an 'administrative nightmare'. It is possible that each division will have to employ at least one full-time person to manage data collection to support these models . . . the value of tracking ABC data on a regular basis is questionable and one-time cost studies might be more reasonable" (Jones 1995).

In addition to speculative cost projections, privatization savings in Indianapolis were exaggerated by the fact that several costs were not figured into the contracts at all:

- costs of contract development, including substantial legal fees,
- costing (scoping costs),
- costs of monitoring performance under the contracts,
- overhead costs in some contracts, and
- lawsuit settlements incurred as a result of the privatization effort.

As Mullins and Zorn concluded, "Furthermore there are few institutional controls to prevent either overstatement of baseline cost figures or the understatement of the contract costs. In fact, the process as it operates today is nearly devoid of independent checks and balances and is thus open to political manipulation" (Mullins and Zorn 1996).

Consultants, Contractors, and Contributors

Hiring outside consultants allowed Goldsmith to lay off or fire dozens of city employees, many of whom spent their lives working for the city and were nearing retirement. The work performed by the dismissed employees was in many instances given to private companies, often under improperly bid contracts. The use of consultants and contractors is a widespread practice in local, state and the federal government. However, the extent of their use in Indianapolis and the circumstances surrounding their use caused critics to express concern.

In response to complaints about the loss of city jobs to well-paid consultants, the Mayor explained, "It's more likely for someone not associated with the city to remain objective about its reform" (Schuckel 1992b).

One criticism that resurfaced often in Indianapolis during the Goldsmith years was the highly selective nature of the administration's devotion to competition. State law in Indiana does not require competitive bidding for so-called "professional services" such as lawyers, engineers, golf pros, and a variety of consultants. However, bidding is required on public works projects and purchases over $75,000 ($25,000 before Goldsmith's HB 1398 was passed in 1995, see Chapter 14). Under Goldsmith, the award of contracts for professional and other services was dogged by repeated criticism to the effect that financial and political support for the Mayor, not qualifications, were the main considerations in the award of contracts. Although bidding was not legally required for professional services, good management practice in more substantive projects would be to issue Requests for Proposals or Requests for Qualifications to ensure that the best value is obtained. Goldsmith comments on his bidding practices in his book, "Occasionally, a professional service provider would bring us a particularly good idea, winning the right to develop it, but almost always we entertained bids" (Goldsmith 1997, 73). A closer look at the major privatization efforts in Indianapolis simply does not support that claim.

During the Goldsmith administration, the city's expenditures for contractual work escalated dramatically. It is difficult to estimate expenditures with certainty, however, because of the way in which categories in the operating budget were shifted, renamed, and expanded. For example, prior to 1996, the city's operating budgets had only one category for "contractual consultants;" however, in 1996 contractual consultants were separated into specific categories such as "architectural and engineering services." In 1994, a new category, "management contracts," appeared to accommodate the management of city services such as the wastewater treatment facilities. The changes in category labels and content complicates any efforts to make historical comparisons, or even to track the use of consultants. The author's efforts to track these changes thus provide only a rough estimate of the use of consulting services under Goldsmith.

It appears that the city's purchase of services (including contractual consultants, legal, third-party contracts and management contracts) rose from about $8.3 million in 1991 to over $90 million in Goldsmith's last year (City of Indianapolis 1994; 2000). Expenditures for "contractual consultants" quadrupled in Goldsmith's first term from about $5.1 million in 1991 to $20.1 million in 1995 (City of Indianapolis 1993; 1995). Third-party contracts rose from less than $2 million in 1991 to nearly $25 million during Goldsmith's last year in office.

One of the many ramifications of this escalation was the inability to provide oversight, largely because the administration did not believe in (or plan for) oversight, which in turn resulted in wasted taxpayer dollars. The vastly increased reliance on contractors in lieu of city employees likewise translated into loss of institutional memory and created problems with continuity and consistency of municipal record keeping. This in turn made it difficult for the administration to respond to periodic allegations of bid rigging and political favoritism.

Throughout his eight years in office, Goldsmith was subject to questions about the relationship between award of contracts and donations to his various political campaigns. Mandatory contributions from city workers to the party in power had been outlawed in Indiana, and while many city workers continued their contributions voluntarily, they were no longer a reliable source of political funding. Furthermore, their small donations went to the Republican party, not to any particular candidate. Private contractors, however, could be "asked" for "voluntary" donations, and those donations could be channeled to a candidate. During the Goldsmith years, it was not a secret that bidders on city contracts were expected to make contributions to the Elect Goldsmith Committee. *NUVO Newsweekly*, a local alternative newspaper, reported allegations that a contractor lost two important contracts with the city because he refused to contribute to Goldsmith's campaign. The contractor claimed city officials told him that his firm had been selected, but the contracts were subsequently awarded to a firm that had made large campaign contributions (Ramos 1996a). One local civil engineer was quoted, "If you want to play the game, you have to make a donation to his campaign . . . that's pretty common knowledge" (Ramos 1996a).

In a 1996 federal lawsuit, over 120 donors from the local construction community were identified as the source of contributions totaling over $600,000. (Tomanovich 1996a, 10) Commenting on the campaign contributions, Goldsmith remarked to reporter Ken Herman, "Some of our vendors in a burst of exuberance after they got the contract have participated and I think that provided some unfortunate targets" (Herman 1999).

Goldsmith had once claimed that a city could be run with "just a mayor, a police chief, a planning director, a purchasing agent and a handful of contract monitors" (Charen 1998) and replacing public workers with consultants was the first priority of his administration. As mentioned previously, overall spending on contractual consultants jumped from $5.1 million in 1991 (the year before Goldsmith took office) to $20.1 million in 1995 (*In-Roads* 1996, 35). According to the operating budgets, consultants alone cost the city an average of $17 million per year during Goldsmith's tenure (City of Indianapolis 1993-2000). This figure significantly underestimates the true cost of consultants because it does not include numerous consultants paid by direct voucher—a practice frowned upon by Hudnut, but one that was quite common during the Goldsmith administration (White 2000)—nor does it include those consultants who were paid out of the capital budget (see discussion below). A few examples are illustrative of the extent of contracting in the Goldsmith years.

- This chapter details the city's experience with Oscar Robertson Smoot (ORS), the company that was used to oversee the city's construction management projects. The contributions that ORS made directly to the Goldsmith campaigns were approximately $42,000 between 1991 and 1996 (Steve Goldsmith Committee 1992-1997; Goldsmith for Governor 1996; Businessmen for Good Government 1992); indirect contributions (through employees and relatives) were impossible to track.

- Goldsmith awarded D&S Investments a no-bid contract of $8,000 to study where and how to build a jail annex to relieve overcrowding. Subsequently, the contractor recommended a building it had never visited as the site of the new jail annex, and it proposed to buy the building, renovate it and lease it back to the city for $190,500 per year. Goldsmith was personally involved in the negotiations for this $2 million deal. When the news of the secret no-bid deal broke, the project was abandoned in favor of another contractor. (Caleca and Gelarden 1994)

- Goldsmith provided $937,728 to the Hudson Institute, a local conservative think tank, for consulting on privatization and other issues from 1994 to 1999 (City of Indianapolis 2000).

- In 1993 Goldsmith spent $400,000 to hire a consultant to analyze and improve the parking situation in Indianapolis. Fellow Republican Gordon Gilmer, chair of the City-County Council's transportation committee observed, "They've hired some expensive people . . . to perhaps tell them what they already know" . . .

Gilmer added dryly, "the city has a parking division." (Schuckel 1993). The Mayor's spokesperson pointed out that the expensive consultants would perform public education, train parking staff in customer relations, and determine parking perceptions and attitudes—tasks that apparently were beyond the scope of the city's staff.

- Goldsmith commissioned a transportation study in 1994 for $150,000 to examine what he called "the nation's worst" bus system and recommend improvements without raising taxes. The study recommended cutting or changing 22 routes, but completely ignored neighborhoods with high population density, no cars and annual incomes of less than $15,000 (Caleca 1994). Subsequently a council of local residents who actually rode the bus was appointed (at no cost) and their report was accepted while the consultant's expensive study languished on Goldsmith's shelf.

- Goldsmith spent $88,000 for a consultant to study the need for a new arena for the Indiana Pacers (owned by the wealthy Simon brothers) (Johnston 1996a). Consultants were also hired to study the building want-lists for the other area pro teams, and by mid-1996 the costs total an additional quarter million dollars.

Privatizing City Legal

The previous mayor, William H. Hudnut III, had spent relatively little public money on private attorneys, relying primarily on the city's own legal department and outsourcing only for highly specialized skills such as labor negotiation and bond work (Franklin 1995). Goldsmith fired most of the city's in-house attorneys and clerks early in his administration. By downsizing the city's litigation section from nine attorneys to two by November 1992, Goldsmith was able to declare "savings" of $350,000 per year (plus benefits). However, these attorneys' salaries had averaged $50,000 per year (or $25 per hour), and even when the cost of clerical support and space in the City-County building were taken into account, the hourly cost was well below the Indianapolis going rate for legal work (Morgan 1992). Their private sector replacements, hired at up to $200 per hour, would cost taxpayers considerably more. Goldsmith initially replaced the city attorneys by contracting with two firms for a flat-fee rate of $14,500 per month (essentially what the city had paid the in-house attorney section.) A Goldsmith spokesperson said, "We're trying to get a little more for our money" (Morgan 1992). This arrangement did not last long and both firms escaped from their contracts complaining that the pay was "inadequate." Private sector salaries for lawyers were higher, and the firms had substantial overhead costs as well; they simply couldn't compete with in-house counsel on the basis of cost.

A 1995 study conducted by the *Indianapolis Star* found Goldsmith's extensive use of contract lawyers was not cost-effective. Goldsmith discounted the newspaper's analysis, and remarkably, even his own claims that outsourcing saved money, when he observed that it was "virtually impossible to evaluate whether handling cases in-house is more cost-effective." A review of city purchase orders shows that over his two terms as mayor, Goldsmith spent $15,678,557 on legal advice from private attorneys. In Goldsmith's last year alone he spent $2,240,959 compared to $750,000 that Hudnut spent in his last year in office (1991). Even adjusting for inflation, Goldsmith's expenditures were significantly higher (Franklin 1995)

The higher fees did not translate into better results, at least in litigation. Legal settlements climbed after Goldsmith became mayor, jumping from $874,000 in 1991 to over $3.5 million in his first year in office (Franklin 1995). Legal settlements averaged $1.4 million per year in Hudnut's last three years and over $3 million per year in Goldsmith's first three (peaking at $3.7 million in 1998) (City of Indianapolis 2000).

The extent to which these additional legal fees represent costs associated with privatization and contracting, or the fallout from those efforts is not known, but it should be noted that contract lawyers and legal costs represent a cost of privatization that Goldsmith neither acknowledged nor accounted for.

One of the legal conflicts of interest issues that emerged during his administration involved the law firm Barnes & Thornburg, which had formerly employed Goldsmith. A senior partner at the firm, Robert Grand, became a close advisor to Goldsmith and campaign contributor (Franklin 1995). In late 1995, Deputy Mayor Joe Loftus resigned from the city to work for Barnes & Thornburg. This firm then contracted for Loftus to become the city's lobbyist on a $7,500 per month retainer. In his public/private capacity, lobbyist Loftus was able to pressure the construction managers of the new Conseco Fieldhouse to give the Sherman R. Smoot Co. (one of the principles in the ORS company discussed in this chapter) a portion of the $3.7 million construction management contract. According to Loftus, Smoot, now a client of Barnes & Thornburg, deserved this $500,000 plum because of all the "fine work" Smoot had done previously for the Goldsmith administration (Cady 1997). When asked about this obvious conflict of interest, Goldsmith commented, "It's not a conflict of interest. It's the opposite of a conflict" (Johnston 1997). Loftus was also instrumental in lobbying the State Legislature for legislation supporting much of Goldsmith's privatization program, and he was extensively involved in the passage of HB 1398, a purchasing law that applied only to Indianapolis and virtually guaranteed that privatization deals could be made without public oversight. This law is discussed in detail in Chapter 15.

"My Investors"

In a 1996 interview, in response to questions posed to candidates about campaign contributions, Goldsmith stated "People should judge me on the basis of my issues and not on the portfolio of my investors" (Lanosga and Johnston 1996a). Goldsmith's relationship to his "investors," however, resulted in persistent questions about conflicts of interest and favoritism.

- A month before the mayoral election in October 1995, the Goldsmith campaign sent out 1,000 invitations to companies that do business with the City of Indianapolis to attend a reception for Goldsmith. The invitation list obtained by a reporter contained names, addresses and phone numbers of 80 companies and the value of their city contracts, suggesting a connection between contributions and the award of public monies (Johnston and Lanosga 1995).
- In 1998, the city was slated to spend $23 million in land improvements for a $90 million project involving the Marriott Hotel. The principals in the enterprise had given a total of $40,000 to Goldsmith, while the two bidders who lost had given nothing. One of the winners was Dean White, a wealthy businessman from northern Indiana and a major a campaign contributor to Goldsmith (Sword 1998).
- United Consulting Engineers, a civil engineering and architectural design firm, received over $4.3 million (City of Indianapolis 2000) in city business during Goldsmith's two terms. The principals of the company contributed over $44,000 from 1992-1996 (Steve Goldsmith Committee 1992-1997; Goldsmith for Governor 1996).
- In 1996, executives of the Indianapolis Water Company, a partner in the White River Environmental Partnership (WREP), threw a

$250 per person fundraiser for gubernatorial candidate Goldsmith. Critics were disturbed that only seventeen days earlier, the WREP had been awarded a $23.6 million city contract to perform sewer maintenance. The WREP already had a contract to run the city's wastewater treatment plants. One of the evening's hosts was Michael Stayton, Goldsmith's former Director of Public Works, who oversaw the privatization award of the wastewater treatment plants to WREP before resigning to become an executive of a water company subsidiary. City-County Councilor Susan Williams, who voted against giving the WREP yet another lucrative contract observed, "This was a done deal from the get-go and everybody knew it. It was a done deal on the wastewater treatment plants. It's beginning to get ludicrous to say any of this is truly competitive." Goldsmith's response to the criticism: "The timing continues to frustrate me. We keep ending up with these proximity issues." (Johnston 1996b)

Contributors who espoused conservative ideology were not looking for public contracts, but their influence locally and on the national political scene in furthering Goldsmith's privatization agenda was also am important benefit to the Mayor. As economist Julia Abedian points out,

> Goldsmith's actions in Indianapolis have ingratiated him to some of the most influential conservative policy makers in the country and they in turn have adopted him as a model of the Republican mayoralty. This relationship benefits both interests. Goldsmith has a powerful public relations vehicle that lends legitimacy to and creates enthusiasm for his agenda. Privatization advocates get to use the mayor of Indianapolis as cases in point in support of their agenda. The relationship also serves as a built-in campaign finance operation . . . .the more attention he gets, the more national financial and political support seems to come his way. (Abedian 1996)

The quotation from Abedian identifies campaign contributors who do not gain materially but whose "small government/ free-market" agenda is advanced by Goldsmith who, in turn, benefits from their support. A few days after winning his second term as mayor in November 1995, Goldsmith revealed his intention to campaign for governor the following year. He proudly announced to a *Chicago Tribune* reporter, "For the past three years I've been CEO of Indianapolis. Now I'd like to privatize all of Indiana." He promised that if elected governor he would make Indiana the first "fully privatized" state in America

(Lanosga 1995a).

One of the biggest backers of Goldsmith's privatization agenda was Richard Gilder, a trustee of the conservative Manhattan Institute, which was founded in 1978 by William Casey, the former Director of the CIA. Gilder is also founder of the Political Club for Growth that "bankrolls the conservative counterestablishment" (Abedian 1996). According to Stefancic, the Institute, for its size, "publishes more op-ed articles . . . than any other thank tank" (1995, 57).

The Manhattan Institute and Goldsmith are closely tied. Goldsmith currently earns $10,000 a year as chair of the Manhattan Institute's Board of the Center for Civic Innovation, and the Institute holds the copyright to his book *The Twenty-First Century City*. Gilder contributed $100,000 to Goldsmith's campaign for governor, while his wife Virginia, gave $10,000 more. Howard Berkowitz, also of the Manhattan Institute, gave another $100,000.

Some of the other contributors who espouse a conservative ideology and could help Goldsmith further his personal agenda include:

- Charles Koch, Chair and CEO of Koch Industries of Wichita, Kansas. Koch gave $7500 to Goldsmith in 1996. The Charles Koch Charitable Trust funds "conservative and free-market organizations" such as pro-privatization think tanks like Citizens for a Sound Economy (Wilcox 1997, 90)

- David Koch contributed $7,500 to Goldsmith in October 1996. He is President of the David H. Koch Charitable Foundation, which awarded over $9 million in grants to libertarian organizations such as Citizens for a Sound Economy, Reason Foundation and Cato Institute. (Wilcox 1997, 121)

- J. Patrick Rooney is the multimillionaire owner of Golden Rule Insurance Company. Rooney, who originated idea of medical savings accounts and supports school privatization, gave Goldsmith $22,800 for his run for governor; Golden Rule Financial and Golden Rule Insurance gave another $7,793 bringing the total to over $30,000 for 1996 alone (Goldsmith for Governor 1996).

Oscar Robertson Smoot

One of the mainstays of Goldsmith's privatization experiment was Oscar Robertson Smoot (ORS). The *Indianapolis Star* reported that Goldsmith "considers the ORS contracts among his best efforts to reinvent government through using the private sector. He consistently champions ORS as a business-savvy watchdog over city construction projects" (Morgan 1995a). Each time an ORS failure or scandal was revealed, Goldsmith would look into the cameras and microphones and intone the same phrase, "Yes, but they've saved us millions." In fact, the ORS joint venture amounted to leasing a very expensive cadre of inexperienced temporary employees. When its contract with the City of Indianapolis expired, ORS ceased to exist and there was no one to hold accountable when the inadequate work crumbled. Worse, there were few qualified public employees available to carry on the day-to-day administrative tasks since so many had been fired or laid off to make room for ORS.

Who was ORS?

Oscar Robertson Smoot was a joint venture created specifically to act as project manager for the $530 million infrastructure building and repair program known as Building Better Neighborhoods. The joint venture resulted from a partnering of Oscar Robertson and Associates (incorporated in 1992) and the Sherman Smoot Co. of Indiana (incorporated in 1991). *The Indianapolis Business Journal* reported during Goldsmith's first month in office, "Oscar Robertson and Associates hopes to nab more of the bigger projects in Indianapolis in the future. The company is hoping a joint venture with the Smoot Corp., a general construction firm based in Columbus, Ohio, will give it the muscle it needs here in Indianapolis. [The joint venture] was formed according to an ORS executive, because, when you start doing work that exceeds $10-$15 million, there are not a lot of minority firms that can compete. . ." (McKenzie 1992). The ORS contract with the City of Indianapolis was signed in March 1993 (ORS-City Contract 1993).

The players in the Oscar Robertson side of ORS—Oscar Robertson, Rodney Bynum and Warren Tyler—partnered in various projects and created a political action committee (PAC) in 1991, Businessmen for Good Government (BMGG) (BMGG 1991). Two days after the PAC was formed, it contributed $10,000 to Mayor Stephen Goldsmith's mayoral race, helping him to win the following month. The PAC and its principles[1] continued to be important contributors to the Goldsmith campaigns. Most of the PAC's contributions went to the Goldsmith campaigns, and the PAC folded after the ORS contract expired in 1997.

Oscar Robertson, the legendary basketball player from Indianapolis, had started a chemical company (Orchem) in Cincinnati, Ohio after retiring from professional sports in 1974. He was a well-regarded figure in the Indianapolis community, primarily by association with his basketball career. When the news stories of problems with the ORS contract began to surface, there were reports that Robertson was not an active participant in ORS. According to *NUVO Newsweekly*, "Robertson seems to have acted as a front man in the ORS partnership, providing his famous name and his minority presence, but little else. . ." (Ullmann 1996). Robertson's partners, Rodney Bynum and banker Warren Tyler, were considered by some to be the active principals.

Rodney Bynum was treasurer of the BMGG PAC, vice-president of Oscar Robertson & Associates, secretary of Oscar Robertson Co. of Indiana, treasurer of ORS and one of its highest paid associates.[2] Robertson and Bynum also partnered in another troubled venture, Opportunity Associates, in which they used a combination of loans, grants and tax credits from the City of Indianapolis to build seventy houses in Oxford Terrace in 1993 (Gelarden, 1999). Bynum was fired in October 1997 when Robertson discovered hundreds of thousands of dollars "missing" from the Oxford Terrace accounts. Robertson sued Bynum in federal court and federal authorities began investigating in early 1999. The case was complicated because Robertson's lawyer, Joe Whitsett, of the law firm Ice Miller Donadio and Ryan, lost key corporation records.

Warren Tyler, a banker from Columbus, Ohio, was also a principal in the formation of BMGG and a contributor to the Goldsmith campaigns. After Goldsmith took office, he gave Tyler (DBA Warmarr Capital, Inc.) a contract ($95 per hour plus expenses) to evaluate the organization of one of the most powerful city departments, the Department of Metropolitan Development (DMD)[3] (Lanosga 1992). Tyler acted as de facto head of DMD, and according to the *Indianapolis Star* his duties included "interviewing a candidate for the top job in the department, reviewing the budget, attending a planning retreat with city staffers, helping develop a request for proposals to privatize inspection functions and meeting with Churchill Downs officials about the potential for a new racetrack Downtown" (Lanosga 1992). Tyler continued to work for DMD, even after he reached his contract cap of $50,000 in June 1992. In late 1992, Goldsmith attempted to increase Tyler's contract to $113,000. When the newspapers began reviewing Tyler's situation, the request was withdrawn. City-County Councilor Rozelle Boyd stated, "There seems to be a scarcity of information. We can't determine what it is that (Tyler) is actually doing and whether he brings to the city a level of skill and expertise that is absolutely unavailable locally and justifies the amount of money going into it" (Lanosga 1992).

Tyler continued to contribute to Goldsmith's campaign fund. Besides the $2,000 he gave to the PAC, Tyler gave an additional $3,500 through 1997 and his employer in Ohio contributed $2,000 in 1996. Tyler was back in the news in 1999—"deeply involved" in the Oxford Terrace scandal along with Oscar Robertson and Rodney Bynum. The State Savings Bank of Ohio, where Tyler was vice-president, had loaned $1.6 million to help build the project. According to a newspaper interview, Robertson charged that Tyler had warned, "Nobody in the bank knows about this loan. Don't fax anything over. . . I'm the only one who can handle this loan." Ultimately the FBI and the IRS took an interest in this situation. The *Indianapolis Star* reported, "The FBI and IRS have served federal grand jury subpoenas seeking records of a $4.6 million real estate deal after the project's leader, Hoosier basketball legend Oscar Robertson, raised financial questions about his partners." (Gelarden, 1999)

The ORS-City Contract

The no-bid contract with ORS was signed in March 1993—without public notice and without debate by the City-County Council.[4] The Letter of Intent and the contract both appear to have been written by ORS itself. Typically, the city writes a Letter of Intent, advising a contractor of its intention to enter into a contract and issue a purchase order. This process allows the contractor to begin spending money for materials before the contract is official. Letters of Intent are not usually advisable if there is no time constraint requiring a "fast track" start because they invite contractor reliance, making the city liable before a final contract is negotiated and signed (Tomanovich, 2000a). In 1995, when interviewed about the Letter of Intent, ORS Vice-President John Muter admitted that it had been written by ORS: "What the hell is the difference? Somebody had to write the Letter of Intent. It's part of the process. The city knew it needed help" (Ramos and Ullmann 1996a). The Letter of Intent allowed ORS to begin drawing cash before the contract was signed, and purchase orders in the amount of $144,000 for December 1992 and January 1993 predate the contract by two months.

Recently, a city official, David Cleaver of the Department of Capital Asset Management (DCAM), reinforced the need to adhere to good management principles with his announcement of a change in management practices in which he stated that "The City of Indianapolis will not issue a purchase order without an executed contract" (Cleaver 2000).

The contract specified that two other companies, Shiel-Sexton and Hilliard Kosene, share the construction management duties as "associates" and six of the twenty-six positions designated in the contract were assigned to them. (ORS-City Contract 1993, Attachment G, Schedule A 2.2). These three firms—ORS, Shiel-Sexton and Hilliard Kosene—shared much in common:

- They had no prior experience managing large public works projects.
- They were not members of the trade association that sets professional standards for and represents construction managers nationally, the Construction Management Association of America (CMAA) (Ramos and Ullmann 1996a).
- They were major campaign contributors to Mayor Stephen Goldsmith, collectively giving him over $84,000 through 1997 (Steve Goldsmith Committee 1992-1997; Goldsmith for Governor 1996).

The contract further specified that ORS and its two associates be paid on a cost-plus basis using a 2.75 multiplier for salaries and raises (ORS-City Contract 1993, Attachment G, Section 1.1). This meant that if ORS paid an employee $50,000 per year, the city would be billed $137,500. This multiplier caused critics to wonder why Goldsmith would say in an interview, "I don't care how much ORS pays its employees as long as ORS does what the city pays it for" (Morgan 1995a). The contract also allowed 3 percent annual raises for ORS employees, which were charged to the city at 8.25 percent (ORS-City Contract 1993, Attachment G, Section 6.1). This generosity was in stark contrast to the Goldsmith administration's handling of an in-house contract award for fleet maintenance. In another case, city workers, who were competing with national companies, agreed to give up pay raises in exchange for "performance-based incentives" (Lanosga 1995b). According to a fact sheet from the SELTIC file, other concessions by employees were actually much larger: "Metro (bus) employees agreed to a three year wage freeze, early retirement programs and an increase in health insurance premiums to win the right to retain 19 routes" (*Indianapolis Star* 1996a; Daniels n.d.).

The 2.75 multiplier was greater than the market rate at the time; it could only be justified if the contractor had paid for all of its own overhead and expenses (Kennedy, 2000). This was not the case with

ORS—the contract also provided that the city would supply "Office space, furniture and fixtures, telephones, including long distance capabilities; copiers, facsimile machines and other necessary office equipment; office supplies; gasoline for vehicles . . . vehicles and/or mileage, as deemed appropriate by owner [City]" (ORS-City Contract 1993, 6). The value of the office space provided by the city can be estimated at $46,000 based on the amount a city department would have to pay to the city's Building Authority for equivalent space, which was located in the City-County building. The ORS employees were also reimbursed for the cost of parking, another $6,240 (DCAM n.d).

What was the scope of work that ORS was to perform for compensation substantially in excess of the existing market for construction management services? Project Managers were to:

- Work with individuals/agencies who would ultimately use the facilities to draft specifications for construction contractors.
- Set up sequence of project work, manage project sites and schedule material deliveries.
- Coordinate work between various departments to eliminate redundancy.
- Monitor contractors.

The entire $9.4 million cost of employing ORS was charged to the capital budget. This allowed the Goldsmith administration to take credit for "saving" over $9 million in the city's operating budget over the life of the contract. Of course, this bit of legerdemain also entailed additional costs. Assuming the city borrowed that $9.4 million for 20 years at 6 percent, it would pay an additional $6.76 million in interest on the borrowed money according to standard amortization tables (Burrell 1998). This would bring the total cost to taxpayers of hiring ORS to $16 million. In other words, once interest costs are factored in, the cost to the Indianapolis taxpayer of the ORS 2.75 multiplier actually becomes 3.50. The cost of construction and other capital improvements that have an extended useful life and are legitimately and routinely bonded is a cost of doing business. On the other hand, firing employees who are paid out of the operating budget and replacing them with contractors who are paid through the capital budget is a deceptive and wasteful practice.

Well-paid contractors tend to be reliable sources of campaign money and ORS was no exception—ORS and its two designated associates (Shiel-Sexton and Hilliard Kosene) contributed $84,000 and other political favors[5] from 1992-1997 to Goldsmith's political campaigns. In addition, the fact that ORS was a minority-owned firm allowed Goldsmith to defend city employment reductions that were perceived by some as targeting minority workers (Boyd 1999). One of the Mayor's reasons for replacing city employees with contract employees such as ORS was that they would bring a "fresh outside perspective." Unfortunately, there was no one monitoring ORS. Early in the administration, Carlton Curry, a Republican City-County Councilor, proposed setting up a system to monitor the performance of ORS (Lanosga and Johnston 1995). Goldsmith supporters on the Council, however, rejected this proposal. For the entire fifty-two month term of its extended contract, ORS was virtually on its own, with no consistent or in-depth monitoring from the Goldsmith administration (especially after city employees who were working with ORS were fired or transferred). The absence of oversight resulted in a significant cost to the taxpayers, monetarily and in loss of services.

ORS Takes Charge of Projects at the Parks Department

One of the reasons given for the privatization efforts at the Indianapolis Department of Parks and Recreation (IDPR) and other city agencies was that work by the private sector would be better and more cost effective. An examination of ORS activities at the Parks Department provides another demonstration that this fundamental assumption—the private sector is provides better and more efficient service than government—is flawed. A 1991 audit of the Parks Department's construction contract administration provides a baseline for the operation of some of the Department's activities before the privatization. The auditors concluded,

> Our examination indicated that controls in place . . . are generally adequate . . . inspections are being conducted and satisfactorily documented. The files were well-organized and included all required documentation. Our review of change orders indicated the presence of acceptable practices. (Internal Audit Agency 1991, 1).

By all accounts, these and other contemporaneous audits indicate that the Parks Department operations that were audited were operating according to acceptable practices, in contrast to the privatized operations that are discussed below.

The story of ORS at the Parks Department began with the firing of

George Tomanovich, a long time Parks Department employee, and encompasses construction management at the city's parks, swimming pools, and housing authority.[6]

George Tomanovich Raises Concerns about ORS

To insure uniformity of outlook in each department, the city's contract with ORS allowed ORS to request the removal of any city worker "who in the opinion of PROGRAM MANAGER (sic) [ORS] does not perform his work in a proper and skillful manner" (ORS-City Contract 1993, Article 3.5, 6). This clause allowed ORS to fire any public employee for any reason, including questioning privatization or ORS' methods. Parks Department employees George Tomanovich, Al Brethauer and Reed Pryor were all demoted or fired at ORS' request (Tomanovich 2000b).

Tomanovich, a professional engineer and a city employee for over 20 years, headed the construction management section of DPR where he managed a total of twenty-five employees in two sections. One of them was the Land Improvement Section. With a reputation for professionalism and outspokenness, Tomanovich was highly respected at city hall and among the contractors he supervised. He always kept meticulous hand-written records and notes of meetings. After ORS took charge of the Parks Department, Tomanovich continued to oversee construction until he was terminated in January 1995. According to Goldsmith, public employees (such as George Tomanovich) could not provide money-saving scrutiny (like ORS) because "they'd be scrutinizing their own work" (Morgan 1995b). Ironically, Tomanovich was a life-long Republican who had knocked on doors to get signatures for Goldsmith's $530 million bond issue to fund the Capital Improvement Program (CIP).

As ORS took charge of projects at the Parks Department, Tomanovich grew increasingly concerned by expensive but poor quality work performed by ORS and its subcontractors. In response to this concern, Tomanovich submitted a "Hot Idea" through proper channels in February 1994—the "Hot Idea" program was a Goldsmith initiative through which city employees were encouraged to submit suggestions on potential savings. Tomanovich recommended that the Parks Department "hire a full time Department of Parks & Recreation (DPR) Construction Field Project Manager" for the term of the Capital Improvement Program which ORS was then overseeing. Tomanovich went on to point out that " . . . the city [would] save approximately

$80,000 per year for the next two years. We now pay consultant firm (ORS) approximately $120,000 per project manager." He concluded, " . . . .the employee would have the security of a two (2) year job (depending on their performance) and be a REAL (sic) DPR employee, not a consultant. Loyalty and commitment would be there to *this* city." (Tomanovich 1996a. Exhibit G)

Anne Shane, Goldsmith's Chief of Staff at the time, told Tomanovich, "I do not believe your proposal can be classified as a Hot Idea. . . I frankly do not feel that there will be any support from the Council, the mayor or other directors to remove an independent supervisor from the process." (Shane 1994) Shane copied her letter to Tomanovich's boss, Julee Jacob, who subsequently wrote to Tomanovich: "I am directing you to discontinue your efforts to pursue this issue" (Jacob 1994). She went on to say that if Tomanovich needed additional help, "I suggest you contact ORS and ask them to pursue hiring . . . the best person for the job . . . " (Jacob 1994). Tomanovich subsequently took his concerns to Parks Department Director Younger, the Mayor, the prosecutor's office and finally to the newspapers, especially *NUVO Newsweekly*.

The lawsuit would provide evidence that Goldsmith:

- Had Tomanovich followed by city investigators. Parks Department Director Younger told the investigators, "We suspect George Tomanovich of leaking information to the news media" (Atterson 1996, 10). The investigators, who were to determine if Tomanovich were leaving work early and whether he was talking to the media, found that he was working considerably more hours than his time records had indicated.

- Threatened other city employees that they would be fired if they had contact with Tomanovich: "If you associate with George Tomanovich" an employee's "future was limited" (Zishka 1996, 10).

- Advised all city officials against talking to *NUVO* reporters. "Several of the city's public relations representatives have since told *NUVO* they will lose their jobs if they answer the newspaper's questions" (Ramos and Ullmann 1996b).

- Refused to provide *NUVO* with copies of public records under the open records law.

In November 1994, over a year after his first complaint, the Parks Department informed Tomanovich that his position had been eliminated. In a letter to Goldsmith, Tomanovich asked the Mayor not to eliminate the Parks Construction Section (Tomanovich 1995), and he propsed retaining his position and that of a full-time project manager, a move that Tomanovich believed would result in substantial savings to the city. Tomanovich reminded Goldsmith that under his leadership (Tomanovich's), the Construction Section had:

- saved $40,000 to $50,000 per year in contract change orders,
- been free of litigation since 1987,
- accomplished oversight of $8 million of construction at a cost of less than 2.5 percent of project costs, and .
- brought institutional memory to projects by virtue of experienced city employees.

He concluded, "We offer you a service at a lower cost than that of a consultant firm, cost effective management with a proven record of accomplishments . . . experience and dedication to our city. Isn't that what you have told this community privatization is all about?" (Tomanovich 1995)

Goldsmith wrote back testily that he would "once again clarify the city's position." Some of his reasons for hiring ORS included: " . . . we wanted a firm that would provide a complete spectrum of program management services, including value engineering . . . staff, budget, contract . . . and design management . . . value enhancement, community relations, etc." and "we wanted a third party scrutinizing our processes to ensure that taxpayers received value for their investment . . . ." Goldsmith had been so impressed with ORS that he went on to say, "We want to continue to have the full range of services provided by a construction manager like ORS in the future . . . ." (Goldsmith 1995)

Tomanovich, who was out of work for one week, was subsequently assigned to another department with a 35 percent reduction in pay and told "he could not be considered for promotion or advancement to a more lucrative position until he proved his loyalty to the mayor and backed the mayor's privatization initiatives" (Tomanovich 1996a, 19).[7] Later the threat escalated to either establish "loyalty to the mayor or be terminated as a city employee" (Tomanovich 1996a, 18).

After Tomanovich went public with his concerns and the local newspapers began covering the story, Goldsmith reacted angrily: "George Tomanovich was trying to keep his job by claiming to blow the whistle on matters that aren't that significant" (Schneider 1996a). Political reporter Mary Beth Schneider of the *Indianapolis Star* echoed the opinion of many when she noted, "Goldsmith's response then displayed a troubling inclination to defensively dismiss criticism rather than constructively address the problem" (Schneider 1996a).

Tomanovich had filed a tort claim in federal court in early 1995 against Goldsmith, Parks Department Director Leon Younger, the Parks Department Board and the City-County Council of Indianapolis. The lawsuit alleged that privatization was an expensive failure. Among the charges made:

ORS staff had no prior golf course experience and was ill equipped to handle these responsibilities (Tomanovich 1996a, 6).

Leon Younger was instructed by the mayor to replace city employees with ORS staff members and told to ignore laws governing the bidding process in order to expedite this work (Tomanovich 1996a, 6).

ORS employees mismanaged various construction projects (Tomanovich 1996a, 7).

ORS employees conducted other business while on company time (Tomanovich 1996a, 7).

ORS employees did not appear to be monitoring compliance with the 'Prevailing Wage Act' . . . as required by ORS' contract . . . but continued . . . charging the city for monitoring compliance with 'prevailing wage laws'. . . . (Tomanovich 1996a, 8).

ORS was falsifying time records and was billing the city for hours spent managing contracts which were in fact being monitored by Tomanovich, not ORS (Tomanovich 1996a, 8).

[ORS employees] were utilizing city facilities and offices to publish and copy Republican literature and conduct other non-city business (Tomanovich 1996a, 8).

ORS claimed responsibility for 'cost savings'. . . which were actually proposed by Parks' staff, not ORS . . . in order to create a false impression that ORS was responsible for 'significant cost savings ideas' and 'value engineering' (Tomanovich 1996a, 9).

[P]rivate contractors and consultants were being shown favoritism in the letting of public work based upon their financial support of the mayor (Tomanovich 1996aa, 10).

[T]he City of Indianapolis as part of its policy and custom ha[d] undertaken an effort to suppress any and all criticism of the mayor's privatization efforts and its use of private contractors to provide public services (Tomanovich 1996a, 17).

The Mayor's office and Parks Dept . . . have also reorganized the Parks Dept in order to isolate ORS from any public criticism or oversight by city employees such as George Tomanovich (Tomanovich 1996a, 13) .

[ORS issued] instructions to alter and falsify engineer's estimates and provide false and inaccurate supporting documentation to the Board of Parks and Recreation[8] (Tomanovich 1996a, 15).

[T]he privatization agenda of the mayor and other city employees is simply a means of providing political patronage and efficiently obtaining financial support from businesses such as ORS and other city contractors who have been allowed to take over functions previously handled by public employees (Tomanovich 1996a, 19).

These were extremely serious charges. Goldsmith minimized the importance of the case as "nothing new and nothing very significant" (Schneider 1996b). However, the city retained an outside law firm to defend the Mayor and other city officials and a trial date of August 26, 1996 was set. Goldsmith successfully fought a request for his deposition stating that he was "simply too busy to sit for a three-hour deposition." While receiving an enthusiastic endorsement from former GOP presidential candidate Steve Forbes, reporters asked Goldsmith about the lawsuit. Goldsmith replied, "I don't see any reason to give a deposition. I'm not a part of the lawsuit. The underlying issues . . . have nothing to do with me" (Schneider 1996b). The situation was perhaps beginning to make Goldsmith regret his 1993 boast, "I'm involved in everything. I just don't micromanage it" (Johnston and Lanosga 1993). The *Indianapolis Star* editorialized, "Coming in the midst of his campaign for governor, Goldsmith has an obligation to respond to the issues raised by this case. He has thus far resisted efforts to force his testimony" (*Indianapolis Star* 1996b).

In May, George Tomanovich had been willing to take $100,000 plus legal fees and be put back to work at his old salary of $51,000 per year, but Goldsmith refused. By June, however, a settlement was reached that satisfied the Mayor. This settlement included:

- legal fees of $45,000 reimbursed to George Tomanovich (Settlement Agreement 1996, 2);
- $25,771 for lost wages and benefits (Settlement Agreement 1996, 2); and

- a 42-month consulting contract at $6,670 per month ($280,000)
  with no more than 25 hours per week to be scheduled, and
  payable whether or not there was work scheduled (Settlement
  Agreement 1996, Professional Services Agreement 1996).

For this price, Goldsmith kept Tomanovich out of his old
construction management job at the Parks Department and avoided
giving sworn testimony about the disturbing charges contained in the
lawsuit. Tomanovich had wanted to take the case to trial, but his
resources were exhausted—he had already paid legal fees of $45,000
by taking a second mortgage on his home. Goldsmith had a distinct
advantage because public funds were paying for his defense. (Even the
expense of the settlement went on the capital budget, rather than being
paid from the line allocated for legal costs in the operating budget.) The
final irony was to come from the DCAM Director, Greg Henneke, who
had earlier warned Tomanovich that he needed to demonstrate to
Henneke and Goldsmith his support for the Mayor's privatization
efforts if Tomanovich wanted to continue with the city (Tomanovich
1996b, 40). Henneke said, "Taxpayers will get something out of the
settlement with Tomanovich, namely *a consultant who does good
work*" (emphasis mine) (Johnston 1996c).

In a postscript to the Tomanovich case, Goldsmith finally
acknowledged Tomanovich's concerns, but at the same time he
appeared to deflect responsibility for Tomanovich's treatment away
from himself with the following statement: "The Parks Department
didn't give George the credit he deserved for caring about details of the
taxpayer dollar." (Johnston 1996d). Mayor Bart Peterson, Goldsmith's
successor, has rehired Tomanovich to work in the Parks Department to
do essentially the same work he had been doing prior to the time he was
fired by Goldsmith.

Prevailing Wage Monitoring

One of ORS' responsibilities was to monitor the prevailing wage on
all construction projects. Prior to the Goldsmith administration, the city
rigorously monitored prevailing wage and ferreted out dozens of
violations each year (Tomanovich 1998a). However, wage monitoring
was never done on the extensive golf course renovations (or for that
matter on any other construction project) managed by ORS, which were
audited internally or by the State Board of Accounts (Indiana State
Board of Accounts 1999, 4-5).

The 1993 contract required ORS to monitor all projects.[9] The Mayor had been an outspoken critic of the prevailing wage law and of the city's need to monitor it. As a consequence, there was no documented monitoring of prevailing wage. In his deposition, Parks Director Younger stated that Goldsmith "felt if the State wanted to enforce prevailing wage, it was their responsibility," not the city's (Younger 1996, 96). Despite the admission that the administration knew the monitoring was not being done, ORS was paid consistently for doing it, and on the usual cost-plus basis.

In July 1995, the ORS contract was amended (twenty-eight months into the contract) to relieve ORS of any contractual duty to do monitoring: "Any services relating to wage or contract compliance shall be deleted from the Agreement" (ORS-City Contract 1995, Amendment No. 5, 2 (item 3)). However, there was no downward adjustment in payment to ORS as a result.

ORS Manages Construction at the City's Parks

The internal audits of the Franklin/Edgewood Park and Northwestway Park projects were released nearly two years after the projects were supposedly completed. This audit dated July 29, 1996, supported Tomanovich's allegations in the federal lawsuit, which the city had settled earlier for over $300,000. The audits were requested by Greg Henneke, Director of the DCAM and the Department of Public Works, to settle the controversy—""was ORS at fault or George Tomanovich?" (Henneke 1996, 93) If the problems had been confined to the golf courses, it would be possible to suggest that this was one discrete area that had not responded to otherwise positive initiatives. But that would be misleading.

The Franklin/Edgewood Park and Northwestway Park projects were fairly modest, involving $219,089 and $446,993 respectively for playgrounds, paths, parking lots and drainage (Internal Audit Agency 1996a, 1). Tomanovich had begun overseeing the project, which had started in the summer of 1994. By late summer, it was nearly completed and Tomanovich walked through the park with the contractor and architect to make a list of work still to be addressed. This list was a legal document called a "punch list" and required the contractor to make good on any unfinished or unsatisfactory work identified on that list (Tomanovich 1998b). All the principals involved at that time decided the project was far enough along to make partial payment to the contractor and allow the city to begin using the park. A Certificate of

Substantial Completion was issued as of August 23, 1994 and signed in October by all parties—the architect, contractor and George Tomanovich (for the city) (Ramos and Ullmann 1996c). This certificate bound the contractors to finish the punch list and to warranty all work for one year. Tomanovich said that under his signature, as was his custom, he wrote a note stipulating that the contractor must complete the work specified on the punch list. In January 1995, Tomanovich was fired along with his entire Parks Department Construction Section. All of his records were turned over to ORS along with follow-up responsibility for the Franklin/Edgewood and Northwestway Park projects (Tomanovich 1998b).

The internal audit was released over Goldsmith's objections after the *Indianapolis Star* sued for its release. The *Star* found that nearly two years after the original project completion date, "there is no evidence that final punch list items have been fully resolved at both park locations" (Internal Audit Agency 1996, 2). The audit also noted, "Final payment and retainage was released to the construction firm for both construction projects without an inspection of the final punch list items by either contract architects at the direction of the city's contract CIP Program Manager" (Internal Audit Agency 1996, 3). (Franklin/Edgewood Park and Northwestway Park had different architects but the same construction company, Brandt.)

The only hours that were billed for this project by ORS were for Mike Skarp who was paid $3,767 for 50 hours of on-site construction management (Indiana State Board of Accounts 1999, 7). However, no one involved with the project—Tomanovich, the architects, or any of the construction workers—ever saw Mike Skarp or any other ORS employee at the Park sites. This fact was disclosed during an inquiry by the State Board of Accounts and ORS excused itself by saying, "ORS employees charged the wrong cost code on their invoices and the $3,767 in question should have been charged to the Riverside Project" (Indiana State Board of Accounts 1999, 7). However, this was extremely unlikely since the Riverside Project had not begun until late 1994, well after the Franklin/Edgewood Project (Tomanovich 2000c).

NUVO Newsweekly did an investigation into the alleged ghost employment of ORS employee, Mike Skarp, and wrote: "As an example of the fiscal complexity of the city's partnership with ORS, the payment ORS claimed for Skarp's work in October, 1994, was a single line in 15 pages of records that ORS sent to the city to support its invoice for $486,000 monthly payment under its contract with the Goldsmith Administration" (Ullmann and Ramos 1996). Billing the city for work not done normally would be considered ghost employment, a felony in Indiana. But contract employees such as Skarp are not considered public employees and are therefore not subject to the laws governing public employees. The Public-Private Agreement Law of 1995, discussed in Chapter 15, removed any possibility of holding these contract employees accountable. Furthermore, by the time of the audit, the city's copy of the certificate of substantial completion had evolved into a completely new document, which was dated February 6, 1995 (four months after the certificate had been signed by the architect and contractor). The revised certificate did not have a note stipulating the work to be done and rather than George Tomanovich's signature, it was signed by ORS' Becky Federwisch. In other words, no city employee had inspected and signed off on the Franklin project. A private contractor, ORS, had vouched for other private contractors without even seeing the work site and had authorized payment of public funds for unfinished and unsatisfactory work

The city had different options available for holding the contractor accountable. For example, it could have had city crews finish and redo the work and bill the contractor, as was the practice before privatization, or it could have demanded that the contractor do the necessary work during the warranty period at no charge. However, Goldsmith told ORS to handle it. (Ramos and Ullmann 1996c). ORS hired another contractor, Harco Paving, to rework and finish the botched Parks Department projects and added the cost to a separate paving contract. It eventually became necessary to hire yet a third contractor to clean up after the second, and even then, as the audit reports, "other items (particularly those associated with the playground area, playground benches and trails—one of which is currently overrun with weeds and washed out in some places) appear to have been either unfinished or ineffectively remedied, in our opinion" (Internal Audit Agency 1996, 3). The audit agency contacted the original contractor about the unfinished work on the project two years later and was told that since the final payment and retainage had been released by ORS, it was entitled to conclude that "all work had been satisfactorily completed" (Internal Audit Agency 1996, 4).

After the second contractor failed to correct the drainage work, the auditors observed, "Our observation of the drainage work completed under the recent contract showed severe deterioration of completed drainage work leading from the parking lot area to a retention pond" (Internal Audit Agency 1996, 4). Follow-up with the Parks Department and ORS by the auditors "about this condition indicated they were unaware of any field inspections having been performed during drainage work or after its completion. No documentation could be provided to us describing the work that was actually performed" (Internal Audit Agency 1996, 4). The audit concluded that $26,200 in work paid for in the original contract had not been completed.

The auditors also noted: "This review was performed without benefit of 'as-built' drawings for both projects, the architect inspection reports, and project meeting minutes for Franklin/Edgewood Park and the Parks Construction Section inspection reports for Northwestway Park, as these documents could not be located during our review. We also could not confirm the completeness of some other documents . . . in regards to having a full set at our disposal" (Internal Audit Agency 1996, 1). George Tomanovich responded in an interview, "My staff did have full inspection files. ORS removed them from the office in 1995" (Tomanovich 1998b).

The *Indianapolis News* editorialized in August, 1996, "Yet another project has been bungled by the people paid by Mayor Stephen Goldsmith to do the job . . . consultant Oscar Robertson/Smoot . . . paid contractors $26,200 for work that never was done." The editorial went on to scold the Mayor by reminding him that "$26,200 is not such a small percentage when one considers that the audit only dealt with $666,025 worth of work" (*Indianapolis News* 1996a). The editorial added, "Thus, an audit of just a tiny fraction of ORS' total activities revealed substantial mismanagement in the form of work done improperly and payment to a contractor for which no work was done. Who knows what audits of additional work overseen by ORS would uncover?" (*Indianapolis News* 1996a).

Former Prosecutor Goldsmith was firm in his dismissal of the incident saying he had "no plans to investigate the allegations of doctored and missing documents because all of the people involved no longer work for the city" (Johnston 1996). The Mayor concluded, "I think I'm going to move past it, because I don't think anything productive can come from it" (Johnston 1996).

ORS Manages Construction at the City's Swimming Pools

Audits of work overseen by ORS were few and far between, but a sampling reveals some disturbing tendencies. This section provides a glimpse of problems that internal audits revealed at construction projects managed by ORS at three of the city's swimming pools: Krannert-King-Brookside, Garfield Aquatic Center and Indy Island Aquatic Center. All of these examples put the spotlight on weaknesses related to the privatization efforts of Mayor Goldsmith.

Krannert-King-Brookside (KKB) Pool Renovation Project

Bid Violations

A proposal for the construction of three pools, Krannert-King-Brookside, was prepared in January 1994. An engineer's estimate was prepared for the KKB project by Jim McKnight for $965,789 (Tomanovich 1996a, Exhibit A, 11a). Only two bids were received for the project and they were within one-half of one percent of each other. George Tomanovich believed that the bid by Hasser Construction, a company that had no experience on pool projects, was a dummy bid to allow the other contractor, Brandt Construction, to win (Tomanovich 2000c). Tomanovich believed this bid violation to be the most serious that he had seen (Ramos 1996a).

An even greater concern was that the bids were for $1.5 million, or 49 percent over the engineer's estimate (Tomanovich 1996a, 11a). Normally, according to the audit, "Each project should have a minimum of three (3) confirmed bidders, with a goal of five (5) as an average" (Internal Audit Agency 1995). With only two bids, one of which was suspicious and both of which were considerably over the engineer's estimate, department policy plainly stated that "a written report must be sent to both Asset Manager and ORS Project Executive" (in this instance the project executive for ORS was John Muter). Furthermore, the Asset Manager, a city employee, must then provide written authority to proceed with the project under these less than ideal conditions (Hefleng 1995). The fact that the bids were 49 percent over the engineer's estimate should automatically have caused the project to be re-bid. However, the proper procedure was not followed. Instead, ORS construction manager, Darryl Coleman, directed engineer McKnight to alter and falsify his estimate upward to coincide with the bids (Tomanovich 1996a, 11a).

Tomanovich took the engineer in to see Parks Director Leon Younger. In Younger's words: "Well, George brought Jim McKnight in and said, 'Leon, I want you to hear this.'" McKnight went on to explain the issues saying he . . . "didn't think it was right that somebody was asking him to change the bid . . . " (Younger 1996, 84). Exhibit C of the

Tomanovich lawsuit is the actual engineer's estimate with figures revised by an ORS employee.

According to Tomanovich, his supervisor, Julee Jacob, was angry because Tomanovich was making such a "big deal" out of the irregularities. He stated that Jacob ripped the engineer's estimate to shreds in front of Tomanovich and his staff and ordered Tomanovich to go home and not attend the Parks Board meeting. Engineer McKnight had been told earlier to stay away by ORS' Darryl Coleman. The outcome of this incident was that Jacob recommended that Brandt get the contract based on a "ballpark figure" called the scoping estimate. The scoping estimate was not based on an engineer's evaluation and in this case was a half-million dollars higher (Tomanovich 2000c).

In a letter to an ORS official, the Internal Audit Agency inquired about the altered engineer's estimate, "We also noted that after the bid opening, the Architect was asked to raise his cost estimate; however, we could locate no documentation regarding the reason(s) precipitating this request. Were there errors or omissions in the design?" (Hefleng 1995)

SELTIC Recommends Privatizing Materials Testing Laboratory

Concrete, and a lot of it, was needed to construct the Krannert-King-Brookside pools. Prior to Goldsmith's privatization efforts, the city ran its own materials testing laboratory to ensure that concrete used in projects such as the KKB construction met the required specifications. The laboratory also had the capability to test structural steel, asphalt, soil and other materials. However, in February 1993, SELTIC, the Mayor's advisory group on privatization, had recommended that the city "get out of the testing business." According to a study by a local consultant, the laboratory needed an upgrade that would cost $45,000 to $70,000 and the annual cost of operating the laboratory was $110,000. If the testing were placed in private hands, these costs could be avoided (Heiken 1993). So, the city's laboratory was privatized, but the costs of upgrading the laboratory were not avoided. In fact, the city actually spent more on the privatized service than it would have on upgrading its laboratory. A contract was signed with SEG Inc. in August 1993 to take over the city's material testing laboratory. The contract specified that SEG receive a maximum of $200,000 per year (Department of Transportation 1993, 3). The city allowed the private testing company to lease the same materials laboratory testing facility, which supposedly needed a costly upgrade (according to SELTIC), for a modest $600 per month. The lease agreement also included the use of the laboratory's equipment, which included two Sartorius Electric Balances, two Troxler Nuclear Gauges and a Forney Compression Testing Machine (DCAM 1996, Exhibit B),

To complicate matters even further, SEG, a private testing company, was also charged with overseeing the separate testing laboratories hired by each individual contractor. So, the new system, which was to replace the supposedly inefficient, pre-privatization system, added another layer of bureaucracy by requiring that each contractor hire its own outside testing laboratory to check its work, and SEG would then perform spot checks of each of the other laboratory's work.

This complicated system allowed the construction contractor to figure cost of this extra laboratory check into its bid, thereby adding further expense to the project, and these secondary and tertiary relationships made it more likely that off-specification concrete would slip through. And, according to the audit report, this is just what happened:

> Fifteen (15) of forty-two (42) concrete test reports showed characteristics of slump, air content, water added and/or delivery time of the materials placed outside the project specification for concrete work. Each of the fifteen pours represent an occasion when project inspectors were unable to attend and observe the pour with testing lab personnel and in each case, loads were not rejected on site by the contractor. The testing lab was a sub-contractor . . . and was not authorized to stop a potentially defective pour. (Internal Audit Agency 1995, 4)

Prior to privatization, the city maintained a uniformly well regarded materials testing laboratory that provided quality, quick turn around and value. In this case, the public agency was preferable to the private one. The public testing laboratory owed no loyalty to the contractor and was not dependent on the contractor's good will. The public laboratory could order the contractor to stop work whenever the test results tests showed a defective pour. The private laboratory could not. The $100,000 in annual cost to operate the public laboratory would appear to be a good use of taxpayer resources compared to the privatized service.

Garfield Park Aquatic Center

The Garfield Aquatic Center audit was completed in July 1997, one year after the renovated facility opened. At the time of the audit, the project costs were $2,640,195, but the final claims had not been submitted at the close of the review (Internal Audit Agency 1997, 1). In this project, the auditors' general conclusion noted the following problems:

- Record keeping on the project was "extremely poor."
- There was no follow-up to assure that all deliverables were received.
- Critical documentation was in many cases missing or incomplete.
- Maintenance manuals and warranties had not been received, even though the facility had opened the previous summer.
- A required inspection prior to the expiration of the warranty period had not been planned. (However, it did take place as a compliance issue attributed to the audit.)
- The resulting warranty inspection and the auditors' observations both indicated items requiring repair under the warranty provisions.

Additional comments included:

- There were only ten daily reports on file for the entire one-year project.
- Documentation for change order pricing was scattered throughout several file folders.
- There were no pre-construction meetings.
- There were no certified payrolls for subcontractors.
- Plaster ceilings are cracking.
- Numerous cracks in concrete around pool.
- Significant cracking in bottom of the leisure pool and one crack at bottom of lap pool.

At a Garfield Park neighborhood meeting in March 1996, residents voiced concerns to a City-County Councilor over the way the whole project was progressing. City-County Councilor Bob Massie, who represented the Garfield area, was angry that city planners responsible for the project (ORS) would not attend this meeting of seventy-five taxpayers. He also complained that he had been unable to find out how the project's $5 million had been spent since project expense lists were unavailable (Bibbs 1996). Approximately $4 million of Garfield money was used to pay for other ORS problem projects such as the Riverside Project, which experienced dozens of change orders (Tomanovich 2000d). The Garfield project was in jeopardy, but a grant of $5 million from the Eli Lilly Endowment allowed its completion. Councilor Massie remarked, "It would have been better to let the place run down. Then you'd only have frustrated people instead of $5 million down the drain" (Bibbs 1996). One resident, Sandy Sigmund, told reporters,

"That aquatic center, to me, looks cheap and does not fit in with the character of the park."

Since its construction, the Garfield facility has experienced a number of problems including leaking roofs, improperly functioning filters and ventilation systems, and structural problems. One of ORS's "value enhancements" at this facility was to save money by not installing drains in the conservatory. As a result, the control room for the conservatory's electrical system flooded causing considerable damage. (Tomanovich 2000d)

Indy Island Aquatic Center

Indy Island Aquatic Center, which offered year round swimming, was opened in 1995 at a cost of $1.9 million (Gelarden 1998). ORS was completely in charge of this project. According to the *Indianapolis Star*, the park experienced problems soon after it opened. The heat, humidity and chlorine seemed oppressive, and the ventilation system did not appear to be working properly. This problem was "solved" by propping open the outside doors and using large exhaust fans to ventilate the pool. Soon rust was forming everywhere in the facility—walls, fountains, doorframes and even stainless steel fixtures. The lack of ventilation and corrosion in the facility was caused by poor design, including the design of a completely inadequately heating, ventilation and cooling system (Gelarden 1998).

Another problem at Indy Island was also the result of Goldsmith's management policies. In his book Goldsmith says, "Our efforts to dissolve traditional job descriptions had two goals: to push authority down to the front lines and to hold every employee responsible for customer satisfaction" (Goldsmith 1997, 69). He continued, "Too many narrowly described jobs reduce effectiveness, increase supervisory costs and demean workers. When employees are set free, great things happen" (Goldsmith 1997, 69). This philosophy led him to eliminate key personnel and job descriptions within the city.

Among the "great things" that happened at Indy Island were that inexperienced lifeguards were managing and performing maintenance in order to save money on the operating budget. Unfortunately, these young employees occasionally forgot to change filters, which clogged up pressure gauges (Howey 1999). Also, when bacteria levels shot up, these inexperienced staffers would at times add chlorine to the pool even though swimmers were still in the water, in violation of the Marion County Health Department regulations. In July 1998, after only three years of operation, the City-County Council voted to provide $250,000 to replace the corroded HVAC system. By the time the rusting stainless steel was repaired or replaced and the facility deoxidized and repainted, the bill came to $500,000 (Gelarden 1998).

ORS Manages Construction at the City's Housing Authority

The most troubled department in the city was the Public Housing Authority. Though riddled with scandal and incompetence and on the federal Department of Housing and Urban Development's (HUD) list of "troubled agencies," this department was subjected to only one internal audit by the city during Goldsmith's eight years as Mayor. The lone audit was performed by the city for a period from July to December 1992. The massive fifty-three page report concluded that all areas being reviewed "are in need of improved efficiency and accountability . . . performance reports being either non-existent or, when available, misleading" (Internal Audit Agency 1993, 1). Follows up audits were not performed during the next seven years.

The impact of ORS on the Housing Authority was considerable, and it eventually triggered a federal audit. In March of 1992, Goldsmith announced a "reorganization of the city's housing and development agency" and layoffs of 55 personnel (Morrison 1992). He also eliminated 47 vacant slots and put a hiring freeze in place. Maintenance and oversight responsibilities were consistently the first positions to be trimmed by Goldsmith, and in the case of the Housing Authority, he had reduced the public housing maintenance staff from 51 to 34 by February 1993. Goldsmith claimed downsizing would save $2.6 million. (The laid off employees first learned of their fate during a news conference; Goldsmith told the shocked employees, "It is impossible to tell people privately what is going to happen a week ahead of time" (Morrison 1992)).

The downsized agency had already been placed on HUD's "troubled agency" list in 1992 and things got worse thereafter. Staff retention at the executive levels was a problem. During the first six years of Goldsmith's administration, the Housing Authority had three executive directors and two acting executive directors (U.S. HUD 1997, 5). In a rare moment of candor during a 1998 interview with journalist Michael Grunwald, Goldsmith admitted that his housing authority was "totally incompetent" (Grunwald 1998). What he did not tell Grunwald is that he had appointed the executive directors and he personally had hired the agency's construction manager, ORS (without competitive bidding).

ORS began supervising construction at various public housing projects in 1993. By fall of 1996, it had billed the city $1.5 million for overseeing renovations at six public housing projects (Lanosga and Johnston 1996b). There would have been more money for ORS, but in June 1996 federal officials blocked the city from handing ORS yet another no-bid contract in the amount of $1.1 million. (*Indianapolis News* 1996b). Officials at HUD told the city that ORS' contract violated federal rules requiring competitive bidding. The *Indianapolis News* reported that when faced with actual competition, "ORS chose not to participate in the subsequent bidding. Spokesman John Muter said the firm was busy with other work" (*Indianapolis News* 1996b).

Mayor Goldsmith told reporters that work done by ORS is "one of the most dramatic success stories in public housing across the United States in 20 years" (*Indianapolis News* 1996b). Not everyone agreed—certainly not the residents and auditors of these projects. In a memo dated June 11, 1996 Charles Spann, Director of Facilities for the Housing Authority, told the Modernization Director of the Housing Authority, Bill Coleman, that ORS projects had "sinkholes, cracked walkways, leaky roofs, damaged ceilings, flawed siding and incomplete security systems" (Lanosga and Johnston 1996b). Spann told the Housing Authority Board in August that two of the recently finished projects will be a "maintenance headache in less than five years because of the poor quality materials used" (Lanosga and Johnston 1996b). In a statement reminiscent of other ORS projects reported on in this chapter, he added that these two communities have "Unfinished apartments, streets, sidewalks and playgrounds and that since the warranties have expired, the city will have to pay for rework and repair" (Lanosga and Johnston 1996b). Marsha Arnold, Community Manager at Hawthorne Place, kept long lists of incomplete, substandard work on apartments that were considered finished by the contractors (Lanosga and Johnston 1996b).

The *Indianapolis Star* reported that HUD was watching ORS even if city auditors were not. "HUD inspection reports in ORS' first two projects, Blackburn Terrace and Hawthorne Place, made repeated references to unqualified subcontractors, bad planning, poor coordination among contractors and poor workmanship." As early as December 1994, HUD had complained to Public Housing Authority Director John Nelson that he needed "to compel ORS to ensure quality craftsmanship." The letter went on, "We recommend the Division assess the capability of planning and the construction management of (ORS). . . . An additional construction management firm should be considered" (Lanosga and Johnston 1996b).

In response to the criticism, ORS blamed the general contractor who in turn blamed an incompetent subcontractor. Three years after the renovations began, change orders were still being submitted by ORS to the Housing Authority Board on the Hawthorne Place renovation. Housing officials charged that the flurry of change orders was caused by improperly written contracts for which ORS was responsible. ORS, in turn, blamed the Housing Authority's administration for requesting so many changes. Public Housing Board Member Aaron Haith scoffed that the administration "wouldn't know to make changes unless the construction manager (ORS) recommended them" (Lanosga and Johnston 1996b). Despite the problems, the Housing Authority Board responded to HUD's suggestions to find another manager in 1995 by putting ORS in charge of even more projects and adding $800,000 to its contract.

ORS faced more embarrassment during the construction of New Ralston Estates. In that project, ORS managers allowed streets and sidewalks to be laid down before sewer and utility hook-ups were made. Susan Williams, the City-County councilor for the district, angrily observed, "The private sector screwed it up, more than any government inefficiencies I've seen in 10 years" (Johnston 1995). The city tried to cover for ORS again, saying "there were no problems beyond what a complicated building project would incur" (Johnston 1995).

The federal audit report, released on June 12, 1997 noted that under Goldsmith's direction the Public Housing Authority's "scores have been decreasing every year since 1994" (U.S. HUD 1997, 1). Other problems with the Housing Authority under Goldsmith included:

> . . . an excessive vacancy rate of 23 percent. The Housing Authority did not have the resources to repair and reoccupy the backlog of vacant units and it did not have a plan to correct the problem (U.S. HUD 1997, 3).

> Took excessive time, 314 days, to repair and lease vacant units (U.S. HUD 1997, 4).

> Maintenance staff's time was not fully accounted for and maintenance personnel were not effectively supervised and evaluated (U.S. HUD 1997, 4).

The average applicant waited between one and three years to receive housing.(U.S. HUD 1997, 4).

The agency awarded contracts without using full and open competition and awarded a contract when a known conflict-of-interest existed (U.S. HUD 1997, 15).

As of December 31, 1996, only 31 of the Agency's 421 vacant units were available for occupancy . . . The Director of Maintenance said he did not have enough maintenance staff to repair the backlog of vacant units in addition to repairing units resulting from normal turnover (U.S. HUD 1997, 10).

During 1996, the vacant units cost the Agency over $389,000 in lost income (U.S. HUD 1997, 9).

Housing Authority officials had numerous ties to ORS. The Modernization Director was Bill Coleman, who had originally worked for Kosene & Kosene, the developers who assisted ORS on earlier projects. (The Kosenes were strong Goldsmith supporters and campaign contributors.) After leaving the Housing Authority, Coleman accepted a job with ORS partner, Sherman R. Smoot Co. (Lanosga and Johnston 1996b).

Edward Jagnandan, another unsuccessful director, was fired in 1997. Since he had been employed for less than a year, the city, after firing him, was forced to pay him $42,500 in addition to a $30,000 consulting contract (*Indianapolis Star* 1997).

What was more troubling was that the new director was to be paid $122,000 per year in salary and benefits while the recently fired director was being retained as a "consultant." The Editor of the *Indianapolis Star* summed it up: "Public housing in Indianapolis is a mess structurally, financially and administratively . . . renovation projects totaling $35 million were plagued by shoddy workmanship and excessive construction changes" (*Indianapolis Star* 1997).

ORS's Philosophy of Value Enhancement: The Difference Between Public and Private Cost Over-runs

One of the reasons Mayor Goldsmith gave George Tomanovich for hiring ORS was that the company was a firm that would provide "value engineering" and "value enhancement," among other services

(Goldsmith. 1995). Early in the ORS contract, officers of ORS associates Shiel-Sexton and Hilliard Kosene had proposed the use of a value planning process—looking for ways to save money. According to a 1993 memorandum from Andrew Shiel to John Muter of ORS, value planning would be used to select projects for the overall Capital Improvement Program, and value engineering would look at materials and methods for efficiencies (Shiel 1993). ORS installed value coordinators in each of the departments to implement the value enhancement program and its cost savings goals. The standard operating procedure for value enhancement was, "Someone must be assigned to think value every minute of every day of every week" (Shiel 1993). The goal for value enhancement was a cost saving of "at least 10% of program dollars" (Gallant et al. 1993).

In a 1996 interview Andrew Shiel explained value engineering to *NUVO Newsweekly*: "Value Engineering, . . . I always use the example of building a five-lane bridge connecting a two lane road. Believe it or not, that type of thing used to occur . . . Not during the current administration, but prior to that. And it's just making sure that you don't do work that's not necessary to be done." (Ramos and Ullmann 1996a). Shiel claimed value engineering had resulted in saving the city "$75 million . . . that wouldn't have been saved otherwise" (Ramos and Ullmann 1996a). Value planning, value engineering and value enhancement did work, to a point—there is no record of the construction of "five-lane bridges connecting two lane roads" during the Goldsmith administration (nor during the Hudnut administration, despite Andrew Shiel's implication). However, the value-added program did cause a number of significant problems.

Many of the ORS-managed projects resulted in cost overruns caused by change orders. A change order is a device to allow the construction contractor to add changes (and charges) to the original contract. Former Director of Administration Don McPherson observed, "You get change orders because the specifications are not written clearly . . . because if you're looking at it from the viewpoint of the contractor who's bidding, their bidding is based on the information that the customer—the city—has provided" (Ramos and Ullmann 1996b). ORS, as construction manager for the city was responsible for producing the specifications on which contractors based their bids. Change orders frequently are issued to accommodate revised specifications and do not need to be bid; they can result in significant cost overruns. Competent, careful construction managers work to avoid change orders.

Change orders were not unusual in ORS projects. For example, in the 1995 Riverside Park Project, ORS was responsible for a total of twelve change orders that increased the costs of a $1.3 million project by $250,000 (20 percent over the original contract). ORS also convinced the Parks Board that the use of four different contractors rather than a single contractor at the Riverside Aquatic Center would save the taxpayers $43,000. The change orders on the project added $163,719 to the project cost. Commenting on the overruns, Goldsmith spokesman, Joe Loftus, told reporters that ORS is a "tremendous success story." (Lanosga and Johnston 1995)

In 1996, *NUVO Newsweekly* compared cost overruns on nine state projects (using public employees) to nine privatized city projects, and its findings included the following:

- Privatized city project cost overruns were as high as 16.3 percent.
- State public project cost overruns were as high as 3.3 percent.
- ORS managed many of the projects with the highest percentage of cost overruns.
- One city project cost 300 percent more than the original bid. (Ramos and Ullmann 1996b)

The significant difference between the state and city projects was that the state had qualified, in-house, public works architects and engineers who managed the projects—the city had ORS. Tom Coulter, Deputy Director of Indiana Public Works Division, told *NUVO Newsweekly* that "rather than privatize the state's construction management, the state has developed cost-effective methods that use state employees and minimize cost overruns . . . the state cuts overruns by working with the contractors before and during the project to eliminate problems before they develop." Coulter said that he had overruns, "but nothing approaching those numbers [for the city's construction projects] . . . We really don't really have the contractors coming to us with an increase." (Ramos and Ullmann 1996b)

Examples of Value Enhancement

George Tomanovich recalled sitting in value enhancement meetings, protesting various "value enhancement" suggestions with long-term consequences. Some examples included:

- "Saving" money on golf cart paths by not placing stone under the asphalt to compensate for freezing and thawing. The asphalt would have broken up after a bad winter so Tomanovich used gravel instead.

- The Engineer recommended 8-10 foot golf cart paths so maintenance vehicles could use them and not tear up the turf and two 4-foot carts could pass one another without running off and rutting the ground. Instead, the "Value Planners" decided on less expensive 6-foot paths.

- The Engineer recommended placing de-watering pumps around the new pool at Riverside, which was to be built on a flood plain. The pump would keep water from getting under the pool and cracking it. ORS vetoed that as too expensive and instead increased the thickness of concrete in the pool bottom to 2 feet. The pool floor cracked the year after the grand opening and remains cracked and leaking. (Tomanovich 2000d)

The October 1993 "Value Enhancement Newsletter" provides additional examples of "savings:" deleted portions of Williams Creek Project (savings - $600,000); repaired roofs at Fire Stations No. 33 and 10 in lieu of replacement (savings = $29,500). Another "Value Enhancement Newsletter" includes actual suggestions submitted at the Mayor's Conference by Goldsmith himself (ORS 1994b). Those suggestions included selling Warren Township Raymond Park land and directing the proceeds to other parks' improvements and delineating a bike path by a stripe along road (rather than constructing a separate path) at the Wayne Township Krannert High School Road Project. The March 1994 newsletter describes additional savings including: reduced project scope (saving $2.5 million), deleted bike path (saving $400,000) and deleted portions of drainage (saving $188,392). The June 1994 newsletter identifies a saving of over $500,000 by eliminating inspection contracts for two resurfacing projects (ORS 1994c). (These suggestions did save money: if a project is not built or inspected, there are no costs for construction or inspection.)

"Volunteerism" was another value enhancement tool that saved money by using "volunteer" public employees (usually salaried) to perform work that would otherwise require payment. For example, Team Building Days generally involved landscaping, clean up, painting, and similar tasks. On June 3, 1994 a Parks Department/ORS team "saved" $20,000 on these activities (ORS 1994c). During the month of June, ORS identified $105,000 of dollars saved through volunteerism (ORS 1994c). In this instance and others, it was made very clear that volunteerism was expected of employees, resulting in several lawsuits against the city for unfair labor practices (Strauss 1999).

When a police substation building project overseen by ORS experienced cost over-runs, the ORS project manager advised the architect to use cheaper materials. According to *NUVO Newsweekly*, ORS Project Manager Brian Miller wrote (on city stationery), "We appreciate your concerns for this project . . . However, in order to meet the entire city's needs, we have been asked to minimize initial costs to the utmost including utilization of materials which will not yield the best life cycle costs" (Ramos and Ullmann 1996b).

Another value enhancement strategy that will have long-term consequences for the community was revealed in early 1996. According to *NUVO* reporter, Fred Ramos, Goldsmith "quietly changed the construction specifications for city sewers by letting contractors use cheaper plastic sewer pipe instead of more expensive concrete pipe" (Ramos 1996b). Several City-County Councilors told Ramos that representatives of the concrete pipe industry had been warned by the Goldsmith administration that if they opposed the switch to plastic, they would get no further contracts for their concrete pipe (Ramos 1996b).

Summary

Parks Director Leon Younger best summed up the city's privatization experiment with ORS and the consequences to the taxpayers of Indianapolis. When asked in his sworn deposition, "What would you guess the total savings was using ORS over these [public] employees?" Younger replied, "Oh, I wouldn't say there was a savings . . . it's strictly a business decision based on our ability to get it [construction management] out of our operating budget and over to our capital improvement side" (Younger 1996, 39).

Notes

[1] Lewis Smoot contributed $3,100 to the PAC in January 1992 (Businessmen for Good Government 1992).

[2] As a community information manager Bynum earned $45.25 per hour, which was billed to the city at $124.44 per hour (ORS 1994a, Attachment).

[3] DMD regulates businesses, zoning, housing and economic development in Indianapolis. According to *Encyclopedia of Indianapolis* DMD was "targeted... [by Goldsmith] for extensive reorganization and many layoffs. It was the only

city-county department for which he chose not to appoint a full time director" (Bodenhamer and Burrows 1994, 629).

[4] The original contract was extended by sixteen months through nine amendments (March 23, 1993 to July 31, 1997) for a total contract time of four years and 4 months.

[5] For example, ORS allegedly printed Goldsmith's political materials in the City-County Building (Tomanovich 1996a, 8) .

[6]The record of ORS activities in the Parks Department is the best documented of the five departments affected by ORS. There is a wealth of sworn testimony and documentation available because of a 1996 federal lawsuit filed by Tomanovich against the City, Mayor Goldsmith and ORS.

[7] Allegation Number 50.

[8] An example of this allegation is provided in the discussion of the Krannert-King-Brookside Pool Project later in this chapter.

[9] "The program Manager for each area shall: Establish and implement all relevant policies/procedures to monitor contractor compliance with EEO (Equal Employment Opportunity) regulation. Procedures will include...Prevailing Wage Compliance Procedure (and). . . Monitor(ing) prevailing wage payments . . . " (ORS-City Contract 1993, Attachment A, 2).

Chapter 15

Privatizing the City's Golf Courses

Jack Miller[1]

Introduction

The Mayor's advisory group on privatization, the Services, Efficiency and Lower Taxes for Indianapolis Commission (SELTIC) recommended the privatization of the city's golf courses. In early 1992, Mayor Stephen Goldsmith began the privatization efforts by hiring Leon Younger from Columbus, Ohio, to assume control of the Indianapolis Department of Parks and Recreation (IDPR). Younger was to oversee the first major privatization initiative, beginning with the twelve public golf courses, and to help the private construction project manager, Oscar Robertson Smoot (ORS), assume control of the Parks Department construction projects. This decision appears to have been made without the benefit of long-term planning and without consideration as to who would do the work if the contract manager were not rehired or did not complete the work. Although ORS was involved in construction projects at the golf courses, the primary focus of this chapter is on the privatization of the golf courses, rather than the involvement of ORS.

Prior to privatization, the golf courses, which were valued at over $80 million, had earned the city over $3 million annually (based on a three-year average for 1989-1991). During the administration of the previous mayor, William H. Hudnut III, much of the excess revenue had been channeled to other parks projects, allowing the condition of the golf courses to decline. Goldsmith claimed privatization was needed because the courses were "not receiving the level of capital investment needed to maintain (and enhance) the level of play" and that private management would bring in more money. Goldsmith believed that the golf courses and other services should be viewed as profit centers that generated revenue through user fees; at a minimum these services should be self-sufficient. Privatization did generate more money, and the reason for the increased income was that greens fees (user fees) were raised and surcharges were instituted on passes. Goldsmith defended the price increases, saying the money would go for "parks programs involving children" (Johnston 1997). Between 1992 and 1999, greens fees were raised five times, and the last increase was requested by the pros to cover higher chemical and labor costs (not for parks programs used by children). The increases amounted to an 84 percent jump in greens fees while surcharges on passes quadrupled during this period (Hurrle 2000). In 1997 the popular "unlimited pass" was eliminated because the pros complained that revenue from season passes (and the surcharge levied with each use) unfairly bypassed them and went directly to the Parks Department (Bell 1995).

When the Goldsmith Administration described the golf course privatization for the media, higher gross revenues were cited as proof of success, but little was said about why revenues increased— consistently higher user fees that could have improved the quality of the courses without privatization. Most of the increase in fees went to the pros after privatization and not to the city. These higher fees also tended to discourage low-income players.

Before privatization, the city paid the pros a flat fee of $9,500 for a nine-hole golf course. Other provisions of their contracts were:

- The pros owned the golf carts and kept most of cart rental fees.
- Pros stocked concessions and kept most of the profits from those sales.
- The city kept all greens fees and a small percentage of cart rental fees and concessions. (Karto 2000)

According to David Karto, the pro who managed the Southwestway course, he would make $50,000 in a good year (Karto 2000). Karto, who refused to contribute to Goldsmith's campaigns, was one of only two pros who lost his bid for a contract. Karto sued the city for failing to notify him of his termination as required in his contract in 1992. He also charged that Parks Department officials led pros to believe they would be given an opportunity to match competing bids. Karto had managed the course for thirteen years and had increased revenues every year at the well-run course (Johnston and Lanosga 1996). His reward for thirteen years of exemplary service was to be told—on Christmas Eve 1992—that he had lost the bid and that he would not be allowed to match the better offer as promised. According to Karto, Goldsmith gave him a week to sell his golf carts and clear out (not surprisingly Karto found little market for golf carts in the dead of winter) (Karto 2000).

Karto won his lawsuit and was awarded $75,000. Depositions in the case demonstrated the arbitrary nature of the contracting process: City-County Councilor Cory O'Dell served on the selection committee and testified that, "The process was full of holes . . ." Former Parks Director Younger testified that applicants were purposely not told what the criteria were "to encourage creativity." Younger had also offered a contract to a person who had not submitted a proposal at all . . . with the Mayor's approval. (Johnston and Lanosga 1996)

One of Goldsmith's comments on the privatization was, "I think golf is a spectacular success . . . ." Concerning Karto, the pro who brought suit, Goldsmith added, "He's a loser" (Johnston and Lanosga 1996).

The other pros who had previously managed the courses for the Parks Department were all Goldsmith contributors, and they were all awarded the private management contracts. This gave the pros access to over $10 million in capital from the Parks Department share of the $530 million in Capital Improvement Program[2] bond money, which previously had not been available for course upgrading. This "hybrid" or semi-privatization began in January 1993.

The succeeding years, which were very costly for taxpayers, represented a windfall for the pros. Contracts were rewritten and amended at least three times for each course to address the latest development, oversight or scandal. The contracts were tailored for each specific golf course so a great deal of legal work was required.

The Privatization Contracts

In the case of the golf course privatization, the courses were not sold outright—the public retained ownership, risk, and expense while the pros avoided paying property taxes, as a truly private operator would have had to do. The city funded most of the capital improvements at the courses and even some utility and maintenance costs.

For example, the 1993 contracts provided:

- All capital improvements were to be paid for by the taxpayers.
- All repairs over $2,500 per year were to be paid for by the taxpayers.
- The pros would administer capital improvement projects with no oversight by the city.
- The pros would keep 97.5 percent of the greens fees and 92 percent of all other revenues. (IDPR 1993a)

This sort of privatization was very good for the pros. They received greens fees, which previously had gone entirely to the city, and free equipment; furthermore, they did not have to shoulder the burden of capital improvements, and they were free of oversight. They made a lot of money.

Competitive Bidding and Permit Requirements Are Ignored

The contracts became effective January 1, 1993 and the pros were "ecstatic" according to the *Indianapolis Star* (Bell 1992). The pros were so ecstatic that from 1993 through 1996 they contributed over $29,000 to the Mayor's campaign fund (Steve Goldsmith Committee 1992-1997). It should be noted that in the year before privatization, only one contribution could be found from a golf pro to Goldsmith—and that was for $30 (Steve Goldsmith Committee 1992-1997).

An internal audit of the golf courses released December 17, 1993 revealed serious problems with the golf privatization effort. One of the violations identified by the auditors for the projects that were examined was that construction contracts were not awarded through an "advertised bid process" as required by state statute for projects exceeding $25,000 (IDPR 1993b, 2). Additional findings included:

- The pros and employees were not bonded.
- The city was continuing to pay for utilities and long distance phone calls.
- Pros were "monitoring" capital improvement projects with no department oversight.
- Two contracts were unsigned.
- Contracts were poorly written and did not clearly define staffing or equipment levels, service plans, maintenance standards or capital improvement priorities.

With respect to one of the more serious findings—that the pros themselves were monitoring capital improvement projects without departmental oversight—the auditors recommended that the "Parks Construction Section be given responsibility for monitoring all golf course capital improvements projects" (IDPR 1993b, 2). Although the Parks Construction Section was slated for elimination, Director Younger replied, "We agree with this recommendation and will have the inspections done by our Construction Managers"—in other words, ORS (IDPR 1993b, 2).

ORS was in charge of golf by the spring of 1994. The previous construction manager at the Parks Department, George Tomanovich, had voiced concerns about ORS and its management and had attempted to prevent some of its actions. He was fired for voicing those concerns and for "not being a team player" with respect to Goldsmith's privatization efforts. Tomanovich, who filed a federal lawsuit against the city, subsequently received a settlement (and a consulting contract) from the city (see Chapter 14) ORS gave its employee, Tom Souter, responsibility for managing the golf projects. Souter was a "hands on" golf administrator who spent as much time as possible on the course—golfing. As Golf Director Reed Pryor noted, "This gentleman played golf, played a lot of golf, but when it came down to having expertise necessary to do the job right, as far as construction on the golf course . . . he had virtually none and I think he was the wrong guy to be working on the golf projects for ORS" (Pryor 1996). When pressed by attorney Richard Cook about Souter's habit of golfing instead of working during the week, Pryor replied, "far and away the number of times I would see him would be during the business day playing golf" (Pryor 1996). (Souter's golfing days were charged to the city at 2.75 times his pay of $25.73 per hour for a total hourly charge of $70.76 (IDPR 1994a, 2)).

To ensure that the courses looked good for the upcoming season, the pros were given free rein. They were ordered to proceed expeditiously with repairs and remodeling and to send the bills to the city because, according to parks Director Younger, "the mayor wanted to demonstrate very quickly to the golfers that there had been major improvements in golf" (Younger 1996, 73). To cut through tiresome red tape and produce fast results, the pros disregarded the statutory requirements for competitive bidding and city/state building inspections and permits. Some even enlisted friends to do the construction and remodeling (Lanosga and Johnston 1993a). As Parks Director Younger told Reed Pryor, Golf Director, "Just do it! It's easier to ask forgiveness than ask permission" (Pryor 1996).

The County Prosecutor investigated the bidding violations. The pros claimed they had been "uninformed" about the state bid laws. Modisett's report in October of 1994 stated that there was "insufficient evidence" to prove that "any criminal laws were knowingly violated" by the pros, Parks Director, or the Mayor and he declined to initiate any criminal prosecutions at that time (Modisett 1994, cover letter). Nevertheless, he was baffled at how such an important legal requirement could be ignored: "We received no real explanation for how so many people, from so many different perspectives within the community, the SELTIC Commission, and the Administration could have overlooked this issue. We also received no satisfactory explanation why minutes of meetings, supported by confirmatory documentation between the participants, were not maintained by government officials for a project affecting millions of taxpayer dollars" (Modisett 1994, 4).

Prosecutor Modisett decided not to file charges in the investigation of bidding violations. Modisett said his decision was made in part because he had been assured by city officials that there would be "no other reimbursement for work that was in progress" (Johnston and Lanosga 1995)—in other words, no further payments would be made for illegal work. In spite of this assurance, according to a top Goldsmith aide further payments totaling $48,650 were made for additional unbid golf course projects in 1996 in order "to close out an unfortunate episode of bidding violations" (Johnston and Lanosga 1995). An angry Modisett told reporters, "I'm concerned. Why are these payments being made after assurances they weren't paid? This is taxpayer money" (Johnston and Lanosga 1995).

In April 1996, during the Tomanovich federal lawsuit, Younger reversed the testimony given in his earlier deposition and testified that he had discussed the oversight management with Goldsmith earlier. Younger stated that he had suggested using a city employee to manage oversight, but that the Mayor had insisted on using a private construction manager (ORS) (Lanosga and Johnston 1996). In a May 1996 newspaper interview, Modisett commented, "Mr. Younger's civil deposition indicates for the first time that he discussed the state bidding law requirements with the mayor during a time when the city was still in a position to ensure compliance with these laws" (Lanosga and Johnston 1996). Modisett called on his successor, Scott Newman, to investigate possible obstruction of justice or to appoint a special prosecutor. Prosecutor Newman, a political ally of the Mayor, quietly let the matter drop.

Another way of streamlining the golf construction projects was to bypass the permitting process for course improvements. From 1993 through 1996 "permits for structural, plumbing, HVAC systems, etc. were bypassed by the Parks Department" (Tomanovich 1998). This left the city exposed to liability if anyone had been injured by defective wiring or structural problems in the construction.

What were the consequences of the rush to show results and ignore the competitive bidding requirements? The city paid $652,000 to reimburse all the illegal, unbid and uninspected work (Johnston and Lanosga 1995). Goldsmith, Park Director Younger, and the pros were all surprised at the extent of the subsequent scandal since, as the Mayor put it, the pros were not "guilty of anything more serious than the sin of enthusiasm" (Goldsmith 1997, 42).

Additional Benefits to the Pros and Contractors

One of the serious problems encountered during the Goldsmith administration's privatization projects involved the transfer of public resources into private hands. In the golf course privatization, the administration gave the pros 200 pieces of free golf equipment that had been paid for by the taxpayers. The original cost of that equipment was $1.5 million. According to a newspaper report, no one in the administration "bothered to determine the fair market value of the equipment before turning it over . . . " (Lanosga and Johnston 1993b).

In another case related to the golf course privatization, heavy equipment in the Land Improvement Division of the Parks Department was sold to contractors at bargain basement prices. The private contractors then leased the equipment back to the city at a profit or charged the city a hefty fee for its use. George Tomanovich subsequently commented on the inexperience that led to this arrangement:

> As manager of the Land Improvement section it was my policy to always have heavy equipment operators shut their engines down when not in use. Private contractors often leave engines idling to run up 'billable hours.' To save wear-and-tear and fuel, park's heavy equipment was always turned off when not in use. When Deputy Mayor Skip Stitt noticed the low hours on this equipment, he assumed it wasn't being used enough to justify the city owning it. So, without asking me or any of the operators about the low hours, Stitt set up an auction. The auction brought about twenty cents on the dollar and made a lot of construction contractors very happy. One contractor made back his bid price by using his new equipment to pulverize soil that he sold back to the Parks Department. He was able to recover the purchase price of the equipment in a few months. (Tomanovich 2000)

Two Golf Courses: Coffin and Whispering Hills

Coffin Golf Course

The history of one golf course is illustrative of the ramifications of privatization at the public golf courses. Coffin Golf Course was the oldest and toughest golf course in the park system. It was the site of the National Publinx Tournament in 1932, 1955 and 1972, and pros such as Walter Hagen and Gene Sarazen played there (Gelarden 1995a). Over the years, Coffin fell into disrepair and closed after the 1992 season.

There was talk of selling Coffin to developers for an apartment project, but instead it was slated for a $2.9 million renovation using city-backed bonds.

New Management for Coffin

The acting pro gave up management of the course so Mayor Goldsmith could form a non-profit corporation to run it (Pickett 1995). The Indianapolis Golf Management Corporation (IGMC) was incorporated in 1994 as a 501C-3 not-for-profit corporation. The Board of Directors included Parks Director Leon Younger and former Deputy Mayor, Joe Loftus.[3] The five-year contract, which was signed September 1, 1994, required IGMC to oversee the renovation and subsequently manage the course. The stated purpose for having a non-profit manage the course was to ensure that maximum revenues from Coffin would go to repaying the renovation costs. Since IGMC had no capital and no previous experience, Goldsmith authorized interest-free loans totaling $350,000 for start-up funds. The contract specified, "The Corporation shall repay such amounts without interest to Department as soon as reasonably possible but in no event later than December 31, 1999" (IDPR 1994b, 14). Three months later, the following addendum was signed, "As consideration for the Corporation's management services during the grow-in (12/1/94 to 7/1/95) the Dept. shall pay $100,000 to the Corporation. . . ." (IDPR 1994c). In return, the contract specified that IGMC "pay the debt service on the City of Indianapolis Parks Project Revenue Bonds, Series 1994 B in accordance with the schedule attached" (IDPR 1994b, 13). In describing the contract, Parks Director Younger said, "We like this because it offers us a good way to ensure that every dollar goes to support the revenue bonds and the improvements made" (Johnston and Lanosga 1994).

Another infusion of cash took place in April, 1995 when the city once again paid IGMC $170,000 to "Coordinate with representatives of the City . . . and Wadsworth Golf Construction Co. to complete wetland plantings; tree trimming; landscaping, etc." (IDPR 1995). The 1995 season required another $100,000 loan to IGMC for "start-up expenses" to be paid back during the 1996 golf season (IDPR 1996). By this time, grants and loans to IGMC totaled $720,000. It did not seem to occur to anyone that this arrangement simply added a layer of bureaucracy, and that the non-profit corporation was merely duplicating the non-profit Parks Department with, however, two notable differences:

- The Department of Parks and Recreation was accountable to the public and IGMC was accountable only to the Mayor.
- IGMC had absolutely no experience renovating or managing golf courses.

Coffin Gets a Facelift

The city hired a top golf architect, Tim Liddy, for $205,845[4] to re-design and remodel the old course, and hopes ran high as new greens, sand bunkers, fairways and cart paths took shape. One optimistic sports writer gushed, "These improvements will occur because the $2.9 million project (in tax-free municipal bonds) will be overseen by IGMC, and chaired by Bob Taylor, a retired Eli Lilly executive" (Picket 1994). To get the best view of the dramatic Indianapolis skyline for the golfers, architect Liddy decided to clear-cut over 70 large, mature trees near the river, which resulted in increased erosion. By 1999, the erosion had advanced to the point that it would require a $221,000 investment to reinforce the riverbank and keep the remaining area from washing away (Rohn 1999).

Work went ahead at a furious pace, with chain saws buzzing, bulldozers rumbling, trees crashing to the ground, and a grand new layout taking shape. As opening day approached, the newspaper headlines announced, "Coffin course to come alive after years of rough times." One reporter waxed poetic in his praise of the pricey architect, "Liddy raised fairways to encourage quick runoff when the river comes calling, included wetlands to please Mother Nature, installed more than 50 bunkers and seeded the tees and greens with best grass . . .He did a whale of a job" (Gelarden 1995b). The renovation price tag had climbed to $3.2 million, but at the grand opening, a beaming Goldsmith assured everyone it was all worth it, "We believe the renovation will permit Coffin to re-enter the ranks of the states' top half dozen public golf courses" (Gelarden 1995b).

Greens fees were raised from $12 to $20 on the weekends, excluding cart fees (Hurrle 2000) and 6,000 golfers teed off in July. Just six weeks later, excuses replaced poetry while prices climbed, "The combination of heavy traffic, new turf and extremes of heat and humidity took its toll on Coffin's tees and greens." The golf course superintendent explained, "This fall we'll reconstruct five tees with sand base and improve the drainage and make them bigger . . . the greens are already improving" (Richards 1995).

A year later when the Indiana Golf Association Amateur Championship Tourney was held at Coffin, the hapless golfers found what sportswriter Phil Richards described: "A ravaged set of tee complexes . . . Thirteen of Coffin's 18 holes were built on floodplain sheltered by a thickly-wooded ridge, circulation is poor, turf grass diseases a constant threat. . . . Fairways only inches above the surface level of adjacent ponds and wetlands" (Richards 1996).

The course superintendent, Ryan Fisher, and his crew had just rebuilt five tee complexes the previous fall and planned to rebuild the rest of the "new" but ravaged tees "replacing topsoil with sand, which affords better drainage and healthier turf" (Richards 1996). Of the year-old facility, Fisher said his twelve-man maintenance crew could only do so much. "I'd love to have the cart paths done, the tees done, everything. I'd love to throw $700,000 at this every year" (Richards 1996). In a scathing April 1996 memo, new golf director Stan Burton evaluated the amateurs of IGMC with a fresh perspective:

> Under the present "system" at Coffin, nothing positive can happen in the short term. I would go so far as to say that the long term success of Coffin is in serious jeopardy. The Indianapolis Golf Management Corporation has not shown the ability to lead or provide direction for the staff to follow . . . This Board has not been held publicly accountable for any of their actions or lack thereof. It seems that the board is more interested in reading about themselves than attacking the hard task of making the golf course something that all of central Indiana can be proud of. (Burton 1996)

Despite the investment of over $1.3 million from 1995 through March 1997 and $270,000 in additional cash payments from the city, the non-profit had been unable to repay any of the 1994 and 1995 loans ($450,000) from the city. The bond debt service remained unpaid also ($261,000 for 1996) because "bad weather forced a late start for the '96 golf season" (Bell 1996).

IGMC Board member and city lobbyist, Joe Loftus, complained that Coffin "needs an infusion of money" and that IGMC could not afford to do it. Where did all the money go? Revenues, loans and grants for the period totaled over $2 million. By late 1996, IGMC had decided to terminate its contract with the city, and R. N. Thompson assumed the remainder of IGMC's contract in April 1997. Thompson minced no words about Coffin's condition, "It was an embarrassment to the city and I thought we needed to get in there and get going. We've started putting about $500,000 into it" (Richards 1997). IGMC was officially released from its contract in April 1998 (Hurrle 1998).

IGMC is Replaced

In 1996, rather than resuming control over Coffin, the city decided to try privatization again, and it issued a request for proposals to run the course and pay off the $3 million in bonds (Bell 1996). The successful bidder would also have to pay for paving the golf paths on the newly renovated course. The city's golf administrator said that Coffin ". . . really needs the paths. It doesn't take a genius to see the course was built on a flood plain" (Bell 1996). Presumably, golf architect Liddy was turning out to be less than a genius for using wood chips on the soggy paths. Burton, the Parks Department Golf Director, agreed in his memo, "The problems at Coffin are due in large part to a poor master plan. The first thing that should be done is to pave ALL of the cart paths with asphalt . . . The total cost would be around $160,000. This will improve the public perception of their rounds of golf over the current intolerable situation . . . Cart paths should have been put in during construction" (Burton 1996).

To improve the chances of finding someone willing to shoulder these costs, the city offered a complex 15-year contract that would allow the contractor to keep all revenue. Despite the rhetoric of "marketization," there was once again no competition. Only one operator even submitted a proposal, and it was accepted. More complications arose when the city had to buy back the $3.4 million in bonds because provisions of the old bond issue would interfere with the new contract, according to the Parks Department Director (Bell 1997). The new manager, Gray Eagle Golf, LLC, would pay the city $33,000 a month for 15 years to retire the bonds and pay back IGMC's $450,000 unpaid loan to the city (IDPR 1998). Gray Eagle was a new company specifically formed to run Coffin by R. N.Thompson and William Mays of Mays Chemical.

As a reward for being the only contractor to "compete," R. N. Thompson & Associates, Inc. (as Gray Eagle) was also awarded a 15-year contract to "integrate certain terms relating to separate agreements for Riverside Municipal Golf Course, the Golf Academy and Coffin

Municipal Golf Course" (IDPR 1998). All golf contracts were reworked and amended at least three times for each course from 1993 to 1999. The cost of contract development was not reflected in these, or any, of the privatization agreements initiated by the Goldsmith administration.

Whispering Hills

Whispering Hills golf course is an example of a more conventional agreement that provides a striking contrast to the contractual agreements at the other golf courses. This privatization agreement was different from the others because of complications from an earlier tax increment funding arrangement. By law, all excess income was required to be invested in the course itself. The 1993 agreement with William Krohne, Inc.[5] stipulated the pro's compensation in the contract ($35,000 in salary plus 3.5 percent of the gross revenue) with no secrecy involved (IDPR 1993c, 15). The net profits did not go to the pro as revenue, rather the contract stipulated that these were to be deposited in an operations account on behalf of the Parks Department and applied to course improvements (IDPR 1993c, 14). Operating and maintenance expenses came out of the revenues generated by the facility, and in June 2000 there was $145,000 in the Whispering Hills "savings account" (Hurrle 2000). This accomplishment is all the more striking when compared to the other courses because Whispering Hills is a nine-hole "oak" course (in the city's rating system, gold courses are the most expensive, followed by silver, bronze, and oak). In 1991 green fees at Whispering Hills were a modest $4.50.

A review of operating records from 1994 through 1999 shows that this unassuming course generated gross revenues of $2,877,775 (Whispering Hills 1994-1999). A net profit of $276,406 was realized after expenses including maintenance, salaries, seed and insurance. (Under the terms of the privatization contracts at the other golf courses, the net profit would have gone to the pro.) In 1999 the Whispering Hills pro earned over $53,000; 36,347 rounds of golf were played; and the course improved remarkably based on customer surveys. Over the years, this course has been well run and golfer satisfaction has been high, according to surveys. The records are clear and available to the public, in stark contrast to the other privatized courses where the pro's income is a well-guarded secret. This contract, which is similar to the pre-privatization structure, is good for taxpayers and golfers, and it should provide a model for future contracts.

Profits and Losses from Privatization

A financial analysis of the privatization of the golf courses provides a different picture than the administration's glowing reports of success. Table 1 provides a financial summary for the golf course operations before privatization (1989-1992) and during privatization (1993-1999) based on data sources including Indianapolis operating budgets and information from the Parks Department.[6] This table identifies total sales (all sales from concessions and green fees) and the Parks Department's total operating expenses for the golf courses (includes salaries, maintenance and utilities, but not capital improvements). The Parks Department's gross profit is determined by taking the difference between total sales and total operating expenses. The net profit (loss) to the Parks Department is determined by the difference between the gross profit and the capital improvements.

From 1989 through 1992, the time during which the city operated the courses, the operating expenses for all the courses averaged $2.75 million per year. This included salaries for an average of 80 public employees, plus equipment, supplies, utilities and similar expenses. The city-operated courses generated a net profit to taxpayers of $702,000 (with an average of $234,000) during each of the three years for which data were available.

When the Goldsmith administration privatized the golf courses, it was able to claim savings of $1.18 million in salaries during the first year of privatization (Lanosga and Johnston 1993c). However, as seen in Table 1, the city still lost over $1.2 million during that first year, and accountability flew out the window. Where did the money go?

Before privatization, the pros had averaged about $50,000 per year in income. After privatization, the lion's share of the greens fees and concessions went to the pros, while the city contributed substantially to the upkeep of the facilities. For example, during 1993, the pros received 97.5 percent of the greens fees and 92 percent of other sales, while the city paid for all "repairs and replacements" in excess of $2,500 for the calendar year, and for all capital improvements. The city also assumed the risk of any casualty losses to any building in excess of insurance proceeds. Under these favorable contract conditions, the pros' risks were nonexistent and their profits correspondingly huge. Determining how much money the pros made managing these public facilities was complicated by the secrecy clauses built into their contracts that prohibited disclosure of this information. No explanation was given as to how this secrecy protected or advanced the public's interests. In fact, it did just the opposite.

**Table 1:	Annual summary for golf course operations before privatization (1989-1992) and during privatization (1993-1999)**

Year	Rounds Played	Greens Fees	Total Sales	Staff	Salaries and Benefits
1989	437,945		$2,939,239	63	$1,159,670
1990	492,649		$3,359,734	79	$1,297,432
1991	448,000		$3,600,439	85	$1,690,373
1992	510,842	$3,399,474			$1,616,353
1993	499,391	$3,642,112	$6,997,299	4	$189,844
1994	531,645	$4,341,673	$8,281,666		$68,701
1995	536,318	$4,832,433	$9,573,429		$52,140
1996	481,866	$4,871,266	$8,573,536		$79,245
1997	523,891	$6,087,691	$10,299,956	2	$67,217
1998	528,808	$6,249,275	$10,984,666	2	$53,007
1999	497,401	$5,951,961	$10,653,837	1	$54,000
Total '93-'99	3,599,320	$35,976,411	$65,364,389		$564,154

Year	Parks Total Operating Expenses	Parks Gross Profit[a]	Capital Improvements	Parks Net Profit (Loss)[b]	Dollars to Pros to Run Courses
1989	$2,510,008	$429,231	$25,834	$403,397	
1990	$2,681,435	$678,299	$21,709	$656,590	
1991	$2,849,037	$751,402	$49,450	$701,952	
1992	$3,096,445		$43,115		
1993	$478,338	$1,137,322	$1,900,000	($1,241,016)	$5,859,977
1994	$412,069	$866,231	$122,357	$331,805	$7,415,435
1995	$576,044	$999,613	$3,634,000	($3,210,421)	$8,573,816
1996	$946,461	$940,663	$513,174	($518,972)	$7,632,873
1997	$254,986	$1,167,613	$602,000	$310,627	$9,132,343
1998	$382,055	$1,057,729	$527,264	$148,410	$9,926,937
1999	$323,806	$723,576	$528,422	($128,652)	$9,930,261
Total '93-'99	$3,373,759	$6,892,747	$7,827,217	($4,308,229)	$58,471,642

Source: Indianapolis Operating Budgets (1991-2000); Hurrle (2000)
[a]Parks Gross Profit = Total Sales - Parks Total Operating Expenses
[b]Parks Net Profit (Loss) = Parks Gross Profit - Capital Improvements

During the period of privatization from 1993 through 1999, the city's share of the $65,364,389 in gross revenue was $6,892,747. When this figure is adjusted for the Parks Department's operating expenses, the city's share drops to $3,518,988. When city-paid capital improvements are factored in, the city actually lost $4,308,229 over the seven years of privatization, while the pros split over $58 million to run the courses. If these figures are expressed in annual averages, the pros required an average of $8.35 million per year to oversee the courses. Even if the city's capital investments in the courses are ignored, the private contractors still required three times as much money to operate the public golf courses as had been required during the time period before the advent of "businesslike" practices under privatization.

Determining City Net Profits before and during Privatization

Another way to look at the profit to the city is to determine the Parks Department's net profit margin and compare it to the net profit/loss after privatization. Table 2 shows pre-privatization net profit margins[7] that averaged about 17.7 percent over the three years during which the city operated the golf courses. After privatization, the net profit margin[8] showed four years of losses that ranged from 1 percent to 34 percent, but only three years of profits and they were quite low (1 percent, 3 percent and 4 percent).

Determining the Profits to the Pros

Determining exactly how much profit the pros received from the $58 million to operate the golf courses was difficult to determine because of the secrecy clause in their contracts, which limits the availability of data. In 1994 R.N. Thompson, who owns several private golf courses and currently manages three public courses, speculated on the profit margins of the pros. Thompson conservatively estimated that profit at Eagle Creek course, the crown jewel of the public courses, was at least $500,000. This estimate was based on revenue of $1,362,645. The city's share of the profits during that year was $39,519 (Johnston 1994).

A profitability analysis for the pros was conducted with the available data to determine if the 1994 estimate was verifiable. Table 3 provides an estimate of the profits received by the pros. The methodology[9] used in this analysis computes the cost of running the golf course before privatization and adjusts those costs for inflation to estimate how much

Table 2: Financial analysis of Parks Department cost per round of golf

Year	Rounds Played	Total Sales	Sales/ Rounds Played	Greens Fees
1989	437,945	$2,939,239	$6.71	
1990	492,649	$3,359,734	$6.82	
1991	448,000	$3,600,439	$8.04	
1992	510,842			$3,399,474
1993	499,391	$6,997,299	$14.01	$3,642,112
1994	531,645	$8,281,666	$15.58	$4,341,673
1995	536,318	$9,573,429	$17.85	$4,832,433
1996	481,866	$8,573,536	$17.79	$4,871,266
1997	523,891	$10,299,956	$19.66	$6,087,691
1998	528,808	$10,984,666	$20.77	$6,249,275
1999	497,401	$10,653,837	$21.42	$5,951,961
Total '93-'99	3,599,320	$65,364,389	$18.16	$35,976,411

Year	Greens Fees per Rounds Played	Parks Net Profit (Loss)[a]	Net Profit as Percent of Total Sales	Net Profit (Loss) Per Round
1989		$403,397	14	$0.92
1990		$656,590	20	$1.33
1991		$701,952	19	$1.57
1992	$6.65			
1993	$7.29	($1,241,016)	-18	($2.49)
1994	$8.17	$331,805	4	$0.62
1995	$9.01	($3,210,421)	-34	($5.99)
1996	$10.11	($518,972)	-6	($1.08)
1997	$11.62	$310,627	3	$0.59
1998	$11.82	$148,410	1	$0.28
1999	$11.97	($128,652)	-1	($0.26)
Total '93-'99	$10.00	($4,308,229)	-7	($1.20)

Source: Indianapolis Operating Budgets (1991-2000); Hurrle (2000)
[a]Parks Net Profit = Parks Gross Profit - Capital Improvements

it should cost to operate the privatized golf courses. The year 1991 was used as the base year since this was the year in which the city's operating costs were the highest ($6.36). This should provide a conservative estimate of the profits for the pros. The base figure was then adjusted for inflation in each subsequent and the resulting cost was multiplied by the rounds per year to estimate the cost of the pros operating the golf courses in each year of privatization.

Table 3: Operating expenses for Parks Department and estimation of profits to pros

Year	Rounds Played	Parks Total Operating Expenses	Parks Operating Expenses/ Round Played
1989	437,945	$2,510,008	$5.73
1990	492,649	$2,681,435	$5.44
1991	448,000	$2,849,037	$6.36[a]
1992	510,842	$3,096,445	$6.06
Total '89-'92	1,889,436	$11,136,925	$5.89 (ave)

Year	Rounds Played	Estimated Operating Cost/ Round Played	Estimated Total Operating Cost	Dollars To Pros To Run Courses
1993	499,391	$6.83	$3,410,841	$5,859,977
1994	531,645	$7.03	$3,737,464	$7,415,435
1995	536,318	$7.21	$3,866,853	$8,573,816
1996	481,866	$7.39	$3,560,990	$7,632,873
1997	523,891	$7.62	$3,992,049	$9,132,343
1998	528,808	$7.75	$4,098,262	$9,926,937
1999	497,401	$7.87	$3,914,546	$9,930,261
Total '93-'99	3,599,320	$7.39	$26,581,005	$58,471,642

Year	Estimated Net Profit to Pros[b]	Dollars to Pros Per Round Played	Estimated Profit to Pros Per Round Played
1993	$2,449,136	$11.73	$4.90
1994	$3,677,971	$13.95	$6.92
1995	$4,706,963	$15.99	$8.78
1996	$4,071,883	$15.84	$8.45
1997	$5,140,294	$17.43	$9.81
1998	$5,828,675	$18.77	$11.02
1999	$6,015,715	$19.96	$12.09
Total '93-'99	$31,890,637		

Source: Indianapolis Operating Budgets (1991-2000); Hurrle (2000)
[a]Used as basis for adjusting operating cost/round for inflation in the years 1993-1999
[b]Estimated Net Profit to Pros = Dollars to Pros to Run Courses - Estimated Total Operating Cost

This figure was then subtracted from the pro's overall share each year in the privatization. This analysis suggests that profit to the pros per round of golf played ranged from $4.90 per round in 1993 to $12.09 per round in 1999. The total profit to the pros (cost per round multiplied by number of rounds) ranged from $2.45 million in 1993 to $6.01 million in 1999 (nominal dollars).

When the pro's estimated profits per round of golf played (see Table 3) are compared to the sales generated per round of golf (see Table 2), it is clear that, despite increasing sales revenues per round of golf and increasing amounts paid to the pros, the privatization of the golf courses lost money for the taxpayers. The private managers received nearly $32 million in profits for seven years of operating these publicly owned golf courses, or over $4.5 million per year in profit. The pros were doing very well, averaging half a million dollars per pro each year, or 10 times their pre-privatization income.

HB 1398—The Trust-Me Law

Prosecutor Modisett investigated possible criminal activity in the privatization of the city's golf courses. The investigation was complicated by the city's lack of documentation; there were absolutely no "memoranda, notes, agendas of meetings between public officials concerning the golf privatization issue" (Modisett 1994, 4). This lack of paper trail is, of course, consistent with Park Director Younger's testimony in 1996 that, "Steve (Goldsmith) doesn't very seldom (sic) put anything in writing" (Younger 1996, 97). As noted previously, the report concluded that while laws were broken, it would be difficult for the state to prove "criminal intent. "

The report stated that Indiana criminal statutes defined conflict of interest, bribery and official misconduct as "all sanctioned acts involving public officials and the abuse of 'property' or 'pecuniary interests'" (Modisett 1994, 9). While the report found "administrative neglect" on the part of city officials, it illustrated two extremely important hurdles in trying to prove criminal behavior by private parties in any privatization deal:

- Can the pros even be considered "public servants"? If not, ethics, bribery, official misconduct, bid laws and conflict of interest statutes are not relevant, and they do not apply.
- Any prosecution "would have to prove more than the simple fact that the golf professionals derived a profit from their unbid projects since privatization, *by definition envisions profit making*" (emphasis mine). (Modisett 1994, 10)

The prosecutor concluded that "Non-compliance with bidding laws is a serious breach of the public trust and should not be tolerated, but without a criminal motive . . . there is insufficient prosecutorial merit in bringing criminal charges" (Modisett 1994, 10). He made the following recommendations:

- The Indiana State Legislature should pass stern penalty provisions for bid law violations "to make sure future privatization participation adheres to the necessity of strictly following public bidding requirements" (Modisett 1994, 11)
- The city should not make further reimbursements for any unbid work.

He concluded, "City officials have assured us that no projects done in violation of the bidding statutes will be compensated, now or in the future" (Modisett 1994, 11).

As it turned out, those "assurances" lasted only until Modisett lost the prosecutor's office in the fall of 1994. With the Democratic prosecutor gone and a Goldsmith protégé, Scott Newman, in the prosecutor's office, the Mayor embarked on a program to make sure no further charges of illegality befell his privatization program.

Instead of moving to correct illegal behavior, however, the Mayor wrote a new law to exempt privatization deals from provisions of over 2000 pages of state laws regulating ethics, prevailing wage, public bidding and the sale of public property (Simpson 1995). The intent of this bill was to simplify and legalize the transfer of taxpayer-financed government services and resources to private companies by exempting them from prevailing wage, competitive bid laws and public scrutiny. Deputy Mayor Joe Loftus tried to comfort skeptical legislators by pointing out that there would still be some accountability because the Mayor and administrators who approved a secret deal would be subject "to public criticism" after the fact (Niederpruem 1995). The *Indianapolis News* editorialized against the bill, saying the Goldsmith administration "has not convinced the public that it can be totally trusted. In its rush to privatize, it has broken laws and run ahead of the public more than once" (*Indianapolis News* 1995).

To Goldsmith Lobbyist Joe Loftus' claim that secrecy was needed to "cut the best deal for the taxpayers," the *Indianapolis Star* editorialized, "Rubbish!" (*Indianapolis Star* 1995a). Loftus finally conceded that the original bill had "inartfully crafted" provisions (Simpson 1995). Open-government advocates and labor contested the bill, but after a great deal of "artful" crafting and compromise, it was passed and signed into law in May 1995 by Governor Evan Bayh. As Mullins and Zorn pointed out: "Late nineteenth and early twentieth century American urban history suggests that closed negotiations do not guarantee results consistent with the broader public interest. Therefore the Goldsmith administration's sponsorship of this privatization legislation raises questions about willingness to be accountable to the public" (Mullins and Zorn 1996). Table 4 shows some of the major differences between the pre-1995 state purchasing law and the Goldsmith statute.

Because of these Goldsmith-engineered changes to state law, much of the wrongdoing alleged in a 1999 citizens' petition to the Indiana State Board of Accounts concerning golf privatization was now legal. For example, the petitioners had alleged: "The golf pros have and still continue to negotiate and execute new construction projects without adhering to city open bidding ordinances." The State Board of Accounts responded that "Public Works Law requires certain public works projects to be awarded through a competitive bidding process," but "this chapter does not apply to a person that has entered an operating agreement . . . with an agency under IC5-23." In other words, competitive bidding does not apply to privatization deals. (Indiana State Board of Accounts 2000)

The passage of HB 1398 seems incongruous with the previous statements made by Goldsmith and his administration regarding the importance of competition:

> You don't ever stop competing the work. The only way is to measure yourself in the marketplace every day (Mitch Roob, former director of DCAM and close Goldsmith advisor, January 1994) (Morgan 1994).

> We are basically trying to force this model—performance-based, competitively-based service delivery—on every dollar we spend (Mayor Stephen Goldsmith, March 1995) (Gelarden 1995c).

> Competition empowers workers and inspires an entrepreneurial spirit in city government down to the front-line employee level (Mayor Stephen Goldsmith, 1997) (Goldsmith 1997, 54).

Another important change in purchasing practices was that "money received by any person managing or operating a public facility" under a public-private agreement is no longer considered to be public money. Taxpayer dollars are not considered public dollars when spent by private contractors in privatization deals. With these major changes in the law in place, the State Board of Accounts report notes that "On August 1, 1995, the city and course operators amended and restated the twelve agreements to be governed by the public-private agreement law" (Indiana State Board of Accounts 2000, 4). After August 1995, the pros could legally hire anyone they wanted to do construction, *without* competitive bidding, and send the bill to the city just as they had done in 1993 when it was illegal. Only now, there would be no scandal.

House Bill 1398 was a major victory for Goldsmith's approach, which did not include concepts of "public-ness," "shared purpose" and democracy. It also gave privatization in Indianapolis the blessing of state government. Interestingly,

- The 1995 law applied solely to Indianapolis after a Republican State senator blocked statewide application complaining that "Indianapolis should keep its experiments with government to itself" (*Indianapolis Star* 1995b).
- The new law allowed secret negotiations in privatization deals as long as the public is given one week to comment on the completed deal.

Table 4: Synopsis of purchasing law changes, before and after HB 1398.

Citation	Pre-HB 1398	HB 1398
§36-1-9-1(a)(2)	Purchasing laws apply to all purchases made from a public fund.	Purchasing law applies to purchases made by political subdivisions or agencies from a public fund.
§36-1-9-1(b)(7)&:(8)	none	Purchasing laws do not apply if goods are purchased with non-public funds, *nor do they apply to public/private agreements.*
§36-1-9-3(a)&(b)	Public bids required when annual purchases exceed $25,000 for each line or class of materials.	Public bids only required when annual purchases exceed $75,000 for each line or class of materials.
§36-1-9-4(a)&(b)	Either three written quotes or open market allowed when annual purchases are under $25,000.	Three written quotes required when annual purchases are between $25,000 and $75,000. Open market purchases allowed if no valid quotes are received.
§36-1-9-4.5(a)&(b)	none	Any procedure acceptable when annual purchases are under $25,000 (written or oral quote or open market allowed).

Citation	Pre-HB 1398	HB 1398
§36-1-9-6(a)	Only bid bond or certified check is acceptable for bids exceeding $100,000.	Any other evidence of financial responsibility is acceptable for bids exceeding $100,000 if so specified in the bid notice.
§36-1-9-13(a)(3)	None.	Sole source purchases allowed upon purchasing agent's written recommendation.
§36-1-9-16	None.	*Special procurements allowed without following bid laws in emergencies, if unique chance for savings exist and so forth, upon purchasing agent's written determination.*
§36-1-12-4(a)&(b)	Bids on public work projects required if cost exceeds $25,000.	Bids on public work projects required if cost exceeds $75,000.
§36-1-12-5(a)&(b)	Three written quotes needed if cost of public work project is under $25,000.	Three written quotes needed if cost of public work project is under $25,000, but open market allowed if all quotes rejected and reasons are noted.
§36-1-12-13.1(a)	Payment bond required on public work project if cost exceeds $75,000.	Payment bond required on public work project if cost exceeds $100,000.
§5-16-7-1(k)	None.	Prevailing wage does not apply to public work project if the cost is under $150,000.

Source: Deglopper 1995.

Summary

   The Goldsmith Administration claimed that the efficiencies of privatization had resulted in remarkable improvements to the golf courses and facilities at no cost to the taxpayers. "Instead of paying the expenses of the golf courses, the city received . . . close to a million dollars a year—from the pros (Goldsmith 1997, 41). However, the financial data and profitability analyses demonstrate that the privatization of the city's golf courses was costly for both taxpayers and golfers.

Privatization of the golf courses ignored bid laws, bypassed the permitting process, destroyed institutional memory, and wasted public resources by giving away city equipment. The city lost money despite firing 42 full-time and 40 part-time employees from the golf division at the Parks Department. The city lost money even though it raised user fees 80 percent and quadrupled surcharges. The city also lost golf customers because of the user fee increases, and by 1999 attendance was below pre-privatization levels.

Revenues at the golf courses increased, but the private operators received most of the profits, while taxpayers retained millions in expenses for capital improvements and other costs. During the seven years of private management, the taxpayers spent $4 million more than they received despite total revenues of $65 million. Private contractors were allowed to divide over $58 million to manage these public courses.

By disposing of the city's golf course equipment and personnel, the administration also effectively closed the door on any public sector bid against the private operators in the future. This action lent a quality of permanence to the privatization that will make it difficult for a future administration to reassert city control without a significant financial commitment.

Notes

[1] The author gratefully acknowledges the assistance of Lou Campagna, Research Director, Alliance for Democracy, in the analysis of profitability.

[2] The Capital Improvement Program was intended to rebuild the city's crumbling infrastructure, and it encompassed streets, sewers, sidewalks, parks and so forth (see also Chapter 14).

[3] Loftus became the Mayor's chief lobbyist and an attorney with a private law firm in late 1995.

[4] City of Indianapolis and Marion County Purchase Orders between May 1993 and December 1994.

[5] Krohne also contributed $1,270 in 1994, the first year of his contract (Steve Goldsmith Committee 1992-1997).

[6] It should be noted that there are significant information gaps about the history of golf privatization during the Goldsmith Administration. These gaps are due in part to the lack of institutional memory caused by the massive firings at the Parks Department. Only by piecing together information from newspaper articles, operating budgets and interviews with former employees was it possible to fill in many pre-1997 blanks (1997 was the year the current golf director was hired). After a six month search, the golf administrator was unable to locate records for: 1) total sales at golf courses for 1992, 2) amount of capital

improvements paid by the City during 1993-1994, 3) number of rounds played in 1992, 4) amount of money greens fees generated prior to 1992, and the city's share of revenues for 1992.

[7] *Net Profit Margins for the City before Privatization*

For the years 1989-1991, divide the total sales by each round of golf played to determine the sales generated per round of golf under the Parks Department management. Calculate the cost of each round of golf by dividing the total operating expenses by the rounds of golf played. For example, in 1989, sales generated per round of golf was $6.71 (Table 2) and operating cost per round of golf was $5.73 (Table 3).

The Parks Department's net share of revenues (after capital improvements) divided by the number of rounds provides the city's profit per round of golf. The net profit percentage for the city is then calculated by dividing the net share of revenues by the total sales. For example, in 1989 the net profit to the Parks Department was $403,397 (14 percent of total sales) and the net profit per round was $.92.

[8] *Net Profits to the City after Privatization*

After 1993, the data for sales and number of rounds played is complete. The city's total operating expenses as privatization took hold declined dramatically. At the same time, the sales generated per round of golf increased. The cost per round of golf is not known since the golf pros do not divulge this information. For example, in 1989 the sales generated per round of golf played was $14.01 (Table 2).

As noted previously, the pros who ran the courses after 1992 were not required to divulge their income statements or balance sheets, but the total amount paid to the pros to run the courses is known. For example, the total amount paid to the pros during 1993 was $5,859,977 (Table 3). Dividing this figure by the rounds played yields the amount paid to the pros per round of gold ($11.73 in 1993, Table 3).

Logically, one would expect that since the sales per round is now greater under "privatization" than when the city ran courses that the city would be making healthy net profits along with the pros. However, this assumption would be wrong. Once the effects of city-paid capital improvements are subtracted out of the Parks Department's gross income, the golf courses actually lost money in almost every year. Even during the years that the golf program had a net profit, the profit margins are far below the profit margins under the city's management. For example, in 1993 the Parks Department realized a loss of $1,241,016 based on a loss of $2.49 per round played (Table 2).

[9] *Determining the Amount Paid to Pros*

Because the golf pros were not required to divulge their incomes, there are no available data for their expenses. However, the expenses (operating costs per round of golf) can be estimated from the city's total operating expenses (exclusive of capital improvements) during the pre-privatization period. To be conservative, the year with the highest cost, 1991, was selected for the analysis of the pros profits. Table 3 shows that the city's operating cost in 1991 was $6.36 (does not include the capital improvement expenses). This figure is used to approximate the pros operating expenses by first adjusting the 1991 operating cost for inflation in each of the succeeding years.

Next, the total operating cost to the pros is calculated by multiplying the estimated operating cost per round of golf by the total number of rounds. For example, the operating cost per round played in 1993 was $6.83 (Table 3). Multiplying this by the rounds played yields a total operating cost of $3,410,841 (Table 3).

Then, the estimated profit to the pros is calculated by subtracting the total operating costs from the payment to the pros to operate the golf courses. The estimated net profit to the pros divided by the number of rounds played provides the estimated profit per round. The estimated total profit to the pros was $2,449,136, and the estimated profit per round of golf was $4.90 (Table 3).

Chapter 16

Privatizing the City's Swimming Pools—Splash, Inc.

Jack Miller

Introduction

An important aspect of the privatization philosophy espoused by Mayor Stephen Goldsmith was that public services can and should be self-supporting. In his book, *The Twenty-First Century City*, Goldsmith says, "We planned to shift many of our costs from taxes to user fees, so that our customers could let us know if we were providing poor services" (Goldsmith 1997, 24). This approach, which could be characterized as exchanging citizen rights for customer privileges, raises philosophical problems because it excludes those with little or no money and flies in the face of the whole concept of "public services." By the Mayor's own standards, privatizing the pools resulted in particularly poor service since attendance fell from 48,667 to 34,044 (a 30 percent decrease) by the end of the three year Splash experiment (IDPR 1996a, 12; IDPR 1996b).

The Privatization Experiment

The Indianapolis Department of Parks and Recreation (Parks Department; also called IndyParks) maintains nineteen swimming pools in Marion County. Preparation for contracting out the management of three of these pools "began in 1992 and negotiations were finalized throughout 1993" according to the Parks Department (IDPR 1996b). Splash, Inc. was chosen from three companies that responded to the city's request for proposals, and a one-year renewable contract was signed in the spring of 1994.

The experiment, which lasted for three years, demonstrates how difficult it is to run a public service at affordable prices and still turn a profit. It also demonstrates that people who cannot afford the increased user fees necessary for profitability are excluded, and that accountability suffers when the lines of responsibility are unclear, as they so often are when another layer of bureaucracy is required and added to manage the privatization effort. Ironically, privatization is intended to streamline and reduce bureaucracy, but the opposite can occur. The Mayor's privatization committee, Service, Efficiency and Lower Taxes for Indianapolis Commission (SELTIC), was a key player in the decision to privatize the pools, and this decision was based on wildly exaggerated statements of the cost of operating the pools. The *Indianapolis Star* reported that according to SELTIC "The three pools cost the city more than $330,000 to operate last year [1993] . . . they took in $115,000 in receipts." Based on this analysis, SELTIC naturally recommended the move to private management." However, according to the Parks Department's own figures, SELTIC had over-estimated the cost of running these three public pools by nearly 100 percent (Johnston and Lanosga 1994). This mistake would turn out to be costly for the taxpayers.

1993, Pre-Privatization

In 1993, the year prior to privatization, the three public pools (Gustafson, Broad Ripple, and Sahm) had revenues of $134,996 from admissions, facility rentals, concessions and lessons, and the actual cost to the Parks Department to operate the pools was $192,935 (IDPR 1996a, 8). Therefore, total losses for the 1993 season were $57,939. In 1993, admission fees (user fees) had not yet been increased in an effort to shift the cost of operation to the users, and the fee structure at all three pools was: ages 0-3 (free); ages 4-12 ($1.00); ages 13-17 ($1.50); ages 18-64 ($2.00); and over 65 ($1.50). The fee structure was the same at all of the public pools. Swimming lessons were provided at a nominal fee.

1994, First Year of Privatization

The contract for 1994 specified that Splash, Inc. was to be responsible for operating the three pools on a daily basis, performing routine maintenance and operating the concessions. Splash was to assume all costs of chemicals and utilities. In return, the city would pay Splash an annual base fee of $33,032,[1] and allow the company to "retain all net revenues from concessions, admissions and the like up to $122,426.00," a figure derived from receipts of the previous year. (Johnston and Lanosga 1994).

The city would receive "18% of all gross sales, after sales taxes, on all proceeds in excess of $122,460.00" (IDPR 1994a, 12) and would be responsible for repairs, marketing and the opening and closing costs for the summer season. Parks Director Leon Younger told the *Indianapolis Star*, "It'd be awful hard to put that on a contractor. We would have had those expenses regardless" (Johnston and Lanosga 1994). What he did not mention was that the city's expenses were offset by revenues prior to privatization. Parks Director Younger confidently predicted that Splash would save the city money, ". . . based on how much heat we have. If we stay in the 80's and 90's, we'll have a good summer and they'll have a good summer" (Johnston and Lanosga 1994). As events unfolded, the weather was the least of Younger's worries.

The premier 1994 season was kicked off with a price increase in admission fees to shift operational costs to users in keeping with Mayor Goldsmith's philosophy of making services self-sufficient. The new fee structure included two categories, youth (age 18 and under) and adults (over 18), and the fees were adjusted based on the quality of the pools. Sahm was considered to be a higher quality facility than Gustafson and Broad Ripple. Although the actual price increase may appear nominal because the amounts are relatively small, the increases were significant to users, many of whom represented lower income levels. The increase in fees for adults was 12.5 percent at Gustafson and Broad Ripple and 50 percent at Sahm. The increase for children is more difficult to represent because the age categories changed from three in 1993 to one in 1994 and subsequent years. However, based on an average of the 1993 youth categories, the fees for youth increased by 50 percent at Gustafson and Broad Ripple and by 140 percent at Sahm.

An immediate savings to Splash was realized by eliminating security officers from the staff because, according to Splash's President, Melinda Ziegler, "they scare swimmers away" (Johnston and Lanosga 1994). She went on to say, "if there's a security problem at any of the pools, the company will simply call the police" (Johnston and Lanosga 1994). This saved Splash the $8,000 per season previously paid by the Parks Department for security officers. A Parks Department audit did agree that ". . . an IPD officer can generally be found at or near each of the pool sites. This serves as a deterrent to illegal activity near the family-oriented pools" (IDPR 1996b, 5). Unfortunately for Splash, the likely presence of an IPD officer "at or near" the pools did not deter all illegal activity, and the attempt to save money by eliminating security may have resulted in greater costs for the company.

A Parks Department review after the 1994 season found certain "unanswered irregularities in bookkeeping." The 1995 season saw $6,525 disappear from receipts while in 1996 another $16,744 was stolen in seven separate incidents. The Parks Department audit mentioned a cryptic note attached to one of Splash's cash reports: "money stolen. . . no deposit" (IDPR 1996a, 9). The audit went on to state that ". . . since there is no documentation (police report, thief (sic) report), we recommend that Splash be responsible for these funds" (IDPR 1996a, 9).

A major provision in the 1994 contract required that the Parks Department "will bill contractor for utility costs (electric, water, natural gas)" and that Splash "purchase and stock adequate quality and quantity of pool water sanitation chemicals" (IDPR 1994a, 9). By the end of the season however, Splash had spent $16,572 more than it had expected on chemicals and requested reimbursement from the city (IDPR 1994b). According to Splash, the increased costs were caused by 1) pressure from the Marion County Health Department to chlorinate the water more frequently (Glasson 1999) and use a "more expensive method of chlorine treatment which the company advised against" (Lanosga and Johnston, 1994b) and 2) massive water leaks causing the usage of chemicals, water and utilities to soar. A sternly worded memorandum from the Parks Department pointed out that, "It is IDPR's belief that by entering this contract, Splash assumed *some* (emphasis mine) risk associated with the cost of operating the public pools" (IDPR 1994b). In spite of what appeared to be straightforward contractual language, the Parks Department decided to split the additional expense with Splash.

As a result of these problems, the first year's balance sheet showed the city's operating losses had increased compared to the time when the Parks Department operated the pools. The basis for this comparison includes 1993 losses of $57,939 reported by the Parks Department (IDPR 1996a) and 1994 losses reported by the *Indianapolis News* of $55,002 (Lanosga and Johnston 1994) plus the $8,286 added for unexpected chemical use figured in later (IDPR 1994b). The total loss (in spite of the increase in user fees) to the city in 1994 was $63,288, or a 9.2 percent increase over 1993 losses.

The 1994 Pool Contract Wrap-Up Summary stated that the Parks Department was also "disturbed" by a 24 percent drop in program registration (swimming lessons). This decrease in lessons appeared to be due to a 73 percent increase in lesson fees over 1993 (from an average $10.15 per student to $17.55). Receipts in 1994 were up by 31 percent, but program enrollment fell from 1,239 to 941. Officials were also concerned that in spite of a 12 percent increase in attendance, pool revenues were up only 7 percent and concessions had fallen by an alarming 22 percent. The author of the Wrap-Up Summary noted, "after a test of the bank deposits and other financial records, questions remain unanswered. This is disconcerting." (IDPR 1994b)

Melinda Ziegler claimed that her "company didn't make any money on the deal either" (Lanosga and Johnston 1994) despite revenues and reimbursements in excess of $180,000 (IDPR 1994b). Ziegler felt this was due to the previously mentioned unanticipated expenses. At one point in 1994, responding to Splash's request for capital improvement money to increase patron satisfaction, the Parks Department responded: "We would encourage and expect Splash as entrepreneurs, to initiate and implement a system of purchasing and renting lounge chairs to further generate revenue and profit" (Taylor, 1994). Besides giving Splash advice on lucrative chair rentals, the city took additional steps to ensure that if anyone were going to lose money in 1995, it would *not* be the contractor.

1995, Second Year of Privatization

The 1995 contract provided for the city to assume *all* responsibility for utility bills and chemical costs (IDPR 1995a, Exhibit B). This contract raised admission fees again, and it increased the base compensation for Splash from $33,032 to $39,400. Compared to the pre-privatization situation, admission fees for adults were now 25 percent higher at the two lower-priced pools and 100 percent higher at the third pool. Youth prices also increased; they were 80 percent higher at the two lower-priced pools and 260 percent higher at the third pool. These increases generated a 12 percent increase in gross receipts; however, open swim attendance fell by 17 percent from the previous year (9,365 fewer swimmers).

The increased revenue generated from user fees did not, however, help taxpayers, and a year-end financial analysis (see Table 1) showed that the city losses climbed to $135,632—a 113 percent increase in cost compared to pre-privatization expenses (IDPR 1995b). The $38,152 profit shown for Splash resulted primarily because the city shouldered nearly $72,000 in utilities and chemical costs, which were the contractor's responsibility in the original contract.

Table 1: Financial analysis of the privatization of three swimming pools for the 1995 season (summary of Parks Department's Pool Contract Wrap Up)

Parks Department
Expenses:

Contract payment to Splash, Inc. to operate 3 facilities		$ 31,440
Facility maintenance: (open, closing, and general repairs)		$ 26,945
Utilities		$ 35,392
Chemical costs		$ 36,445
Marketing (% of total for all pools)		$ 5,475
Supplies		$ 1,096
	Total Expenses	$136,793

Revenue:

From Splash contract		$ 1,161
	Net Loss	($135,632)

Splash
Expenses:

Payroll: (staff, management, administration)		$120,690
Cost of goods sold		$ 16,791
Operating expenses		$ 18,809
	Total Expenses	$149,189

Revenue:

From Parks Department (to manage 3 pools)[a]		$ 31,440
Admission, program, and concessions		$155,901
	Total Revenues[b]	$187,341
	Net Gain	$ 38,152

Source: IDPR 1995b.

[a]Adjusted from income of $39,400 by the Parks Department to reflect penalty for Splash not meeting its obligation to contribute its total amount to the Parks Department foundation.

[b]Utilities and chemicals were assigned to Splash in the original contract. In 1995, the contract was amended to assign all of the utilities and chemical expenses back to the Parks Department. The net gain for Splash does not reflect the true costs of the pool operations. Accordingly, Splash would have assumed a net loss.

The privatization experiment suffered other setbacks in the summer of 1995. According to the *Indianapolis Star*, two Splash lifeguards at one of the privatized pools, "improperly poured five gallons of liquid chlorine into a 55 gallon drum of muriatic acid (*Indianapolis Star*, 1995)." The fumes overcame twenty people at the pool and sent six of them to the hospital.

A former Parks Department employee, Ron Graham, said that he, "warned Splash repeatedly to use less chlorine" and that chronic over-chlorination could also damage the pools and pumps (Graham, 1999). However, as before, a Splash representative contended that the Marion County Health Department was forcing the company to use more chlorine.

An inspector at the Marion County Health Department, Dennis Jenkins, provides a different story. Jenkins noted that Splash had performance problems over the period that they operated the pools. Jenkins remembered one instance when he had tested the pool water and found high bacteria levels. As was his custom, he advised the Splash manager that she could either "shock" the pool with chlorine or he would have to close the pool down so it could be treated. Normally, the chlorine must be routed through the pumping system, but shocking was allowed if high bacterial levels were encountered. A heated debate followed in which the Splash operator berated the inspector for making such a "big deal" out of cloudy water (cloudy water is an indication that chlorination is inadequate). While they were talking, Splash assistants were busy pouring five-gallon drums of liquid chlorine into the pool. Jenkins said they must have poured "half their summer's supply into the water in just a few minutes" (Jenkins 2000). Questions about excessive chemical use and operator training would plague the project up to the end.

Over-chlorination by inexperienced personnel caused customers to complain of bleached swimming suits. The excess chlorine also caused a more significant problem—deterioration of the liner at the Gustafson pool. The liner, which was installed in 1988 and warranted for 25 years, had to be replaced at a cost of $50,930 the year after the Splash contract terminated. The city paid for the replacement cost, which was not covered by the warranty because of misuse (Indianapolis 1997, 2). A new filter system, costing $52,570 was also installed at the Broad Ripple pool (Indianapolis 1997, 1).

1996, Third Year of Privatization

In an effort to stem the city's losses, the 1996 contract was renegotiated yet again, using a so-called "reversed-tiered revenue system." This system gave the Parks Department 7 percent of the first $50,000 of revenue after taxes, 5 percent of the second $50,000, and 3.5 percent of the final $30,000 in generated revenue (Board of Parks and Recreation 1995, Addendum #1). All proceeds in excess of $130,000 in this contract were to be retained by Splash. This innovative approach "was initiated with the intent of increasing revenues for both Splash and DPR," according to a management review of the pools by the Parks Department (IDPR 1996b, 3). The review went on to explain, "DPR would benefit since they would receive a percentage of revenues once Splash reached certain levels rather than if they reached the one, final goal (as in the previous contracts). Splash would benefit because it would receive all revenue past a certain figure . . . an incentive for Splash to reach and exceed that goal . . . " (IDPR 1996b, 3).

Another change in the contract was that the Parks Department gave Splash a chlorine allowance of $29,000 for two pools, and costs over this amount were to be reimbursed to Splash if there were a "significant water loss." Chemical use at the third pool was to be paid entirely by Splash. Once again, the Parks Department had raised admission prices. The two less expensive pools had admission prices that remained the same as for the previous year (representing an increase of 25 percent over the pre-privatization levels), but the third pool peaked at $4.50 for adults (125 percent over 1993 prices of $2.00) (IDPR 1996c, 16). The increase for youth at the two less expensive pools was 111 percent over 1993 average prices, and it was 322 percent at the more expensive pool. The increases took their toll on 1996 pool attendance, which ended the season down a dramatic 30 percent from 1993 (IDPR 1996a).

This poor performance lent a certain irony to the words Parks Director Leon Younger had uttered in 1994, "a major factor in negotiating the Splash contract was the city's desire to keep the prices of admissions low." Younger went on to say that the admission prices at the pools could not simply be increased as they could at the golf courses because "we look at the pools as a core service." (Johnston and Lanosga 1994)

The total revenues for three Splash pools also sagged in 1996, down 9 percent from the previous year. Even the "incentives" provided by the reverse-tier system failed to generate any income to the Parks Department. The final audit of 1996 noted that after various credits were applied, "the net effect of this structure [reverse-tier system] will cause the Dept. to owe Splash $452" (IDPR 1996a, 13). When the cost of chemicals, utilities,[2] base compensation, maintenance labor/supplies and marketing are added, the 1996 season cost the taxpayers $111,772 or 93 percent more than before privatization (IDPR 1996a; Clark 1996).

Wrapping It Up

Throughout it all, the Parks Department tried to put a positive spin on the experiment by pointing out that privatization:

1) [R]educed Administrative duties and increased gross revenue (IDPR 1994b).
2) Demonstrated how "private enterprise" can operate and manage through less bureaucratic systems with more flexibility (IDPR 1996b).
3) Provides "the opportunity to compete or compare our city's aquatic management services with a private business . . . an invaluable managerial experience" (IDPR 1995c).

In a report reviewing the three-year Splash program, Ryan Puckett, Special Projects Coordinator for Mayor Goldsmith's Regulatory Study Commission ignored the 30 percent drop in attendance and the 9 percent drop in revenues to effuse: "The continued increase in revenues is a promising sign for the competitive management of DPR Pools, proving that a partnership between the local business and the city can work within the Aquatic Department." Puckett continued, "we recommend that DPR continue to operate these three pools on a contractual basis." (IDPR 1996b, 7)

In response to the ongoing Splash failure to bring concession revenues back up to the 1993 levels a hopeful Puckett wrote, "We further recommend that Splash and DPR evaluate the option of using another contractor to run concessions for the three contracted pools" (IDPR 1996b, 7). Puckett apparently was unaware of the contractor's feelings about the previous three-year "partnership between local business and the city." Beth Glasson, Vice-President of Splash, fumed in a letter to the *Indianapolis Star* in 1997, "The company lost over $90,000.00 due to the misrepresentations by the Parks Department and a deaf ear from the mayor and his office" (Glasson, 1997).

Many of the problems which the city experienced with Splash—from the "chlorine cloud" of 1995 to the lower concession revenues—could have happened whether the pools were privatized or not. However, the

Parks Department's own comparison (see Table 2) shows that the Splash-operated pools were consistently more expensive to operate per swimmer. The Parks Department analysis compares each of the Splash operated pools with a comparable pool (in terms of square footage and attendance) that the Department operated. In each case, the operational costs and the cost per swimmer at the Splash-operated pools was higher than at the pools operated by the Parks Department.

Table 2:   1995 performance comparison between pools operated by Splash Inc. and the Parks Department

Comparison Item	Splash-Operated Pools	Parks Department-Operated Pools[a]
Pools	Gustafson	Douglass
Expenses[b]	$ 67,823	$ 42,008
Attendance	15,177	9,330
Cost per swimmer	$ 4.77	$ 4.50
Pools	Broad Ripple	Wes Montgomery
Expenses	$ 63,223	$ 49,115
Attendance	16,326	13,030
Cost per swimmer	$ 3.87	$ 3.77
Pools	Sahm	Ellenberger
Expenses	$189,662	$ 72,133
Attendance	27,807	23,788
Cost per swimmer	$ 6.82	$ 3.03

Source: IDPR 1995b.
[a]The comparison pools were chosen by the Parks Department to compare the Parks Department self-operated pools against the Splash-operated pools. The comparison pools are similar in pool square footage and attendance figures.
[b]Expenses for Splash-operated pools are the total Parks Department expenses plus Splash payroll expenses. This gives an even comparison with the Parks Department self-operated expenses.

Summary

Privatization apologists could not hide the fact that the three-year experiment had been a complete failure, not only for the city and Splash, but most importantly, for the swimmers who were priced out of using public pools and for the taxpayers who footed the bills for increased costs, decreased service and uncompensated damage to public property. By the end of the privatization experiment, the city's costs shot up over 90 percent; admissions fees and programs fees had escalated as much as 125 percent; concession revenues remained at 25 percent below 1993 levels; swim attendance and lessons fell precipitously; and a new pool liner and pump costing $103,500 was required for two of the Splash-operated pools, while nothing comparable occurred at the city-run pools selected by the Parks Department to develop comparison data.

Goldsmith attempted no further pool privatizations after 1996, and the user fees, which had been increased to turn the pools into profit centers, were reduced in response to the drop in attendance. By the 1999 season the admission prices at the two less expensive pools went back to the pre-privatization prices. The prices at the more expensive pool stayed at the 1996 levels.

Notes

[1]Based on Splash's ability to raise $10,000 for the IndyParks Foundation. The contract stipulated that those portions of the money not raised would be charged against Splash's base pay. For example, if Splash raised only $1,000, the Parks Department would subtract $9,000 from the company's base pay. Splash was not able to raise the stipulated amounts during any of the contract years.

[2]Utilities were paid at Sahm and Gustafson pools by the Parks Department.

Chapter 17

Indianapolis International Airport: A Success Story

Dennis Rosebrough

Philosophy and Process

On October 1, 1995, a new chapter in American airport management began when Indianapolis International Airport became the largest privately managed airport in the United States. Under the terms of a performance-based management contract, BAA Indianapolis LLC, a newly formed subsidiary company of London-based BAA plc, assumed full management responsibility for the five airports and one heliport owned by the Indianapolis Airport Authority (IAA) (BAA plc 1994).

The start of the contract culminated a two-year process during which the philosophical and practical issues of private airport management were formulated into a Request for Proposal issued by the Indianapolis Airport Authority Board[1] in September of 1994 (IAA 1994). The selection of BAA was announced on May 11, 1995, followed by contract signing on September 12, 1995 (IAA 1995).

The Airport Authority's largest and most significant holding is the Indianapolis International Airport. The airport is classified as a medium hub airport that has grown to serve 7.5 million passengers each year. The main complex includes a 500,000 square foot passenger terminal with thirty-one gates and 10,000 parking spaces in both garage and surface parking. In 1999 there were eighteen airlines operating 185 daily departures to forty-five destinations with non-stop service. The primary air service market catchment area includes a large portion of Indiana, although passengers regularly come to the airport from Ohio, Illinois and Kentucky (Airport Authority 2000).

In addition to providing traditional passenger service, Indianapolis International Airport has become one of the world's major air cargo airports, serving as home for the second largest sorting hub in the FedEx system and sole sorting hub for United States Postal Service Priority and Express Mail products. A total of 109 cargo aircraft land and take off each weekday in a major night sort and a smaller day sort operation. Total cargo volume increased by 23 percent in 1998 making Indianapolis the eighth largest cargo airport in the United States and the sixteenth largest in the world (Airport Authority 2000).

A new dimension aviation activity came to the airport in a big way in 1991 when United Airlines selected Indianapolis as the site of its new $800 million maintenance center. The successful package included $300 million in combined financial incentives from the State of Indiana, the City of Indianapolis and Hendricks County (the county adjacent to the airport on the west) and an immediately available building site on the airport with infrastructure in place. Other major aircraft maintenance operations on the airport are operated by American Trans Air and FedEx (Airport Authority 2000).

Much of the success at the airport can be credited to a tradition of airport planning that is traced back to the original site selection for the city's new municipal airport in 1929. The present terminal complex is on the first 900 acres of land purchased for the airport. Careful planning continued throughout the steady growth of the airport that paralleled the growing commercial aviation industry, especially after World War II and into the early 1960s when jet aircraft entered the commercial airline market. Looking at the projections for substantial passenger growth, the Airport Authority prepared a comprehensive master plan for the airport. That master plan, adopted in 1975, has been the blueprint for all development of the airport. The plan provided ample land for aviation related uses, such as FedEx, the Postal Service Hub, the United Airlines Maintenance Center, American Trans Air and others. The plan also recommended an airfield layout with two widely spaced parallel runways and a non-intersecting crosswind runway for maximum capacity and operational reliability. The crowning, but remaining, element to complete the master is the new midfield terminal complex to replace the present terminal (Airport Authority 2000).

With the highly successful development of Indianapolis International Airport and a complementary array of four general aviation facilities and a downtown heliport, why would the Airport Authority Board consider private management? To understand the issue, it is necessary to examine the "unusual" financial structure under which American airports operate. Historically, as airports around the country needed to develop facilities, the airport owners (cities or states or special authorities) looked to the airlines for financial backing of bonded debt. This relationship provided the airlines with veto authority over major capital projects as a *quid pro quo* for their willingness to back the bonds. In most cases, the airlines' financial commitment to an airport included the funding of operational and maintenance expenses as well as the debt service. The amount of money paid by the airlines to the airports is based on the portion of the airport budget that is not funded by non-airline sources such as parking, concessions and property rental (Airport Authority 2000). The airline charges (space rental and landing fees) are therefore a function of the airport's debt service payments, operation/maintenance expenses and the amount of non-airline revenue generated by the airport operator.

It is important to note that the Federal Aviation Administration (FAA) has also promulgated regulations restricting the flow of funds at airports. United States Code Section 47107 absolutely prohibits the diversion of revenue from airport sponsors for non-aviation purposes (U.S. Code 2000a). This is an important procedural safeguard against misapplication of funds, as is federal oversight generally. The federal government became involved with airport financing through a series of grant programs for capital development administered by the FAA. In general terms, the FAA collects a tax on airline tickets that goes into the Aviation Trust Fund (U.S. Code 2000b). Money is distributed from this fund back to local airports through various grant programs. A portion of the trust fund is also used to support FAA functions such as air traffic control. The involvement of the Federal government has resulted in many regulations and grant assurances that airports must obey to remain eligible for grants. The fundamental tenet that prohibits airport revenues from being used for "non-airport" purposes means that a city cannot use excess airport revenues or "profits" to fund schools, parks, police or other government services.

As important as these fiscal safeguards are, they create an environment in which there are no direct financial rewards to the airport operator or other local government agencies for efficient or innovative airport management, since the airline financial agreements guarantee a "balanced budget" for the airport and there is no ability to use excess airport revenue for other purposes. Incentives are further diminished because almost all airports operate as monopolies with no real competition in their markets to drive improvements.

Although Indianapolis International Airport was one of the best developed facilities in the country and was considered one of the better managed airports, the Airport Authority Board began to notice that non-airline revenue at the airport was not growing at an acceptable rate and that overall customer services were not keeping pace with new airport industry standards. The net effect was an increasing cost for the airlines to operate at Indianapolis International Airport (Airport Authority 2000). The situation was not critical, but the trend was not good. The Airport Authority Board was particularly sensitive to airline costs because a number of "low-fare and "start-up" airlines currently serve Indianapolis, providing one of the lowest average ticket prices of any airport in the United States. Controlling costs, including airport charges, is critical to the success of these carriers that often operate on slim profit margins. The Board looked for ways to correct the course. Noting the publicized successes of Mayor Stephen Goldsmith's "managed competition" initiatives in other government functions, later the subject of his book (Goldsmith 1997), the Board decided to explore private management options for the airport.

From the beginning, the goal of the Airport Authority Board was to bring the forces of competition and financial reward into airport management, with success measured by the twin goals of controlling the airlines' costs and improving customer service. Since the Board was introducing a new process for American airports, there were no prescribed implementation plans or specific models to be followed. The Board moved cautiously and sought advice from experts in the burgeoning field of airport privatization, bringing in national consultants such as Infrastructure Management Group (IMG), based in Washington, D.C. The challenge was to devise a process that specified the desired results, while not limiting potential managers by imposing too-restrictive specifications. The plan adopted by the Board called for an initial solicitation of general concepts followed by a more specific Request for Proposal (RFP 1994).

The first solicitation was issued in March of 1994, but it only succeeded in letting the market know what was happening in Indianapolis. The Airport Authority Board found that the potential bidders did not want to reveal their individual concepts and plans until the official proposal process. The formal Request for Proposals was issued in September of 1994. Staying true to the concept of competition, the Board invited the current Airport Authority management staff to submit a proposal and provided funds for its preparation, in order to put the staff on a level playing field with private companies. The Board wanted the competition process to stimulate management creativity among all potential operators. If the current staff had the best proposal, the process still worked.

Five proposals were submitted to the Board, four from private companies and one from the staff. Three proposals, including the staff's, received further consideration. After a series of interviews, the selection of BAA was announced on May 11, 1995. BAA had committed to controlling airport operating costs while significantly increasing non-airline revenue, the combination of which contributes to lowering airport costs to the airlines. Relevant language from the BAA response illustrates the approach to be taken:

> Measurement of performance would be against quantified baseline benchmarks. Performance may be defined as a combination of cost improvements, revenue generation and service standard improvements while maintaining the highest levels of safety and security.

> The key here is to establish objective knowledge of what the airport customers themselves require (as opposed to what the airport operator *believes* customers require). Our approach would be to introduce the whole range of service performance indicators currently in use at our airports in the United Kingdom and in our Pittsburgh retail operation.

> Notwithstanding these proposed organizational changes and any activities subcontracted, BAA pledges that there will be no compulsory redundancies resulting from restructuring (BAA plc 1994).

While BAA's performance in the United Kingdom and Pittsburgh provided important data, allowing a "background check," it is also very important to note that BAA backed its proposal with a financial guarantee. It posted a $50 million dollar letter of credit insuring performance and promised an initial investment of $500,000 of its own funds in the airport's retail operations. The willingness of BAA to assume substantial risk was a major factor in the award of the contract (Airport Authority 2000).

The next step in the process was to negotiate the actual contract that would incorporate all of the desired concepts and define the relationship between the Airport Authority as owner and BAA as the airport manager. Also to be devised was a formula to calculate compensation paid to BAA that would be consistent with the Airport

Authority Board's initial goal of controlling airlines' costs and improving customer service. Both the Board and BAA wanted to assure that rewards would be based on BAA's actual accomplishments and, conversely, that those financial impacts beyond BAA's control would not unfairly reduce compensation. The accepted solution was agreement on a baseline that took the costs in 1994 and projected them forward, assuming "normal" passenger increases and "normal" inflation. If BAA succeeded in achieving a net cost per passenger below that baseline, the compensation would be 33 percent of the amount saved. The contract did not specify how the net number would be reached, that is, whether it would be accomplished by cost-controls or revenue enhancements, or both. BAA could also earn a customer service quality bonus of 5 percent based on mutually agreed performance criteria (Airport Authority 2000).

The contract also incorporated the major elements of the BAA proposal to the Airport Authority. The company guaranteed savings of $32 million over the ten-year life of the contract, backing that guarantee with the $50 million letter of credit. BAA also committed to hiring all current airport employees with the same or improved wages and benefits (Airport Authority 2000).

BAA plc and BAA Indianapolis LLC

BAA plc is the largest private airport company in the world. The company traces its origins back to the mid-1960s when the British government created the British Airports Authority to manage its gateway international airports, which included the three London airports—Heathrow, Gatwick and Stansted and Prestwick in Scotland. The situation changed in the mid-1980s when Prime Minister Margaret Thatcher was implementing her program to return or move to the private sector some of the previously nationalized industries or traditional government functions. The government authorized the Authority to transition to a corporate structure in 1986 preparatory to being floated on the London Stock Exchange in 1987. The process worked smoothly and the stock sale was an overwhelming success. The company selected the name BAA plc since the former British Airports Authority was already called "BAA" by many people and in the media. BAA's own experience of moving from a government agency to a private company provided valuable insight for the airport management transition in Indianapolis.

As a private company, BAA plc now owns outright the three London airports as well as Glasgow, Edinburgh and Aberdeen airports in Scotland and Southampton Airport on the south coast of England. The company must finance all operational and capital expenses for these airports without any government funds. In this truly privatized system, the company is constantly challenged to develop revenue sources that will not only cover operational costs, but also provide adequate resources for securing large amounts of capital. Because BAA can be perceived as a monopoly, the British privatization plan provided for a governmental review of the airline charges levied by the company every five years as well as a solicitation of airport customers' opinions of the company's performance. Government-imposed caps on the airline charges, at less than the rate of inflation, have challenged the company to maximize the non-airline revenue stream even more (Airport Authority 2000).

In the early 1990s the company realized that continued growth and increased value to its shareholders was limited if activity were confined to the domestic British market. Over the years the company had developed significant expertise in airport management. The combination of these factors led the company to launch an international marketing effort, initially in consultancy work with other airports and then more fully, seeking airport ownership or management contracts. The market appeared to include a mixture of airports, some whose management company was owned by the government and some whose governments wanted to raise funds by leasing or selling their airports. In developing countries, in particular, there appeared to be a need for both capital and management expertise.

The first opportunity for BAA in the United States was at Pittsburgh where a new terminal was being built. Pittsburgh officials and their consultants had looked at a variety of airports as they considered design options. They learned that BAA had advanced the concept of airport retailing and was familiar with standards of customer service and satisfaction, skills driven by the need to raise non-airline funds. The new terminal project would provide an excellent opportunity for Pittsburgh to distinguish its airport by incorporating aspects of the BAA approach. After a competitive bid process, BAA was awarded a fifteen-year contract to develop and manage the retail and food/beverage operations at Pittsburgh International Airport. The Pittsburgh contract was a "master concessionaire" lease, not a contract for total airport management. The plan has been a success both in terms of revenue for Pittsburgh Airport and in establishing Pittsburgh as a new standard by which all American airports are measured for retailing and food/beverage service (Airport Authority 2000).

Management Responsibilities at Indianapolis

The final contract between the Airport Authority and BAA Indianapolis LLC, the new subsidiary company, established the formula for compensation and the terms of the relationship between the two entities. The Airport Authority remained the owner of all airport assets and retained responsibility for budget approval and capital development. BAA Indianapolis LLC would implement polices adopted by the Airport Authority Board and would have full responsibility for the on-going management of the facilities. The company would prepare budgets and make recommendations to the Board concerning the operations and development of the airport. All Airport Authority personnel became employees of BAA Indianapolis and were governed by the company wage, benefit and personnel policies (Airport Authority 2000).

Throughout the first year the company focused on shifting employees from a governmental to a private employee approach. A short-term transition team led the effort for the first six months, and then a small core of BAA veterans who had accepted two- and three-year assignments in Indianapolis followed. Experiences in BAA's own transition from public to private just ten years prior provided valuable lessons in the development of a new corporate culture. The employee program included large group orientation meetings and small group sessions. The transition plan, which was actually crafted by the existing airport management team working with BAA's leadership, was intended to move at a comfortable pace, yet challenge the employees to think differently. At the time that the Indianapolis contract was beginning, a new employee involvement and empowerment program was being implemented at BAA's airports in the United Kingdom. Incorporating the elements of the United Kingdom program at Indianapolis proved to be a very successful part of the orientation to BAA. With input gathered through employee meetings and informal interaction, the management team established "project boards" to address some key issues. Each project board included front line employees with an interest or knowledge in the issue. This approach to problem solving had not been used under the more traditional former public management and the lack of involvement in decision-making had been a source of irritation with a number of employees. The new "project boards" represented a positive change and contributed greatly to the overall acceptance of BAA among the workforce.

To capture the new private sector mentality, the employees were asked to change their vocabularies. For example: "The airport is now a *business*, not a utility. The airport no longer has passengers and visitors, but *customers*. The airport has *business partners*, not tenants" (Airport Authority 2000).

In addition to accomplishing changes in workforce attitudes, BAA and the Airport Authority Board wanted to make some physical changes at the airport to demonstrate the new approach to airport management. The retail offering at the airport was one area where substantial improvements could be made relatively quickly. In its proposal, BAA had committed to investing $500,000 of its own money to "jump start" a retail project. In the first year, thirteen new brand name retail shops were opened in modified existing spaces and planning began for the creation of a retail court with an 8,500 square foot expansion of an existing terminal walkway. This new space would house nine new retailers in a brightly-lit shopping center environment.

During the first year of the contract, the management structure of the airport was reviewed, both internally and externally, with the goal of matching the organization to meet the business objectives. For example, a retail department was created for the development and management of the expanding retail activities. Parking was redefined as a retail function and put in the new department, eliminating a level of management. The personnel function was enhanced with a training coordinator to implement the corporate commitments to staff development. The airport's first minority affairs manager was appointed to centralize initiatives for employee recruitment and business activities with minority-owned businesses (Airport Authority 2000).

The review also resulted in the reorganization and streamlining of some functions. Separate building and airfield maintenance departments were combined into one airport maintenance function within the engineering department. In each of these cases, the number of front line employees remained the same or actually increased while the supervisory staff was reduced. Employees saw these changes as evidence that the company's commitment to "empowered" employees was genuine.

Although the savings in operating costs and the increased non-airline revenue were critical elements of the contract, there was also the goal of improving customer service. BAA had introduced a Quality of Service (QSM) program at the United Kingdom airports several years prior to the Indianapolis contract. QSM is an intercept interview program where customers are queried about a variety of quality issues during their airport experience. Each year over 600,000 interviews are conducted at the seven airports in the United Kingdom. The results are tabulated and widely published among the entire workforce. In some areas the QSM results can be the basis for salary increases. In all cases the results are analyzed carefully and become the basis for management decisions including major capital expenditures.

The QSM program was implemented immediately in Indianapolis with a sample size of 6,000 interviews based on total passenger traffic. The Indianapolis staff is now keenly aware of the QSM results. The survey results are also supplemented by a feedback card program initiated by BAA that features self-mailing comment cards. In combination, the two programs provide valuable and timely customer input for the BAA staff. The Airport Authority Board has incorporated some of the QSM results in calculating the annual quality bonus for BAA.

Having operated airports in areas where environmental issues were highly emotional, BAA had adopted a proactive approach to mitigating the environmental impact of its airports. BAA applied those same principles to Indianapolis and implemented one of the nation's first comprehensive airport environmental management systems (EMS). The EMS required an environmental assessment of the entire airport, including the facilities of business partners on the airport. Issues such as underground storage tanks, hazardous chemicals and recovery programs were evaluated. A timeline for corrections and on-going monitoring was established. New contract language for future leases was developed to prevent future problems (Airport Authority 2000).

The challenge for BAA has been to sustain the enthusiasm and initial force for change that came with the launch of the new venture. As an ongoing business, BAA is aware that maintaining enthusiasm is far more difficult than initially generating it. The dynamic nature of the airport industry and a recurring message that continuous improvement will result in financial and personal rewards have been sufficient motivators for most of the BAA staff thus far. Recent examples of continuous improvements include the new pay-on-foot automated parking system and a new credit card access business traveler parking lot. In the terminal, a totally new food and beverage program is has been completed, bringing fifteen new "brand name" restaurants to the airport. (TGI Fridays, California Pizza Kitchen, Au Bon Pain, Ben and Jerry's and Starbucks are new additions.) Less visible, but important improvements have occurred in the computer and management information systems and in facility maintenance programming.

The Bottom Line

The question is whether all of these changes and improvements have enabled BAA to achieve the contractual goal of reducing the airlines' operating cost while enhancing customer service at the airport. The list of customer service improvements and the customer reaction to them as validated by formal (QSM and feedback cards) and informal reaction attest to success in that area (Airport Authority 2000). Equally convincing are the financial results for the first three full years of the private management contract.

A key measurable financial factor is the net non-airline revenue per passenger, which is the total non-airline revenue available after covering operation and maintenance costs. This result is significant because it captures the success of BAA in increasing non-airline revenue and the success of BAA in controlling operating expenses. This number is meaningful to the airlines because these are the funds available to reduce landing fees and space rental costs that factor into the airport fees charged to the airlines. When more net non-airline revenue is available to cover airport costs, fewer funds are needed from the airlines.

Net non-airline revenue per passenger has increased from $2.08 in 1994 to $3.74 in 1998 and was $4.26 in 1999 based on the Authority's financial reports (IAA 1994-1999). These results are the net difference between non-airline revenue that has increased from $8.45 per passenger in 1994 to $10.42 in 1999 and the operation and maintenance expenses that have decreased from $6.37 per passenger in 1994 to $6.16 in 1999 (IAA 1994-1999). Net non-airline revenue has thus shown significant increases. The private management contract with BAA resulted in cumulative savings of $19 million in the first three years of the contract. Conservative estimates project total savings in excess of $173 million over the 13-year life of the contract (Airport Authority 2000).

A unique characteristic of the original management agreement was an article entitled "Spirit of Agreement." This article provided the language that "It is the intent of the Authority and Contractor (BAA) that both parties shall benefit from the execution and performance of this Agreement." As BAA's compensation was calculated for the first year, differences in interpretation of the contract, especially with respect to parking fees, led to a review of the methodology outlined in the original agreement. Negotiations between the Airport Authority and BAA resulted in removing parking revenue from the compensation calculations while both altering the percentage of savings paid to BAA and extending the term of the Agreement by three years. (Airport Authority 2000). The resolution of the issue reflected both the parties' commitment to the "spirit" article and the initial success of the relationship between the Airport Authority and BAA.

Summary

The first four years of private airport management in Indianapolis have been a learning experience not only for the Indianapolis Airport Authority and BAA, but also for the airport industry throughout the world. The early successes have clearly demonstration that private management can yield benefits to all airport customers. By introducing competition and the profit motive, the incentives of the market are applied to a critically important part of the country's commercial infrastructure to meet the demands into the 21st century. But there are other important lessons to be learned from the success of this partnership:

- The Indianapolis Airport Authority Board exercised appropriate and consistent oversight. It did its homework at the beginning, conducted careful and independent evaluation of the original bids, imposed careful standards and procedures, and demanded adequate fiscal guarantees. It has also continued to monitor performance independently.
- BAA's willingness to guarantee its performance with substantial financial resources meant that the Indianapolis Airport Authority Board could have confidence that its contractor was at risk and that any failures would not be borne by the taxpayers.
- The existence of federal constraints on how airport revenues could be applied was yet another safeguard for the taxpayers.
- Last, but most definitely not least, BAA's commitment to slow and careful implementation of the transition was critical. This approach minimized disruption and change and showed concern for issues of employee morale. That approach paid big dividends by creating motivated and positive employees.

The experience of the Indianapolis Airport Authority demonstrates that market incentives, when implemented thoughtfully and with due regard for process and oversight, can pay significant dividends.

Notes

[1] The Airport Authority Board has seven members who serve staggered four-year terms. Five members are appointed by the Mayor of Indianapolis, one by the ex-officio Marion County Commissioners and one by the Hendricks County Commissioners. (The Indianapolis Airport lies on the line between the two counties.)

Of the mayoral appointees, no more than three may be of the same political party and one must be a resident of either Wayne or Decatur Township, the townships where the airport is located. The Airport Authority statute also provides for an advisory member appointed by the county commissioners of any other county where the Airport Authority owns property. These statutory requirements ensure representation by those most immediately affected by Airport planning and development issues. (Airport Authority 2000).

Afterword

Summing Up

Stephen Goldsmith wanted to "shake up" city government. He succeeded—but how did reality in Indianapolis measure up to the extravagant claims made by Goldsmith for his privatization experiment? What does the foregoing examination suggest about the "marketization" of Indianapolis, and what can it teach us about the current "reinvention" movement in general?

The Indianapolis Experience

What were Goldsmith's claims, and what were the facts? What results have the authors of the foregoing chapters documented?

- *Claim*: Privatization was first and foremost a commitment to fiscal prudence. The facts show Goldsmith dramatically increased municipal debt and that we wasted millions of tax dollars on consultants, poor-quality construction, and a variety of poorly managed municipal experiments. For example, Goldsmith reduced the workforce by 62 percent during his two terms as mayor, "saving" the taxpayers $149 million in salaries and benefits (constant 1991 dollars)—however, Goldsmith fails to mention that shifting these jobs and functions to the private sector cost taxpayers $290 million (constant 1991 dollars over the same period.[1]

- *Claim*: The administration practiced "compassionate conservatism." The facts show that Goldsmith attempted to gut regulations that protect poor people from slumlords and he "marketized" parks that priced poor families out of city swimming pools and golf courses.

- *Claim*: The City's neighborhoods were "empowered." The facts show that Goldsmith made staffing and policy decisions that most neighborhoods adamantly opposed.

- *Claim*: "Marketization" meant "customer service." The facts show that Goldsmith demonstrated a consistent disregard for public opinion, democratic process and political accountability.

- *Claim*: The administration spent a billion dollars on the city's infrastructure. The facts show that, although antiquated sewers were by far the most pressing infrastructure problem when Goldsmith took office, sewer overflows were not addressed, and discharges of raw sewage continue to pollute local rivers and streams.

- *Claim*: Privatization meant more efficient and effective government. The facts show Goldsmith left Indianapolis with more debt, more crime, more confusion and more civic polarization.

Based on Goldsmith's many claims, one would expect the Indianapolis economy to be strong and have experienced significant growth during his tenure. Morton Marcus, Director of the Indiana Business Research Center, has conducted a long-term economic analysis during the period 1969 to 1997 based on U.S. Bureau of Economic Analysis data. Morton examined aggregate aspects of economic performance: population, employment or jobs, real personal income, earnings, real per capita personal income and earnings per job. During the period of analysis, the Indianapolis metro area had mediocre growth compared to the nation and to its peer metro areas. Morton found that the greatest gains in earnings (4.7 percent) and employment (3.8 percent) during the period of analysis came in the service sector. In 1969, Indianapolis ranked 27th in total employment among 316 metro areas in the United States. By 1997, it had declined to 32nd. When Indianapolis was compared to 39 other metro areas that are similar in size and structure, Indianapolis ranked 25th among the 40 metro areas in employment growth from 1969 to 1997. According to Morton, "Thus, in comparison to the nation, Indianapolis is not a great success story . . . Overall, it lost market share" (Marcus 1999[2]).

If there is an irony to these results, it is Goldsmith's persistent use of a pro-business rhetoric in service of policies that no successful business would employ.

- Successful businesses carefully examine core functions to determine what works and what does not. These businesses strive for continual improvement. The Goldsmith administration assumed nothing worked and operated under a "management *du jour*" approach that changed with each new idea on the market.
- No prudent business incurs debt to pay operating expenses, yet the Goldsmith administration consistently bonded for personnel costs and other expenditures that should have been paid from the operating budget.
- Good business depends upon good internal controls. State Board of Account audits, as well as sworn evidence in the Tomanovich lawsuit, demonstrated the absence of such controls in Indianapolis under Goldsmith.
- Effective business practices include establishment of clear lines of authority and responsibility. The eight years of the Goldsmith administration were marked by constant change and confusion over responsibility for city services.
- Businesses that ignore applicable laws and regulations incur substantial costs, if they survive at all. Open disdain for bid procedures, disclosure and open door requirements and prevailing wage laws was a hallmark of the Goldsmith administration.
- No business can long afford to ignore its shareholders and investors. The Goldsmith administration was unaccountable to its citizen-shareholders and ungrateful to its rank-and-file political investors (albeit more sensitive to those political supporters who contributed cash).
- Successful businesses learn from mistakes and change business plans that do not work. The Goldsmith administration was prepared to change anything and everything—*except* its insistence on reinvention. It was unable to identify problems and when it did, it was unable to make needed changes.

Above all, successful businesses that are concerned about the future do not expect instant results. They take the long view. When change is necessary, as it often is, these businesses factor in the very real costs involved—from employee turnover, to customer confusion, to loss of institutional memory and capacity.

The administration that Stephen Goldsmith inherited was far from perfect, but Indianapolis was, by all measures, a well-managed city. It was, as Goldsmith's predecessor was fond of saying, "a city that works." Rather than approach that inheritance as a trust, as an infrastructure to be both maintained and improved, Goldsmith opted to tear the structure apart and rebuild it according to his own vision. Rather than building consensus for specific improvements, he instituted wholesale and constant—some would say obsessive—change that proved to be inconsistent with the conduct of orderly and responsive government. Indeed, the only thing that *didn't* change during the Goldsmith years was his insistence upon doing it his way, no matter how much hostility he engendered and no matter how dismal the results.

Broader Lessons for Privatization of Government Services

The lessons learned in Indianapolis do not differ significantly from those enumerated in Chapter 1, although the scope and intensity of the Indianapolis experiment meant that we may have learned a greater number of them.

- The goals of public service are larger than merely providing a service at the lowest possible cost.
- Great care must be taken lest government contracts be viewed—or become—simply another form of patronage.
- Privatization efforts must begin with planning for the future in the event a contractor cannot or will not fulfill its contractual obligations.
- It is very easy to manipulate (inflate) the "true cost" to government of providing a service, in order to make a privatization decision look prudent.
- Oversight is a significant cost of privatization that must be taken into account. While it can be expensive to provide, it can be even more expensive to omit.
- Privatization comes with a cost in terms of upheaval, risk and unforeseen consequences.
- Privatization can mean loss of government expertise and equipment, and a reduced ability to respond in the future.
- In the absence of a uniform process with substantive requirements that all bidders must meet, a sufficient number of bidders and an independent evaluative agency, there will be no accountability and no savings. (It is worth noting in this context that the one privatization initiative that seems to work in Indianapolis is at the airport, where an independent board

handled oversight and federal regulations constrained decisions and the application of funds.)

There is a fundamental difference between government *procurement* and reinvention as it was practiced in Indianapolis. Governments have purchased goods and services in the market for many years, and will certainly find it beneficial to continue to do so. There is also a difference between competition and simply contracting with private companies to do the government's business, as Goldsmith himself has recognized—in his book and his speeches, if not in his actions. A private monopoly is not inherently superior to a public one, and it may be significantly less accountable.

There is, finally, a crucial difference between insisting that government operate in a business-like fashion, and trying to turn government into a business.

Conclusion

The Indianapolis experiment is yet another episode in a long series of true stories featuring America's love affair with ideological simplicity and easy answers. Real-world public policy is rarely so simple. Mantras such as "cut taxes and government bloat" and "run government like a business" are appealing. But, as the Indianapolis experiment shows, efforts to "reinvent" can have far-reaching deleterious effects and must be undertaken with great care to preserve existing levels of service and allow for continual improvement in the future.

The issue is not "should local government contract for services" but "when and under what circumstances should government contract with private providers, and what precautions should we insist upon?" What is red tape to one observer will be prudent management of tax dollars to another. How best to achieve a balance between accountability and efficiency has long been one of the central concerns of public administration. The most poignant lesson to be learned from the "reinvention experiment" in Indianapolis is that accountability and the democratic process can be seriously compromised without any corresponding improvement in efficiency or improved services.

Ingrid Ritchie & Sheila Suess Kennedy

September 2000

Notes

[1]Personal communication, Jack Miller. Savings and shifted costs calculated based on Indianapolis operating budgets 1991-2000. Shifted costs include costs of privatizing, consultants, contractual services, legal services, third party contracts, management contracts and overtime.

[2] The source of the summarized data are: Morton J. Marcus. 1999. "The Indianapolis Economy in Perspective" (draft manuscript). Indianapolis, IN: Indiana University, Kelly School of Business.

Bibliography

Preface

Brant, Martha. 2000. "The Sage of Indianapolis." *Newsweek Magazine*. 03 January.

Boyd, Rozelle, Susan Williams, Monroe Gray and Jeffrey Golc. 1996. "Letter to the Editor." *Indianapolis Star*. 25 August.

Goldsmith, Stephen. 1997. *The Twenty-First Century City*. Washington, D.C.: Regnery Publishing, Inc.

Howey, Brian. 1999. "Peeling the Goldsmith Onion." *NUVO Newsweekly*. 10 June.

Indianapolis News. 1994. "Privatization Run Amuck." 30 August.

Indianapolis Star. 1999. "Goldsmith Reflects On Record, Offers Insights to His Successor." 22 December.

Chapter 1

Alaska Session Laws. 1999. 62.

Alaska Statutes. 1999. Sections 36.30.005, 010.

Arizona Revised Statutes. 1999. Sections 41-2771(1)(9), 2772(A), 2773(1), (4), (5), (6)(d); 46-300.1, 342, 343, 344, 345.

Arkansas Acts. 1999. 17.

Brenner, Elsa. 1997. "Westchester Briefs–Privatization Setback." *New York Times*. 16 November.

Cohen, David. 1998. "Blackout in Auckland Not Something to Make Light Of." *Straits Times*. Singapore. 27 February.

Colorado Revised Statutes. 1998. Sections 24-50-501, 503(1)(d), (f)(I)-(III), (2).

Corley, Cheryl and Bob Edwards. 1997. "Tennessee Private Prisons Debate." *NPR Morning Edition*. 13 November.

DeNucci, A. Joseph. 1996. "Privatization Should Deliver Ample Benefits." *Telegram & Gazette*. Worcester, Massachusetts. 22 March.

District of Columbia Code. 1999. Sections 1-1181.5b(a)(1), (3), (5), (6), (8), (9); 1-1191.3(b)(6).

Ellis, Virginia. 1997. "Bankrupt Firm Allegedly Kept State Park Fees." *Los Angeles Times.*31 December.

Eugebretson, Gary D. 2000. "Prepared Testimony Before the House Committee on Government Reform Subcommittee on Government Management, Information and Technology." 16 March.

Fernandez, Kurt, et al. 1997. "Labor Cheers,

Texas Jeers HHS Decision Limiting Privatization of Texas Welfare Plan" *BNA Daily Labor Reporter.* 07 May. D9.

Florida Statutes Annotated. 1996. Section 288.901, 957.07

Flynn, Joan M. 1997. "Outsourcing Proposal for Government Encounters Criticism from White House." *BNA Daily Labor Reporter.* 23 June. D17.

Flynn, Joe. 2000. "Prepared Testimony Before the House Committee on Appropriations Subcommittee on Defense." 29 March.

Georgia Code Annotated. 1996. Sections 36-86-4, 45-12-178.

Gray, James 1998a. "PAC: Electricity Slowly Returns to NZ's Biggest City." *AAP Newsfeed.* 22 February.

_____. 1998b. "PAC: Mercury Under Fire For Auckland Power Crisis." *AAP Newsfeed.* 22 February.

Green, Rick. 1997. "EAI Rebounds With a New Name: The Fortunes of Education Alternatives Inc., The For-Profit School Management Firm That Left Hartford About Two Years Ago After a High-Profile Failure, Appear to Be on The Rise Again." *Hartford Courant.* 18 December. A16.

Hanna, Chris. 1997. "Unions Say Contracting Out Cuts Services, Saves No Money." *BNA Daily Labor Reporter,* 02 October. D20.

Heilbroner, Robert and Lester Thurow. 1994. *Economics Explained: Everything You Need to Know about How the Economy Works and Where It's Going.* New York, NY: Touchstone.

Holloway, Lynette. 1997. "Shelters Improve Under Private Groups, Raising a New Worry." *New York Times.* 12 November. B-1.

Hutton, Will. 1998. "Darkness at the Heart of Privatization." *London Observer.* O8 March.

Jensen, Geraldine. 1997. "Prepared Statement before the House Government Reform and Oversight Committee Human Resources Subcommittee." *Federal News Service.* 04 November.

Jordan, Robert A. 1997. "DeNucci Resists False Lure of Transportation Privatization." *Boston Globe.* 18 May. C-4.

Kansas Statutes Annotated. 1996. Sections 12-5505, 5508, 5509; 75-3759(2)(a), (4)(a).

Kentucky Revised Statutes Annotated. 1998. Section 11A.130.

Kolker, Ken. 2000a. "Inmates shifted to Meet State Law." *Grand Rapids Press.* 19 May.

_____. 2000b. "Changes Ahead for Troubled Prison." *Grand Rapids Press.* 20 May.

Lincoln Park Zoological Soc'y v. NLRB, 116 F.3d 216 (7th Cir. 1997)

London Independent. 1997. "Private Water Health Risks Hushed Up." 09 March. 2.

Los Angeles Times. 1991. "County Cancels Biggest Contract in Wake of Audit." 06 March.

_____. 1998a. "A Tighter Rein on Privatization." 04 January. M-4.

_____. 1998b. "Phone Line to Reserve Campsites in State Parks Reopens Today." 28 January. A-18.

Louisiana Revised Statutes. 1999. Sections 24:522(C),(D).

Massachusetts Annotated Laws. 1996. Chapter 7, Sections 52, 54(1)-(5), (7); Chapter 268A, Section 5.

McNabb, Denise and Yvonne Martin. 1998. "Blacking Out a City." *Wellington Dominion.* 23 February. 11.

Merina, Victor. 1998. "L.A. County Pact with Holmes & Narver Is Upheld Despite Federal Probe of Firm." *Los Angeles Times.* 20 July. 4-6.

Mississippi Code Annotated. 1998. Section 27-103-209(2).

Montana Code Annotated. 1998. Sections 2-8-302, 303(1)(d)-(i), 304(1),(2); 2-18-1206.

Nadel, Mark V. 1997. "Prepared Statement Before the House Committee on Government Reform and Oversight Subcommittee on Human Resources and Intergovernmental Relations, on Child Support Enforcement Privatization: Challenges in Ensuring Accountability for Program Results." *Federal News Service.* 04 November.

New Jersey Statutes. 1999. Section 30:1-7.4.

Oklahoma Statutes. 1999. Section 595.3.

Palast, Gregory. 2000. "Profit and Education Don't Mix: Britain Should Learn a Lesson from the US." *London Observer.* 26 March. 7.

Pasternak, Judy. 1989a. "County Coughs up $1.2 Million Extra For Fleet." *Los Angeles Times.* 22 December. B-1.

_____. 1989b. "County Vehicle Firm Wants More Money: Government: Request for an Additional $2.8 Million Comes Amid a Spurt of Complaints Against the Private Maintenance Contractor." *Los Angeles Times.* 10 November. B-1.

Poulter, Sean. 1999. "In Wake of *E.Coli* Tragedy, Water Firms Come under Fire." *London Daily Mail.* 18 August. 5.

Professional Engineers in California Government v. Department of Transportation, 936 P.2d 473 (Cal. 1997).

Putnam, Judy. 2000. "UAW Sues to Stop Prison Health-Care Plan." *Ann Arbor Press.* 26 May.

Reid, Graham. 1998. "Last One Out, Please Turn the Lights Back On." *London Observer.* 08 March. 9.

Richards, Craig, Rima Shor, and Max Sawicky. 1996. *Risky Business: Private Management of Public Schools.* Washington, D.C. Economic Policy Institute Press.

Rudd, Don. 1997. "Will Privatization Cause Costs to Soar?" *St. Louis Post-Dispatch.* 26 November. B7.

Shenk, Joshua Wolf. 1995. "The Perils of Privatization." *Washington Monthly.*

27:16. May.

Sclar, Elliott D., et al. 1989. *The Emperor's New Clothes: Transit Privatization and Public Policy*. Washington, D.C. Economic Policy Institute.

———. 2000. *You Don't Always Get What You Pay For: The Economics of Privatization*. Ithaca, NY: Cornell University Press.

Shays, Christopher. 1997. "Prepared Statement of Before The House Government Reform And Oversight Committee Human Resources Subcommittee." *Federal News Service*. 04 November.

Starr, Paul. n.d. *The Limits of Privatization*. Washington, D.C. Economic Policy Institute.

Stevens, L. Nye. 1996. "Federal Contracting: Comments on S.1724, The Freedom From Government Competition Act." 24 September.

———. 1997. "Privatization and Competition: Comments on S.314, The Freedom From Government Competition Act." 29 September.

Stienstra, Tom. 1998. "It's Almost Reservation Time at Parks." *San Francisco Examiner*, 28 January. C-7.

Thomson, Jean. 1995. "Cutoff of EAI Saves Little: Scrapped Contract Does Not Resolve Schools' Money Crisis." *Baltimore Sun*. 23 November. 1A.

U. S. Department of Housing and Urban Development. 1984. "Delivering Municipal Services Efficiently: A Comparison of Municipal and Private Service Delivery."

U.S. General Accounting Office. 1996. "Private and Public Prisons: Studies Comparing Operational Costs and/or Quality of Service." Rep. No.96-158.

———. 1997. "Privatization: Lessons Learned by State and Local Governments." Report Number 97-48.

U.S. Newswire. 1997. "Lockheed Martin Forecasts Growth in Child Support Privatization." 04 November.

Utah Code Annotated. 1999. Sections 63-55a-2, 3(1)(b),(e):63- 95-102(7), 103-105.

Virgin Islands Code Annotated. 1996. Section 73.

Virginia Code Annotated. 1996. Section 9-342.

Wallin, Bruce A. 1997. "The Need for a Privatization Process: Lessons from Development and Implementation." *Public Administration Review*. 57:11.

Wessel, Robert H. 1995. "Privatization in the United States." *Business Economics*. 30:45

Wollett, Donald H. et al. 1993. *Collective Bargaining in Public Employment* (4th ed.) St. Paul, Minnesota. West Publishing Company.

Chapter 2

William Blomquist and Roger Parks, "Fiscal, Service, and Political Impacts of Indianapolis-Marion County's Unigov." *Publius: The Journal of Federalism*. 25:4.

Geib, George W. and Miriam K. Geib. 1990. *Indianapolis First*. Indianapolis, IN: Indianapolis Chamber of Commerce.

———. "Empowering Boosterism: The Indianapolis Unigov Experiment."

Ohio Valley History Conference, refereed paper.
Gurwit, Rob. 1994. "Indianapolis and the Republican Future." *Governing Magazine.* 7:2
Marion County Election Board. "Certificate and Memorandum of Votes Cast." November 1991, November 1995. Indianapolis, IN.
_____. 1991-1999. "Marion County Republican Central Committee Financial Reports." November.
Marion County Republican Central Committee Archives. 1972-1999.
Marion County Republican Central Committee. 1991. *Republican Committeemen: An Analysis.* Indianapolis, IN.
Owen, C. James and York Wilbern. 1985. *Governing Metropolitan Indianapolis: The Politics of Unigov.* Berkeley, CA: University of California Press.
Walcott, Susan M. 1999. "Bustbelt to Boomtown: Regime Succession and the Transformation of Downtown Indianapolis." *Urban Geography.* 20:7.
Wilbern, York. 1976. "Indianapolis: City and County Together." *New York Affairs.* 3:3.

Chapter 3

Annee, Paul. 1999. Interview by Sheila Suess Kennedy. 10 May.
Armstrong, Fred. 1999. Interview by Sheila Suess Kennedy. 08 June.
Blomquist, William A. 1994. "Government." 86-93. IN: *The Encyclopedia of Indianapolis.* Edited by D. J. Bodenhamer and R. G. Barrows. Bloomington, IN: Indiana University Press.
Brown, Amos. 1999. "Is the city's financial house of cards about to crash?" *Indianapolis Recorder.* 21 May.
Geib,George W. 1994. "Politics." In *The Encyclopedia of Indianapolis.* Edited by D. J. Bodenhamer and R. G. Barrows, 161-169. Bloomington, IN: Indiana University Press.
_____. 1999. Interview by Sheila Suess Kennedy. 18 November.
Gilmer, Gordon. 1999. Interview by Sheila Suess Kennedy. 14 November.
Goldsmith, Stephen. 1997. *The Twenty-First Century City.* Washington, D.C.: Regnery Publishing, Inc.
_____. 1999. Letter to the Editor. *Indianapolis Business Journal.* 26 April.
Grunwald, M. 1998. "The Myth of the Supermayor." *The American Prospect.* 40: 20-27.
Hale, M. D. 1994. "Administration of William H. Hudnut III." 717-720. IN: *The Encyclopedia of Indianapolis.* Edited by D. J. Bodenhamer and R. G. Barrows. Bloomington, IN: Indiana University Press.
Hudnut, William H III. 1995. *The Hudnut Years in Indianapolis, 1976-1991.* Bloomington, IN: Indiana University Press.
_____. 1998. *Cities on the Rebound: A Vision for Urban America.* Washington, D.C.: The Urban Land Institute.
_____. 1999. Interview by Sheila Suess Kennedy. 08 June.
Lugar, Richard G. 1972. "The Second Inaugural Address." 09 January.

_____. 1974. "Developments in Indianapolis During the Lugar Administration."

_____. 1968. "Mayor's Report to the People." 09 April.

Reed, C. M. 1999. "Managerialism and Social Welfare: A Challenge to Public Administration." *Public Administration Review*. 59: 263-266.

Rosentraub, Mark S. 2000. "The Fiscal Burdens of Economic Development: Governance, Structure, and the Consequences of Indianapolis's Partial Consolidation." *State and Local Government Review*. (forthcoming).

Sawyers, Paula Parker. 1999. Interview by Sheila Suess Kennedy. 10 November.

Sweezy, John. 1999. Interview by Sheila Suess Kennedy. 14 November.

Ullmann, Harrison J. 1999. "Revolution! A city where the people are the problem." *NUVO Newsweekly*. 27 May.

Walls, John W. 1994. "Administration of Richard G. Lugar." 935-937. IN: *The Encyclopedia of Indianapolis*. Edited by D. J. and R. G. Barrows. Bloomington, IN: Indiana University Press.

Chapter 4

Blomquist, William, Roger B. Parks, and Mark S. Rosentraub with Drew Klacik. 1992. *Municipal Federalism: A Program for Neighborhood Governance and Communities*. Publication Number 93-U02. Indianapolis, IN: Center for Urban Policy and the Environment.

City of Indianapolis. 1994. Comprehensive Annual Financial Report. 31 December.

_____. 1997. Comprehensive Annual Financial Report. 31 December.

_____. <http://www.indygov.org>

Fahy, Joe. 1992. "Goldsmith Asks Churches for Help." *Indianapolis News*. 05 February

Franklin, Erica. 1992. "Lines of Communication Remain Open, Mayor's Aide Tells Neighborhood Leaders." *Indianapolis Star*. 29 April. D-4.

Goldsmith, Stephen. 1997. *The Twenty-First Century City*. Washington, D.C.: Regnery Publishing, Inc.

_____. 1998. Letter accompanying Comprehensive Annual Financial Report of the City of Indianapolis. 30 June.

Harvard Business School. 1983. "Downtown Indianapolis Rejuvenation Project," Case Study 0-583-165.

Heikens, Norm. 1993. "Neighborhood Parks Idea Rebuffed; High Hopes for New Pilot Program." *Indianapolis Business Journal*. 26 July 26. 3A+.

Indianapolis News. 1991. Editorial. "The Bus Indy Missed." 19 September. A-8.

Lanosga, Gerry. 1992a. "Goldsmith Takes Reins, Prepares for Changes." *Indianapolis News*. 01 January. A-1+.

_____. 1992b. "Merger of City, County Operations Studied." *Indianapolis News*. 06 January. A-1+.

_____. 1992c. "Daniels to Head Efficiency Panel." *Indianapolis News*. 31

January. C-1+.

_____. 1992d. "Goldsmith Studies Briefing Books." *Indianapolis News.* 03 February. C-3.

_____. 1992e. "Mayor's Team Opened Wallets." *Indianapolis News.* 03 February. C-1+.

_____. 1992f. "Council Asks for Consultation." *Indianapolis News.* 11 February. 1992. B-1+.

Lanosga, Gerry and Kathleen Schuckel. 1992. "90 City Employees Lose Jobs." *Indianapolis News.* 05 February. D-1+.

Lathrop, Ann. 1998. Indianapolis City Controller, Letter accompanying Comprehensive Annual Financial Report of the City of Indianapolis. 30 June.

Marion County Alliance of Neighborhood Associations. 1993. *Common Ground.* April. 1(6).

Morgan, Kevin. 1992. "Neighborhood Leaders Blast City Development Overhaul." *Indianapolis Star.* 01 April. B-3.

Penner, Diana. 1992. "City Considering Training Academy for Neighborhoods." *Indianapolis Star.* 09 December. D-1.

Schuckel, Kathleen. 1992a. "Police Department Revamped." *Indianapolis News.* 09 January. A-1+.

_____. 1992b. "Metro Changes Show Goldsmith Plays Key Role in Transit Issues." *Indianapolis News.* 22 January. B-3.

_____. 1992c. "Mayor Has Neighborhood Plan." *Indianapolis News.* 30 January. B-1.

_____. 1992d. "Neighborhoods Differ on Privatizing Services." *Indianapolis News.* 17 February 17. C-2.

_____. 1992e. "Council, Mayor Differ on Figures." *Indianapolis News.* 25 February. C-1+.

_____. 1992f. "City Plans to Lay Off 100 More." *Indianapolis News.* 26 February. A-1+.

_____. 1992g. "Leaders Feel Left Out of Decisions." *Indianapolis News.* 02 April.

_____. 1992h. "Administrator Brings Expertise in Health to City." *Indianapolis News.* 03 April. A-4.

_____. 1992i. "City Workers Cite Frustration." *Indianapolis News.* 21 December. B-1+.

Schuckel, Kathleen and Gerry Lanosga. 1992. "55 Losing Jobs in DMD Shuffle." *Indianapolis News.* 17 March. B-1+.

Chapter 5

Anderson, B. 1993. "Performance accountability system: identifying services and costs." *KPMG Peat Marwick Government Services Newsletter.* May.

Bartik, T.J. 1991. *Who Benefits From State and Local Economic Development Policies?* Kalamazoo, MI: W.E. Upjohn Institute.

Bodenhamer, D.J. and R.G. Barrows 1994. Editors. *The Encyclopedia of*

Indianapolis. Bloomington, IN: Indiana University Press.

City of Indianapolis. 1987. *Component Unit Financial Report, Year Ended December 31, 1986*. Indianapolis Department of Administration, Division of Finance.

_____. 1988. *Component Unit Financial Report, Year Ended December 31, 1987*. Indianapolis Department of Administration, Division of Finance.

_____. 1989. *Component Unit Financial Report, Year Ended December 31, 1988*. Indianapolis Department of Administration, Division of Finance.

_____. 1990. *Component Unit Financial Report, Year Ended December 31, 1989*. Indianapolis Department of Administration, Division of Finance.

_____. 1991. *Component Unit Financial Report, Year Ended December 31, 1990*. Indianapolis Department of Administration, Division of Finance.

_____. 1992. *Component Unit Financial Report, Year Ended December 31, 1991*. Indianapolis Department of Administration, Division of Finance.

_____. 1993. *Component Unit Financial Report, Year Ended December 31, 1992*. Indianapolis Office of the City Controller.

_____. 1994. *Component Unit Financial Report, Year Ended December 31, 1993*. Indianapolis Office of the City Controller.

_____. 1995. *Component Unit Financial Report, Year Ended December 31, 1994*. Indianapolis Office of the City Controller.

_____. 1996. *Component Unit Financial Report, Year Ended December 31, 1995*. Indianapolis Office of the City Controller.

_____. 1997. *Component Unit Financial Report, Year Ended December 31, 1996*. Indianapolis Office of the City Controller.

_____. 1998. *Component Unit Financial Report, Year Ended December 31, 1997*. Indianapolis Office of the City Controller.

_____. 1999. *Component Unit Financial Report, Year Ended December 31, 1998*. Indianapolis Office of the City Controller.

Fuchs, E. R. 1992. *Mayors and Money*. Chicago, IL: University of Chicago Press.

Geib, G.W. 1994. "Politics." 161-169. IN: *The Encyclopedia of Indianapolis*. Edited by D.J. Bodenhamer and R.G. Barrows. Bloomington, IN: Indiana University Press.

Goldsmith, Stephen. 1992. "Moving municipal services into the marketplace," *Carnegie Council Privatization Project*, No. 14. New York. 20 November.

_____. 1997. *The Twenty-First Century City*. Washington, D.C.: Regnery Publishing, Inc.

Henn, Jr., C. (Editor). 1992. *Here is Your Indiana Government*. Indianapolis, IN: Indianapolis Chamber of Commerce.

Hudnut, III, William. 1993. Letter to Bruce Hubbell, KPMG Peat Marwick, Indianapolis, IN. 08 June.

Husock, H. *Organizing Competition in Indianapolis: Mayor Stephen Goldsmith and the Quest for Lower Costs*. Case 18-95-1269.0. Kennedy School of Government Case Program. Cambridge, MA: Harvard College.

Judd, D. 1988. *The Politics of American Cities: Private Power and Public*

Policy. New York, NY: Harper-Collins.

Levine, C.H. (Editor). 1980. *Managing Fiscal Stress: The Crisis in the Public Sector.* Chatham, NJ: Chatham House Publishers, Inc.

Logan, J. 1993. "Cycles and trends in the globalization of real estate." 33-54. IN: *The Restless Urban Landscape.* Edited by P.L. Knox. Englewood Cliffs, NJ.

Montgomery, William and Samuel Nunn. 1996. "Privatization, participation, and the planning process: a case study of wastewater treatment infrastructure." *Public Works Management and Policy.* 1(1): 43-59. July.

Osborne, D. and T. Gaebler. 1992. *Reinventing Government: How the Entrepreneurial Spirit Is Transforming the Public Sector.* Reading, MA: Addison-Wesley.

Potapchuk, W.R., J.P. Crocker, and B. Schechter. "Systems reform in two cities: Indianapolis, Indiana and Charlotte, North Carolina." *National Civic Review.* 87(3): 213-226.

Reed, B.J. and J.W. Swain. 1990. *Public Finance Administration.* Englewood Cliffs, NJ: Prentice-Hall.

Sharp, E.B. 1990. *Urban Politics and Administration: From Service Delivery to Economic Development.* New York, NY: Longman.

Chapter 6

Blomquist, William. 1999. Interview by Sheila Suess Kennedy. 23 January.

Boaz, D. 1997. *Libertarianism: A Primer.* New York, NY: The Free Press.

Boyd, R., et. al. 1996. Letter to the Editor. *Indianapolis Star.* 25 August.

Boyd, Rozelle. 1999. Interview by Sheila Suess Kennedy. 08 February.

Brant, Martha. 2000. "The Sage of Indianapolis." *Newsweek Magazine.* 03 January.

"Comprehensive Annual Financial Reports (CAFR)." City of Indianapolis. 31 December 1992, 1993, 1994, 1995, 1996, 1997, 1998.

Davis, Kathy. 2000. Interview by Sheila Suess Kennedy. 23 May.

Elkin, S. L., and K. E. Soltan. 1993. *A New Constitutionalism.* Chicago, IL: University of Chicago Press.

Epstein, R. A. 1995. *Simple Rules for a Complex World.* Cambridge, MA: Harvard University Press.

Goldsmith, S. 1997. *The Twenty-First Century City.* Washington, D.C.: Regnery Publishing, Inc.

Gregory, R. J. 1999. "Social Capital Theory and Administrative Reform: Maintaining Ethical Probity in Public Service." *Public Administration Review.* 59: 63-75.

Haase, D. L. 1996. "Goldsmith Says City Innovation Has Its Price." *Indianapolis Star.* 04 December. C1.

Hardin, R. 1998. "Trust in Government." In *Trust and Governance.* Edited by V. Braithwaite and M. Levi. New York: Russell Sage Foundation.

Hennessey, J. T. 1998. "'Reinventing' Government: Does Leadership Make the Difference?" *Public Administration Review.* 58: 522-532.

Howey, B. A. 1998. "Peeling the Goldsmith Onion: The Mayor Brought Dramatic Changes to City Government, But What it Cost and What We Got is a Mystery." *NUVO Newsweekly.* 03 December.

_____. 1999a. "Are Goldsmith's Books Crooked?" *NUVO Newsweekly*, 14 January.

_____. 1999b. "Goldsmith's Community Credit Card." *NUVO Newsweekly.* 20 May.

Howey, B. A., and M. Schoeff Jr. 1998. "Inside the Stunning '98 Indiana Election." *The Howey Political Report*, November.

Hudnut, W. H. 1998. *Cities on the Rebound: A Vision for Urban America.* Washington, D.C.: The Urban Land Institute.

_____. 1999. Interview by Sheila Suess Kennedy. 18 February.

Indianapolis Star. 1994. "Privatization Run Amuck." 30 August.

_____. 1999. "Debt Load for City is Becoming a Key Issue." 29 June.

Jacobs, J. 1992. *Systems of Survival.* New York, NY: Random House.

Johnston, K. 1996. "Critics Question the Propriety of Fundraiser for Goldsmith." *Indianapolis Star.* 14 July.

Kettl, D. F. 1993. *Sharing Power: Public Governance and Private Markets.* Washington, D.C.: The Brookings Institution.

Kirlin, J. J. 1996. "What Government Must Do Well: Creating Value for Society." *Journal of Public Administration Research and Theory.* 1: 161-185.

Krull, John. 1999. Interview by Sheila Suess Kennedy. 27 January.

Lowi, T. J. 1995. *The End of the Republican Era.* Norman, OK: University of Oklahoma Press.

Miller, Jack. Chapters 14, 15 and 16, this volume.

Montgomery, W, and Sam Nunn. 1996. "Privatization, Participation, and the Planning Process: A Case Study of Wastewater Treatment Infrastructure." *Public Works Management and Policy.* 1: 43-59.

Morgan, Kevin. 1993. "Family Feud: Hudnut Raps Goldsmith." *Indianapolis Star.* 25 November.

Nytes, Jacqueline, City-County Council. 2000. E-mail response to Sheila Suess Kennedy. 19 June.

O'Laughlin, Beth. 2000. Interview by Sheila Suess Kennedy. 28 June.

Remondini, David. 1991. "Goldsmith Looking to Cut City Force by Twenty-five Percent." *Indianapolis Star.* 26 November.

Romine, Van. 1998. "Civic Participation, Social Capital and Leadership." LaJolla Institute. <www.lajollainstitute.org>

Rosenbloom, David H., James D. Carroll and Jonathan D. Carroll. 2000. *Constitutional Competence for Public Managers: Cases and Commentary.* Itasca, IL: F.E. Peacock Publishers, Inc.

Smith, S. R., and M. Lipsky. 1993. *Nonprofits for Hire.* Cambridge, MA: Harvard University Press.

Spicer, M. W. 1995. *The Founders, the Constitution, and Public Administration: A Conflict in World Views.* Washington, D.C.: Georgetown University Press.

State Board of Accounts. 1999a. "Special Report of Construction Projects for Municipal Gardens Recreation Center and Carson Park Recreation Center." 16 September.

_____. 1999b. "Special Report of Construction Projects for Franklin-Edgewood Park, Krannert-King-Brookside Aquatic Centers, and Perry Park Ice Rink and Aquatic Facility." 16 September.

Stern, William M. 1994. "We got real efficient real quick." *Forbes.* 20 June.

Ullmann, Harrison. 1998. "Revolution: A City Where the People are the Problem." *NUVO Newsweekly.* 27 May.

_____. 1999. Interview by Sheila Suess Kennedy. 23 January.

Washington Post. 1993. "A Mayor Shows Gore's Team the Way." 25 August.

Williams, Brian. 1999. "Our Fiscal Future Will Be Challenge For Next Mayor." Indianapolis Business Journal, 1-7 November.

Yankelovick, D. 1991. *Coming to Public Judgment: Making Democracy Work in a Complex World.* Syracuse, NY: Syracuse University Press.

Zore, Gerald. 2000. Interview by Sheila Suess Kennedy. 20 June.

Chapter 7

Bodenhamer, David and William Doherty. 1995. "The Police Department." *The Hudnut Years.* Bloomington, IN: Indiana University Press.

Bratton, William. 2000. "The Legacy of Detective Sipovisc." *Time Magazine.* 06 March.

Campbell, James, John Bent and Chris Dahlke. 1999. Interviewed by Paul Annee. 14 June and 03 August.

City of Indianapolis. 1998. "Comprehensive Annual Financial Report." City of Indianapolis. 31 December.

Controller, City of Indianapolis. 2000. Response to Freedom of Information Act Request by Sheila Suess Kennedy. 29 June.

Federal Bureau of Investigation (FBI). 1992-1999. "Uniform Crime Reports." Washington, D.C.

Gelardin, Joseph. 1996. "Police brawl is under review." *Indianapolis Star.* 30 August.

Goldsmith, Stephen. 1997. *The Twenty-First Century City.* Washington, D.C.: Regnery Publishing, Inc.

Grunwald, Michael. 1998a. "The Myth of the Supermayor." *The American Prospect.* September-October.

_____. 1998b. "'Nap Town' wakes up to homicide." *Boston Globe.* 04 January.

Indianapolis Police Department. 1992-1999a. "Annual Reports."

_____.1992-1999b. "Staffing Statistics."

Indianapolis Star. 1992a. "Crew goes from raising barn to razing it." 19 February.

_____. 1992b. "Changes coming in police services." 23 February.

_____. 1992c. "Police union seeks answers to reorganization queries." 02 June.

_____. 1992d. "Confusion at IPD prompts delay in new policing plan." 09 June.

_____. 1994. "At IPD, Who's the Boss?" 06 August

_____. 1995. "Looking for experts." 26 May.

Lanosga, Gerry and Kathleen Johnston. 1995. "Suggestions arise from gun dispute." *Indianapolis Star.* 19 May.

O'Laughlin, Beth. 2000. E-mail response to inquiry by Sheila Suess Kennedy. 13 June.

Patterson, James. 1992. "Calls to 911 face new scrutiny." *Indianapolis Star.* 29 June.

Peterson, Bart. 1999. *The Peterson Plan.* Indianapolis, IN: Peterson for Mayor Campaign. September.

Richardson, James F. 1974. *Urban Police in the United States.* Port Washington, NY: Kennikat Press.

Rosenbaum, D.P. Editor. 1994. *The Challenges of Community Policing: Testing the Promises.* Newbury Park, CA: Sage.

Shramm, Susan. 1993. "Some critics still aren't sold on community policing plan." 25 January.

Shuckel, Kathleen. 1992. "Police Reform Heightens Tensions." *Indianapolis Star.* 11 May.

White, Charles. 2000. Telephone interview by Sheila Suess Kennedy. 30 June.

Wilson, James Q. and George Kelling. 1982. "Broken Windows: The Police and Neighborhood Safety." *Atlantic Monthly.* March.

U.S. Advisory Commission on Intergovernmental Relations. 1971. *For a More Perfect Union—Police Reform.* Washington, D.C.: U.S. Government Printing Office.

Chapter 8

Alley, Ann. (Federal Grants Administrator, Department of Metropolitan Development1995-1998). 1999. Interview by Lamont Hulse. 30 September.

Amerson, Lydia et al. 1995. "Turning Toward Neighborhoods: A Progress Report." Indianapolis, IN: Center for Urban Policy and the Environment.

Annala, Ellen K, President and Chief Executive Officer of United Way of Central Indiana, Inc. (Former Executive Director of Community Service Council/United Way of Central Indiana, Inc.). 1999. Interview by Lamont Hulse. 30 September.

Blomquist, William A. 1994. "Unigov, Creation of." IN: *The Encyclopedia of Indianapolis.* Edited by D. J. Bodenhamer and R. G. Barrows. Bloomington, IN: Indiana University Press.

Crawford, Sue, et al. 1994. "Turning Toward Neighborhoods: A Preliminary Report." Indianapolis, IN: Center for Urban Policy and the Environment.

Cunningham, Cynthia, (former Neighborhood Planner with Indianapolis Department of Metropolitan Development, 1989-1996). 1999. Interview by Lamont Hulse. 01 October.

Ehret, Lisa. 1994. "Indianapolis Neighborhood Housing Partnership (INHP)." IN: *The Encyclopedia of Indianapolis*. Edited by D. J. Bodenhamer and R. G. Barrows. Bloomington, IN: Indiana University Press.

Gelarden, R. Joseph. 1986. "Goldsmith: ambitious Boy Scout." *Indianapolis Star*. 08 June.

_____. 1992. "Changing of the Guard." *Indianapolis Star*. 26 July. F1.

Goldsmith, Stephen.1997. *The Twenty-First Century City*. Washington, D.C.: Regnery Publishing, Inc.

Harris, Art. 1984. "Prosecutor Stephen Goldsmith: A master of the Media." *Indianapolis News*. 01 October. A1.

Haerle, George, Member, Nora-Northside Community Council, Inc. and Marion County Alliance of Neighborhood Associations. 2000. Interview by Lamont Hulse. 21 March.

Hayes, Ruth, President of the Nora-Northside Neighborhood Association. 1999. Interview by Lamont Hulse. 27 September.

Heikens, Norm. 1994. "DMD revolving door sweeps in Elaine Bedel." *Indianapolis Business Journal*. 01 August.

Hulse, Lamont J. "Neighborhoods and Communities." 139-140. IN: *The Encyclopedia of Indianapolis*. Edited by D. J. Bodenhamer and R. G. Barrows. Bloomington, IN.: Indiana University Press.

Jackson, D.D. 1987. "Indy's image is aglow." *Smithsonian*. June.

Johnston, Kathleen M. 1991. "Mayor-to-be's dream turning into reality." *Indianapolis News*. 28 November.

_____. 1995. "New chief named to head metropolitan development agency." *Indianapolis Star*. 16 November. C4.

King, Jerry, (Former President of Near Eastside Community Organization and former member of Urban Neighborhoods of Indianapolis). 1999. Interview by Lamont Hulse. 17 September.

Lanosga, Gerry and Kathleen Johnston. 1994. "Metropolitan Development gets a new leader." *Indianapolis News*. 21 July.

Morgan, Kevin. 1992. "Goldsmith's wife more than candid when it comes to aiding mayor." *Indianapolis Star*. 21 June. A1.

_____. 1993. "A year full of lessons." *Indianapolis Star*. 01 January.

Morgan, Kevin and Patrick Morrison. 1992a. "The Disorganization Man." *Indianapolis Star*. 21 June.

_____. 1992b. "Wife leads influential 'kitchen cabinet.'" *Indianapolis Star*. 21 June.

Neal, John, Department of Metropolitan Development. 1999. Interview by Lamont Hulse. 30 September.

O'Neil, John R. 1991a. "Goldsmith's neighborhood plan relies on advocates." *Indianapolis Star*. 22 October. C2.

_____. 1991b. "Putting Ideas into Action." *Indianapolis Star*. 29 December. A1.

Perkins, Estelle, (former President of Fountain Square Neighborhood Association). 1995. Interview by Ted Slutz and Vivetta Kiasmore. 05 July.

Polis Center. 1996. *The Near Westside: A Timeline of Faith and Community*.

Indianapolis, IN.

Porter, Greg, Indiana State Representative from Indianapolis (former staff, Westside Cooperative Organization late 1980s and early 1990s) 1999. Interview by Lamont Hulse. 28 October.

Remondini, David J. 1992. "Goldsmith's mayoral days begin: Vows tenure geared to city's neighborhoods." *Indianapolis Star.* 2 January. A1.

Rogers, Nancy Silver, (former Deputy Mayor of Neighborhoods, City of Indianapolis). 1999. Interview by Lamont Hulse. 29 September.

Schuckel, Kathleen. 1991. "Mayor-elect's ambassadors begin their work." *Indianapolis News.* 26 November.

_____. 1992a. "Neighborhoods differ on privatizing services." *Indianapolis Star.* 17 February. C1.

_____. 1992b. "Leaders feel left out of decisions." *Indianapolis News.* 02 April. C1.

_____. 1992c. "Communities target of plan: Goal to improve services, neighborhood infrastructure." *Indianapolis News.* 10 September.

Schuckel, Kathleen and Gerry Lanosga. 1993. "Mayor's hard work sometimes pays." *Indianapolis News.* 15 March.

Stackhouse, Steve. 1991. "Steve & Louie: What's the difference?" *NUVO Newsweekly.* 30 October-06 November.

Swindell, David and Roger Parks. 1995. "Neighborhoods and Unigov." IN: *The Hudnut Years: Indianapolis 1976-1991.* Bloomington, IN: Indiana University Press.

Traub, Patrick. 1991a. "A City at the Crossroads." *Indianapolis Star.* 04 November.

_____. 1991b. "How will they manage?" *Indianapolis Star.* 27 October. F1.

Walls, John W. 1994. "Lugar, Richard G., Administration of." 935-937. IN: *The Encyclopedia of Indianapolis.* Edited by D. J. Bodenhamer and R. G. Barrows. Bloomington, IN: Indiana University Press.

West, Dennis. 1995. IN: *The Hudnut Years: Indianapolis 1976-1991.* Bloomington, IN: Indiana University Press.

Wilson, David. 1993. "Everyday Life, Spatiality, and Inner Disinvestment in a US City." *The International Journal of Urban and Regional Research.* 17(4).

Chapter 9

Amerson, Lydia. 1995. *Turning Toward Neighborhoods: A Progress Report.* Indianapolis, IN: Center for Urban Policy and the Environment.

Annala, Ellen K, President and Chief Executive Officer of United Way of Central Indiana, Inc. (Former Executive Director of Community Service Council/United Way of Central Indiana, Inc.). 1999. Interview by Lamont Hulse. 30 September.

Arnold, Diane, Community Director of the Hawthorne Community Center. 1999. Interview by the Lamont Hulse. 01 October.

Aspen Institute. 1999. *Voices from the Field 2:Dynamic Tensions in Early CCI*

Practice: The Product-Process Tension. Washington, D.C.

Bell, Robert. 1997. "Mayor launches Front Porch Alliance." *Indianapolis Star.* 17 September. D03.

Blomquist, William A. 1993. *Municipal Federalism: A Program for Neighborhood Governance and Communities.* Indianapolis, IN: Center for Urban Policy and the Environment.

Cisneros, Henry. 1996. *Higher Ground: Faith Communities and Community Building.* Washington, D.C.: U. S. Dept. of Housing and Urban Development.

Crawford, Sue, et al. 1994. *Turning Toward Neighborhoods: A Preliminary Report.* Indianapolis, IN: Center for Urban Policy and the Environment.

Farnsley, Arthur E. 2000. "Ten Good Questions About Faith-based Partnerships and Welfare Reform." Indianapolis, IN: *The Polis Center at IUPUI.*

Goldsmith, Stephen. 1992. "Bureaucracy Shackles the Urban Poor." *Wall Street Journal.* 10 June. 1A14.

_____. 1994. Letter quoted in Crawford, Sue et. al. "Turning Toward Neighborhoods: A Preliminary Report." Indianapolis, IN: Center for Urban Policy and the Environment.

_____. 1997. *The Twenty-First Century City.* Washington, D. C.: The Manhattan Institute.

Higgens, Will. 1996. "Churches bring hope to families." *Indianapolis Star.* 11 June. B02.

Horne, Terry. 1994. "Budget OK may affect 14 centers." *Indianapolis News.* 28 September. F10.

Indianapolis Police Department, Marion County Prosecutor, Health and Hospital Corporation of Marion County, et al. 1997. *Memorandum of Understanding: A Plan to Eradicate Neighborhood Drug Markets.* 27 March.

Indianapolis Star. 1994. "A Healthy Tension." 21 January. A20.

_____. 1996. "A role for churches." 21 January. D2.

King, Jerry, (Former President of Near Eastside Community Organization and former member of Urban Neighborhoods of Indianapolis). 1999. Interview by Lamont Hulse. 17 September.

Lanosga, Gerry. 1995. "Critics see red over green-space swapping." *Indianapolis Star.* 21 September. F01.

_____. 1996. "City is set to spend millions on projects." *Indianapolis Star.* 26 August. B01.

Lanosga, Gerry and Kathleen Johnston. 1996. "Goldsmith turns sights back to city he governs." *Indianapolis Star.* 11 November. A01.

Malone, Hope, (former Executive Director of the Indianapolis Resource Center (1997-1999). Interview by Lamont Hulse. 22 September.

Morgan, Kevin. 1994a. "Council to stand up to mayor on welfare." *Indianapolis Star.* 12 December. C01.

_____. 1994b. "Job Training Funds for Agency Okd." *Indianapolis Star.* 13 December. D2.

Neal, Andrea. 1999. "Goldsmith reflects on Indy." *Indianapolis Star.* 4 November. A 24.

Penner, Diana. 1994. "City called 'a laboratory for neighborhood revival.'" *Indianapolis Star.* 14 January. B05.

_____. 1995. "Funding debate leaves agencies in quandary." *Indianapolis Star.* 04 January.

Polin, Al, Neighborhood Coordinator, Mapleton-Fall Creek. 1999. Interview by the Lamont Hulse. 01 October.

Polis Center at IUPUI. 1999. *Final Evaluation of the Front Porch Alliance.* Indianapolis, IN.

Rogers, Nancy Silver, (former Deputy Mayor of Neighborhoods, City of Indianapolis). 1999. Interview by Lamont Hulse. 29 September.

Schuckel, Kathleen and Gerry Lanosga. 1993. "Mayor's hard work sometimes pays." *Indianapolis News.* 15 March.

Smith, Scott. 1995. "Neighborhood group finally heard." *Indianapolis Star.* 19 September. B03.

Smock, Kristina. 1997. "Comprehensive Community Initiatives: A New Generation of Urban Revitalization Strategies." *Comm-Org Working Papers Web Page.* 15 October.

Sword, Doug. 2000. "Front Porch Alliance relegated to the sidelines." *Indianapolis Star.* 14 February. A1.

Tom, Reverend Phil (former Director of Community Development Corporations at Indianapolis Neighborhood Housing Partnership (1990-1993), Consultant through Local Initiatives Support Corporation (LISC) contract to eight targeted neighborhoods (1994-1999). 1999. Interview by Lamont Hulse. 01 October.

U.S. Department of Housing and Urban Development (HUD). 1998. *HUD Blue-Ribbon Practices in Housing and Community Development-John Gunther Awards, City of Indianapolis, IN: The Front Porch Alliance.* Washington, D.C.: U.S. Department of Housing and Urban Development.

Williams, Olgen. 1999. Interview by Lamont Hulse. 01 October.

Chapter 10

Chubb, John E. and Terry M. Moe. 1990. *Politics, Markets & America's Schools.* ashington, D.C.: The Brookings Institution.

Garber, Michael P., et al. 2000. *Indiana Education: On Shaky Ground.* Indianapolis, IN: Hudson Institute, Education Policy Center.

Goldsmith, Stephen. 1997. *The Twenty-First Century City.* Washington, D.C.: Regnery Publishing, Inc.

_____. 2000. "Reform is missing in Indiana." *Indianapolis Star.* 17 July. A6.

Hanushek, Eric A. 1981. "Throwing Money at Schools." *Journal of Public Policy Analysis and Management.* 1 (1): 19-41.

Indianapolis Public Schools. 1997. *IPS Academic Achievement Plan: Operating Guidelines for Schools, 1997-98 School Year.* Indianapolis, IN, A.P. Office.

Lehnen, Robert G. 1992. "Constructing State Education Performance Indicators from ACT and SAT Scores." *Policy Studies Journal.* 20 (1): 22-40.

Lehnen, Robert G. and Carlyn E. Johnson. 1989. *Financing Indiana's Public Schools: Update 1989.* Indianapolis, IN: Indiana University School of Public and Environmental Affairs.

Ullmann, Harrison J. 1999a. "School 44: A Good School in a Hard Place." *NUVO Newsweekly.* 15 April.
<http://www.nuvo.net/archive/041599/041599_acover.html.>

_____. 1999b. "Think About It! Part II: Getting Madder And Getting Smarter." *NUVO Newsweekly.* 18 February.
< http://www.nuvo.net/archive/02189921899_aullmann.html.>

_____. 1999c. "Think About It! Part III: Living Badly Is The Worst Revenge." *NUVO Newsweekly.* 25 February.
< http://www.nuvo.net/archive/022599/025599_aullmann.html.>

_____. 1999d. "To Duncan "Pat" Pritchett, " *NUVO Newsweekly.* 18 March.
<http://www.nuvo.net/archive/031899/031899_aullmann.html.>

_____. 2000. "The ISTEP: When half the truth is worse than no truth." *NUVO Newsweekly.* 24 February.
<http://www.nuvo.net/archive/022400/street/022400_street_c.html.>

U.S. Chamber of Commerce. n.d. *Final Report to the Lilly Endowment, Inc. on the Center for Workforce Preparation and Quality Education School Finance Project: Executive Summary.* Washington, D.C.: U.S. Chamber of Commerce, Center for Workforce Preparation and Quality Education.

Wolf, Jr., Charles. 1994. *Markets or Governments: Choosing between Imperfect Alternatives, Second Edition.* Cambridge, MA: The MIT Press.

Young, David. 2000. Interview by Robert Lehnen. 18 July.

Chapter 11

Brooks-Gunn, Jeanne and Greg Duncan. 1997. "The Effects of Poverty on Children," *The Future of Children.* Los Altos, California: The David and Lucille Packard Foundation.

Carpenter, Dan. 1995. "The Price of Poverty." *Indianapolis Star.* 06 April. A01.

Goldsmith, S. 1997. *The Twenty-First Century City.* Washington, D.C.: Regnery Publishing, Inc.

Indiana Department of Education. 1999. <http://doe.state.in.us/>

Indianapolis Housing Agency. 2000. "Marion County Center for Housing Opportunities Monthly Report, June 5-July 7, 2000."

Indianapolis Public Schools, Planning Department. 1991. "Litigation Summary." March.

Indianapolis Public Schools. 1999. Internal records.

Indianapolis Star. 1991. "Goldsmith proposes greater police presence for schools." 08 October.

_____. 1992. "City backs IPS school choice plan." 28 July.

_____. 1993a. "Mayor seeks more control on approval of tax hikes." 03

December.

———. 1993b. "Mayor defends lower tax valuation for mall." 05 August.

———. 1994a. "Board president fights splitting up IPS." 31 December.

———. 1994b. "Mayor to push for school reforms." 30 December.

———. 1994c. "Mayor rips into schools." 23 December.

———. 1994d. "Mayor calls planned IPS tax hike 'disaster.'" 22 November.

———. 1994e. "Mayor says he'll fight plan to hike school tax." 23 November.

———. 1994f. "Mayor opposes tax hike for IPS." 23 November.

———. 1994g. "School chief, mayor differ on tax cuts for business." 30 April.

———. 1994h. "Mayor wants big change in IPS." 03 February.

———. 1994i. "Alliance moves irk other IPS hopefuls." 27 April.

———. 1994j. "School hopefuls cry foul." 27 April.

———. 1995a. "Mayor, IPS again at odds." 14 June.

———. 1995b. "Mayor to push for charter schools, vouchers." 15 October.

———. 1995c. "Execs five $350,000 to schools." 02 March.

———. 1995d. "IPS teachers give Goldsmith an 'F'." 27 February.

———. 1995e. "Voucher plan for IPS fails test in Senate." 23 February.

———. 1995f. "Controversial IPS reform bill may be too extreme to pass." 03 February.

———. 1995g. "Goldsmith pitches IPS plan." 30 January.

———. 1995h. "Goldsmith draws fire over plan to fix IPS." 30 January.

———. 1995i. "Bill seeks to split IPS." 28 January.

———. 1995j. "Goldsmith poised to reinvent IPS." 23 January.

———. 1995k. "Mayor didn't consult IPS allies on plan." 23 January. A05.

———. 1995l. "Mayor blasted for soloing IPS plan." 31 January.

———. 1995m. "Goldsmith's style irks one-time ally." 31 January.

———. 1995n. "Mayoral control over IPS." 09 February.

———. 1995o. "Mayor denies power play." 13 February.

———. 1996. "Audience asks board to cut carefully." 22 October. B01.

———. 1997a. "Mayor touts reforming IPS as way to solve city's woes." 28 September.

———. 1997b. "Mayor lobbies legislators to overhaul IPS board." 30 January.

———. 1997c. "Parents offer thoughts on how to improve IPS." 28 October. B01.

———. 1998. "Controversial Steward ousted after 16 years." 06 May. A01.

———. 1999. "Near Northside area close to Fall Creek could see rebirth with new, rebuilt homes." 24 March.

Lewit, Eugene M., et al. 1997. "Children and Poverty: Analysis and Recommendations," *The Future of Children*. Los Altos, California: The David and Lucille Packard Foundation

Maher, Timothy, Bobby Potters and Jane Blankman-Hetrick. 1999. *IPS Facilities Survey: Public Perceptions and Future Directions in the Post-Busing Era*. University of Indianapolis.

Metcalf, Kim. 1999. "Evaluation of the Cleveland Scholarship and Tutoring Grant Program 1996-1999." 01 September.

Rose, Lowell. 1999. "Briefing on the Student Mobility Factor for the Indiana Education Roundtable." *Indiana Urban School Association.* 23 November.

Rosentraub, Mark S. 2000. "City-County Consolidation and the Rebuilding of A Downtown Area and a City's Image: The Fiscal Lessons from Indianapolis' Unigov Program." *State and Local Government Review.* Forthcoming.

Rosentraub, Mark S. and Samuel R. Nunn. 1994. "City and Suburbs: Linkages, Benefits, and Shared Responsibilities." Indianapolis, IN: Center for Urban Policy and the Environment, Indiana University.

Rosentraub, Mark S. et al. 1996. "Building the Economic Future of Metropolitan Indianapolis: A Proposal for Regional Cooperation and Finance." Indianapolis: Center for Urban Policy and the Environment, Indiana University.

Ullmann, Harrison J. 1998a. "The Sins of the Fathers." *NUVO Newsweekly.* 29 October-5 November.

_____. 1998b. "Think About It!" Three part series. *NUVO Newsweekly.*

United States of America v. Board of School Commissioners of the City of Indianapolis, 483 F.2d 1406 (1972).

Chapter 12

AWT. 1993. Agreement for the Operation and Maintenance of the City of Indianapolis, Indiana, Advanced Wastewater Treatment Facilities. 20 December.

AWT. 1994. Six Months Update. *White River Environmental Partnership.* August.

Browning, E.S. 1994. "French companies pour into U.S. Waterworks market." *Wall Street Journal.* 25 February. B04.

Environmental Policy Work Group, City of Indianapolis. 1993. "Environmental Policy Papers." Photocopied.

Francis, Mary. 1994. "Air pollution board blocks city's threat to close lead plant." *Indianapolis Star.* 31 December.

Gelarden, R. Joseph. 1993. "Public works board hires private company to treat city wastewater." 21 December. C01.

Goldsmith, Stephen, Mayor, City of Indianapolis. 1992. Letter to David E. Lakin, Groups Advocating Greenspace Environments (GAUGE). 24 March.

_____. 1997. *The Twenty-First Century City.* Washington, D.C.: Regnery Publishing, Inc.

_____. 1999. "The high cost of 'swimmable' waters." *Indianapolis News.* 20 October.

Harris, Welton (Art). 1993a. "Private firm to operate sewage works." *Indianapolis News.* 13 November. C01.

_____. 1993b. "Environmentalist fears wastewater changes." *Indianapolis*

News. 10 November. C01.

_____. 1993c. "City refutes union's report on wastewater." *Indianapolis News.* 14 December. D02.

_____. 1993d. "Sewage plant monitoring gets cool reception." *Indianapolis News.* 18 December. C01.

_____. 1994a. "No response from city on environmental policy." *Indianapolis News.* 28 July.

_____. 1994b. "Water company pollution charged." *Indianapolis News.* 10 January. C01.

Ignarski, Laura. 1996a. "Council Oks sewer system privatization." *Indianapolis Star.* 25 June. B03.

_____. 1996b. "Environmentalists protest Goldsmith fundraiser." *Indianapolis Star.* 18 July. C06.

Indiana Department of Environmental Management (IDEM). 1998. "Demo/Reno Asbestos Inspection Field Checklist." 06 October.

_____. 1999. Certified Letter to Randall McMillan, President, Kleen All of American, Inc. and Bruce Wallace, President, Alliance Environmental, Inc. RE: Commissioner of the Department of Environmental Management v Kleen All of American, Inc. and Alliance Environmental, Inc. Cause No. A-4310 and 4361. 05 January.

_____. n.d. "Indianapolis Air Pollution Control Board. Asbestos Regulation Background Information Document." Department of Public Works.

_____. 1992. "Regulation XIII. Asbestos Abatement. Preliminarily Adopted - June 12, 1992."

Indianapolis Chamber of Commerce. n.d. "A Business Agenda 1996 - 1999, Strategies for a Successful Community." Indianapolis, Indiana.

Indianapolis News. 1993a. "Watching over wastewater." 02 December. A08.

_____. 1993b. "NAACP opposes privatization." 04 December.

_____. 1994. "Privatization run amuck." 30 August. A06.

Indianapolis Star. 2000. Editorial. "Peterson's CSO plan." 12 July. A14.

Jordan, David R., Assistant Administrator Air Pollution Control Section, Department of Public Works. 1993. Memorandum to Barry Baer, Director of Public Works. RE: "Regulatory Study Commission Asbestos Information and Analysis Statement." 1 February.

Kahlo, Clarke. 1998. "Indy Parks' eagerness to cut trees." *Indianapolis Star/News.* 15 October. A19.

_____. 2000. E-mail communication to Ingrid Ritchie. 20 July.

Kaplan, Lori F. 1999a. "It's time to reduce sewage overflows." *Indianapolis Star.* 26 September. D03.

_____. 1999b. "High time to fix raw sewage problem." *Indianapolis Star.* 12 November. A23.

Lakin, David E., Groups Advocating Urban Greenspace Environments (GAUGE). 1992. Letter to Mayor Stephen Goldsmith. 23 January.

Lanosga, Gerry. 1994. "Emotions still run high on treatment plant deal." *Indianapolis News.* 28 January. B02.

Lanosga, Gerry and Kathleen Johnston. 1994. "Privatization hits snag."

Indianapolis Star. 18 August. A01.

Lausch, Gene and Tom Rose. 1992. Memorandum to Interested Parties and Persons in the Regulatory Review Process. 30 December.

MacIntyre, Larry. 1996. "Goldsmith agenda falters in Statehouse." *Indianapolis Star*. 2 February. B01.

Maloney, Tim, Executive Director of the Hoosier Environmental Council. 2000. Interview by Andy Knott. 17 July.

Mason, Douglas. 1993. "Plan to privatize city's AWT plants all wet." *Indianapolis News*. 08 December. A13.

McClaren, George. 1999a. "City sues state to delay crackdown on wastewater." *Indianapolis Star/News*. 31 August.

_____. 1999b. "Mayor blasts environmental groups; Goldsmith says racism allegations in city's sewer dispute are ridiculous." *Indianapolis Star/News*. 06 October.

Miller, Don, Stewardship Section, Indianapolis Department of Parks and Recreation. 2000. Interview by Clarke Kahlo and e-mail communication to Ingrid Ritchie. 20 July.

Morgan, Kevin. 1993. "Group that may treat city sewage is linked to '92 dumping case." *Indianapolis Star*. 11 December. A01.

_____. 1994a. "Administration forgoes public input." *Indianapolis Star*. 31 January. D01.

_____. 1994b. "Despite a done deal, council sets hearing on water plants." *Indianapolis Star*. 11 January. B01.

_____. 1994c. "Grand jury plans to examine sewage spills that killed fish." *Indianapolis Star*. 08 December. B01.

_____. 1995. "Firm avoids shutdown by accepting penalties." *Indianapolis Star*. 12 January.

Montgomery, William and Samuel Nunn. 1996. "Privatization, Participation and the Planning Process: A Case Study of Wastewater Treatment Infrastructure." *Public Works Management and Policy*. 1(1): 43-59.

Mullins, Daniel and C. Kurt Zorn. 1996. "Privatization in Indianapolis: A Closer Look at the Savings and the Wastewater Treatment Facility." *In-Roads, A Quarterly Journal of the Sycamore Institute*. Fall.

Niederpruem, Kyle. 1993. "State boosts regulation of asbestos." *Indianapolis Star*. 28 April.

_____. 1994a. "GOP councilman wants to save more trees from the ax," *Indianapolis Star*. 2 July. A1.

_____. 1994b. "City gives lead plant cleanup deadline." *Indianapolis Star*. 24 December.

_____. 1994c. "Rules on asbestos prompt question of conflict of board." *Indianapolis Star*. 19 May.

_____. 1996a. "Goo, gunk overwhelm testers. State looking at sending samples to outside contractors to pare backlog." *Indianapolis Star*. 18 February.

_____. 1996b. "Demos say vote sets stage for rollback in water-quality standards." *Indianapolis Star*. 19 January. B06.

_____. 1997. "For mayor, it won't be easy to be green." *Indianapolis Star/News*. 20 April. B01.

Regulatory Study Commission. n. d. "Information and Analysis Statement. Asbestos Regulation XIII." Attachment to Sommer 1993b.

Rohn, David. 2000a. "Indiana flush with aging septic system." *Indianapolis Star*. 17 July.

_____. 2000b. "Problems lurk just below surface." *Indianapolis Star*. 26 January.

Schramm, Susan. 1994. "Sewer rates to be frozen during '94, mayor says." *Indianapolis Star*. 10 January. C01.

Sommer, James K., Chairman, Regulatory Study Commission. 1993a. Letter to Dr. Robert Daly, President, Indianapolis Air Pollution Control Board. 16 April.

_____. 1993b. Letter to Barry Baer, Director, Department of Public Works and Dr. Robert Daly, Chairman, Air Pollution Control Board. 28 January.

Strauss, John. 1999. "City nears deal with state officials . . . " *Indianapolis Star/News*. 11 September.

Sword, Doug. 1999. "City-State White River feud spills over on local airwaves." *Indianapolis Star/News*. 14 October.

Truell, Peter. 1994. "Scandals crimp business for French firms." *Wall Street Journal*.

20 October. A18.

Ullmann 1995. "There's something fishy about the Belmont Street sewer plant." *NUVO Newsweekly*. 5-12 October.

Zogg, Jeff. 1995. "Company agrees to pay fine, cut emissions." *Indianapolis News*. 11 January.

Chapter 13

Ashley, Bob. 1995. "Pulling the Plug on Health and Hospital Corporation," *Indianapolis C.E.O.* November. 9: 12-18.

Brookside Neighborhood Association et al. 1996. Memorandum to Regulatory Review Commission. 03 July.

Burton, Cathy, M. L. Coleman, and Mary Walker. 1996. Memorandum to All Health and Hospital Corporation Regulatory Review Commissioners. 09 April.

Butler Tarkington Neighborhood Association (BTNA). n. d. "MCANA - Marion County Alliance of Neighborhood Associations: What are they doing for you?"

Fahy, Joe. 1994. "Wishard layoffs unlikely in '95. Official says streamlining can cut hospital deficit." *Indianapolis News*. 19 July. B1.

Fahy, Joe. 1996a. "Handling of regulation reviews worries group." *Indianapolis Star*. 06 June.

_____. 1996b. "County targets poor areas to cut housing inspections." *Indianapolis Star*. 24 May. A2.

Goldsmith, Steve, Mayor, City of Indianapolis. 1995a. Memorandum to Gene

Lausch, 17 January.

_____. 1995b. Letter to Jack Whelan, Chairman, Board of Trustees, Health and Hospital Corporation of Marion County, and Mitchell Roob, Jr., President and Executive Director, Health and Hospital Corporation of Marion County. 25 October.

_____. 1997. *The Twenty-First Century City.* Washington, D.C.: Regnery Publishing, Inc.

Health and Hospital Corporation of Marion County. n. d. a. "Occupied Housing and Sanitation Code Enforcement Benefits."

_____. n. d. b. "Housing code enforcement checks and balances."

_____. 1975. "Our Corporate History." *HealtH [sic] Capsule.* April.

_____. 1980. Housing and Environmental Standards Ordinance. Chapter 10.

_____. 1995a. General Ordinance No. 7-1995(A).

_____. 1996a. "Minutes of the Regulatory Review Commission." Attachment, "Framework, final draft." 10 January.

_____. 1996b. "Regulatory Review Work Groups." 19 January.

_____. 1996c. Memorandum to Members of the Housing Workgroup. RE: "HHC Staff Response to Part I of the Housing Workgroup Report, Draft 5-30-96." 05 June.

_____. 1996d. "Health and Hospital Staff Comments Regarding the Housing Report Draft." 15 May.

_____. 1996e. "Cost Summaries of Repairs."

Horseman, Karen S. 1996. Memorandum to Housing Workgroup. RE: "Request to the Housing Workgroup at their meeting of May 30, 1996." 29 May.

Indiana. 1951. Chapter 287. H.82.

Indianapolis Business Journal. 1995. Editorial. "Regulatory review is good government." 20-26 November.

Indianapolis Chamber of Commerce. n.d. "A Business Agenda 1996 - 1999, Strategies for a Successful Community." Indianapolis, Indiana.

Indianapolis News. 1995a. Editorial. "Time for H&H review overdue." 14 November.

_____. 1996. Editorial. "Encourage public input." 22 January. A06.

Indianapolis Star, 1995a. Editorial. "Regulation Review." 14 November.

_____. 1995b. Editorial. "Open it up." 19 December.

_____. 1996a. "Agency head mutes chats with reporter." 19 May.

Indianapolis Star/News. 1997. "Behind Closed Doors: An inside look at Hoosier politics and power." 16 November. B03.

King, Jerry. President, Marion County Alliance of Neighborhood Associations, Dixie Ray, President, Near Eastside Community Organization, Karen Horseman, Attorney. 1996. Memorandum to Housing Workgroup. RE: "Parts I and II of the Housing Workgroup Report." 04 June.

Lausch, Gene. 1996. Memorandum to Al Hubbard. RE: "Housing Report." 01 July.

Marion County Health Department, Department of Housing and Neighborhood Health. 1996. "Environmental Health Specialist Competency Needs."

Mood, Eric W. 1986. *APHA—CDC Recommended Minimum Housing Standards*. Washington, D.C.: American Public Health Association.

Morgan, Kevin. 1994. "Privatizing goes public." *Indianapolis Star*. 30 January. B1.

Nanavaty, Deputy Chief, East District. 1996. Letter to Marsha Branson, Marion County Health Department. 27 June.

Nancrede, Sally Falk. 1996. "City Allocates $2.3 million for housing project." *Indianapolis News*. 09 March.

Niederpruem, Kyle. 1995. "Neighborhood alliance slams closed sessions for rules review." *Indianapolis Star*. 16 December .

_____. 1996. "Regulatory review now open to public." *Indianapolis Star*. 05 January.

Pontious, Jeanne M., Board Member and Treasurer, Citizens Neighborhood Coalition, Inc. 1996. Letter to Steve West *et al.* 20 May.

Price, Nelson. 1994a. "Healthy outlook. a confident Mitch Roob takes charge of Wishard, county health department." *Indianapolis News*. 25 June. A1.

Ray, Dixie, President of Near Eastside Community Organization (NESCO). 1996. Testimony to Regulatory Review Commission. 21 May.

Regulatory Review Commission. 1996a, "Housing Workgroup Report to the Regulatory Review Commission: Part B - Background and Analysis Drafted by the Moderator." Review Draft for the Housing Workgroup. 19 June.

_____. 1996b. "H&H Housing Code Study Outline." 31 January.

_____. 1996c. "Report of the Workgroup on Housing, Review Draft for Housing Workgroup." 11 May.

_____. 1996d. "Report of the Workgroup on Housing," Review Draft for Housing Workgroup. 14 May.

_____. 1996fe "Report of the Workgroup on Housing," Review Draft for the Public. 17 May.

_____. 1996f. "Housing Workgroup Report to the Regulatory Review Commission Part II: Recommendations and Discussion Issues," Review Draft for the Housing Workgroup. 29May.

_____. 1996g. "Housing Workgroup Report to the Regulatory Review Commission Part I: Background and Analysis," Review Draft for the Housing Workgroup. 30 May.

_____. 1996h. "Housing Workgroup Report to the Regulatory Review Commission Part A: Discussion Issues," Review Draft for the Housing Workgroup. 07 June.

_____. 1996i. "Housing Workgroup Report to the Regulatory Review Commission Part B: Background and Analysis," Review Draft for the Housing Workgroup. 11 June.

_____. 1996j. "Housing Workgroup Report to the Regulatory Review Commission Part A: Discussion Issues," Review Draft for the Housing Workgroup. 17 June.

_____. 1996k. "Housing Workgroup Report to the Regulatory Review Commission Part B: Background and Analysis," Review Draft for the

Housing Workgroup. 17 June.

———. 1996l. "Housing Workgroup Report to the Regulatory Review Commission Part A: Discussion Issues Drafted by the Moderator," Review Draft for the Housing Workgroup. 19 June.

———. 1996m. "Housing Workgroup Report to the Regulatory Review Commission: Executive Summary, Drafted by the Moderator."

———. 1996n. "Health and Hospital Regulatory Review Information." December.

———. 1996o. "Health and Hospital Corporation Regulatory Review, Public Swimming Pool, Spa and Beaches Regulation." 02 May.

Regulatory Study Commission. 1996. "Regulatory Study Commission Review Standards."

Ritchie, Ingrid and Stephen J. Martin. 1994. *The Healthy Home Kit*. Chicago, IL: Dearborn Financial Publishing, Inc.

Salvato, Joseph A. 1992. *Environmental Engineering and Sanitation*, Fourth Edition. Somerset, NJ: Wiley Interscience, John Wiley & Sons, Inc.

Schoch, Eric B. 1994a. "Health agency chief vows change. New executive director of the corporation that runs Wishard plans to introduce competition." *Indianapolis Star*. 21 January. B7.

———. 1994b. "Roob is ready to rock health agency's budget." *Indianapolis Star*. 14 May. B1.

———. 1995. "Commission tackles local health rules," *Indianapolis Star*. 14 December. B-2.

Smith, Keith D., Chief Indianapolis Fire Department. 1996. Letter to Alan Moberly, Marion County Health Department. 07 June.

Spillane, Lori A. 1996. Memorandum to Eugene Lausch. RE: "Overlap of Enforcement Efforts of Other Local Government Agencies with H&H Enforcement Efforts Under Chapter 10 and Dependency of Other Agencies on H&H Chapter 10 Enforcement." 03 April.

Tucker, William. 1978. "How housing regulations cause homelessness." *The Public Interest*. 102 : 78-88.

Uhl, Sue. 1995. Memorandum to Interested Persons. RE: "Health and Hospital Regulatory Review Process Work Groups Structure and Function/Opportunity for Public Input." 29 December.

U.S. Department of Health, Education and Welfare, Public Health Service. 1976 (reprinted 1979). *Basic Housing Inspection*. Atlanta, GA: U.S. Department of Health, Education and Welfare.

Walker, Mary L. 1996a. Memorandum to Members of the Regulatory Review Commission. RE: "Housing Report to the Regulatory Review Commission." 05 July.

———. 1996b. Memorandum to Dr. Henry Bock, Chairman, Public Health Committee, HHC Board of Trustees. 17 July. Memorandum to Members of the Board of Trustees, Marion County Health and Hospital Corporation. RE: "Concerns About the Environmental Code Regulatory Review Process." 18 July.

———, member Housing Workgroup, representing Marion County Alliance of Neighborhood Associations. 1996c. Memorandum to Commissioner Yvonne Shaheen and Commissioner Jamie Street. RE: "Neighborhoods' responses to some suggestions by de-regulators." 26 July.

_____. 2000. Telephone interview by Ingrid Ritchie. 12 and 14 July.

Williams, Kathryn M., Public Policy Director, Indiana Coalition on Housing and Homeless Issues, Inc. 1996. Letter to Gene Lausch and Members of the Housing Code Workgroup, RE: "5/17/96 Draft Report of the Workgroup on Housing and Issues Identified." 24 May.

Zahn, Tamara, President, Indianapolis Downtown, Inc. 1996. Letter to Al Hubbard, Commissioner, Regulatory Review. 25 July.

Chapter 14

Abedian, Julia. 1996. "Reinvented Government? Privatization in Two Midwestern Cities." *In-Roads, A Quarterly Journal of the Sycamore Institute*. Fall.

Atterson, Lloyd. 1996. Sworn Deposition of Lloyd Atterson in Tomanovich v City of Indianapolis et al. 25 January.

Bibbs, Rebecca. 1996. "Garfield Park area residents air concerns." *Indianapolis Star*. 20 March.

Bodenhamer, D. J. and R. G. Burrows. Editors. 1994. *The Encyclopedia of Indianapolis*. Bloomington, IN: Indiana University Press.

Boyd, 1999. Interview by Sheila Suess Kennedy. 08 February.

Burrell. 1998. "Home and Business Reference." Springfield, MA: Merriam-Webster, Inc.

Businessmen for Good Government PAC. 1991. "Statement of Organization for Political Action Committee, Indiana State Election Board; Businessmen for Good Government, filed October 3, 1991."

_____ PAC. 1992. "Report of Receipts and Expenditures of Political Action Committee, Businessmen for Good Government, Schedule A."

Cady, Dick. 1997. "Prosecutor may want to probe the wonders of no bid contracts." *Indianapolis Star/News.* 22 July.

Caleca, Linda Graham. 1994. "More obstacles confront overhaul of bus system." *Indianapolis Star*. 18 June.

Caleca, Linda Graham and Joseph Gelarden. 1994. "Jail annex on hold . . . " *Indianapolis Star*. 02 March

Charen, Mona. 1998. "The Goldsmith key to city success." *Indianapolis Star*. 20 June.

City of Indianapolis. 1993-2000. "Operating Budgets."

City of Indianapolis, Office of the Controller. 2000. "Purchase Order Spreadsheets, 1992-1999."

Cleaver, David, DCAM. 2000. Facsimile to Jack Miller. 26 May.

Cohen, Adam. 1997. "City boosters: A new breed of activist mayors is making City Hall a hothouse for innovation." *Time*. 18 August.

Daniels, Mitch. n.d. Facsimile to SELTIC file. From Chamber of Commerce to Clarke Kahlo.

Department of Capital Asset Management (DCAM), City of Indianapolis. n.d. "Lease DECAM Move Cost Analysis." 1993-1994 spreadsheets.

_____, City of Indianapolis. 1996. "Amendment to Lease for DCAM Testing Laboratory, Exhibit B Laboratory Equipment, Inventory Listing." 31 December.

Department of Transportation, City of Indianapolis. 1993. "Contract between the Department of Transportation, City of Indianapolis and Snell Environmental Group, Inc." 25 August.

Franklin, Erica. 1995. "Attorney fees may be downside to downsizing: high-priced law firms are cashing in on Goldsmith's push toward privatization." *Indianapolis Star.* 28 May.

Gallant, Greg, John Muter and Clay Whitmire. 1993. Confidential Draft to Lisa Gilman, Greg Henneke and Julee Jacob. RE: "CIP Policy Directives." 14 July.

Gelarden, R. Joseph. 1998. "Indy Island to reopen by Dec. 15 after repairs." *Indianapolis Star.* 4 December.

Gelarden, Joe. 1999. "Feds probe Robertson housing development," *Indianapolis Star.* 29 March.

Goldsmith, Stephen, Mayor of Indianapolis. 1995. Letter to George Tomanovich. 12 January.

_____. 1997. *The Twenty-First Century City.* Washington, D.C.: Regnery Publishing, Inc.

_____. 1998. Transcript of a speech at the Allegheny Institute for Public Policy Luncheon. Pittsburgh, PA. 18 March.

Goldsmith for Governor. 1996. "Report of Receipts and Expenditures of a Political Committee." 1996 Reports.

Grunwald, Michael. 1998. "Myth of the Supermayor." *The American Prospect.* 40: September-October.

Hefleng, Mary, Internal Audit Agency. 1995. Letter to Becky Federwisch, OR/S. 31 January.

Heiken, Norm. 1993. "SELTIC predicts savings of more than $1 million for latest initiatives."

Henneke, Greg. 1996. Sworn Deposition of Greg Henneke in Tomanovich v City of Indianapolis et al. 23 April.

Herman, Ken. 1999. "Indianapolis mayor taps experience to advise Bush." *American Statesman.* 22 July.

Howey, Brian. 1999. "Chaos In The Nation's 'Most Audited City." *NUVO Newsweekly.* 25 March-1 April.

Indiana State Board of Accounts. 1999. "Special Report of Construction Projects for Franklin-Edgewood Park, Krannert-King-Brookside Aquatic Centers, and Perry Park Ice Rink and Aquatic Facility." 16 September.

Indiana State Election Board.1991. "Statement of Organization for Political Action Committee." filed by Businessmen for Good Government PAC. Filed 03 October.

Indianapolis News. 1996a. Editorial. "A city contractor goofs again." 03 August.

_____. 1996b. "Firm backed out of contract after HUD ruling." 24 September.

Indianapolis Star. 1996a. "Privatization under Goldsmith." 01 November.

_____. 1996b. "Paranoia at City Hall." 07 June.

_____. 1997. Editorial. "Public Housing Chaos." 12 May.

In-Roads, A Quarterly Journal of the Sycamore Institute. "Hoosier Index, Privatization in Indianapolis." Fall 1996.

Internal Audit Agency, City of Indianapolis. 1991. "Final Report Construction Contract Administration, Department of Parks and Recreation." 20 December.

_____. 1993. "Final Report Division of Housing, Department of Metropolitan Development." 18 June.

_____. 1995. "Final Report Krannert, King & Brookside Aquatic Centers, Capital Improvement Program, Department of Parks and Recreation." 21 July.

_____. 1996. "Franklin/Edgewood and Northwestway Park Construction Projects." 29 July.

_____. 1997. "Final Report Garfield Aquatic Center, Department of Parks and Recreation." 10 December.

Jacob, Julee, 1994. Memorandum to George Tomanovich, RE: "Hot Idea." 10 June.

Johnston, Kathleen. 1996a. "Advice on new arena site to cost $88,000." *Indianapolis Star.* 03 July.

_____. 1996b. "Critics question propriety of fund-raiser for Goldsmith." *Indianapolis Star.* 14 July.

_____. 1996c. "Council discusses funding restrictions . . ." *Indianapolis Start.* 18 July.

_____. 1996d. "Employee says his year long suit against city was a 'living hell.'" *Indianapolis Star.* 14 June.

_____. 1995. "City accused of hiding housing blunder." *Indianapolis News.* 27 January.

_____. 1996. "City consultants paid for work that wasn't done, audit shows." *Indianapolis Star.* 30 July.

_____. 1997. "Smoot given lucrative arena contract. Ex-deputy mayor, now firm's attorney, recommended Goldsmith donor whose past work had been criticized." *Indianapolis Star/News.* 17 July.

Johnston, Kathleen and Gerry Lanosga. 1993. "Mayor's hard work sometimes pays." *Indianapolis News.* 15 March.

_____. 1995. "Fund-raiser by Goldsmith is questioned." *Indianapolis Star.* 15 October.

Kennedy, Robert. 2000. Interview by Sheila Suess Kennedy. July.

Lanosga, Gerry. 1992. "Questions put consultant on hot seat," *Indianapolis News.* 29 December.

_____. 1995a. "Story says mayor wants all of state privatized." *Indianapolis Star.* 07 November.

_____. 1995b. "Goldsmith rival to stage forum. . . " *Indianapolis News.* 07

July.

Lanosga, Gerry and Kathleen Johnston. 1995. "Riverside project overruns common." *Indianapolis Star*, 10 December.

———. 1996a. "Candidates of the people relying on big donors." *Indianapolis Star*. 24 March.

———. 1996b. "City contractor criticized for housing work . . . " *Indianapolis Star*, 24 September.

McKenzie, Coral. 1992. "A piece of the action." *Indianapolis Business Journal*. 27 January.

Modisett, Jeffrey, Marion County Prosecutor. 1994. Letter to Mayor Goldsmith. RE: "Investigation of Parks Department—Findings and Conclusions." 27 September.

Morgan, Kevin. 1992. "Four lawyers for city lose their jobs; staff reduction to result from mayor's privatization movement." *Indianapolis Star*. 03 November.

———. 1995a. "Goldsmith denies campaign donations are tied to partnership's city contracts." *Indianapolis Star*. 13 February.

———. 1995b. "After 18 years on job, worker watches city privatize it away," *Indianapolis Star*. 04 January.

Morrison, Patrick. 1992. "Goldsmith alters housing agency; 55 lose jobs." *Indianapolis Star*. 17 March.

Mullins, Daniel and C. Kurt Zorn. 1996. "Privatization in Indianapolis, a closer look at savings and the wastewater treatment facility." *In-Roads, A Quarterly Journal of the Sycamore Institute*. 1(3): 17.

ORS. 1994a. Letter to Clay Whitmire, City of Indianapolis. RE: "Capital Improvement Program." Attachment: "Oscar Robertson Smoot Joint Venture Monthly Invoice No. 94-11."

———. 1994b. "Value Enhancement Newsletter." 4th Edition. 28 March.

———. 1994c. "Value Enhancement Newsletter." 5th Edition. 17 June.

ORS-City Contract. 1993. "Program Management Agreement between the Oscar Robertson Company of Indiana and the Sherman R. Smoot Company of Indiana, A Joint Venture (Collectively Known as "Program Manager") and the City of Indianapolis by and through the Department of Parks and Recreation, the Department of Metropolitan Development, the Department of Public Safety, the Department of Public Works and the Department of Transportation (Collectively Known as "Owner") and the City of Indianapolis by and through its Department of Transportation (Owner)." 25 March

———. 1995. "Amendment No. 5 - DPR for Program Management between Oscar Robertson Co. of Indiana & Sherman Smoot Co. of Indiana, A Joint Venture & Department of Parks & Recreation." July.

Professional Services Agreement between the Indianapolis Department of Capital Asset Management ("Department") and George Tomanovich ("Contractor") 13 June 1996 to 14 December 1999.

Ramos, Fred. 1996a. "Goldsmith escapes FBI scrutiny." *NUVO Newsweekly* 5-12 September.

_____. 1996b. "Money down the drain." *NUVO Newsweekly*. 8-15 April.

Ramos, Fred and Harrison Ullmann. 1996a. "Building Better Neighborhoods—ORS does it at twice the cost with half the results." *NUVO Newsweekly*. 11-18 January.

_____. 1996b. "Building Better Neighborhoods: another public private partnership gives ORS the key to the city." *NUVO Newsweekly*. 4-11 January.

_____. 1996c. "Hidden audit challenges Goldsmith's claim that privatization saves money." *NUVO Newsweekly*. July 18-25.

Schneider, Mary Beth. 1996a. "Democrat critics cloud Goldsmith's political future." *Indianapolis Star*. 13 July.

_____. 1996b. "Goldsmith says case about golf course pact is mostly insignificant." *Indianapolis Star*. 08 June.

Schuckel, Kathleen. 1993. "City to pay for parking study: $400,000 will buy analysis of downtown." *Indianapolis News*.25 November.

Settlement Agreement ("Agreement") between George Tomanovich ("Mr. Tomanovich") and the Consolidated City of Indianapolis ("Indianapolis"); Stephen Goldsmith, Mayor; Leon Younger, former Director of Indianapolis Parks and Recreation; Board of IndyParks and Recreation of Indianapolis, Indiana; and City-County Council of Indianapolis-Marion County, Indiana. 12 June 1996.

Shane, Anne, City of Indianapolis. 1994. Letter to George Tomanovich. 04 June.

Shiel, Andy, Shiel-Sexton. 1993. Memorandum to John Muter, ORS. 14 July.

Stefancic, Jean. 1995. *No Mercy—How Conservatives Think Tanks and Foundations Changed American's Social Agenda*. Philadelphia, PA: Temple University Press.

Stern, William M. 1994. "We got real efficient real quick." *Forbes*. 20 June.

Steve Goldsmith Committee. 1992-1997. "Report of Receipts and Expenditures of a Political Committee." 1992-1997 Reports.

Strauss, John. 1999. "Suit claims city forced staff to work unpaid overtime." *Indianapolis Star*. 13 January.

Sword, Doug. 1998. "Winning hotelier had donated to mayor." *Indianapolis Star/News*. 18 September.

Tomanovich, George. 1995. Letter to Mayor Stephen Goldsmith. 03 January.

_____. 1996. "George Tomanovich Plaintiff v City of Indianapolis; Stephen Goldsmith, Mayor, of the City of Indpls.; Leon Younger, Director of the IndyParks and Recreation, Board of IndyParks and Recreation of Indianapolis, Indiana; City-County Council of Indianapolis—Marion County, Indiana; Defendants." Cause No. IP 95-0872-C M/S. Filed in U.S. District Court, Southern Judicial District, Indianapolis Division. 29 April.

_____. 1996b. Sworn Deposition of George Tomanovich in Tomanovich vs. City of Indianapolis et al. 16 May.

_____. 1998a. Letter to Jack Miller. 06 October.

_____. 1998b. Interview by Jack Miller. 07 October.

_____. 2000a. Telephone interview by Jack Miller. 12 May.

_____. 2000b. Telephone interview by Jack Miller. 26 June.

_____. 2000c. Telephone interview by Jack Miller. 01 May.

_____. 2000d. Telephone interview by Jack Miller. 25 July.

Ullmann, Harrison. 1996. "If Goldsmith privatized himself. . . " NUVO Newsweekly. 22 August.

Ullmann, Harrison and Fred Ramos. 1996. "City workers charge ORS with ghost employment." *NUVO Newsweekly.* 4-11 July.

U.S. Department of Housing and Urban Development (HUD). 1997. "Audit Report, Office of Inspector General, Department Housing and Urban Development." 12 June.

White, Charles. 2000. Telephone interview by Sheila Suess Kennedy. 30 June.

Wilcox, Derk, Editor. 1997. *The Right Guide: A Guide to Conservative and Right-of-Center Organizations.* Ann Arbor, MI: Economic American, Inc.

Younger, Leon. 1996. Deposition. George Tomanovich, Plaintiff v City of Indianapolis et al., Defendants. Cause No. IP 95-0872-C M/S. Filed in U.S. District Court, Southern Judicial District, Indianapolis Division, 19 April.

Zishka, Sharon. 1996. Sworn Deposition of Sharon Zishka in Tomanovich vs. City of Indianapolis et al. 23 January.

Chapter 15

Bell, Robert. 1992. "Golf course plan makes pitch for more green." *Indianapolis Star.* 13 August.

_____. 1995. "Municipal golf courses giving less green." *Indianapolis Star.* 5 February.

_____. 1996. "City to seek bids on Coffin Golf course . . ." *Indianapolis Star/News.* 28 December.

_____. 1997. "Coffin Golf course operation all set . . . " *Indianapolis Star/News.* 31 July.

Burton, Stan, Golf Director, Indianapolis Department of Parks and Recreation. 1996. Memorandum to Ray Wallace, Director, IDPR. RE: "Coffin Golf course, Indianapolis Golf Management Corporation Assessment as of 4/30/96." 30 April.

Deglopper, Douglas. Assistant Corporation Counsel, City of Indianapolis. 1995. "Synopsis Of 1995 Purchasing Law Changes." 17 July.

Gelarden, Joe. 1995a. "As city golfers return to reborn Coffin." *Indianapolis Star.* 20 July.

_____. 1995b. "Coffin course to come alive after years of rough times." *Indianapolis Star.* 29 June.

_____. 1995c. "Mayor Stephen Goldsmith's term in office . . ." *Indianapolis Star.* 26 March.

Goldsmith for Governor. 1996. "Report of Receipts and Expenditures of a Political Committee." 1996 Reports.

Goldsmith, Stephen. 1997. *The Twenty-First Century City.* Washington, D.C.: Regnery Publishing, Inc.

Hurrle, Lou, Golf Director, Indianapolis Department of Parks and Recreation. 1998. Letter to Robert Taylor, Chairman IGMC. 23 March.

_____. 2000. Memorandum to Jack Miller. RE: "Fee history of golf courses 1990-1999." 14 June.

Indianapolis Department of Parks and Recreation (IDPR). 1993a. "Amended and Restated City of Indianapolis, Department of Parks and Recreation, Golf Professional Agreement, Effective as of the first day of January 1993 between the Department of Parks and Recreation of the City of Indianapolis and Jerry Hayslett, Inc." 01 January.

_____. 1993b. "Agreement between Indianapolis DPR and William Krohne, Inc., January 1, 1993."

_____. 1994a. "Oscar Robertson Smoot Monthly Invoice No. 94-07, 9/19/94 Period: July 27, 1994 through August 30, 1994."

_____. 1994b. "City of Indianapolis, Department of Parks and Recreation, Golf Course Management Agreement." 01 September.

_____. 1994c. "First Amendment to Management Agreement." 01 December.

_____. 1995. "Second Amendment to Management Agreement." 25 April.

_____. 1996. "Third Amendment to Management Agreement." March.

_____. 1998. "Coffin Municipal Golf Course Management Agreement, March 1 1998 Between DPR of the City of Indianapolis (Department) and Gray Eagle Golf, LLC, an Indiana Limited Liability Company ("Manager")." 01 March.

Indiana State Board of Accounts. 2000. "Special Report of Municipal Golf Course Management Contracts, City of Indianapolis, Marion County, Indiana." 07 January.

Indianapolis News. 1995. Editorial. "Secretized government." 20 February.

Indianapolis Star. 1995a. Editorial. "No to Secrecy." 22 February.

_____. 1995b. Staff Report. "Focused privatization bill advances in senate." 07 April.

Internal Audit Agency. 1993. "The Final Report Golf Management Contracts, Department of Parks and Recreation." 17 December.

Johnston, Kathleen. 1994. "Businessman offers to run golf course." *Indianapolis News.* 09 December.

_____. 1997. "Four Indianapolis golf courses fees are going up," *Indianapolis Star/News.* 14 December.

Johnston, Kathleen and Gerry Lanosga. 1994. "Coffin work delayed." *Indianapolis News.* 07 April.

_____. 1995. "Payments bother Modisett." *Indianapolis News.* 05 June.

_____. 1996. "Lawsuit challenges golf course contracts." *Indianapolis Star.* 20 August.

Karto, David. 2000. Telephone interview by Jack Miller. 10 July.

Lanosga, Gerry and Kathleen Johnston. 1993a. "Not up to par—privatization hits the rough series 1. Golf pros broke the law." *Indianapolis News.* 21 December.

_____. 1993b. "Not up to par—privatization hits the rough series 2. Abusing city equipment" *Indianapolis News*. 22 December.

_____. 1993c. "City still bleeds green to maintain its courses." *Indianapolis News*. 22 December.

_____. 1995. "Payments bother Modisett." *Indianapolis News*. 05 June.

_____. 1996. "Lawsuit depositions suggest firm missed city connection." *Indianapolis Star*. 07 June.

Modisett, Jeffrey, Marion County Prosecutor. 1994. Letter to Mayor Goldsmith. Re: "Investigation of Parks Department—Findings and Conclusions." 29 September.

Morgan, Kevin. 1994. "Privatizing goes public." *Indianapolis Star*. 30 January.

Mullins, Daniel and C. Kurt Zorn. 1996. "Privatization in Indianapolis, a closer look at savings and the wastewater treatment facility." *In-Roads, A Quarterly Journal. of the Sycamore Institute*. Fall.

Niederpruem, Kyle. 1995. "Bill to let city deal in secret passes panel." *Indianapolis Star*. 15 December.

Pickett, Bill. 1994. "Renovated Coffin should be ready in '95." *Indianapolis Star*. 07 August.

_____. 1995. "Essig, city golf scene still part of each other . . . *Indianapolis Star*. 09 July.

Pryor, Reed. 1996. Transcription of interview by Richard Cook, Attorney. 30 April.

Richards, Phil. 1995. "Golf Scene." *Indianapolis Star*. 20 August.

_____. 1996. "Golf Club moves to improve maintenance." *Indianapolis Star*. 22 August.

_____. 1997. "Coffin Golf Course to receive needed improvements." *Indianapolis Star/News*. 24 April.

Rohn, David. 1999. "Indy Parks will build erosion barrier." *Indianapolis Star*. 02 December.

Simpson, Cam. 1995. "Mayoral staff to rework bill . . ." *Indianapolis News*. 10 February.

Steve Goldsmith Committee. 1992-1997. "Report of Receipts and Expenditures of a Political Committee." 1992-1997 Reports.

Tomanovich, George. 1998. Letter to Jack Miller. 06 October.

_____. 2000. Interview by Jack Miller. 12 July.

Whispering Hills Golf Club. 1994-1999. "Report of Results, 1998-1999." "The William Krohne, Inc. Income Statement 1994-1997." "Evaluation Forms." Indianapolis, IN.

Younger, Leon. 1996. Deposition. "George Tomanovich, Plaintiff v City of Indianapolis et al., Defendants." Cause No. IP 95-0872-C M/S. Filed in U.S. District Court, Southern Judicial District, Indianapolis Division, 19 April.

Chapter 16

Board of Parks and Recreation, Consolidated City of Indianapolis, IN. 1995. General Resolution No. 57A, 1995.

482   To Market, To Market: Reinventing Indianapolis

Clark, Leslie, Magnet Park Administrator, Indianapolis Department of Parks
and Recreation. 1996. Letter to Mindy Ziegler and Beth Glasson, Splash,
Inc. 13 December.

Glasson, Beth, Vice-President, Splash, Inc. 1997. Letter to the Editor, "Parks
problems." *Indianapolis Star/News*. 20 August.

_____. 1999. Telephone interview by Jack Miller. 09 September.

Goldsmith, Stephen. 1997. *The Twenty-First Century City*. Washington, D.C.:
Regnery Publishing, Inc.

Graham, Ron. 1999. Telephone interview by Jack Miller. 09 September.

Jenkins, Dennis, Environmental Health Specialist. Marion County Health
Department. 2000. Telephone interview by Jack Miller. 24 July.

Indianapolis, City of. 1997. "City Cum Status as of 10/14/97."

Indianapolis Department of Parks and Recreation (IDPR). 1994a. "Contractual
Services Agreement Indianapolis Department of Parks and Recreation and
SPLASH, Inc." 01 April.

_____. 1994b. "Memorandum 1994 Pool Contract Wrap-up Summary."

_____. 1995a. "Contractual Services Agreement." 15 May.

_____. 1995b. "Memorandum 1995 Pool Contract Wrap-up Summary."

_____. 1995c. "1995 Pool Management Contract Evaluation Indy-
Parks/Splash, Inc. Relationship."

_____. 1996a. "IndyParks Final Audit Report." 1 November.

_____. 1996b. "Initiative Management Review DPR Pools." 24 October.

_____. 1996c. "Contractual Services Agreement Indianapolis Department of
Parks and Recreation and Splash, Inc." 30 May.

Indianapolis Star. 1995. "20 are overcome by fumes at Sahm Park swimming
pool," 29 July.

Johnston, Kathleen and Gerry Lanosga, 1994. "Firm is hired to run 3 pools."
Indianapolis News. 14 June.

Lanosga, Gerry and Kathleen Johnston. 1994. "3 City pools cost taxpayers less;
Pilot privatization project produces mixed results." *Indianapolis News*. 23
December.

Taylor, Tracy. 1994. Memorandum to Leon Younger. RE: "Response to
Splash, Inc. Letter of 9/27/94." 09 November.

Chapter 17

Airport Authority of Indianapolis. 2000. Internal documents.

BAA plc. 1994. "Managed Competition Proposal."

Goldsmith, Stephen. 1997. *The Twenty-First Century City*. Washington, D.C.:
Regnery Publishing, Inc.

Indianapolis Airport Authority (IAA). 1994. "Requests for Proposals."
September.

_____. 1994-1999. "Financial Reports."

_____. 1995. "Contract for the Management of the Indianapolis Airport
between BAA Indianapolis LLC and the Airport Authority of
Indianapolis."

U.S. Code. 2000a. 49 U.S.C. Section 4107 (2000).
_____. 26 U.S.C. Section 9502 (2000).

Index

Hayes, Ruth, 182, 185-86, 190,
192
HB 1398, 151, 408-12
Health and Hospital Corporation
of Marion County (*see also*
regulatory review), 297-319,
324-43, 420-23
downsizing, 305, 349, 356, 382,
390n3
environmental health programs,
299-301
housing code enforcement, 301-
05
independence, loss of, 305
investment in housing stock,
334-35
regulatory review arguments
against housing code
enforcement
effect on housing, 329-29
ability to enforce, 329-31
landlord and tenants, 331-33,
relationship to health, 324-27
targeted for regulatory review,
309-14
Henneke, Greg, 372-73
Herman, Ken, 254
histoplasmosis, 305, 339n8
homicide rate, Indianapolis, 211
Hoosier Environmental Council,
269, 271, 295n1
Housing and Urban Development,
Department of, 367, 382-85
Howard, Glenn, 167-68
Howey, Brian, xvi, 140, 143
Hubbard, Allan, 311, 314, 321
HUD, *see* Housing and Urban
Development, Department of
Hudnut, William H. III (*see also*
governing), 143, 147, 148, 176,
213, 355-57, 386, 392
downtown development, 177-
78, 181
environmental issues, 270-01,
275-84, 296n8
fiscal management, 104-37

governing profile, 66-69
governing contrast to Goldsmith
and Lugar, 70-74
neighborhood programs, 176-
78, 181, 183, 185, 189
policing, 160, 165-66, 172-73n1
Republican Party, history of, 60
Hudson Institute, 162, 355

I

IBJ, *see Indianapolis Business
Journal*
IEA, *see* Indiana Education
Association
IGMC, *see* Indianapolis Golf
Management Association
Indiana Education Association
(IEA), 224-46; 261
union busting, 246
Indiana University Purdue
University Indianapolis
(IUPUI), 66, 68, 90, 177, 183,
191, 199
*Indianapolis Business Journal
(IBJ)*, quotes
on city finances, 153
on Housing Authority, 385
on neighborhood issues, 190
on ORS, 361
on regulatory review and
environmental code
enforcement, 312
Indianapolis Chamber of
Commerce,
environmental issues, 275, 282
regulatory review, 308, 313-14,
317, 339n10
Indianapolis, economic
development, 446
Indianapolis Golf Management
Corporation (IGMC), 398-401
Indianapolis Housing
Neighborhood Partnership, 207,
213
Indianapolis International Airport
(IAA), privatization of, 429-41

SerVaas, Buert, 59, 192
Service, Efficiency, and Lower
    Taxes for Indianapolis
    Commission (SELTIC),
    79, 89, 91-92, 95, 101n9, 105,
    121, 288, 350, 364, 378, 391-
    96, 418
sewers, *see also* infrastructure
Shane, Anne, 188, 368
Sherman, Lawrence, 162
Shiel, Andrew, 386
Shiel-Sexton, 364-65, 386
sidewalks, *see also* infrastructure
Silvers, Nancy, 84-86, 92-93,
    100n5
Skarp, Mike 374-75
Smith, David, 277
Smith, Keith D., 340n20
Smoot, Sherman R. and Co., 357-
    58, 361, 385, 389n1
Souter, Tom, 395
Southeast Community
    Organization (SECO), 198
Southeast Neighborhood
    Development (SEND), 196-98
Southeast Umbrella Organization
    (SUMO), 198
Southeastern Neighborhood, 197
Spann, Charles, 383
Spicer, Michael, 139-41, 144, 146,
    149
Spillane, Lori, 341n25
Splash, Inc., 417-27 (*see also*
    Parks and Recreation,
    Department of)
Stanczykiewicz, Bill, 219
Stayton, Michael, 359
Stitt, Skip, 315, 328, 352, 397
strategic tools, 213, 351
streets, *see* infrastructure
sunsetting regulations, 298, 310,
    313, 314, 338n2
Sweeney, Michael, 81
Sweezy, John, 61
swimming pools, privatization of,
    417-27

Styring, William, 314, 317, 339

T
targeted neighborhoods, *see also*
    Citizen's, Mapleton Fall Creek,
    Martindale-Brightwood,
    NESCO, Southeastern, UNWA,
    WESCO,
    194-96, 198-99, 203-09, 211-
    14, 216-17, 221, 223-25
Tate, Chester Jr., 326
Tate, Rev. Douglass, 204
taxes (*see* fiscal issues)
Taylor, bob, 399
The Twenty-First Century City,
    city employees, 98
    education, 235, 245
    empowering neighborhoods,
    206, 208, 212-14, 218, 225
    environment, 278, 293
    library controversy and free
    speech, 71
    Metropolitan Development,
    Department of, 86
    regulation, 297
    success stories, 98
    targeting neighborhoods, 196,
    199
    user fees, 417
Thompson, R.N., 401, 405
TIFed properties and taxes (*see
    also* fiscal issues), 128-129,
    131-33, 136, 254-55
Toler, Jim 159, 169, 171
Tomanovich, George and lawsuit,
    150, 363, 367, 378, 385, 387,
    390n5-n6, 395-97
Township Administrator, 86, 91,
    192-93
Township Team Leader, *see*
    Township Administrator
Transportation, Department of
(*see* also Metro Bus)
    downsizing, 79
    privatization of services, 95-99
    reorganization of, 82, 87

About the Editors and Contributors

Editors

Ingrid Ritchie, Ph.D. is an Associate Professor in the School of Public and Environmental Affairs at Indiana University Purdue University at Indianapolis where she teaches courses in environmental had hazardous materials management. She received her doctoral and master's degrees in environmental health from the University of Minnesota. With over twenty years of experience in government, academia, and consulting, Dr. Ritchie's areas of expertise include the management of air, water and land pollutants; hazardous materials; worker health and safety; risk assessment; and policy analysis. Dr. Ritchie is the author of technical reports and publications in scholarly journals, two United States Environmental Protection Agency publications on the investigation of indoor air quality, and two books on the management of environmental hazards in businesses and homes. Dr. Ritchie's extensive community service includes serving on the Indianapolis Air Pollution Control Board, the body responsible for regulating air pollution, during both the Goldsmith and Hudnut administrations.

Sheila Suess Kennedy, J.D. is an Assistant Professor in the School of Public and Environmental Affairs at Indiana University Purdue University at Indianapolis where she teaches courses in public policy and law. She received her law degree from the Indiana University School of Law. Professor Kennedy has over twenty years of legal experience in government, academia and private practice. Prior to joining the University, Ms. Kennedy was Executive Director of the

Indiana Civil Liberties Union; she also served as Corporation Counsel for the City of Indianapolis during the Hudnut administration and was a Republican candidate for the United States Congress in 1980. Professor Kennedy's scholarly articles and books focus on civil liberties and legal issues in the public domain. Professor Kennedy is the author of a book on her experiences at the ACLU and a book documenting the history of free expression in America. Professor Kennedy's public service activities include a wide variety of local community boards. She is also a regular guest columnist for the *Indianapolis Star* and *The Indiana Word.*.

Contributors

Paul Annee spent thirty years as an officer with the Indianapolis Police Department, and he was the Chief of Police during the last administration of former Mayor William H. Hudnut III. He currently manages midwest regional security operations for National City Bank.

Kelly Bentley is a member of the Indianapolis Public Schools' Board of School Commissioners. Elected in 1998, she currently serves as the Board's Vice-President. A past business owner, she is now focused on improving educational opportunities within the public school system.

William Blomquist, Ph.D. is the Chairman of the Department of Political Science at Indiana University Purdue University Indianapolis. He is the author scholarly publications in the area of policy process and the management of common-pool resources, particularly surface and groundwater resources. Dr. Blomquist's publications also include works on the fiscal, service and political impacts of local government.

Ellen Dannin, J.D. is Professor of Law, California Western School of Law and the author of numerous articles on collective bargaining, labor-management cooperation and New Zealand labor law, as well as privatization.

George W. Geib, Ph.D. is Professor of History at Butler University in Indianapolis. He is a specialist in the early American Republic and the American Midwest, with particular interest in urban, military and political studies. Dr. Geib's publications include three books on Indiana history.

Lamont Hulse is the Executive Director of the Indianapolis Neighborhood Resource Center (INRC). The INRC promotes training, organizational and leadership development for citizens and community based organizations in Indianapolis. Mr. Hulse currently serves on the Neighborhoods and Community Development Impact Council for the United Way of Central Indiana and on the Indianapolis Steering Team for the Strengthening Families Initiative with the Annie E. Casey Foundation.

Robert G. Lehnen, Ph.D. is Professor of Public and Environmental Affairs at the Indiana University School of Public and Environmental Affairs at IUPUI. He has analyzed education policy in Indiana for more than twenty years and was the former director of the Education Policy Office, established with support from the Lilly Endowment. The Education Policy Office provided policy research on reforming Indiana's primary and secondary education system to Indiana's principle education decision makers, the Indiana Education Council composed of Indiana's seven education commissioners. Dr. Lehnen has published extensively in the area of school finance and performance.

Jack Miller, D.D.S., a retired dentist, is a long-time political activist and critic. He serves as the Coordinator of the Alliance for Democracy of Indiana, a non-profit organization seeking to reinvigorate the principles of democracy in society, and as a board member of the Hoosier Environmental Council, Indiana's largest environmental organization providing research and advocacy on a broad range of environmental issues. During 1999, he contributed an article on privatization to *The Progressive Populist*.

Samuel Nunn, Ph.D. is Associate Professor of Public and Environmental Affairs at Indiana University Purdue University Indianapolis and Associate Director of the Center for Urban Policy and the Environment. Dr. Nunn's areas of expertise include public and fiscal management and planning. He has published scholarly articles on public-private partnerships, public finance, and economic development. Dr. Nunn was formerly a municipal administrator with the City of Fort Worth.

Dennis Rosebrough is currently the Public Affairs Director at the Indianapolis International Airport, the same job he held prior to the time that airport management was contracted out to BAA. Prior to assuming his position with the Airport Authority, he was a public information officer for the City of Indianapolis during the Hudnut administration. He has been active in the Marion County Republican Party.

Ray Suarez is an internationally renowned reporter, producer, and host of radio and television programming. He is a Senior Correspondent for the acclaimed NewsHour with Jim Lehrer on PBS. Prior to accepting this position, Mr. Suarez was the host of NPR's popular interview and call-in program, Talk of the Nation. He is the author of *The Old Neighborhood: What We Lost in the Great Suburban Migration, 1966-1999*.